better business

second canadian edition

michael solomon

mary anne poatsy

kendall martin

jeff short
Humber College

sandra wellman
Seneca College

kerri shields
Centennial College

PEARSON

Toronto

Editor-in-Chief: Claudine O'Donnell
Acquisitions Editor: Carolin Sweig
Marketing Manager: Jessica Saso
Program Manager: Karen Townsend
Project Manager: Jessica Hellen
Developmental Editor: Paul Donnelly
Media Editor: Nicole Mellow
Media Producer: Daniel Szabo
Production Services: Aptara®, Inc.
Permissions Project Manager: Joanne Tang
Photo Permissions Research: Dimple Bhorwal, Aptara®, Inc.
Text Permissions Research: Phyllis Padula, Aptara®, Inc.
Interior Designer: Aptara®, Inc.
Cover Designer: Anthony Leung
Cover Image: Fotolia

Credits and acknowledgments for material borrowed from other sources and reproduced, with permission, in this textbook appear on the appropriate page within the text.

10 9 8 7 6 5 4 3 2 V0TX

Library and Archives Canada Cataloguing in Publication
Poatsy, Mary Anne, author
Better business/Michael R. Solomon, contributing editor; Mary Anne Poatsy, Kendall Martin, Jeff Short, Humber College, Sandra Wellman, Seneca College. — Second Canadian edition.
Includes index.
Revision of: Better business/Michael R. Solomon, contributing editor; Mary Anne Poatsy, Kendall Martin, Kerri Shields, Centennial College. — Canadian edition. — Toronto: Pearson Canada, 2012.
ISBN 978-0-13-381097-4 (pbk.)
1. Industrial management. 2. Business. 3. Entrepreneurship. 4. Commerce. I. Solomon, Michael R., editor II. Martin, Kendall, author III. Short, Jeff (Professor of business), author IV. Wellman, Sandra, author V. Title.
HD31.P62 2015 658 C2014-904909-9

ISBN 978-0-13-381097-4

Brief Contents

Chapter

Contents

To Students

How can you use *Better Business* as an effective learning tool?

Read Actively

Do you ever find that you need to reread a text many times before you fully understand it? Do you ever have trouble remembering what you read?

As a student, you are expected to read regularly. As an employee, reading to develop your skills and knowledge will likely be an important part of your job. Before you begin reading anything, you should determine your reading objective—what is it you want to gain from reading? When you read a newspaper or magazine, for example, you might simply skim over the material to discover the main points. But when you read a textbook, you must read carefully (that is, read every word), make notes, and question what you are reading.

You can use the SQ3R technique to improve your understanding of a text:[1]

- Survey (or skim)
- Question (ask yourself questions about what you are reading)
- Read
- Recall (identify major points and answer questions from Q)
- Review (review all sections)

When you are reading for a course, you need to make sure you're actively involved in the text. Active readers predict, make inferences, and draw conclusions; they ask questions while they read and stop often to check for understanding. Fortunately, *Better Business* provides in-text questions throughout every chapter, giving you built-in cues to make your study active, promote deeper thought, and engage your critical thinking skills. For example, instead of simply listing the tasks that managers perform, *Better Business* asks you, "What tasks do managers perform?" and gives you the information to answer that question.

If you think that active reading will take too much time, think again. Active reading saves time because it improves reading comprehension and retention—it helps you understand and remember what you've read, meaning you won't have to reread material again and again. Reading actively takes only a little effort, but it produces big results.

Better Business strives to engage you in the material, pique your interest, drive your curiosity, and promote active reading. Active reading assists you in doing what you came to university or college to learn how to do—think deeply about issues of importance in our society. Ultimately, the process of active reading helps you understand and retain what you read and assists you in mastering academic reading. This mastery leads to a successful educational experience and will also serve you well in your future profession.

Use the Learning Style That Works Best for You

Better Business provides you with multiple ways to learn. Each of us has a preferred learning "style"; some like to *watch* and learn (visual), others like to *do* and learn (kinesthetic), and still others like to *listen* and learn (auditory). So, while simply reading a textbook is a good start to learning, most of us will remember more and remember longer by learning in multiple ways. For auditory, visual, and kinesthetic learners, the MyBizLab online learning system is packed with interactive online lesson presentations, self-study tools, videos, glossary flashcards, business case simulations, and much more. You can explore a media-rich eText, strengthen your understanding of key topics through engaging online lessons, and test your mastery of each chapter through a robust Study Plan. No matter what your preferred learning style, MyBizLab will provide you with a wealth of study tools and opportunities to explore and learn.

You have likely completed a learning styles inventory in the past, but if you haven't, it would be beneficial for you to complete the "Multiple Pathways to Learning" activity on MyBizLab, which will help you determine your preferred learning style. Knowing your learning style will help you compensate for your weaknesses and capitalize on your strengths. With the question-driven learning strategy implemented in the textbook and the wealth of learning resources at your disposal in MyBizLab, you will be well on your way to academic and career success.

To Instructors

About the Second Canadian Edition

What makes *Better Business* an effective teaching resource?

Question-Driven Learning

We all use questions to learn and to gain a better understanding of the knowledge that we need in our careers, our studies, and our lives. The importance of question-driven learning cannot be overstated—the brain creates pathways to information in response to questions. Strong questions motivate and encourage students to achieve deeper understanding of any topic. *Better Business* applies the principles of question-driven learning by using in-text questions as the driving force for acquiring knowledge. The interactive writing style of this book makes it an easy-to-read, engaging text for students.

Multiple Levels of Thinking

Better Business reflects Benjamin Bloom's question-based philosophy by providing a suite of discussion questions, application exercises, and critical thinking questions that may be used to teach and test not only students' knowledge, comprehension, and application of specific concepts, but also their higher-level thinking skills (analysis, synthesis, and evaluation). Bloom's classification of educational objectives, popularly known as *Bloom's taxonomy*, can help educators better assess student learning and thinking skills. In the absence of such a classification system, educators may inadvertently emphasize memorization of facts instead of other (likely more important) learned capabilities. Questions in the Instructor's Manual and the electronic test bank are associated with specific levels of Bloom's taxonomy. Instructors can select questions from *Better Business* and its online resources that reflect and reinforce each lesson plan's objective.

Multiple Modalities of Learning

Studies have shown that learning is more effective when it is multimodal. For example, using visuals alongside verbal or textual learning can yield significant benefits for the learner. A Metiri Group research study on multimodal learning recommended that instructors create multimodal and interactive or collaborative lessons in order to engage students' thinking in a variety of ways, using whatever media is best suited to the student and the material.[2] *Better Business* follows this approach with the inclusion of MyBizLab, Pearson's revolutionary online learning system. It gives professors and students easy access to a variety of online lessons, media, and activities that get students interacting with business and not just reading about it.

What's New in the Second Canadian Edition

There is much that is new and improved in this edition to ensure clarity, concision, and currency of presentation. Here are some of the key changes:

- Content has been reorganized and streamlined, from 13 to 12 chapters: Chapter 1, "Business Fundamentals," has been substantially overhauled; the chapter on Global Business now appears at the end of the text; and the former Chapter 9, "Business Technology," has been removed with key content from it being redistributed to other chapters.
- Chapter 2, "The Environment of Business," is new to this edition, incorporating material from the former Chapter 1 ("Business Fundamentals) and Chapter 3 ("Legal, Ethical, and Responsible Business"), focusing on the environments of business (PEST) and competition (Five Forces, and types of competition).
- Chapter 3 now features a discussion of the Legatum Prosperity Index, an annual ranking of 142 countries based on factors such as wealth, economic growth, and the quality of life; it also includes a report from the *Fraser Institute*, a Canadian agency that studies the impact of competitive markets and government intervention on individuals and societies, to include on the "*Economic Freedom of the World*." This provides some context for the existence of capitalist markets around the world.
- Chapter 4 features an updated discussion of the reasons to start a business; it also includes new information about Internet entrepreneurs and home-based entrepreneurs in the section about types of entrepreneurs.
- Chapter 7 features two new "Top Ten" boxes: "The 10 Skills Employers Most Want in 20-Something Employees" and "Ways to Get Promoted."

- Chapter 8 now features a discussion of how marketing benefits consumers by providing time, form, task, place, and ownership utility.
- In Chapter 9, we explore how packaging affects the environment.
- Chapter 10 includes a discussion of the new ISO Standard—ISO 14067, Carbon footprint of product, as well as a new section on sustainability in manufacturing.
- Chapter 12 contains a new section on global business trends.
- More Canadian content and examples have been added throughout.
- New and updated visuals can be found throughout.
- New and updated opening discussions can be found in many chapters.
- New and updated closing cases can be found in many chapters.

Pedagogical Features

How do the *Better Business* chapters enhance teaching and learning?

Each chapter is packed with real, relevant, and timely examples that reinforce key concepts. A wealth of chapter-opening, in-chapter, and end-of-chapter features help students learn, link, and apply major concepts:

Opening Discussions Each chapter begins with an engaging Opening Discussion that sets the stage for the chapter. These brief introductory case studies discuss real-world organizations and countries, introducing students to critical issues and business concepts. They include questions to inspire class discussion, prompt thinking, and generate interest in the chapter content.

whyhire.me

LEARNING OBJECTIVES

After studying this chapter, you should be able to:

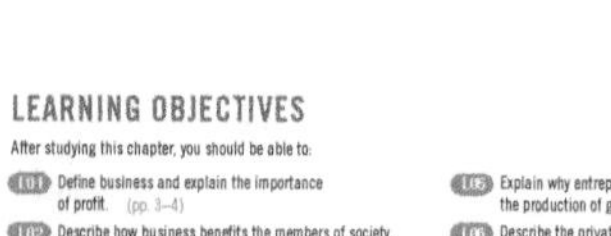

LO1 Define business and explain the importance of profit. (pp. 3–4)

LO2 Describe how business benefits the members of society. (pp. 4–5)

LO3 Explain the difference between for-profit and nonprofit organizational goals. (pp. 5–7)

LO4 Describe the factors of production. (pp. 7–9)

LO5 Explain why entrepreneurs and technology are essential to the production of goods and services. (p. 9)

LO6 Describe the private enterprise system and how competition affects business in Canada. (pp. 9–10)

LO7 Identify and describe the main purposes of the functional areas of most businesses. (pp. 10–14)

OPENING DISCUSSION: STARTING A NEW BUSINESS

The WhyHire.me Innovation

As Facebook, LinkedIn, Twitter, and myriad other online social media sites become increasingly prevalent, more employers are scrutinizing these networking sites to screen potential employees. In a 2009 CareerBuilder survey, 45 percent of the 2600 employers surveyed reported that they research job candidates through social media.[1] Because of content found on social networking sites, 35 percent of employers reported that they chose *not to hire* candidates. Obviously, it is becoming imperative for job seekers to ensure their online image is not diminishing their job opportunities.

While teaching career positioning to a marketing class in 2008, Patti Church realized that students needed to start thinking about this topic sooner rather than later. At the same time, Andy Church and Robert Saric were discussing the value of having an established online personal brand when looking for employment after noticing the tremendous positive impact it had on their own job search efforts. Patti brought to Robert's and Andy's attention the point that many university and college students do not realize how transparent they are on the web. The three entrepreneurs formed a legal partnership and set out to develop a social media tool that would not only educate students about professional personal branding, but also provide a venue whereby students could safely build an online career portfolio to showcase their skills, abilities, and knowledge; establish a positive online reputation; and proactively position themselves to get hired! It was time to start using digital tools for a digital generation.

Their efforts resulted in WhyHire.me, a career success platform where students can create a professional and unique online brand presence.[2] As head of curriculum design, Patti leads the development of learning materials and overall student learning experience. With his considerable experience in education technology 2.0, stakeholder management, and growing global brands for publishers, Andy is responsible for the development of product requirements and go-to-market planning. Robert—a right-brained engineer and head of digital—is responsible for the strategy and development of all online career success services and solutions.

Additional WhyHire.me facts (as of 2011):

On Target Boxes, Off the Mark Boxes, and Top 10 Lists Each chapter includes either an On Target or Off the Mark box. These boxed features illustrate positive and negative outcomes of business ventures related to chapter material. They are accompanied by questions to inspire classroom discussions and further understanding of the topics. These features, along with various Top 10 lists, help fuel in-class dialogue.

top10

Richest People in Canada (2014) (CDN$)

1. Thomson family: Thomson Reuters, Woodbridge Co. Ltd. (media, information, distribution) — $26.1 billion
2. Galen Weston: George Weston Ltd., Loblaw Companies Ltd., Holt Renfrew (food, groceries, retail, real estate) — $10.4 billion
3. Irving family: Irving Oil Ltd. (oil, forestry products, gas stations, media, transportation, real estate) — $7.85 billion
4. Rogers family: Rogers Communications Inc. (cable TV, communications, media, pro sports) — $7.6 billion
5. James Pattison: Jim Pattison Group (auto sales, food, media, forestry products, entertainment, export services) — $7.39 billion
6. Saputo family: Saputo Inc. (food, real estate, transportation) — $5.24 billion
7. Estate of Paul Desmarais: Power Corporation of Canada (financial services, media) — $4.93 billion
8. Jeffrey Skoll: eBay Inc. Participant Media (Internet, media) — $4.92 billion
9. Richardson family: James Richardson & Sons Ltd. (financial management) — $4.45 billion
10. Carlo Fidani: Orlando Corp. (real estate) — $4.08 billion

Source: "Canada's 100 Wealthiest People, 2014 Edition," *Canadian Business*, November 21, 2013, accessed March 31, 2014, http://www.canadianbusiness.com/companies-and-industries/richest-people-in-canada-2013-2/?gallery_page=26#gallery_top.

Newman Forge & Pattern: Turning a Hobby into a Business

"A business plan? I'm not an MBA—I don't do those things," jokes John Newman. In reality, the no-nonsense entrepreneur from Hamilton, Ontario, has massive plans for his blacksmithing and pattern-making shop, Newman Forge & Pattern. When his employer downsized in 2003, rather than look for another job John decided to turn his hobby into a business. After years of blacksmithing in his home garage, he purchased a proper shop in an industrial area and opened for business. Although nerve-racking, John says starting his own shop was the best decision he could have made: "The only time I had second thoughts was when I was at the shop at two or three in the morning, pulling all-nighters to meet a delivery. But it's definitely been worth it."

Turning a hobby into a career isn't as fun as you'd think, he asserts—it can take some of the enjoyment out of it, because it's no longer your escape from work. "But you can start your business at a more gradual pace, and you already have a lot of the equipment, which helps." John says the best thing about working alone and being his own boss is flexibility: "If it snows, I can sometimes skip work and go skiing!" However, there are downsides. "There's no one to collaborate with, and it can be lonely at

John Newman

Discussion Questions

1. **Do you think the initial capital investment John needed to start his business was very large? How do you think he might have got the money to start this business?**
2. **When John decided to start his own business, what**

Dream Team or Nightmare?

If we look at Michael Eisner, the former Disney chief executive officer (CEO), we see that for his first 10 years at Disney (Research), he and chief operating officer (COO) Frank Wells were a great team. Under their guidance, Disney revived its famous animation tradition and the movie business prospered. Eisner and Wells not only saved a legendary company, but they also made shareholders rich. When Wells died, Eisner then formed one of the most famously ill-fated teams in recent history.[47]

In 1995, Michael Ovitz—one of Hollywood's most powerful talent agents and the founder of Creative Artists Agency—was brought on as Disney president under CEO and board chair Michael Eisner. Ovitz quickly grew frustrated with his role and vague definition of duties.[48] After a tumultuous 14 months as Disney's second-in-command, he was dismissed by Eisner. Disney shareholders later sued Eisner and Disney's board of directors for awarding Ovitz roughly US$140 million in severance. The 2005 trial lasted three months, with the judge ruling that Eisner and the other directors properly carried out their fiduciary duties. Although Disney won, the case aired some embarrassing testimony about the "Machiavellian atmosphere inside the Magic Kingdom."[49] Eisner stepped down as CEO that same year.

In analyzing what went wrong; the overriding answer is conflicting business and personal agendas. Ovitz wanted to put big money into projects that Eisner dismissed as "off strategy," such as buying a National Football League franchise. Eisner also did not approve of Ovitz spending US$2 million renovating his own office. This team failure cost Disney enormously—in both money and reputation.[50]

Discussion Questions

1. **What steps can companies take to ensure they don't hire someone who won't work well with the team?**
2. **Does thinking differently mean two people won't get along? Why or why not?**
3. **How much time and money did Disney lose over this situation?**

BizChat Boxes *BizChat boxes* include questions that can spark thoughtful in-class discussions or online writing assignments via MyBizLab. BizChat boxes explore "hot topics" in business to help connect the chapter material to what's happening in business today.

Apple: Taking a Bite Out of Microsoft?

Apple and Microsoft have a history of bitter rivalry revolving around the desire to dominate the personal computer market. The main point of contention between these companies is the graphical user interface (GUI), which is the user interface for the main program that runs personal computers. Apple released the first GUI to include folders and long file names in 1983. When Microsoft released Windows 2.0 in 1988, Apple took Microsoft to court, complaining that the "look and feel" of the Windows interface was stolen from the Apple interface. This suit continued until 1992, when Apple finally lost.

Microsoft led the competition in the early 1990s. It became industry standard to have Windows operating systems preinstalled on most PCs, which were dominating the personal computer market at the time. The 10-year battle finally ended when Apple announced an official alliance with Microsoft in 1997. Microsoft and Apple agreed to a five-year deal in which Microsoft would continue to develop Office software for Apple computers, and Apple agreed to bundle Microsoft's Internet Explorer in all its operating systems.[27]

The computer industry went through some tough times around the turn of the century, but Apple and Microsoft remained two of the most successful companies in the world. The element of competition between these companies drove them to succeed, and perhaps led to the production of higher-quality operating software.

Discussion Questions

1. **Some people say that Microsoft imitated Apple's "look and feel" in their user interface. Why might they do that?**
2. **You likely remember the TV commercials that pitted the cool Mac guy against the awkward PC nerd. Are these ads effective in illustrating the competition between the two companies? Why or why not?**
3. **Are you a Mac or PC person? How do you think you developed this preference?**

LEARNING OBJECTIVES

After studying this chapter, you should be able to:

LO1 Understand how the globalization of markets and production has affected business. (pp. 304–306)

LO2 Explain why globalization has accelerated so rapidly. (pp. 306–309)

LO3 Explain the meaning of *comparative advantage* and *absolute advantage* and describe the benefits and costs of international trade. (pp. 309–311)

LO4 Define free trade and summarize the different types of trade barriers used to protect domestic industries from foreign competition. (pp. 311–314)

LO5 Describe the organizations that facilitate trade and attempt to eliminate trade barriers. (pp. 314–318)

LO6 Distinguish among the three basic strategies of international business. (pp. 318–319)

LO7 Outline the ways international firms can successfully enter foreign markets. (pp. 319–321)

LO8 Define exchange rates and explain how they affect international business. (pp. 321–325)

LO9 List the economic factors and challenges that play a role in conducting business on a global scale. (p. 325)

LO10 Summarize the sociocultural, political, legal, and ethical challenges to conducting business in a global marketplace. (pp. 325–328)

1 Learning Objectives, Key Terms, and Chapter Synopsis Tied directly to the synopsis at the end of the chapter and to the TestGen questions, each chapter's Learning Objectives preview the main points students should know after studying the chapter. Throughout the chapter, Key Terms are defined in marginal notes. At the end of each chapter, the Chapter Synopsis reminds students of the chapter's Learning Objectives and summarizes the main concepts discussed within the chapter.

CHAPTER SYNOPSIS

LO1 Define business and explain the importance of profit. (pp. 3–4)

Business is any activity that provides goods or services for the purpose of earning profit. Some businesses produce physical/tangible goods, while other businesses offer services. Every business needs to sell its products to a sufficient number of customers who are willing to buy the products at a price that enables the business to earn a profit. A **profit** is earned when a company's **revenue** (the total amount of money received for goods and services provided) is greater than its **expenses** (the costs incurred to produce and sell the goods or services offered by the business). A **loss** occurs when a company's revenue is less than its expenses.

More often than not, profit is the driving force behind a business's growth. As more profit is generated, a company is able to reward its employees, increase its productivity, or expand its business into new areas. Profit provides an incentive and rewards businesspeople for taking the risks involved in developing and selling new goods and services that consumers value. In other words, profit is what motivates entrepreneurs to start and operate a business.

LO2 Describe how business benefits the members of society. (pp. 4–5)

only the material standard of living, but also the more intangible aspects that make up human life, such as environmental quality, good health, social interactions, leisure time, and a general belief that "life is good."

LO3 Explain the difference between for-profit and nonprofit organizational goals. (pp. 5–7)

The main objective of a for-profit business is to offer goods and services to customers to earn a profit. Nonprofit organizations, however, do not go into business to pursue profits. Instead, a **nonprofit** (also referred to as a not-for-profit) organization seeks to serve its community through social, educational, or political means. Organizations such as universities, hospitals, environmental groups, and charities are nonprofit organizations. Any excess revenue they generate is used to further their stated mission. They often direct their activities toward shaping the quality of our lives and our communities.

LO4 Describe the factors of production. (pp. 7–9)

The **factors of production** are the resources used to produce goods and services. They include labour, natural resources, capital, entrepreneurial talent, and technology.

primary data Raw data collected by the researcher. The data are frequently collected through observation, questionnaires, surveys (via mail, email, or telephone), focus groups, interviews, customer feedback, samples, and controlled experiments.

focus group Typically a group of eight to ten potential customers who are asked for feedback on a good or service, advertisement, idea, or packaging.

secondary data Data that have already been collected and processed. An example of secondary data is census data.

Better Business, Better World Vignettes In many chapters, the Better Business, Better World vignettes illustrate how businesses are engaging in the solutions to sustainable development challenges, global citizenship and equity, and social responsibility. The vignettes contain discussion questions to enhance students' understanding of the topic and help initiate classroom discussion.

Better Business Better World

Do You Prefer to Do Business with Companies You Can Trust?

The Council of Better Business Bureaus (CBBB) is the North American umbrella organization for all Better Business Bureaus (BBB). Both the CBBB and BBB are dedicated to cultivating honest, responsive relationships between businesses and consumers, instilling consumer confidence and contributing to a trustworthy marketplace. Founded in 1912, the BBB has grown to 128 bureaus serving communities across North America, evaluating and monitoring more than 3 million local and national businesses and charities.[12]

Financed by the private business sector, the BBB is a nonprofit, unbiased public service organization that establishes and maintains high standards for fair and honest business behaviour. Businesses that earn BBB-accredited status contractually agree and adhere to the organization's

- *Be transparent.* Openly identify the nature, location, and ownership of the business, and clearly disclose all policies, guarantees, and procedures that bear on a customer's decision to buy.
- *Honour promises.* Abide by all written agreements and verbal representations.
- *Be responsive.* Address marketplace disputes quickly, professionally, and in good faith.
- *Safeguard privacy.* Protect any data collected against mishandling and fraud, collect personal information only as needed, and respect the preferences of customers regarding the use of their information.
- *Embody integrity.* Approach all business dealings, marketplace transactions, and commitments with integrity.

The BBB provides objective advice, free Reliability Reports on businesses and Wise Giving reports on charities, and educational information on topics affecting marketplace trust. To further promote trust, the BBB also

Critical Thinking Questions End-of-chapter Critical Thinking Questions are designed to get students to think about how the material they are studying applies to them as individuals, community members, and global citizens.

CRITICAL THINKING QUESTIONS

1. Consider all of the factors of production: labour, natural resources, capital, entrepreneurs, and technology. Is each of these resources a vital part of the school you attend or the company you work for? Which factors do you believe are most important to the goods and services provided by your organization? Why?
2. Give examples of the ways in which each of the five factors of production can affect the business performance of McDonald's or Walmart.
3. If firms competing in the same industry have access to the same labour market, how can a company use employees to create a competitive advantage over rivals?
4. Considering the rapid increase in ecommerce, it is likely that you have purchased or sold some sort of product online. If not, you have probably browsed the webpages of eBay or your favourite clothing store. Can you list a few companies or organizations that do not offer their products or services online? How does their status and growth compare with similar companies who do offer goods and services online?

Team Time Exercises End-of-chapter Team Time Exercises have students work in teams to improve their collaboration and problem-solving skills.

TEAM TIME

The Competitive Edge

Competition arises when two or more businesses compete to attract consumers and gain an advantage over one another. Divide into three groups: Company A, Company B, and Consumers.

SCENARIO

Companies A and B: Collectively decide what type of business you want to represent (e.g., sports apparel company, beauty salon, or pet care agency), then choose a product or service applicable to that type of business. (Both groups should choose the same type of business and product or service.)

PROCESS

Step 1. *Companies A and B:* Decide how you will present your product to your consumers. Focus on the following factors: packaging/presentation, price/budget, quality. *Consumers:* Compile a list of what is important to you when choosing this product or service.

Step 2. *Companies A and B:* Provide a brief presentation to your competition and consumers. *Consumers:* Provide in-depth feedback to both companies about how they could improve; consider the initial list you created in Step 1.

Step 3. *Companies A and B:* Use the consumer feedback to alter your product or service to gain advantage over your competition.

ETHICS AND RESPONSIBILITY

Standard of Living versus Quality of Life

Standard of living mainly focuses on productivity and increasing financial wealth, while quality of life seems to include a broader range of issues, although some of these appear to negatively impact standard of living.

Process

Step 1. Divide the class into small discussion groups. Half of the class should develop a case that supports the following argument: Canadians would be better off if society focused on productivity to maximize standard of living. The second half of the class will develop a case supporting the position that Canadians would be better off if society prioritized issues that would maximize our quality of life.

Step 2. Once the small groups have had sufficient opportunity to develop their arguments, pair each group with an opposing group. These groups should take turns making their arguments, trying to convince the opposing team to come to their side.

Step 3. With the whole class, discuss the following questions:

a. What are the strongest arguments in support of focusing on standard of living? What do you think we can do to increase standard of living in Canada?
b. What are the strongest arguments in support of focusing on quality of life? What can we do to improve quality of life for Canadians?
c. Is it possible to have both? What could we do to create a balance between standard of living and quality of life?

Ethics and Responsibility Exercises End-of-chapter Ethics and Responsibility Exercises are designed to increase students' understanding of business ethics and corporate social responsibility.

Closing Cases The Closing Case wraps up the chapter material by relating the experience of a company to the business topics discussed within the chapter.

CLOSING CASE

GE's Imagination Is a Factor of Production

Traditionally, the name Thomas Edison is synonymous with the word *ingenious*. Similarly, his invention of the carbon filament incandescent lamp, or light bulb, is symbolic of all things innovative. This ingenuity and innovation created the building blocks for General Electric (GE). GE is a business that started 130 years ago with a bright idea that developed into a world-changing product. The commercial light bulb not only had a profound impact on people's daily lives, it also gave birth to a business that would eventually grow into one of the world's largest corporations.

first national television network when its station, WRGB, became the first to relay a national broadcast from New Yo City. Each of these individual achievements produced the opportunity to develop new areas of business.[14]

Despite GE's years of successful growth, like any bus it must continue to ask itself, "Why are we here? What do have to offer?" When GE was first established, its purpose to bring electric energy and light to the masses through pr ucts such as dynamos and electric lamps. Today, GE has a what broader purpose. The company says, "We exist to so problems for our customers, our communities and societie ourselves."[15]

MyBizLab Resources

MyBizLab delivers **proven results** in helping individual students succeed. It provides **engaging experiences** that personalize, stimulate, and measure learning for each student. For the second Canadian edition, MyBizLab includes powerful new learning resources, including a new set of online lesson presentations to help students work through and master key business topics, a completely restructured Study Plan for student self-study, and a wealth of engaging assessment and teaching aids to help students and instructors explore unique learning pathways. MyBizLab online resources include:

- **NEW Interactive Lesson Presentations.** Students can now study key chapter topics and work through interactive assessments to test their knowledge and mastery of business concepts. Each presentation allows students to explore through expertly designed steps of reading, practising, and testing to ensure that students not only experience the content, but truly engage with each topic. Instructors also have the ability to assign quizzes, projects, and follow-up discussion questions relating to the online lessons to further develop the valuable learning experiences from the presentations.
- **NEW Study Plan.** MyBizLab offers students an engaging and focused self-study experience that is driven by a powerful new Study Plan. Students work through assessments in each chapter to gauge their understanding and target the topics that require additional practice. Along the way, they are recognized for their mastery of each topic and guided toward resources in areas that they might be struggling to understand.
- **NEW Dynamic Study Modules.** These new study modules allow students to work through groups of questions and check their understanding of foundational business topics. As students work through questions, the Dynamic Study Modules assess their knowledge and only show questions that still require practice. Dynamic Study Modules can be completed online using your computer, tablet, or mobile device.
- **BizSkills and Decision-Making Simulations.** BizSkills are real-world scenarios that invite students to assume the role of a decision maker at a company to apply the concepts they have just learned. Decision-Making Mini-Simulations walk students through key business decision-making scenarios to help them understand how business decisions are made. Students are asked to make important decisions relating to core business concepts. At each point, students receive feedback to help them understand the implications of their choices in the business environment. Both types of simulations can now be assigned by instructors and graded directly through MyBizLab.
- **NEW Business Today Video Database.** Business Today is a dynamic and expanding database of videos that covers the disciplines of business, marketing, management, and more. In addition to the videos that have been specifically correlated to this text, you will find new videos posted regularly. Check back regularly to see up-to-date video examples that are perfect for classroom use.
- **BizChat Writing Assignments.** Each assisted-graded writing assignment is based on a BizChat Discussion Question from the text and provides the perfect framework for instructors to efficiently assign, review, and grade students' written work. Questions are accompanied by a clickable rubric that allows instructors to review written work, provide immediate feedback, and assign a grade quickly and consistently.
- **NEW Learning Catalytics.** Learning Catalytics is a "bring your own device" student engagement, assessment, and classroom intelligence system. It allows instructors to engage students in class with a variety of question types designed to gauge student understanding.

- **Glossary Flashcards.** The Glossary Flashcards provide a targeted review of the Key Terms in each chapter. They allow learners to select the specific terms and chapters that they would like to study. The cards can also be sorted by Key Term or by definition to give students greater flexibility when studying.
- **Business Plan Project**. A simple, concise Business Plan Project is available on MyBizLab for instructors to share with their students.
- **NEW Canadian Sketch Animation Series.** Explore a NEW animation series that presents key marketing and business concepts from a uniquely Canadian perspective. This interesting and lively series of videos will help your students grasp course concepts that they find difficult.

Instructor Supplements

Better Business includes an innovative supplement package for instructors. These supplements can be downloaded directly from Pearson Canada's online catalogue.

- **Instructor's Manual**. This valuable resource includes chapter outlines, teaching tips, weblinks, supplemental activities, a chapter–video correlation guide, and answers to discussion and end-of-chapter questions. Each answer is tagged with the appropriate level of Bloom's taxonomy.
- **PowerPoint® Slides**. Each chapter presentation includes 25 to 30 high-quality slides. The PowerPoint Slides highlight key points from the text and are fully customizable.
- **TestGen and Test Item File**. TestGen is a powerful online assessment-generation program that helps instructors easily create and print quizzes, tests, and exams, as well as homework or practice handouts. The *Better Business* TestGen contains multiple-choice, true/false, short answer, and essay questions—approximately 150 questions in total per chapter. Questions and tests can all be authored online, allowing instructors ultimate flexibility and the ability to efficiently manage assessments at any time, from anywhere. A Test Item File in Microsoft Word® is also available.
- **Image Library**. The Image Library contains image files for all numbered figures and tables from the textbook.
- Pearson's **Learning Solutions Managers** work with faculty and campus course designers to ensure that Pearson technology products, assessment tools, and online course materials are tailored to meet your specific needs. This highly qualified team is dedicated to helping schools take full advantage of a wide range of educational resources by assisting in the integration of a variety of instructional materials and media formats. Your local Pearson Canada sales representative can provide you with more details about this service program.

Pearson Custom Library

For enrolments of at least 25 students, you can create your own textbook by choosing the chapters that best suit your own course needs. To begin building your custom text, visit www.pearsoncustomlibrary.com. You may also work with your local Pearson Canada sales representative to create your ideal text—publishing your own original content or mixing and matching Pearson content.

About the Authors

Michael Solomon

Michael R. Solomon, Ph.D., is Professor of Marketing and Director of the Center for Consumer Research in the Haub School of Business at Saint Joseph's University in Philadelphia. He also is Professor of Consumer Behaviour at the Manchester School of Business, the University of Manchester, U.K. Prof. Solomon's primary research and consulting interests include consumer behaviour, branding, and marketing applications of virtual worlds. He has written several textbook and trade books; his *Consumer Behaviour* text is the most widely used in the world. Michael often speaks to business groups about new trends in consumer behaviour and marketing strategy.

Mary Anne Poatsy, MBA, CFP

Mary Anne is a senior faculty member at Montgomery County Community College, teaching various computer application and concepts courses in face-to-face and online environments. She holds a BA in psychology and education from Mount Holyoke College and an MBA in finance from Northwestern University's Kellogg Graduate School of Management. Mary Anne has more than 11 years of educational experience, ranging from elementary and secondary education to Montgomery County Community College, Muhlenberg College, and Bucks County Community College, as well as training in the professional environment. Before teaching, she was a vice-president at Shearson Lehman Hutton in the Municipal Bond Investment Banking Department.

mpoatsy@comcast.net

Kendall Martin, Ph.D.

Kendall has been teaching since 1988 at a number of institutions, including Villanova University, DeSales University, Arcadia University, Ursinus College, County College of Morris, and Montgomery County Community College at both the undergraduate and graduate levels. Kendall's education includes a BSc in electrical engineering from the University of Rochester and an MSc and Ph.D. in engineering from the University of Pennsylvania. She has industrial experience in research and development environments (AT&T Bell Laboratories) as well as experience with several start-up technology firms. At Ursinus College, Kendall developed a successful faculty training program for distance education instructors. She makes conference presentations throughout the year.

kmartin@mc3.edu

Jeff Short

Jeff Short is a Professor of Management and Strategy at Humber College who makes Introduction to Business a fun and practical experience. Jeff's students learn through experimentation and apply their new knowledge by playing business simulations, participating in small group discussions and planning meetings, and extensive reflection over their results. Jeff holds an MBA from the Schulich School of Business at York University, a degree in psychology, professional designations in human resources management and industrial relations, and is a Certified Master Trainer. Prior to beginning his teaching career, Jeff held several consulting and leadership roles with the Government of Canada, presided over a national youth volunteer network, and operated his own small business.

jeff.short@humber.ca

Sandra Wellman

Sandra Wellman has been a professor at Seneca College for the past 18 years. Prior to joining the faculty at Seneca, she taught economics, finance, and risk management at the Schulich School of Business at York University at both the graduate and undergraduate levels. Sandra has also taught purchasing and supply chain management and retail management online for OntarioLearn for the past eight years. Sandra completed her undergraduate degree in economics at Queen's University and her graduate work at the University of Western Ontario. She is the co-author of *Macroeconomics*, Second Canadian Edition, with Elijah James, as well as the author of many instructor supplements in the areas of economics, operations management, retail management, international business, and marketing.

sandra.wellman@senecacollege.ca

Kerri Shields

Kerri is a college professor who enjoys learning as much as she enjoys teaching. Her education includes a Computer Programmer Diploma from Centennial College, a Bachelor of General Studies (Arts and Science) from Athabasca University, and an MBA (Marketing and Finance) from Columbia Southern University. She has taught information systems, office administration, and business courses at Centennial College, St. Lawrence College Saint-Laurent, Seneca College, and Loyalist College, both in the face-to-face and online learning environments. Before becoming a professor at Centennial College she worked as a consultant and project manager for a multinational workforce solutions provider where she held positions in training and development, information technology, management, recruitment and selection, sales and marketing, customer service, and quality control. The breadth of her work experiences and her ability to transfer learning and knowledge from one field to another is what makes her a unique and effective professor. As a result of student nominations, Kerri was selected from a prestigious group of contenders as the recipient of the Government of Ontario's Leadership in Faculty Teaching (LIFT) Award and the Centennial College Board of Governors Teaching Excellence Award.

kerrishields@rogers.com

Acknowledgements

Thanks are due to the team at Pearson Canada, including Carolin Sweig, Acquisitions Editor; Karen Townsend, Program Manager; Paul Donnelly, Developmental Editor; and Jessica Hellen, Project Manager.

And a big "thank you" to each of the reviewers who provided invaluable feedback that helped shape the content of the textbook and the online resources that accompany it:

John Amendola, Seneca College
Laurentiu David, Centennial College
Edmund DelSol, Centennial College
Geoff Dewar, George Brown College
Sandi Findlay-Thompson, Mount Saint Vincent University
Dave Fleming, George Brown College
Gina Grandy, Mount Allison University
Patrick Hung, University of Ontario Institute of Technology
Karyn Mart, Southern Alberta Institute of Technology
Craig Stephenson, Conestoga College/McMaster University
Peter Tingling, Simon Fraser University

1 Business Fundamentals

whyhire.me

LEARNING OBJECTIVES

After studying this chapter, you should be able to:

- **LO1** Define business and explain the importance of profit. (pp. 3–4)
- **LO2** Describe how business benefits the members of society. (pp. 4–5)
- **LO3** Explain the difference between for-profit and nonprofit organizational goals. (pp. 5–7)
- **LO4** Describe the factors of production. (pp. 7–9)
- **LO5** Explain why entrepreneurs and technology are essential to the production of goods and services. (p. 9)
- **LO6** Describe the private enterprise system and how competition affects business in Canada. (pp. 9–10)
- **LO7** Identify and describe the main purposes of the functional areas of most businesses. (pp. 10–14)

OPENING DISCUSSION: STARTING A NEW BUSINESS

The WhyHire.me Innovation

As Facebook, LinkedIn, Twitter, and myriad other online social media sites become increasingly prevalent, more employers are scrutinizing these networking sites to screen potential employees. In a 2009 CareerBuilder survey, 45 percent of the 2600 employers surveyed reported that they research job candidates through social media.[1] Because of content found on social networking sites, 35 percent of employers reported that they chose *not to hire* candidates. Obviously, it is becoming imperative for job seekers to ensure their online image is not diminishing their job opportunities.

While teaching career positioning to a marketing class in 2008, Patti Church realized that students needed to start thinking about this topic sooner rather than later. At the same time, Andy Church and Robert Saric were discussing the value of having an established online personal brand when looking for employment after noticing the tremendous positive impact it had on their own job search efforts. Patti brought to Robert's and Andy's attention the point that many university and college students do not realize how transparent they are on the web. The three entrepreneurs formed a legal partnership and set out to develop a social media tool that would not only educate students about professional personal branding, but also provide a venue whereby students could safely build an online career portfolio to showcase their skills, abilities, and knowledge; establish a positive online reputation; and proactively position themselves to get hired! It was time to start using digital tools for a digital generation.

Their efforts resulted in WhyHire.me, a career success platform where students can create a professional and unique online brand presence.[2] As head of curriculum design, Patti leads the development of learning materials and overall student learning experience. With his considerable experience in education technology 2.0, stakeholder management, and growing global brands for publishers, Andy is responsible for the development of product requirements and go-to-market planning. Robert—a right-brained engineer and head of digital—is responsible for the strategy and development of all online career success services and solutions.

Additional WhyHire.me facts (as of 2011):

- The entrepreneurial team funded the new venture from personal capital, up-front money paid by their first client in support of developing the prototype, and government grants.
- WhyHire.me's mission statement is "To create a safe learning space for post-secondary students to experiment and learn about the power of social media as a personal marketing tool."[3]
- The ongoing development process will never stop. The team is constantly applying user feedback to consider possible system enhancements, developments, and new features offered by the open-source community.
- Each entrepreneurial team member is working two jobs. At different times, each of them has a different emphasis on WhyHire.me and their other contract work. It is a delicate balancing act when self-financing your own business.
- Sales and marketing are done by all three team members, but contractors are used for various functions, including accounting, legal, graphic design, specialty programming, and sales lead generation.
- The entrepreneurial team is not being paid because all revenue goes toward programming and other contracting costs.
- Social media (i.e., Twitter, blogging, social channels) and personal selling have been the entrepreneurial team's primary marketing tools and have opened the doors to the clients they currently have.

Patti says, "It's very hard to stay ahead of the competition, especially when there are free tools in the marketplace which people often compare us to. Understanding our positioning is key and being able to clearly communicate it is important also."[4]

DISCUSSION QUESTIONS

1. Visit the WhyHire.me website and compare this social media tool to others. Do you think this was a good business idea? What are the risks?
2. Do you think WhyHire.me could become as popular as LinkedIn or Facebook? Why or why not? What can these partners do to grow their business?
3. What types of issues or problems do you think these entrepreneurs have had to deal with or will have to deal with?

WHAT IS BUSINESS?

LO1 Define business and explain the importance of profit.

Business is any activity that provides goods or services for the purpose of earning profit. Some businesses produce physical/tangible **goods**, such as clothing, automobiles, or computers, while other businesses offer **services**, such as auto repair, health care, or live entertainment. Some businesses, such as restaurants or home renovation, provide both goods and services—food prepared and delivered with a smile, or a new swimming pool installed in your backyard. Every business needs to sell its products to a sufficient number of customers who are willing to buy the products at a price that enables the business to earn a profit. A **profit** is earned when a company's **revenue** (the total amount of money received for goods and services provided) is greater than its **expenses** (costs incurred to produce and sell the goods or services offered by the business). A **loss** occurs when a company's revenue is less than its expenses.

business Any activity that provides goods or services for the purpose of earning profit.

goods Any physical products offered by a business.

services Intangible products that are bought or sold.

profit A profit is earned when a company's revenue is greater than its expenses.

revenue The total amount of money received for goods and services provided.

expenses Costs incurred to produce and sell the goods or services offered by a business.

loss A loss occurs when a company's revenue is less than its expenses.

Donskarpo/Shutterstock

Example Profit Calculation

Example: Calculating Profit

Bob's T-shirt Hut sells T-shirts at a local shopping mall. Last month Bob sold 400 custom T-shirts at a price of $20 each. Bob purchased the plain unprinted cotton shirts from a supplier at a cost of $5 each, and his cost for the artwork that was printed on each shirt sold was $1 per shirt. Bob paid his employee $10 per hour and she worked 160 hours last month. In addition, Bob paid $1000 rent to the mall.

How much profit did Bob's T-shirt Hut earn last month?

Profit	=	Revenue	−	Expenses	
		400 shirts sold × $20 per shirt = $8000		Unprinted shirts: 400 shirts × $5 each	$2000
				Artwork: 400 shirts × $1 per print	$400
				Wages: $10 per hour × 160 hours	$1600
				Rent:	$1000
				Total expenses:	$5000

Profit = Revenue − Expenses
= $8000 − $5000
= $3000

Therefore, Bob's T-shirt Hut earned a profit of $3000 last month.

Richest People in Canada (2014) (CDN$)

1. Thomson family: Thomson Reuters, Woodbridge Co. Ltd. (media, information, distribution) — $26.1 billion
2. Galen Weston: George Weston Ltd., Loblaw Companies Ltd., Holt Renfrew (food, groceries, retail, real estate) — $10.4 billion
3. Irving family: Irving Oil Ltd. (oil, forestry products, gas stations, media, transportation, real estate) — $7.85 billion
4. Rogers family: Rogers Communications Inc. (cable TV, communications, media, pro sports) — $7.6 billion
5. James Pattison: Jim Pattison Group (auto sales, food, media, forestry products, entertainment, export services) — $7.39 billion
6. Saputo family: Saputo Inc. (food, real estate, transportation) — $5.24 billion
7. Estate of Paul Desmarais: Power Corporation of Canada (financial services, media) — $4.93 billion
8. Jeffrey Skoll: eBay Inc. Participant Media (Internet, media) — $4.92 billion
9. Richardson family: James Richardson & Sons Ltd. (financial management) — $4.45 billion
10. Carlo Fidani: Orlando Corp. (real estate) — $4.08 billion

Source: "Top 25 richest people in Canada 2014".

Why Is Profit Important?

More often than not, profit is the driving force behind a business' growth. As more profit is generated, a company is able to reward its employees, increase its productivity, or expand its business into new areas. Profit provides incentive and rewards businesspeople for taking the risks involved in developing and selling new goods and services that consumers value. In other words, profit is what motivates entrepreneurs to start and operate a business.

How Does Business Benefit Society?

LO2 Describe how business benefits the members of society.

The proprietor of a business is not the only one who benefits from earned profits and business success. A successful business provides the goods and services people need and want, provides employment opportunities for members of the community, pays taxes, and generates income and spending in the economy. Socially responsible firms contribute even more by actively advocating for the well-being of the society that generates their success.

Successful businesses help to raise a country's standard of living and improve the quality of life. A country's **standard of living** is the level of wealth, comfort, material goods, and necessities available to its people. It is the ease by which people living in a time or place are able to satisfy their needs and wants. It is generally measured by standards such as income per person and poverty rate. Other measures are also used, such as access to and quality of health care, income-growth inequality, availability of employment, environmental quality, and educational standards. One measure of the standard of living is the United Nations Human Development Index (HDI). High ratings for health care, educational attainment, public safety, environmental sustainability, and social development in terms of gender equality helped Canada place eleventh out of 169 countries on the 2012 HDI.[5]

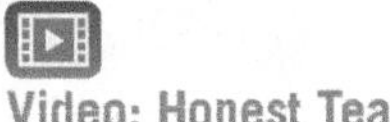
Video: Honest Tea

standard of living The level of wealth, comfort, material goods, and necessities available to a country's people. It is the ease by which people living in a time or place are able to satisfy their needs and wants. It is generally measured by standards such as income per person and poverty rate.

Highest Standard of Living

According to the United Nations Human Development Index, these are the top 10 countries with the highest standard of living in 2014:

1. Norway
2. Australia
3. Switzerland
4. Netherlands
5. United States
6. Germany
7. New Zealand
8. Canada
9. Singapore
10. Denmark

Source: United Nations Development Programme, "Human Development Index (HDI)," Copyright © 2011 by Human Development Report Office. Used by the permission of Human Development Report Office.

The idea of a country's "standard" of living may be contrasted with the **quality of life**, which is more subjective and intangible. It takes into account not only the material standard of living, but also more intangible aspects that make up human life, such as environmental quality, good health, social interactions, leisure time, and a general belief that "life is good." According to the Organisation for Economic Co-operation and Development's (OECD) 2011 Better Life Initiative survey, Canada ranked second (after Australia) out of 34 countries in terms of having the best quality of life.[6]

quality of life A subjective and intangible measure that takes into account not only a country's material standard of living, but also more intangible aspects that make up human life, such as environmental quality, good health, social interactions, leisure time, and a general belief that "life is good."

Do All Businesses Operate to Create a Profit?

LO3 Explain the difference between for-profit and nonprofit organizational goals.

Not every organization that generates revenue and pays expenses is considered a for-profit business. They may operate like a business, but **nonprofit organizations** do not go into business to pursue profits. Instead, a nonprofit, also referred to as a not-for-profit, organization seeks to serve its community through social, educational, or political means. Organizations such as universities, hospitals, environmental groups, and charities are nonprofit organizations (such as the Canadian Diabetes Association, Canadian Cancer Society, and Canadian Red Cross). Any excess revenue they generate is used to further their stated mission. Nonprofit and voluntary organizations are an extension of the millions of Canadians who direct and support their activities, shaping the quality of our lives and our communities.

Business Sectors

What is the difference between the public and private business sectors?

Businesses are often categorized into specific groupings called sectors, which can be based on business activities, how profits are managed, or the industry in which the business operates.

The **public business sector** includes goods and services produced, delivered, and allocated by the government and public sector organizations (publicly controlled

public business sector Includes goods and services produced, delivered, and allocated by the government and public sector organizations (publicly controlled government business enterprises).

Canadian Diabetes Association

Manitoban Louise Yurchak is one of the many dedicated volunteers who support the nonprofit Canadian Diabetes Association.

government business enterprises). The government sector includes all federal, provincial, territorial, and municipal government ministries and departments. It also includes public school boards, public universities and colleges, and public health and social service institutions. Public sector organizations operate in the marketplace, often in competition with privately owned organizations. Government may have direct or indirect control over public sector organizations, which are also referred to as Crown corporations. The aim of the public sector is to provide services that benefit the public as a whole, either because it would be difficult to charge people for the goods and services concerned or because people might not be able to afford to pay for them. The government can provide these goods and services at a lower price than if they were provided by a for-profit company. Examples include public utilities (such as water and sewage, electricity, and gas) and nationalized industries (such as coal and steel).

private business sector Includes goods and services produced and delivered by private individuals or groups as a means of enterprise for profit.

The **private business sector** includes goods and services produced and delivered by private individuals or groups as a means of enterprise for profit. The sector is not controlled by government. These businesses can be small firms owned by just one person or large multinational businesses that operate globally. Large businesses may have many thousands of owners. A public (or publicly traded) company within the private business sector is not part of the public sector (government-provided services and government-owned organizations); it is a particular kind of private sector company that can offer its shares for sale to the general public (e.g., Microsoft, Apple, BlackBerry, Rogers Communications).

nonprofit and voluntary sector Includes nongovernmental, nonprofit organizations that receive support from individual Canadians, governments, and businesses.

The **nonprofit and voluntary sector** includes nongovernmental, nonprofit organizations that receive support from individual citizens, governments, and businesses. Nonprofit organizations (NPOs) are also referred to as private voluntary organizations (PVOs), not-for-profit organizations (NFPOs), or nongovernmental organizations (NGOs). In the global business world, there is inconsistency in how these terms are defined. A nonprofit organization could be a not-for-profit corporation or an unincorporated association. A not-for-profit corporation is usually created with a specific purpose in mind and could be a foundation or charity or other type of nonprofit organization. A private voluntary association is a group of volunteers who enter into an agreement to form an organized body to accomplish a purpose. In this textbook, not-for-profit corporations, private voluntary organizations, and nongovernmental organizations are classified in the nonprofit and voluntary sector as nonprofit organizations.

Nonprofit organizations have the ability to respond to issues more quickly than government and are usually formed or expanded in reaction to a community need not being met by the government. The Canadian government recognizes the importance of the nonprofit sector as a key partner in building a stronger Canada, and it supports the sector in a number of ways, such as partnering, streamlining funding practices and accountability, and developing knowledge on the nonprofit sector.[7] The nonprofit sector often relies heavily on the government for funding.[8]

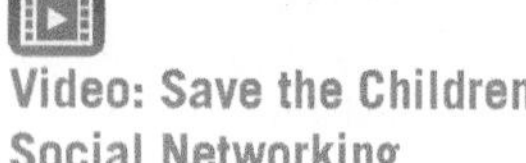

Video: Save the Children: Social Networking

Nonprofit organizations operate in a variety of areas, including sports, religion, arts, culture, fundraising, and housing. The various organizations include hospitals, universities and colleges, education and research organizations, business and professional associations, and unions—CARE, Save the Children, Habitat for Humanity, Greenpeace, and World Vision are all nonprofit organizations. People who work in nonprofit organizations

Kurhan/Shutterstock

Since 1985, volunteers working with Habitat for Humanity have helped over 2200 families in Canada get a safe, decent, and affordable place to call home.[9]

may be paid employees or unpaid volunteers, which is why the sector is called the "nonprofit and voluntary sector."

factors of production The resources used to produce goods and services.

In 2003, Statistics Canada conducted a national survey of nonprofit and voluntary organizations. At that time, approximately 161 000 nonprofit organizations were formally registered or incorporated in Canada, of which about 80 000 were registered charities. Charities registered with the federal government are exempt from a variety of taxes and enable donors to claim tax credits for the donations they make. Collectively, these charities reported annual revenues of $112 billion and employed more than 2 million people. With the exclusion of hospitals, universities, and colleges, the sector had $75 billion in revenues and 1.3 million employees.[10]

Factors of Production

LO4 Describe the factors of production.

What resources are needed to produce goods or services? To understand fully how a business operates, you must consider the **factors of production**, which are the resources (inputs) used to produce goods and services (outputs). For years, businesses focused on four traditional factors: labour, natural resources, capital, and entrepreneurial talent (see **Figure 1.1**). However, in the

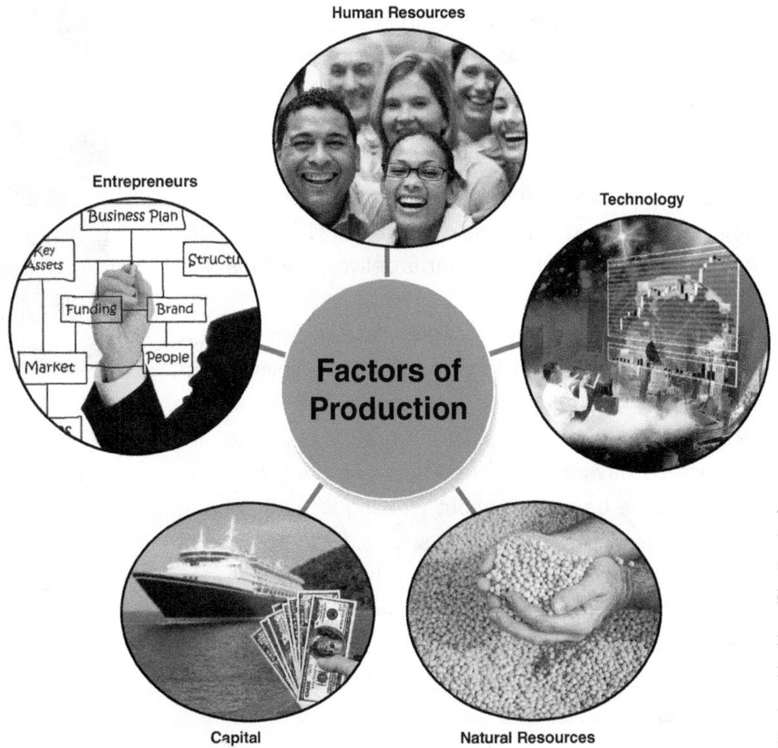

Stephen VanHorn/Shutterstock

Figure 1.1 Factors of Production

economy of the twenty-first century, an additional factor has become increasingly important: technology.

labour The human resource that refers to any physical or intellectual work people contribute to business production.

natural resources The raw materials provided by nature and used to produce goods and services.

real capital The physical facilities used to produce goods and services.

financial capital Money used to facilitate a business enterprise.

- *Labour.* Businesses need people to get things produced. **Labour** is the human resource that refers to any physical or intellectual work people contribute to business production and includes all people who work to produce goods and services. Human resources can be a key element of a company's success, and as such companies invest great effort in hiring and motivating effective employees.
- *Natural resources.* Most workers who provide the labour to produce a good need something tangible to work with. **Natural resources** are the raw materials provided by nature and used to produce goods and services. Soil used in agricultural production; trees used for lumber to build houses; and coal, oil, and natural gas used to create energy are all examples of natural resources.
- *Capital.* There are two types of capital: real capital and financial capital. **Real capital** refers to the physical facilities used to produce goods and services. **Financial capital** is the money used to facilitate a business enterprise. In Canada, financial capital can

On Target

Newman Forge & Pattern: Turning a Hobby into a Business

"A business plan? I'm not an MBA—I don't do those things," jokes John Newman. In reality, the no-nonsense entrepreneur from Hamilton, Ontario, has massive plans for his blacksmithing and pattern-making shop, Newman Forge & Pattern. When his employer downsized in 2003, rather than look for another job John decided to turn his hobby into a business. After years of blacksmithing in his home garage, he purchased a proper shop in an industrial area and opened for business. Although nerve-racking, John says starting his own shop was the best decision he could have made: "The only time I had second thoughts was when I was at the shop at two or three in the morning, pulling all-nighters to meet a delivery. But it's definitely been worth it."

Turning a hobby into a career isn't as fun as you'd think, he asserts—it can take some of the enjoyment out of it, because it's no longer your escape from work. "But you can start your business at a more gradual pace, and you already have a lot of the equipment, which helps." John says the best thing about working alone and being his own boss is flexibility: "If it snows, I can sometimes skip work and go skiing!" However, there are downsides. "There's no one to collaborate with, and it can be lonely at times." Soon John plans to expand his shop and add a few employees, but for now it's just him. "I set out a plan, and I don't leave until I get it done."[11]

John Newman

Discussion Questions

1. **Do you think the initial capital investment John needed to start his business was very large? How do you think he might have got the money to start this business?**
2. **When John decided to start his own business, what factors of production do you think he required?**
3. **How do you think technology might help John expand his business?**

be acquired through business loans, from investors, or through other forms of fundraising, or even by tapping into personal savings.

- *Entrepreneurs.* An **entrepreneur** is someone who assumes the risk of creating, organizing, and operating a business and who directs all the business resources. Entrepreneurs are a human resource, just like labour, but what sets entrepreneurs apart from labour is their willingness to take risks and their ability to manage an enterprise to bring their ideas to market. Successful entrepreneurs are rewarded with profits for bearing risks and for their expertise in creating goods and services that consumers are willing to pay for.
- *Technology.* **Technology** includes human knowledge, work methods, physical equipment, electronics and telecommunications, and various processing systems used to perform business activities. Technology also refers to items and services such as smartphones, computer software, and digital broadcasting that make businesses more efficient and productive. Successful companies are able to keep pace with technological progress and harness new knowledge, information, and strategies. Unsuccessful organizations typically fail because they have not kept pace with the latest technology and techniques.

entrepreneur Someone who assumes the risk of creating, organizing, and operating a business and who directs all the business resources.

technology Includes human knowledge, work methods, physical equipment, electronics and telecommunications, and various processing systems used to perform business activities.

LO5 Explain why entrepreneurs and technology are essential to the production of goods and services.

Video: Muttville: Seven Key Business Rules in the Pursuit of Success

Why are entrepreneurs so important? Entrepreneurs are the innovators who create business ideas and start businesses from those ideas. They attempt to make a profit by combining the factors of production (inputs) to create goods and services (outputs). For example, the factors of production used to produce a pizza in a pizza restaurant would include

- the land that the pizza restaurant is located on, the electricity used to run the store, and the wheat and other food products from which the pizza is made;
- the labourers who make the pizzas;
- the store and equipment used to make the pizza, and the money used to operate the business;
- the technology used to gather customer information, market to customers, deliver to customers, track inventory, and reorder supplies; and
- the entrepreneurship skills used to coordinate the other factors of production to initiate the production process.

Why is technology a key factor in production? Companies do not require technology for the sake of technology alone. Rather, technology has become a critical factor for obtaining and managing **information and knowledge**, which are quickly becoming the key factors of production as the new competitive business environment places a premium on these factors. Not only do companies need technology to obtain and manage information, they need human resources (knowledge workers) with the skills to manipulate the information and turn it into knowledge that the company can use for competitive advantage. Knowledge is a tricky thing to manage, but companies can translate their information assets into real value for the business by learning from past successes or failures, identifying opportunities to improve profitability, or simply enabling teams to become more productive. With increased mobility of information and the global workforce, information and knowledge can be transported around the world.

information and knowledge Quickly becoming the key factors of production as the new competitive business environment places a premium on these factors.

Video: MINI: Working in a Virtual World

THE PRIVATE ENTERPRISE SYSTEM

LO6 Describe the private enterprise system and how competition affects business in Canada.

How Is Business Conducted in Canada?

Although Canada's economic system is a mixed market economy, where government intervenes to protect the interests of society (this is described in greater depth in Chapter 3), the founding principles upon which business and consumers in Canada exchange goods and

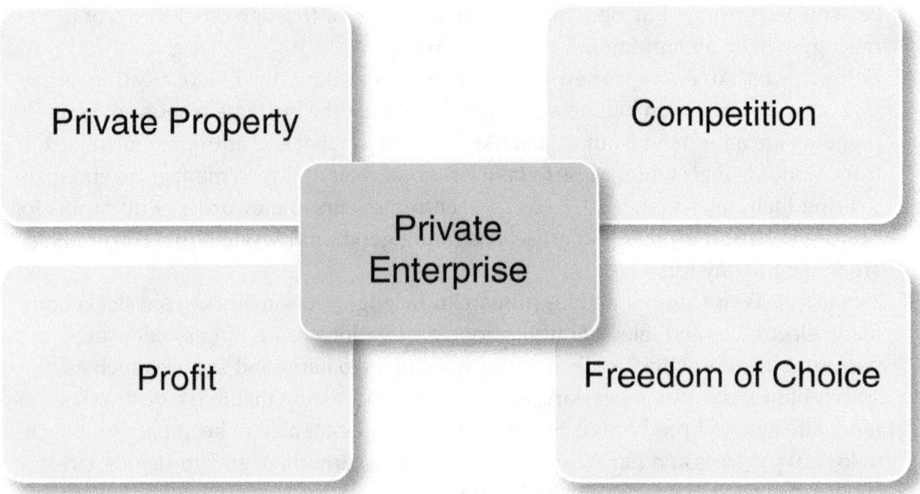

Figure 1.2 Four Basic Rights of Private Enterprise

services for money is based on the private enterprise system (also referred to as *capitalism* or a *market economy*). This system allows individuals and businesses to make their own economic choices.

Competition is the basis of the private enterprise system. Businesses that best satisfy the needs of consumers are rewarded with profit, and businesses that fail to satisfy the needs of customers do not survive. To be successful, businesses must satisfy their customer's needs better than their rivals by either offering a superior product or by offering a good product at a lower price. The competitive nature of the private enterprise system requires businesses to constantly monitor the preferences and needs of customers and the competitive moves of rivals so that they can remain competitive. This benefits consumers because businesses develop new or better-quality products and offer greater value as they compete to attract customers.

The private enterprise system is based on four basic rights (shown in **Figure 1.2**):

- *Private property.* The right to own, buy, sell, or leave as an inheritance private property, including land, patents on inventions, and private possessions.
- *Competition.* The right to fair competition in the marketplace.
- *Profits.* The right to all after-tax profits earned through business activities.
- *Freedom of choice.* The right to own and conduct business, change jobs, negotiate wages, and choose which products to buy.

Functional Areas of Business

LO7 Identify and describe the main purposes of the functional areas of most businesses.

functional areas Separate departments where business activities are grouped by similar tasks or skills.

What activities are needed to operate a business? **Functional areas** in businesses are often separate departments where business activities are grouped by similar tasks or skills. In larger, more complex organizations these departments have responsibility for carrying out specific activities to ensure that the business operates efficiently to achieve its objectives. Each department often employs people who have specialized training and expertise in these areas. For example, the accounting and finance departments employ people with accounting designations, human resources will include experts with specialized training and who often have credentials in human resources, and sales and marketing will include employees with the necessary knowledge and talent to develop new markets and maximize sales of the company's products. This kind of specialization allows employees to focus their efforts on developing higher levels of expertise in their chosen careers.

Figure 1.3 Functional Areas of Business

Smaller businesses must conduct the same business functions but on a smaller scale, so they do not always have separate departments for each functional area. For example, in most new small businesses, the owner may be involved in running all aspects of the company on his or her own. However, as the business grows, the volume and difficulty of the activities become too difficult for one person to manage, so more of the specific tasks will need to be assigned to different employees, and as the company grows further and more employees are hired, the owner may decide to create different departments to take responsibility for certain activities. People are organized in different ways in different organizations, depending on factors such as the size of the organization, the culture of the organization, the nature of the industry, and the preferred structures of the managers.

The main functional areas you will often see in businesses are sales and marketing, operations, customer service, accounting and finance, human resources, research and development, and information technology (see **Figure 1.3**). Each of the functional areas of business will be discussed in more detail.

The sales and marketing function For any business to exist it must sell its products to customers, so sales and marketing are necessary functions for all businesses. Marketing involves researching to identify potential opportunities to develop and sell products that will satisfy the needs of certain types of customers. Marketers are involved in recommending which products the company should develop, what price to charge, determining how best to get the products to the customer, and creating strategies to promote customer awareness and demand for the company's products. The marketing function is closely linked with sales. Sales representatives are the direct link to the customer, so they not only need to be friendly, they must also be knowledgeable about the products and able to demonstrate how the product will best satisfy the customer's needs. In some industries, sales representatives are involved in negotiating the terms of a sale with a customer and may need to travel to meet potential clients or to make sure that existing customers are satisfied.

The operations function All businesses are involved in the production of goods or services. The operations function is responsible for managing the resources used to produce and deliver the company's products and services. Operations are a core aspect of the business; it is how physical goods are manufactured or services are delivered to customers. Production staff ensures that goods are produced on time, are of the right quality, and that service procedures are developed and implemented to meet customer expectations. In manufacturing, operations staff are involved in identifying and contracting with suppliers of raw materials and managing inventory levels to minimize unnecessary costs of production. The operations function involves designing and determining the best way to produce and deliver goods and services. Today, many production processes are automated using machines or robots to do the routine tasks; however, production employees are also involved and frequently work in teams to ensure that goods are produced on time and at appropriate quality standards. In service companies, operations staff are likely frontline workers and have direct contact with customers on a daily basis; as such, they represent the company and directly impact the customer's experience.

The customer service function For a business to remain successful in the long term, it must work to ensure that customers are satisfied with the goods and services purchased from the company. When customers experience problems with the product or have complaints or questions, they expect a polite, quick, and helpful response from the company. If the level of service is poor, they will not only take future business elsewhere, they will likely tell others about their dissatisfaction and possibly cause additional lost sales. To help manage a positive relationship with customers, many businesses have a customer service department, where trained staff attempt to resolve customer enquiries and complaints. The interaction between customer service representatives and customers is most often done over the telephone; however, online chat has grown in popularity. Depending on the industry, customer service representatives not only require excellent people skills so they can help unhappy customers, but also often require a high level of technical skills and product knowledge to be able to address customer concerns.

Video: Dunkin' Donuts

Video: Stew Leonards

The accounting and finance function All businesses need to keep track of their financial situation to ensure that they are profitable and able to pay their bills. Accounting and finance staff keep track of the money coming into and going out of the business. Employees in finance and accounting are involved in keeping financial records, paying for items the company purchases, and following up with customers who may be late making payments, and they may also prepare staff payroll. An important function of accounting and finance is the production of financial reports that managers use to know how much profit (or loss) is being made by the business's activities. Senior managers use the information provided by these reports to make critical decisions about the direction the business should take. Finally, accounting and finance staff develop plans to help the company determine how to pay for expansion plans and investment in new equipment that will be used long into the future.

The human resources (HR) function The human resources of a business are its employees, and the quality of these employees directly impacts the long-term success of the company. The human resources function is responsible for conducting research to ensure that the organization's current and future labour demands are satisfied. People involved in the human resources function are responsible for recruiting and hiring qualified employees, who are needed to achieve the organization's objectives. They also ensure that employees are properly trained and able to complete their work efficiently, effectively, and safely. Because employees are so valuable to the business, human resources attempts to ensure that the company retains good, experienced staff by creating policies outlining fair treatment and compensation while also making sure that working conditions balance productivity concerns with employee well-being. Human resources is also involved when employees need to be let go from the company, either because the company has too many employees and needs to downsize or because of performance issues. In all jurisdictions, organizations are subject to laws that protect the employment rights of workers as well as set health and safety standards. A critical role for staff involved in the human resources function is to understand and stay up to date with changes to relevant laws to ensure that the business complies with these requirements.

The research and development (R&D) function Research and development is a long-term investment that supports the company's future growth by improving existing products and developing new products that the company can produce and sell to customers. In most companies, R&D staff work to develop practical products that consumers will want to buy. R&D attempts to find the best ways to design products so they can be manufactured at a reasonable cost and therefore sold at a competitive price. R&D not only influences the products available to consumers, but also the ways in which the business operates. For example, technological advances in computers have increased efficiency and changed the ways that companies do business (online sales, management information systems, email, etc.), and the development of technologies such as robotics have completely changed how many products are manufactured. Depending on the industry, the types of activities vary greatly: For example, drug research by a pharmaceutical company is very different from trying to improve the speed of a computer chip or create a new flavour of ice cream. So R&D departments employ staff who are often very specialized, such as designers, scientists, engineers, software developers, or technologists.

Video: Sports Drinks Science: Is It Hype?

The information technology (IT) function The information technology function is vital to a business because most business tasks are done using a computer. IT staff support the organization's employees by answering questions and fixing technical problems that arise. Larger organizations often connect employees through a computer network, so staff involved in information technology are involved in maintaining servers and installing hardware and software. Experts working in information technology also advise company managers on opportunities to use new technologies that can benefit the

Simulation: Technology Direction

LDprod/Shutterstock

In 2012, Canadians spent $18.9 billion online for goods and services.[12]

business and are typically involved in acquiring and installing new computer equipment. Many businesses use the Internet to manage relationships with suppliers, and for some businesses their online presence is their only connection with their customers, so reliable information technology is vital. Considering the critical nature of the organization's data and the growing importance of privacy, a top priority for the information technology function is system security. Staff working in the information technology function are diligent about protecting the system from viruses and hackers, and invest a great deal of effort to devise plans for backing up data so that it can be restored if ever lost because of a disaster.

Why do the different functional areas need to work collaboratively? In larger organizations, where people are physically separated by departments, coordinating the business's efforts is a challenge for management. For a business to achieve its objectives, all of the functional areas must work closely together. There must be regular communication between departmental managers and staff, because each department has information that the others need to make effective decisions. For example, R&D needs to work closely with marketing to know what products consumers want to buy; operations needs to know sales forecasts so they can create production schedules to satisfy customer orders on time; and customer service needs to share the details of customer complaints that might affect production or marketing. Alignment between the various functional areas is critical for any organization to achieve its goals.

CHAPTER SYNOPSIS

LO1 Define business and explain the importance of profit. *(pp. 3–4)*

Business is any activity that provides goods or services for the purpose of earning profit. Some businesses produce physical/tangible goods, while other businesses offer services. Every business needs to sell its products to a sufficient number of customers who are willing to buy the products at a price that enables the business to earn a profit. A **profit** is earned when a company's **revenue** (the total amount of money received for goods and services provided) is greater than its **expenses** (the costs incurred to produce and sell the goods or services offered by the business). A **loss** occurs when a company's revenue is less than its expenses.

More often than not, profit is the driving force behind a business's growth. As more profit is generated, a company is able to reward its employees, increase its productivity, or expand its business into new areas. Profit provides an incentive and rewards businesspeople for taking the risks involved in developing and selling new goods and services that consumers value. In other words, profit is what motivates entrepreneurs to start and operate a business.

LO2 Describe how business benefits the members of society. *(pp. 4–5)*

The proprietor of a business is not the only one who benefits from earned profits and business success. A successful business provides the goods and services people need and want, provides employment opportunities for members of the community, pays taxes, and generates income and spending in the economy. Socially responsible firms contribute even more by actively advocating for the well-being of the society that generates their success. Successful businesses help raise a country's standard of living and improve the quality of life. A country's **standard of living** is the level of wealth, comfort, material goods, and necessities available to its people; it is the ease by which people living in a time or place are able to satisfy their needs and wants. **Quality of life** is subjective and intangible. It takes into account not only the material standard of living, but also the more intangible aspects that make up human life, such as environmental quality, good health, social interactions, leisure time, and a general belief that "life is good."

LO3 Explain the difference between for-profit and nonprofit organizational goals. *(pp. 5–7)*

The main objective of a for-profit business is to offer goods and services to customers to earn a profit. Nonprofit organizations, however, do not go into business to pursue profits. Instead, a **nonprofit** (also referred to as a not-for-profit) organization seeks to serve its community through social, educational, or political means. Organizations such as universities, hospitals, environmental groups, and charities are nonprofit organizations. Any excess revenue they generate is used to further their stated mission. They often direct their activities toward shaping the quality of our lives and our communities.

LO4 Describe the factors of production. *(pp. 7–9)*

The **factors of production** are the resources used to produce goods and services. They include labour, natural resources, capital, entrepreneurial talent, and technology.

- **Labour** is the human resource that refers to any physical or intellectual work people contribute to business production.
- **Natural resources** are the raw materials provided by nature and used to produce goods and services.
- Capital includes both **real capital** (the physical facilities used to produce goods and services) and **financial capital** (the money used to facilitate a business enterprise).
- **Entrepreneurs** are people who assume the risk of creating, organizing, and operating a business and who direct all of the business's resources.
- **Technology** includes human knowledge, work methods, physical equipment, electronics and telecommunications, and various processing systems used to perform business activities.

LO5 Explain why entrepreneurs and technology are essential to the production of goods and services. (p. 9)

Entrepreneurs are the innovators who create business ideas and start businesses from those ideas. They invest in bringing their business ideas to life and attempt to make a profit by combining the factors of production to create goods and services. Without entrepreneurs no business would start, and the goods and services society values would not exist.

Technology refers to items and services such as smartphones, computer software, and digital broadcasting that make businesses more efficient and productive. Successful companies are able to keep pace with technological progress and harness new knowledge, information, and strategies. **Information and knowledge** are quickly becoming the key factors of production because the new competitive business environment places a premium on these factors. Successful companies use technology to create real value for the business by learning from past successes or failures, identifying opportunities to improve profitability, or simply improving productivity.

LO6 Describe the private enterprise system and how competition affects business in Canada. (pp. 9–10)

The founding principles upon which businesses and consumers in Canada exchange goods and services for money is based on the private enterprise system (also referred to as capitalism or a market economy). This system allows individuals and businesses to make their own economic choices. Competition is the basis of the private enterprise system. Businesses that best satisfy the needs of consumers are rewarded with profit, and businesses that fail to do so do not survive. To be successful, businesses must satisfy their customer's needs better than rivals by either offering a superior product or offering a good product at a lower price. The competitive nature of the private enterprise system requires businesses to constantly monitor the preferences and needs of customers and the competitive moves of rivals to remain competitive.

LO7 Identify and describe the main purposes of the functional areas of most businesses. (pp. 10–14)

Functional areas in businesses are often separate departments where business activities are grouped by similar tasks or skills, allowing employees to focus their efforts on developing higher levels of expertise in their chosen careers. The main functional areas you will often see in businesses are sales and marketing, operations, customer service, accounting and finance, human resources, research and development, and information technology.

- *Sales and marketing.* Marketing involves identifying opportunities to develop and sell products that will satisfy the needs of certain types of customers and creating strategies to promote customer awareness and demand for the company's products. The marketing function is closely linked with sales; sales representatives are the direct link to the customer.
- *Operations.* The operations function is responsible for managing the resources used to produce and deliver the company's products and services.

Functional Areas of Business

- *Customer service.* To help manage a positive relationship with customers, many businesses have a customer service department, where trained staff attempt to resolve customer enquiries and complaints.
- *Accounting and finance.* Employees in finance and accounting are involved in keeping financial records, paying for items the company purchases, and following up with customers who may be late making payments, and they may also prepare staff payroll. Other important functions of this department are producing financial reports and developing plans to help the company make strategic, financially sound decisions.
- *Human resources (HR).* The human resources function is responsible for ensuring that the organization hires, develops, and retains the talent needed so that it can achieve its objectives. A critical role for HR staff is ensuring that the organization complies with complicated laws related to worker rights and health and safety.
- *Research and development (R&D).* Research and development is a long-term investment that supports the company's future growth by improving existing products and developing new products. R&D also attempts to find the best ways to design products so they can be manufactured at a reasonable cost and therefore sold at a competitive price.
- *Information technology (IT).* IT is vital to a business because most business tasks are done using a computer. IT staff support the organization by helping employees use technology effectively, advising management on new technology opportunities, and ensuring the company's data and systems are protected.

MyBizLab

Study, practise, and explore real business situations with these helpful resources:

- **Interactive Lesson Presentations:** Work through interactive presentations and assessments to test your knowledge of business concepts.
- **Study Plan:** Check your understanding of chapter concepts with self-study quizzes.
- **Dynamic Study Modules:** Work through adaptive study modules on your computer, tablet, or mobile device.
- **Simulations:** Practise decision-making in simulated business environments.

KEY TERMS

business *(p. 3)*
entrepreneur *(p. 9)*
expenses *(p. 3)*
factors of production *(p. 7)*
financial capital *(p. 8)*
functional areas *(p. 10)*
goods *(p. 3)*
information and knowledge *(p. 9)*
labour *(p. 8)*
loss *(p. 3)*
natural resources *(p. 8)*
nonprofit and voluntary sector *(p. 6)*
private business sector *(p. 6)*
profit *(p. 3)*
public business sector *(p. 5)*
quality of life *(p. 5)*
real capital *(p. 8)*
revenue *(p. 3)*
services *(p. 3)*
standard of living *(p. 5)*
technology *(p. 9)*

CRITICAL THINKING QUESTIONS

1. Consider all of the factors of production: labour, natural resources, capital, entrepreneurs, and technology. Is each of these resources a vital part of the school you attend or the company you work for? Which factors do you believe are most important to the goods and services provided by your organization? Why?
2. Give examples of the ways in which each of the five factors of production can affect the business performance of McDonald's or Walmart.
3. If firms competing in the same industry have access to the same labour market, how can a company use employees to create a competitive advantage over rivals?
4. Considering the rapid increase in ecommerce, it is likely that you have purchased or sold some sort of product online. If not, you have probably browsed the webpages of eBay or your favourite clothing store. Can you list a few companies or organizations that do not offer their products or services online? How does their status and growth compare with similar companies who do offer goods and services online?

APPLICATION EXERCISES

1. **Calculating profit.** The Bagel Bar is a small restaurant located in the food court of a local shopping mall. Last month the restaurant sold 2000 bagels at a price of $3 each. The Bagel Barn purchases their bagels from a supplier at a cost of 50¢ each and spent $500 for cream cheese, butter, and other assorted toppings. The two employees are paid $10 per hour and they each worked 160 hours last month. In addition, The Bagel Bar paid $1000 rent to the mall. How much profit did The Bagel Bar earn last month?
2. **The private enterprise system.** Canada's version of capitalism allows for freedom of choice, competition, the right to own private property, and the right to keep profits. Go to Industry Canada's website at www.ic.gc.ca and create a brief summary of some of the ways that government helps to support fair competition in Canada.
3. **Entrepreneurs.** Did you know that there are services available to help people start new businesses? Go online and find out what business incubators are available near your community, and write a brief summary of the kinds of services they offer.
4. **Customer service.** Think about the last time you received excellent customer service. What were some of the reasons you feel that the service was so good? Make up a business and write a brief policy that you believe will guide your employees to ensure that customers experience excellent service. Share your policy with the class.
5. **Functional areas of business.** Assume that you are the CEO of a midsize sporting goods company. Describe what kinds of functional areas you would set up, what each would do to support the company in achieving its goals, and how you would ensure there is coordination between each area.

TEAM TIME

The Competitive Edge

Competition arises when two or more businesses compete to attract consumers and gain an advantage over one another. Divide into three groups: Company A, Company B, and Consumers.

SCENARIO

Companies A and B: Collectively decide what type of business you want to represent (e.g., sports apparel company, beauty salon, or pet care agency), then choose a product or service applicable to that type of business. (Both groups should choose the same type of business and product or service.)

PROCESS

Step 1. ***Companies A and B:*** Decide how you will present your product to your consumers. Focus on the following factors: packaging/presentation, price/budget, quality. *Consumers:* Compile a list of what is important to you when choosing this product or service.

Step 2. ***Companies A and B:*** Provide a brief presentation to your competition and consumers. *Consumers*: Provide in-depth feedback to both companies about how they could improve; consider the initial list you created in Step 1.

Step 3. ***Companies A and B:*** Use the consumer feedback to alter your product or service to gain advantage over your competition.

Consumers: Discuss how the two companies compared to real-life companies offering similar products or services. Would you consider purchasing from either of these two companies? Why or why not?
Step 4. ***Companies A and B:*** Present your product again. Explain why your product or service surpasses that of your competition.
Step 5. ***Consumers:*** Discuss the changes made by both companies and consider how they accommodated your needs. Did each company effectively incorporate your feedback into its revised presentation? Choose one company that you think gained the competitive advantage.
Step 6. ***Entire class:*** Openly discuss the factors real companies must face in competition. Were these factors considered in the challenge?

ETHICS AND RESPONSIBILITY

Standard of Living versus Quality of Life
Standard of living mainly focuses on productivity and increasing financial wealth, while quality of life seems to include a broader range of issues, although some of these appear to negatively impact standard of living.

Process
Step 1. Divide the class into small discussion groups. Half of the class should develop a case that supports the following argument: Canadians would be better off if society focused on productivity to maximize standard of living. The second half of the class will develop a case supporting the position that Canadians would be better off if society prioritized issues that would maximize our quality of life.
Step 2. Once the small groups have had sufficient opportunity to develop their arguments, pair each group with an opposing group. These groups should take turns making their arguments, trying to convince the opposing team to come to their side.
Step 3. With the whole class, discuss the following questions:

a. What are the strongest arguments in support of focusing on standard of living? What do you think we can do to increase standard of living in Canada?
b. What are the strongest arguments in support of focusing on quality of life? What can we do to improve quality of life for Canadians?
c. Is it possible to have both? What could we do to create a balance between standard of living and quality of life?

CLOSING CASE

GE's Imagination Is a Factor of Production

Traditionally, the name Thomas Edison is synonymous with the word *ingenious*. Similarly, his invention of the carbon filament incandescent lamp, or light bulb, is symbolic of all things innovative. This ingenuity and innovation created the building blocks for General Electric (GE). GE is a business that started 130 years ago with a bright idea that developed into a world-changing product. The commercial light bulb not only had a profound impact on people's daily lives, it also gave birth to a business that would eventually grow into one of the world's largest corporations.

The roots of GE started to form in 1876 when Thomas Edison opened a laboratory to experiment with electricity and electric devices. These experiments resulted in the invention of the light bulb. By 1890, Edison had established the Edison General Electric Company. During this time, a competing business, the Thomas-Houston Company, was quickly becoming a leader in the field of electrical technology. Both Edison and Thomas-Houston's head, Charles A. Coffin, realized that with each organization's patents and technologies combined, they could create a successful and innovative company. So in 1892 the two companies merged to create the General Electric Company.[13]

From that initial configuration, GE developed into a massive conglomerate that encompasses six different companies located in 160 countries with more than 300 000 employees worldwide. The company's multifaceted structure was formed by its ability to turn ideas into industry. In 1896, GE introduced the X-ray machine, which represented GE's ability to use important scientific discoveries in a practical manner. This product laid the groundwork for GE Healthcare. Likewise, the first electric fan, invented in 1902, was the first of many modern conveniences that helped develop GE Industrial. GE also formed the first national television network when its station, WRGB, became the first to relay a national broadcast from New York City. Each of these individual achievements produced the opportunity to develop new areas of business.[14]

Despite GE's years of successful growth, like any business it must continue to ask itself, "Why are we here? What do we have to offer?" When GE was first established, its purpose was to bring electric energy and light to the masses through products such as dynamos and electric lamps. Today, GE has a somewhat broader purpose. The company says, "We exist to solve problems for our customers, our communities and societies, and ourselves."[15]

GE considers imagination to be its greatest commodity. While imagination is not a good that you can box up and sell in a store or a service you can order online or over the phone, it is something that GE uses as a factor of production. An active imagination can conjure up innovative goods and services. GE hopes that these goods and services will fuel the global economy and improve people's lives.

Another benefit of imagination is that it has allowed GE to keep up with social and cultural changes. GE has developed high-tech imaging systems to detect cancer in the country's aging population, energy-efficient appliances to combat global warming and help consumers save money, and large-scale infrastructures to help developing countries. Staying in touch with the wants and needs of the market has made GE a successful business for 130 years. Since its inception, GE has tailored its imagination to produce innovative products that are useful to the world. "Anything that won't sell, I don't want to invent. Its sale is proof of utility, and utility is success," stated Thomas Edison. That philosophy is what has allowed GE to turn its imagination into industry, and industry into profits.

DISCUSSION QUESTIONS

1. How important do you think it is for a business to be innovative? Is the newest idea always the best idea? Do you think GE would still be a successful company today if it continued to focus solely on electrical technologies?
2. Why did Edison Electric Company and the Thomas-Houston Company merge? What challenges might each company have encountered if they had remained competitors? Why is it sometimes beneficial for businesses, particularly technology-based businesses, to merge?
3. Thomas Edison is often credited with being the inventor of the light bulb because he created the first light bulb that was appropriate for use in a person's home. Is it important for a business to create products that are practical? Why or why not?

2 The Environment of Business

(left) Darrin Henry/Shutterstock; (right) Kzenon/Shutterstock

LEARNING OBJECTIVES

After studying this chapter, you should be able to:

- **LO1** Describe the macro business environment and explain why managers must be aware of changes taking place. (p. 21)
- **LO2** Explain how managers use the PEST model to analyze external business opportunities and threats. (pp. 21–25)
- **LO3** Explain how sociocultural and technological forces can impact the profitability of a business. (pp. 25–29)
- **LO4** Describe how Porter's five forces model is used to analyze the ways competition affects an industry. (pp. 30–32)
- **LO5** Summarize the four degrees (levels) of competition that may exist within an industry. (pp. 32–33)
- **LO6** Explain why government in Canada allows some monopolies to exist and how consumer interests are protected. (p. 33)
- **LO7** Explain the impact that perfect competition has on selling price. (pp. 33–34)

OPENING DISCUSSION: COFFEE, ECONOMICS, AND FAIR TRADE

Every morning about 28 million Canadians start their day with a cup (often cups) of the world's most popular beverage. No, not beer . . . coffee![1] Worldwide, over 400 billion cups of coffee are consumed every year[2]—enough to fill over 47 000 Olympic-sized swimming pools, or, if each cup were lined up side by side, enough to circle Earth 962 times. Coffee is the second most-traded commodity in the world, preceded only by crude oil. Annually, the coffee industry generates sales in excess of $100 billion—ahead of other commodities such as natural gas, gold, and sugar.[3] In Canada, as in many parts of the industrialized world, "coffee culture" has become central to society, shaping our language, habits, and even our national identity: At work, we "take a coffee break"; we scope out new romantic relationships by "going for coffee"; and as Canadians, Tim Hortons is a national icon (most non-Canadians have no idea what a large double-double is).

With coffee growing only in the tropics, you'd think that Brazil, Vietnam, and Colombia would be prospering as the world's leading producers, but this is far from the case. The majority of the world's coffee is grown on small family-operated farms that have no more than five to seven acres of land. Entire communities come together and usually harvest the coffee beans by hand. It is a long and meticulous process. To be paid the full market price, farmers must transport the beans to nearby cities where roasters purchase them; however, because coffee is grown in remote mountainous locations and few farmers can afford their own truck, they are often forced to sell to middlemen (referred to as "Coyotes") who generally pay them half the market price. The result is that farmers usually bring in a cash income of only $500–$1000 a year.[4]

So who benefits from the $100 billion coffee industry? At Starbucks, one pound of Dark Roast sells for $16.95. One pound can also brew 26 tall-size cups at $1.85 each and will generate revenues of $89. Obviously coffee shops in Canada have expenses related to roasting, importing, handling, labour, and rent, but overall 90 percent of the profits from the coffee industry go to the traders and retailers.[5]

The basic economics of the coffee crop is a major source of this inequity. As a commodity, the market price of coffee is extremely volatile. For example, despite the impressive amount of coffee being consumed, global production exceeded demand by almost 7 million 132-pound bags in 2013. This surplus caused coffee prices to drop to less than $1.50 per pound, but it costs the farmers more than that to grow and harvest the beans.[6]

This is where fair trade comes in. The basic concept is that farmers are guaranteed to receive a minimum price that is intended to cover production costs and allow for a fair wage for their effort. When market prices are low, farmers are guaranteed the floor price; however, when market prices are higher participating buyers agree to pay the higher amount. In addition to the fair trade price, there is an additional sum of money called a fair trade premium. This money is used to improve the social, economic, and environmental conditions in the farmers' communities.[7]

Understanding that their success is tied to the existence of thousands of coffee farmers, the three biggest coffee companies in Canada have begun investing in responsible coffee purchasing practices to ensure a long-term supply of high-quality coffee. Tim Hortons, for example, is involved in a partnership program focused on creating sustainable coffee farming communities, McDonald's sells 100% fair trade espresso and 25% fair trade coffee, and Starbucks has been buying fair trade coffee since 2000 and has plans to only sell ethically sourced coffee by 2015.[8] Although these kinds of initiatives increase costs for coffee companies, it seems likely that the benefit goes beyond ethical motives—it may also make good business sense.

DISCUSSION QUESTIONS

1. Why do you think coffee has become so central to our culture? Can you think of any other current social–cultural issues that might be shaping our society?

2. Thousands of small coffee farmers are victims of the volatility of coffee prices. What could these small farmers do to strengthen their bargaining position and increase their profitability?
3. Why do companies like Starbucks and Tim Hortons participate in fair trade programs when it forces them to pay more for coffee? How might this be good for business?

ENVIRONMENTS OF BUSINESS

Video: Soda Wars Heat Up

Describe the macro business environment and explain why managers must be aware of changes taking place.

The Macro Business Environment

What strategic issues are outside of management's control? Imagine playing a game of chess where, without warning, the rules could change. At any time a third or fourth competitor could enter the game or players could even team up, the size of the game board could increase or decrease, new game pieces with different "powers" could be added, or the objective could switch from taking your opponent's king to some other random piece. In some ways, you might think about the environments of business as "the rules of the game," and these rules are always changing. Using certain analytical tools, organizations attempt to predict these changes and then create or modify strategies in the hopes of achieving positive results.

A **business environment** refers to forces outside the business that can affect the firm's industry and competitive environment. These forces include government regulations and policies, the economy, social and cultural issues, demographic shifts, as well as evolving technologies. Competition in particular has a large impact on all businesses, and this not only includes the strength of rivals but also factors affecting customers, suppliers, distributors, and even products offered by other industries that may not be obvious competitors.

business environment The forces outside the business that can affect the firm's industry and competitive environment.

What are the different business environments in which organizations operate? Organizations operate within a macro business environment and are also affected by their competitive environment. Both affect their potential for success.

The **macro environment** is the external environment over which the organization can exert little influence. This environment is often referred to by the acronym *PEST* (political–legal, economic, sociocultural, and technological). These factors create opportunities for and pose threats to the organization. For example, changes in government policy, fluctuations in the economy, social change, and new technologies can all have a significant effect on a company's success.

macro environment The external environment over which the organization can exert little influence. This environment is often referred to by the acronym *PEST* (political–legal, economic, sociocultural, and technological).

The **competitive environment** includes groups and organizations that have a direct relationship with the business. For example, suppliers, distributors, competitors, and external customers deal with the firm regularly and have a direct interest in the activities of the company because they are clearly affected by its actions.

competitive environment The groups and organizations that have a direct relationship with the business and have an interest in the activities of the company because they are clearly affected by its actions.

THE PEST MODEL

Explain how managers use the PEST model to analyze external business opportunities and threats.

Organizations must continuously consider the environments within which they operate because changes in these environments feed all aspects of corporate planning. Measuring changes in business environments allows organizations to take actions to sustain the company or gain a competitive advantage.

To help analyze the macro environment, managers use several analysis processes to gather, analyze, and dispense information for tactical or strategic purposes. One option is

Kheng Guan Toh/Fotolia

to analyze external factors using the **PEST model**. This classification distinguishes among the following factors:

PEST model A model used to measure changes in the external business environment that might affect the company's ability to prosper. Stands for political–legal, economic, sociocultural, and technological.

- *Political–legal factors.* Government policy and political decisions can affect many vital areas of business. Factors may include ethical considerations, employment laws, competition laws, product regulations, consumer laws, sustainable environmental practices, and health and safety legislation.
- *Economic factors.* Changes in the local, national, or global economy can affect business operations. Factors may include interest rates, economic growth, industry changes, inflation and exchange rates, and taxation changes.
- *Sociocultural factors.* Consumer behaviour and preferences will affect decisions about product offerings. For example, environmentally friendly business processes affect demand patterns and create business opportunities. Other factors may include social trends, demographics, and ethical considerations.
- *Technological factors.* As technology changes, companies must adjust business practices to compete in the global business world. Factors include new technologies, online shopping, research and development, and global access.

There are several variations of the PEST model. Other forms you may encounter include SLEPT analysis (social, legal, economic, political, and technological) or STEEPLE analysis (social/demographic, technological, economic, environmental (nature), political, legal, and ethical), and sometimes PESTLE or PESTEL and PESTLIED (where the *I* represents international). The PEST model used above incorporates all these factors.

Video: Subaru America: The External Environment

Managers regularly analyze the changes measured by the PEST model (see **Table 2.1**) on local, national, and global scales so they can make informed decisions, set goals, and implement strategies to increase business revenue. These factors may include changes in government, popular opinion, fashion trends, weather, and new technology. In addition, changes in one external environment can have an impact on the other external environments. For example, cigarette smoking has steadily declined over the past five decades. In 1965 over 50 percent of Canadians smoked, versus less than 20 percent in 2011.[9] No-smoking laws, higher taxes on cigarettes, and the social stigma attached to smoking have all contributed to this decline in sales. Recognizing these threats, tobacco giant Philip Morris entered the e-cigarette market at the end of 2013. Electronic cigarette sales are projected to surpass regular cigarettes by 2047.[10] PEST analysis is a useful tool for understanding market demand or decline, current business position, and potential threats and opportunities.

Scyther5/Shutterstock

Electronic cigarettes are devices that simulate the sensation of smoking. As many Canadians try to quit smoking, e-cigarettes are becoming increasingly popular and are expected to surpass regular cigarettes in sales by 2047.

Table 2.1 PEST Model for Analysis

Political–Legal	Economic	Sociocultural	Technological
Government type and stability	Levels of disposable income (after paying taxes) and income distribution	Cultural aspects, health consciousness, population growth rate, age, distribution	Maturity of technology, rate of obsolescence, and competing technologies
World trade agreements, regulations, and restrictions	Interest rates, taxes, and inflation	Migration flows—labour mobility	Research and technological breakthroughs and improvements
Environmental regulations and protection	Overseas economic growth and emerging markets	Consumer demand for environmentally safe business practices	Government spending on research and development
Freedom of press, rule of law, and levels of bureaucracy and corruption	Current and projected economic growth	Lifestyle changes and trends	Industry focus on technology
Tax policies and trade and tariff controls	Stage in the business cycle	Demographics: gender, age, family size, etc.	Energy use and costs
Consumer protection laws, employment laws, health and safety laws and regulations	Impact of technological changes on the economy	Living conditions, level of education, and earning capacity	Information technology, Internet, and mobile technology
Political stability	Government spending	Work–life balance attitudes	Global and local communications
Competition laws and regulations	Unemployment and supply of labour	Ethical and moral standards governing the practices of business—customer values, market values, stakeholder values	Technology access, licensing, intellectual property issues, and advances in manufacturing
Government organization and attitude	Labour costs and supply		Waste removal and recycling

Political–Legal Environment

How do politics affect an organization? The **political–legal environment** reflects the government's relationship with business. It is often a direct consequence of the political parties in power, which represent the popular opinion of the citizens of a region. Organizations hire lobbyists to influence legislation and run advocacy ads that state their point of view on public issues. Special interest groups have grown in number and power, putting more constraints on marketers. The public is placing high expectations on organizations to be ethical and responsible. Politicians work to get re-elected by listening to the concerns of their citizens, which can affect businesses in many ways. For example, if citizens protest having a new shopping mall built in their neighbourhood because they will lose a playground, the shopping mall may be forced to relocate.

political–legal environment The government's relationship with business.

Political decisions that affect the education of the workforce, the health of the nation, and the quality of an economy's infrastructure (such as roads and rail systems) can have an impact on many vital areas of a business. Here are three examples of how political decisions might affect a business:

1. If less of the workforce receives higher education because education fees rise, then qualified employees could be more difficult for businesses to find. Once found, these employees could demand higher wages, which would increase business costs.
2. If the cost of health care rises for individuals, then households will have less money to spend on the goods and services that they may have otherwise purchased from businesses, which would decrease business profits.
3. If roads and rail systems are not kept in good repair because the government decides to spend tax money elsewhere, businesses may be forced to choose alternate transport methods or increase transport time by travelling a longer route, which would increase business costs.

Video: Talking Politics in the Workplace

Syda Productions/Fotolia

One of the many purposes of laws and regulations is to protect consumers. One example is the CRTC's recent changes to the wireless code, making it easier for consumers to change wireless providers and find out details about their programs.

Political stability is also an important consideration, especially for international firms. Many companies would not be willing to do business in a country where there is political unrest or where trade relationships are not defined and stable. For example, Canadian firms are more likely to do business with the United States, Mexico, and England than with Afghanistan or Haiti.

How does the law affect an organization? Laws pertaining to taxes, competition, consumers, products, and the environment (land, air, and water) are some of the laws that organizations need to be aware of. For example, in Canada, there are strict regulations about advertising for alcohol, tobacco, and broadcasting. In December 2013, The Canadian Radio-television and Telecommunications Commission (CRTC) implemented a new "wireless code" in response to many complaints from Canadians about their wireless service providers. This new code attempts to better protect consumers by allowing them to cancel contracts with no charge after two years, placing limits on roaming and data overage charges, and ensuring that contracts are written in plain language that clearly describes the services.[11]

Laws and regulations tell organizations what they can and cannot do, and companies that do not abide might be fined, have their managers imprisoned, or have their businesses closed for noncompliance with the law.

Video: Tylenol Creators Release New Medical Warning

economic environment Consists of factors that affect consumer purchasing power and spending patterns.

Economic Environment

How does the economic environment affect an organization? The **economic environment** consists of factors that affect consumer purchasing power and spending patterns. Such factors might include the changing value of the Canadian dollar, a skilled-labour shortage, and environmental sustainability. When there is a period of low sales, low employment, and low productivity (a recession), many people are out of work and household incomes are lower, thus consumer spending is lower. Less consumer spending means less revenue for businesses, which means businesses cannot afford to expand operations, hire additional employees, or spend money on researching and developing new products. When there is a period of high sales, high employment, and high productivity (business, and therefore the economy, are said to be "booming"), most people have jobs and make a good income, thus consumer spending rises. Economic change can also have a strong impact on a firm's behaviour. For example, higher interest rates can deter businesses from obtaining loans to expand their operations, a strong domestic currency might make exporting more difficult if it increases prices in terms of foreign currencies, and inflation might provoke higher wage demands from employees and increase operating costs.

globalization The movement toward a more interconnected and interdependent world economy.

Video: The New Global Challengers

Video: MINI: Globalization

How does globalization affect business? **Globalization** is the movement toward a more interconnected and interdependent world economy. This means that economies around the world are merging as technology, goods and services, labour, and capital move back and forth across international borders. The effects of globalization on the business world vary, from economic transformation in India to the shutting down of major manufacturing plants in Canada.

The Internet and modern technological advances are making it possible for a company of any size from anywhere in the world to compete globally. Competition between businesses consists of trying to get the customer to buy one company's product instead of the one offered by its competitor. They compete to see which company has the greater market share (percentage of sales of a particular product or service in a given region) and thus is more successful. While Canada competes with its traditional economic partners and international allies, the United States and the United Kingdom, it must also compete with new emerging economies, such as China and India. To remain competitive in the global arena, Canada's competitiveness policies will have to strengthen the economic relationships with its traditional allies while at the same time developing sustainable and competitive economic relationships with emerging economies.

sociocultural environment An interconnected system of different demographic factors such as race, ethnicity, gender, age, income distribution, sexual orientation, and other characteristics.

Sociocultural Environment

LO3 Explain how sociocultural and technological forces can impact the profitability of a business.

How does the sociocultural environment affect an organization? A **sociocultural environment** is made up of different demographic factors such as race, ethnicity, gender, age, income distribution, sexual orientation, and other characteristics. Social, economic, and political movements and trends cause the social environment to change constantly;

Video: Burger King Markets New Fries as Healthier

Better Business Better World

Do You Prefer to Do Business with Companies You Can Trust?

The Council of Better Business Bureaus (CBBB) is the North American umbrella organization for all Better Business Bureaus (BBB). Both the CBBB and BBB are dedicated to cultivating honest, responsive relationships between businesses and consumers, instilling consumer confidence and contributing to a trustworthy marketplace. Founded in 1912, the BBB has grown to 128 bureaus serving communities across North America, evaluating and monitoring more than 3 million local and national businesses and charities.[12]

Financed by the private business sector, the BBB is a nonprofit, unbiased public service organization that establishes and maintains high standards for fair and honest business behaviour. Businesses that earn BBB-accredited status contractually agree and adhere to the organization's high standards of ethical business behaviour. BBB accreditation does not mean that the business's products or services have been evaluated or endorsed by the BBB, or that the BBB has made a determination as to the business's product quality or competency in performing services. To be accredited by the BBB, a business or organization affirms that it meets and will abide by the following standards:[13]

- *Build trust.* Establish and maintain a positive track record in the marketplace.
- *Advertise honestly.* Adhere to established standards of advertising and selling.
- *Tell the truth.* Honestly represent products and services, including clear and adequate disclosures of all material terms.
- *Be transparent.* Openly identify the nature, location, and ownership of the business, and clearly disclose all policies, guarantees, and procedures that bear on a customer's decision to buy.
- *Honour promises.* Abide by all written agreements and verbal representations.
- *Be responsive.* Address marketplace disputes quickly, professionally, and in good faith.
- *Safeguard privacy.* Protect any data collected against mishandling and fraud, collect personal information only as needed, and respect the preferences of customers regarding the use of their information.
- *Embody integrity.* Approach all business dealings, marketplace transactions, and commitments with integrity.

The BBB provides objective advice, free Reliability Reports on businesses and Wise Giving reports on charities, and educational information on topics affecting marketplace trust. To further promote trust, the BBB also offers compliance- and dispute-resolution support for consumers and businesses when there is a difference in viewpoints.

Discussion Questions

1. **Why is it important for businesses to build trust with consumers? Why is it important that consumers can trust the businesses they buy from?**
2. **Why would a business want to obtain BBB accreditation? Does this accreditation mean that consumers can trust the products the business sells to be high quality?**
3. **Have you ever been "scammed" by a business? What was the situation and what did you do about it? Did you go to the BBB for help? Why or why not?**

an influx of immigrants can change racial demographics, or an economic slump can change income distribution demographics. These changes affect where people live, what they buy, and how they choose to spend their money. To best serve employees, customers, and the community, businesses must consider shifts and changes in the social environment when making decisions.

How does an aging population affect business? Changing demographics—age, gender, family size, income level, educational level—can change patterns in consumer demand. An aging population presents challenges as well as opportunities. Not only are older Canadians living longer, healthier lives, they are also better educated, wealthier, and have achieved a higher standard of living than previous generations. Baby boomers, the generation born between 1943 and 1960, represent the majority of the aging Canadian population. By 2020, they will be 60 to 75 years old, and most of them will have begun their retirement. Over the past 50 years, the median age of Canadians has risen from 27.2 to 38.8 years, while the share of those aged 65 and older has increased from 7.7 to 13.2 percent. According to Statistics Canada, by 2026—when most baby boomers will have retired—the median age of Canadians will rise to 43.3 years and seniors will make up 21.2 percent of the population. By 2051, these figures are estimated to rise to 46.8 years and 26.4 percent, respectively.[14]

Opportunities exist for businesses to market to baby boomers as they age. As boomers become empty-nesters, they will most likely move to smaller homes or condominiums closer to the cities, where they can be close to shopping, restaurants, and entertainment. Boomers are also tech savvy and will continue to use the Internet, satellite connections, and other electronic devices. Many companies market specific product lines to boomers. For example, cosmetics company Revlon is targeting the aging population with an anti-aging beauty line aimed at baby boomer women. Revlon is hoping this product line will generate US$200 million in new sales.[15]

Although an aging population presents many opportunities for corporations, it also presents challenges for the Canadian economy. As the ratio of the nonworking population to the working population increases, problems could occur, such as increased health care needs, higher taxes, and a reduction in government spending on pensions and health care.

According to Statistics Canada, by 2056 seniors will account for 25 to 30 percent of the Canadian population. While the senior segment is increasing, children and young people make up a decreasing segment of the Canadian population. As many older Canadians retire, relatively fewer young people are moving into the workforce to replace them, which means there will be a decreasing number of people available to provide social and economic support for seniors. In 2006 there were five working-age people (aged 20 to 64) for every senior, down from seven in 1971. By 2056, it is estimated (medium-growth scenario) that there will be only two working-age people for every senior in Canada.[16] As shown in **Figure 2.1**, the result of such a trend could be a severe labour shortage for many years.

Despite these challenges, catering to the needs of an older population will ultimately present businesses with

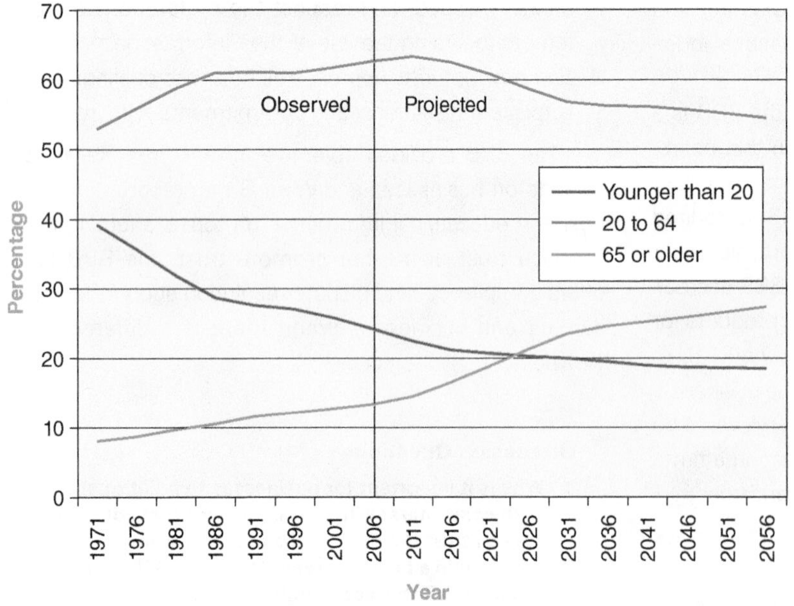

Figure 2.1 Change in Age Demographics

Source: Data points from Statistics Canada, "Observed and Projected Percentage of Youth, Working Age Population, and Seniors, Canada, 1971 to 2056," accessed February 10, 2011, http://www.statcan.gc.ca/pub/82-229-x/2009001/demo/desc/poc-desc1.2-eng.htm.

opportunities for growth—especially in the health care, pharmaceutical, and travel industries, as a bigger population translates to a larger market for these goods and services.

How does diversity affect business? As Canada becomes more diverse, it is important for businesses to reflect that diversity in their workforce. By 2031, between 25 and 28 percent of the population could consist of people born outside of Canada. Between 29 and 32 percent of the population could belong to a visible minority group, as defined by the Employment Equity Act. By 2031, visible minority groups could comprise 63 percent of the population in Toronto, 59 percent in Vancouver, and 31 percent in Montreal.[17] This means that in some companies, visible minorities could account for the majority of the workforce. RBC has more than 52 000 full-time employees in Canada, with 26 percent of employees being visible minorities. Boeing Canada has close to 1500 employees, with 26 percent of employees being visible minorities.[18]

However, in today's business climate, increasing and managing a company's diversity involves more than just employing an ethnically diverse workforce. Companies must develop a **diversity initiative**, which outlines their goals and objectives for managing, retaining, and promoting a diverse workforce. A diversity initiative might include a nondiscrimination policy, minority network, or diversity education. According to Harvard sociology professor Frank Dobbin, "To increase diversity, executives must treat it like any other business goal."[19]

diversity initiative Outlines a company's goals and objectives for managing, retaining, and promoting a diverse workforce. It might include a nondiscrimination policy, minority network, or diversity education.

Although the inclusion and advancement of racial minorities in the workplace is an important step in establishing a diverse workforce, it is only part of the process. Today, the term *minority* applies to more than just people of different ethnicities. Some minority groups represent a person's gender, culture, religion, sexual orientation, or disability. Companies must include these minority groups in their diversity initiative to ensure that all minority employees are treated fairly by management and co-workers.

Video: Communicating in a World of Diversity-Hewlett Packard

How does the "green movement" affect business? In a 2007 United Nations study, many of the world's most respected environmental scientists reported that the threat of global warming and climate change is real.[20] As environmental anxieties become prevalent throughout society, it is important for businesses to get involved in a **green economy**—one that factors ecological concerns into business decisions. Businesses that manufacture products that contribute to higher emissions of carbon dioxide and consume inordinate amounts of fossil fuels must adapt to this new environmental awareness if

green economy When ecological concerns are taken into account in business decisions.

Stephen Meese/Shutterstock

A focus on environmental issues is opening up markets, such as wind turbines, that will become increasingly important in the future.

they want to be relevant in a green economy. As an example, Toyota has seen its sales increase largely because of its Prius hybrid vehicles, which run on electricity as well as gasoline. Hybrid vehicles have not only become strong sellers, they have become part of our popular culture.[21]

A focus on environmental issues also creates a new market that will be increasingly important in the future. The demand for more green products presents new opportunities for entrepreneurs to meet those needs, and "green-collar" jobs could revitalize the currently decimated Canadian and US manufacturing economies. Creating wind energy turbines, installing solar panels, and weatherproofing houses and office buildings are going to be necessary businesses of the twenty-first century.

Technological Environment

technological environment Includes human knowledge, work methods, physical equipment, electronics and telecommunications, and various processing systems used to perform business activities.

How do technological changes affect the business environment? The **technological environment** includes human knowledge, work methods, physical equipment, electronics and telecommunications, and various processing systems used to perform business activities. Over the past 20 years, advancements in information technology (IT) have been revolutionary. In today's business world, it is a necessity to stay on the cutting edge of technology to remain competitive. Regardless of the type of business, technology can be used to keep a company flexible, organized, and well connected—with either customers or employees.

Product and service technologies are used for creating products and services for customers. Organizations must constantly be watching for technological breakthroughs that might make their products or services better than those of their competitors. Organizations also have to be mindful of technologies that might make their products or services obsolete and thereby threaten their survival. For example, when DVDs hit the market, VHS sales dropped; now VHS is no longer on the market, and online streaming is quickly replacing DVDs and Blu-ray discs. For some companies (such as IBM, Apple, Microsoft, Rogers, and Dell), technology is the basis for competition; because these companies market themselves as being technological leaders, they need to invest large amounts in research and development to stay ahead—or even just to keep up.

Research and development technologies are being used to create new products, services, and processes. For example, SunChips uses solar energy at one of its eight manufacturing plants to produce snacks that are not only better for the consumer, but better for the planet as well. Technological improvements and innovation in general are important to the economic development of a country.

How expensive is it to keep up with technology? There is no question that keeping up with the pace of technology is an expensive and time-consuming task. The rapid pace of technological innovation means that computers are outdated after three years and obsolete after five years.[22] In addition, there is the cost of applicable software, training, and infrastructure, which often makes IT the largest expense in many companies.[23] However, cost is not the only aspect of technology to consider. In the same way that robotics completely revolutionized the automotive industry, advancements in computer and telecommunications technology are completely changing the foundation and focus of how many businesses are run.

Technology, when used and implemented effectively, can help streamline businesses; cut costs; increase productivity, security, and transparency; and improve communication with customers. Giving employees the technology they need to get their work done more efficiently and effectively is the simplest way to increase productivity. If employees can get more work done in a shorter time, productivity goes up. When employees are more productive, they are more valuable. This, in turn, makes the whole company more valuable. In addition, the right technology can help streamline a business's internal operations, so the business can be more effective, efficient, and productive.

Thirty years ago, businesses were often centrally located with all employees in one building. Today, this is less common. Technology is making it possible for employees to telecommute, or work from home or another location away from the office. The "virtual global workforce," or telecommuters who work on a global scale, expands the pool of potential employees, so that the right employee can be found for the job regardless of where he or she lives.[24] Teleconferencing (and videoconferencing) is keeping CEOs and other corporate representatives from having to travel constantly for meetings. It is also allowing companies to communicate more easily, regardless of distance. These advancements are saving money on what used to be necessary expenses. With less travel, there is less money spent on plane tickets, hotel rooms, and food, and with more employees telecommuting, many businesses can operate out of smaller offices, which are cheaper and easier to manage.

How has the Internet changed the way business is done? While IT is the tool that is changing the function of business, the Internet is the tool that is changing the scope. The Internet is a global data communications system. It offers a way for consumers and businesses to communicate with each other, as well as a way for businesses to communicate with other businesses and consumers to communicate with other consumers. Using the Internet to conduct online business is a concept known as ecommerce or ebusiness. Although IT by itself would be extremely influential for the business world, the Internet makes it truly revolutionary. In 1995, the Internet was just starting to proliferate. Even though it had been commercially available for years at that point, the Internet had only recently become viable after the advent of the World Wide Web a few years before. Many people were intimidated by this new technology, and companies that operated solely on the Internet were not expected to do well. This changed in 1995, when both eBay.com and Amazon.com launched. These companies showed that Internet-based businesses were not only possible, but also potentially lucrative. Their high-profile success paved the way for today's ebusiness merchant.[25]

Video: HSN: Retailing and Wholesaling

Video: ZipCar: Business Technology

Many businesses that exist in the bricks-and-mortar (physical store) world of commerce are now finding they also need to have an Internet presence to compete for customer loyalty. Many new business startups begin as online stores, with no physical location where consumers can shop. Every year, conducting business over the Internet becomes a more significant element of the overall economy. As it becomes easier for consumers to find even the most obscure items at competitive prices, the sale of goods and services online will continue to be a driving force in our economy. As the Internet and its influence continue to grow, so will its economic importance and necessity for businesses. However, the prevalence of the Internet also presents dangers and concerns for business.

One important concern is privacy. Emails, internal documents, and chat transcripts all contain private information not intended for public viewing. Nevertheless, many of these documents can be accessed online, because online storage has become a convenient alternative to hard drives. Web-based email and documents ("the cloud") are also becoming more common. Even gaining access to a work or home computer from a remote location is a simple process that is becoming more popular. With this universal access, it is increasingly difficult to ensure that information remains private. Web-based storage and services offer many benefits to business, yet privacy and security concerns cannot be overlooked.

Goodshoot/Getty Images

Technology makes it possible to work from virtually anywhere. Is that a good thing?

THE COMPETITIVE ENVIRONMENT

LO4 Describe how Porter's five forces model is used to analyze the ways competition affects an industry.

competition When two or more businesses contend with one another to attract customers and gain an advantage.

How does competition influence business? In a market-based economy, such as those of the Canada and the United States, there is an emphasis on individual economic freedom and a limit on governmental intervention—although Canada's government interacts with business and the economy to a greater degree than the US government does. In a market economy, competition is the driving force. **Competition** arises when two or more businesses (local, national, or global) compete with one another to attract customers and gain an advantage. Canada's private enterprise system is based on the belief that competition benefits consumers by motivating businesses to produce a greater variety of better and cheaper goods and services. Competition is good for consumers, good for the economy, and can be good for businesses. For example, 7UP created a new market because of extremely fierce competition in the cola industry. It positioned itself as the "un-cola," and with the launch of Cherry 7UP and Diet Cherry 7UP, the company secured its third-place spot in the soft drink industry in early 1987. The two new "light, refreshing" drinks seized 1.4 percent of the more than US$40 billion total soft drink market in their first year and boosted 7UP's total share to 6.2 percent.[26]

Porter's five forces model A model used to depict the five forces that affect industry competition: threat of new entrants, threat of substitutes, bargaining power of buyers, bargaining power of suppliers, and rivalry among existing competitors.

Competition varies within industries and has a big influence on how companies operate. Competing for a finite number of consumers means that less-efficient companies and less-desirable products are usually eliminated from the marketplace. Because profit is the ultimate goal, it is the job of a successful business to convince customers that its product is either better or less expensive than that of its competitors. For example, there is currently competition among cable TV services (e.g., Rogers), satellite TV services (e.g., Bell), and Internet TV services (e.g., Netflix). How serious a threat is streaming content over the Internet? Sales of Internet-connected TVs, such as Apple TV, are growing. In addition, there are already devices such as Blu-ray DVD players, video game consoles, and network media players that provide Internet access. With Internet TV, consumers can pay for the services they want without all the other packaged services, offering consumers a low-cost and focused option. Are satellite and cable companies going to offer the same option? Can satellite and cable companies continue if consumers don't want to pay for a multitude of channels they don't watch? It will be interesting to see what happens.

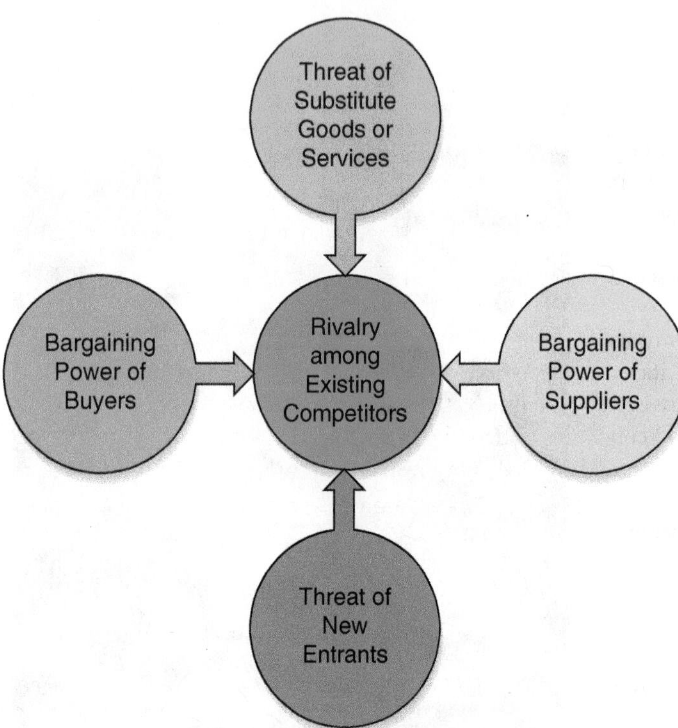

Figure 2.2 Michael Porter's Five Forces Model: The Five Forces That Shape Industry Competition

Source: "Michael Porter's Five Forces Model: The Five Forces That Shape Industry Competition" by Michael Porter from Five Competetive Forces Model Porter. Copyright © 2010. Published by the author.

Porter's Five Forces Model

One of the most important external factors that affects most companies is the degree of industry competition—how fiercely businesses compete for the same customers, the same resources, or with products or services that are very similar to each other. To be effective, managers must understand the company's competitive situation and then develop competitive strategies to take advantage of opportunities and combat threats in the industry. One tool used by managers to analyze competitive situations is **Porter's five forces model**, which depicts the five forces that affect industry competition (see **Figure 2.2**).

Let's examine these five forces in more detail.

1. *Threat of new entrants.* How easy is it for new entrants to start competing? Some industries, such as automotive manufacturing, require huge capital investments and therefore are extremely difficult to enter. Other industries, such as home cleaning or lawn care, require very little capital and therefore are relatively easy to enter. Government regulations may restrict entrance until certain criteria are met. The threat of entry of new competitors is high when brand names are not well known, capital investment is low, government regulation is not restrictive, and there is little differentiation between products.
2. *Threat of substitutes.* How easily can customer needs be satisfied by the products or services offered by other industries? For example, newspapers keep subscribers informed about daily events, but so can television and Internet sources. Coffee provides a morning caffeine rush, but so do tea and Red Bull. If there are many substitutes available, the industry is more competitive and the profit potential for the firms in the industry is decreased. To combat the threat of substitutes, companies try to differentiate their products and services in many ways, some of which may include price (Walmart's lowest-price guarantee), quality (Maytag says you'll never need to call the repairman), service (WestJet is known for superior service), or image (the now iconic "hip Mac" versus "stuffy PC" commercials). The threat of substitutes is high if consumers can easily switch to the products of another industry that are cheaper, can find a substitute that has better quality or performance, or can switch at a low personal cost.
3. *Bargaining power of buyers.* How strong is the position of buyers? Can they order large volumes to push the cost down? When there are only a few buyers and many suppliers the buyers have a great deal of bargaining power, but when there are only a few suppliers and many buyers the buyers have little bargaining power. The bargaining power of buyers is high when buyers purchase products in high volume, buyer switching costs are low, and substitutes are available.
4. *Bargaining power of suppliers.* Do many potential suppliers exist or only a few? If there are many suppliers from which a company can order its supplies, then the suppliers do not have much bargaining power (the company has the power). When there are

Apple: Taking a Bite Out of Microsoft?

Apple and Microsoft have a history of bitter rivalry revolving around the desire to dominate the personal computer market. The main point of contention between these companies is the graphical user interface (GUI), which is the user interface for the main program that runs personal computers. Apple released the first GUI to include folders and long file names in 1983. When Microsoft released Windows 2.0 in 1988, Apple took Microsoft to court, complaining that the "look and feel" of the Windows interface was stolen from the Apple interface. This suit continued until 1992, when Apple finally lost.

Microsoft led the competition in the early 1990s. It became industry standard to have Windows operating systems preinstalled on most PCs, which were dominating the personal computer market at the time. The 10-year battle finally ended when Apple announced an official alliance with Microsoft in 1997. Microsoft and Apple agreed to a five-year deal in which Microsoft would continue to develop Office software for Apple computers, and Apple agreed to bundle Microsoft's Internet Explorer in all its operating systems.[27]

The computer industry went through some tough times around the turn of the century, but Apple and Microsoft remained two of the most successful companies in the world. The element of competition between these companies drove them to succeed, and perhaps led to the production of higher-quality operating software.

Discussion Questions

1. **Some people say that Microsoft imitated Apple's "look and feel" in their user interface. Why might they do that?**
2. **You likely remember the TV commercials that pitted the cool Mac guy against the awkward PC nerd. Are these ads effective in illustrating the competition between the two companies? Why or why not?**
3. **Are you a Mac or PC person? How do you think you developed this preference?**

only a few suppliers from which a company can order the supplies it needs to do business, then the suppliers have a great deal of bargaining power. The bargaining power of suppliers is high when the product is highly differentiated or substitutes are unavailable.

5. *Rivalry among existing competitors.* Does a strong competition between the existing players exist? Is one player dominant, or are they mostly equal in strength and size? Companies are always trying to increase market share (more sales and more customers). To do this, they must devise creative marketing strategies, cut costs, and improve customer service and product quality. Some companies focus on quality, image, or service (e.g., BMW), while others focus on lower prices (e.g., Walmart). The intensity of rivalry is high when there are many competitors, competitors have equal size or market share, there is little differentiation between products, or consumers have no preference for a particular brand.

Video: iPhone-Mania: How Long Can It Last?

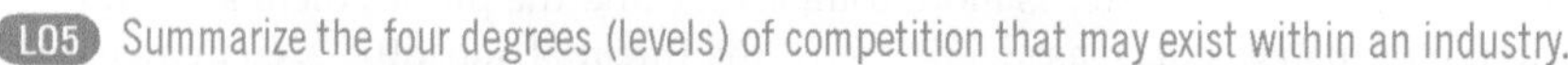

The Degrees (Levels) of Competition

Some products or services have no substitutes, whereas others share the market with many similar products. Various industries experience different degrees of competition, ranging from many competitors to few or no competitors. The number of substitutes for a certain product or service determines the degree (level) of competition. Economists have identified **four degrees of competition**:

four degrees of competition The four levels of competition in business: monopoly, oligopoly, monopolistic competition, and perfect competition.

- monopoly
- oligopoly
- monopolistic competition
- perfect competition

These degrees of competition are four points on a scale, not absolute measures (see **Figure 2.3**). For example, many industries fall somewhere between monopolistic competition and oligopoly.

Is there any competition if there is only one seller? If one Internet company were the sole provider of Internet services, that company would be considered a monopoly. Likewise, if Eddie's Coffee Kiosk is the only place students can buy coffee on campus, then Eddie has a monopoly. A **monopoly** occurs when there is only one provider of a service or product and no substitutes for the product exist. In Canada as well as in other countries, large monopolies are rarely allowed. In fact, Canada's Competition Bureau reviews all mergers in all sectors to determine whether they will likely result in substantial lessening or prevention of competition. For example, Rogers Communications acquired Atria Networks following approval from the Competition Bureau. But Canada's Competition Bureau denied Interac's request to become a for-profit organization, and has challenged the Canadian Real Estate Association over rules they say limit consumer choices.[28] In November 2013, the Competition Bureau issued a "no-action letter" with

monopoly A form of competition where there is only one provider of a service or product and no substitutes for the product exist.

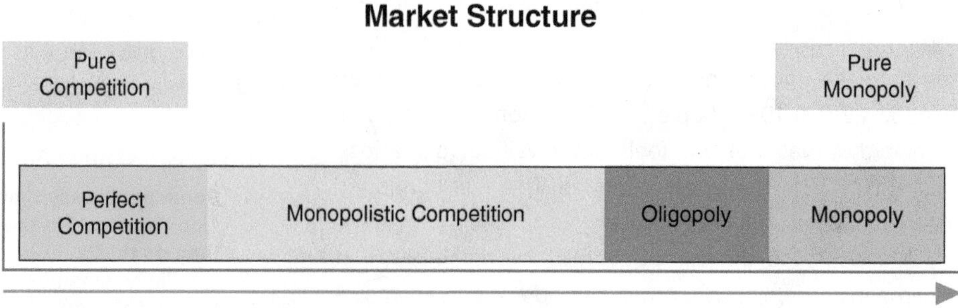

Figure 2.3 Degrees of Competition: The Further Right on the Scale, the Greater the Monopoly Power

respect to TELUS's proposed purchase of Public Mobile after determining that the acquisition would unlikely reduce or prevent competition in the mobile wireless industry of Southern Ontario and Greater Montreal. A no-action letter confirms that the Bureau has reviewed a specific proposed transaction and concluded that it will not, at this time, challenge that proposed transaction before the Competition Tribunal under the merger provisions of the Competition Act.[29]

LO6 Explain why government in Canada allows some monopolies to exist and how consumer interests are protected.

Natural monopolies include public utilities, such as those that sell gas or water. These organizations require huge investments, and it would be inefficient to duplicate the products they provide; therefore, they may be permitted to hold monopolies in an effort to conserve natural resources. However, the government regulates the prices for these goods and services. **Legal monopolies** occur when a company receives a patent giving it exclusive use of an invented product or process. Polaroid held a patent on instant photography technology for a number of years (patents exist for a predetermined amount of time). During this time, Polaroid benefited from having no competition and was able to recover the high costs of bringing the new technology to the market. Without competition, the company enjoyed a monopolistic position with regard to pricing.

natural monopolies Monopolies that include public utilities, such as those that sell gas or water. These organizations require huge investments, and it would be inefficient to duplicate the products they provide.

legal monopolies Monopolies that occur when a company receives a patent giving it exclusive use of an invented product or process.

What happens when another seller enters a monopoly? An oligopoly may be formed when another company enters a monopoly. An **oligopoly** is a form of competition in which only a few sellers exist. In the example of Eddie's Coffee Kiosk, a bookstore on campus might open a café that offers coffee to the students. Students now have a choice to buy coffee either at the bookstore or at Eddie's Coffee Kiosk. The situation has now changed from a monopoly to an oligopoly. When there are few sellers in a given market, each seller has a fairly large share of the market. Typically, oligopolies occur in industries in which there is a high investment to enter, so oligopolies are often major corporations in the airline, pharmaceutical, high-tech, automobile, and tobacco industries.

oligopoly A form of competition in which only a few sellers exist.

Because there is little differentiation among products, competition is strong in an oligopoly and prices differ only slightly, if at all, among the few suppliers. If one company cuts prices, its action is usually matched quickly by the competition. Therefore, competition in an oligopoly is centred on product differentiation (making one product stand out from another) more than on price.

What if there are many sellers with little difference between their products, but buyers perceive them as different? **Monopolistic competition** occurs when there are many buyers and sellers and little differentiation between the products, but consumers perceive there to be a difference so they favour one product offering over another. As an example, assume that the campus cafeteria begins to offer Tim Hortons brand coffee. Also assume that the perception among students is that Tim Hortons coffee is superior to Eddie's and the bookstore's coffee. The added choice of a perceived superior product creates monopolistic competition. Eddie's Coffee Kiosk faces new competition that is perceived to be better than his product, and demand for his coffee decreases.

monopolistic competition A form of competition where there are many buyers and sellers and little differentiation between the products, but consumers perceive there to be a difference so they favour one product offering over another.

Monopolistic competition is everywhere. It exists in the shoe industry among Nike, Adidas, Under Armour, and others; in the coffee industry among Tim Hortons, Starbucks, Country Style, and others; and in the ice cream industry among Breyers, Häagen-Dazs, and Chapman's, to name a few. These are traditional monopolistic competitive businesses because there are many buyers and sellers and the products are similar but not identical.

LO7 Explain the impact that perfect competition has on selling price.

What if there are many sellers and each seller's products are almost identical? **Perfect competition** occurs when many buyers and sellers of products are virtually identical and any seller can easily enter and exit the market. When these conditions exist, no single supplier can influence the price. Selling price will be determined by the market based on available supply and existing demand for the product. In reality, there are few, if

perfect competition A form of competition where there are many buyers and sellers of products that are virtually identical, and any seller can easily enter and exit the market.

On Target

All Kinds of Tablets

Welcome to the world of tablets. Worldwide tablet orders continue to grow, reaching 142.5 percent growth year over year in the first quarter of 2013. But let's go back to the beginning for a moment—Apple's initial release of the iPad, a tablet device designed for media engagement and light content creation. In April 2010, the iPad was greeted by eager consumers and its introduction resulted in surging sales. Within a week of the launch of the basic model, an estimated 450 000 units were sold, and 3 million were sold within three months. By the end of 2010, nearly 15 million iPads had been sold worldwide. After the iPad 2 was launched, Apple reported combined sales for all iPads of more than 15 million in just the last three months of 2011! Compare this to the initial sales for Amazon's ebook reader, the Kindle. The Kindle was first introduced to the market nearly two-and-a-half years earlier than the iPad and sold approximately 250 000 units in the first year.[30]

Fast forward to 2013, several iPad generations later (at a recent Apple conference, chief executive Tim Cook revealed that Apple has sold 170 million iPad units since the product's inception), with competition heating up in the industry to include Samsung's Galaxy, ASUS's Nexus device, and Microsoft's Surface and Surface Pro tablets, among others. At the end of the second quarter of 2013, Amazon's share of the global tablet market was 2.3 percent.

Shutterstock

Apple remains the dominant player with the iPad, but Samsung has made the most gains in the space, rising from a 7.5 percent share in 2012 to 18.9 percent in the second quarter of 2013. ASUS, Acer, and Lenovo have also made gains, and now rank above Amazon Kindle in terms of market share.

Discussion Questions

1. **A market that was once thought of as a pure monopoly by Apple has now opened up to some interesting competition. Or do you think Apple and Samsung have a lock in the tablet market?**
2. **In what ways has increased competition in the tablet market benefited consumers?**
3. **How do the manufacturers of tablets attempt to differentiate their products to compete for sales?**

any, examples of perfect competition. However, agricultural products, such as grains, fruits, and vegetables, come close.

Competition encourages businesses to make creative decisions and gives customers options. Because of this need for competition, the Canadian government keeps a close watch on monopolies and ensures that no single seller drastically influences the price of a certain service or product.

CHAPTER SYNOPSIS

LO1 Describe the macro business environment and explain why managers must be aware of changes taking place. (p. 21)

The **business environment** refers to forces outside the business that can affect the firm's industry and **competitive environment**. These forces include government regulations and policies, the economy, social and cultural issues, demographic shifts, as well as evolving technologies. Competition in particular has a large impact on all businesses, and this not only includes the strength of rivals, but also factors affecting customers, suppliers, distributors, and even products offered by other industries that may not be obvious competitors. The business environment is constantly changing, so managers must be aware of how these changes may affect their industry so that they can develop strategies to pursue opportunities and protect the company from emerging threats.

LO2 Explain how managers use the PEST model to analyze external business opportunities and threats. (pp. 21–25)

To help understand the business environment, one option for managers is to analyze external factors using the **PEST model**, which is a useful tool for understanding market demand or decline, current business position, and potential opportunities and obstacles. PEST helps guide managers to focus on emerging issues and trends in categories related to *political–legal, economic, sociocultural,* and *technological* factors.

LO3 Explain how sociocultural and technological forces can impact the profitability of a business. *(pp. 25–29)*

Sociocultural factors refer to things such as social trends, population, demographics, and ethical considerations, all of which can directly impact consumer behaviour and preferences, which will ultimately affect decisions about product offerings. For example, environmentally friendly business processes are affecting demand patterns and creating business opportunities.

As technology changes, companies must adjust business practices to compete in the global business world. Factors include new technologies, online shopping, research and development, and global access, all of which affect how business is conducted, the costs of doing business, and may even cause the formation of entirely new industries.

LO4 Describe how Porter's five forces model is used to analyze the ways competition affects an industry. *(pp. 30–32)*

Competition arises when two or more businesses compete with one another to attract customers and gain an advantage. **Porter's five forces model** depicts the five forces that affect industry competition: threat of new entrants, threat of substitutes, bargaining power of buyers, bargaining power of suppliers, and rivalry among existing competitors. The intensity of the competition within an industry has a big influence on how a company operates.

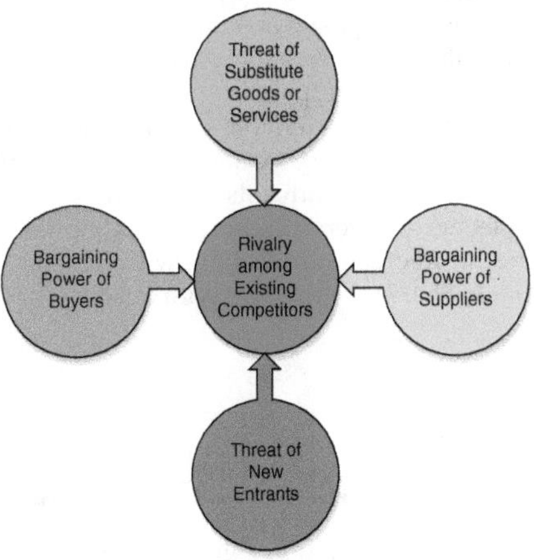

Michael Porter's Five Forces Model: The Five Forces That Shape Industry Competition

LO5 Summarize the four degrees (levels) of competition that may exist within an industry. *(pp. 32–33)*

The number of substitutes for a certain product or service determines the degree (level) of competition. The **four degrees of competition** are **monopoly, oligopoly, monopolistic competition**, and **perfect competition**.

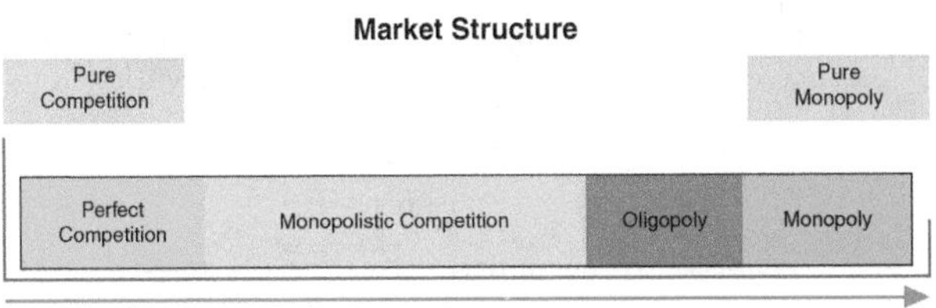

Degrees of Competition: The Further Right on the Scale, the Greater the Monopoly Power

LO6 Explain why government in Canada allows some monopolies to exist and how consumer interests are protected. *(p. 33)*

Natural monopolies include public utilities, such as those that sell gas or water. These organizations require huge investments, and it would be inefficient to duplicate the products they provide. Therefore, they may be permitted to hold monopolies in an effort to conserve natural resources. However, the government regulates the prices for these goods and services.

Legal monopolies occur when a company receives a patent giving it exclusive use of an invented product or process. This temporary period of reduced competition gives innovative firms the opportunity to recover the high costs of bringing the new technology to the market.

LO7 Explain the impact that perfect competition has on selling price. *(pp. 33–34)*

Perfect competition occurs when there are many buyers and sellers of products that are virtually identical, and any seller can easily enter and exit the market. When these conditions exist, no single supplier can influence the price. Selling price will be determined by the market based on available supply and existing demand for the product.

MyBizLab Study, practise, and explore real business situations with these helpful resources:

- **Interactive Lesson Presentations:** Work through interactive presentations and assessments to test your knowledge of business concepts.
- **Study Plan:** Check your understanding of chapter concepts with self-study quizzes.
- **Dynamic Study Modules:** Work through adaptive study modules on your computer, tablet, or mobile device.
- **Simulations:** Practise decision-making in simulated business environments.

KEY TERMS

business environment *(p. 21)*
competition *(p. 30)*
competitive environment *(p. 21)*
diversity initiative *(p. 27)*
economic environment *(p. 24)*
four degrees of competition *(p. 32)*
globalization *(p. 24)*
green economy *(p. 27)*
legal monopolies *(p. 33)*
macro environment *(p. 21)*
monopolistic competition *(p. 33)*
monopoly *(p. 32)*
natural monopolies *(p. 33)*
oligopoly *(p. 33)*
perfect competition *(p. 33)*
PEST model *(p. 22)*
political–legal environment *(p. 23)*
Porter's five forces model *(p. 30)*
sociocultural environment *(p. 25)*
technological environment *(p. 28)*

CRITICAL THINKING QUESTIONS

1. It is not unusual to encounter businesses that have streamlined their activities to accommodate for environmental forces. Can you think of examples of businesses that might be forced to alter their business decisions based on how they are impacting the environment? How might these decisions affect their profits?
2. Most business owners agree that keeping up with the pace of technological change is a challenging task. Imagine you are the owner of a new restaurant business and must decide what technology would best suit your needs. From what types of technology would this business benefit?
3. You are considering the possibility of opening a grocery store. What kinds of government regulations do you think will impact your business? What are the advantages and disadvantages of government regulation of business?

APPLICATION EXERCISES

1. **Demographics.** Imagine you are starting a new retail clothing business in the city where you attend school. To what demographic area would you market? Think about the following factors: race, ethnicity, gender, age, income, and sexual orientation. Visit www.statcan.gc.ca to locate reports on the demographic area in which you are interested. Do you believe your business can thrive in this area? If not, what area would be conducive to your obtaining future customers? Would you have to change your retail clothing products in any way for the demographic market?
2. **Languages of the global marketplace.** As globalization increases and the world markets become more intertwined, language barriers become important. Investigate online resources for automated translation tools. What happens if you want to read a webpage posted by a German firm? Can you make online purchases from a company based in Asia? What resources are there for translating telephone conversations in real time? Investigate Babelfish.com and personal interpreter services such as LanguageLine.com.
3. **Ecommerce.** Did you know there are websites dedicated to keeping businesses and consumers up to date on the latest ecommerce news and trends? Check out www.ecommercetimes.com, find a recent ecommerce trend, and write a brief summary.
4. **Political–legal environment.** The political–legal environment of business affects business operations in many ways. For instance, many provincial governments have changed the consumer tax structure into a single federally administered tax, the harmonized sales tax (HST). You will find information online at www.cra-arc.gc.ca and www.retailcouncil.org/quickfacts/taxrates. Previously, businesses applied a goods and services tax (GST) and a provincial sales tax (PST) to most sales transactions. How might this change affect business operations? Does HST apply to all provinces, all businesses, and all consumers?
5. **Sociocultural environment.** Public opinion has a huge impact on how companies and the Canadian government act. Conduct online research to find a recent news event that discusses consumers responding negatively to some business venture or change. For example, communities often respond negatively to garbage dumps and nuclear power plants being placed in their neighbourhoods. They protest through rallies, writing letters to government, posting online discussions and opinions, word of mouth, meetings with company leaders, and emails. Share your findings with the class.

TEAM TIME

Cultural Awareness: An Unwritten Law

There are many challenges facing multinational companies where diversity and cultural awareness are concerned.

PROCESS

Step 1. Divide into six groups, each representing one of the following countries: China, France, Germany, Japan, Mexico, and Canada. Examine the cultural practices, customs, and values of the country you will represent. This may be done in class if you have Internet access or as homework.

Step 2. Each group should pair together with a second group as follows: Canada with Japan, Mexico with Germany, and China with France.

Step 3. Each group should produce one scenario of a business transaction that would be affected by cultural differences found in your research. Fabricate specific companies, characters, interactions, and resolutions.

Step 4. Answer these questions and discuss with the class: What were some challenges encountered in your business scenario and how did you overcome them? Why is it important for multinational companies to research a foreign country with which they intend to conduct business?

CLOSING CASE

How Much Snooping Is Too Much Snooping?

BlackBerry, founded in 1984 as Research In Motion and led by Mike Lazaridis and Jim Balsillie, is headquartered in Waterloo, Ontario, with offices throughout North America, Asia-Pacific, and Europe. In addition to designing and manufacturing the BlackBerry smartphone, the company also creates software for businesses and the operating system that allows the BlackBerry to provide mobile access to email, instant messaging (IM), smartphone applications (apps), media files, and the Internet.

In the past several years, BlackBerry has been facing challenges from the governments of India, United Arab Emirates, and Saudi Arabia. In the name of national security, these countries have been demanding access to the company's secure customer data, as they see such access as a necessary tool in their fight against terrorists. Each of these countries threatened to ban BlackBerry service unless the company complied.

Concerned that terrorists may exploit the encryption in smartphones to plan illegal activity, the Indian government is urging telecommunications companies to devise solutions to meet its security needs. The government said it would ask BlackBerry, Google, Skype, and other service providers to establish local servers and authorize security agencies to monitor email traffic. "They have to install servers in India," Home Secretary G.K. Pillai told reporters in New Delhi, adding, "This applies to all." He said notices would be sent to the companies for "lawful access" by India's security agencies.[31] Companies that do not comply could be banned. For BlackBerry, more than a million of its smartphone users would be affected by a ban, and the company would have to halt expansion into the world's second-biggest mobile phone market.[32]

DISCUSSION QUESTIONS

1. Do you think it is an invasion of privacy for a government to want to monitor digital communications? Is it the government's right to do so? Why or why not?
2. What political–legal and sociocultural pressures is BlackBerry dealing with?
3. What might happen to BlackBerry's sales if is permits monitoring of digital communications? If the communications service provider does not oblige the Indian government, do you think the country would ban the service? Why or why not?

3 Economics and Banking

AND Inc/Shutterstock

LEARNING OBJECTIVES

After studying this chapter, you should be able to:

LO1 Define economics and describe the different types of economic systems. (pp. 40–43)

LO2 Describe the laws of supply and demand and how equilibrium price is determined. (pp. 43–49)

LO3 Understand how economic indicators, including gross domestic product (GDP), price indexes, the unemployment rate, and productivity, reflect the economic health of a country. (pp. 50–53)

LO4 List and describe the four stages of the business cycle. (pp. 53–54)

LO5 Summarize how the government uses both monetary and fiscal policies to stabilize the economy as a result of business cycle fluctuations. (pp. 54–59)

OPENING DISCUSSION: EMERGING ECONOMIES

Which Emerging Economies Are Gaining Global Economic Power?

To strengthen international cooperation, country leaders have established several forums as mechanisms to bring together developed and emerging economies in informal discussions to achieve stable, sustainable, and mutually beneficial growth. For example, the G7 is a forum bringing together the finance ministers from the world's wealthiest, most developed nations—Canada, the United States, France, Germany, Italy, Japan, and the United Kingdom—which meets periodically to achieve cooperation on international economic and monetary issues. The G7 holds an annual meeting of heads of government to discuss issues such as the global economic outlook and macroeconomic management, international trade, energy, climate change, political–security issues, and relations with developing countries. The G20 is an informal forum that advocates open, constructive discussion between industrial and emerging-market countries on key issues in the global economy. The members of the G20 include Argentina, Australia, Brazil, Canada, China, France, Germany, India, Indonesia, Italy, Japan, Republic of Korea, Mexico, Russia, Saudi Arabia, South Africa, Turkey, the United Kingdom, the United States, and the European Union. Together, G20 members represent around 85 percent of global gross domestic product, over 75 percent of global trade, and two-thirds of the world's population.[1]

In recent years, there has been a shift in global economic power away from the developed G7 economies toward the developing world. The emerging countries, known as the E7 countries, include the BRIC (Brazil, Russia, India, and China), Mexico, Indonesia, and Turkey. Although South Africa lags behind the other members in terms of economic growth, China formally invited it to join the BRIC in 2010, hence the change in acronym to BRICS. It is predicted that by 2018, the E7's combined wealth will overtake that of the G7 nations, and China is on course to succeed the United States as the world's largest economy.[2]

"India's growth may accelerate to 9.5 percent between 2011 and 2015," Morgan Stanley economist Chetan Ahya recently said in an interview. "India's gross domestic product has expanded at an average 7.1 percent over the decade through the third quarter of 2009, compared with 9.1 percent in China, which surpassed Japan as the second-largest economy last quarter."[3]

John Hawksworth, chief economist at PriceWaterhouseCoopers, said, "In many ways, the renewed dominance by 2050 of China and India, with their much larger populations, is a return to the historical norm prior to the Industrial Revolution of the late eighteenth and nineteenth centuries that caused a shift in global economic power from Asia to Western Europe and the United States—this temporary shift in power is now going into reverse. This changing world order poses challenges and opportunities for businesses in the current advanced economies."[4]

Rising international economic integration—or *globalization,* as it is commonly known—offers many opportunities. However, the public often associates globalization with job losses and downward pressure on wages and working conditions.

DISCUSSION QUESTIONS

1. Why do you think Canadians might associate globalization with job loss and lower wages?
2. What opportunities and challenges might arise for Canadian businesses as a result of emerging economies? Consider both small and large firms.
3. In your opinion, has a global marketplace changed the way we work, our business laws, or the technology required to do business? If so, how?

BASICS OF ECONOMICS

LO1 Define economics and describe the different types of economic systems.

Economics Defined

economics The study of how individuals, businesses, and government make decisions about how to allocate limited (scarce) resources to best satisfy people's wants, needs, and desires.

What is economics? Do you ever wonder what makes the price of oil rise, why unemployment climbs, or how rising prices may affect you? Certainly you are aware that some occupations pay more than others, but have you ever wondered why? Why do tuition fees keep rising, or why is rent higher in some parts of the country? Studying economics can help you answer these questions. **Economics** is the study of how individuals, businesses, and governments make decisions about how to allocate limited (scarce) resources to best satisfy people's wants, needs, and desires. It is about businesses making goods (such as books, pizza, or computers) or supplying services (such as giving haircuts, painting houses, or installing home entertainment networks) that people want or need to buy. The resources—labour, capital, natural resources (i.e., land), entrepreneurship, and technology—are known as economic resources or factors of production because they are the required inputs that help businesses produce outputs (goods and services).

scarcity The economic problem of how to reconcile unlimited human wants and desires with limited economic resources.

Because resources are scarce and businesses do not have enough tools, money, or products to provide all the books, pizza, or haircuts that we want, businesses must decide what and how much to make. Not everyone will be able to have what he or she wants because of the limited resources (such as money, space, or time) and supplies—this is the fundamental economic problem known as **scarcity**. Therefore, economists look at how resources are distributed in the marketplace and how equitably and efficiently those resources are disbursed. Economics examines capitalism versus socialism, management of inflation and unemployment, economic development of poor countries, pollution and global warming, energy policies, national defence, international trade and finance, old age security, and many specific government policies (such as minimum wage, agricultural price supports, and rent control).

circular flow An economic cycle in which businesses and households provide government with tax payments generated from revenue and wages, and government uses the tax money to provide businesses and households with incentives, programs, and services.

How do government, businesses, and households interact? Households provide businesses with inputs to production: labour (as workers), land and buildings (as landlords), entrepreneurs, and capital (as investors). Businesses use those inputs to produce goods and services (outputs), which they provide to government and households. Government and households buy those goods and services, which provides businesses with revenue. The revenue obtained by businesses is then used to buy additional resources. Businesses and households provide government with tax payments. Government uses the tax money to provide businesses and households with incentives, services, and programs (e.g., health care, roads, and community programs). This cycle is known as the **circular flow** of Canada's economy (see **Figure 3.1**).

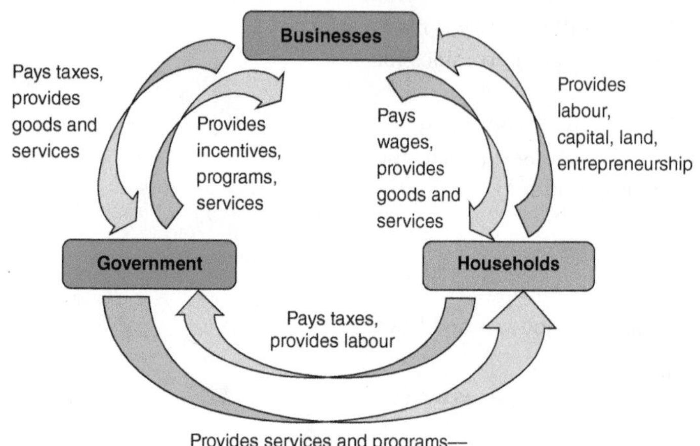

Figure 3.1 Circular Flow of Canada's Economy

Why is it important to study economics? There are many reasons to study economics, but one of the most important is to understand how people get the goods and services they need and want. Studying economics will help us interpret the impact of government decisions on firms, industries, and nations. It helps us understand the effect international trade has on a global and national level. Studying economics is also important because it allows us to make better decisions in our personal and professional lives; understand business cycles, investments, and standards of living; and solve problems. There are two broad branches in economics: *microeconomics* and *macroeconomics*.

What is microeconomics? **Microeconomics** is the study of how individual businesses, households, and consumers decide to allocate their limited resources in exchange for goods and services. When an automobile parts manufacturer analyzes how a change in steel prices might affect production costs, he or she is using the microeconomic principles of supply and demand.

Changes in interest rates impact demand in the housing market–this is a topic considered in macroeconomics.

What is macroeconomics? **Macroeconomics** looks at the bigger picture. It is the study of the behaviour of the overall economy, or aggregates. Broader variables, such as changes in the unemployment rate, interest rates, and prices, are considered in the study of macroeconomics. For example, macroeconomics examines how a change in interest rates affects the demand for housing, or how a change in the housing market affects the overall economy. The government and individuals in a society also affect how resources are allocated and define the economic system in which goods and services are allocated.

microeconomics The study of how individual businesses, households, and consumers decide to allocate their limited resources in exchange for goods and services.

macroeconomics The study of the behaviour of the overall economy. Broader, aggregate variables, such as changes in the unemployment rate, interest rates, and prices, are considered in the study of macroeconomics.

Economic Systems

What is an economic system? An **economic system** describes the organization or economic structure of a country; it refers to the way in which an economy allocates its scarce economic resources and how it produces and distributes its output. These economic systems include the following:

- traditional economies
- planned (or controlled) economies
- market economies
- mixed economies

Traditional economies were found in earlier agrarian communities, which were primitive in nature, relying on agriculture for survival. Traditional economies were grounded in the strength of the family and a strong social network. Very few traditional economies exist today. Most economies today represent some form of a mixed economic system or a market economic system. **Table 3.1** summarizes the features of the three most common basic economic systems.

economic system The organization or economic structure of a country; it refers to the way in which an economy allocates its scarce economic resources and how it produces and distributes its output.

Table 3.1 World Economic Systems

Type of Economy	What to Produce	How to Produce	For Whom to Produce
Planned (Controlled)	Government or other centralized group determines what to produce.	Government or other centralized group determines and controls the resources and means of production.	Government or other centralized group determines wages and sets prices. Resources and products are distributed to a common group.
Market	Individuals and private firms make decisions based on consumer needs and wants.	Individuals and private firms determine the production methods. The focus is on efficiency and profitability.	Individual income ultimately controls purchasing decisions.
Mixed	Individuals determine what to produce with some level of government involvement.	Individuals and government control resources and determine production methods.	Government distributes some goods and services through selected social programs. Individual income determines purchasing decisions for other goods and services.

planned economic system A system in which the government plays an important role in determining what goods and services are provided and how they are produced and distributed. Both *communism* and *socialism* are examples of planned economic systems.

communism An economic system in which government makes all economic decisions and controls all the social services and many of the major resources required for the production of goods and services.

socialism An economic system in which the government plans and controls many important industries, but there does exist a form of capitalism whereby individuals are permitted ownership of resources and less crucial industries.

privatization The conversion of government-owned production and services to privately owned, profit-seeking enterprises.

capitalism An economic system that allows freedom of choice and encourages private ownership of the resources required to make and provide goods and services consumers enjoy. Also called a market economy, free market, or free enterprise.

Video: Fresher Than Fresh: Economics

What is a planned economic system? In a **planned economic system**, the government plays an important role in determining what goods and services are provided and how they are produced and distributed. Both communism and socialism are examples of planned economic systems.

Communism is an economic system in which government makes all economic decisions and controls all the social services and many of the major resources required for the production of goods and services. Karl Marx, the originator of communist principles in his book *The Communist Manifesto*, envisioned the workers themselves eventually taking over the government's responsibilities to provide the services. No communist country has achieved this level of Marx's vision. Existing communist states, including North Korea and Cuba, are failing economically. One of the main problems with communist systems are shortages of goods and services. In fact, in the later years of the twentieth century, most former Soviet states and Eastern European countries, as well as China, turned from a communist-based economy to a market economy to combat these problems.

Socialism describes an economy where the government plans and controls many important industries. It is similar to communism but allows for some capitalism (individual ownership). In socialist economic systems, governments traditionally run some of the essential industries, such as social services, education, health care, retirement, and unemployment, as well as other necessary businesses, such as utility companies (telephone, electric, water, sewer). The government charges high tax rates to pay for the services it provides. For example, according to the Legatum Prosperity Index, an annual ranking of 142 countries based on factors such as wealth, economic growth, and quality of life, Norway ranked first in 2013.[5] That same year, the marginal tax rate in Norway ranked among the highest in the world at 47.8 percent.[6] Canada ranked third on the prosperity index, and the marginal tax rate was 48 percent.[7] Although citizens of socialist countries pay higher tax rates, they benefit from social programs that tax proceeds are used to fund. Many Western European countries, such as France and Sweden, have adopted a socialist planned economy. Generally, workers in socialist economies work fewer hours, have longer vacations, and receive more health, education, and childcare benefits than do workers in purely capitalist economies.

Although many feel government-controlled and government-supplied social services provide a fair and equitable distribution of such services, a concern with true socialism is a diminishing motivation for workers. In a true socialist system, workers turn over their earnings and profits to the state rather than keep their own earnings, thus reducing the incentive to work hard. Therefore, it is difficult to find purely socialist economies. Many socialist and communist countries are beginning to change to market-based economies through the practice of **privatization**—the conversion of government-owned production and services to privately owned, profit-seeking enterprises.

What is a market economy? In a market economy, individuals are able to make their own economic decisions. For example, there may be several frozen yogurt shops in your town, and each one may sell yogurt at different prices—no one is restricting the number of frozen yogurt shops, nor is anyone controlling what price they can charge. Similarly, people are free to choose any variety of frozen yogurt they would like to buy. This freedom of choice for both the buyer and seller defines a free market economy. The United Kingdom, the United States, and Japan are examples of market economies.

Capitalism, also known as a market economy, free market, or free enterprise, is the economic system that allows such freedom of choice and encourages private ownership of the resources required to make and provide goods and services. Capitalism has become a major influence in the Western world's economic system. In a capitalist economy, the production and pricing of goods and services are determined through the operation of a market—the mechanism by which buyers and sellers exchange goods and services.

Although there is no current example of a country that demonstrates pure capitalism, the Fraser Institute, a Canadian agency that studies the impact of competitive markets and government intervention on individuals and societies, produces an annual report called the *Economic Freedom of the World*. According to the 2013 report, the following countries

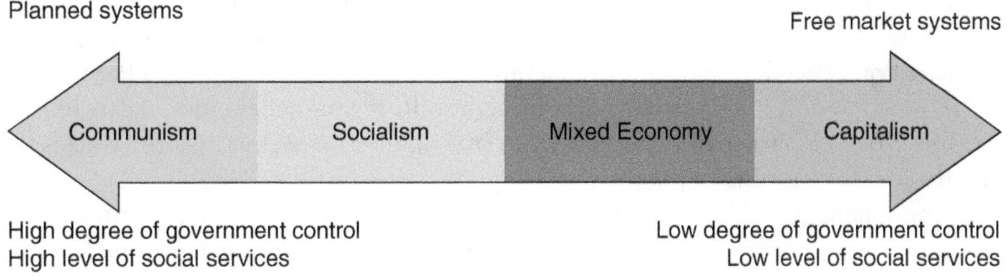

Figure 3.2 Continuum of Economic Systems: Degree of Government Control

have been assessed as the "freest" economies in the world, so we can infer that they most closely resemble a capitalist economy:[8]

1. Hong Kong
2. Singapore
3. New Zealand
4. Switzerland
5. United Arab Emirates
6. Mauritius
7. Finland
8. Bahrain
9. Canada
10. Australia

You will notice that the United States did not rank in the top 10: "Unfortunately for the United States, we've seen overspending, weakening rule of law, and regulatory overkill on the part of the U.S. government, causing its economic freedom score to plummet in recent years. This is a stark contrast from 2000, when the U.S. was considered a bastion of economic freedom and ranked second globally."[9]

What is a mixed economy? Today, most economic systems are **mixed economies**, meaning they are a blend of market and planned economies. Most Western European countries, for example, operate with a mixed economy of privately owned businesses and government control of selected social programs, such as health care. Although Canada's system operates largely on the principles of a free market, some aspects of it are consistent with socialist characteristics. Canada Post, the Canadian Broadcasting Corporation (CBC), and the Royal Canadian Mint are examples of **Crown corporations**—businesses owned by the federal government that provide important services to Canadians—which offer evidence of a certain degree of government involvement in the Canadian economy. Canada's generous social programs, including employment insurance, health care, and pension benefits, are afforded because of the tax revenue collected by the government. These examples demonstrate that although individuals have the right to privately own resources and the market is driven primarily by the forces of supply and demand, the presence of the government in various critical industries makes Canada's economic system a mixed economy.

One way to think about the various mixed economies and how they relate to either a market or planned economic system is to place them on a continuum, as shown in **Figure 3.2**.

mixed economies A blend of market and planned economies with a mixed economy of privately owned businesses and government control of selected social programs, such as health care.

Crown corporations Businesses owned by the federal government that provide important services to Canadians, such as Canada Post, the Canadian Broadcasting Corporation (CBC), and the Royal Canadian Mint.

BUSINESS AND ECONOMICS

LO2 Describe the laws of supply and demand and how equilibrium price is determined.

Supply and Demand

Why do business managers need to have an understanding of economics?

Business managers and owners must understand the basic principles of economics, particularly the concepts of supply and demand, because the survival of their business is largely determined by the activities in the market. Without any consumer demand, businesses will fail. Businesses need to be able to accurately estimate demand and understand the forces that affect the price of their offerings. For example, as the demand for fuel-efficient cars rises, automobile manufacturers such as General Motors and Ford need to make decisions about their product offerings: introducing new, fuel-efficient cars to satisfy this growing market and finding ways to re-engineer larger, family-size vehicles to reduce the level of gas consumption.

Business managers also need to be aware of the potential impact that government decisions, such as changing interest rates, have on their business decisions. The general health of the economy, in particular inflation and unemployment, will inevitably impact individual business and the entire industry in which they operate. Understanding economics, how prices are determined, the relationship between supply and demand, and the involvement of government is instrumental to operating a successful business.

bartering People trading goods or services without a medium of exchange. The "price" of something is determined by the needs of each person in the bartering exchange and what they are willing to trade.

medium of exchange Something such as money that is generally accepted in exchange for goods and services.

double coincidence of wants A situation that requires all parties in the exchange to have an item that the other wants in order to accomplish trade.

currency A medium of exchange for the transfer of goods and services that provides a consistent and equitable standard, the value of which is based on an underlying commodity, such as gold.

supply and demand A complicated process involving multiple factors, such as income levels, tastes, and the amount of competition in the market. The willingness and ability to purchase an item is called demand, and the willingness and availability to provide that item is called supply.

How do supply and demand affect business? In the era of **bartering**, when people traded goods or services without a **medium of exchange**, the "price" of something was determined by the needs of each person in the bartering exchange and what they were willing to trade. For example, if you wanted milk and had no cow, but you did have chickens, you were willing to give up eggs for milk—you would look for someone who wanted to trade his or her milk for your eggs. At the end of the trade, everyone was happy—you got the milk you needed and the other person got the eggs he or she needed.

However, there were problems with the bartering system. Bartering can be inefficient and inconsistent and requires a **double coincidence of wants**. What if the person who had the cow did not need eggs, or what if the owner of the cow thought the milk was worth a chicken, but you thought it was worth only a dozen eggs? To offset some of the difficulties of bartering, the concept of currency, or money, was developed—that is, money became the medium of exchange. **Currency**, a medium of exchange for the transfer of goods and services, provides a consistent and equitable standard, the value of which is based on an underlying commodity, such as gold.

In a system using currency, items such as milk, eggs, and chickens are assigned a price, or a value, based on how much the item is worth against the standard. Today, although we do have currency, ultimately the price for a product or service is determined by two fundamental economic concepts: supply and demand.

Supply and demand is actually a very complicated process because of the myriad factors involved. Income levels, tastes, and the amount of competition in the market all play an important role in the determination of supply and demand. However, if we ignore those factors for the moment (and economists do this all the time—it's called *ceteris paribus,* meaning "all else held constant") and just examine the fundamentals, we find that the market price for a product or service is the price at which everyone who wants the item can get it without anyone wanting more or without any of the item being left over. The willingness and ability to purchase an item is called demand, and the willingness and availability to provide that item is called supply.

Yong Hian Lim/Fotolia

Currency provides a medium of exchange and removes the necessity of achieving a double coincidence of wants inherent in a barter economy.

The closest real-world example of determining a market price that is based on pure supply and demand is the **auction process**, like that found on eBay. In an auction process, bidders state the price they are willing to pay for a particular item. The price increases depending on the demand: The greater the demand, the higher the price the bidders are willing to pay. Supply also affects price: If similar or identical items are available for auction, the price is kept lower. When a unique item is auctioned, prices tend to be higher because demand is higher and supply is lower. Eventually, the winning bid establishes the market price.

What does supply mean? **Supply** refers to how much of a product or service is available for purchase at any given time. It is dependent on the resources required to produce the product or offer the service, such as land, labour, and capital (buildings and machinery), and the quantity of similar products that can be easily substituted for the product and that are competing for the consumer's attention. However, if all of these factors are ignored or held constant (recall the assumption of *ceteris paribus*) then supply is directly affected by price (selling price).

Supply is derived from a producer's desire to maximize profits. The more money a business can get for its good or service, the more of its product it is willing to supply. In economic terms, the **law of supply** states that there is a direct relationship between price and quantity: The amount supplied will increase as the price increases, and if the price is lower a lower quantity of the product will be supplied.

Consider the following example: If Eddie opens a coffee kiosk in the middle of campus, he will want to supply more cups of coffee at the price of $2.00 per cup than at the price of $0.50 per cup. This makes intuitive sense: *He will have a greater incentive to supply coffee at the higher price.* To illustrate this point, let's assume the cost for Eddie to make a cup of coffee is $0.30, factoring in the cost of labour, supplies, equipment, and rent. Selling a cup of coffee at $0.50 means Eddie makes $0.20 profit, but selling a cup of coffee at $2.00 means Eddie makes $1.70 profit—that's a big incentive when you multiple that profit by hundreds of cups per day. Notice in **Table 3.2** that Eddie supplies only 10 cups of coffee at $0.50 per cup. However, if Eddie can charge $1.25, he has a greater incentive to supply more cups of coffee, so he produces 70 cups. At the price of $2.00, Eddie wants to supply even more cups of coffee, and his supply increases to 115. The more he can charge, the more he will want to supply. This relationship between supply and price can be illustrated in a graph, which economists call a supply curve, like the one shown in **Figure 3.3**. However, the demand for coffee has a very different reaction to price.

What does demand refer to? **Demand** refers to how much of a product or a service people want to buy at any given time. People are willing to buy as much as they need, but they have limited resources (money). Therefore, the **law of demand** states that people will buy more of an item at a lower price than at a higher price. In our coffee example, as shown in **Table 3.3**, students buy 12 cups of coffee when Eddie charges $2.00 a cup, but they buy 120 cups of coffee from Eddie at $0.50 a cup. In other words, as price decreases, demand increases. Economists illustrate the relationship between demand and price with a graph that they call a demand curve, as shown in **Figure 3.4**.

What factors determine price? As shown in the example of Eddie's Coffee Kiosk, there is an obvious conflict when setting a price. The *higher the price*, the more the product is likely to be supplied, but the *lower the price*, the more customers will likely purchase, or demand. If these two concepts of pricing are at odds with each other, then what determines the final price? Holding all other factors constant, prices are set at a point where supply equals demand. The supply–demand relationship is one of the fundamental concepts of economics. At Eddie's Coffee Kiosk, for example, at some point supply and demand will be equal. Although Eddie would love to sell

SELF CHECK Imagine you are a chef and have just realized your dream of opening your own gourmet Italian food restaurant. Do you know enough about supply and demand? You can test yourself by taking the following quiz.

1. You purchase a pasta machine that makes pasta three times faster than your current process. Your supply of fresh pasta will go
   A. up
   B. down
2. The price of flour skyrockets. Your supply of pasta will go
   A. up
   B. down
3. A highly publicized scientific study claims that low-carb diets help people lose weight faster than any other type of diet. The demand for your fresh pasta will go
   A. up
   B. down
4. A highly publicized scientific study claims that high-carb diets help people lose weight faster than any other type of diet. The demand for your fresh pasta will go
   A. up
   B. down

Answers: 1. A; 2. B; 3. B; 4. A

If you got ...
0 or 1 answer(s) correct: You're not supply-and-demand savvy yet. This section will help.
2 or 3 answers correct: You're semi-savvy in the fundamentals of supply and demand. Read this section carefully to build on your knowledge base.
4 answers correct: You're supply and demand savvy. Read this section to learn even more.

auction process A system that exemplifies price determination as bidders state their willingness to pay a price for an item based on demand. Supply factors into the price determination since multiple items available for sale will result in a lower price.

supply How much of a product or service is available for purchase at any given time.

law of supply States that there is a direct relationship between price and quantity: The amount supplied will increase as the price increases, and if the price is lower a lower quantity of the product will be supplied.

demand How much of a product or a service people want to buy at any given time.

law of demand States that people will buy more of an item at a lower price than at a higher price.

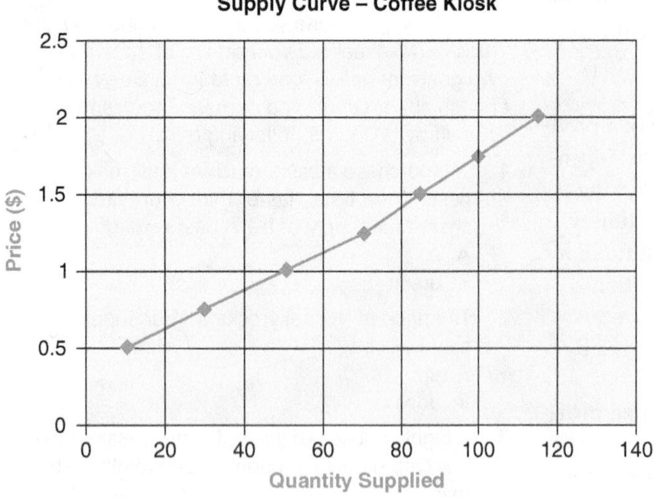

Figure 3.3 Supply Curve

The supply curve illustrates the incentive to supply more of an item as prices increase.

Table 3.2 The Relationship between Price and Quantity Supplied

Price ($)	Quantity Supplied (cups)
0.50	10
0.75	30
1.00	50
1.25	70
1.50	85
1.75	100
2.00	115

coffee at $2.00 a cup, he realizes that not many students are willing to buy coffee at that price. At the price of $2.00 a cup, Eddie would not use up his entire supply, creating a **surplus**, which occurs when sellers supply more of a product than buyers are willing to purchase.

surplus Occurs when sellers supply more of a product than buyers are willing to purchase.

As Eddie begins to lower his price, he finds that more students are willing to buy his coffee. However, if Eddie lowers his price too much—to $0.50 a cup, for example—then the demand would be so great that Eddie would run out before he was able to satisfy all the students who wanted coffee. This would create a **shortage**, which occurs when sellers do not produce enough of a product to satisfy demand.

shortage Occurs when sellers do not produce enough of a product to satisfy demand.

Ideally, Eddie will determine a price at which he is willing to supply the coffee and at which students are willing to demand the coffee without anyone wanting more or without any coffee being left over. The price at which supply equals demand is the **equilibrium price**, or market price. The equilibrium price is illustrated in a supply-and-demand

equilibrium price The market price at which supply is exactly equal to demand.

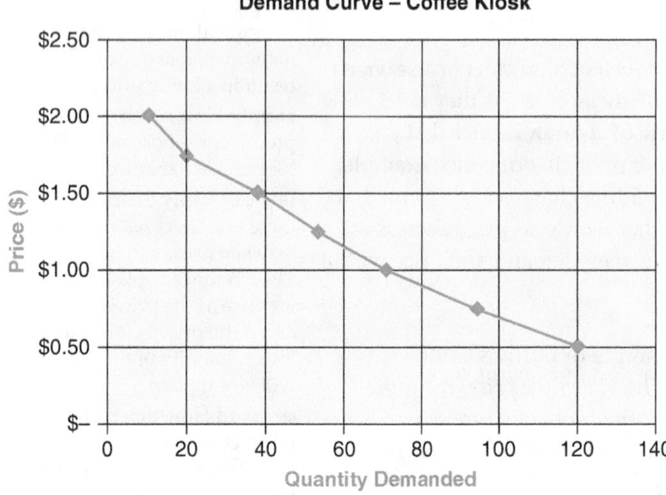

Figure 3.4 Demand Curve

The demand curve illustrates that demand increases as prices decrease.

Table 3.3 The Relationship between Price and Quantity Demanded

Price ($)	Quantity Demanded (cups)
0.50	120
0.75	95
1.00	72
1.25	55
1.50	38
1.75	23
2.00	12

curve, as shown in **Figure 3.5**. In this case, 60 cups of coffee is the equilibrium quantity associated with an equilibrium price of $1.15.

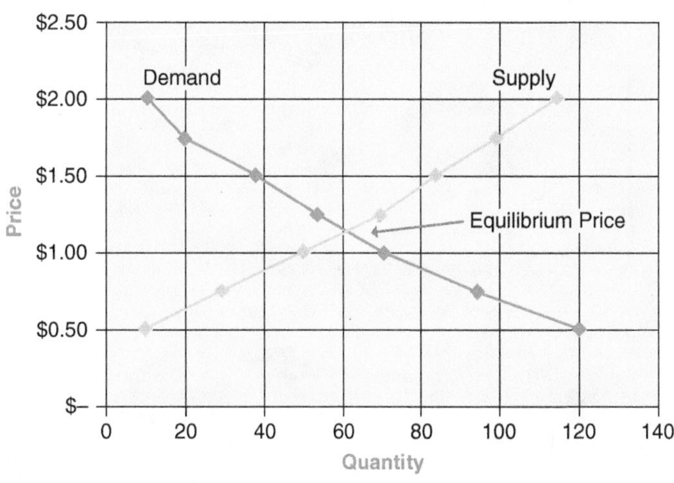

Figure 3.5 Equilibrium Price

The equilibrium or market price is the price at which supply equals demand.

What factors affect supply? Imagine you are the owner of a retail specialty shop specializing in unique silver jewellery or low-calorie homemade jams. What would happen if your supplier of these exquisite jewellery pieces increased the price they charged you to obtain them? What would happen if your supplier of homemade jams opened up a factory to make the same jam products faster and in more abundance? Both of these situations would affect your supply. Many factors can create a change in supply. These factors, known as the determinants of supply, are

- technology changes
- changes in resource prices
- price expectations
- number of suppliers in the market
- the price of substitute goods

Changes in any of these factors can shift the supply curve to the left (reducing supply) or to the right (increasing supply). **Table 3.4** summarizes the key determinants of supply.

Let's examine each key determinant in more detail.

Technology Changes Improvements in technology enable suppliers to produce their goods or services more efficiently and with fewer costs. For example, a jewellery maker with new tools is able to create unique pieces of jewellery in less time.

Changes in Resource Prices The price of the resources used to produce a good or service affects the cost of production. An increase in resource prices increases the cost of production and reduces profits, which lowers the incentive to supply a product. An increase in the price of silver, for example, will increase the price of a necklace or bracelet.

Price Expectations Price expectations reflect the producer's best guess at the future price of a good. Current supply may be increased or decreased depending on expectations of future prices. If prices are expected to increase in the future, the supplier may reduce supply now to supply more later at higher prices. If prices are expected to decrease in the future, the supplier may make every attempt to deplete supplies now at the higher price.

Table 3.4 Examples of Determinants of Supply

Determinant of Supply	Example
Technology changes	Continuing improvements in technology result in lower costs of production and create a higher level of productivity, which increases quantity and lowers price.
Changes in resource prices	A decrease in the cost of lumber increases the number of new homes built.
Price expectations	An anticipated lowering of interest rates may indicate a future increase in new housing contracts.
Number of suppliers in the market	An increase in homebuilders increases the supply of new homes and decreases the cost of new homes.
Price of substitute goods	Construction of apartment buildings is an alternate construction project to building new single-family residences.

Bayne Stanley/Alamy

The price of fuel affects how much you pay for an airline ticket. If fuel prices increase, so will the cost of your plane ticket.

Number of Suppliers in the Market The supply of a product or service increases as the number of competitors increases. It makes sense that the number of suppliers often increases in more profitable industries. For example, although Tim Hortons remains the leader in the retail coffee market, many companies, such as Starbucks and McDonald's, are marketing to coffee drinkers because of Tim Hortons' success, thus increasing the supply of coffee. Similarly, as an industry becomes less popular, maybe due to a change in technology, the number of suppliers decreases. When the digital camera became popular, the number of suppliers of film cameras decreased.

Price of Substitute Goods The price of comparable substitute goods also affects the supply of a product. If there are other equally comparable goods available at a lower price, the supply of the higher-priced goods will be affected. For example, if margarine, a substitute for butter, is priced lower than butter, then the supply of butter could be affected by consumers switching from butter to margarine.

Assuming that everything else is held constant, a change in any of these determinants of supply will affect the supply of a product and shift the demand curve. If the change is a positive effect, thereby increasing supply, the supply curve shifts to the right. Negative changes decrease supply and shift the supply curve to the left.

What factors affect demand? Just as there are factors that affect supply, there are also factors that affect demand for a product. These factors, known as the determinants of demand, are

- changes in income levels
- population changes
- consumer preferences
- complementary goods
- substitute goods

A positive change in any of these determinants of demand shifts the demand curve to the right, and negative changes shift the demand curve to the left. **Table 3.5** summarizes the determinants of demand.

Let's examine each of these key determinants in more detail.

Changes in Income Levels When income levels rise, people are able to buy more products. Conversely, when income levels fall, most people cut back on spending and buy fewer products. Therefore, when the economy enters a recession and people begin to lose their jobs, the demand for some goods and services decreases. An improving economy will bring an increase in spending as more people find jobs and create an increase in demand for some goods and services. Change in income levels is one factor that affects the housing market, for example. With an increase in income, people can afford to buy a home for the first time or can afford to upgrade to a bigger, more expensive home if they already own.

Population Changes Vacation rentals in resort communities experience demand shifts when populations fluctuate due to seasonal changes. Increases in population create greater demand for utilities (telephone, electricity, sewer, and water services) and public and consumer services (banks, drugstores, and grocery stores).

Table 3.5 Determinants of Demand

Determinants of Demand	Example
Changes in income levels	Job loss will reduce discretionary income and decrease the amount of coffee one buys. A promotion may allow a homeowner to buy a larger house or a house in a better neighbourhood.
Population changes	An increase in young, working professionals in a neighbourhood may increase the demand for coffee shops and single-family homes.
Consumer preferences	Needs and wants change based on fads and often manipulation by advertisers. A health alert concerning the negative effects of caffeine might reduce the demand for coffee.
Complementary goods	If the construction of new houses is in demand, complementary goods such as appliances and other home goods are also in demand. A reduction in new housing would negatively affect these other industries.
Substitute goods	These are products or services that can be used in place of another. In the housing industry, modular housing or trailers can be substituted for building a new home from scratch.

Consumer Preferences Demand for a product can change based on what is "cool" or "popular" at any given moment. Rainbow Loom bracelet makers, Xbox One gaming consoles, and the Apple iPhone 6 are all products that had high initial demand. As the demand for these items increases, there is a shift in the demand curve to the right. As demand begins to decrease, the demand curve shifts to the left.

For example, there has been an explosion in high-definition television (HDTV) sales over the last few years. Consumer demand for flat-panel TVs came from the developed TV markets, such as North America, Japan, and Western Europe, as well as from emerging markets. Because more manufacturers and retailers have entered the HDTV market, prices for sets continue to decrease. Prices have continued to decline but at the expense of profitability for many in the supply chain, especially at the brand and reseller level; however, increased sales usually mean additional customers and market share. Because of consumer demand, it is expected that Internet connectivity will rapidly become a standard feature on all but the lowest-priced TV models, just as 120 Hz has become standard for most LCD HDTV models.

Complementary Goods Products or services that complement each other and are consumed together, such as iPods and iTunes, are considered complementary goods. The demand for iTunes is great as long as consumers are buying and using iPods. If a new technology renders the iPod obsolete, the demand for iTunes will decrease, shifting the demand curve for iTunes to the left.

Substitute Goods Goods that can be used in place of other goods, such as Coca-Cola for Pepsi or a McDonald's Quarter Pounder for a Burger King Whopper, are substitute goods. Suppose, for example, someone reported getting violently ill after eating a McDonald's Quarter Pounder. The demand for the Burger King Whopper might increase, shifting the Whopper's demand curve to the right.

Imagine you are the owner of a bakery. How would you determine prices for your goods? At this point in the chapter, you should be able to answer this question. Your prices are a factor of supply and demand. A higher price provides you with an incentive to supply more baked goods. Conversely, a lower price will increase demand for these goods. The simple solution is to set prices at a point at which supply equals demand. Ideally, you would determine a price at which you are willing to supply various baked goods and at which customers are willing to purchase the goods without creating either a surplus or a shortage.

Simulation: Supply and Demand (Moondogs Coffee)

Video: Gas Prices Plummeting

ECONOMIC INDICATORS

LO3 Identify how economic indicators, including gross domestic product (GDP), price indexes, the unemployment rate, and productivity, reflect the economic health of a country.

Economic Growth

How do we determine whether the economy is growing? Businesses must monitor changes in the economy so they can plan accordingly. Let's look at the example of Greg Johnson's lumber company. Greg needs to decide how much inventory to purchase for his lumber company. He has seen new housing starts decline over the past several months, but he knows that if conditions change he could be supplying lumber for another housing boom in the near future. His staffing needs can change as quickly as his inventory requirements. Without any knowledge of future housing demand, it is difficult for Greg to determine appropriate inventory or staff levels. As a business owner, Greg knows his business is subject to fluctuations in the economy. In Greg's situation, the economy is struggling and new housing starts are declining. People are not in a position to buy real estate. This affects the number of new housing starts and, in turn, Greg's business. Which aspects of the economy should Greg watch to help him make his business decisions? How can he determine the health of the economy?

economic indicators Indicators such as gross domestic product (GDP), consumer and producer price indexes (which measure inflation), and the unemployment rate are used by economists to determine how well businesses are performing overall.

gross domestic product (GDP) Measures economic activity—the overall market value of final goods and services produced in a country in a year.

nominal GDP A measure of economic activity that includes all of the changes that have occurred in market prices during the year from inflation and deflation.

real GDP A measure of economic activity that attempts to remove the effects of inflation by using constant prices in some base year, thus allowing for comparisons against historical periods.

purchasing power parity (PPP) A measure to compare GDP between countries to determine living standards that takes into account the relative cost of living and the inflation rates of the countries, rather than just exchange rates, which might distort the real differences in income.

gross national product (GNP) Attributes earnings to the country where the firm is *owned*, not where the product is manufactured.

In the previous section, you learned about several factors that affect supply and demand. The overall state of the economy will affect supply and demand as well. In a healthy, stable economy, demand for consumer goods is high and businesses are typically expanding. In a struggling economy, the opposite is true. Consumers are not spending, demand is low, and businesses are often laying off workers and suffering from declining revenues. So the level of economic activity is a good indicator of business activity. Because changes in the economy can affect a business, managers need to be aware of a number of key economic indicators and how they relate to business. Economists primarily use the following three **economic indicators** to determine how well businesses are performing overall:

- gross domestic product (GDP)
- consumer and producer price indexes
- the unemployment rate

We'll look at these economic indicators, as well as productivity, in this section.

There are three broad economic goals shared by economies around the world: economic growth, price stability, and full employment. The broadest measure of the health of any country's economy is the size of its **gross domestic product (GDP)**. This indicator measures the level of economic activity—the overall market value of final goods and services produced in a country in a year. **Nominal GDP** includes all of the changes that have occurred in market prices during the year from inflation and deflation. **Real GDP** is a measure of economic activity that attempts to remove the effects of inflation by using constant prices in some base year, thus allowing for comparisons against historical periods.

Only goods actually produced *in the country* are counted in the country's GDP (hence the use of the word *domestic*). When comparing GDP between countries to determine standards of living, calculations are based on **purchasing power parity (PPP)**. PPP takes into account the relative cost of living and the inflation rates of the countries, rather than just exchange rates, which might distort the real differences in income.

Gross national product (GNP) attributes earnings to the country where a firm is *owned*, not where a product is manufactured. GDP can be contrasted with GNP in that GDP defines its scope *according to location* while GNP defines its scope *according to ownership*. For example, the Canadian-based aircraft manufacturer Bombardier has a significant presence in China, Japan, India, Russia, Europe, and the Middle East. The market value (selling price) of all products produced at all of Bombardier's locations is included in Canada's GNP. However, the market value of all products produced at Bombardier in China is included in China's GDP, but not in Canada's GDP. So the GNP measures the Canadian income resulting from production, whereas the GDP measures production in Canada regardless of country of ownership. Canada ranked fourteenth in GDP in 2012 with a GDP of US$1 474 000 000 000.[10]

How does the GDP act as an indicator of economic growth? When GDP goes up, the indication is that the economy is in a healthy state; goods and services are being produced and businesses are active. A declining GDP indicates a sluggish, contracting economy where fewer goods are being produced, fewer services are being sold, and businesses are relatively inactive. The eventual outcome is that employees are laid off, hours are reduced, or the business shuts its doors altogether. Therefore, business owners use GDP data to forecast sales and adjust production and investment in inventory. GDP is an aggregate figure, though, and does not account for differing sizes of nations. You are correct to assume that GDP in the United States is roughly 10 times that of Canada—it has 10 times the population. When comparing countries' relative GDP positions, it is useful to look at **GDP per capita** (per person), in which total GDP is divided by a country's population.

Countries by GDP (2013)

Country	GDP (PPP)
1. European Union	$ 16.95 trillion
2. United States	$ 16.72 trillion
3. China	$ 9.33 trillion
4. Japan	$ 5.007 trillion
5. Germany	$ 3.593 trillion
6. France	$ 2.739 trillion
7. United Kingdom	$ 2.49 trillion
8. Brazil	$ 2.19 trillion
9. Russia	$ 2.113 trillion
10. Italy	$ 2.068 trillion

Source: Based on Central Intelligence Agency, *The World Fact-book 2013*, https://www.cia.gov/library/publications/the-world-factbook/fields/2195.html.

How does producing more goods and services result in lower costs? In its broadest terms, **productivity** measures the quantity of goods and services that human and physical resources can produce in a given time. Many factors go into measuring productivity. For example, comparing output to the amount of labour used is one popular measure.

However it is measured, productivity is an indicator of a business's health. An increase in productivity indicates that existing resources are producing more goods or services in the same amount of time. Therefore, higher productivity often results in lower costs and lower prices, which generates more income and more profitability. Companies can reinvest the economic benefits of productivity growth by increasing wages and improving working conditions, reducing prices for customers, increasing shareholder value, and increasing tax revenue to the government, thus improving GDP. Therefore, overall productivity is an important economic indicator of the economy's health.

GDP per capita Measures the country's total GDP divided by the country's population.

productivity Measures the quantity of goods and services that human and physical resources can produce in a given time.

Inflation

How is price stability measured? There are two price indexes commonly used as economic indicators of inflation: the consumer price index and the producer price index. A consistent *increase* in either indicator indicates **inflation**, which is a rise in the general level of prices over time. A *decrease* in the rate of inflation is **disinflation**, and a continuous decrease in prices over time is **deflation**. The government also uses these indicators to make monetary policy decisions to control inflation and deflation (which is discussed later in this chapter).

inflation A rise in the general level of prices over time.

disinflation A decrease in the rate of inflation.

deflation A continuous decrease in prices over time.

How are changes in the price of consumer goods measured? The **consumer price index (CPI)** is a benchmark used to track changes in prices over time. The CPI measures price changes by creating a "market basket" of a specified set of goods and services (including taxes) that represent the average buying pattern of urban households. Through the monthly CPI, Statistics Canada tracks the retail price of a representative shopping basket of about 600 goods and services from an average household's expenditures: food, housing, transportation, furniture, clothing, and recreation. The basket of goods and services is evaluated by the Canadian government to ensure that it reflects current consumer buying habits. The value of this market basket is determined by the combined prices of these goods and services, which is then compared to its value in a previous period (generally a month), and the change is noted. Monthly CPI figures track the changes in prices of goods and services purchased by households (see **Figure 3.6**). The **cost of living** is the average monetary cost of the goods and services required to maintain a particular standard of living. It is closely related to the CPI. Statistics Canada uses 2002 as a base year to measure CPI changes, so in 2002 the CPI was equal to 100. This means that the basket of goods in 2002 cost Canadians $100. The CPI in November 2013 was measured at 123.0, meaning that the same basket of goods that cost $100 in 2002 cost $123.00 in November 2013.

consumer price index (CPI) A benchmark used to track changes in prices over time. It measures price changes by creating a "market basket" of a specified set of goods and services (including taxes) that represent the average buying pattern of urban households.

cost of living The average monetary cost of the goods and services required to maintain a particular standard of living. It is closely related to the CPI.

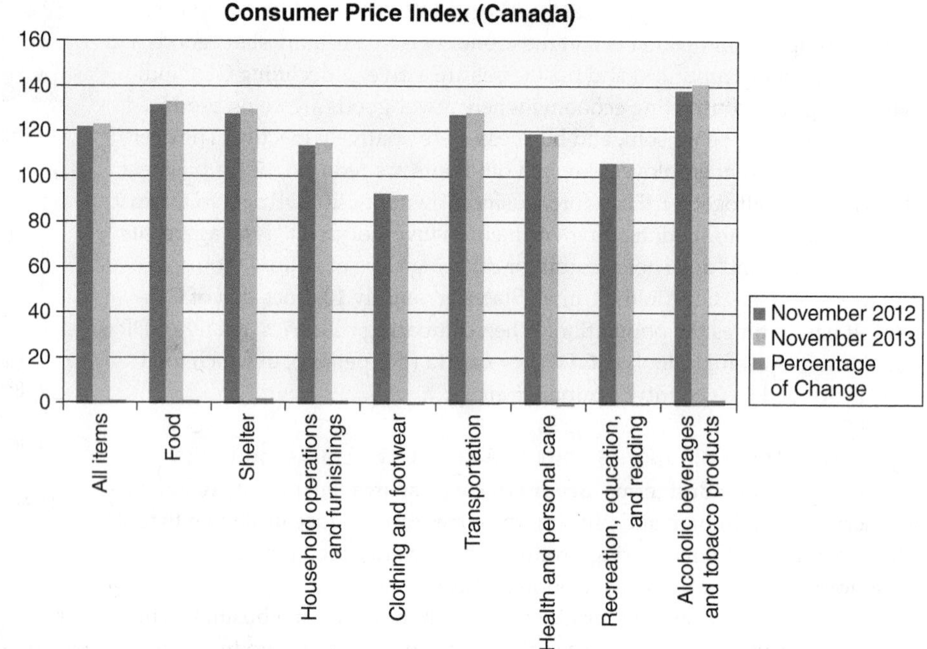

Figure 3.6 CPI Changes from November 2012 to November 2013

Source: Data points from Statistics Canada, "Consumer Price Index, by Province (Monthly)," accessed January 13, 2014, http://www.statcan.gc.ca/tables-tableaux/sum-som/l01/cst01/cpis01a-eng.htm.

Does the CPI measure changes in all prices? The CPI measures changes in prices of *consumer goods* only. It does not measure changes in prices of goods used to create consumer goods, such as capital and resource expenditures. The **producer price index (PPI)** tracks the average change in prices at the wholesale level (from the seller's perspective). Therefore, it tracks prices of goods sellers use to create their products or services, such as raw materials, product components that require further processing, and finished goods sold to retailers. The PPI excludes energy prices and prices for services.

producer price index (PPI) A benchmark used to track the average change in prices at the wholesale level (from the seller's perspective). Therefore, it tracks prices of goods sellers use to create their products or services, such as raw materials, product components that require further processing, and finished goods sold to retailers. The PPI excludes energy prices and prices for services.

Why are price indexes important? A change in prices is an important economic indicator. It is a measurement of purchasing power, and it triggers certain business decisions. During periods of increasing prices as reflected by the CPI, the purchasing power of a dollar decreases, meaning that less is bought with a dollar today than could have been bought with the same dollar yesterday. To compensate for such price increases, wages eventually need to be increased. In turn, businesses must eventually increase prices to compensate for the higher cost of labour. Similarly, if the price to produce goods or services increases, businesses will need to pass on those cost increases in the form of higher prices, again decreasing the consumer's purchasing power. Therefore, business leaders watch the CPI and PPI to determine the rate at which consumer and wholesale prices change, respectively.

Unemployment

What other indicators are used to measure the economy? The **unemployment rate** measures the number of people who are at least 15 years old, are seeking work, and are currently unemployed.[11] Because there are different reasons that people are not working, there are several different measurements of unemployment:

unemployment rate Measures the number of people who are at least 15 years old, are seeking work, and are currently unemployed.

- *Frictional unemployment* measures temporary unemployment in which workers move between jobs, careers, and locations.
- *Structural unemployment* measures permanent unemployment that happens when an industry changes in such a way that jobs are terminated completely. Many steel workers and miners lost jobs because of declines in those industries. More recently, many bank tellers have been replaced by automated teller machines (ATMs). These workers can learn new skills or receive additional training in an effort to keep their jobs or find new ones. Often this kind of unemployment, which is created when technological advancements displace traditional human workers, is referred to as *technological unemployment*.

- *Cyclical unemployment* measures unemployment caused by businesses not having enough demand for labour to employ those who want to work. This generally results from fluctuations in the business cycle (hence the use of the word *cyclical*). Companies must cut back their workforce when there is a downturn in the business cycle. Once the demand for goods and services increases, companies begin to hire again. When economic output falls, as measured by GDP, the business cycle is low and cyclical unemployment will rise.
- *Seasonal unemployment* measures those who are out of work during the "off season," for instance, people employed in snow- or beach-related industries, agriculture, or tourism activities.

Why is unemployment an important economic measure? Businesses, as well as government policymakers, pay close attention to unemployment rates. High unemployment levels in Canada are a concern for the government since it results in an increase in unemployment benefits and government spending on social programs, such as welfare and health care. High unemployment can also result in increases in mental stresses and physical illnesses and is associated with higher incidences of crime and domestic violence. It is costly for businesses to lay off workers and then hire and train new workers as the economy eventually improves. In a declining economy, businesses prefer to reduce their workforce through retirement and natural attrition, which takes considerable planning. However, if the unemployment rate drops too low, the concern is that more workers have increased buying power and spend more, which ultimately causes prices to increase, resulting in a higher inflation rate. Therefore, the challenge is to keep both inflation and unemployment low—a difficult task since they seem to have an inverse relationship.

How do economic indicators help businesses make decisions? Earlier in this chapter we looked at the example of Greg Johnson's lumber company. After ensuring there is inventory to fill current needs, Greg keeps a close eye on all economic indicators, especially the CPI and unemployment rate, to help guide his future buying decisions. He knows that movements in the CPI determine the trend of current prices. Such trends can help Greg determine whether it is better to stock up now at lower prices or wait to buy later if prices are expected to fall.

Equally important is the unemployment rate. Greg's business is tied closely to the new housing industry. Unfortunately, Greg is feeling the pressures of a sagging housing industry and a declining economy. Because there is less for his employees to do, he has already laid off workers. A continued downturn in the housing industry will increase the unemployment rate as more and more construction workers are laid off. This indicates to Greg that consumers are not likely to be planning to purchase a new home. For Greg, this translates into the probability that his inventory of lumber and other building materials is not likely to move quickly. Watching these indicators over time and understanding how to interpret them allows Greg to have a better understanding of the health of the economic environment in which he operates. Certainly Greg will benefit from this knowledge, because he will be better able to make smart business decisions, forecasts, and future plans.

Video: Job Search Help for Young Workers

GOVERNMENT AND THE ECONOMY

The Business Cycle

LO4 List and describe the four stages of the business cycle.

What are fluctuations in the economy? As the CPI rises, the annual rate of inflation rises. Canada's annual rate of inflation, which reached a high of 12.5 percent in 1981, has remained quite stable, staying within the Bank of Canada's target range of 1 to 3 percent since it implemented a noticeable shift in its focus toward price level stability in the mid-1990s.[12] Over time, the economy naturally fluctuates, which means it goes through periods of increased growth (expansion) and decreased growth (contraction). Economists refer to these increases and decreases as the **business cycle**.

business cycle Describes how the economy fluctuates over time, going through periods of increased growth (expansion) and decreased growth (contraction).

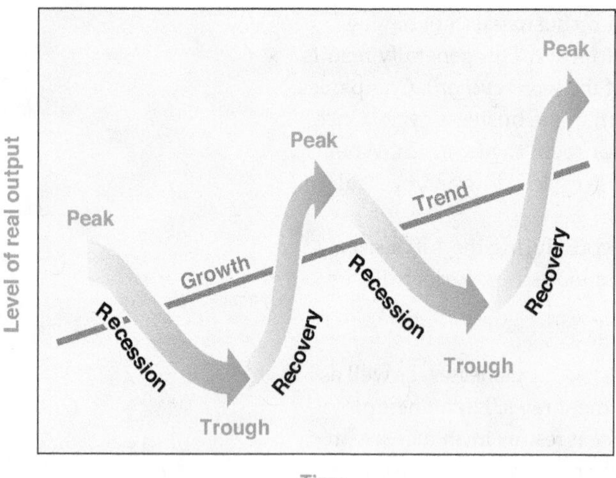

Figure 3.7 Business Cycle

There are four stages of the business cycle, as illustrated in **Figure 3.7**.

- *Peak:* This stage occurs when the economy is at its most robust point. The peak occurs after the expansionary phase and before the recessionary phase. It is characterized by high levels of economic activity, high levels of consumer spending, high output (GDP), low unemployment rates, and eventually rising prices.
- *Recession:* By definition, a **recession** is a decline in the GDP for two or more consecutive quarters of a year. In recessionary times, corporate profits decline, unemployment increases, and the stock market reacts with large selling sessions that result in decreasing stock prices. A severe or prolonged recession is a **depression**. Depressions are usually associated with falling prices (deflation). After the onset of the Great Depression of 1929, the government used policies to control the economy to avoid another Great Depression.
- *Trough:* A trough occurs when the recession hits bottom and the economy begins to expand again.
- *Expansion or recovery:* After a recession or even a depression, the economy eventually hits a trough and begins to grow again. It enters into an expansionary or recovery phase. The recovery will eventually hit a peak, and the cycle begins again.

recession A decline in the GDP for two or more consecutive quarters of a year.

depression A severe or prolonged recession.

Controlling Fluctuations in the Economy

LO5 Summarize how the government uses both monetary and fiscal policies to stabilize the economy as a result of business cycle fluctuations.

How does the government control fluctuations in the economy? Ideally, the economy could stay near its peak all the time, where consumers enjoy high spending and high income and businesses enjoy high sales and high revenues. But left to its own forces and in reaction to external actions on the economic system, such as wars and weather variations, the economy will inevitably cycle through peaks and troughs. To smooth out the fluctuations in the business cycle, the government influences the economy through its **fiscal policy**, in which the government determines the appropriate level of taxes and spending, and through its **monetary policy**, in which the government manages the supply of money and interest rates.

fiscal policy The way in which the government determines the appropriate level of taxes and spending to smooth out fluctuations in the business cycle and stabilize the economy.

monetary policy The way in which the government manages the supply of money and interest rates to smooth out fluctuations in the business cycle and stabilize the economy.

contractionary fiscal measures Fiscal policy measures that include increasing taxes and decreasing government spending in an attempt to slow the economy.

Why does the government increase taxes in a fiscal response? The government increases taxes as part of its fiscal policy in an attempt to offset rising inflation. Higher taxes reduce consumers' personal disposable income, which translates into lower consumer spending. This slows the growth of businesses and slows down the economy by reducing the amount of money in the system. Decreasing taxes does not have quite the opposite effect on the economy as increasing taxes. It would seem that if increasing taxes would slow down an economy, a tax cut would help stimulate the economy. Although that is partially true, the amount of money entering the system depends on how much of the tax reduction consumers spend and how much they save. Money put into savings does not help stimulate the economy immediately. **Contractionary fiscal measures** include increasing taxes and decreasing government spending in an attempt to slow the economy.

How does government spending help stimulate the economy? Increasing government spending is a fiscal policy response that the government uses to help fuel a lagging economy. The government spends money on a variety of projects, such as infrastructure improvements and projects that benefit the military, education, and health care. Government spending increases cash flow to the economy faster than decreasing taxes because it provides an immediate injection of funds into the system. Often, government spending creates additional jobs, which also helps stimulate the economy. During periods of high economic growth, the government may decrease its spending. **Expansionary fiscal measures** include decreasing taxes and increasing government spending to stimulate the economy and put money back into the hands of businesses and consumers, encouraging businesses to expand and consumers to buy more goods and services.

expansionary fiscal measures Fiscal policy measures that include decreasing taxes and increasing government spending to stimulate the economy and put money back into the hands of businesses and consumers, encouraging businesses to expand and consumers to buy more goods and services.

Money Supply

In addition to fiscal policy, how else can the government stabilize the economy?

The **Bank of Canada** acts as the federal government's financial adviser and is responsible for promoting the economic and financial well-being of Canada. The Bank of Canada manages the country's money supply through its monetary policy to control inflation. In addition to setting monetary policy, the Bank of Canada provides banking services to member banks and to the federal government. It is headed by a board of directors that has the power to increase or decrease the money supply and raise or lower short-term interest rates, therefore affecting credit availability.

The Bank of Canada has set a target rate for inflation in the range of 1 to 3 percent. When inflation is present in the economy and is approaching or exceeding the 3 percent rate, the Bank of Canada will take contractionary measures to decrease the money supply and raise interest rates (causing people to borrow less and save more, which reduces the amount of money in the economy). To counter a recession, the Bank of Canada will take expansionary measures to increase the supply of money and lower interest rates on borrowing money (causing people to save less and borrow more, which increases the amount of money in the economy).

Bank of Canada Acts as the federal government's financial adviser and is responsible for promoting the economic and financial well-being of Canada. It manages the country's money supply through its monetary policy to control inflation.

What is a budget surplus? Every year the government creates a budget—a financial plan that outlines expected revenues from taxes and fees and projects forecasted government spending. If the money the government takes in (through taxes and fees) exceeds the money the government spends (for things such as social services, defence, and transportation), the result is a **budget surplus**. **Figure 3.8** illustrates the various revenue and

budget surplus Occurs when the money coming into the government exceeds the money being spent by the government.

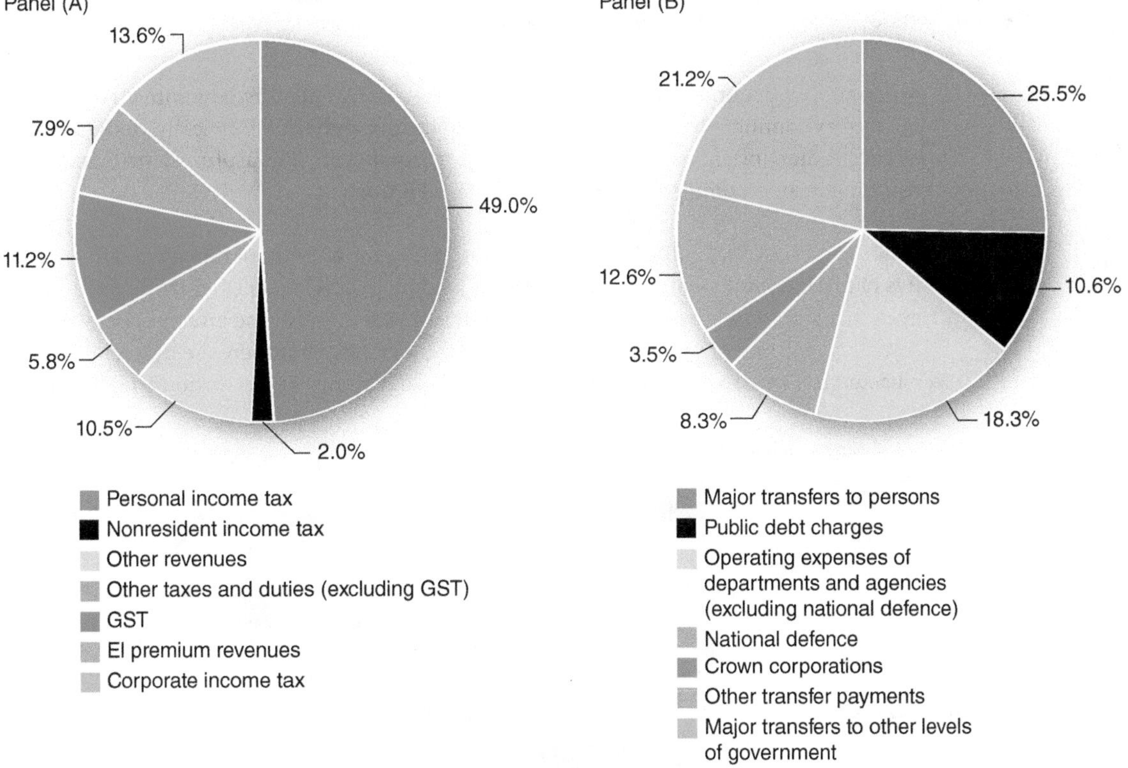

Figure 3.8 Composition of Revenues and Expenses for 2012–2013

Source: Data from Department of Finance Canada, *Annual Financial Report of the Government of Canada: Fiscal Year 2012–2013*, accessed January 13, 2014, http://www.fin.gc.ca/afr-rfa/2013/report-rapport-eng.asp#a3.

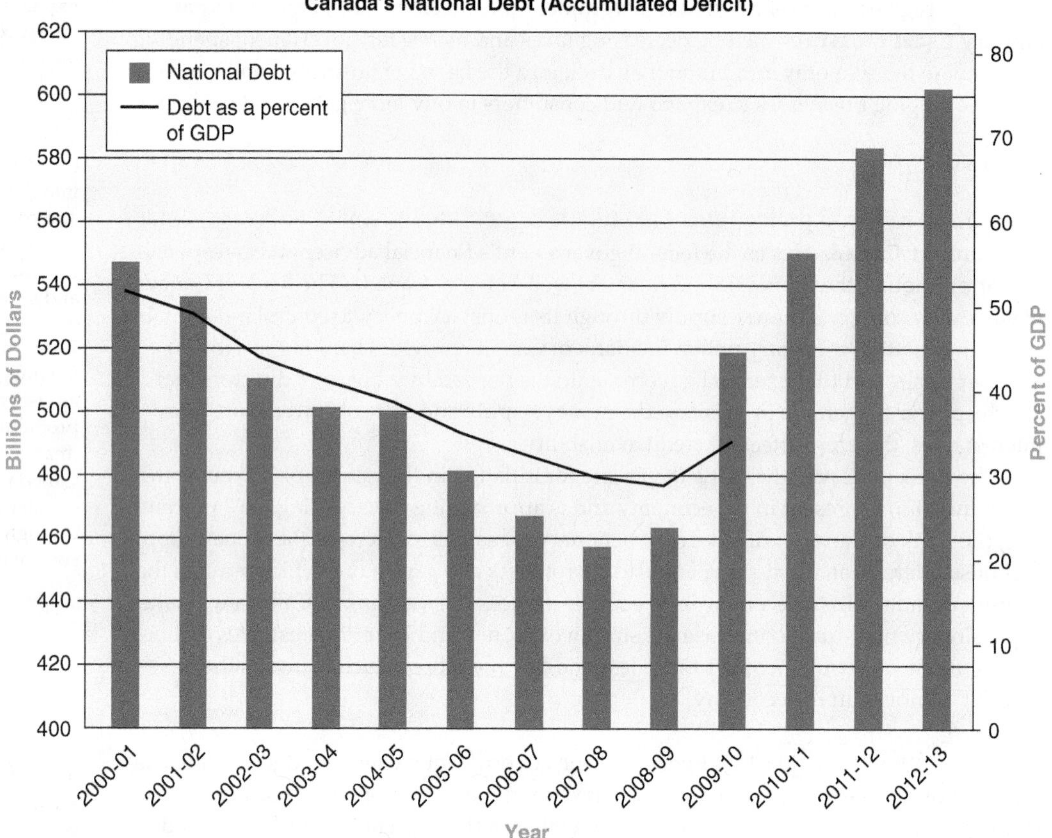

Figure 3.9 Canada's National Debt (Accumulated Deficit)

Source: Data from Department of Finance Canada, *Annual Financial Report of the Government of Canada: Fiscal Year 2012–2013,* accessed January 13, 2014, http://www.fin.gc.ca/afr-rfa/2013/report-rapport-eng.asp#a3.

budget deficit Occurs when the money being spent by the government exceeds the money coming into the government.

national debt The accumulated total yearly deficits.

expenditure categories for 2012–2013. If the money being spent by government exceeds the money coming into government, there is a **budget deficit**. Historically, budget deficits occur more often than surpluses, and the yearly deficits (or surpluses) are totalled, resulting in an accumulated **national debt** (see **Figure 3.9**).

What is the money supply? When determining the amount of money in our system, it is natural to think of all the coins and bills held by people, businesses, and banks. However, that would only represent a portion of the money supply. The money supply is the combined amount of money available within the economy, but there are different ways to measure it. The standard measures usually include currency in circulation and demand

Canadian currency includes many security features. This image outlines the features included on the $20 bill.

Table 3.6 Bank of Canada Measures of Money

M1+ (gross)	Currency outside the banks plus all chequable deposits held at chartered banks, trust and mortgage loan companies, credit unions, and caisses populaires (excluding deposits of these institutions); plus continuity adjustments. Coins, bills, travellers' cheques, and chequing accounts constitute the narrowest measure of our money supply. These assets are the most liquid in that they are already in the form of cash or are the easiest to change into cash.
M1++ (gross)	M1+ (gross) plus all nonchequable deposits (other than fixed-term deposits) held at chartered banks, trust and mortgage loan companies, credit unions, and caisses populaires; less interbank deposits; plus continuity adjustments.
M2 (gross)	Currency outside banks plus bank personal deposits, bank nonpersonal demand and notice deposits; less interbank deposits; plus continuity adjustments.
M3 (gross)	M2 (gross) plus bank nonpersonal term deposits and foreign-currency deposits of residents; less interbank deposits; plus continuity adjustments.
M2+ (gross)	M2 (gross) plus deposits at trust and mortgage loan companies and at government savings institutions; deposits and shares at credit unions and caisses populaires; life insurance company individual annuities; money market mutual funds; plus continuity adjustments and other adjustments.
M2++ (gross)	M2+ (gross) plus Canada Savings Bonds and other retail debt instruments; plus non-money market mutual funds.

Source: Bank of Canada, "Canada's Money Supply," accessed January 13, 2014, http://www.bankofcanada.ca/wp-content/uploads/2010/11/canada_money_supply.pdf. Used by Permission of Bank of Canada.

deposits (depositors' easily accessed assets on the books of financial institutions). Some of the other measures are called *monetary aggregates* (see **Table 3.6**). As of November 2013, Canada's money supply was $644 732 million M1 (gross), $1 231 996 million M2, and $1 747 622 million M3.[13]

Why is controlling the money supply important? Money has a direct effect on the economy, because the more money consumers have, the more they tend to spend. When consumers spend more, businesses do better. Demand for resources, labour, and capital increases because of the stimulated business activity and, in general, the economy improves. However, there can be too much of a good thing. When the money supply continues to expand, eventually there might not be enough goods and services to satisfy demand, and when demand is high, prices will rise. (Remember the demand curve? It shifts to the right.) Sometimes this situation is described as "too much money chasing too few goods."

The opposite can also happen when the supply of money becomes limited following a decrease in economic activity. When the economy begins to slow down because of decreased spending, either disinflation or deflation results. The Bank of Canada uses monetary policy to help keep inflation within the inflation-control target range of 1 to 3 percent. To help avoid price level instability (the presence of inflation or deflation) the Bank of Canada uses a variety of monetary tools (see **Table 3.7**) to affect the

Table 3.7 Bank of Canada's Monetary Tools and Their Effects

Tool	Action	Measure	Effect on Money Supply	Effect on Interest Rates	Effect on Economic Activity
Open Market Operations	Buy government securities	Expansionary (money is put into circulation)	Increases	Lowers	Increases
	Sell government securities	Contractionary (money is taken out of circulation)	Decreases	Raises	Decreases
Overnight Rate	Raise overnight rate	Contractionary (interest rates go up, dollar goes up)	Decreases	Raises	Decreases
	Lower overnight rate	Expansionary (interest rates go down, dollar goes down)	Increases	Lowers	Increases

money supply. Among these tools we will discuss two: open market operations and the overnight rate.

What are open market operations? One of the main tools the Bank of Canada uses in its monetary policy is open market operations, which is the buying and selling of government securities (bonds and Treasury bills or other financial instruments). Monetary targets such as inflation, interest rates, or exchange rates are used to guide these transactions. When the Bank of Canada buys or sells Canadian securities, it is changing the level of reserves in the banking system. When it buys securities, it adds reserves to the system, money is said to be "easy," and interest rates drop. Lower interest rates help stimulate the economy by decreasing the desire to save and increasing the demand for loans such as home mortgages. Since new homebuyers would benefit by getting a mortgage with the lowest interest rate possible, they should watch for reports that would indicate what the Bank of Canada intends to do with its open market operations.

What is the overnight rate? The Bank of Canada carries out monetary policy by influencing short-term interest rates. The overnight rate is the interest rate at which major financial institutions borrow and lend one-day (or "overnight") funds among themselves; the Bank of Canada sets a target level for that rate. The bank rate is the rate of interest that the Bank of Canada charges on short-term loans to financial institutions. It is adjusted in accordance with changes to the overnight rate and is used to administer monetary policy.[14] To help ensure that inflation remains low for sustained economic growth and job creation, the bank rate is adjusted from time to time. Banks usually increase the rate they charge their customers, the prime rate, whenever the Bank of Canada raises the overnight rate. Changes to the overnight rate not only influence interest rates that customers pay on loans and mortgages, but it might also affect interest rates consumers receive on investments.

By lowering the overnight rate, commercial banks are encouraged to borrow funds from the Bank of Canada. The commercial banks then lend money to businesses, thereby stimulating the economy by putting funds into the economic system. When prime rates are low, demand increases for more expensive items, such as housing, furniture, automobiles, and appliances, because businesses and households can borrow money at lower interest rates. When interest rates are low, businesses and households also tend to spend more and save (or invest) less, because they are not receiving a big return on their invested money. If the economy is too robust, the Bank of Canada can increase the overnight rate, which discourages banks from borrowing additional funds. Businesses are then discouraged from borrowing because of the higher interest rates.

As demand for goods and services and spending increase, the Canadian dollar appreciates, which increases the cost of Canadian products relative to foreign ones, thus leading to adjustments in spending. Specifically, the demand by foreign consumers for Canadian products decreases (fewer exports) and the demand by Canadians for foreign products increases (more imports).

When you deposit money into a bank, the money does not sit in a vault waiting for the time when you want to withdraw it. Instead, banks use your deposited money to make loans to others: people, small businesses, corporations, and other banks. Banks make money by the interest charged on those loans. However, the bank must be able to give you back your money when you demand it. Therefore, banks do not lend out the entire balance of deposits, but instead they retain a portion of it—a reserve—that is sufficient to cover any demands by customers for funds on any given day. This includes trips to ATM machines, use of debit cards, requests for loans, and payment of cheques that customers write. If the banks do not have enough funds to cover daily demands, customers might get nervous that the bank will lose their money and might withdraw all their funds.

It is important to be aware of the overall state of the economy when making decisions on large investments. Because the government's actions affect the economy, it is also important to know what these actions are and what effect they will have. For example, in making a decision about whether to buy a home, you should observe whether the Bank of Canada is buying or selling securities. If the Bank of Canada buys securities, it is putting money back into the economy in an attempt to stimulate or boost the economy (expansionary measure); therefore, it is likely that interest rates for mortgage loans will decrease (expansionary measure).

CHAPTER SYNOPSIS

LO1 Define economics and describe the different types of economic systems. *(pp. 40–43)*

Economics is the study of how individuals, businesses, and government make decisions about how to allocate limited (scarce) resources to best satisfy the wants, needs, and desires of people.

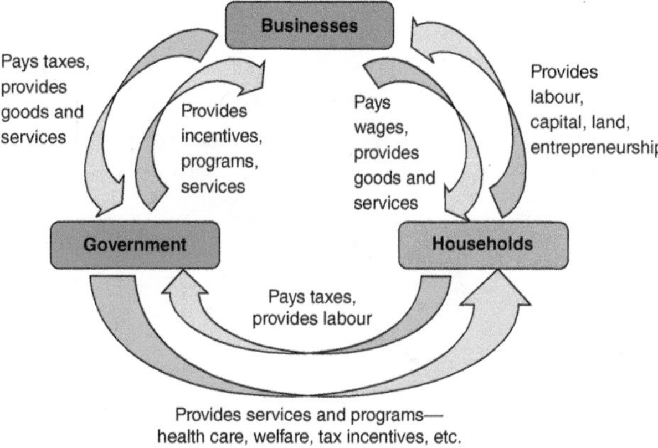

Circular Flow of Canada's Economy

Microeconomics is the study of how individual businesses, households, and consumers make decisions to allocate their limited resources in the exchange of goods and services.

Macroeconomics is the study of the behaviour of the overall economy. Broader, aggregate variables, such as changes in the unemployment rate, interest rates, and prices, are considered in the study of macroeconomics.

In a **planned economic system**, the government plays an important role in determining what goods and services are provided and how they are produced and distributed. Both communism and socialism are planned economic systems.

Communism is an economic system in which government makes all economic decisions and controls all the social services and many of the major resources required for the production of goods and services.

Socialism describes an economy where the government plans and controls many important industries, but there does exist a form of capitalism whereby individuals are permitted ownership of resources and less crucial industries.

Capitalism, also called a market economy, free market, or free enterprise, allows freedom of choice and encourages private ownership of the resources required to make and provide the goods and services consumers enjoy.

Today, most countries use a **mixed economy**, which is a blend of market and planned economies. Most Western European countries, for example, operate with a mixed economy of privately owned businesses and government control of selected social programs, such as health care.

LO2 Describe the laws of supply and demand and how the equilibrium price is determined. *(pp. 43–49)*

Supply and demand are complicated concepts because many factors are involved, such as income levels, tastes, and the amount of competition in the market, to name a few. The ability and willingness to buy an item is called demand, whereas the willingness and availability to bring that item to the market is called supply.

Supply refers to how much of a product or service is available for purchase at any given time. In economic terms, the **law of supply** states that the amount supplied will increase as the price increases; if the price is lower, less of the product is supplied.

Demand refers to how much of a product or a service people want to buy at any given time. Therefore, the **law of demand** states that people will buy more of an item at a lower price than at a higher price.

Factors or determinants of supply include

- technology changes
- changes in resource prices

World Economic Systems

Type of Economy	What to Produce	How to Produce	For Whom to Produce
Planned (Controlled)	Government or other centralized group determines what to produce.	Government or other centralized group determines and controls the resources and means of production.	Government or other centralized group determines wages and sets prices. Resources and products are distributed to the common group.
Market	Individuals and private firms make decisions based on consumer needs and wants.	Individuals and private firms determine the production methods. The focus is on efficiency and profitability.	Individual income ultimately controls purchasing decisions.
Mixed	Individuals determine what to produce with some level of government involvement.	Individuals and government control resources and determine production methods.	Government distributes some goods and services through selected social programs. Individual income determines purchasing decisions for other goods and services.

- price expectations
- number of suppliers in the market
- the price of substitute goods

Factors or determinants of demand include

- changes in income levels
- population changes
- consumer preferences
- complementary goods
- substitute goods

When sellers supply more of a product than buyers are willing to purchase there is a **surplus**. When sellers do not produce enough of a product to satisfy demand there is a **shortage**. The price at which supply equals demand is the **equilibrium price**, or market price.

Equilibrium Price

Inflation is a rise in the general level of prices over time. A decrease in the rate of inflation is **disinflation**, and a continuous decrease in prices over time is **deflation**.

The **consumer price index (CPI)** is a benchmark used to track changes in prices over time. The CPI measures price changes by creating a "market basket" of a specified set of goods and services (including taxes) that represent the average buying pattern of urban households.

The **cost of living** is the average monetary cost of the goods and services required to maintain a particular standard of living. It is closely related to the CPI.

LO4 List and describe the four stages of the business cycle. *(pp. 53–54)*

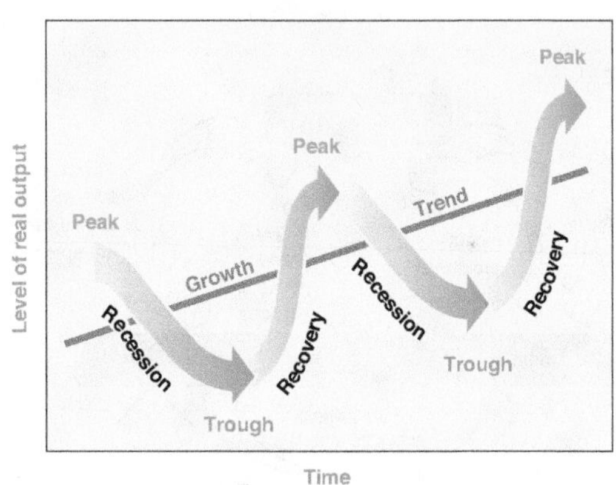

Business Cycle

LO3 Understand how economic indicators, including gross domestic product (GDP), price indexes, the unemployment rate, and productivity, reflect the economic health of a country. *(pp. 50–53)*

Economists primarily use the following three **economic indicators** to determine how well the economy is performing overall: gross domestic product (GDP), consumer and **producer price indexes** (CPI and PPI), and the **unemployment rate**.

When **GDP** goes up, it indicates that the economy is in a positive state. Goods and services are being produced and businesses are doing well. A declining GDP indicates a sluggish, contracting economy where fewer goods are being produced, fewer services are being sold, and businesses are relatively inactive. The eventual outcome is that employees are laid off, hours are reduced, or the business shuts its doors altogether.

In its broadest terms, **productivity** measures the quantity of goods and services that human and physical resources can produce in a given time.

LO5 Summarize how the government uses both monetary and fiscal policies to stabilize the economy as a result of business cycle fluctuations. *(pp. 54–59)*

To smooth out the fluctuations in the business cycle, the government influences the economy through its **fiscal policy**, in which the government determines the appropriate level of taxes and spending, and through its **monetary policy**, in which the government manages the supply of money and interest rates.

Contractionary fiscal measures include increasing taxes and decreasing government spending in an attempt to slow the economy. **Expansionary fiscal measures** include decreasing taxes and increasing government spending to stimulate the economy and put money back into the hands of businesses and consumers, encouraging businesses to expand and consumers to buy more goods and services.

MyBizLab Study, practise, and explore real business situations with these helpful resources:

- **Interactive Lesson Presentations:** Work through interactive presentations and assessments to test your knowledge of business concepts.
- **Study Plan:** Check your understanding of chapter concepts with self-study quizzes.
- **Dynamic Study Modules:** Work through adaptive study modules on your computer, tablet, or mobile device.
- **Simulations:** Practise decision-making in simulated business environments.

KEY TERMS

auction process *(p. 45)*
Bank of Canada *(p. 55)*
bartering *(p. 44)*
budget deficit *(p. 56)*
budget surplus *(p. 55)*
business cycle *(p. 53)*
capitalism *(p. 42)*
circular flow *(p. 40)*
communism *(p. 42)*
consumer price index (CPI) *(p. 51)*
contractionary fiscal measures *(p. 54)*
cost of living *(p. 51)*
Crown corporations *(p. 43)*
currency *(p. 44)*
deflation *(p. 51)*
demand *(p. 45)*
depression *(p. 54)*
disinflation *(p. 51)*
double coincidence of wants *(p. 44)*
economic indicators *(p. 50)*
economic system *(p. 41)*
economics *(p. 40)*
equilibrium price *(p. 46)*
expansionary fiscal measures *(p. 55)*
fiscal policy *(p. 54)*
GDP per capita *(p. 51)*
gross domestic product (GDP) *(p. 50)*
gross national product (GNP) *(p. 50)*
inflation *(p. 51)*
law of demand *(p. 45)*
law of supply *(p. 45)*
macroeconomics *(p. 41)*
medium of exchange *(p. 44)*
microeconomics *(p. 41)*
mixed economies *(p. 43)*
monetary policy *(p. 54)*
national debt *(p. 56)*
nominal GDP *(p. 50)*
planned economic system *(p. 42)*
privatization *(p. 42)*
producer price index (PPI) *(p. 52)*
productivity *(p. 51)*
purchasing power parity (PPP) *(p. 50)*
real GDP *(p. 50)*
recession *(p. 54)*
scarcity *(p. 40)*
shortage *(p. 46)*
socialism *(p. 42)*
supply *(p. 45)*
supply and demand *(p. 44)*
surplus *(p. 46)*
unemployment rate *(p. 52)*

CRITICAL THINKING QUESTIONS

1. What might happen if the government did not attempt to control inflation? Inflation can be both a good thing and a bad thing. Explain.
2. The text discusses the unemployment rate as a measure of economic performance. Another way to gauge economic performance is to count the number of people *employed* in the economy. Is it possible for the unemployment rate to rise and the number of people employed to rise at the same time? Is either measurement better than the other?
3. Look in the newspaper or on the Internet to find the most current economic indicators, such as GDP, unemployment rate, and CPI. Statistics Canada is a good place to start. What forces are working to improve or worsen the economy? If you are interested, you can visit the Bank of Canada's website. Once there, you can access the latest report on monetary policy, which is filled with valuable information that relates directly to this chapter.
4. What are the advantages of capitalism? What are the advantages of socialism? What are the disadvantages of each? How does this information relate to your everyday life?
5. The text defines GDP as the measurement of economic activity—the market value of products and services produced in a country in a year. Think about other things that might "help" GDP that are really not good for our society in general, such as the economic activity required to clean up oil spills or increases in consumer debt to buy more goods. Other situations could also "hurt" GDP by limiting expenditures on items, but help the overall good of society, such as reusing plastic bags or installing solar water heaters (thus limiting spending on oil, gas, and electricity). Does the definition of GDP need to be revised?

TEAM TIME

The Great Debate

Your instructor will divide the class into three groups and assign each group one of the following debate topics. Once in your group, divide the group into two smaller groups to prepare stances on your assigned debate issues.

DEBATE TOPICS

1. Walmart is interested in creating a commercial bank in Montreal. What are the implications of having a retail giant enter the banking industry? Should this be allowed?
2. What impact does increasing the minimum wage have on unemployment? Does increasing the minimum wage benefit the worker, or does it ultimately result in higher unemployment? Hint: Consider using a demand and supply model (where labour is the "product" and employees are represented by the supply curve).
3. Taxation and tax cuts cause volatile debate among political leaders. Many say that tax cuts help strengthen the economy by freeing up money to increase spending. Others say that past tax cuts have not had a positive effect on the economy and have only caused greater stress on the government budget and reduced the government's ability to spend on important public needs. Do tax cuts benefit the economy?

PROCESS

Step 1. After dividing your group into two debate sides, meet separately to discuss the issues of the debate.
Step 2. Group members should then individually prepare their responses to their side of the debate issue.
Step 3. Gather your smaller groups and go over the responses provided by each group member. Develop a single list of responses.
Step 4. Determine who will be the group's primary spokesperson for the debate.
Step 5. Each group will be given five minutes to present its side of the issue. After each group has presented its argument, each team will be given five minutes to prepare a rebuttal and then three minutes to present the rebuttal.
Step 6. Repeat this process with the other groups.

ETHICS AND RESPONSIBILITY

Economic Inequality

Economic inequality refers to the differences of assets and income between groups. It has long been the subject of great discussion and can refer to the inequality between individuals, urban versus rural areas, countries, or economic structures. As a class or on an individual basis, discuss the following:

1. How do you define economic equality? For example, is economic equality simply making sure everyone has equal income, or is it enough to provide all citizens with an equal *opportunity* to earn income?
2. Is economic equality feasible? Would other problems result from economic equality?
3. One method used to measure differences in national income equality around the world is the national Gini coefficient. Research the Gini coefficient online. Which countries have the greatest economic equality? Which have greater inequality?
4. What other methods could be used to measure economic equality?

CLOSING CASE

Lingering Effects of the Great Recession

Canada survived the Great Recession. The recession of 2008–2009 was the most serious since 1930. It was not without consequence, however, and for many the effects are still lingering. This recession hit individuals with severe results. A Statistics Canada report from March 2013 calculates that the average household owed a record $164.97 in market debt for every $100 of disposable, after-tax income they earned in the fourth quarter of 2012.[15] That is only a few percentage points shy of where US household debt levels were before that country's real estate market collapsed, and was a key reason why Finance Minister Jim Flaherty tightened mortgage rules in July 2012.[16]

The amount of accumulated personal debt became unmanageable as wage increases began to slow down and layoffs began to rise. Total insolvencies reported by the Office of the Superintendent of Bankruptcy Canada were 123 234 in 2008 and 158 441 in 2009, an increase of 28.6 percent.[17] The average bankruptcy profile reflects those who have lost jobs or have experienced a serious health problem.[18] In a bad economy, workers find it tougher to pay their bills; unpaid bills reduce a company's revenues, causing greater negative pressure on an already struggling economy—it's a vicious cycle.

The federal government struggles with increasing debt loads as well. Prior to the Great Recession, the Canadian government was on a focused path of debt reduction. In 1997 the size of the national debt (Canada's accumulated debt, or the sum of its budget deficits) was $609 billion, and the cost to service this debt was extraordinary. Canada's interest payments as a percentage of government spending topped out at 29.8 percent in 1996–1997.[19] Embarking on a reversal of this trend, the federal government was effectively able to run 10 years of successful budget surpluses, reducing the size of the debt to $516.3 billion in 2008. Peaking at $49.4 billion in 1995–1996, Canada's debt service payments slid consistently to $30.99 billion by 2008–2009. That reduction represented a drop of 37 percent.[20]

Then the recession hit, and regrettably 10 years of fiscal restraint were erased—like a cloud of smoke, the gains were

Christopher Pike/QMI Agency

The Canadian Taxpayers Federation installed a massive ticking debt clock on Parliament Hill in 1993, constantly reminding Canadians of the ever-mounting debt on both a national and personal level.

gone. The fiscal year 2009–2010 was the worst year on record, erasing of the gains made during 2001 and 2008. The budget deficit in 2010 was $55.6 billion. The Economic Action Plan devised by the government provided fiscal stimulus to a struggling economy coupled with increasing transfers and a greater dependence on the employment insurance program. The debt was back up to $582.5 billion in 2010. The following two years experienced continued annual deficits, and by the end of 2013 the Canadian national debt had risen to $673.1 billion.

This story is disheartening, but just how bad is it, you might wonder? The answer depends on who you ask. But the picture is not complete without considering these debt levels in terms of GDP. Canada's national debt translates into about 30 percent of the total GDP. That makes the country a shining star among struggling G7 economies and represents a drastic decline from the mid-1990s when the federal debt-to-GDP ratio hit nearly 70 percent.[21]

DISCUSSION QUESTIONS

1. What kind of monetary policy was the Bank of Canada pursuing in 2008–2009 during the Great Recession? Discuss how the Bank of Canada would use the two tools of monetary policy, the overnight rate and open market operations, during that time.
2. How do interest rate decisions made by the Bank of Canada affect the public service charges made on the national debt?
3. How does Canada's rising debt burden private citizens in their personal lives? How does it burden small businesses?
4. Looking at the period from 1998 to 2008 when the Canadian government was able to run a budget surplus and pay down the debt, consider what sacrifices had to be made to achieve these gains. Do you think Canadian citizens would be willing to make these sacrifices today to reduce the debt load and associated interest charges for future generations?

4 Entrepreneurship, Small Business, and New Venture Creation

CBC TV

LEARNING OBJECTIVES

After studying this chapter, you should be able to:

LO1 List the traits of an effective entrepreneur, and describe how these characteristics often lead to business success. (pp. 66–70)

LO2 Describe the factors that lead to small business failure, and explain why a business plan is crucial to small business success. (pp. 70–73)

LO3 Compare the advantages and disadvantages of starting a business from scratch to buying an existing business. (pp. 73–75)

LO4 Outline the advantages and disadvantages of franchising. (pp. 75–79)

LO5 Summarize the potential benefits and drawbacks of each major source of small business financing. (pp. 79–80)

LO6 Explain the advantages and disadvantages of sole proprietorship. (pp. 80–82)

LO7 Explain the advantages and disadvantages of partnership and describe the importance of partnership agreements. (pp. 82–84)

LO8 Explain how a corporation is formed and how it compares with sole proprietorships and partnerships. (pp. 84–85)

LO9 Describe the characteristics of nonprofit corporations and cooperatives. (pp. 86–87)

LO10 Summarize the different types of mergers and acquisitions and explain why they occur. (pp. 87–88)

OPENING DISCUSSION: STARTING A NEW BUSINESS

It's often said that necessity is the mother of all invention, and Lee Renshaw brings this sentiment to life. While he was studying industrial design at Humber College, Renshaw lived an hour away in Kitchener, Ontario. As a result, he spent the majority of his school nights couch-surfing with friends and living out of a duffel bag: "It was a nightmare—my clothes were literally in a huge ball all the time. I wanted some way not to look like I was living out of a laundry basket," he says. From this aversion to wrinkled trousers arose Rise and Hang Travel Gear, his organizational travel gear line. In other words, a better kind of luggage.

Rise and Hang Travel Gear rose to fame on a 2013 episode of CBC's *Dragons' Den*. Clad in nothing but their fluorescent underwear, Lee and brother/co-owner Sean demonstrated their product's ability to keep clothing clean and neat by taking clothes out of the Rise and Hang and dressing neatly in front of the panel. After catching the Dragons' attention, it was up to Lee's presentation skills to seal the deal. The brothers ended up securing $100 000 for a 50 percent stake in their company with Arlene Dickinson and David Chilton.

Before starting Rise and Hang Travel Gear, Lee developed many skills and abilities both through part-time jobs and as a college student that he says helped him to refine Rise and Hang both as a company and a product. "I got a tonne of experience communicating my ideas and receiving positive and negative feedback . . . and then being able to use it constructively. Everyone has an opinion, but the trick is to be able to sort out what is useful and what is not. I like getting negative feedback because it means that I . . . might gain an insight that my competitors don't know about. [Using this skill, I] did a lot of market research to determine what our customers liked and didn't like and used that knowledge to develop our product line."

To begin, he and Sean wrote a business plan, but he stresses the importance of its adaptability. "A business plan is good to figure out that the basics are in check when starting. After that, all you really have is assumptions until you get real data." Initially, they had intended to market Rise and Hang to the retail mass market on their own, but realizing the need for publicity they changed their plan quickly. Part of his grander plan was choosing a perfectly matched partner in brother Sean. Optimistic Lee had the design and sales skills, while his more realistic brother was a pro at project management. "While we have different strengths and weaknesses, at the core we share the same vision for our brand and keep each other accountable." They complement one another, as all great partners do.

His top advice for budding entrepreneurs? Start young. You need lots of time to build a business. He also explains that even if, like him, your product may be more innovative than the standard Adidas hold-all, this alone won't make it more popular. "Without sales, you have no business, no matter how good your 'mousetrap' is. Anything you do in life comes down to being able to sell." If you can't sell, hire somebody who can. Luckily, the Renshaw brothers hit the mark dead on: not only a good mousetrap, but "Don Drapers" in the *Dragons' Den*, too.[1]

DISCUSSION QUESTIONS

1. Lee mentioned that the experience he gained from past jobs and what he learned at college helps him in his business. What experiences do you have or what are you learning in school that you think could help you be successful in business?
2. What do you think are some of the biggest advantages and disadvantages of working with a partner?
3. What types of issues do you think Lee and Sean have had to deal with to start and grow their business?

ENTREPRENEURSHIP: WHAT'S IN IT FOR ME?

LO1 List the traits of an effective entrepreneur, and describe how these characteristics often lead to business success.

The Traits of Successful Entrepreneurs

entrepreneur Someone who assumes the risk of creating, organizing, and operating a business and who directs all the business resources.

opportunity niche A need in the marketplace that is not being adequately fulfilled.

What is an entrepreneur? We've all heard of Starbucks, Nike, and Microsoft, but you probably don't associate these big-name companies with small business. But at one point, each of these companies was a small business started by **entrepreneurs**—people who assume the risk of creating, organizing, and operating a business. Not all small businesses are entrepreneurial. What makes a new venture entrepreneurial is that the idea behind the business is innovative or change oriented. Entrepreneurs most often start a business to satisfy an **opportunity niche**—a need in the marketplace that is not being adequately fulfilled.

The brothers who started McDonald's spotted an opportunity niche. Realizing that the hamburger was the bestseller in their California restaurant, they created an assembly line that allowed them to produce burgers quickly and inexpensively, and business boomed. It expanded even more when Ray Kroc, who was selling milkshake machines in California, convinced the brothers not only to use his milkshake machines but also to let him open another McDonald's restaurant in Chicago. Seeing the opportunity niche in fast food, Kroc later bought the McDonald's restaurants from the McDonald brothers. The company now operates more than 32 000 restaurants in 117 countries, generating more than US$20 billion in revenue annually.[2]

Video: New Toy Company Inspires Little Girls to Build Houses

What are the traits of successful entrepreneurs? Wayne Huizenga started Waste Management Inc., now a leader in the waste and environmental services industry, by buying a single garbage truck in 1968. He expanded the company by buying other trash collection services, and by 1983 the company had grown into the largest of its kind in the United States. But Huizenga didn't stop there. He also started Blockbuster Video, as well as AutoNation, the behemoth automotive dealer.[3] How can some entrepreneurs like Huizenga begin many successful businesses while others have a difficult time getting their ideas off the ground? How do successful entrepreneurs see an opportunity niche and know exactly what they need to do to seize the opportunity and succeed?

Video: Fruit Breeder Invents Cotton Candy Flavoured Grapes

Video: Convertible Heels: Shoe Transforms for Day, Night

Although luck and timing play a large role in entrepreneurial success, research has also shown that successful entrepreneurs

- are innovative
- take risks
- are motivated to succeed
- are flexible and self-directed
- work well with others and possess good leadership skills
- are "system thinkers," seeing the whole process rather than just individual pieces of it

Whitebox media/Mediablitzimages/Alamy

All businesses have to start somewhere. Even McDonald's, which is one of the biggest businesses in the world today, started out as just a single restaurant in California.

How are entrepreneurs innovative? Successful entrepreneurs see problems to be solved or opportunities that aren't being addressed in the marketplace—they recognize opportunity niches. They also make improvements to existing products or systems, or they introduce something new and make profitable solutions out of problems. Renowned management and business thinker Peter Drucker noted that successful entrepreneurs "exploit change as an opportunity for a different business or a different service."[4] For example, Henry Ford did not invent the automobile—he just found a better way to build them. His improvement was not only in creating a new machine (the Model T), but also in developing an assembly line process by which his company could make multiple automobiles more efficiently, allowing Ford to dramatically lower

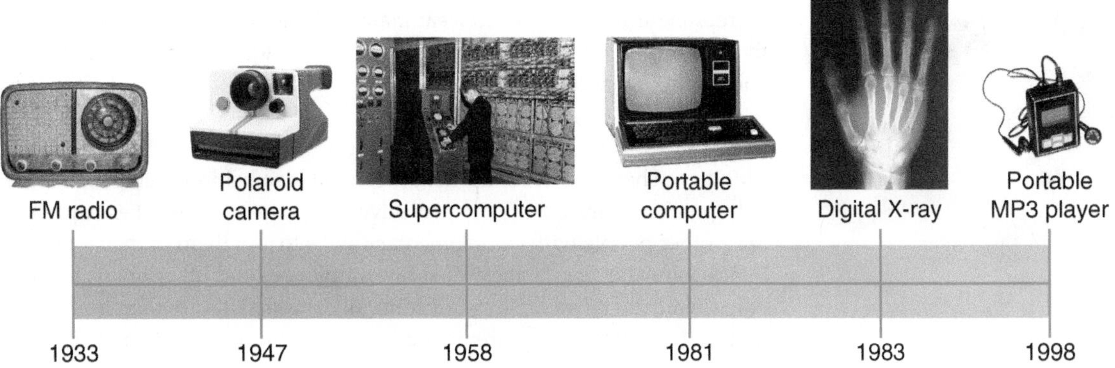

Figure 4.1 Twentieth-Century Entrepreneurial Innovations

Image Sources, left to right: Klikk/Fotolia; yossarian6/Fotolia; Sovfoto Universal Images Group/Newscom; Rudybaby/Fotolia; Contrail/Fotolia; Alexander Potapov/Fotolia.

the price and thus make automobile ownership affordable to the average worker. Ford's innovative assembly process became the standard for efficient manufacturing. Think about other entrepreneurs and the innovation behind their success. Ben Cohen and Jerry Greenfield of Ben & Jerry's Ice Cream didn't invent ice cream; rather, they capitalized on people's growing desire for high-quality food products and used the best and biggest chunks of nuts, fruits, candy, and cookies in their ice cream.[5] **Figure 4.1** lists some other important innovations by entrepreneurs in the twentieth century.[6]

How do entrepreneurs take risks? Being an entrepreneur involves risk—the risk of failure, the risk of losing one's career, and of course financial risks. Because entrepreneurs are often creating new and innovative products, the processes they develop are often untried and therefore involve risk. Successful entrepreneurs are aware of these risks, recognize that they can influence events but do not have complete control over them, and are willing to accept the knowledge that they may fail. Successful entrepreneurs therefore take calculated risks—that is, they consider the likelihood of success before deciding whether to take a particular risk.

What makes entrepreneurs motivated to succeed? Entrepreneurs are motivated by many different factors. Some entrepreneurs are motivated to provide for themselves or their families. These individuals may be driven to pursue multiple ventures before uncovering a successful idea. Other entrepreneurs are motivated to succeed by the personal fulfillment they feel upon successfully launching a business.

Entrepreneurs' keen desire to succeed has led one entrepreneur, Ted Kennedy, to start a company rooted in this notion. Kennedy noticed that many participants in the Ironman triathlon were corporate executives. He also noticed that these executive triathletes sought above-average accommodations prior to and during their competition. So he formed CEO Challenges, a company that organizes luxury sports experiences for corporate executives. CEO Challenges provides luxury accommodations the night before a race, ensures family members and friends are positioned alongside the race to have the perfect view of their racer, and offers other amenities an executive might want when competing in physical challenges.[7]

Why do successful entrepreneurs need to be flexible and self-directed? Because entrepreneurial ventures are subject to uncertainty and risk, entrepreneurs need to be able to react quickly to new and unexpected situations. And because entrepreneurs are

SELF CHECK Becoming a successful entrepreneur involves a complex blend of skill, savvy, and luck. Before embarking on such an endeavour, however, you'll need to familiarize yourself with a few concepts. Test your entrepreneurial vocabulary with the following quiz.

1. "It's all about fulfilling an opportunity niche!" Liza, a budding entrepreneur, exclaims. Liza is likely referring to
   A. a need in the market.
   B. a storage nook.
   C. a sense of belonging.
2. A system thinker is someone who
   A. contemplates the technological side of a business.
   B. focuses on the entire process of turning an idea into a reality.
   C. designs methods of doing things.
3. Micropreneurs are likely to
   A. be petite.
   B. hire thousands of employees.
   C. enjoy running a small business.
4. When you hear the word *gazelle*, you think
   A. antelope.
   B. fast-growing business.
   C. graceful.

Answers: 1. A; 2. B; 3. C; 4. B

Are you confident in your understanding of entrepreneurial lingo? Or do you need a primer in the use of these terms? Whatever the case, read on for in-depth information on entrepreneur basics, types of entrepreneurs, and what it takes to be an entrepreneur.

their own bosses, they need to be able to make their own decisions. An entrepreneur must be able to wear many hats, acting not only as the executive but also as the sales manager, financial director, administrative assistant, and mailroom clerk.

Maridav/Shutterstock

Entrepreneurs are self-directed and innovative, but they rarely work alone. At some point everyone needs someone else with complementary skills to help in the venture.

Why are people skills and leadership skills important to entrepreneurs? They may come up with the initial idea behind their business, but entrepreneurs rarely work by themselves. At some point most entrepreneurs need other people with complementary skills to join them in their venture. If their business expands, they must hire employees and other managers to help them run it. Leadership and communication skills are therefore important traits of successful entrepreneurs who must motivate others to feel as passionately about the entrepreneurial enterprise as they do.

What does it mean for entrepreneurs to be "system" thinkers? Although entrepreneurs develop companies from an idea, they must focus on the entire process of turning their idea into a business to succeed. Successful entrepreneurs are able to see the whole picture when they set up their businesses. They determine how to resolve a problem or capitalize on an opportunity by developing a solid plan, including the production, financing, marketing, and distribution of the service or product. For example, while on a canoe trip in northern Ontario, Greg Taylor, Cam Heaps, and Greg Cromwell sat around a campfire dreaming of running their own brewery one day. This dream became a reality when they wrote a business plan and attracted investors with their vision and passion. In 2000 they opened Steam Whistle Brewing in Toronto, brewing a premium pilsner that competes with the best in the world. The three friends saw the opportunity and began the process of creating their company not with just an idea but with a system: Use quality natural ingredients, employ "good beer folks," and "do one thing really really, really well." In 2013 Steam Whistle won a number of awards including the Ontario Craft Brewers Centre of Excellence awards in Product Quality and Process Innovation, and Sustainability Accomplishments.[8]

Types of Entrepreneurs

Are there different types of entrepreneurs? Beyond the traditional entrepreneurs described in the previous sections, other entrepreneurial categories have begun to crop up:

- lifestyle entrepreneurs
- micropreneurs
- home-based entrepreneurs
- Internet entrepreneurs
- growth entrepreneurs
- intrapreneurs

lifestyle entrepreneurs
Entrepreneurs who look for more than profit potential when they begin a business.

What are lifestyle entrepreneurs? **Lifestyle entrepreneurs** look for more than profit potential when they begin a business. Some lifestyle entrepreneurs are looking for freedom from corporate bureaucracy or the opportunity to work at home or in a location other than an office. Others are looking for more flexibility in work hours or travel schedules.

micropreneurs
Entrepreneurs who start their own business but are satisfied with keeping the business small in an effort to achieve a balanced lifestyle.

What are micropreneurs? **Micropreneurs** start their own business but are satisfied with keeping the business small in an effort to achieve a balanced lifestyle. For example, a micropreneur might open a single restaurant and be satisfied with running only that one restaurant, instead of expanding as Ray Kroc did with the McDonald brothers' restaurant. Micropreneurs, or small business people, have no aspirations of growing large or hiring hundreds or thousands of employees. Businesses such as dog-walking services, painters, and special-occasion cake bakers would all be considered micropreneurial opportunities.

What are home-based entrepreneurs? As the name suggests, **home-based entrepreneurs** are entrepreneurs who run their businesses out of their homes. Sheena Edwards was a stay-at-home mom who was looking for a creative outlet. She decided to start making crystal-embellished women's flip-flops and now runs Lizzie Lou Shoes from her home. Production of the shoes is managed by Edwards's cousin in New Delhi, India. "I love owning my own business, as it gives me the creative outlet I crave while still allowing me to be home with my kids and not miss a thing (with the exception of sleep!)," says Edwards.[9]

home-based entrepreneurs Entrepreneurs who run their businesses out of their homes.

In addition to offering lifestyle advantages, such as being able to stay at home with children, home-based businesses offer several financial advantages. Staying at home eliminates commuting time and costs, as well as office rent and other overhead expenses. Also, home-based entrepreneurs can take advantage of tax deductions for part of their rent or mortgage payment, property taxes, insurance, utilities, and home repairs and improvements.

What are Internet entrepreneurs? Advances in technology have spawned another type of entrepreneur, the **Internet entrepreneur**, who creates businesses that operate solely online. The advent of Web 2.0 technologies (e.g., blogging and social networking), smartphone apps, contextual web-based advertising (e.g., Google Ads) that helps to provide revenue, along with faster broadband connections has meant that a greater number of successful online businesses are being established. Some of the most famous Internet entrepreneurs include Mark Zuckerberg (Facebook), Jeff Bezos (Amazon), Pierre Omidyar and John Donahoe (eBay), Sergey Brin and Larry Page (Google), and Jimmy Wales (Wikipedia).

Internet entrepreneurs Entrepreneurs who create businesses that operate solely online.

Youth may have an advantage in this entrepreneurial genre because success requires little investment, some spare time, and a good understanding of what their peers are looking for. For example, David and Catherine Cook and their older brother Geoff started MeetMe (formerly MyYearbook.com) over spring break in 2005. The social networking site invites members to meet new people through playing games, chatting, and sending virtual gifts purchased with Lunch Money, the site's virtual currency. Members are also given the opportunity to donate Lunch Money to their favourite charity through their charity application. MeetMe has over 1 billion page views on mobile devices and 1.2 billion page views on the web each month. In 2013, the social networking company had revenue of approximately $39 million.[10]

growth entrepreneurs Entrepreneurs who strive to create fast-growing businesses and look forward to expansion.

intrapreneurs Employees who work in an entrepreneurial way within the organizational environment.

What are growth entrepreneurs? **Growth entrepreneurs** strive to create fast-growing businesses and look forward to expansion. The companies that these types of entrepreneurs create are known as gazelles. Typically, a gazelle business has at least 20 percent sales growth every year for five years, starting with a base of at least $100 000.[11] It is hard to recognize a gazelle business during its rapidly growing period, though companies such as eBay and Google can clearly be identified in retrospect as having been gazelles in their early years.

What are intrapreneurs? You don't necessarily have to leave your company to have an entrepreneurial experience. Some companies are fostering **intrapreneurs**—employees who work in an entrepreneurial way within the organizational environment. At the home appliance company Whirlpool, for example, developing intrapreneurs is an important part of corporate success. The company's success depends on producing creative solutions to household problems. Instead of relying solely

Andrew Miller/Newscom

Catherine Cook, at the age of 17, co-created the wildly successful website MeetMe with her older brothers Dave and Geoff during spring break.

On Target

Facebook's Mark Zuckerberg

When Mark Zuckerberg, a Harvard student, came up with the idea for Facebook, he didn't realize that he was spearheading a billion-dollar organization. The idea behind "The Facebook," as it was originally called, was to provide a forum for students on the Harvard campus to network and display pictures of themselves and their friends. The site was launched on February 4, 2004, and within a month half of the undergraduates on the Harvard campus were users of the site. Expansion came quickly, as Dustin Moskovitz and Chris Hughes joined Zuckerberg to help promote the site. Within two months, the entire Ivy League was included in the Facebook network. In September 2005, these entrepreneurs decided to allow high schools to join the network. Finally, on September 11, 2006, the public was allowed to join Facebook, so long as all potential members had a valid email address and were at least 13 years old.

Yaacov Dagan/Alamy

On May 18, 2012, Facebook sold shares to the public for the first time, which proved to be highly controversial.[14] The IPO (initial public offering) was one of the biggest in technology history, and certainly the biggest in Internet history, with a peak market capitalization of over $100 billion.[15] A lot of "hype" in the media likely contributed to inflating share prices. Shortly after the stock peaked its value began to drop quickly, and within three months the company's stock had fallen by 50 percent, wiping out $50 billion in shareholder value.[16] Despite the controversy, the site has more than 1.6 billion monthly users worldwide and is constantly expanding, so many analysts still see Facebook as a good investment.[17]

Discussion Questions

1. **Why do you think Facebook is so popular? Is it without problems?**
2. **How was Facebook able to grow so quickly? What marketing strategy was used?**
3. **Research Mark Zuckerberg on the Internet and read about the history of Facebook. What characteristics does Zuckerberg have that relate to those of entrepreneurs?**

on the traditional research and development (R&D) process, Whirlpool management is tapping the creative juices of their employees by encouraging them to generate ideas that will enhance the company's existing products. Although employees are not separately compensated for their ideas, they are pleased that the company asks for their ideas and have responded enthusiastically. By the end of the first year of the program, 60 ideas were in the prototype stage and 190 were close to entering the marketplace.[12,13]

Starting Your Own Business

LO2 Describe the factors that lead to small business failure, and explain why a business plan is crucial to small business success.

Why would I want to start my own business? People start small businesses for many different reasons (see **Figure 4.2**):

1. *Opportunity knocks.* An idea for a new company often starts when someone envisions a product or a service that isn't being offered yet. Other people create opportunities from their own obstacles. For example, a father frustrated at watching his autistic

Opportunity & Innovation
New ideas and needs bring new businesses.

Control
More control of business decisions; do not want to work for someone else.

Financial Independence
Owners feel they can make more money operating their own business.

Schedule Flexibility
Looking for a better work–life balance.

Unemployment
Seeking income due to job loss.

Figure 4.2 Reasons to Start a Small Business

Image Sources: top to bottom, left to right: Carsten Reisinger/Fotolia; alphaspirit/Fotolia; tiero/Fotolia; almagami/Fotolia; alphaspirit/Fotolia

child try to communicate with others founded the Animated Speech Corporation, a company that develops software-based conversational language learning systems to help autistic children communicate.[18]

2. *Financial independence.* Many people begin a small business because they want financial independence, though this should not be the sole reason. Most small businesses don't start out as profitable ventures. Traditionally, it takes three to five years for new businesses to become profitable.
3. *Control.* Many people starting their own business state that they want more control over business decisions than their current position allows. Others know that they aren't satisfied working for someone else.
4. *Flexibility.* Many small business owners appreciate the work–life balance that owning their own business affords. Many also feel working in a small business is more rewarding than working for a larger company. Small business owners believe their companies offer less bureaucracy and more flexibility than larger firms. With fewer channels to go through when decisions need to be made, small business owners can react more quickly to take advantage of immediate opportunities. In addition, small business owners say running their own business gives them the flexibility to adjust their work to their particular situations.
5. *Unemployment.* Whereas most individuals start their own businesses for the reasons mentioned previously, some are pushed into starting their own business because they have no other employment opportunities. "Life begins when you get fired," was exactly the case for Bruce Freeman, owner of ProLine Communications, Inc. Three months after being fired, he couldn't think of what to do next. Then, encouraged by a friend, Bruce started his own business. His first client was a company he worked with in his previous job. Now, over 10 years later, he's making more money than he ever could have in his old job.[19]

What are the advantages and disadvantages of owning a business? Operating a business is a lot of hard work and comes with no guarantee for success. Small business survival rates in Canada decline over time. About 96 percent of small businesses that enter the marketplace survive for one full year, 85 percent survive for three years, and 70 percent survive for five years.[20]

Substantial benefits await the successful entrepreneur, including financial rewards (profit), social rewards (pride, making a difference, worthwhile cause), and independence (work for yourself, at your own pace).

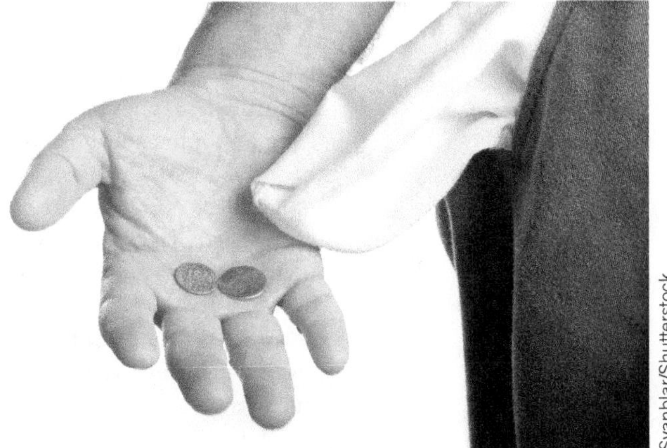

Svanblar/Shutterstock

Sometimes being fired is the best thing that could happen to you! Some entrepreneurs get started when they have no other employment opportunities.

Amy Walters/Shutterstock

Staring your own business is not without risk. Unfortunately, many small businesses fail, and failure can mean substantial financial loss for the owner.

However, with these rewards come potential risks:[21]

- *Financial risk.* Substantial financial loss and even bankruptcy are possible results of business failure. Business owners also have to take taxes and insurance costs into consideration, such as a health insurance plan to cover employees. They also need liability insurance, which will protect the company in the event of stolen or damaged property or if an employee is injured on the job. For example, if a local jewellery store is broken into and inventory is stolen, liability insurance will cover the cost of the broken window and the stolen property. If the jewellery store is not insured, the business could go bankrupt if the owner can't afford to cover the loss and damages.
- *Social risk.* Due to the excessive amount of time an entrepreneur has to devote to a new business venture, he or she has less time for family, friends, and social events, so the potential for losing a friend or even a marriage is very real.
- *Career risk.* Entrepreneurs usually quit their jobs to pursue their own startup, but if things go wrong in the new business venture it may be difficult to resume a career.
- *Psychological risk.* Owning your own business can be rather stressful. There is a difference between good stress (eustress), which gives a person enough adrenalin to handle difficult situations in a positive way, and bad stress (distress), which can hurt the entrepreneur and the business. Some factors that may cause distress are having too much worry, working too hard for long periods, and having no one to turn to for help when feeling overstressed.

While many entrepreneurs feel that the rewards of owning their own business are worth the risks, it's important to be aware of why businesses fail. These reasons include

- accumulating too much debt
- inexperienced management
- poor planning

Let's look at each of these reasons for failure in more detail.

What causes excessive debt accumulation? One reason many new businesses fail is that they accumulate too much debt. Most begin a new business by borrowing funds. Regardless of whether the loan comes from a bank, an outside investor, or a credit card company, if the new business does not generate returns quickly enough to begin to pay back the initial loan, there is temptation to take on more debt to keep the business running. Interest on loans can accumulate quickly, causing an owner to become further entrenched in a potentially unrecoverable situation. What's worse is that some business owners borrow against their personal assets, putting them at risk of personal bankruptcy.

How does inexperienced management lead to failure? Although entrepreneurs and small business owners are good at coming up with ideas, they may not be great at managing the books and their employees. Many inexperienced business owners ignore the signs of a business beginning to fail or attribute the failure to the wrong reasons. In addition, although owners need to build a team they can't hand over all control. Good management stays on top of all aspects of the business and makes the tough decisions when necessary. As Nina Riley, CEO and founder of Water Sensations, a company that

Figure 4.3 A Business Plan Outlines a Company's Goals and Strategies

makes clear-liquid flavour enhancers for water, says, "When things go bad—at the first indication—you gotta nip it in the bud, wrestle it to the ground to fix it. You just can't let it go. If this is your own company, you have to strive to be perfect."[22]

How important is planning to business success? Accumulating debt and poor business management happen after the business has developed. One of the biggest reasons businesses fail is that there was no formal plan in place to begin with. Planning is sometimes harder than doing because it takes time, brainwork, and requires delaying your personal gratification, but the old adage is true: "Businesses that fail to plan, plan to fail." The good news is that poor planning is completely avoidable once you know what kinds of planning you should do before you start your small business.

A **business plan** is a formal document that states the goals of the business as well as the plan for reaching those goals. A business plan should tell the story of your business concept—it is a blueprint for the company, and it is an indispensable tool in attracting investors or obtaining loans. Preparing a business plan takes a lot of time, but it is time well spent because your business plan is an ongoing guide. You use it to acquire startup capital as well as to assess your company's progress, as long as you remember to update it periodically.

business plan A formal document that states the goals of the business as well as the plan for reaching those goals.

A realistic business plan forces you to think critically about your proposed business and reduces your risk of failure. Business plan templates are available online, and the Royal Bank of Canada (RBC) has a very useful site (www.rbcroyalbank.com/sme/) for entrepreneurs starting a business, which includes sample business plans and templates.

Business plans vary in format and number of sections. The main components in most business plans are shown in **Figure 4.3** and include the company's mission statement, history, and the qualifications of the owners and management team and any resources they might have to contribute to the business. It also includes a marketing plan, an operational plan, a financial plan, a risk analysis, and identifies the competition and highlights opportunities for success.

Video: Wild Planet: The Entrepreneurial Spirit

STARTING A SMALL BUSINESS

LO3 Compare the advantages and disadvantages of starting a business from scratch to buying an existing business.

Entrepreneurs usually start a small business by starting from scratch (building a new business), buying an existing business, or buying a franchise.

Starting a Business from Scratch

What are the advantages of starting a business from scratch? Although starting from scratch is the riskiest way to take ownership of a business, most entrepreneurs choose this option because there are a number of attractive benefits:

- *Freedom to do what you want.* When building something new there is opportunity to make all the important decisions such as location, equipment, staff selection, and supplier relationships.
- *You can start small and grow the business over time.* Buying an existing business can be costly, but starting from scratch, particularly if it's a home-based business, may be possible with a modest investment.
- *The satisfaction of building something from nothing.* Many entrepreneurs are inspired by the challenge of creating something new and are passionate about bringing their ideas to life.
- *You can create the image and reputation you want.* There is no negative impact of a previous owner's bad decisions when you start a business from scratch, so you have a blank slate and can build your own reputation.

Video: Toms

What are the disadvantages of starting a business from scratch? Starting a business from scratch is not an easy proposition. There is a lot of hard work involved, and it is very risky. Some of the disadvantages of starting a business from scratch include the following:

- *The business has no proven track record.* A new business has not produced any results, so it is uncertain if the business plan will lead to actual profits. Although the plan should be based on significant market research, the success of the business is always a gamble until proven by real results.
- *It takes time to build a good reputation.* A new business is unknown to customers, so a great deal of effort is needed to develop relationships and build a strong brand. This takes years.
- *Nothing is established—you need to do everything.* Equipment must be purchased, locations determined, facilities set up, staff hired, procedures developed, and supplier relationships established. Although these decisions are critical, they consume many weeks.
- *There is no existing cash flow, and it can take a long time before the business begins to earn a profit.* A new business starts with no customer base and zero sales. It usually takes several years before the business begins to earn a profit, so during this time owners need to have access to large amounts of cash to keep the business operating until it can support itself.
- *It can be difficult to obtain financing.* For all the reasons stated above, starting a business from scratch is extremely risky. Since financial institutions are highly risk averse, it can be difficult to secure loans or even credit from suppliers until the business has proven to be viable.

Buying an Existing Business

What are the advantages of buying an existing business? While starting from scratch is a popular way to begin a business, another way is to buy a pre-existing business. Many experts recommend buying an existing business because this option has certain important advantages:

- *Ease of startup.* It's often simpler to buy an existing business than to start one from scratch. For example, there is a reduction in startup time and energy when you purchase an operational business that has no serious problems. This means that suppliers, existing staff and management, and equipment and inventory are all in place to help facilitate the transition.
- *Existing customer base.* An existing business may have a satisfied customer base already in place. If no significant changes are made to drive away current customers, the business can continue to run and provide immediate cash flow.

Video: Domino's Pizza: Franchising

- *Financing opportunities.* If the business has had a positive track record, it might be easier to obtain financing to purchase the existing business.

Table 4.1 Things to Consider before Buying a Business

Initial Questions to Ask
Why is the business for sale?
What do current customers say?
How much time does the current owner put into the business?
Are there opportunities for growth?
Who is the competition?
Due Diligence Checklist
Get an independent valuation of inventory and equipment.
Have an accountant go over financial statements for the past three years.
Have a lawyer analyze pertinent business documents (property leases, employment contracts, etc.).
Talk to suppliers to see if they will continue to supply the business when ownership changes hands.
Check for lingering or festering hazardous waste problems—they'll become your responsibility as the new owner.

What are the disadvantages of buying an existing business? There are also disadvantages to buying an existing business:

- *High purchase price.* Because you may need to buy the owner out of the business, the initial purchase price may be high. This can be more than the immediate upfront costs associated with a startup, but not necessarily any different from a franchise. Although you can easily determine the value of the physical business and its assets, it is more difficult to determine the true value of the previous owner's goodwill—the intangible assets represented by the business's name, customer service, employee morale, and other factors—that might be lost with a change in ownership. Often the intangible assets are overvalued, making the business cost more than it is worth.
- *Inheriting the previous owner's mistakes.* If the previous owner made some poor choices, you may have to deal with the ramifications. For instance, you might inherit dissatisfied customers, bad debt, and unhappy distributors or purchasing agents. You'll need to work to change the minds of people who have had a bad experience with the previous ownership.
- *The Unknowns.* There is no guarantee that existing employees, management, customers, suppliers, or distributors will continue to work with the business once new ownership takes over. If staff does stay, you might be inheriting unanticipated problems.

What do you need to check before you buy a business? Existing businesses are sold for many reasons. Before buying an existing business, make sure you perform **due diligence**—research and analyze the business to uncover any hidden problems associated with it. You want to avoid buying a company with a dissatisfied customer base or with a large amount of unpaid bills. **Table 4.1** provides a brief checklist of things you should look into before buying a business. However, not all businesses for sale have problems. For example, some family-run businesses run out of family members to pass the business on to, so the owners might be left with no choice but to sell the business. Whether you buy an existing business or franchise or begin a business of your own, you'll be joining a large group of small business owners who make a significant contribution to the Canadian economy.

due diligence Researching and analyzing the business to uncover any hidden problems associated with it.

Buying a Franchise

LO4 Outline the advantages and disadvantages of franchising.

What is a franchise? A **franchise** is a method of doing business whereby the business (the franchisor) grants the purchaser (the franchisee) the right to use its brand name and to sell its goods and services for a specified time. In return, the franchisee provides a

franchise A method of doing business whereby the business (the franchisor) grants the buyer (the franchisee) the right to use its brand name and to sell its goods and services for a specified time.

Table 4.2 Helpful Websites for Potential Franchisees

www.betheboss.ca	BeTheBoss.ca is an information and resource directory for buying a franchise in Canada.
www.cfa.ca	The Canadian Franchise Association educates Canadians about franchising, specific franchise opportunities, and proper due diligence.
www.canadabusiness.ca/eng	The Canada Business Network offers government services for entrepreneurs, information about grants and loans, and links to many other resources.
www.entrepreneur.com/franchises/index.html	Entrepreneur.com's Franchise Zone allows users to search a directory of franchising opportunities and provides tips on buying a franchise. This site also ranks the top franchises in terms of growth, cost, global appeal, and other aspects.
www.franchise.org	The International Franchise Association provides answers to frequently asked questions about franchising and resources for potential and current franchisees. This site also hosts a directory of franchising opportunities in various industries.
www.franchiseinfo.ca	*Canadian Business Franchise Magazine* offers a unique, behind-the-scenes look at those entrepreneurs who have embraced the franchise lifestyle.

share of the income back to the franchisor. Franchising is one of the more popular business venture concepts in Canada. According to the Canadian Franchise Association (CFA), the average term of a franchise agreement in Canada is five years, although franchise agreements come in several fixed periods, including 10 and 20 years.[23] **Table 4.2** lists some helpful websites for potential franchisees.

What are the advantages of franchising? For many, franchising is an easier, less risky means of starting a business. Since the franchisor provides much of the marketing and financial tools needed to run the business, all the franchisee is expected to bring to the table is management and marketing skills, time, and money. In addition to a recognized brand name, there are many other advantages of owning a franchise:

- *It is a proven system of operation.* Instead of wading through the muddy waters of new business ownership by themselves, franchisees benefit from the collective experience of the franchise company. The franchisor has determined, through trial and error, the best system of daily operations for the established business. New franchisees can therefore avoid many of the common startup mistakes made by new business owners since they will be working with standardized products, systems, and financial and accounting systems.
- *There is strength in numbers.* You are not alone when you buy a franchise. Because as a franchisee you belong to a group, you might benefit from economies of scale achieved by purchasing materials, supplies, and services at discounted group rates. In addition, it is often easier to get approval for business loans when running a franchise, as the lending institution associates less risk with a franchise.
- *Initial training is part of the deal.* The beauty of franchising is that you're in business for yourself but not by yourself. The franchisor offers initial training to ensure a successful store opening and might offer ongoing training if new products or services are being incorporated into the franchise line.
- *Marketing support is provided.* As a franchisee, you are often given marketing materials generated at the corporate level and have the benefit of any national advertising programs that are created. Although you are expected to run your own local marketing efforts, you have the support of other franchisees in the area and the recognition of an established brand to help you in your efforts.

- *Market research is often provided.* Good franchisors do considerable market research and can generally conclude whether there is demand for the product or service in the area before selling the franchisee a franchise. The franchisor should also help identify the competition and offer strategies to differentiate the franchise from them.

ZUMA Press, Inc./Alamy

There are many benefits of owning a franchise. Tim Hortons is one of the most recognizable brands in Canada, and some say that owning a Tim Hortons franchise is like having a licence to print money! However, this kind of brand awareness comes with significant costs attached.

What are the disadvantages of franchising?

Although buying a franchise provides the franchisee with many benefits, there are some disadvantages too:

- *Lack of control.* There is not much opportunity to contribute creatively to the franchise since the franchisor often controls the look of the store and the product or service. The franchisee, however, is expected to bring the necessary drive and spirit to make the franchise a success.
- *Startup costs.* More than 70 percent of all franchises require more than \$50 000 to start. In addition, franchisees must pay a monthly royalty fee to the franchisor. The royalty fees are due regardless of how the business is doing and can be a huge overhead expense. Other costs the franchisee might incur include real estate purchase or rental, equipment purchase or rental, extra signage, and opening inventory. For example, a Tim Hortons franchise in Canada costs \$480 000 to \$510 000, with at least \$153 000 of this being liquid or cash assets. In addition, a franchisee must have at least \$50 000 in startup cash. Royalty fees of 4.5 percent on gross sales are paid each week, advertising fees of 4 percent on gross sales are paid each month, and rental fees of 8.5 percent of gross sales are paid each month.[24]
- *Internal competition.* Some franchises do not restrict the location or number of their franchise locations. In those instances, franchisees could experience serious competition not only from another company but also from other franchisees in the same franchise organization.
- *Share common problems.* If the franchisor or another franchisee is having problems, all franchisees will feel its pain. For example, when a Wendy's restaurant was falsely accused of serving chili with a human thumb mixed in, business in all Wendy's restaurants plummeted.

What are things to watch out for when considering buying a franchise? The most common piece of advice offered to anyone interested in buying a franchise is to do your homework up front. Although a lot of the startup process is done for you, you are still buying a business that will require your time and money and is not guaranteed to succeed. **Table 4.3** shows suggested questions to ask the company that you are buying the franchise from (franchisor) and other people who have bought franchises from the company (franchisees) before you take the plunge.

Video: My Gym: Organizing the Business

Video: Fun Facts about Franchsisng

Small Business Support

Where can small business owners go for help? There are several sources of help that a small business owner can turn to.

Government of Canada, Canada Business Network This government resource (www.canadabusiness.ca/eng) offers startup services for entrepreneurs, including developing a business plan, naming and registering a business, buying a business, and financing a business.

Provincial Small Business Enterprise Centres The Small Business Enterprise Centres (SBECs) across Canada provide entrepreneurs with all the necessary startup and development tools. Each centre can help entrepreneurs determine what they need to do

Table 4.3 Questions to Ask before Buying a Franchise

	Questions to Ask the Franchisor	Questions to Ask Other Franchisees
Competition	• What is the competitive advantage of the product/service? • What makes the business more attractive to an owner and more attractive to a customer?	• How is your system better than competitors'? • How does your business match up? • Who are your competitors?
Franchise System	• How time tested and standardized is the franchise system? • What franchise system is used and how does it work? • How long has the franchise been in business and what improvements has it made recently?	• How long have you been in business? • Does your location meet your customers' needs? • Who selected the site?
Support and Training	• How much support does the franchisor give the franchisee? • What is the initial and ongoing training? • Are there toll-free help lines, field support, annual meetings, local meetings, purchasing programs, and marketing promotion?	• How is your relationship with the franchisor? • How is the initial training, ongoing training, and ongoing support? • How are the marketing, advertising, and promotional programs handled?
Financial Strength	• What is the financial strength of the company and the experience of management? • How much revenue comes from franchise fees and how much revenue comes from royalties? • How has the stock performed?	• Are you pleased with earnings? • Is volume growing?
Franchise Relationships	• How important is the franchisee to the franchise? • How can they describe the relationship with the franchisor? • Have there been any lawsuits/arbitration? • If so, how have they been resolved?	• Do you have second thoughts (would you do this again)? • Would you own more units?

Source: Based on "Checklist of Questions to Answer Before You Buy a Franchise," PowerHomeBiz.com, http://www.powerhomebiz.com/vol2/franchise-checklist.htm.

before, during, and after launching their business. Business support also exists for specific groups, such as Aboriginal entrepreneurs, female entrepreneurs, and young entrepreneurs. (See www.ontario.ca/business-and-economy/small-business-advice-support-services-regulations.)

Industry Canada The business section of Industry Canada's website (www.ic.gc.ca/eic/site/icgc.nsf/eng/h_07064.html) offers business owners many resources (e.g., financing program, internship program) and information on topics such as statistics, research, and regulations.

Small Business Association of Canada (SBA Canada) A nonprofit organization, SBA Canada (www.sba-canada.ca) provides growth and development opportunities to small businesses through networking, mentorship, collaboration, self-development, and education.

business incubators Organizations that support startup businesses by offering resources such as administrative services, technical support, business networking, and sources of financing that a group of startup companies share.

Entrepreneurs' Organization (EO) EO (www.eonetwork.org/) provides individual mentoring by connecting business owners with experts in their industry. Although EO is for those who are currently in a viable operation (its requirements are that you must be a founder, cofounder, owner, or controlling shareholder of a business with a minimum of $1 million in annual gross sales and you must be younger than 50 years old), such mentoring services can be helpful to second-stage small business owners.

Simulation: Getting Your Business Off the Ground

Business Incubators **Business incubators** are organizations that support startup businesses by offering resources such as administrative services, technical support, business networking, and sources of financing that a group of startup companies share.

There are several benefits to incubation beyond sharing a receptionist and copy machine. Business incubators are often run by colleges, universities, and technical schools, and many are sponsored by economic development organizations, cities, or countries. The Canadian Association of Business Incubation (CABI) is a vital national body of organizations dedicated to supporting the growth of new and emerging businesses.

Mario beauregard/Fotolia

Finding the money required to finance your business venture can be challenging. Many business owners use their own personal savings.

FINANCING CONSIDERATIONS

LO5 Summarize the potential benefits and drawbacks of each major source of small business financing.

Personal Financing

Where can I get the money to start a business? Most new ventures need some capital to purchase inventory, secure a physical location, and begin some modest marketing efforts. Most business owners tap into their own personal savings when they initially invest in their business. Friends and family are generally secondary sources of cash. Such contacts are often good sources for financing because, unlike banks or other lending institutions, they often do not require a high rate of return or demand to see the business turn a quick profit. However, it's important when borrowing from friends and family that you treat them as professionally as possible. Make sure you give them a document with an indication of how you intend to pay them back and some sort of a contingency plan if things go wrong. In addition, they should be kept informed of any risks of the venture—both upfront and ongoing.

Can I use credit cards to finance my business? Credit cards offer a convenient way to obtain funds quickly, especially with some of the zero percent financing available. If used wisely, credit cards are a convenient means of acquiring short-term cash, and nearly 50 percent of small business owners use personal credit cards as a source of financing for their small business. However, credit cards should be used only if you can pay the balance completely every month. The risk associated with using credit cards for your initial business financing is the high rate of interest charged on unpaid balances. According to the Financial Consumer Agency of Canada, if you had a $1000 balance on a credit card with an 18 percent interest rate and made the minimum monthly payment, it would take you 10 years to pay off this debt and you would actually pay $1800 in total.[25] The credit card option is expensive if you cannot pay the balance every month.

SELF CHECK Which of the following is a *do* and which is a *don't*?

When financing a business . . .

1. Do or Don't: Give friends and family who you borrow from a document indicating how and when you intend to pay them back.
2. Do or Don't: Rely heavily on credit cards if you can't pay the balance completely every month.
3. Do or Don't: Borrow against your own assets without fully understanding the potentially severe personal consequences of business failure.
4. Do or Don't: Consider applying for a startup loan or line of credit from your bank.
5. Do or Don't: Seek financing from a venture capitalist if the idea of relinquishing any control over your business does not appeal to you.

Answers: 1. Do; 2. Don't; 3. Don't; 4. Do; 5. Don't

Loans and Grants

What if I need more money than I can provide myself? For larger amounts, new business owners sometimes obtain a loan by borrowing against their own assets, such as the equity in their house or against their retirement account, but the consequences of the business failing are very severe. If you're purchasing an existing business or a franchise, banks and other financial institutions often provide funding. In fact, roughly half of all small businesses use bank loans and lines of credit as part of their financing strategy. These institutions offer startup loans and lines of credit to help businesses make payroll during slower periods as well as capital loans to buy equipment or machinery. The Business Development Bank of Canada (BDC) promotes entrepreneurship by providing highly tailored financing, venture capital, and consulting services to entrepreneurs.

grants Financial awards usually offered by federal and provincial governments and some private organizations.

Can I apply for grants to help start a business? **Grants** are financial awards usually offered by federal and provincial governments and some private organizations. The Canadian government realizes that small businesses are a significant part of our economic growth; therefore, the government's Centre for Small Business Financing (www.grants-loans.org/small-business-grants.php) provides the necessary financial resources to facilitate this. The government set aside more than $21 billion in 2011 for small businesses in grants (which are nonrepayable), low- or no-interest loans (repayable), tax refunds or credits, guaranteed loans, financial insurance against business risks, and repayable contributions.[26]

Venture Capital and Other Forms of Financing

What if I need additional sources of funds through investors? There are other sources of funding for your business, such as venture capital, angel investors, or small business investment companies (SBIC):

venture capitalists Investors who contribute money to your business in return for some form of equity—a piece of ownership.

- *Venture capitalists.* Unlike banks, where there is a contractual agreement to pay back the money, **venture capitalists** contribute money to your business in return for some form of equity—a piece of ownership. Venture capitalists are very picky about the projects in which they invest. They look for the potential of a public stock offering; therefore, such financing is generally only available to those businesses that have been operating for several years and that have the potential to become larger regional or national companies. To protect their investment, venture capitalists sometimes require that they play an active role in the management of the company, so business owners must be open to the idea of relinquishing some control when they seek venture capital funding.

angel investors Wealthy individuals who are willing to put their own money into your business in hopes of a profit return later on.

- *Angel investors.* **Angel investors** are wealthy individuals who are willing to put up their own money in hopes of a profit return later on. Angel capital fills the gap in startup financing between "friends and family" who help provide you with startup money and venture capital. Angel investors are often retired entrepreneurs or executives who may be interested in angel investing for reasons that go beyond purely monetary returns.

Small Business Investment Companies (SBIC) Private venture capital firms that make equity capital or long-term loans available to small companies.

- *SBIC program.* If venture capital is not available or suitable, an alternative is the **Small Business Investment Company (SBIC)** program. SBICs are private venture capital firms that make equity capital or long-term loans available to small companies. Canada's Venture Capital and Private Equity Association (CVCA) represents the majority of private equity companies in Canada, with more than 1800 members.

Keep in mind that, to protect their investments, outside investors are often looking for some controlling or managerial role in the business. Funding a business is a task fraught with challenges and difficult decisions. When a great deal of money is on the line, the stakes—personal, professional, and financial—are quite high. Thorough research and careful planning are essential to navigating these tricky issues. By understanding the available options and being prepared to deal with financial predicaments, business owners give themselves the best chance at success.

FORMS OF BUSINESS OWNERSHIP

LO6 Explain the advantages and disadvantages of sole proprietorship.

Sole Proprietorships

What is it called when one person owns a business? Whether they intend to run large factories, small retail stores, or ebusinesses, entrepreneurs must decide which form of legal ownership best suits their goals: sole proprietorship, partnership, corporation, or cooperative.

sole proprietorship A business owned by one person and not protected by limited liability.

A **sole proprietorship** is a business that is owned by one person. A sole proprietorship does not need to register with the government and it is not legally separated from

What's in a Name?

Naming a business should be fun, but it can also be stressful, especially if you make some of the more common mistakes:

Mistake 1 | Involving friends, family, employees, or clients in the naming decision. You want to make the name communicate the key elements of your business, not the combined efforts of your friends and family.

Mistake 2 | Description + Product = Name. Although it seems catchy at the time, the result of company names that try to marry description with product is forced and often trite. A service franchise named QualiServe or a day spa named TranquiSpa ultimately aren't the right choices.

Mistake 3 | Using generic names. Gone are the days when General Electric or ACME Foods work as corporate names. In such highly competitive times, when new products or services are fighting for attention, it is best to choose a unique name.

Mistake 4 | Making up a name. While using generic names may not be good, be careful to avoid names that are obscure, hard to pronounce, or hard to spell unless there is solid market research behind it.

Mistake 5 | Using geographic names. Unless you plan to stay local, including a specific geographic name may imply that you won't go beyond that regional territory.

TIP: You might need to hire a company to create a name for you. Acura, Flixx, and Compac are all names that were created by experts.

Discussion Questions

1. **Can you think of a company name that you are not fond of? Do you shop there? Do you wonder why the owner gave it that name?**
2. **Can you think of a company name that is difficult for you to pronounce? Do you think this causes a loss of business for the company?**
3. **Why do you think some business owners name their companies starting with an "A" or an "AA" or sometimes even an "AAA"? Does this make it easy for customers to remember? Can it be confusing for customers?**

the owner. This means the company's debts are the responsibility of the owner, and the owner pays personal income tax on his or her profits rather than corporate taxes. A sole proprietorship is simpler to operate and is under less government regulation than other businesses, but there is also more risk involved. If the company is sued, the owner is liable. If the company owes a debt that the business can't afford to pay, the creditors can legally collect personal assets, such as funds from the owner's retirement accounts, property, or cars. A sole proprietorship is not protected by *limited liability*, which would require owners to be responsible only for losses up to the amount they invested. **Limited liability** safeguards personal assets from being seized as payment for debts or claims.

limited liability Safeguards personal assets from being seized as payment for debts or claims.

How do I start a sole proprietorship? The minute you begin doing business by yourself—that is, collecting income as a result of performing a service or creating a product—you are operating as a sole proprietor. There are no special forms to fill out, nor any special filing requirements with the federal or provincial government. At a minimum, you might need to obtain local licences or permits, or you might have to ensure that you're operating in an area zoned for such business activity.

What are the advantages of being a sole proprietor? There are several advantages to forming your business as a sole proprietorship, the first of which is ease of formation. With only one person making all the decisions and no need to consult other owners or interested parties, sole proprietors have greater control and more flexibility to act quickly. Another advantage is that there are no specific corporate records to keep or reports to file, including tax reporting. Since there is no legal distinction between the owner and the business, no separate tax return is required. As a result, the income and expenses of a sole proprietorship flow through the owner's personal tax return. For example, imagine you run a landscaping business during the summer in addition to your regular job. If the lawn mower breaks down and needs to be replaced, that expense could be more than all the earnings you collected, generating a loss for your lawn mowing business. You can subtract that loss from the income earned from your regular job, reducing your income tax obligation.

What are the disadvantages of being a sole proprietor? If the type of business you're running has the potential for someone to sue you because of errors on your part, you may not want to operate as a sole proprietorship. A sole proprietor is personally responsible for all the debts and liabilities of the business. A **liability** is the obligation to pay a debt such as an account payable or a loan.

liability The obligation to pay a debt such as an account payable or a loan.

A sole proprietor may also incur a liability if he or she becomes responsible for paying for any damages or personal injuries the owner's employees cause. While there may be an unlimited number of employees in a sole proprietorship, there is also unlimited liability for their actions. **Unlimited liability** means that if business assets aren't enough to pay business debts, then personal assets, such as the sole proprietor's house, personal investments, or retirement plans, can be used to pay the balance. In other words, the proprietor can lose an unlimited amount of money.

unlimited liability If business assets aren't enough to pay business debts, then personal assets, such as the sole proprietor's house, personal investments, or retirement plans, can be used to pay the balance.

Imagine that you're running a catering business, and while you're preparing food in someone's house, the oven catches fire because you forgot to take the egg rolls off the paper tray. You are personally responsible, or liable, for paying for any damages if your business assets are not sufficient to cover the damages. If the damages are severe enough—perhaps your client's entire house burns down—you could lose all your assets, including your own home and savings.

Another drawback of a sole proprietorship is the potential difficulty in borrowing money to help your business grow. Banks will be lending to you personally, not to your business, so they will be more reluctant to lend large amounts, and the loan will be limited to the amount of your personal assets.

Partnerships

LO7 Explain the advantages and disadvantages of partnership and describe the importance of partnership agreements.

What are the advantages of bringing in a partner? Sometimes running a business by yourself can be a daunting task, and adding one or more owners can help share the responsibilities. A **partnership** is a type of business entity in which two or more owners (or partners) share the ownership and the profits and losses of the business. There are several reasons why joining with someone else in starting a business makes sense. More owners help contribute to both the starting and ongoing capital of the business. Multiple people are involved in partnerships, so there is more time available to increase sales, market the business, and generate income. Sharing the financial responsibility brings on more people who are interested in the company's overall profitability and are as highly motivated as you are to make the business succeed. Therefore, additional owners, unlike employees, are more likely to be willing to work long hours and go the extra mile.

partnership A type of business entity in which two or more owners (or partners) share the ownership and the profits and losses of the business.

Adding partners to help share the workload also allows for coverage for vacations, illness, or personal issues. Moreover, if partners have complementary skills, they create a collaboration that can be quite advantageous. Partners can help discuss ideas and projects as well as make the big decisions. For example, if you're great at numbers but hate to make sales calls, bringing in a partner who loves to knock on doors would be beneficial for your business.

The two most common partnership forms include general partnerships and limited partnerships. A **general partnership** is similar to the sole proprietorship in that all the (general) partners are jointly liable for the obligations of the business. The **general partners** are full owners of the business, are responsible for all the day-to-day business decisions, and remain liable for all the debts and obligations of the business. Sometimes a business can bring on additional "limited" partners, mostly to provide capital and earn a share in the profits, but not to operate the business. **Limited partners** don't participate actively in the business—they are simply investors and their liability is limited to the

general partnership A type of partnership that is similar to the sole proprietorship in that all the (general) partners are jointly liable for the obligations of the business.

general partners Partners who are full owners of the business and are responsible for all the day-to-day business decisions and remain liable for all the debts and obligations of the business.

limited partners Partners who don't participate actively in the business, and their liability is limited to the amount they invested in the partnership.

amount they invested in the partnership. **Limited partnerships** consist of at least one general partner (who has unlimited liability) and one or more limited partners who cannot participate in the day-to-day activities of the business or they will risk losing their limited liability status.

Stephen Coburn/Shutterstock

Bringing in one or more partners to your business can be beneficial, especially if they have complementary skills to your own. However, choosing a partner is a lot like choosing a spouse: The wrong decision can bring you a lot of challenges and grief.

What are the disadvantages to adding partners?

For every advantage a partner can bring, adding the wrong partner can be equally problematic. Obviously, adding partners means sharing profits and control. A potential partner may have different work habits and styles from you, and if the partner's style isn't complementary the differences can prove challenging. In addition, as the business begins to grow and change, your partner might want to take the business in a different direction than you do. Like entering into a marriage, you want to consider carefully the person(s) with whom you will be sharing your business.

As a form of business ownership, how does a partnership compare to a sole proprietorship? Partnerships and sole proprietorships are very similar; in fact, the biggest difference between the two is the number of people contributing resources and sharing the profits and the liabilities. It's just as easy to form a partnership as a sole proprietorship. The government does not require any special forms or reports—although some local restrictions may apply for licences and permits. For example, if you and your brother-in-law form a small partnership called "All in the Family Electricians," before you are able to do business you might have to apply for a licence, but you do not need any special papers to create the partnership itself. Also, like a sole proprietorship, partnerships do not file a separate tax return. All profits and losses of the partnership flow directly through each partner's own tax return.

limited partnerships A type of partnership that consists of at least one general partner (who has unlimited liability) and one or more limited partners who cannot participate in the day-to-day activities of the business or they will risk losing their limited liability status.

What goes into a partnership agreement? Although no formal documentation is required to create a partnership, it's a good idea to draw up an agreement. A partnership can begin with a handshake, and many of them do, but it is best for all involved parties that a written document, called a *partnership agreement*, formalizes the relationship between business partners. Think of a partnership agreement as a business prenuptial agreement. It helps to settle conflicts when they arise and may discourage small misunderstandings from erupting into larger disagreements. Many points can be included in a partnership agreement; however, the following items should always be included in the agreement:

1. *Capital contributions.* The amount of **capital**, or investments in the form of money, equipment, supplies, computers, and any other tangible thing of value, that each partner contributes to begin the business should be noted in the partnership agreement. In addition, the agreement should also address how additional capital can be added to the business—who will contribute it and whether there will be a limit to a partner's overall capital contribution.
2. *Responsibilities of each partner.* To avoid the possibility of one partner doing more or less work than others, or a conflict arising over one partner assuming a more controlling role than others, it's best to outline the responsibilities of each partner from the beginning. Unless otherwise specified, any partner can bind the partnership to any debt or contract without the consent of the other partners. Therefore, it's especially important to spell out the policy regarding who assumes responsibility for entering into key financial or contractual arrangements.
3. *Decision-making process.* It is important to consider how decisions will be made. Knowing whether decisions will be the result of mutual consent of all or several partners, or whether just one or two partners will make the key decisions is essential to help partners avoid disagreements. What constitutes a "key" decision should also be defined in the agreement. In a partnership of two, where the possibility of a deadlock is likely, some partnerships provide for a trusted associate to act as a third partner whose sole responsibility is to act as the tiebreaker.

capital Investments in the form of money, equipment, supplies, computers, and any other tangible thing of value.

4. *Shares of profits or losses.* Not only should the agreement specify how to divide profits and losses between the partners, but it should also specify how frequently this will be done. One partnership agreement might stipulate that the profits and losses will be proportional to each partner's initial contribution to the partnership, whereas another partnership agreement might just split the profits evenly. It's also important to detail how adjustments to the distributions will be made—if any at all—as the partnership matures and changes.
5. *Departure of partners.* Eventually, the composition of partners will change; original partners will leave and new partners will come aboard. The partnership agreement should have rules for a partner's exit, whether it's voluntary, involuntary, or due to death or divorce. Provisions to remove a partner's ownership interest are necessary so the business does not need to liquidate. The agreement should include how to determine the amount of ownership interest and to whom the departing partner is permitted to transfer his or her interest. It's important to consider whether a partner can transfer his or her ownership solely to the remaining partners or whether individuals outside the existing partnership can buy the departing partner's share.
6. *Addition of partners.* The partnership agreement also helps spell out the requirements for new partners entering the partnership. How the profits will be allocated and whether there will be a "junior partner" period during which the new partner can prove him or herself before obtaining full partner status should also be included.

Corporations

LO8 Explain how a corporation is formed and how it compares with sole proprietorships and partnerships.

What is a corporation? When you think of corporations, you might think of large companies such as Canadian Tire, BlackBerry, or Air Canada, but any-sized company can incorporate. A **corporation** is a specific form of business organization that is a separate legal entity, that is liable for its own debts, and whose owners' liability is limited to their investment in the company. Because a corporation is considered a separate entity apart from its owners, it has legal rights like an individual, so a corporation can own property, assume liability, pay taxes, enter into contracts, and can sue and be sued—just like any other individual. Unlike partnerships and sole proprietorships, corporations provide business owners with better protection of their personal assets.

corporation A specific form of business organization that is a separate legal entity, that is liable for its own debts, and whose owners' liability is limited to their investment in the company.

How do corporations raise capital? Sole proprietorships and partnerships, by their nature, are dependent on their founding owners. When an owner dies or otherwise leaves, the partnership or sole proprietorship is usually terminated. On the other hand, shareholders own a corporation, so its existence doesn't depend on its founding members. Shares of ownership are easily exchanged, so the corporation will continue to exist should the owner die or wish to sell his or her interest in the business. In theory, a corporation is capable of continuing forever.

Elena Elisseeva/Shutterstock

People usually think of big companies when they think of corporations, but any-sized business can incorporate, including a one-person consulting firm.

Incorporating offers a business greater flexibility when raising money. Banks and venture capitalists are more likely to lend money to a business that is incorporated. In times when greater sources of funds are needed than venture capital or bank loans can raise, a corporation can extend its ownership by "going public"—selling shares of ownership in the corporation to the public on the stock exchange. A stock certificate is tangible evidence of investment and for some

Figure 4.4 Steps in Forming a Corporation

investors that is very important. Corporations are said to be **public corporations** when shares of stock are widely held and available for sale to the public—such as Bombardier and Petro-Canada. The stock of a **private corporation** is held by only a few people and is not generally available for sale—such as Cirque du Soleil and The Jim Pattison Group.

public corporations Companies whose shares of stock are widely held and available for sale to the public.

private corporations Companies whose shares of stock are held by only a few people and are not generally available for sale.

How is a corporation formed?

If a company intends to do business in more than one province, it must incorporate under the federal Canada Business Corporations Act. If a company intends to do business in only one province, it may incorporate under that province's corporation act. Generally, a corporation files **articles of incorporation** with the government, laying out the general nature of the corporation, the name of the corporation and its directors, the type and number of shares to be issued, and the location of the company's operations. Once the articles are approved, the corporation's directors meet to create bylaws that govern the internal functions of the corporation (see **Figure 4.4**). Specific duties of the board of directors and individual board members, committees, and officers are set out in the corporate bylaws. The **bylaws** are the rules of a corporation, established by the board of directors during the process of starting a corporation. All corporations must attach the word "Incorporated" (Inc.), "Limited" (Ltd./Ltée), or "Corporation" (Corp.) to the company name.

articles of incorporation Lay out the general nature of the corporation, the name of the corporation and its directors, the type and number of shares to be issued, and the location of the company's operations.

bylaws The rules of a corporation, established by the board of directors during the process of starting a corporation.

How is a corporation structured?

Shareholders—investors who buy shares of ownership in the form of stock—are the real owners of a corporation. Dividends are payments made by a corporation to its shareholders. When a corporation earns a profit, it can either reinvest that profit in the business (called retained earnings) or it can be paid to the shareholders as a dividend. Many corporations retain a portion of earnings and pay the remainder in dividends. A dividend is allocated as a fixed amount per share; therefore, a shareholder receives dividends in proportion to their shareholdings (the more shares, the more dividends). Shareholders can attend annual meetings, elect a board of directors, and vote on matters that affect the corporation, in accordance with its charter and bylaws. Each share or stock generally carries only one vote. The shareholders elect a **board of directors** to govern and handle the overall management of the corporation. A corporate board has great power and great responsibility: the board must act with the corporation's best interests in mind. The directors set corporate goals and policies, hire corporate officers (e.g., president, vice-president, CEO, CFO, COO, CIO), and oversee the firm's operations and finances.

shareholders Investors in a corporation who buy shares of ownership in the form of stock.

board of directors A group of people who are elected by shareholders to govern and handle the overall management of the corporation.

What are the advantages of incorporation?

Aside from the obvious, biggest advantage of the corporate structure of limited liability, continuity is another advantage. In theory, a corporation could continue forever because shares of stock may be sold or passed on to heirs. As mentioned above, corporations also have an advantage when raising money.

What are the disadvantages of incorporation?

It is costly to incorporate and there are many government regulations. Because a corporation is a separate legal entity, many requirements must be fulfilled to maintain the corporate status. For example, all companies must file an annual report and maintain written minutes of annual and other periodic board of director and shareholder meetings. Double taxation is also considered a disadvantage of incorporation. **Double taxation** means that the corporation must pay income taxes on its profits, and the shareholders must pay personal income taxes on the dividends they receive from the corporation.

double taxation Means that the corporation must pay income taxes on its profits, and the shareholders must pay personal income taxes on the dividends they receive from the corporation.

Nonprofit Corporations

LO9 Describe the characteristics of nonprofit corporations and cooperatives.

Must a nonprofit corporation be legally incorporated? Some organizations don't fit the mould of sole proprietorship, partnership, or corporation. When this occurs, business owners might form nonprofit organizations or cooperatives. Legally, a nonprofit corporation is an incorporated business that does not seek a net profit and instead uses revenue available after normal operating expenses for the corporation's declared social or educational goals. Incorporation is not necessary, but to receive limited liability protection a nonprofit organization must file incorporation papers and become established as a separate legal entity.

Similar to a for-profit corporation, a nonprofit corporation is required to hold board of director meetings and to keep complete books and records. The greatest difference from a for-profit corporation is that a nonprofit organization cannot be organized for any person's private gain. Nonprofit organizations do not issue shares of stock, and their members may not receive personal financial benefit from the organization's profits (other than salary as an employee). In addition, should the nonprofit dissolve, the organization's assets must go to a similar nonprofit group.

Do nonprofit corporations generate profits? Nonprofit corporations are not in business to generate a profit. Nonprofit organizations generate their revenue primarily through fundraising and donations. To maintain their tax-exempt status, nonprofit organizations must demonstrate that a substantial portion of their income or revenue is spent on services to achieve their goals. Nonprofit corporations must apply for charitable status to benefit from tax-exempt status and to issue tax-deductible receipts to donors. The Canada Revenue Agency (CRA) is the government department responsible for granting organizations charitable tax status.

What are the benefits of being tax-exempt? As a corporation that has received tax-exempt status, the donations that are the organization's primary source of revenue are tax deductible to the donor, which encourages funding. Other benefits of tax-exempt status are that the nonprofit is exempt from paying most federal and provincial corporate income taxes and may be exempt from provincial sales and property taxes. Such organizations are able to apply for grants and other public or private distributions, as well as discounts on postal rates and other services.

Cooperatives

How do cooperatives differ from the other forms of business ownership? Cooperatives differ from other forms of business because they have a different purpose, control structure, and allocation of profit. A **cooperative** is a business owned and governed by members who use its products or services, not by outside investors. The primary purpose of cooperatives is to meet the common needs of their members. For instance, Mountain Equipment Co-op is Canada's largest retailer cooperative, which sells outdoor gear, clothing, and offers services to its members. Cooperatives exist in virtually every sector of the economy, from agriculture, retail, and financial services to housing, childcare, funeral services, and renewable energy. See **Table 4.4** for a comparison of the forms of business ownership.

cooperative A business owned and governed by members who use its products or services, not by outside investors.

Video: Elm City Market: Organizational Structure

How are cooperatives structured? Cooperatives depend on their members to volunteer for projects supported by the co-op and serve on boards and committees. The control structure in a cooperative differs from that of a corporation in that each member receives one vote, not one vote per share. This helps cooperatives serve the common need rather than the individual need. Profits are shared among the members based on how much they use the co-op, not on how many shares they hold. Some people may consider the democratic voting arrangement and dividends based purely on patronage a disadvantage and may be discouraged from forming or joining a cooperative.

Table 4.4 Comparison of Forms of Business Ownership

Characteristic	Sole Proprietorship	Partnership	Corporation	Cooperative
Ease of formation	High	High	Medium	Medium
Continuity	Low	Low	High	High
Protection against liability	Low	Low	High	High
Tax advantages	High	High	Low	High
Ease of raising money	Low	Medium	High	High
Government regulation	Low	Low	High	Medium

Business Combinations: Mergers and Acquisitions

LO10 Summarize the different types of mergers and acquisitions and explain why they occur.

What are mergers and acquisitions? Sometimes, in the evolution of a business or in response to market forces, companies seek opportunities to expand by adding new product lines, spreading out into different geographic areas, or growing the company to increase its competitive advantage. Often product or market expansion is done gradually by slowly adding new product lines or penetrating new areas. However, it takes time and investment to research and develop new products or to locate and build in new areas. Often, especially to remain competitive, expansion needs to happen more quickly. In that case, it's easier to integrate another established business through the process of mergers or acquisitions.

A **merger** occurs when two or more firms combine to form one new company, which often takes on a new corporate identity. Generally, a merger implies that the two companies involved are about the same size and have mutually agreed to form a new combined company. When a "merger of equals" happens, both merging companies cease to exist and one new company takes over. For example, in 2009 Suncor Energy merged with Petro-Canada, stating that by merging the two oil companies would create Canada's largest energy company, which would provide protection against potential foreign buyouts.[27]

merger Occurs when two or more firms combine to form one new company, which often takes on a new corporate identity.

Under the Competition Act, mergers of all sizes and in all sectors of Canada's economy are subject to review by the Competition Bureau to determine whether they will likely result in a substantial lessening or prevention of competition. For instance, when TD Bank wanted to acquire Canada Trust in 2000, the Competition Bureau concluded that the merger would likely lessen competition and affect consumers negatively. To remedy the bureau's concerns, TD Bank proposed to sell the branches in the identified problematic markets and either convert its Visa credit card portfolio to MasterCard or sell the Canada Trust MasterCard portfolio. The bureau announced that the government had approved the Canada Trust acquisition contingent upon the proposed remedies being fully implemented.[28]

An **acquisition**, on the other hand, occurs when one company or investor group buys a corporation and the identity of the acquired company might be lost. Often the purchased company ceases to exist, and it operates and trades under the buying company's name. A company can also acquire divisions or subsidiaries of another firm.

acquisition Occurs when one company or investor group buys a corporation and the identity of the acquired company might be lost.

When the acquisition is supported by the target company's management and board of directors, it is called a **friendly takeover**, but if the takeover goes against the wishes of the target company's management and board of directors, it is called a **hostile takeover**. Hostile takeovers are usually accomplished through a *proxy fight*, whereby the acquiring company quietly purchases enough stock on the open market to gain a controlling interest in the company and affect a change in management. Another method used in hostile acquisition occurs through a *tender offer*, where the acquiring firm offers to buy the target company's stock at a price higher than its current value, which is meant to induce shareholders into selling.

friendly takeover Occurs when the target company's management and board of directors support an acquisition.

hostile takeover Occurs when a takeover goes against the wishes of the target company's management and board of directors.

Horizontal Merger

merges with

Vertical Merger

merges with

Product Extension Merger

merges with
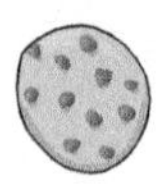

Market Extension

merges with

Conglomeration

merges with

Figure 4.5 Different Types of Mergers

Companies merge for different strategic reasons. Sometimes companies merge to enter new markets, whereas others want to expand into new fields and save costs.

Why do mergers and acquisitions occur? *Synergy* is the business buzzword often used to justify a merger or an acquisition. **Synergy** is the achieved effect when two companies combine and the result is better than each company could achieve individually. Synergistic value is created when the new company can realize operating or financial economies of scale (the cost advantage that a business obtains from expansion). Combined firms often lower costs by trimming redundancies in staff, sharing resources, and obtaining discounts accessible only to a larger firm. Often, companies join together to gain a greater competitive advantage or become the dominant force in their market.

Are there different types of mergers? The rationale and strategy behind every merger is different but, as illustrated in **Figure 4.5**, there are some consistencies that are distinguished by the relationship between the two companies that are merging:

- *Horizontal merger.* Two companies that share the same product lines and markets and are in direct competition with each other, such as a soft drink company and a mineral water company, are merging horizontally.
- *Vertical merger.* Two companies that have a company/customer relationship or a company/supplier relationship, such as Walt Disney and Pixar or eBay and PayPal, are merging vertically.
- *Product extension merger.* Two companies selling different but related products in the same market, such as the 2005 merger between Adobe and Macromedia, are forming a product extension merger.
- *Market extension merger.* Two companies that sell the same products in different markets, such as Morrison and Safeway supermarkets, are forming a market extension merger. Although both Morrison and Safeway are in the United Kingdom, Morrison is mainly in Great Britain and Safeway is mainly in Scotland.
- *Conglomeration.* Two companies that have no common business areas merge to obtain diversification, such as Citicorp, a banking services firm, and Travelers Group Inc., an insurance underwriting company, which combined to form one of the world's largest financial services group, Citigroup Inc.

synergy The achieved effect when two companies combine and the result is better than each company could achieve individually.

Are there disadvantages with mergers? Although cost cutting may be the initial focus of some mergers, revenues and profits ultimately suffer because day-to-day activities are neglected. Additionally, corporate cultures may clash, and communications may break down if the new division of responsibilities is vague. Conflicts may also arise from divided loyalties, hidden agendas, or power struggles within the newly combined management team. Employees may be nervous because most mergers result in the elimination of jobs and some may actually leave the company, feeling their jobs are in jeopardy and seeking a more stable environment.

CHAPTER SYNOPSIS

LO1 List the traits of an effective entrepreneur, and describe how these characteristics often lead to business success. *(pp. 66–70)*

Successful **entrepreneurs**

- are innovative
- take risks
- are motivated to succeed
- are flexible and self-directed
- work well with others and possess good leadership skills
- are "system thinkers," seeing the whole process rather than just individual pieces of it

Successful entrepreneurs see problems to be solved or opportunities that aren't being addressed in the marketplace—

they recognize **opportunity niches**. They also make improvements to existing products or systems, or they introduce something new and make profitable solutions out of problems.

LO2 Describe the factors that lead to small business failure, and explain why a business plan is crucial to small business success. *(pp. 70–73)*

A **business plan** is a formal document that states the goals of the business as well as the plan for reaching those goals. A business plan should tell the story of your business concept—it is a blueprint for the company, and it is an indispensable tool in attracting investors or obtaining loans. Preparing a business plan takes a lot of time, but it is time well spent because your business plan is an ongoing guide. You use it to acquire startup capital as well as to assess your company's progress, as long as you remember to update it periodically. A realistic business plan forces you to think critically about your proposed business and reduces your risk of failure.

Businesses fail because of the following reasons:

- accumulating too much debt
- inexperienced management
- poor planning

LO3 Compare the advantages and disadvantages of starting a business from scratch to buying an existing business. *(pp. 73–75)*

	Starting from Scratch	Purchasing an Existing Business
Advantages	• Freedom to do what you want • Can start small and grow • Satisfaction of building something new • Can create the kind of image and reputation you want	• Ease of startup • Existing customer base and revenue • May be easier to secure loans because the business has a proven track record
Disadvantages	• It's risky! • The business has no proven track record • It takes time to build a good reputation • Nothing is established; you need to do everything • There is no existing cash flow • It can be difficult to obtain financing	• High purchase price • May inherit previous owners mistakes • There are unknowns

LO4 Outline the advantages and disadvantages of franchising. *(pp. 75–79)*

For many, buying a **franchise** is an easier, less risky means of starting a business. Since the franchisor provides much of the marketing and financial tools needed to run the business, all the franchisee is expected to bring to the table is management and marketing skills, time, and money. In addition to a recognized brand name, other advantages include a proven system of operation, strength in numbers, initial training, marketing support, and market research is often provided as well.

Although buying a franchise provides the franchisee with many benefits, other disadvantages include lack of control, heavy workload, competition, shared common problems, high startup costs, and franchisees must pay a monthly royalty fee to the franchisor. Other costs the franchisee might incur include real estate purchase or rental, equipment purchase or rental, extra signage, and opening inventory.

LO5 Summarize the potential benefits and drawbacks of each major source of small business financing. *(pp. 79–80)*

For larger amounts, new business owners sometimes obtain a loan by borrowing against their own assets, such as the equity in their house or against their retirement account, but the consequences of the business failing are very severe. **Grants** are financial awards that are usually offered by federal and provincial governments and some private organizations. **Venture capitalists** are another source of funding. Unlike banks, where there is a contractual agreement to pay back the money, venture capitalists contribute money to your business in return for some form of equity—a piece of ownership. **Angel investors** are wealthy individuals willing to put up their own money in hopes of a profit return later on.

Often, outside investors are looking for some controlling or managerial role in the business. When a great deal of money is on the line, the stakes—personal, professional, and financial—are quite high. By understanding the available options and being prepared to deal with financial predicaments, business owners give themselves the best chance at success.

LO6 Explain the advantages and disadvantages of sole proprietorship. *(pp. 80–82)*

There are several advantages to forming your business as a **sole proprietorship**, the first of which is ease of formation. With only one person making all the decisions and no need to consult other owners or interested parties, sole proprietors have greater control and more flexibility to act quickly. Another advantage is that there are no specific corporate records to keep or reports to file, including tax reporting. Since there is no legal distinction between the owner and the business, no separate tax return is required. As a result, the income and expenses of a sole proprietorship flow through the owner's personal tax return.

A sole proprietor is personally responsible for all the debts and liabilities of the business. **Unlimited liability** means that if business assets aren't enough to pay business debts, then personal assets, such as the sole proprietor's house, personal investments, or retirement plans, can be used to pay the balance. Another drawback of a sole proprietorship is the potential difficulty in borrowing money to help your business grow.

LO7 Explain the advantages and disadvantages of partnership and describe the importance of partnership agreements. *(pp. 82–84)*

Since a **partnership** has more owners, there are more available contributions to both the starting and ongoing capital of the business. Sharing the financial responsibility means all the owners are interested in the company's overall profitability and are as highly motivated as you are to make the business succeed. Therefore, additional owners, unlike employees, are more likely to be willing to work long hours and go the extra mile.

Adding partners to help share the workload also allows for coverage for vacations, illness, or personal issues. Moreover, if partners have complementary skills, they create a collaboration that can be quite advantageous. Partners can help discuss ideas and projects as well as make the big decisions. Partners can help in sales and marketing to generate income.

For every advantage a partner can bring, adding the wrong partner can be equally problematic. Obviously, adding partners means sharing profits and control. A potential partner may have different work habits and styles from you, and if the partner's style isn't complementary, the differences can prove challenging. In addition, as the business begins to grow and change, your partner might want to take the business in a different direction than you do, so preparing a partnership agreement can help to clarify the partners' expectations of how to run their business and how they plan to resolve any possible disagreements.

LO8 Explain how a corporation is formed and how it compares with sole proprietorships and partnerships. *(pp. 84–85)*

A **corporation** is a separate legal entity, liable for its own debts, and whose owners' liability is limited to their investment in the company. Because a corporation is considered a separate entity apart from its owners, it has legal rights like an individual, so a corporation can own property, assume liability, pay taxes, enter into contracts, and can sue and be sued—just like any other individual. Unlike partnerships and sole proprietorships, corporations provide business owners with better protection of their personal assets.

If a company intends to do business in more than one province, it must incorporate under the federal Canada Business Corporations Act. If a company intends to do business in only one province, it may incorporate under that province's corporation act.

LO9 Describe the characteristics of nonprofit corporations and cooperatives. *(pp. 86–87)*

Legally, a nonprofit corporation is an incorporated business that does not seek a net profit and instead uses revenue available after normal operating expenses for the corporation's declared social or educational goals.

Cooperatives differ from other forms of business because they have a different purpose, control structure, and allocation of profit. A cooperative is a business owned and governed by members who use its products or services, not by outside investors. The primary purpose of cooperatives is to meet the common needs of their members.

LO10 Summarize the different types of mergers and acquisitions and explain why they occur. *(pp. 87–88)*

Sometimes, in the evolution of a business or in response to market forces, companies seek opportunities to expand by adding new product lines, spreading out into different geographic areas, or growing the company to increase their competitive advantage. Often, especially to remain competitive, this expansion needs to happen quickly. In that case, it's easier to integrate another established business through the process of **mergers** or **acquisitions** than try to add new product lines or expand into new areas.

- *Horizontal merger:* two companies that share the same product lines and markets and are in direct competition with each other, such as a soft drink company and a mineral water company.
- *Vertical merger:* two companies that have a company/customer relationship or a company/supplier relationship, such as Walt Disney and Pixar or eBay and PayPal.
- *Product extension merger:* two companies selling different but related products in the same market, such as the 2005 merger between Adobe and Macromedia.
- *Market extension merger:* two companies that sell the same products in different markets, for example, Morrison supermarket and Safeway. Although both are in the United Kingdom, Morrison is mainly in Great Britain and Safeway is mainly in Scotland.
- *Conglomeration:* two companies that have no common business areas merge to obtain diversification, such as Citicorp, a banking services firm, and Travelers Group Inc., an insurance underwriting company, combining to form one of the world's largest financial services group, Citigroup Inc.

MyBizLab Study, practise, and explore real business situations with these helpful resources:

- **Interactive Lesson Presentations:** Work through interactive presentations and assessments to test your knowledge of business concepts.
- **Study Plan:** Check your understanding of chapter concepts with self-study quizzes.
- **Dynamic Study Modules:** Work through adaptive study modules on your computer, tablet, or mobile device.
- **Simulations:** Practise decision-making in simulated business environments.

KEY TERMS

acquisition *(p. 87)*
angel investors *(p. 80)*
articles of incorporation *(p. 85)*
board of directors *(p. 85)*
business incubators *(p. 78)*
business plan *(p. 73)*
bylaws *(p. 85)*
capital *(p. 83)*
cooperative *(p. 86)*
corporation *(p. 84)*
double taxation *(p. 85)*
due diligence *(p. 75)*
entrepreneurial team *(p. xx)*
entrepreneur *(p. 66)*
franchise *(p. 75)*
friendly takeover *(p. 87)*
general partners *(p. 82)*
general partnership *(p. 82)*
grants *(p. 80)*
growth entrepreneurs *(p. 69)*
home-based entrepreneurs *(p. 69)*
hostile takeover *(p. 87)*
Internet entrepreneurs *(p. 69)*
intrapreneurs *(p. 69)*
liability *(p. 82)*
lifestyle entrepreneurs *(p. 68)*
limited liability *(p. 81)*
limited partners *(p. 82)*
limited partnerships *(p. 83)*
merger *(p. 87)*
micropreneurs *(p. 68)*
opportunity niche *(p. 66)*
partnership *(p. 82)*
private corporations *(p. 85)*
public corporations *(p. 85)*
shareholders *(p. 85)*
Small Business Investment Company (SBIC) *(p. 80)*
sole proprietorship *(p. 80)*
synergy *(p. 88)*
unlimited liability *(p. 82)*
venture capitalists *(p. 80)*

CRITICAL THINKING QUESTIONS

1. Bill Gates, Donald Trump, and Oprah Winfrey are some well-known successful entrepreneurs. What common traits do these individuals possess that have led to their success?
2. Compare the different sources of funding available to small business owners. Which sources of funding seem best when a business is just starting? Which sources of funding seem best once the business is established and is looking to expand?
3. Imagine that you are planning to open a new business in partnership with a close friend. Briefly describe the skills and abilities that your new partner can offer that you lack. What

are the pros and cons of partnering with this person? What kinds of issues do you anticipate might potentially cause disagreement with this person? Write examples of terms you could include in a partnership agreement that would help the business run more smoothly.

4. Discuss the different risks facing someone creating a new business from scratch and someone buying an existing small business. What risks will both new business owners face? Compare the advantages and disadvantages of each option. Which would you rather do and why?
5. Businesses, especially small businesses, often compete for customers through customer experience—customer service, quality of the experience, or exceeding the customer expectations. Imagine that you open your own business. Identify how you could build a competitive advantage by offering a better customer experience. Be specific. What would your business offer customers that would entice them to buy from you instead of your competitors?

APPLICATION EXERCISES

1. **A closer look at franchising.** Using the Internet, research a franchise that you think would be a viable investment opportunity for you. Put together a brief report that outlines the following information about your chosen franchise: fees (initial and ongoing), location/site assistance, training and ongoing support, marketing assistance, competition (both from other businesses and additional franchises within the organization), and the pros and cons of starting a business with this franchise.
2. **Microfinancing: A little $ can go a long way.** Visit www.kiva.org and click on the "Lend" tab to view the list of entrepreneurs. Use the drop-down menus in the "Find Loans" search bar to locate an entrepreneur or entrepreneurial team you would consider lending money to. In a brief report, discuss the entrepreneur or group you chose, including information on the loan amount requested, the percentage of funds raised, the entrepreneur's country of origin, and a summary of the entrepreneur's business venture. In your report, explain your reasons for choosing to loan to this particular entrepreneur.
3. **Do you have what it takes to be an entrepreneur?** Visit the Business Development Bank of Canada's (BDC) website at www.bdc.ca. Go to the Advice Centre, Tools, and complete the Entrepreneurial self-assessment. What aspects of your personality make you a good candidate to be an entrepreneur? What is holding you back?
4. **Business combinations.** Look on the Internet for a current example of a business merger, takeover, or acquisition. Explain the circumstances of the event. What companies are involved? Was the event friendly or hostile? What are the reasons given for the combination? What is your opinion of this business combination? Do you think it is a good business decision? Why or why not?
5. **Small business owners.** In the results of the 2011 Census, Milton, Ontario, was named the fastest-growing community in Canada. Imagine that you want to start a catering business in Milton (or another fast-growing community). You see that a catering business is for sale in Milton for $150 000. The company specializes in catering business events. The owner, currently operating the business from home, is moving to another country and wants to sell. You will need outside investors to help you purchase the business. Develop questions to ask the owner about the business. What other types of information would you need before making a decision to buy this company? Either you will purchase this existing business or start a catering business of your own, therefore you should investigate the feasibility of each option. Once you've gathered the necessary information, visit Sample Business Plans (www.bplans.com) and search for a sample catering business plan and review it. Use the example you found as a starting point to draft an executive summary that will attract investors for your business.

ETHICS AND RESPONSIBILITY

Social Responsibility: Forming a Plan of Action

Milton Hershey, founder of Hershey Chocolate Company, dedicated himself to caring about his customers, his employees, and his community at large. Hershey felt that giving back to the community was not only his moral obligation but also a crucial part of his success.

Step 1. Imagine that you operate a business in your community (choose from a restaurant, a landscaping service, or a beauty salon).

Step 2. As a class or in smaller groups, discuss the ways in which your business can contribute to customers, employees, and the community in socially responsible ways. Write down a list of ideas that your group came up with.

Step 3. Create a social responsibility plan for your company. In the document, describe your business and the ways in which your business can contribute to specific organizations in your community. Be as specific with your plan as possible. Your instructor may ask you to submit your work or discuss it with the class.

CLOSING CASE

The Fish That Pulled Him Under

Born in Europe, avid angler Kevin Hengeveld immigrated to Canada in the early 1980s. In the 1990s, Hengeveld started an import/export wholesale business in Ontario whereby he would import products not currently sold in the Canadian market and sell them to fishing stores all over Ontario. There was a big demand for this type of equipment, especially from Canadians of European descent. He dealt with many fishing storeowners and learned much about how the retail fishing industry worked.

Hengeveld created an online store called Fish in the Net where he could sell his imported goods directly to customers, acquiring many loyal customers. He was very knowledgeable about many types of fishing (i.e., float fishing, carp fishing, sport fishing, ice fishing) and published a fishing magazine in two languages.

During the second year of business, Hengeveld noticed that many stores were not paying on time, but the products were selling well. For many years, Hengeveld had thought about opening his own fishing equipment store. Recreational fishing/angling was a passion of his since he was a small child, so when a retail space became available in 2003 in a wealthy area of town, Hengeveld decided to rent it and start his own brick-and-mortar retail business. The store specialized in European-style fishing and float fishing and sold equipment and bait. Hengeveld continued his wholesale operations, but focused on his new venture. He held seminars at the store and provided information to customers regarding new and current fishing techniques. The business was established as a sole proprietorship, and Hengeveld initially financed the startup of the business through personal savings of $20 000 and a $25 000 line of credit. Later he obtained another $75 000 line of credit. He never did have enough time to write his business plan fully.

The live bait the store sold generated a big percentage of the income, but it also generated a big percentage of the expenses. Not only were storage tanks, refrigerated tanks, and fridges needed, but the government had many regulations pertaining to the type of bait a store could sell and the reporting that must be done. Due to the hours anglers would go fishing, the store had to be open very early in the mornings and 24 hours on the weekends. Staff had to be trained on how to handle live bait. There was a 40 percent loss in bait product, and suppliers insisted on cash payments on delivery with no returns.

The store also sold fishing licences, which required monthly reporting to the Ministry of Natural Resources (MNR) but also attracted customers. A yearly live bait sales report was also required by the MNR, which was very time consuming to create because it detailed the number of fish sold. The business was audited once by the Canada Revenue Agency and it went well because Hengeveld had hired an accountant to be sure all payroll deductions, special reporting, and income tax calculations were accurate and complete.

There was not a lot of competition in the area, just a few small, family-operated stores. Hengeveld's wife helped with the bookkeeping and the purchases and reporting processes when she could, but she also had a full-time career. Hengeveld soon was doing enough business that he actually purchased a second store, taking over his main competitor of the family-operated stores. Hengeveld was doing so well in this second store location that he decided to close the first store, as he was feeling a bit stretched running between the two stores and trying to be a good husband and father. He felt the original store's business was only about half that of the second store so it was best to focus his efforts on the second store, even though the second store was not in as good a neighbourhood and the operating costs were somewhat higher. The property owner had Hengeveld sign a lease that included a clause stating that the lessee was responsible for all repairs and for paying the hydro bills for both the store space as well as the apartment upstairs. To Hengeveld's dismay, the store space was dilapidated, and he found out later that he was responsible for many more repairs than he initially thought.

Hengeveld hired a programmer to update the business website since this was his primary marketing tool, and soon it became the first of its kind for sports anglers in Canada. Customers could order online, use message boards, chat with each other, and arrange to meet at the store and go fishing together. The site offered an interactive experience for customers and brought many new customers not only from Canada but also from the United States.

He installed a security system in his store, and had an alarm system in place because the store was open 24 hours on weekends. Hengeveld had a difficult time finding qualified staff that he could rely on to show up for work and not steal from the store. He had a couple of employees who did not deal with customers well and customers had complained about them to Hengeveld. Part-time staff consisted of mostly college students taking a break from their studies; while most had good customer service skills, they proved unreliable in other ways.

In 2005, a major outdoors store, Bass Pro, opened within a 20-kilometre range, and Hengeveld estimated that he lost around 25 percent of his revenue after the mega store moved in. Business started to slow in 2007 just before the recession hit in 2008. In the beginning, Hengeveld's business was not making a profit, but he was able to cover expenses and repay creditors. During the last few years, the store was losing money. In the end, Hengeveld decided to close his brick-and-mortar store but continue to operate his online store as more of a part-time pursuit.

DISCUSSION QUESTIONS

1. What entrepreneurial traits does Hengeveld have? What made him want to start his own business?
2. Analyze the situation. What do you think went wrong? Did Hengeveld make mistakes? If so, what were they?
3. What might Hengeveld had done differently to continue his business success? Search for one or more sample business plans for a retail fishing store (you should find at least one at www.bplans.com). Review it. What stands out in your mind about the plan? Do you think Hengeveld could have done better with his business if he had a business plan to start with? Why or why not?

5 Business Management

Jon Holowachuk

LEARNING OBJECTIVES

After studying this chapter, you should be able to:

LO1 Describe the ways managers apply technical, interpersonal, decision-making, conceptual, and time management skills to business. (pp. 95–98)

LO2 Explain how corporate vision and a mission statement help to keep the company focused on achieving its goals and objectives. (pp. 98–102)

LO3 Describe the implications of tactical plans, operational plans, and contingency plans within the context of management. (pp. 102–103)

LO4 Explain the significance of organizing and how most organizations are organized. (pp. 103–105)

LO5 Distinguish among vertical organizations, horizontal organizations, and network organizations. (pp. 105–107)

LO6 Describe what makes a good leader and the various styles of leadership. (pp. 107–110)

LO7 Explain the importance of control within a business. (pp. 111–112)

OPENING DISCUSSION: EFFECTIVE MANAGEMENT

Creating an Experience to Remember

Although it is impossible to know for sure, rough estimates suggest that we are exposed to approximately 5000 marketing messages every day, including billboards, television commercials, popups, and even logos printed on products.[1] If we actually processed everything we saw throughout the day, our brains would explode! Okay, maybe that's a bit extreme, but for sure we'd be overloaded and quickly become overwhelmed. Luckily our powerful brains have found a way to filter the information we need and ignore what we don't. This subconscious process of selective perception and selective memory suggests that we only pay attention to things that are relevant—in other words, things that we are personally interested in. This raises questions about the effectiveness of traditional advertising.

Here's where Jon Holowachuk (photo appearing on the previous page) comes in. Jon is the senior site coordinator at eventSing Promotions Inc., avid snowboarder, and supporter of men's health though the Movember campaign. eventSing is a Canada's largest action sports event and entertainment production company, and it specializes in planning and running action sports–oriented events and experiential marketing. For the past 10 years they have worked with clients such as Disney, Molson Coors, Billabong, and Red Bull, promoting their philosophy: "eventSing makes action sports easy."[2]

In February 2014, Jon and his team organized the Red Bull Jib Cup at Wilfrid Laurier University, an event that attracted snowboarders and skiers from across Ontario to answer the question, "What colleges and universities have the best talent in the snow?" According to Jon, "Our goal was to design and deliver an event that represented Red Bull's premium, energetic image—and do this within budget." The setup included a 10-foot scaffolding drop built for riders to get their speed up before they chose between three features: two rails and one wall ride. Jon relies on his planning and organizing skills to make this happen: "Before the event we lay out the course design and build it. We're setting up umbrellas, arches, tables, and coolers, ensuring that our client's assets are in place and look great." Once the event started, Jon and his team took a backseat to Red Bull staff who ran the event, but they stayed close by to assist as needed. After the contest, they took down the site, packed up the assets, and left the location spotless.

For an event like Red Bull's Jib Cup to be successful, Jon depends on members of his team to do their jobs well. A core team works on smaller, reoccurring events: "They are great because I can rely on them to represent eventSing and our client's brands to the highest level possible," says Jon. Keeping employees motivated is a challenge for every manager, but according to Jon his core team is already motivated because "they have a vested interest in eventSing and in our clients."

Some of the larger events are too big for the core team to handle on their own. In these cases Jon hires students and temp workers to help, but "contract workers are a little harder to motivate because they are unsure what to do and don't always feel the same level of commitment to eventSing and our clients as the rest of us do," says Jon. With these workers Jon has to be more hands on and actually works alongside them to show them what do to and to model the standards and work ethic he expects. Regardless of whether the employee is a core member of the team or a temp, Jon believes that everyone must be treated with respect: "Please and thank you go a long way to getting the most from people."

As a manager in the event marketing industry, Jon says there is no "typical" day: "I can be planning asset delivery and site design for Belvedere Vodka and receive a phone call from McDonald's asking us to visit a Ronald McDonald House to read stories to children. You need to be flexible and adapt to each situation." For people who are driven to achieve goals, managing others can be very rewarding. For Jon, "the best part of my job is the great sense of pride and accomplishment I feel when staff come together to build an unforgettable event for our clients and participants." On that note, Jon says that this year's Jib Cup was a success: "We built an excellent site that was more exciting than the previous year, and most importantly competitors had a great day and our client Red Bull was pleased."[3]

DISCUSSION QUESTIONS

1. What are some of the most important skills needed by a manager like Jon?
2. Why do you think Jon says it is more difficult to manage temporary workers than his usual core team?
3. What do you think managers should do to make sure their employees are highly motivated?

SKILLS OF SUCCESSFUL MANAGERS

LO1 Describe the ways managers apply technical, interpersonal, decision-making, conceptual, and time management skills to business.

Working with People and Resources

Who are managers? Have you ever been in a team situation in which one person has been instrumental in making the group work more effectively? That person could have been a peer or a superior, but somehow he or she knew exactly what had to be accomplished, assessed the resources available to achieve the goal, and organized and led other group members to accomplish the goal. If so, you've seen management in action.

Management is the process of working with people and resources to accomplish the goals of the organization. The organization can be a simple working group, a corporate department, or a multibillion-dollar company. The size of the group doesn't matter, but the skills of a manager and the process a manager goes through are similar across all management levels (low-level or first-line managers, middle-level managers, and top-level managers—all of which are discussed later in this chapter).

management The process of working with people and resources to accomplish the goals of the organization.

What skills do managers need? Since managers are involved in many tasks, a successful manager needs to possess a variety of skills, including *technical, interpersonal, conceptual, decision-making,* and *time management skills.* It is a rare person who is master of all these skills. Moreover, because they are responsible for a variety of jobs, and because these jobs can change quite rapidly, managers must assess the skills required in any given situation. Managers must also be willing to acquire these skills quickly if necessary.

Technical Skills Every job has a specific set of technical skills that are important for managers to possess. **Technical skills** include the abilities and knowledge that enable an employee to carry out the specific tasks required of a job, such as drafting skills for an architect, programming skills for a software developer, or market analysis skills for a marketing manager. Technical skills may also include how to operate certain machinery. Managers must be comfortable with technology and possess good analytical skills to interpret a variety of data. In addition to having the skills pertinent to their own jobs, managers must also know how to perform, or at least have a good understanding of, the skills required of the employees they supervise.

technical skills The abilities and knowledge that enable an employee to carry out the specific tasks required of a job.

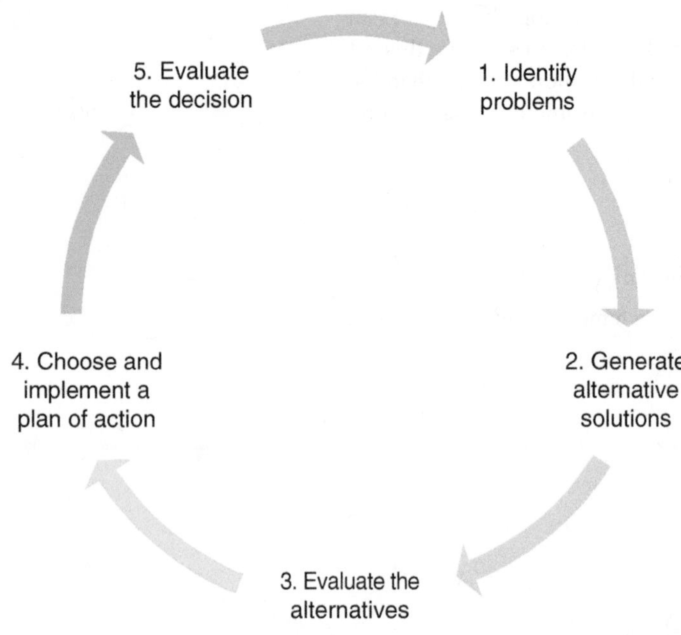

Figure 5.1 Stages of Decision Making

Interpersonal Skills Managers achieve goals working with people both inside and outside the organization, so it's important that they possess good interpersonal or human relations skills. **Interpersonal skills** enable a manager to interact with other people to motivate them. It's important that a manager develop trust and loyalty with the people he or she interacts with often and that the manager can motivate and encourage employees to work together.

Interpersonal skills are important skills at any management level. Top managers must be able to communicate with the board of directors, investors, and other leaders in the business community. They must also communicate with middle managers to understand clearly the goals and strategies of the organization. Middle managers must communicate with all levels of management and act as liaisons among groups. Lower-level managers must be able to motivate employees, build morale, and train and support those who perform the daily tasks of the organization.

Video: Southwest Airlines: Leadership and Decision Making

interpersonal skills Skills that enable a manager to interact with other people to motivate them.

decision-making skills The ability to identify and analyze a problem, examine the alternatives, choose and implement the best plan of action, and evaluate the results.

Video: CH2MHill: Decision Making

Decision-Making Skills It is critical that a manager has good problem-solving and **decision-making skills**—the ability to identify and analyze a problem, examine the alternatives, choose and implement the best plan of action, and evaluate the results. When making important decisions, managers often go through a formal decision-making process similar to that shown in **Figure 5.1.** The steps in such a process are as follows:

1. In analyzing any situation or case, managers *identify problems* or opportunities by analyzing data and searching for trends. Such problems may include poor growth in sales, an increase in customer dissatisfaction, or excess inventory buildup. The same situations may also be opportunities in disguise. For instance, excess inventory may offer an opportunity to offer a special sale to customers.
2. Once a problem is defined, managers then *generate alternative solutions.*
3. Once they have identified several alternatives, managers *evaluate the alternatives* based on various criteria, such as cost, feasibility, time, resources needed, market acceptance, and compatibility with the company's mission, values, and goals. Managers often rank the evaluated alternatives by various criteria. This evaluation process can be tedious, but identifying and evaluating alternatives is critical to making a good decision. Many times the best routes are not taken because management has not taken the time to explore all alternatives thoroughly.
4. Once managers have evaluated all alternatives, they *choose the best plan of action.* As a final check, management may seek customer or market opinion on the chosen plan of action before completely committing to this choice. In some instances, if the market or customer feedback is not positive, management will look to pursue another alternative. When the final choice has been made, plans are put in place to *implement the plan of action.*
5. Managers also *evaluate the decision* to ensure it is carried out correctly and meets the goals of the organization. If the goals are not being met, the decision-making process may become cyclical, beginning again with *identifying problems.*

conceptual skills The ability to think abstractly, picture the organization as a whole, and understand its relationship to the rest of the business community.

Conceptual Skills To make good decisions, a good manager must also have **conceptual skills**—the ability to think abstractly, picture the organization as a whole, and understand its relationship to the rest of the business community. Such skills also include understanding the relationships among the parts of the organization itself. Whenever new market opportunities or potential threats arise, managers rely on their conceptual skills to help them analyze the impending outcomes of their decisions. Conceptual skills are extremely important for top-level managers and are often developed with time and experience.

Time Management Skills **Time management skills** refer to the ability to achieve the maximum amount of productivity in a set amount of time. A manager may possess all the skills discussed above, but that may not be enough to manage a successful business. For example, say that the manager of a small deli built his business from humble beginnings; he had a vision and expanded from there. His knowledge of business logistics is superb, and every day he makes important decisions. He spends hours each day talking with his employees and has gained their respect. Taking all of this into consideration, you would think that his deli would be successful. But this is not the case.

time management skills The ability to achieve the maximum amount of productivity in a set amount of time.

Although this manager has vision, knowledge, and interpersonal skills, he does not make efficient use of his time. For example, instead of socializing with his employees on Friday, he could manage a workshop to help them sharpen their customer service skills. Time management requires that managers have the ability to recognize specific ways in which they can make every task or situation productive. The following steps are crucial to effective time management for almost any manager:

1. *Determine the level of urgency of paperwork.* Some paperwork, such as billing, may be more important than others, such as a quarterly report due in three months. Managers must separate paperwork according to due dates and clearly label each pile. Keeping a schedule—either electronically or on a calendar—and crossing off each task when completed are important time management skills.
2. *Create folders for email.* Managers receive plenty of email, which can be a tremendous time drain. To manage email effectively, managers should filter spam to a specific folder and create other folders based on subject, such as "advertising samples," "employee requests," and so on. Effective managers leave the messages requiring an immediate reply in their inbox and address urgent messages right away. Otherwise, managers designate a time each day that they will address all other messages.
3. *Designate a time for telephone calls.* Of course, as is the case with email, there may be urgent calls that a manager must take immediately. However, effective managers have an office assistant take messages and allocate a specific time to return calls.
4. *Identify clear agendas for meetings.* Time can be easily wasted if a meeting agenda is not clear and goals are not set. Effective managers distribute an agenda to all attendees before a meeting that specifies the goals the meeting must achieve. An agenda helps everyone stay on task and end the meeting on time.

By following steps such as these, managers find that their productivity levels increase and more time is freed up for completing other tasks required of the job.

BizChat

Social Media: How Do Web-Based Tools Make Time Management Easier?

Calendars have traditionally been a tool used by individuals to manage their personal schedules. But with modern social media tools, Web-based calendars can provide an easy exchange of information and synchronization of schedules. Various Web-based planning tools are available that allow multiple viewers to add new content to the calendar, thus making the scheduling of meetings more effective. For example, Meeting Wizard is a product that sends out email invitations with a poll of suggested meeting times. It then creates a report for you with the group responses and will send a confirmation email of the final time chosen to all participants. NeedToMeet is another application that allows you to have the entire group enter their available times on a Web-based calendar. Doodle (also available for iPhone or Android) is scheduling software that lets you check the yes/no votes for suggested meeting times, even on your phone.

Discussion Questions

1. **Such tools have proven useful to many managers, but some people argue that Web-based tools can make simple tasks more complicated and can actually make us less productive. What do you think?**
2. **Some employees complain that this kind of technology blurs the line between work and home life. In what ways do you think this technology could interfere with work–life balance?**
3. **How effective are the tools you use to manage your time?**

What tasks do managers perform? Management is the process of organizing people and resources efficiently to direct activities toward common goals and objectives. It includes making major decisions such as setting long-term goals for the organization, determining which products or services the organization will produce, deciding how employees will be organized, and developing strategies for effective, efficient, and successful business operations. All managers engage in a common set of functions to meet the organization's goals. These include planning, organizing, leading (directing), and controlling.

FUNCTIONS OF MANAGEMENT

LO2 Explain how corporate vision and a mission statement help to keep the company focused on achieving its goals and objectives.

Planning

Why do managers need to plan? As illustrated in **Figure 5.2**, management involves four primary functions: planning, organizing, leading, and controlling. These functions integrate all of the company's resources, including human, financial, and technological.

In today's busy world, it's easy to get distracted. Goals and plans help to keep you on task. **Planning** is the process of establishing goals and objectives and determining the best ways to accomplish them. **Goals** are broad, long-term accomplishments an organization wants to achieve within a certain period—in most companies, this is about five years. **Objectives** are the short-term targets designed to help achieve these goals.

planning The process of establishing goals and objectives and determining the best ways to accomplish them.

goals Broad, long-term accomplishments an organization wants to achieve within a certain period.

objectives The short-term targets designed to help achieve goals.

strategic plan The main course of action created by top-level managers that sets the approach for achieving the long-term goals and objectives of the organization.

Video: Acer vs. HP: Can Acer Surpass HP?

Strategic Planning

What is the highest level of planning in an organization? A **strategic plan** is the main course of action created by top-level managers that sets the approach for achieving the long-term goals and objectives of an organization. Simply put, a strategic plan points an organization to where it wants to be in the future and identifies how it will get there. A strategic plan helps to answer three questions:

1. Where is the company going?
2. What should the company focus on?
3. How will the company achieve its goals?

To be effective, a strategic plan should be realistic and obtainable and should look at the big picture. Although individual goals sometimes contribute to the plan, the overall strategic plan is focused on an entire organization or an entire department.

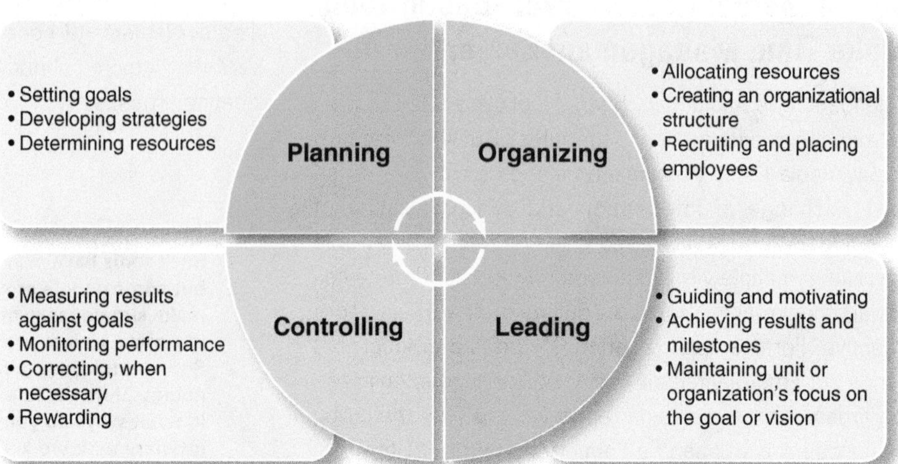

Figure 5.2 The Four Functions of Management

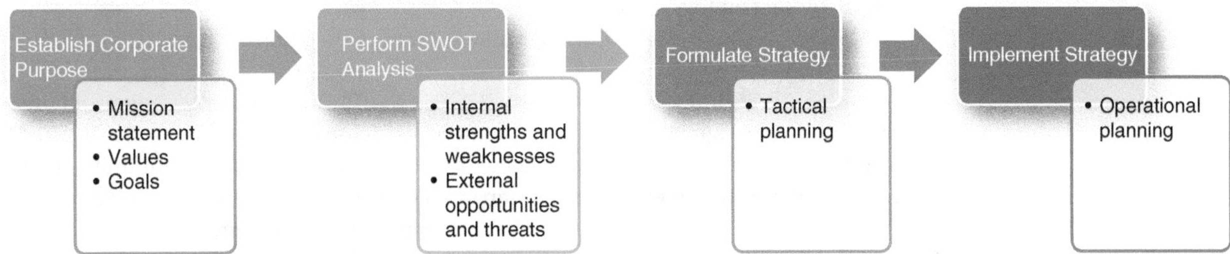

Figure 5.3 Strategic Planning Process

How is a strategic plan developed? A good strategic plan reflects what is happening inside and outside an organization and shows how those conditions and changes will affect the organization in the future. Those making strategic plans must pay attention to the capabilities and resources of an organization, as well as changes in the environment. There are several steps to the process of developing a strategic plan, as shown in **Figure 5.3**.

Vision and Mission Statement

What helps define the direction of a business? The first step in creating a strategic plan is to establish a corporate purpose through a clearly defined *vision*. A **vision** identifies what the business wants to be in the future—what you would like to see as the end result of all your work. The vision should be made clear to all employees and stakeholders. The vision statement for General Electric (GE) under the former CEO Jack Welch read as follows: "To become the most competitive enterprise in the world by being number one or number two in every business in which we compete."[4] A single clear vision worked for GE—during the 20 years Welch was CEO, the company's market value went from US$14 billion to more than US$410 billion.[5]

vision Identifies what the business wants to be in the future.

What helps define the purpose of a business? People often confuse the vision of a company with its mission statement. The vision statement sets the long-term objective of a company and tells where the company is headed. A **mission statement** is a more current description of an organization's purpose, basic goals, and philosophies. A mission statement not only helps management remain focused but also lets employees understand the core values of the company they work for.

mission statement A description of the organization's purpose, basic goals, and philosophies.

Mission statements reflect the personality of a company, so even companies in the same industry can have mission statements that vary greatly in design and content. Some use scientific jargon in a no-nonsense manner directed specifically to a certain target audience. Others may try to reach a larger audience by using a simple, direct statement that inspires the average consumer. You may find that a company uses its mission statement to highlight its environmental awareness or to set an abstract goal for the firm's employees, like working to make the world better able to communicate. Other companies may discuss only their own business goals. The mission statement is a chance for consumers and employees to get a peek into the central values of a company.

What makes an effective mission statement? If employees feel an owner's passion for the business through the mission statement, it has a positive impact. Employees then incorporate the goals and objectives of the mission into their daily work and pass these on to customers and suppliers through their words and actions. A clear message of mission throughout a company tends to strengthen a company's position.

What are some benefits of well-defined vision and mission statements? The vision and mission statements lead to important benefits, such as

- keeping management on track by ensuring strategies are consistent with the organization's goals,

- inspiring employees, and
- giving investors insight into the values of the organization.

Are mission statements only for businesses with a profit? No. Nonprofit organizations also have a mission statement, but because these organizations are not centred on investor return, their mission statements focus their outreach on the community or a specific public service. For example, the Canadian Cancer Society's mission statement states, "The Canadian Cancer Society is a national, community-based organization of volunteers whose mission is the eradication of cancer and the enhancement of the quality of life of people with cancer."[6] This statement reflects the organization's commitment to serving the community.

Both the vision and mission statement are usually posted on an organization's website. However, because the mission statement is directed toward customers—unlike the vision, which is directed toward employees—it is often used alone on advertising materials or on the actual product. A mission statement describes the true essence of what the company does, while a vision is what the company wants to do in the future. A vision challenges a company to grow. The vision and mission statement are critically important as they help keep management on track, inspire employees working for an organization, and indicate to investors or consumers what type of organization they are involved with. They also provide a guide for management as they evaluate alternative plans and strategies to ensure they are consistent with the organization's current and future direction.

How do managers define a company's values? As you have learned, management creates a mission statement and vision to keep them focused on corporate strategy and objectives. The mission statement and vision also help create the "feel" or workplace environment, also known as the corporate culture. The **corporate culture** is a collection of values, norms, and behaviour shared by management and workers that defines the character of the organization. Google, for example, has a unique culture, set by a corporate philosophy that includes statements such as "You can make money without doing evil" and "You can be serious without a suit."[7]

corporate culture A collection of values, norms, and behaviour shared by management and workers that defines the character of the organization.

In a corporation in which the culture is not well defined or, even worse, supports questionable behaviour, problems result. This was the case for the natural-gas giant Enron, which eventually went bankrupt because of significant lack of control and poor ethical behaviour from top management. On the other hand, when the corporate culture is strong, and all employees accept the culture as their own, they are motivated to maintain it and monitor their own behaviour.

After defining a mission and vision statement, companies often define core values or principles. **Core values**—the fundamental beliefs about what is important and appropriate when conducting company activities—affect a company's overall planning processes and operations. For the mission and vision statements to be enacted upon, they must reflect the values of the company. They serve as guidelines for conduct and behaviour as a company works toward its vision. Values may be embedded in a company's code of conduct, code of ethics, code of business conduct, or other such document.

core values The fundamental beliefs about what is important and appropriate when conducting company activities, which affect a company's overall planning processes and operations.

Here are a few examples of core values that help define workplace culture:

- *Coca-Cola:* "Our inclusive culture is defined by our seven core values: leadership, passion, integrity, collaboration, diversity, quality, and accountability."[8]
- *Volvo Cars:* "Cars are driven by people. The guiding principle behind everything we make at Volvo is—and must remain—safety."[9]
- *Cara Foods:* The strength of Cara is built on five core values. "They are the essence of Cara, cherished by all teammates. People, Self-responsibility, Integrity, Passion for Winning, Quality."[10]
- *Canadian Tire:* "Integrity, honesty and respect are core values at Canadian Tire."[11] These values are embedded into the company's code of business conduct, and Canadian Tire expects all employees to abide by the code's principles and expectations when conducting business on behalf of the company.

Video: Life Is Good: Marketing Ethics and Social Responsibility

SWOT Analysis

How does the management team begin to move a company toward achieving its vision? Once a company's vision and mission statements have been articulated, management must assess the company's own strengths and weaknesses as well as its position among its competitors. In addition, management must assess what changes are anticipated to occur both inside and outside the organization and determine whether the company is poised appropriately to respond to such changes.

What is a SWOT analysis? This analysis of strengths, weaknesses, and anticipated changes is called a **SWOT analysis** and helps determine the strategic fit between an organization's internal, distinctive capabilities and external possibilities relative to the business and economic environments. SWOT stands for

SWOT (Strengths, Weaknesses, Opportunities, and Threats) analysis A situational analysis of strengths, weaknesses, and anticipated changes that helps determine the strategic fit between an organization's internal, distinctive capabilities, and external possibilities relative to the business and economic environments.

Strengths,
Weaknesses,
Opportunities, and
Threats.

Figure 5.4 gives a brief explanation of each component of the SWOT analysis.

In evaluating a company's internal *strengths* and *weaknesses,* management must analyze a company's internal resources, including such elements as its financial health; the strengths of its employees; and its marketing, operations, and technological resources. For example, a company's strength might be its strong marketing department, but its weakness could be an unfavourable location.

To evaluate a company's external *threats* and *opportunities,* management should assess various external elements, such as economic, political, and regulatory environments as well as social, demographic, macroeconomic, and technological factors that could affect the company and industry. It also must perform analyses on the state of the industry and market as well as the company's competitors. For example, a recession could threaten an alternative energy company, whereas increasing awareness of global warming may provide greater opportunity for market growth.

What happens after a SWOT analysis is completed? After conducting a SWOT analysis, managers establish a set of goals and objectives. In defining exactly what a

SWOT Analysis

Internal Strengths	**Internal Weaknesses**
Potential internal assets that give a company a competitive advantage **Examples for Walmart:** • Powerful brand • Reputation for value, convenience • Wide range of products in one store	Lack of internal capability or expertise compared to the competition **Examples for Walmart:** • Not as flexible as competitors who sell just one type of product (clothing) • Global but still in only a few countries
External Opportunities	**External Threats**
Foreseeable external changes that could favourably affect a company's competitive capability **Examples for Walmart:** • Expand to new locations and new types of stores • Take over or form alliances with other global retailers in Europe or China	External conditions that could negatively affect a company's competitive capability **Examples for Walmart:** • Intense price competition increasing • Global retail exposes Walmart to political problems in the countries where it operates • Being number one makes Walmart the target of competition

Figure 5.4 SWOT Analysis

Source: Based on Tim Friesner, "SWOT Analysis Wal-Mart," May 8, 2014, accessed July 25, 2011, http://www.marketingteacher.com/walmart-swot/.

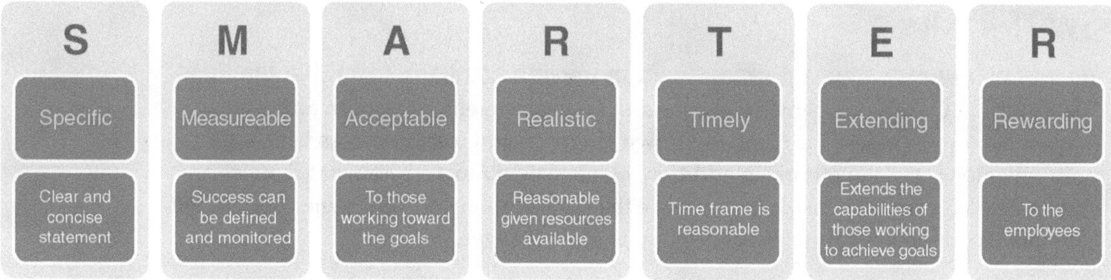

Figure 5.5 SMARTER Design of Goals

Source: Based on Carter McNamara, "Strategic Planning (in Nonprofit or For-Profit Organizations)," *Free Management Library*, accessed March 30, 2011, http://managementhelp.org/planning/index.htm#anchor1384873.

specific goal is, it is best to make sure clear deadlines are specified and measureable outcomes are included. The acronym SMARTER is helpful when designing and wording goals and objectives. Goals should be **S**pecific, **M**easurable, **A**cceptable (to those working to achieve the goals), **R**ealistic, **T**imely, **E**xtending (the capabilities of those working to achieve the goals), and **R**ewarding to the employees as well (see **Figure 5.5**).[12]

Tactical, Operational, and Contingency Planning

LO3 Describe the implications of tactical plans, operational plans, and contingency plans within the context of management.

tactical plans Plans that specifically determine the resources and the actions required to implement particular aspects of the strategic plan.

How does management decide how to execute a strategic plan? The next part of the process of creating a strategic plan is to have middle management generate *tactical plans* to carry out the goals of a company. **Tactical plans** specifically determine the resources and the actions required to implement particular aspects of a strategic plan. Whereas strategic plans have a long-term focus, tactical plans are made with a one- to three-year horizon in mind. Determining a company's annual budget, for example, is one function of a tactical plan. Let's say one goal of the strategic plan of a paper supply company is to sell more products to large offices on the west coast. One part of this company's tactical plan might be to determine how much money should be allocated to advertising in that area.

operational plans Plans that determine the process by which tactical plans can be achieved.

How is a tactical plan translated into instructions for employees? The specifics of carrying out tactical plans are *operational plans*. In an **operational plan**, first-line managers precisely determine the process by which tactical plans can be achieved. Operational plans depend on daily or weekly schedules and focus on specific departments or employees. For example, once the paper supply company determines how much of its budget can be allocated to advertising, specific department managers might have to determine which employees will travel to advertise the product.

contingency planning A set of plans that ensures that the organization will run as smoothly as possible during an unexpected disruption.

What if unforeseen events occur? **Contingency planning** is a set of plans that ensures that an organization will run as smoothly as possible during an unexpected disruption. Sometimes extreme circumstances occur that force a company to move outside of their plans and find alternative means to survive. We have seen all too frequently the effects that natural disasters can have on businesses. The massive earthquake and tsunami that devastated Japan in 2011 led to power shortages, disrupted supply chains, and drastically impacted factory output. The resulting shortage of semiconductors led to worldwide disruption of manufacturing facilities that relied on Japanese parts.[13]

We have also seen companies quickly fall into disfavour because of unexpected failures in product quality, such as the lead paint found on Mattel toys that resulted in millions of toys being recalled. All the best corporate strategies can be negated quickly if an unexpected crisis occurs and a plan is not in place to deal with it adequately. What happens if a company suddenly has more sales than production can handle, or if the best-selling product is recalled because of a defect? Who would run the company if the CEO or the company owner unexpectedly died? How should a company fight off an unpredictable takeover threat from a competitor or a rapidly spreading computer virus that threatens to shut down all internal and external lines of communication?

Strategic Plan — **Top Management**
- Sets the approach for achieving an organization's long-term goals and objectives
- Acts as a framework for decisions
- Assists in setting corporate benchmarks

Tactical Plan — **Middle Management**
- Determines resources and actions necessary to implement the strategic plan
- Made with a one- to three-year horizon in mind

Contingency Plan — **Middle Management**
- Keeps an organization running in the event of a disruption
- Details internal and external communication procedures for such an event
- Determines which departments are most vital to an organization during a crisis

Operational Plan — **First-Line Management**
- Involves planning the execution of the tactical plan
- Depends on daily or weekly schedules
- Focuses on specific department or employees

Figure 5.6 The Four Types of Management Plans

How can planning help companies weather unexpected events? Contingency planning encompasses how management will communicate, both internally and externally. Internally, management must inform its employees how they should continue to do their jobs. Externally, an organization must have a plan in place to deal with requests for information either from employees, the families of employees, or even the media. Contingency planning involves determining what departments within a company are vital to the immediate needs of the organization when an unexpected crisis occurs. The particulars of each plan differ depending on the size and function of a company and the magnitude of the crisis the plan is needed for.

Simulation: Plan for Success

Figure 5.6 summarizes the types of plans that companies use to carry out their goals.

Organizing

LO4 Explain the significance of organizing and how most organizations are organized.

How are plans put into action? Once goals have been finalized and plans have been made, the next step in the management process is to put those plans into action. **Organizing** is the process of structuring the capital, personnel, raw materials, and other resources to carry out the plans in a way that best matches the nature of the work. Part of organizing is to establish an organizational structure. Organizational structure depends on a variety of factors, such as the number of employees in the organization, the speed at which decisions need to be made, the subjectivity of the business to rapid change, and the collaborative nature of the work. Planning and organizing are two of a manager's most important responsibilities. How a manager goes about accomplishing these tasks has a tremendous impact on every aspect of the company. Every company, regardless of its size or specialty, needs a solid organizational structure. Without one, employees may have trouble making decisions and assigning responsibility.

organizing The process of structuring the capital, personnel, raw materials, and other resources to carry out the organization's plans in a way that best matches the nature of the work.

Video: azTeen Magazine

Are most companies organized in the same way? Not all corporations are organized in the same way. The traditional way of organizing management falls into a vertical, hierarchical structure. **Figure 5.7** shows a traditional vertically structured managerial pyramid.

At the peak of the pyramid, **top-level managers** are the corporate officers responsible for the organization as a whole. Most established corporations determine the corporate officers, especially the chief executive officer (CEO) or president. Depending on the size and organizational complexity of the company, top management can also include the chief financial officer (CFO), chief operations officer (COO), and chief information officer (CIO). Top managers generate the strategic plans, long-term goals, mission statement, and vision for the organization. They establish the culture of the organization and inspire employees to adopt senior management's vision. In smaller corporations, especially small startup companies, top managers may also be responsible for planning and

top-level managers The corporate officers responsible for the organization as a whole.

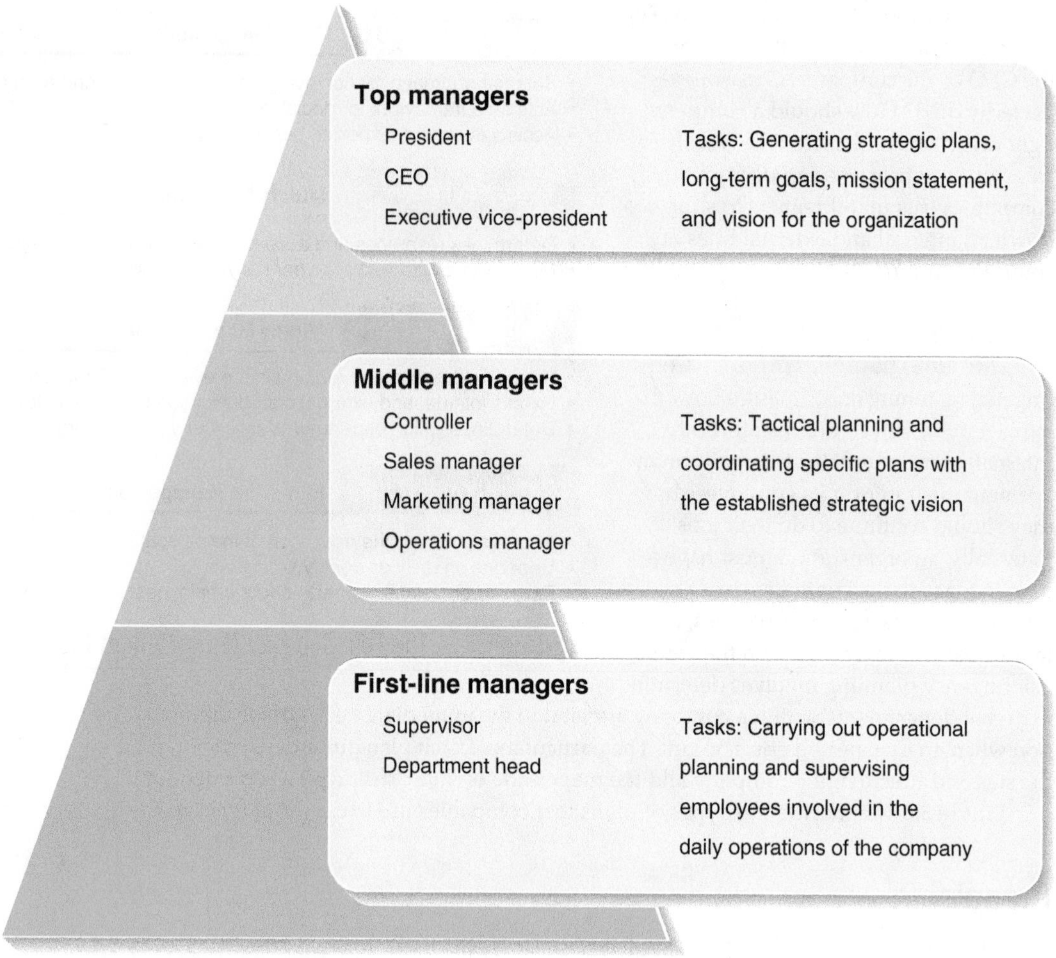

Figure 5.7 The Managerial Pyramid

carrying out the day-to-day tasks of the company. But as the business grows, such companies will need to add more employees and divide the work into smaller tasks and areas of specialty.

middle-level managers Top managers for only one division or a part of an organization.

Middle-level managers can be thought of as top managers for only one division or a part of an organization. As such, middle-level managers are responsible for tactical planning and for creating more specific plans that coordinate with the strategic vision set by the top managers. Included in this management layer are positions such as division managers (finance, marketing, sales, operations, and IT) or team leaders who are not arranged by function but are responsible for a group of employees who must carry out specific tasks for the organization.

first-line managers The managers who carry out operational planning.

The bottom of the managerial pyramid includes **first-line managers**, who carry out operational planning. These managers fill a supervisory role over those employees who carry out the day-to-day operations of the company.

Not all companies have all three layers of management—some have more and some have less. Typically, you'll find the "extra" layers are middle managers. However, the organizational pattern of a vertically structured business generally can be represented by the managerial pyramid.

organizational chart A chart that shows how groups of employees fit into the larger organizational structure.

Smaller companies that have relatively few employees tend to be organized differently than large corporations. Small companies tend to have much simpler structures compared with large companies. Regardless, to accomplish many tasks at the same time, organizations must have some division of labour and allocate work into smaller tasks. An **organizational chart**, such as the one in **Figure 5.8**, shows how groups of employees fit into the larger organizational structure.

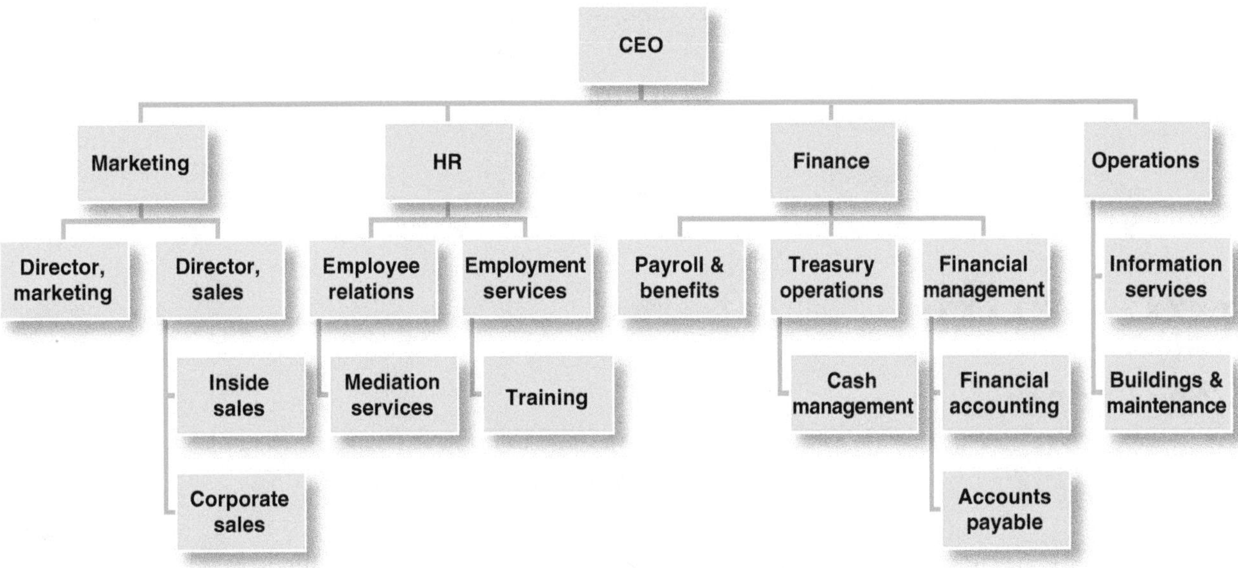

Figure 5.8 Organizational Chart

An organizational chart is used to display the division of labour and organizational structure within a company.

LO5 Distinguish among vertical organizations, horizontal organizations, and network organizations.

What is a vertical organization? In a **vertical organization** (or tall organization), the company is organized by specific function, such as marketing, finance, purchasing, information technology, and human resources. In such organizational structures, levels of expertise within functions are developed and managers can better keep track of economic and environmental conditions that affect their functional area. Potential problems may arise, however, because integration between functions and divisions is not always easy. Vertical organization usually calls for long lines of communication and "reporting up." This makes it difficult for a company to respond quickly to changes in a market or to provide innovation because keeping each division updated means spending time doing so.

vertical organization A company that is organized by specific function, such as marketing, finance, purchasing, information technology, and human resources. Also called a tall organization.

What are the differences between a vertical and horizontal organizational structure? Vertical organization has been the primary structure of business since the Industrial Revolution. Although such traditional pyramidal management has its benefits, in the early 1990s vertical organizational structures were criticized as being overspecialized, fragmented, and inflexible. Some businesses, such as Ford Motor Company, Xerox, Motorola, and Barclays Bank, found that they were more successful when they organized in a horizontal structure and formed management groups around areas of specific production or product units.[14] In a **horizontal organization** (or flat organization), the traditional managerial pyramid is flattened and the management layers are collapsed. A horizontally structured organization still has some of the pyramidal aspects, including a CEO and perhaps another layer of middle management, but then the organization concentrates the majority of the remaining employees into working teams or groups. **Figure 5.9** illustrates the basic differences in organizational charts of a vertically structured organization and a horizontally structured organization.

The benefit of a horizontal organization is that each team has more responsibility for the outcome of its work. There are fewer layers of management, so fewer reporting issues arise, and if needed the boss's approval can be sought and received much faster. The company can be more responsive since individuals in a horizontal organization are more empowered to make decisions. Horizontal structures have been deemed the "model for the knowledge age." They are suitable for industries that require rapid responses to quick changes.

horizontal organization An organization where the traditional managerial pyramid is flattened and the management layers are collapsed. Also called a flat organization.

Video: CH2MHill: Organizational Structure

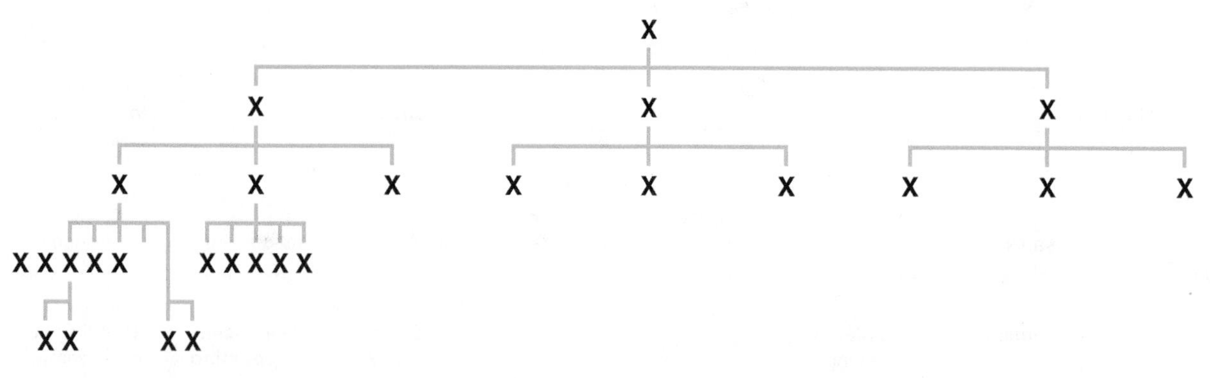

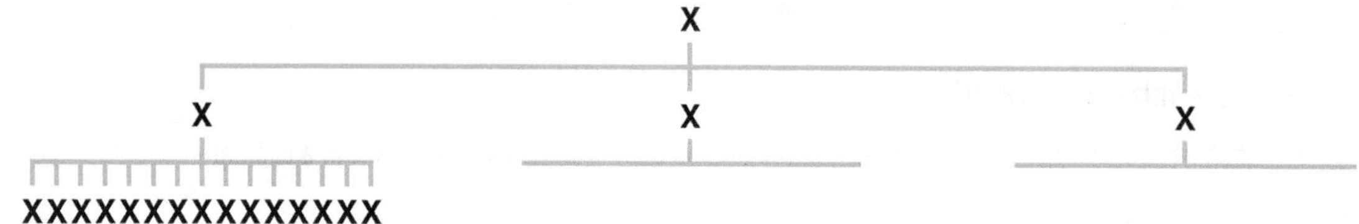

Figure 5.9 Vertically and Horizontally Structured Organizations

Occasionally, when companies have grown so large that the variety of product lines, geographic regions, or manufacturing processes can be difficult to manage, they restructure from a vertical organization to a horizontal one. In these circumstances, managers often try to streamline functions to make management easier. For example, they might structure the organization into divisions of employees who work on just one product line. Or they might divide the company into teams in which each team specializes in just one geographic region or works through just one manufacturing process. In essence, these divisions work like separate mini-companies. Each division has its own set of functional expertise, so separate managers are in charge of finance, marketing, human resources, information technology, and so on. The groups work autonomously and are highly differentiated—so much so that they create barriers to coordination across functions. In today's business environment, there are fewer and fewer organizations structured vertically by function.

Video: Rudi's Bakery: Organizational Structure

What other types of organizational structures are there? Although the majority of companies are structured with the more traditional vertical structure or the group-oriented horizontal structure, a new business structure is emerging. Instead of the customary means of producing a product or service in which one company is responsible for all functions, **network organizations** are collections of independent, mostly single-function firms that collaborate on a product or service. For example, Boeing recently completed production of its latest airplane, the Boeing 787. In the past, airplanes were assembled in one hangar. This time, however, Boeing relied on the expertise of hundreds of manufacturers worldwide to independently manufacture the components of the plane and ship the individual pieces for assembly in its main plant. The wings and landing gear are assembled in Italy, and the nose and cockpit are assembled in Wichita, Kansas. Individual or combined elements are then shipped to Everett, Washington, where they are finally assembled into a single 787 plane.

network organizations Collections of independent, mostly single-function firms that collaborate on a product or service.

In addition to Boeing, other companies are using a network arrangement, including Nike, which only owns one manufacturing plant, and Reebok, which only designs and markets but does not produce any of its products. A network structure is not suitable for every company, but it may be successful for companies that need

- to be as flexible and innovative as possible
- to respond quickly to threats and opportunities
- to save time
- to reduce costs and risk

Leading

LO6 Describe what makes a good leader and the various styles of leadership.

Why does an organization need leaders? An organization is often successful when employees have a leader to demonstrate what it takes for a company to achieve its goals. **Leading** is the process of influencing, motivating, and enabling others to contribute to the success and effectiveness of the organization by achieving its goals. Therefore, the quality of leadership exhibited by managers is a critical determinant of organizational success.

leading The process of influencing, motivating, and enabling others to contribute to the success and effectiveness of the organization by achieving its goals.

Are all managers leaders? Famed management researcher and author Peter Drucker once noted that "management is doing things right; leadership is doing the right things."[15] Both leaders and managers strive to motivate people, but they have different scopes. Typically, managers spend their time making sure that specific tasks are done well and completed on time. The leadership of a company, on the other hand, is focused on setting the long-term vision and strategies a company will need to survive and flourish. Truly great leaders are able to be both managers and leaders: They define a vision, foster agreement across the company, and then implement the strategy. As illustrated in **Figure 5.10**, the best leaders are defined as those who do the following:

1. *Challenge the process* by not always accepting conventional beliefs and practices as the only way to accomplish tasks.
2. *Model the way* by serving as a living example of the ideals in which they are asking their employees to share.
3. *Inspire a shared vision* and appeal to people's values and motivate them to care about the corporate goals or an important mission.
4. *Encourage the heart* by showing appreciation, providing rewards, and so on to motivate people in positive ways.
5. *Enable others to act* by giving people access to information and empowering them to perform to their fullest potential.[16]

What are the traits of a good leader? In addition to these five means of effective leadership, most leadership analysts agree that good leaders share several traits:

- *Determination.* Leaders need to achieve and are constantly striving for improvement. They have a high energy level and are ambitious and persistent in the face of obstacles. Leaders don't give up easily. True leadership drive, however, does not come at the expense of others; therefore, leaders delegate authority and responsibility to others to promote their success also. They are the catalysts for positive action.

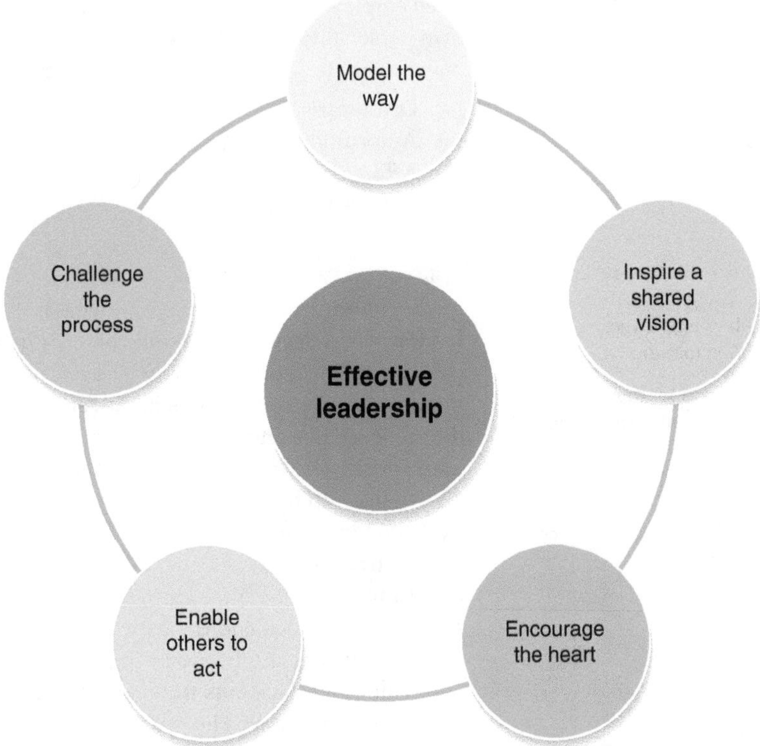

Figure 5.10 Traits of Effective Leadership

SELF CHECK When it comes to the concepts of leadership and control within the business context, myths abound. Can you separate the facts from the fiction? Test your knowledge with the quiz below.

1. Fact or Fiction: All managers are good leaders.
2. Fact or Fiction: There is a difference between a successful manager and an effective manager.
3. Fact or Fiction: Good leaders don't challenge conventional beliefs because that would undermine their authority.
4. Fact or Fiction: Autocratic leadership—making decisions without consulting others—is never a good idea.
5. Fact or Fiction: Lack of controlling can cause companies to implode.
6. Fact or Fiction: Bureaucratic reporting tools have no real purpose.
7. Fact or Fiction: Corporate culture has a big impact on control.

Answers: 1. Fiction; 2. Fact; 3. Fiction; 4. Fiction; 5. Fact; 6. Fiction; 7. Fact

How did you do? Do you have your facts straight? Read on to learn the truth about leadership and control.

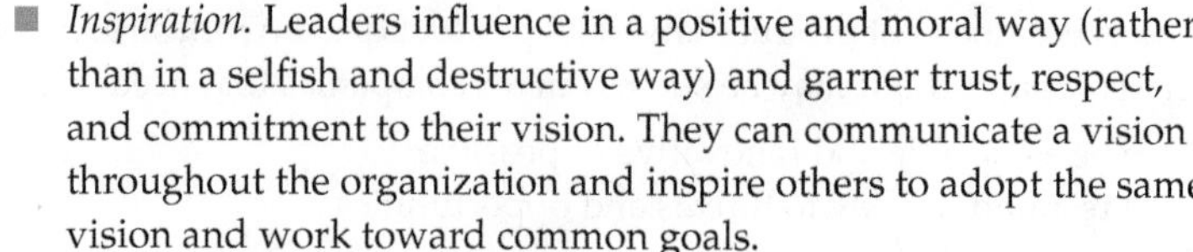

- *Inspiration.* Leaders influence in a positive and moral way (rather than in a selfish and destructive way) and garner trust, respect, and commitment to their vision. They can communicate a vision throughout the organization and inspire others to adopt the same vision and work toward common goals.
- *Flexibility and empathy.* Leaders are good listeners, can perceive the need for a change in tactics, and if necessary can adjust their leadership style to fit the current environment, people, and situation. Leaders must take into account the overall well-being of others and be mindful of their values and feelings.
- *Innovativeness.* Leaders set goals and have a vision of the future that may be different from the norm. Leaders are not afraid to alter their methods, plans, or even thinking if the situation calls for change. In addition, leaders exemplify resourcefulness as they continually brainstorm for solutions to problems and more effective ways of reaching goals.
- *Honesty.* Leaders are honest and credible. Employees can trust that the leader will deal with them in a fair and equitable manner.
- *Self-confidence.* Leaders have the confidence to overcome inevitable obstacles and to make tough decisions despite uncertainty. A leader's confidence promotes calm in stressful situations.
- *Knowledge and competence.* Leaders have a good handle on their business and industry. They are willing to admit mistakes and constantly seek more information to make informed and reasoned decisions. Good leaders base their decisions on facts. They are well organized and detail oriented.

These traits are essential to effective leadership and are common to most good leaders.

Video: Red Frog Events: Leadership and Managing People

What styles of leadership exist? Many different leadership styles exist, and leaders often employ different styles in a given situation depending on a complex mix of their own personality, the corporate culture, the type of company, and the employees they manage. **Table 5.1** lists four of the most common leadership styles:

- Democratic
- Autocratic
- Affiliative (laissez-faire)
- Visionary

democratic leader A leader who delegates authority and involves employees in decision making.

autocratic leader A leader who makes decisions without consulting others.

What are democratic and autocratic leaders like? A **democratic leader** delegates authority and involves employees in the decision-making process. An **autocratic leader** makes decisions without consulting others.

Consider Henry Chang, who runs the kitchen of a large restaurant. Henry allows his staff to offer opinions as he develops the menu. He also lets them experiment with different recipes and food presentations and features their work on the main menu when possible. The kitchen staff members love working with Henry because he allows them to be creative and innovative. He also encourages them to cultivate the skills they need to run their own restaurant some day. However, Henry's restaurant often attracts important political dignitaries and famous entertainers. Sometimes the restaurant becomes unexpectedly busy. In these circumstances, Henry doesn't leave anything to chance and dictates exactly what needs to be done and who should do it. Henry knows he might hurt someone's feelings, but ultimately his staff trust him to make the right decisions to obtain the best results for the restaurant.

For the most part, Henry is a democratic leader because he knows that by involving his employees they become more invested in the process. The tradeoff, Henry recognizes, is that his democratic style of leadership requires more time and advanced planning.

Table 5.1 Styles of Leadership

	Democratic	Autocratic	Affiliative (Laissez-Faire)	Visionary
	VOTE tribalium81/Fotolia	kikkerdirk/Fotolia	NLshop/Fotolia	freshidea/Fotolia
Leader characteristics	• Listens well • Is a team worker • Collaborates • Influences	• Commands—"Do it because I say so" • Threatens • Has tight control • Monitors studiously • Creates dissonance • Contaminates everyone's mood • Drives away talent	• Promotes harmony • Empathizes with others • Boosts morale • Solves conflicts	• Inspires • Believes in own vision • Is empathetic • Explains how and why people's efforts contribute to the "dream"
Benefits to style	Values people's input and gets commitment through participation	Soothes fear by giving clear direction in an emergency	Creates harmony by connecting people to one another	Moves people toward shared dreams
When style is appropriate	To build buy-in or consensus or get valuable input from employees	In a crisis, to kick start an urgent turnaround; with problem employees; traditional military	To heal rifts in a team; motivate during stressful times; strengthen connections	When changes require a new vision or when a clear direction is needed; radical change

When such time is not available, Henry must take complete charge. In those instances, he becomes an autocratic leader. A good leader knows that such commanding leadership can be an effective style in certain circumstances when quick decisions need to be made or when it seems as if the group cannot come to a consensus.

affiliative (or laissez-faire) leader A leader who encourages employees to contribute ideas rather than specifically directive their tasks.

visionary leader A leader who is able to inspire others, believes in their own vision, and moves people toward a shared dream.

What are affiliative leaders?

Some leaders take a more hands-off approach to management and act more as consultants than participants. **Affiliative (or laissez-faire) leaders** are more advisory in style, encouraging employees to contribute ideas rather than specifically directing their tasks. This style of leadership is often best used with groups and teams. Affiliative leadership implemented properly can give employees a sense of challenge, commitment, and renewed energy as they are left to handle tasks on their own. As businesses continue to reduce the layers of management, affiliative and democratic styles are becoming the leadership styles of choice. However, it is possible for affiliative leaders to become too uninvolved in the group's processes. If the group or team members feel that management is virtually absent, team members may choose actions and strategies that are easy and not in line with the goals of a company.

Jeremy Sutton H/Alamy

Gordon Ramsey is an accomplished chef, famous for an autocratic style of leadership in his restaurant kitchens.

What makes a leader a visionary?

Visionary leaders are able to inspire others, believe in their own vision, and move people toward a shared dream. John Lasseter was an animator in Disney's computer animation

Video: Herman Miller: Managers as Leaders

department when George Lucas's company Lucasfilm opened a computer animation division. Lasseter was drawn to the vision of what might be possible with the advances in technology he saw in use at Lucasfilm, so he left Disney in 1984 to spend a month at Industrial Light and Magic (ILM), a division of Lucasfilm. He has been there ever since. In 1986 that division was purchased by Steve Jobs and became its own company, Pixar. Lasseter is currently Pixar's chief creative officer. He has assembled a uniquely creative collection of employees and led them to producing a series of new classics in animated film—including *Toy Story*, *A Bug's Life*, and *Cars*.

As a visionary leader, Lasseter had to create the special environment that would allow creative people the freedom to be inventive but also the structure to meet the deadlines required on a multimillion-dollar film schedule. One example of his leadership is in the production of *Toy Story*. At that time, Pixar had never produced anything longer than a short, five-minute film; it was not clear whether the company could actually produce a full-length film. *Toy Story* was being produced and distributed by Disney (in a partnership with Pixar), and Disney executives called a meeting to see a segment. Disney wanted to make sure the film had the quality it wanted from its new partner. Lasseter remembers the meeting: "I was pretty much embarrassed by what was on the screen. I had made it. I directed everybody to do this . . . but it was a story filled with the most unhappy, mean people." Disney wanted to shut down production and fire staff. But Lasseter negotiated a two-week reprieve and returned to lead his team of cowriters and animators. "Let's make the movie we wanted to make," he told them, and the story took on a gentler, sweeter tone. The team had to work nonstop for the two-week reprieve, with the threat of massive layoffs over their heads. The ending of the story is well known: *Toy Story* went on to achieve $190 million in domestic box office receipts, and Lasseter earned an Honorary Oscar for the achievement. Lasseter has since used visionary leadership to guide the studio to successes with many movies.[17]

contingency leadership A more adaptive style of leadership in which managers recognize that they need to be flexible and use whatever style works best for the particular situation.

As in the case with Henry and his restaurant, no one style of leadership will work in every situation. In reality, managers recognize that they need to be flexible and use whatever style works best for the particular situation. You can think of this adaptive style of leadership as **contingency leadership**. Contingency leadership places a range of leadership styles on a continuum, such as the one in **Figure 5.11**. Those who opt for contingency leadership recognize that forces in today's business environment change, and management may need to respond to different situations in different ways.

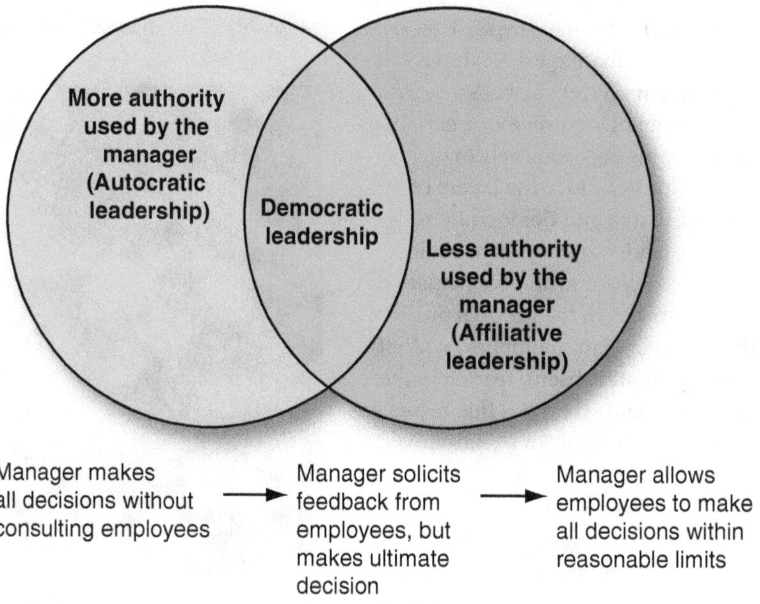

Figure 5.11 Continuum of Leadership Behaviour

Controlling

LO7 Explain the importance of control within a business.

The best-laid plans are meaningless if they aren't put into place effectively. As managers form plans and carry out strategies to meet the goals of an organization, they must also determine whether their plans and strategies are generating the desired results.

Why does a company need to adapt to stay on course? **Controlling** (also called monitoring) is the process by which managers measure performance and make sure the company's plans and strategies are being or have been properly carried out. Through the control process, managers ensure that the direction a company is moving toward aligns with its short- and long-term plans. The controlling process can also detect errors in systems, so if a plan is not meeting its goals it can be modified.

controlling Ensures that the plans and strategies set in place by management are properly carried out.

Video: Controlling

How do managers measure performance? Most companies have control systems that help measure the plans they set in place to carry out the goals of the organization. In general, the control system forms a cycle, as shown in **Figure 5.12**: Performance standards are set and actual performance is measured and compared against the standard. To measure performance, reporting tools such as financial statements and sales reports are used. These reports help determine whether the products are competitive, are using capital wisely, and are being produced efficiently.

In addition to meeting financial, production, and sales measures, another measure of performance is quality so that the products or services the company provides meet or exceed customer requirements. Many managers use **total quality management**, an integrated approach focusing on quality from the beginning of the production process up through managerial involvement to detect and correct problems. Another quality initiative that is receiving much attention is **Six Sigma**, a statistically based, proactive, long-term process designed to look at the overall business process to prevent problems. To achieve the Six Sigma standard, a business must not allow more than 3.4 defects per million opportunities. Based on the results, adjustments are made and the cycle begins again.

total quality management An integrated approach focusing on quality from the beginning of the production process up through managerial involvement to detect and correct problems.

Six Sigma A method that seeks to eliminate defects by removing variation in outcomes and measuring and analyzing manufacturing processes to see if standards are being met.

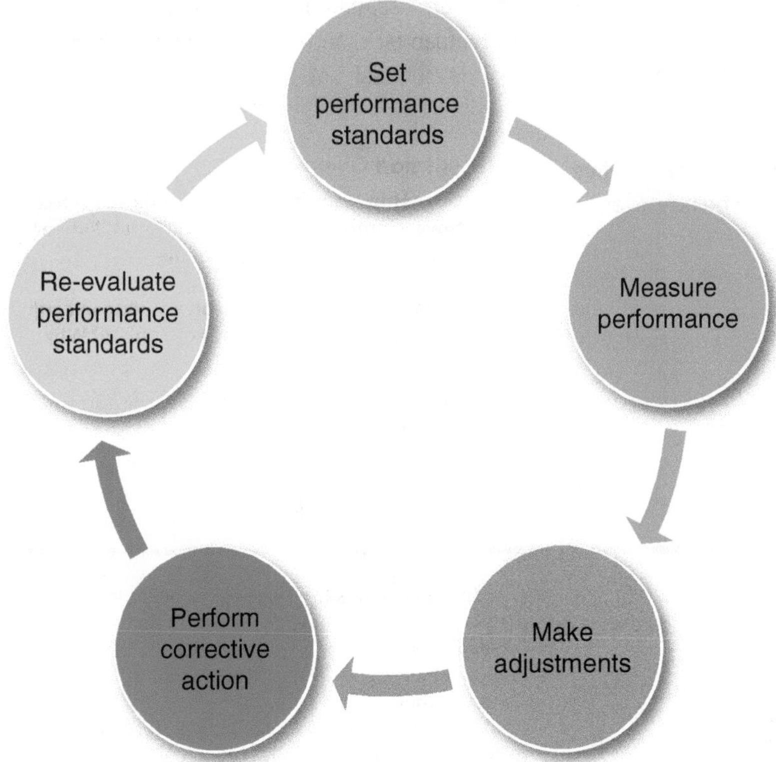

Figure 5.12 The Monitoring/Control Cycle

Video: Pizza Hut: Functions and Skills of Management

On Target

Loblaw's Restructuring[18]

Craig Hutchison is the easygoing senior vice-president of marketing at Loblaw Companies Limited. As such, he's responsible for all marketing activities at Canada's largest food distributor and leading provider of general merchandise products, drugstore, and financial products and services. Loblaw's more than 139 000 full-time and part-time employees execute its strategy, which is developed under three core themes: simplify, innovate, and grow. The company has more than 1000 corporate and franchised stores across Canada and is one of Canada's largest private sector employers. Loblaw strives to be consumer focused, community focused, cost effective, proactive in corporate citizenship, and agile, with the goal of achieving long-term growth for its many stakeholders.[19]

In 2007, however, experiencing infrastructure challenges and increased competition, Loblaw Companies reported its first annual loss in more than 20 years. Coupled with management changes in 2008, the company suffered in the media and the eyes of shareholders. Loblaw countered Walmart's entry into the fresh food business by building larger stores that carried more general merchandise, but the strategy did not help Loblaw compete against the low-price giant, particularly in Ontario, and Loblaw stopped building Superstores in Ontario until they could get the format right.[20]

In 2008, Hutchison stepped in to provide a central marketing voice and restructured the company into five teams: the Joe Fresh and PC Home team, brands, events, the retail team, and a dedicated flyer team. "During the 18 months I was trying to get these people in place I probably had 50 of the 80 people reporting directly to me at one point or another," he says. "So it gave me an opportunity to get to know the team intimately, to know what their strengths were, where they want to grow. A little challenging having 21 direct reports, but it was really a great experience." Hutchison considers the reorganization his greatest accomplishment during that time.

Hutchison's management style is very hands on, and part of the restructuring included a delayering of the organization. "[From] the first person in marketing up to me there are only three layers, so it's a very flat organization and one where ideas are shared very seamlessly."

To ensure that seamlessness, Hutchison visits stores every Wednesday, engaging with consumers and employees and tackling issues. On the executive level, he reviews weekly sales numbers with senior management every Monday to generate timely responses to consumer behaviour fluctuations. "I've always been a very quick marketer, but to be able to see that attention to detail, especially during this economic situation, allowed us to develop much faster insights and put our Spidey radar up early."

David Rosenberg, whose Toronto-based advertising agency, Bensimon Byrne, has worked with Loblaw since 2002, says Hutchison has brought a sharper focus to the brand. "Loblaw is a complex, multifaceted organization that often has to turn on a dime," he says. "To get the whole organization aligned behind a direction is a pretty gargantuan task, and he seems to be able to manage that very difficult task unbelievably well."

Discussion Questions

1. **Does Hutchison's leadership style seem to lean toward autocratic, democratic, or affiliative?**
2. **What are the advantages of flattening the organization?**
3. **Does it seem that Hutchison is acting in conjunction with the three core themes of Loblaw? Why or why not?**

CHAPTER SYNOPSIS

LO1 Describe the ways managers apply technical, interpersonal, decision-making, conceptual, and time management skills to business. *(pp. 95–98)*

Technical skills include the abilities and knowledge that enable an employee to carry out the specific tasks required of a discipline or department. Managers must be comfortable with technology and possess good analytical skills to interpret a variety of data. Managers must also know how to perform, or at least have a good understanding of, the skills required of the employees they supervise.

Interpersonal skills enable a manager to interact with other people to motivate them. It's important that a manager develop trust and loyalty with the people he or she interacts with often and that the manager can motivate and encourage employees to work together.

It is critical that a manager has good problem-solving and **decision-making skills**—the ability to identify and analyze a problem, examine the alternatives, choose and implement the best plan of action, and evaluate the results.

A manager may have the three skills just described, but without **time management skills**, the ability to achieve the maximum amount of productivity in a set amount of time, he or she will not be successful.

LO2 Explain how corporate vision and a mission statement help to keep the company focused on achieving its goals and objectives. *(pp. 98–102)*

As managers carry out the strategic plan, it's important that they ensure their decisions continue to match the overall objectives of the organization. The first step in creating a strategic plan is to establish a corporate purpose through a *vision* and a *mission statement*. A **vision** identifies what the business wants to be in the future. The **mission statement** is a description of the organization's purpose, basic goals, and philosophies. A mission statement not only helps management remain focused, but also lets employees understand the **core values** of the company they work for.

The vision and mission statement are critically important because they help keep management on track, help inspire employees working for an organization, and indicate to investors or consumers what type of organization they are investing in. They also provide a guide for management as they evaluate alternative plans and strategies to ensure they are consistent with the organization's current and future direction.

Managers perform **SWOT analysis** to help determine the strategic fit between an organization's internal, distinctive capabilities, and external possibilities relative to the business and economic environments.

LO3 Describe the implications of tactical plans, operational plans, and contingency plans within the context of management. *(pp. 102–103)*

Once the strategic planning process is complete and long-term goals and objectives have been determined, middle management generates *tactical plans* to carry out the goals determined by the strategic plan. **Tactical plans** specifically determine the resources and the actions required to implement particular aspects of the strategic plan. Whereas strategic plans have a long-term focus, tactical plans are made with a one- to three-year horizon in mind.

The specifics of carrying out tactical plans are *operational plans*. In **operational plans**, first-line managers precisely determine the process by which tactical plans can be achieved. Operational plans depend on daily or weekly schedules and focus on specific departments or employees.

Contingency planning ensures that the organization will run as smoothly as possible during an unexpected disruption. Such planning encompasses how management will communicate, both internally and externally. Internally, management must inform its employees how they should continue to do their jobs. Externally, an organization must have a plan in place to deal with requests for information from either employees, the families of employees, or even the media. Contingency planning involves determining what departments within the company are vital to the immediate needs of the organization when an unexpected crisis occurs.

LO4 Explain the significance of organizing and how most organizations are organized. *(pp. 103–105)*

Once goals have been finalized and plans have been made, the next step in the management process is to put those plans into action. **Organizing** is the process of structuring the capital, personnel, raw materials, and other resources to carry out the plans in a way that best matches the nature of the work. Part of organizing is to establish an organizational structure. Organizational structure depends on a variety of factors, such as the number of employees in the organization, the speed at which decisions need to be made, the subjectivity of the business to rapid change, and the collaborative nature of the work.

Not all corporations are organized in the same way. The traditional way of organizing management falls into a vertical, hierarchical structure, much like the pyramid shown below.

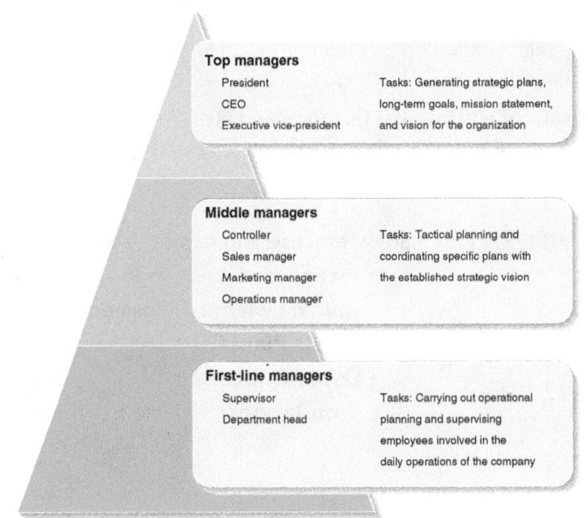

The Managerial Pyramid

LO5 Distinguish among vertical organizations, horizontal organizations, and network organizations. *(pp. 105–107)*

In a **vertical organization** (or tall organization), the company is organized by specific function, such as marketing, finance, purchasing, information technology, and human resources.

In a **horizontal organization** (or flat organization), the traditional managerial pyramid is flattened and the management layers are collapsed.

Instead of the customary means of producing a product or service in which one company is responsible for all functions, **network organizations** are collections of independent, mostly single-function firms that collaborate on a product or service.

LO6 Describe what makes a good leader and the various styles of leadership. *(pp. 107–110)*

Leading is the process of influencing, motivating, and enabling others to contribute to the success and effectiveness of the organization by achieving its goals. The traits of effective leadership are shown in the figure below.

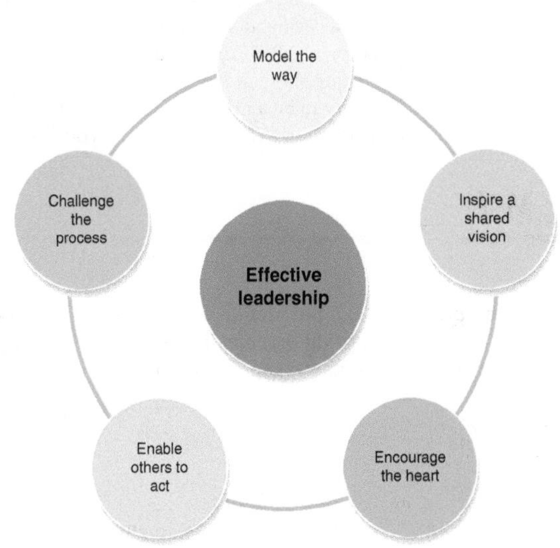

Traits of Effective Leadership

In addition to these five means of effective leadership, most leadership analysts agree that good leaders share several traits: determination, inspiration, flexibility and empathy, innovativeness, honesty, self-confidence, and knowledge and competence.

LO7 Explain the importance of control within a business. *(pp. 111–112)*

Controlling ensures that the plans and strategies set in place by management are properly carried out. Controlling helps to identify and correct weaknesses and errors in the system. Such weaknesses and errors, left uncorrected, can hurt an organization and have caused large companies to implode with illegal or immoral behaviours. Making sure that people are doing what they should and acting appropriately is a primary rationale for instituting control functions in an organization. Controls also pick up errors in the system, so if a plan is not meeting its goals, it can be modified.

MyBizLab Study, practise, and explore real business situations with these helpful resources:

- **Interactive Lesson Presentations:** Work through interactive presentations and assessments to test your knowledge of business concepts.
- **Study Plan:** Check your understanding of chapter concepts with self-study quizzes.
- **Dynamic Study Modules:** Work through adaptive study modules on your computer, tablet, or mobile device.
- **Simulations:** Practise decision-making in simulated business environments.

KEY TERMS

affiliative (or laissez-faire) leader *(p. 109)*
autocratic leader *(p. 108)*
conceptual skills *(p. 96)*
contingency leadership *(p. 110)*
contingency planning *(p. 102)*
controlling *(p. 111)*
core values *(p. 100)*
corporate culture *(p. 100)*
decision-making skills *(p. 96)*
democratic leader *(p. 108)*
first-line managers *(p. 104)*
goals *(p. 98)*
horizontal organization *(p. 105)*
interpersonal skills *(p. 96)*
leading *(p. 107)*
management *(p. 95)*
middle-level managers *(p. 104)*
mission statement *(p. 99)*
network organizations *(p. 106)*
objectives *(p. 98)*
operational plans *(p. 102)*
organizational chart *(p. 104)*
organizing *(p. 103)*
planning *(p. 98)*
Six Sigma *(p. 111)*
strategic plan *(p. 98)*
SWOT (Strengths, Weaknesses, Opportunities, and Threats) analysis *(p. 101)*
tactical plans *(p. 102)*
technical skills *(p. 95)*
time management skills *(p. 97)*
top-level managers *(p. 103)*
total quality management *(p. 111)*
vertical organization *(p. 105)*
vision *(p. 99)*
visionary leader *(p. 109)*

CRITICAL THINKING QUESTIONS

1. Contingency plans are important in any business. Discuss what kinds of plans your school might have in place. How would these plans differ, if at all, from those of a local business in your area? What are a few possible scenarios that would require contingency plans in your school or at a local business?
2. How do you rank leadership qualities? Rank the following qualities and compare your results with your classmates: honest, loyal, competent, caring, determined, ambitious, inspiring, forward-looking, self-confident, and imaginative. What are the top three qualities?
3. Analyze your own ability to be a manager. What already polished skills do you have now? What skills would you need to improve? What skills would you still need to acquire? How could you go about acquiring or improving those skills you do not have?
4. What differences might you expect to find in the corporate cultures of Google and CIBC? Do you think there would there be any similarities?
5. Perform a basic SWOT analysis for the school you are currently attending. Identify at least five strengths, weaknesses, opportunities, and threats. Suggest several ways your school can take advantage of opportunities by using its strengths and several ways in which your school can protect itself from threats and overcome its weaknesses.

TEAM TIME

On a Mission

Research and print several mission statements. Be sure to choose statements from both nonprofit organizations and for-profit organizations. Bring these mission statements to class.

PROCESS

Step 1. Assemble into groups of four or five.
Step 2. As a group, evaluate the mission statements you've chosen for similar components, such as a statement of the product, service, or primary market; an indication of commitment to quality; an indication of a commitment to social responsibility; and a declaration of corporate philosophy.
Step 3. Make notes of the components included in the majority of mission statements and those that are included in only a few mission statements.
Step 4. As a group, decide which mission statement is the most inspiring. Why? Which is the least inspiring? Why?
Step 5. As a class, compare the statements deemed most inspiring from each group and determine which of those is the most effective. Finally, openly discuss with your classmates how the winning statement would affect their inclination to work for or buy from this organization.

ETHICS AND RESPONSIBILITY

Assessing Social Responsibility

One of the functions of management is control, which includes measuring financial performance. But how often and with what tools does a manager assess an organization's social responsibility?

Process

Step 1. In small discussion groups, discuss the following:

- The planning and organizational changes that might need to be implemented
- The controls that a manager might use to measure and monitor the results of his or her social responsibility initiatives
- Any changes in leadership styles that might result from a focus on social responsibility

Step 2. After this discussion, research companies that are known for their social responsibility efforts. Discuss what impact their efforts have had on management.

CLOSING CASE

The Toyota Way of Management[21]

The Toyota Motor Corporation has implemented "The Toyota Way," a management philosophy based on criticism rather than compliance. Every Toyota executive, manager, and employee is taught to criticize their day-to-day processes and constantly look for ways to improve. It is not that Toyota is an overbearing company that critiques its employees' every move; rather, it works to achieve a democratic corporate culture that allows every employee to question if he or she, or that employee's supervisor, is using the most effective methods to do his or her job.

"The Toyota Way" comprises two main principles: continuous improvement and human respect. The idea of continuous improvement is summed up in the Japanese word *kaizen*, which Toyota defines as "a system of continuous improvements in which instances of waste are eliminated one-by-one at minimal cost."[22] Management practises *kaizen* by recognizing mistakes and failures. Toyota knows that managers can't solve problems unless they admit to them. By putting problems before successes, managers can work together to find ways to improve their processes.

Toyota looks to every employee to find problems and suggest improvements. "People in the workplace take the initiative of proposing ideas for improvements. Management respects their input and acts on their suggestions."[23] If an employee knows of a more efficient way to install seatbelts, that person is asked to share his or her idea and possibly use it on the production line. Giving employees the authority to make improvements creates a culture in which every person is invested in the success of the final product. Toyota enlists a type of clan control that encourages employees to examine their work and the work of fellow employees. Managers would like workers to look at their jobs as a combination of three roles: making cars, making better cars, and teaching others how to make better cars.

Toyota recognizes the difference between a successful manager and an effective manager. The company strives to keep management effective by making sure it is completely involved in the work process. Supervisors and managers are not set up to be viewed as "bosses" but as people responsible for finding ways to work more efficiently. Toyota wants its management to be hands on. Even executives must keep one foot in the workplace. By staying on the front line, management is able to implement *kaizen*. The idea of constantly looking for improvements is not supposed to be viewed as micromanagement but as creating a work process that is as efficient and effective as possible.

Today, "The Toyota Way" has proven to be successful. Staying true to the *kaizen* philosophy, Toyota does not measure its success in growth. It knows that getting bigger holds no value unless you get better. For Toyota, getting better means a total commitment in the workplace and a desire to make continuous improvements.

DISCUSSION QUESTIONS

1. Explain "The Toyota Way" of management. How is it related to *kaizen*? How can *kaizen* be used in other types of companies, particularly those that are not manufacturers?
2. Imagine yourself as a manager at a Toyota factory. How would you look for ways to continually improve the work processes of your employees? How would focusing on what doesn't work, as opposed to what does, help you look for ways to improve?
3. Would you consider "The Toyota Way" of management as laissez-faire? Why or why not? What problems might a company such as Toyota face with a laissez-faire style? Is there such a thing as giving employees too much power?

6 Motivation and Teamwork

1-800-GOT-JUNK?

LEARNING OBJECTIVES

After studying this chapter, you should be able to:

LO1 Describe several ways that you can improve your own level of motivation. (pp. 117–119)

LO2 Explain the benefits of having engaged employees and the problems organizations face when employees are not engaged. (pp. 119–120)

LO3 Describe the intricacies of Maslow's hierarchy of needs, McClelland's "three needs" theory, and Herzberg's motivator–hygiene theory. (pp. 120–123)

LO4 Distinguish between extrinsic and intrinsic motivators. (pp. 123–124)

LO5 Summarize the implications of Theory X, Theory Y, Theory Z, and the Vroom models. (pp. 124–128)

LO6 Describe the various tools employers can use to assess personality traits and explain how this knowledge can improve employee satisfaction and productivity. (pp. 128–131)

LO7 Explain the advantages of using teams in the workplace and outline the best practices to create and manage effective teams. (pp. 132–133)

LO8 Describe the roles that members of effective teams play to help the team achieve its goals. (pp. 134–135)

LO9 Explain what you can do to become a more valuable team member. (pp. 135–136)

OPENING DISCUSSION: EMPLOYEE ENGAGEMENT

It's All about People

Engaged employees are good for business. When employees feel engaged, they are more likely to want to work with colleagues and management to find ways to improve the company. Great customer service is one sign that employees are engaged, because engaged employees create a pleasant work environment, making everyone who comes to the workplace (customers included) feel more welcome. All of these benefits can be vital to business success.

Brian Scudamore, founder and CEO of 1-800-GOT-JUNK? totally gets it. His company has grown from a single used pickup truck operating from his parents' home in Vancouver, to an organization that now has more than 220 franchise locations in North America and Australia. Scudamore attributes much of this success to his engaged employees, and in 2013 the company was recognized by Achievers as one of the 50 Most Engaged Workplaces in Canada.[1]

According to Scudamore, "1-800-GOT-JUNK? makes the ordinary business of junk removal exceptional. We create space and peace of mind when junk gets in the way."[2] "There are companies out there that do this sort of thing. They just don't do it like we do. Our uniformed drivers show up in their shiny trucks at a scheduled time, with a standardized price sheet in hand. The level of professionalism that we have adopted is what differentiates us from the competition."[3]

This high level of employee engagement did not just happen; it's part of a purposeful strategy that seems to be working. According to Scudamore, "My vision has always been to build a company in which people are engaged—because with engagement comes performance, loyalty, teamwork, and happiness. In an engaged workplace, everyone wins, from the employees to the customers."[4]

The starting point of the strategy is hiring the right people. 1-800-GOT-JUNK? looks for talented people with the right skills, but new employees also need to have the personality and character to fit within the culture of the company. The company then uses employee referrals as a way to hire other great employees.[5]

But engaged employees need a purpose. Scudamore says that "a vision can engage people to believe in something bigger that they are creating as a team." At least once a quarter, 1-800-GOT-JUNK? employees meet as a team and read their vision aloud to keep it clear and alive in their minds. Employees actually engage in debate about it and come up with new ways to achieve it. A daily team "huddle" also gives the team opportunities to recognize individual successes and to thank people for their great work. Often the best way to engage someone is with a sincere thank you. According to Scudamore, "gratitude goes a long way toward building team engagement, loyalty and, of course, happiness."[6]

At the company's head office, a quote is posted that says "It's all about people." "When people see that quote, it's something we can hold ourselves accountable to," says Scudamore. "It's all about finding the right people, and treating those people right."[7]

DISCUSSION QUESTIONS

1. How can having engaged employees help a business become more successful?
2. Scudamore says that hiring the right people is critical. How would you describe "the right people" for a company like 1-800-GOT-JUNK?
3. If you were a CEO, what would you do to try to engage your employees?

MOTIVATION: THE BASICS

LO1 Describe several ways that you can improve your own level of motivation.

We hear the word *motivation* often. When students seek out extra learning opportunities that go beyond a course's basic requirements, they are described as motivated learners.

But what does motivation have to do with working in a business? Are all of a business owner's actions motivated solely by profit? Does an employer who pays well always have strongly motivated employees? In this section, we'll examine motivation in detail and look at techniques used in the past and the present to motivate employees.

Personal Motivation

personal motivation What drives us internally and externally to succeed in our goals.

What drives you to do your personal best?

Do you ever feel driven and inspired to complete a task? This is what it means to be motivated. **Personal motivation** is what drives us internally and externally to achieve our goals. Think of times that you have pushed to be your best, whether at school, in sports, or in other activities. Is it easier for you to build enthusiasm for tasks that you're sure you can accomplish? Or do you set difficult goals and draw energy from the challenge of attaining them? Some people need immediate gratification or success to stay motivated. Others are able to postpone short-term success in pursuit of long-term gains. Do you need to be rewarded immediately for what you do or are you more motivated by long-term benefits?

Now think about how hard you work when you receive a lot of positive feedback (either financial or emotional). Is getting praise or money for a job important to you? Or are you driven more by the values of the place where you work, your beliefs, or in doing a job well? For some people, being part of the accomplishments of a team is what motivates them. Are you one of those people?

Tyler Olson/Shutterstock

What motivates you? Do you love a physical or mental challenge? Do you get a feeling of satisfaction when you reach one of your goals? People are motivated by different mechanisms, but we can all improve our motivation to succeed.

How can you improve your motivation?

Think of what you could achieve if you were more motivated to succeed and had more energy and more determination on a daily basis. Here are a few ways to improve your motivation:

- *Avoid negative experiences and people.* Emotionally draining situations, pessimistic people, and interpersonal conflicts are unnecessary setbacks that cause you to lose focus on your pursuits and productivity. Instead, find other motivated, positive people to affiliate with.
- *Become passionate about your mission.* Enthusiasm can be a powerful personal motivator because it keeps you energized, so if you are not enthusiastic about the work you are currently doing, find ways to incorporate aspects of what you enjoy doing into your daily life. Sometimes this may mean changing your point of view or attitude toward something so that you look for ways to make tasks you'd rather not do (but that must be done) interesting, rewarding, meaningful, and maybe a little fun.
- *Feel good about yourself.* Personal motivation is not something that happens overnight; you may have to work at it and you might need outside help. Listening to self-help CDs, reading material on the subject, or meeting with a counsellor or life coach might be just what you need to start a successful life.
- *Give yourself a reward.* Personal motivation comes from within, and no one can give you the motivation you need to start, work on, or complete a project. The motivation itself depends on the reward and whether it satisfies your needs or wants. Set goals or milestones (mini-targets) for you to reach each day or along the way during a long-term project, and then reward yourself as you reach each milestone. For

many, this may be a tangible reward, such as money, but for others this may be an intangible, intrinsic reward, such as the self-satisfaction gained from a job well done or mastery of a skill.

Motivation, Engagement, and Flow

LO2 Explain the benefits of having engaged employees and the problems organizations face when employees are not engaged.

Does time fly by when you are engaged in your work? Have you ever been working on a project and you were so immersed in what you were doing that when you looked at your watch four hours had gone by? Psychologist Mihaly Csikszentmihalyi refers to this state of captivated attention as *flow*.[8] A **flow state** happens when you are completely involved and focused on what you are doing. Often people produce their best work, make the best use of their skills, and feel the most pleasure when they are in such a flow state. They are engaged in an activity when they feel a strong match between their own abilities and the challenge of a task—it is neither too difficult, which can lead to frustration, nor too simple, which can lead to boredom. They report a sense of control over what is happening and a feeling of effortlessness in their work. Creating a workplace that fosters the kind of motivation required to engage employees in their work and help get them to into a state of flow is the subject of **organizational psychology**—the study of how to create a workplace that fosters motivation and productivity among employees.

How motivated is North America's workforce? The Q12 is a 12-question survey of employee engagement administered by Gallup. According to Q12 survey results, 69 percent of Canadian and U.S. employees are not engaged or are actively disengaged in their work. Based on respondents' answers to a series of questions, the Q12 classifies employees as "engaged," "not engaged," or "actively disengaged"[9] (see **Table 6.1**). Imagine a workplace in which three out of four employees are complaining or even disrupting activities during the day.

SELF CHECK Feeling motivated often involves the achievement of an intangible yet valuable state called *flow*. Are you a flow starter? Or does the flow state float right past you? Take this quiz to find out.

1. When completing a task, I feel completely involved and focused on what I'm doing.
   A. Always
   B. Sometimes
   C. Never
2. I lose track of time when I'm working on a project or assignment.
   A. Always
   B. Sometimes
   C. Never
3. I feel like tasks are challenging yet doable.
   A. Always
   B. Sometimes
   C. Never
4. I feel like work isn't really "work"; it seems natural and effortless.
   A. Always
   B. Sometimes
   C. Never
5. I feel in control and content when tackling a project.
   A. Always
   B. Sometimes
   C. Never

Answers: If you answered . . .
Mostly As . . . You are a flow starter of the highest degree.
Mostly Bs . . . You foray into flow state on occasion.
Mostly Cs . . . Your familiarity with flow state is almost nonexistent.

What engages employees? In 2007–2008, Towers Watson (formerly Towers Perrin), a professional services firm, conducted a Global Workforce Study, the largest of its kind, to identify the drivers of attraction, retention, and engagement through the eyes of employees at midsize to large organizations worldwide.[10] An **engaged employee** is one who is fully involved in and enthusiastic about his or her work and thus will act to further their organization's interests. The study measured employees'

flow state A state that happens when you are completely involved and focused on what you are doing. Often people produce their best work, make the best use of their skills, and feel the most pleasure when they are in such a flow state.

organizational psychology Studies how to create a workplace that fosters motivation and productivity among employees.

engaged employee An employee who is fully involved in and enthusiastic about his or her work, and thus will act in a way that furthers their organization's interests.

Table 6.1 Motivation Levels of Employees

Engaged	Not Engaged	Actively Disengaged
• Works with passion	• Works with minimal effort	• Works in a disruptive manner
• Feels connected and obligated to the company	• Is indifferent to the company	• Is unhappy with the company
• Adds to the success of the company	• Makes little or no contribution to the company	• Combats the efforts of engaged workers

Source: Based on Gallup, "Employee Engagement," June 25, 2012, http://www.gallup.com.

Best Companies to Work for (2013)

These are fast-growing Canadian companies that offer tremendous career advancement opportunities together with leading-edge employee perks and benefits.

1. Aecon Group Inc.
2. Golder Associates Ltd.
3. Nuance Communications Canada
4. OpenText Corporation
5. Potash Corporation of Saskatchewan Inc.
6. Shell Canada Ltd.
7. TD Bank Group
8. Technip Canada Ltd.
9. Toyota Motors Manufacturing Canada Inc.
10. West Fraser Timber Co. Ltd.

Source: *Financial Post*, "Ten Best Companies to Work for," accessed August 4, 2014, http://www.canadastop100.com/fp10/. Used by permission of Mediacorp Canada Inc.

rational, emotional, and motivational connections to their companies and jobs to calculate their level of engagement and better understand how engagement affects behaviour and performance. The study's results showed that employee engagement rises when employees

- experience a combination of effective and caring leadership,
- are involved in interesting work,
- are assigned appealing development opportunities, and
- receive both tangible and intangible rewards.[11]

The study also found that companies with the highest levels of employee engagement achieve better financial results and are more successful in retaining their most valued employees than companies with lower levels of engagement.[12]

Three of the study's key insights were as follows: (1) Employees are eager to invest more of themselves to help the company succeed but want to understand what's in it for them; (2) senior leaders need to make the leap to a more inspirational and engaging style of leadership to help drive higher engagement; and (3) companies need to understand their employees as well as they understand their customers to design a work environment and experience that will drive higher engagement and performance.[13] The survey showed that senior leadership has a significant impact on engagement. The top engagement driver is employees' belief that senior management has their best interests at heart. Yet only about four out of ten respondents believed this was true in their organization. The challenge for senior management is to recognize the value of employees' untapped potential and to channel it in ways that yield real improvements in business performance. These results make it clear that encouraging flow in the workplace is a challenge.[14]

What are the benefits of keeping employees motivated? Both employers and employees benefit from a motivated workforce. Employers find workers are more productive, more creative, and have much better retention levels when care is taken to provide a motivating environment and tasks. Employees often spend the majority of their waking day at their jobs, and their quality of life and overall happiness are enhanced when they feel excited about the work they contribute. The Global Workforce Study (mentioned earlier) found that firms with the highest percentage of engaged employees collectively increased operating income by 19 percent and earnings per share by 28 percent year to year.[15] If there were 100 employees averaging 70 percent engagement, it would take 116 employees averaging 60 percent engagement to achieve the same results as those 100 employees at 70 percent.[16] The cost of 16 employees working 37.5 hours per week at approximately $14.50 per hour is $8700, so the price of 10 percent disengagement per annum is $452 400! If those employees were senior employees or managers and were receiving a much higher pay level, the cost of disengagement could potentially put a company out of business. Not only does employee disengagement hurt companies financially, but it also may lead to poor company reputation, poor customer service, and lower quality output.

Video: CH2MHill: Motivation

Konstantin Chagin/Shutterstock

Engaged workers are more productive workers, which translates into better bottom-line results for employers.

Early Theories of Motivation

LO3 Describe the intricacies of Maslow's hierarchy of needs, McClelland's "three needs" theory, and Herzberg's motivator–hygiene theory.

Do basic needs for food or shelter motivate us to certain actions? Several theories explain how and why people are motivated. One of the most popular theories was created by an early researcher in the area of human motivation, Abraham Maslow (1908–1970), who published the

How Does a Work Environment Encourage "Flow"?

There is no fixed recipe, but there are companies who have succeeded in building motivated, engaged environments that support workers and support the creative experience of flow.

One such company is SAS, a business software firm in North Carolina. With an incredibly low employee turnover rate of just 2–5 percent[17] and annual revenues of over $2.7 billion,[18] the company has created such an atmosphere in part thanks to the policies of CEO Jim Goodnight. Goodnight lists the following as ways in which SAS works to foster a creative environment:

- It keeps employees intellectually engaged.
- It removes distractions so employees can do their best work.
- It makes managers responsible for sparking creativity.
- It has managers eliminate the arbitrary distinctions between administrative "suits" and more abstract "creatives."
- It engages customers as creative partners.

In addition to fostering strong professional lives, SAS supports its employees in their private lives as well. On the SAS campus, you'll find medical facilities for employees and their families, a Montessori daycare centre, and a cafeteria where families can eat lunch together. "The corporate philosophy is, if your fifth grader is in his first school play, you should be there to see it," says Goodnight.[19] Such a philosophy has led to SAS earning a spot on *Fortune* magazine's Best Companies to Work for list and a spot on *Working Mother* magazine's list of best companies.[20]

Discussion Questions

1. **Why do you think that engaging customers as creative partners helps to increase employee flow?**
2. **What kind of distractions might inhibit employees from being creative?**
3. **How does supporting employee's private lives benefit the company?**

book *The Hierarchy of Needs* in 1954. **Maslow's hierarchy of needs** suggests that our primary needs are met first before our higher-level needs are addressed (see **Figure 6.1**). Maslow suggested that different people find themselves at different places in the hierarchy, so their motivations may be different. While an offer of overtime pay may be a successful motivator for a person concerned with safety needs, it might be the opposite of what someone working to satisfy their need for self-actualization finds motivating.

Maslow's hierarchy of needs A theory that suggests our primary needs are met first before our higher-level needs are addressed.

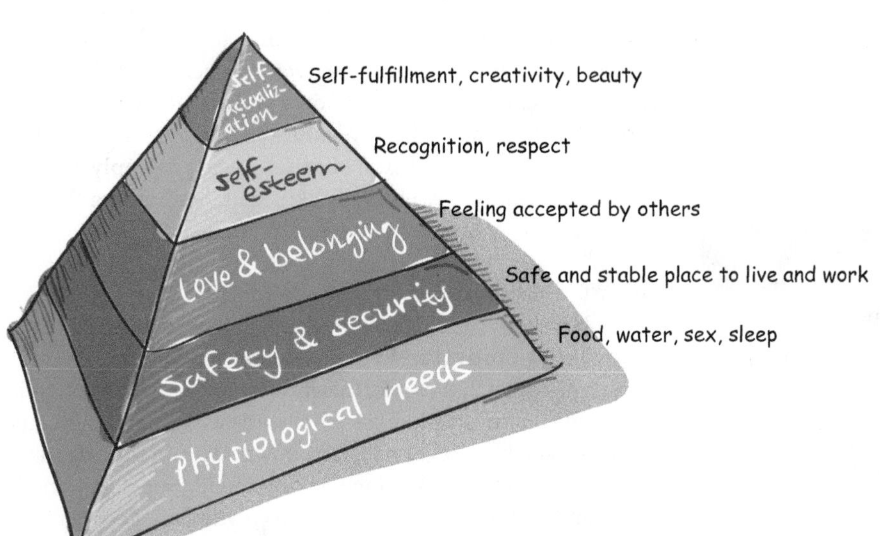

Figure 6.1 Maslow's Hierarchy of Needs

Source: Vitezslav Valka/Alamy

- *Physiological needs.* The first needs to be met are inborn, basic needs—called *physiological needs*—such as the need for water, food, sleep, and shelter. This means that before we can think about anything else in our lives we must ensure that these basic physiological needs are met. Physiological motivation in the workplace may include lunch breaks and paying salaries that enable workers to buy life's essentials.
- *Safety needs.* Once our physiological needs have been met, Maslow's theory holds that we strive to satisfy safety needs, including establishing safe and stable places to live and work (medical insurance, financial savings, relative job security, nonbullying workplace, or living in a safe area).
- *Social needs.* Once both physiological and safety needs have been met, we can consider social or belonging needs. This includes the need to belong to a group and to feel accepted by others. Social motivators in the workplace may include a culture of acceptance, belonging, and community.
- *Esteem needs.* The next level in Maslow's hierarchy includes esteem needs, which are satisfied by the mastery of a skill and by the attention and recognition of others. Some examples of esteem needs are recognition (external motivator), social status (external motivator), accomplishment (internal motivator), and self-respect (internal motivator).
- *Self-actualization needs.* Finally, at the top of the hierarchy are self-actualization needs that cannot be addressed unless and until the lower-level needs have been adequately met. These needs include the desire to maximize our own potential through education, self-fulfillment, as well as experiences of beauty and spirituality. Self-actualized people tend to have motivators such as truth, justice, wisdom, and meaning. Challenging and meaningful work assignments that enable innovation and creativity would motivate someone in the self-actualization level of Maslow's hierarchy of needs.

McClelland's "three needs" theory A theory that suggests there are three main motivators: (1) the need for achievement (to accomplish something difficult on your own), (2) the need for affiliation (to form close personal relationships), and (3) the need for power (to be able to control the behaviour of others).

Herzberg's motivator–hygiene theory A theory that suggests two factors influence a person's motivation: hygiene factors (which cause job dissatisfaction) and motivation factors (which cause job satisfaction).

Do we need to form close personal relationships in the workplace? Other researchers have proposed different models to map human needs to motivation. Psychologist David McClelland (1917–1998) suggested there are three main motivators, a theory known as **McClelland's "three needs" theory**.

1. *The need for achievement*— to accomplish something difficult on your own
2. *The need for affiliation*— to form close personal relationships
3. *The need for power*— to be able to control the behaviour of others

According to McClelland, which need we try to satisfy depends on a variety of complex factors, including our cultural background. Although an individual may have multiple needs, McClelland suggests that one tends to be dominant over the others. In a workplace, this theory could account for differences in motivation among co-workers. For example, a person whose main need is for affiliation may have little motivation to perform a solitary task, whereas a person with a high need for achievement may be highly motivated to perform a difficult task alone. This theory is easy to understand and it gives managers critical insights about human nature so they can improve the impact of their motivational efforts. It is easy to apply because successful leaders are naturally skilled at determining the three needs profile of their employees.

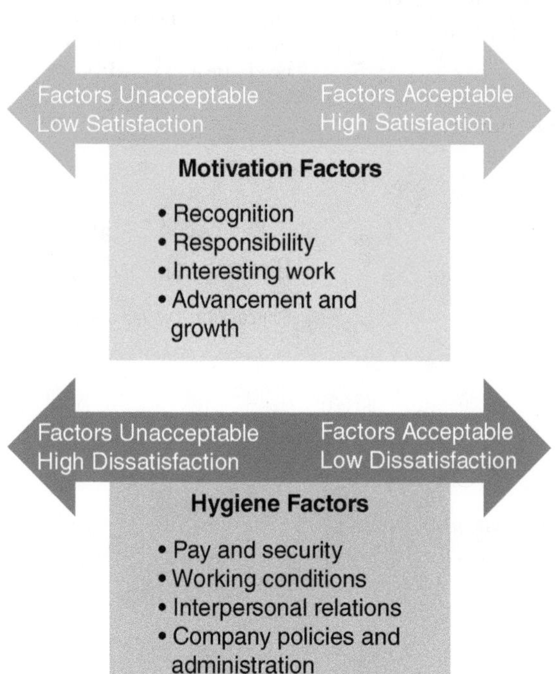

Figure 6.2 Herzberg's Motivator–Hygiene Theory

Do we need a safe work environment? Psychologist Frederick Herzberg (1923–2000) developed a theory in 1959 known as **Herzberg's motivator–hygiene theory** (or *two-factor theory*), which suggests that two factors influence a person's motivation: hygiene factors (which cause job dissatisfaction) and motivation factors (which cause job satisfaction) (see **Figure 6.2**). Hygiene factors include a safe working environment, proper pay and benefits, and positive relationships with co-workers. People rarely notice hygiene factors if they are present. However, if hygiene factors are absent or inadequate, people tend to be dissatisfied. Consider basic working conditions, benefits, or other company policies. If there suddenly is no heat in the place where you work or if your pay is cut, you may be motivated to find a way to meet these needs outside of the company. But if these are already in place, they are taken for granted and may not serve to motivate you.

The second set of factors in Herzberg's theory are motivation factors, which include a sense of responsibility, recognition, promotion, and job growth. Consider the self-actualization needs from Maslow's hierarchy. If there is no path for growth in your job or little recognition of your achievements, you probably would not immediately quit, but it would create a set of conditions that fail to motivate you.

Review the flow state quiz you took earlier in this chapter. Do you understand now what a flow state is and why it is important? What are the benefits of flow state in the workplace? And how can the different theories of motivation account for your achievement, or lack thereof, of flow state?

MOTIVATION: BUSINESS APPLICATIONS

LO4 Distinguish between extrinsic and intrinsic motivators.

Do managers actually use theories of motivation? How can a manager of an assembly line at an automotive plant or a team leader of a software development company take what researchers know about human behaviour and use it to increase productivity and employee satisfaction? The theories of human motivation you have just read about have given rise to a number of different approaches to organize and motivate people in the workplace. Using motivational theories to address the practical matters of motivation in the workplace is no easy task. Finding a way to inspire employees often requires patience and persistence. Fortunately, there are a number of motivational theories that specifically take into account the dynamics of the business environment, giving managers many options to choose from.

extrinsic motivators Motivating factors that are within managers' control, including such things as pay, promotion, and verbal praise.

intrinsic motivators Motivating factors that are outside managers' control because they are internal to each individual employee, such as the sense of purpose or value a person derives from his or her work.

What could a manager do to enhance employee motivation? Managers need to ensure that their employees are productive and eager to do the best job possible. Yet every organization has employees who simply do not produce work of the quality they are capable of providing. Of all the functions managers perform, motivating employees is probably the most complex. This is due, in part, to the fact that what employees are motivated by changes constantly. In the workplace, managers can control some external motivating factors. These motivators, called **extrinsic motivators**, include such things as pay, promotion, and verbal praise. Other factors, called **intrinsic motivators**, are outside the set of factors under a manager's control because they are internal to each individual employee. The examples of these motivating influences shown in **Figure 6.3** are based on a person's actual interest in his or her work and stem from the sense of purpose or value a person derives from his or her work.

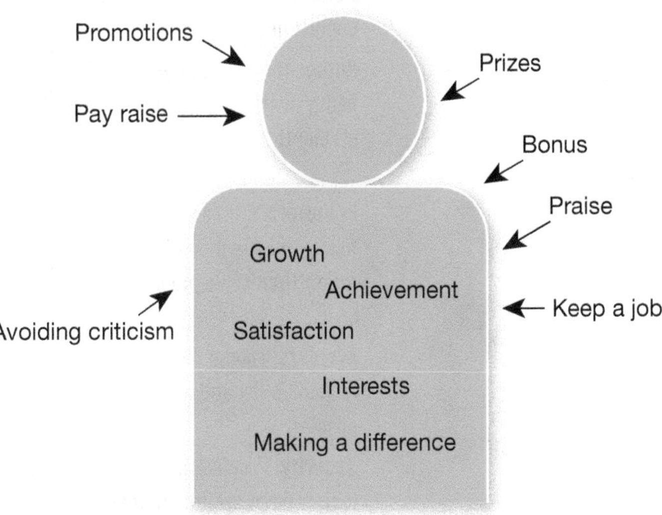

Figure 6.3 Intrinsic and Extrinsic Motivators

In 2006, an educational study in England showed the differences between these two types of motivators.[21] Children from a boys' school and a girls' school were asked to make a poster about their lives. One group was told its poster would decorate a local hospital for sick children. The other group was told it would be paid for its work. Which group of children would produce the better work—those who perceived the task as being worthwhile or those who were promised payment? In this case, much more sophisticated and detailed work came from the group that was working for free. The children were motivated more by the knowledge that they would be helping sick children than by financial reward.

Different people have different balances between intrinsic and extrinsic motivators. So how can business managers best motivate all their employees? An individual motivated intrinsically is working for his or her own satisfaction and may value challenging work he or she perceives as meaningful to the company more than extrinsic factors such as pay. So, for example, a boss who offers unsatisfying work, even though he or she offers bonuses and promotions, will have difficulty motivating an intrinsically motivated worker.

When you are first entering the workforce, money may motivate you as you save for a new car, house, or other things you'd like to buy. As you gain work experience and seniority in your job, money may not motivate you to do *more* in your job, but it may help motivate you *not* to do less. At this career point, you may be better motivated by recognition, promotions, interesting work projects, authority, health benefits, time away from work to spend with family, or other nonmonetary incentives. Some workers are motivated by an increase in pay, while others are motivated by a flexible work schedule (e.g., a compressed workweek or the opportunity to work from home), and still others might be motivated by rewards the employer has not yet offered. Employees are often motivated by work that engages them: They need to like what they are doing and be inspired by their work. Other factors, such as a good work–life balance, also play a role in motivating or demotivating employees, which affects quality of work, productivity, and customer relations. Managers need to ask employees what they want then find a cost-effective way to offer it to them while at the same time increasing company productivity.

Motivational Models Used in Business

LO5 Summarize the implications of Theory X, Theory Y, Theory Z, and the Vroom models.

Besides early theories of motivation, what other models are there? In addition to the theories proposed by Maslow, McClelland, and Herzberg, several models (which are detailed below) provide theoretical explanations of what motivates employees specifically in a business or workplace context.

McGregor's Theory X A theory that suggests people inherently dislike work and want to avoid it.

Do most people dislike work? In 1960, social psychologist Douglas McGregor proposed the Theory X and Theory Y models (see **Table 6.2**). **McGregor's Theory X**

Table 6.2 Comparison of Theory X and Theory Y

Theory X		Theory Y
Not motivated: People naturally dislike working and avoid it when given the opportunity.	***Motivation***	**Naturally motivated:** People see work as a natural part of life.
Authoritarian: Managers must use heavy controls to get people to work efficiently.	***Management***	**Democratic:** Managers need not use heavy controls. Managers allow employees to create their own motivation.
Followers: Employees would prefer to follow the direction of management rather than solve problems on their own.	***Leadership***	**Leaders:** People are creative problem solvers whose ideas can be used in the workplace.
Avoiders: People do not want responsibility and avoid it whenever possible.	***Responsibility***	**Seekers:** People inherently seek responsibility and are willing to accept it when asked.
Security: People are not complex and mainly want security in their jobs.	***Needs***	**Creativity:** People need to be intellectually stimulated and feel that their ideas are utilized.

suggests that people inherently dislike work and want to avoid it. Because of this view, **Theory X management** proposes that employees have to be coerced and controlled by management to be productive. This leads to an authoritarian, hardline management style. In contrast, **McGregor's Theory Y** suggests that people view work as being as natural as playing and resting. People are naturally motivated and will direct themselves to work for the aims of the organization if they are satisfied with their jobs. **Theory Y management** assumes that, on average, people will accept and seek out responsibility. Such managers have a softer style of management that involves the participation of many.

Clearly, Theories X and Y would not work equally well in any given situation. Theory X management—which is authoritarian and hard line—is often seen in large-scale operations such as mass manufacturing or when it is important that orders are carried out immediately and exactly, such as in the military. In the knowledge industry, in which there is a mix of professionals working together to solve complex problems, Theory Y management is more likely to be seen with its participative, gentler style.

Do most people like to be included in decision making? In 1981, William Ouchi put forward a **Theory Z**, based on a Japanese management style that relied heavily on collaborative decision making. In many corporations in Japan in the 1980s, one person might be responsible for many different aspects of a single project. Employees tended to become generalists rather than specialists, who were trained in a very narrow set of tasks. **Theory Z management** is a combination of American and Japanese management philosophies characterized by long-term employment security, consensual decision making, and slow evaluation and promotion procedures, with an emphasis on individual responsibility within a group context. Workers tend to show a desire to cooperate and be loyal to the organization. As a result, companies that apply Theory Z management often reap the benefits of low turnover, high productivity, and strong morale among the workforce. Morale (a sense of purpose and enthusiasm toward one's work) is an important factor in an employee's level of motivation.

Does working hard result in a better outcome for the employee? Although Maslow's hierarchy and other theories describe human motivation, they do so in terms of an overall model for all employees. In 1964, Victor Vroom proposed his expectancy theory, which has since been developed by other researchers. **Vroom's expectancy theory** suggests an individual's motivation in any given situation can be described by the relationship among three psychological forces, illustrated in the formula

$$\text{Motivation} = \text{Expectancy} \times \text{Instrumentality} \times \text{Valence}$$

Expectancy theory suggests that people are motivated to work toward rewards they want and which they believe they have a reasonable chance—or expectancy—of obtaining.[22] A reward that seems out of reach, for example, is not likely to be a motivator.

Expectancy is the idea that a person's effort has an appreciable effect on a situation's result, whether it is a success or failure. Does working harder lead to a more positive outcome for the employee or the company? Or does it not make a difference? This is what expectancy measures.

Instrumentality refers to the idea that the outcome of a situation is related to rewards or punishment. For those who are extrinsically motivated, instrumentality answers the question, "What are the chances I'm going to be rewarded if I do a good job?" Expectancy theory helps to explain why some people do not work as hard as they can when their salaries are based purely on seniority. For those who are intrinsically motivated, instrumentality answers the question, "How good will I feel if I can accomplish this task?"

Valence is the importance that the individual places on the expected outcome of a situation. It answers questions such as "How great a reward will there be if my performance is exemplary?" and "How serious a punishment do I expect if I underperform?" Put simply, Vroom's formulas for high and low motivations read as follows:

High Motivation = (My work actually affects the outcome) × (There's a good chance I'll get a reward if this works out) × (If it works out, it'll be a really big reward!)

Theory X management A style of management that proposes employees have to be coerced and controlled by management to be productive. This leads to an authoritarian, hardline management style.

McGregor's Theory Y A theory that suggests people view work as being as natural as playing and resting.

Theory Y management A style of management that assumes, on average, that people will accept and seek out responsibility. Such managers have a softer style of management that involves the participation of many.

Theory Z A theory based on a Japanese management style that relies heavily on collaborative decision making.

Theory Z management A style of management that is a combination of American and Japanese management philosophies characterized by long-term employment security, consensual decision making, and slow evaluation and promotion procedures, with an emphasis on individual responsibility within a group context.

Vroom's expectancy theory A theory that suggests an individual's motivation in any given situation can be described by the relationship among three psychological forces, illustrated in the formula Motivation = Expectancy × Instrumentality × Valence.

Low Motivation = (Nothing I do is going to impact this situation) × (Even if it does go well, I probably won't see any benefit) × (The only reward from this will be incredibly small)

The Vroom formula can be used to analyze factors including how satisfied employees are at their jobs, how likely it is they will remain at their jobs, and how hard they will work at their jobs. In addition, unlike Maslow's and McClelland's models, which address typical needs across large groups of people, Vroom's model, with its three independent variables measuring the specific levels of expectancy, instrumentality, and valence, can generate a much more specialized result that is attuned to the mental state of a specific individual.

Video: Whole Foods: Teamwork, Motivation, and Communication

equity theory A theory that focuses on social comparisons—people evaluating their treatment by the organization relative to the treatment of others.

How can employees' perception of fair treatment affect motivation? **Equity theory** focuses on social comparisons—people evaluating their treatment by the organization relative to the treatment of others. Employees begin to analyze what they contribute to the company (experience, skills, effort, time, education, etc.) relative to what they get in return (salary, benefits, security, friendly work culture, recognition, power, etc.). The result is a ratio of contribution to return. Employees then compare their own ratios to the ratios they have calculated for other employees. If they feel there is an inequity, such that they contribute more than someone else does yet are paid less, then they try to restore fairness. They may ask for a pay raise, reduce their level of work effort, or complain more about work and begin to become disengaged. They may try to rationalize their situation by finding another person to compare ratios with, or they may simply quit.

participative management and empowerment A management style that involves encouraging employees to become engaged in their jobs and remain loyal to the company by inspiring them to be self-motivated and giving them responsibility with the power (empowerment) to make decisions.

management by objectives (MBO) A performance goal-setting method in which management and employees work together to set goals and evaluate performance.

How can employers encourage workers to be self-motivated? **Participative management and empowerment** involves encouraging employees to become engaged in their jobs and remain loyal to the company by inspiring them to be self-motivated and giving them responsibility with the power (empowerment) to make decisions. The 2013 WorldBlu List of Most Democratic Workplaces comprises 44 organizations from various industries and several countries. Canada had a few companies make the list, including Chaordix (Calgary), LEARN (Laval), NRI Distribution (Kamloops), and TakingITGlobal (Toronto).[23] Many other Canadian companies embrace empowerment and participative management. At WestJet, for example, call centre agents booking flights can override fees and extend special discounts if the customer has a compelling reason (personal tragedy), and ticket agents can immediately reroute passengers without supervisory intervention.[24] The philosophy is to produce satisfied customers; by not having to wait for supervisory approval, customer service is expedited. Employees feel they are important to the company and their decisions affect customers directly.

Sergey Nivens/Shutterstock

Equity theory is all about comparison: Is my situation fair compared to that of my co-workers?

How can employers motivate employees through goal setting? One of the most popular methods for setting performance goals is called **management by objectives (MBO)**, in which management and employees work together to set goals and evaluate performance. This gives employees a clear understanding of their roles and responsibilities within the organization and how their activities relate to the achievement of overall organizational goals. Employees feel that they are important and empowered, resulting in improved motivation, job satisfaction, and commitment. The use of MBO must be carefully aligned with the culture of the organization. While MBO programs are no longer as popular as they were in the late 1980s and early 1990s, they still has their place in management today.

Should management invest in employee skills development? Management often works to help employees improve skills in areas in which they are weak. But is this the best investment of resources for a corporation? **Strength-based management** is a system based on the belief that, rather than improve weak skills, the best way to help employees develop is to determine their strengths and build on them.[25] This system is supported by research that shows that people can learn the most about areas in which they already have a strong foundation. Strength-based programs identify employees' current talents and skills and then provide additional training and support to develop them into areas of excellence. When people are not operating (at work) from their strengths, they usually dislike going to work and talk negatively about the company they work for, interact more negatively than positively with co-workers, deal with customers/clients poorly, and accomplish less on a daily basis.[26]

strength-based management A system based on the belief that, rather than improve weak skills, the best way to help employees develop is to determine their strengths and build on them.

Evolution of Motivational Theories in Business

How have motivational theories changed? In the early twentieth century, as the Industrial Age saw the creation of large corporations, issues of efficiency and labour costs became critical. Researchers such as Frederick Taylor (1856–1915) began to study how to manage people optimally. In 1911, Taylor published his findings in *The Principles of Scientific Management*, proposing ways that managers could increase productivity. He encouraged managers to use scientific study to determine the best methods to complete tasks and then to train employees in these methods. Many of his ideas were implemented in factories.

Taylor's theory became known as **scientific management**, which comprised methods aimed at determining the one best way for a job to be done.[27] By the 1920s and 1930s, a field of academic study called **industrial psychology** was created to further study scientifically how to manage employees and work optimally. Other researchers, such as Frank and Lillian Gilbreth, used photography to study employee work patterns and then analyzed these patterns to increase productivity. For example, they used time-motion studies to analyze factory jobs and then train workers in the precise sequence of steps that would make them most productive. As scientific management theory spread widely, plant managers were hiring time-motion experts to perform the first "scientific" studies that attempted to break jobs down into easily repeated components and to devise more efficient tools and machines for performing them.

scientific management A management theory that comprises methods aimed at determining the one best way for a job to be done.

industrial psychology The scientific study of how to manage employees and work optimally.

Another famous study of the period was Harvard professor Elton Mayo's work at the Hawthorne plant of the Western Electric Company in Illinois. Between 1927 and 1932, Mayo examined physical influences on the workplace (such as lighting and humidity) as well as psychological aspects (such as group pressure and working hours). The major finding, known as the Hawthorne effect, was that *regardless of the experimental changes made*, the production of the workers improved. Researchers concluded that the increase in productivity was based on the attention the workers were receiving. Because they knew they were being studied, the employees felt special and produced more, regardless of the conditions Hawthorne studied. Today the **Hawthorne effect** is used to describe the increase in productivity caused by workers being given special attention. The results of the Hawthorne study launched the radically new human relations movement, in which researchers studied more complicated motivation theories and the emotional world of the worker.[28] After World War II, the direction of research in management theory shifted from management of an individual worker toward management of the entire organization, its structure, and policies.

Hawthorne effect Describes the increase in productivity caused by workers being given special attention.

What motivational theories fit the modern workplace? The fields of organizational psychology and industrial psychology are still very active, and new theories of management practices continue to appear. A motivational theory that is important for the modern workplace comes from examining the open-source movement (software projects that are developed, tested, and maintained for free by a worldwide network of volunteers). Sample open-source projects include Wikipedia and the Linux operating system. These have been hugely successful and were created by professional people working many hours for free—outside their regular jobs. What is causing people to behave this way?

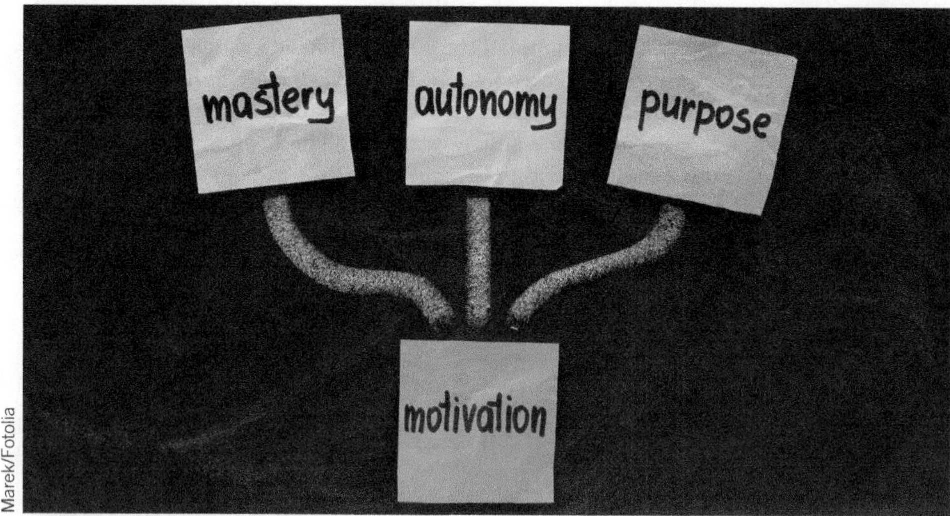

For knowledge workers, autonomy, mastery of skills, and a sense of purpose in their work are key motivators.

Four academic economists explored this by running an experiment where people were recruited to perform a range of tasks—some that required motor skills, some creative, and some needing concentration. Monetary rewards were promised for three levels of performance, with the top performers receiving the equivalent of five months' pay! The result was that the higher the incentives, the *worse* the performance. Similar results were seen when the London School of Economics reviewed corporate pay-for-performance plans.[29] Using economic rewards to motivate employees can actually lead to poorer performance when the work is a creative, cognitive task.

Additional study has shown that modern knowledge workers value three commodities much more highly than money:[30]

- *Autonomy*—having some control over the key decisions in their work lives
- *Mastery*—having a sense of skill and having time to develop and improve skills
- *Purpose*—wanting their lives and work to have a higher meaning

Top-performing companies in our modern knowledge-based environment will need to find ways to offer opportunities for autonomy, mastery, and purpose to their employees. Companies that can adjust their incentive structure to recognize this will see great benefits.

Personality Traits

LO6 Describe the various tools employers can use to assess personality traits and explain how this knowledge can improve employee satisfaction and productivity.

Can we measure someone's personality? Personality assessment tools can help employers determine whether a candidate will "fit" the corporate culture and work well with the team. Personality assessments can help leaders determine their personality tendencies; once identified, they can consciously adjust their leadership style as the situation dictates. Personality assessments measure specific metrics in people's personalities, quantify them, categorize them, and indicate which traits make up an individual's personality. There are various personality models in use today, and while no one model is recognized as the perfect tool, all of these personality assessments or type indicators produce reports that may give us a better understanding of the personality traits required to be successful in a variety of roles, including leadership.

Big Five One of the most widely accepted models of personality. The model categorizes most human personality traits into five broad dimensions and then assigns people a score for each dimension: openness, conscientiousness, extraversion, agreeableness, and neuroticism (emotional stability). Also called the Five-Factor Model.

How can we categorize human personality traits? The **Big Five**, also referred to as the Five-Factor Model, is one of the most widely accepted models of personality.[31] The model categorizes most human personality traits into five broad dimensions and then assigns people a score for each dimension (see **Table 6.3**).

Table 6.3 Big Five Personality Traits

Trait	High Degree	Low Degree
Openness	• Curious • Intellectual • Creative • Open to new ideas	• Consistent • Cautious
Conscientiousness	• Organized • Responsible • Systematic • Self-disciplined • Thorough • Dependable	• Easygoing • Careless • Spontaneous • Not self-disciplined
Extraversion	• Sociable • Talkative • Assertive • Open to new relationships	• Reserved • Quiet time alone • Need less social stimulation
Agreeableness	• Tolerant • Cooperative • Understanding • Trusting • Sensitive to the needs of others	• Cold • Unkind • Suspicious • Antagonistic
Neuroticism (degree of emotional stability)	• Irritable • Moody • Anxious • Experience unpleasant emotions easily	• Secure • Confident • Emotionally stable

When the Big Five test is scored for individual feedback, it is usually presented in a percentile form. For example, if a person scores in the thirtieth percentile for extraversion, they most likely tend to shy away from social situations. A person scoring in the eightieth percentile for conscientiousness most likely has a strong sense of responsibility and orderliness.

What are the implications of the Big Five model in the workplace?[32] People with a high degree of openness perform well in situations that require learning new skills and they often hold unconventional beliefs. In the workplace, they adjust quickly to new jobs and adapt well to change because they seek information and feedback. People with lower scores in openness tend to have more conventional, traditional interests and prefer the straightforward and obvious over the complex and ambiguous. Knowing the degree to which someone is open can give a manager some insight to creating interesting and engaging work for the employee. It also helps those hiring determine how well the individual might fit into the corporate culture and work environment.

Conscientious people are less likely to quit the job or be absent from work and are more likely to have high performance levels and work in a safe manner. Businesses started by highly conscientious people have longer survival rates compared to those who are not as conscientious. People with high scores of conscientiousness prefer planned rather than spontaneous behaviour and have a tendency to act dutifully and measure their performance against external expectations.

Extraverts tend to thrive in jobs involving sales or marketing and are effective as managers, demonstrating inspirational leadership behaviours. They enjoy being with people and are often perceived as having lots of energy. They do well in job interviews and have an easier time than introverts when settling in to a new job. In jobs without social interaction, however, extraverts do not necessarily perform well. They tend to be absent from work more often, potentially because they may miss a workday to attend to the needs of their friends.

People who are high in *agreeableness* are likeable and get along well with others. They are valuable team members who may be effective leaders because they create a fair environment when they are in a leadership role. They lean toward compassion and cooperation rather than suspicion and antagonism toward others. Agreeable people have an optimistic view of human nature, but they are less likely to engage in constructive, change-oriented communication because disagreeing with the status quo may create conflict, which, in most instances, they'd rather not do. Conflict creates change in many cases, however, and changes may bring improvements (unions, government regulations, etc.), so not-so-agreeable personality types are needed in society and in the workplace as well. When hiring a lawyer, what degree of agreeableness would you prefer them to have?

People very high in *neuroticism* experience a number of problems at work, such as relationship difficulties (not getting along with others). They tend to be unhappy in their jobs and have lower levels of career success. If they do achieve managerial positions, they tend to create an unfair working environment. Those scoring high in neuroticism are vulnerable to stress and they often interpret ordinary situations as threatening. People scoring low in this trait tend to be less emotionally reactive and free from persistent negative feelings (although being free from negative feelings does not conclude that they experience many positive feelings).

Cattell 16 personality factors (16 PF) A theory that suggests each of us has a consistent and constant underlying personality.

Thematic Apperception Test (TAT) A personality test that presents a person with a series of images and interprets his or her responses.

Generally, there is a significant link between the Big Five personality traits and job performance in many jobs. Not all five traits predict job performance in all types of jobs, however. Conscientiousness and extraversion are the two Big Five aspects that always correspond to positive job performance, although conscientiousness is more positively linked.[33] Extraversion is negatively associated when it appears to inspire more absenteeism or when combined with low levels of conscientiousness. Much of the current research is on sales and other occupations in which interacting with people is required, so perhaps researching individuals in jobs that require little human interaction would yield different results.

Dmitry Zimin/Shutterstock

Why do you think this woman is riding a bike?

Do we have a consistent and constant underlying personality? According to the **Cattell 16 personality factors (16 PF)**, another widely used model of personality, each of us has a consistent and constant underlying personality. However, the way we see ourselves is influenced by our intelligence, upbringing, and education. These influences may have taught us to suppress or emphasize certain aspects of our personality. If we can understand our basic personality type, this model suggests, we can make better use of our natural strengths and weaknesses. The 16 PF is often used in hiring or in promotion recommendations as well as to improve relationships. Some sample reports that the 16 PF can produce are shown in **Figure 6.4**.[34] Would this person, report (a), be your choice for a position in the human resources department or in the sales department? The 16 PF can also help with analyzing relationships. Would these two people, report (b), work well on a team? Where might there be conflicts?

How can describing pictures give insight to our personality? The **Thematic Apperception Test (TAT)**, developed by Christiana Morgan and Henry

16 PF Profile

(a)

Sten	Factor	Left meaning	Low 1 2 3 4 / Average 5 6 7 / High 8 9 10	Right meaning
4	Warmth (A)	Reserved		Warm
1	Reasoning (B)	Concrete		Abstract
5	Emotional stability (C)	Reactive		Emotionally stable
2	Dominance (E)	Deferential		Dominant
5	Liveliness (F)	Serious		Lively
5	Rule consciousness (G)	Expedient		Rule conscious
4	Social boldness (H)	Shy		Socially bold
5	Sensitivity (I)	Utilitarian		Sensitive
3	Vigilance (L)	Trusting		Vigilant
6	Abstractedness (M)	Grounded		Abstracted
6	Privateness (N)	Forthright		Private
5	Apprehension (O)	Self-assured		Apprehensive
4	Openness to change (Q1)	Traditional		Open to change
6	Self-reliance (Q2)	Group oriented		Self-reliant
5	Perfectionism (Q3)	Tolerates disorder		Perfectionistic
5	Tension (Q4)	Relaxed		Tense

16 PF Profile

(b)

Client 1	Client 2	Factor	Left meaning	Low 1 2 3 4 / Average 5 6 7 / High 8 9 10	Right meaning
4	4	Warmth (A)	Reserved		Warm
1	6	Reasoning (B)	Concrete		Abstract
5	4	Emotional stability (C)	Reactive		Emotionally stable
2	4	Dominance (E)	Deferential		Dominant
5	5	Liveliness (F)	Serious		Lively
5	2	Rule consciousness (G)	Expedient		Rule conscious
4	5	Social boldness (H)	Shy		Socially bold
5	5	Sensitivity (I)	Utilitarian		Sensitive
3	4	Vigilance (L)	Trusting		Vigilant
6	7	Abstractedness (M)	Grounded		Abstracted
6	5	Privateness (N)	Forthright		Private
5	6	Apprehension (O)	Self-assured		Apprehensive
4	4	Openness to change (Q1)	Traditional		Open to change
6	5	Self-reliance (Q2)	Group oriented		Self-reliant
5	7	Perfectionism (Q3)	Tolerates disorder		Perfectionistic
5	4	Tension (Q4)	Relaxed		Tense

Figure 6.4 Sample 16 PF Personality Reports

Legend: ♦ = Client 1, ◊ = Client 2

Murray of Harvard University in the 1930s, is another personality test. Similar to the well-known Rorschach, or inkblot, test, the TAT presents a person with a series of images and interprets his or her responses. However, instead of ambiguous blots of ink, the TAT shows a subject pictures of persons participating in various activities, such as riding a bike or playing a guitar. The subject is asked to make up a story about the individuals in the pictures to explain why those pictured are engaged in particular acts. These stories are supposed to reveal the subject's needs. If the subject explains that the woman riding a bike is trying to get exercise, that subject might carry a need for physical activity. Another subject may suggest that the woman is riding the bike to save money on gasoline. That subject might carry a need for financial stability.

What is the perfect personality tool? While no one model is recognized as the perfect tool, all these personality tests can help to give us a better understanding of the traits that form the foundation of successful leadership.

TEAMWORK

LO7 Explain the advantages of using teams in the workplace and outline the best practices to create and manage effective teams.

The Advantages of Teams in the Workplace

team A group of people linked in a common purpose.

A **team** comprises a group of people linked in a common purpose. Teams are especially appropriate for conducting tasks high in complexity with many interdependent subtasks. A group in itself does not necessarily constitute a team. While different personalities have the potential to create conflict within a team, they can also create unique ideas. Teams normally have members with complementary skills and generate synergy through a coordinated effort that allows each member to maximize their strengths and minimize their weaknesses.

What is the value of using teams in the workplace? In good, working teams there's agreement on the objectives at hand and the best approach to solve a problem.[35] Teammates depend on one another's ideas and efforts to successfully complete tasks. There is a sense of accountability, and members are committed to one another's success.

One product that benefited from team development is the Microsoft Kinect. A breakthrough product for the video gaming industry, the Kinect is an accessory for the Xbox 360 game console. It allows the player to control the system with voice commands and gestures, without holding any controller at all. The Kinect was not designed by a single team—there were seven teams from seven different disciplines. A very small team began exploring ways to track player's body movements. Another small team of computer vision experts from Microsoft Research worked on the key algorithms. Once demos of the team's work began spreading through the company, engineers began to volunteer to come in and work through the night. Kinect sold 8 million units in its first 60 days and holds the Guinness World Record for the fastest-selling consumer electronics device.[36]

Video: CH2MHill: Work Teams

The Challenges of Teams in the Workplace

Do teams always improve the development process? Although teams have been shown to be effective in many situations, some people suggest that teamwork does not always bring more creative output. Research conducted by Barry Staw at the University of California at Berkeley found that when college students were asked to think of business ideas—either individually or in teams—the individuals came up with more ideas than did the teams. In addition, the individuals' ideas were voted as more creative than were the teams' concepts. Staw concluded that collective thinking does not lead to increased creativity and can, in fact, hamper it. One possible reason, Staw proposes, is that team members often want to "fit in" rather than "stand out," and true creativity and original thinking is largely dependent on one's willingness to stand out and take risks.[37]

groupthink A type of narrow-mindedness that can emerge in a group situation if team members have not been carefully selected for a range of skills and attributes.

If a team is not carefully selected, this behaviour of "wanting to fit in" can lead to narrow-mindedness. This is a phenomenon referred to as **groupthink**. People who are from similar backgrounds and sectors of a company tend to have a set of familiar ideas and work with the same set of unspoken assumptions. This may lead to rejecting different ideas without fair examination. The impact of groupthink can be chilling to the creative output of a team, although this challenge can be minimized with thoughtful design in team membership.

Everett Collection

Not every team performs at its best.

In the twenty-first century, another challenge to successful workplace teams is the fact that there is now a wide mix of generations in the workforce (see **Table 6.4**). In fact, it is possible for there to be three or even four generations assigned to a single team. People from separate generations have grown up with social and educational experiences that are so different they take on distinct styles in the workplace.

Table 6.4 Three Generations in the Workplace

Generation	Birth Years	Famous Man	Famous Woman
Baby boomers	1943–1960	Steven Spielberg	Oprah Winfrey
Generation X	1961–1981	Matt Damon	Jennifer Lopez
Millennials	1982–2002	LeBron James	Miley Cyrus

Source: Neil Howe and William Strauss, Millennials Rising: The Next Great Generation *(New York, NY: Vintage, 2000).*

Are generational differences really that significant? In their book *Millennials Rising: The Next Great Generation,*[38] researchers Neil Howe and William Strauss discuss the three dominant generations in the workplace today:

- *Baby boomers.* Those born between 1943 and 1960. The baby boomers are the veterans in the workforce, and many have been with the same company for more than 30 years.
- *Gen Xers.* Those born between 1961 and 1981. Gen Xers, who are known for their independent thinking and hankering for change, are the first generation of workers to value family life over work life.
- *Millennials.* Those born between 1982 and 2002. Like Gen Xers, Millennials want their jobs to accommodate their personal lives, but they also have very high expectations for achievement in their careers.

Millennials, who are now entering college campuses and the workforce, believe in their self-worth and value—whether deserved or not.[39] They feel they have the capability to change the world and the companies they work for. According to Howe and Strauss, members of this generation expect to make their greatest marks on society by using technology to empower the community. Also important to note is that this generation is the primary focus of marketing efforts because they are the biggest youth spenders in history, most often in "co-purchases" with their parents. Teamwork, good behaviour, and citizenship are much more important to Millennials than to earlier generations, and they see equality between different races and genders.

How will this affect business? Strauss predicts that "Young workers will demand that employers adjust to the needs of workers who wish to build careers and families at the same time and lead lower-stress lives than their parents did. Older employees will admire their skills, confidence, and team spirit, but will question their creativity and toughness."[40]

Best Practices for Teams

What kinds of practices set the stage for the best team performance?

Psychologist Mihaly Csikszentmihalyi has extended his idea of flow, discussed earlier, into the team setting. **Group flow** occurs when a group knows how to work together so that each individual member can achieve flow. The characteristics of such a setting are as follows:

group flow A state that occurs when a group knows how to work together so that each individual member can achieve flow.

1. *Creative spatial arrangements.* Pinning ideas on the walls and using large charts to combine ideas from the entire group tend to lead to the open consideration of ideas. Tables are used less because working while standing and moving promotes more discussion and interaction.
2. *Playground design.* This begins with creating a "safe space," agreeing it is safe to bring out ideas that normally one might just keep to him or herself. Often a large number of charts display information inputs, graphs, and the project summary. Wall space can be used to collect results and lists of open topics.
3. *Constant focus on the target group for the product.* At Amazon.com, CEO Jeff Bezos has the nickname "the empty chair" because he often keeps a seat open at team meetings. The empty seat is the most important one in the room as it represents the customer.[41]
4. *Visualization.* Heavy use of visualization and prototyping are used to construct early models. These are then refined to make the models more efficient.

Table 6.5 Belbin's Nine Team Roles

Role	Personality Traits
Plant	Creative and imaginative
Resource investigator	Extraverted and communicative
Coordinator	Mature and confident
Shaper	Challenging and dynamic
Monitor/evaluator	Serious and strategic
Teamworker	Cooperative and diplomatic
Implementer	Disciplined and reliable
Completer/finisher	Painstaking and conscientious
Specialist	Dedicated and self-starting

Adapted from R. M. Belbin, "Team Role Descriptions," Belbin Associates, www.belbin.com/content/page/731/Belbin_Team_Role_Descriptions.pdf. Adapted with permission from Belbin Associates, www.belbin.com.

LO8 Describe the roles that members of effective teams play to help the team achieve its goals.

How do managers create the best teams? Some important aspects a manager should consider in forming a team include the following:

- *Size.* A team that is too large may struggle with cohesiveness. At the same time, a large group can offer the benefit of diverse perspectives.
- *Time frame.* Some teams may be formulated to work on a specific problem or project within a short time frame, while others may work together for longer time periods on everyday tasks.
- *Status.* A team that is formally created by a company may be required to provide progress reports and updates, and it often has access to company resources. Less formal teams may need to take initiative in maintaining lines of communication.

According to business writer and theorist R. M. Belbin, effective teams comprise people with diverse skills, talents, and points of view. Team members' respective skills and talents should complement one another so the team can perform at an optimum level. For example, what might happen if everyone on a team is extremely creative yet inexperienced in effective time management? What if five of six team members are all aggressive leaders? Clearly, a balance of people who embody different team roles is key in the success of a team.

Simulation: Team Management

Belbin's model of nine team roles is outlined in **Table 6.5**. Considering both these roles and the personality traits of potential members can be helpful when designing teams.

cross-functional teams Teams where members are selected across a range of critical functional divisions of a business.

virtual teams Teams that comprise members located in different physical locations but working together to achieve a goal.

What are cross-functional teams? Traditionally, team members were often chosen from the same department, all reporting to a common supervisor. But today's markets demand such quick response and ability to adapt to changing conditions that a new model is emerging: cross-functional teams. In a **cross-functional team**, members are selected across a range of critical functional divisions of a business. For example, in 2004 the LEGO Group was near bankruptcy.[42] Investments in the LEGO theme parks had failed, and some products like Clikits had struggled in the marketplace. The management created a cross-functional team named the Executive Innovation Governance Group. It consisted of employees who could contribute in product innovation, pricing, business processes, marketing, and community building. The group ushered through modifications to existing product lines as well as new products, such as a series of LEGO board games, which was a new product category for LEGO. In 2010, during a declining toy market overall, LEGO saw a 30 percent increase in revenues.

Niels Poulsen DK/Alamy

A cross-functional team can be thanked for saving the LEGO Group from demise. By bringing together employees from many different functional areas, the company was able to modify existing product lines as well as create entirely new ones.

How might technology affect the design of teams? In a **virtual team**, members are located in different physical locations but work together to achieve a goal. The need for virtual teams grows out of the increased globalization of business. Familiar tools such as conference calls and email have evolved to include videoconferencing and live broadcasting of key meetings and events over the Web. Webcasts can now support interactive participation from the viewing audience.

In real time, audience members can ask questions, exchange their own electronic files with the group, and record the presentation for repeated viewing. Web conferencing software such as WebEx and Microsoft Office Live Meeting allow participants in any geographic location to brainstorm together in real time on a common "virtual whiteboard," to watch demos and presentations live, and to record and annotate these discussions for later playback.

The promise of much higher-speed Internet transfer is also being explored. Many colleges and universities are using virtual teams for student competitions whereby teams are created across the globe and communicate and compete in the virtual world. In 2011, new technology made it possible for Queen's University in Kingston, Ontario, to welcome its first virtual class of executive MBA students from across Canada and Bermuda, delivering Canada's most respected MBA program directly to their desktops.[43] Loyalist College in Belleville, Ontario, has been using Second Life (an online virtual world in which users interact through avatars) to meet and teach students in the virtual world. Students in the customs and immigration program experience working as a border guard virtually because security issues have hampered their placement options.[44] This process helps students learn early on that distance does not have to keep people from communicating and working well together. The potential to connect students and workers from many parts of the world may lead to exciting new possibilities for synergy.

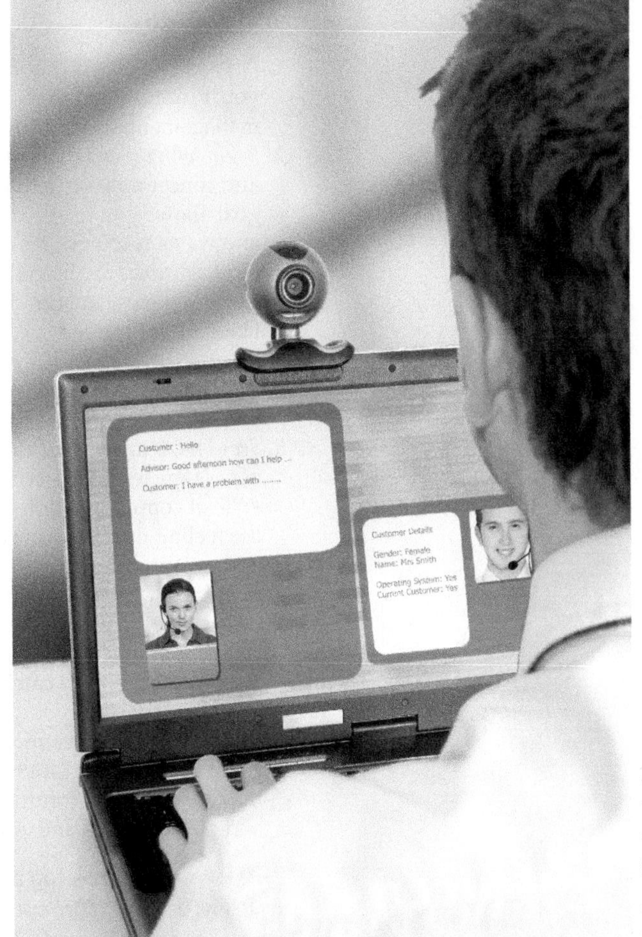

Andresr/Shutterstock

Using Web conferencing software, teams with people in various countries can work together seamlessly.

The best practices for creating strong virtual teams are emerging as virtual teams become a more accepted and useful teaming solution.[45] Most successful virtual teams include some face-to-face meeting time periodically. Very few virtual teams are 100 percent virtual. Although technology allows teams to communicate without ever meeting face to face, it is still important to have the group occasionally meet with one another in the same space to build social connections. Keeping the team connected is a key priority to a virtual team, and it can be difficult to keep contacts strong from a distance. There can be communication delays from working across time zones or using email as a primary mode of communication. Establishing team rules, such as agreeing to respond to email messages within a certain window of time or initiating global office hours, can minimize these problems. Managing a virtual team means managing the whole spectrum of communication strategies and project management techniques as well as human and social processes in ways that support the team.

Video: Mastering Team and Interpersonal Communication – Hewlett Packard

Your Role on a Team

LO9 Explain what you can do to become a more valuable team member.

How can I be a valued team player? It is important to begin now to build the skills that will make you successful in team settings. As we have seen, the best teams are carefully planned and selected and can be the place where some of the most exciting and innovative work in the company is happening. Preparing yourself to contribute in a team setting may be the most important thing you can do to increase your value to an organization, no matter what position you hold.

What habits will give me the best chance to contribute to a team? There are many skills that you can build to enhance your success as a member of a team. One model that organizes these skills is the **Seven Habits model** developed by famed

Seven Habits model A model developed by Stephen Covey that lists the seven habits that successful people exhibits.

management author Stephen Covey.[46] He has found that there are seven habits of behaviour exhibited by successful people:

1. *Be proactive.* This is the ability to control your environment rather than have it control you. Proactive team members are constantly looking "down the road" in terms of time management, work, and obstacles coming that may impede the success of a project.
2. *Begin with the end in mind.* This means that you are able to see the desired outcome and concentrate on activities that help achieve it. Staying focused on the ultimate goal allows you to avoid taking the team in directions that will cause divisiveness and waste resources and energy.
3. *Put first things first.* This skill works together with the second habit in pushing you toward success in your team role. Manage your time and energy so that the required tasks are prioritized.
4. *Think win-win.* This is the most important aspect of interpersonal leadership because most achievements are based on cooperative effort; therefore, the aim needs to be win-win solutions for all.
5. *Seek first to understand and then to be understood.* In communicating with other members of the team, it is critical to develop and maintain positive relationships. This style of communication recommends listening and working to give your teammates the feeling they have been heard as key to your own success in being understood and contributing.
6. *Synergize.* This is the habit of creative cooperation—the principle that collaboration often achieves more than could be achieved by individuals working independently toward attaining a purpose.
7. *Sharpen the saw.* This catch phrase comes from the metaphor of chopping down a tree. If you are constantly sawing and never take time to stop and sharpen the saw, you'll feel as if you're investing tremendous energy, but the results will not be what they could be if you just stopped to sharpen the saw first. Strong team contributors avoid the work mode of continually reacting to crises. Instead, they take time to step back and develop skills and analyze the task at hand so that they can work more efficiently.

If you work to develop and use these habits in your role on teams, you will find that your teams become more successful—and that you are in demand for the next team.

Off the **Mark**

Dream Team or Nightmare?

If we look at Michael Eisner, the former Disney chief executive officer (CEO), we see that for his first 10 years at Disney (Research), he and chief operating officer (COO) Frank Wells were a great team. Under their guidance, Disney revived its famous animation tradition and the movie business prospered. Eisner and Wells not only saved a legendary company, but they also made shareholders rich. When Wells died, Eisner then formed one of the most famously ill-fated teams in recent history.[47]

In 1995, Michael Ovitz—one of Hollywood's most powerful talent agents and the founder of Creative Artists Agency—was brought on as Disney president under CEO and board chair Michael Eisner. Ovitz quickly grew frustrated with his role and vague definition of duties.[48] After a tumultuous 14 months as Disney's second-in-command, he was dismissed by Eisner. Disney shareholders later sued Eisner and Disney's board of directors for awarding Ovitz roughly US$140 million in severance. The 2005 trial lasted three months, with the judge ruling that Eisner and the other directors properly carried out their fiduciary duties. Although Disney won, the case aired some embarrassing testimony about the "Machiavellian atmosphere inside the Magic Kingdom."[49] Eisner stepped down as CEO that same year.

In analyzing what went wrong, the overriding answer is conflicting business and personal agendas. Ovitz wanted to put big money into projects that Eisner dismissed as "off strategy," such as buying a National Football League franchise. Eisner also did not approve of Ovitz spending US$2 million renovating his own office. This team failure cost Disney enormously—in both money and reputation.[50]

Discussion Questions

1. **What steps can companies take to ensure they don't hire someone who won't work well with the team?**
2. **Does thinking differently mean two people won't get along? Why or why not?**
3. **How much time and money did Disney lose over this situation?**

CHAPTER SYNOPSIS

LO1 Describe several ways that you can improve your own level of motivation. *(pp. 117–119)*

- *Avoid negative experiences and people.* Instead, find other motivated, positive people to affiliate with.
- *Become passionate about your mission.* Enthusiasm can be a powerful personal motivator because it keeps you energized.
- *Feel good about yourself.* Listening to self-help CDs, reading material on the subject, or meeting with a counsellor or life coach might be just what you need to start a successful life.
- *Give yourself a reward.* **Personal motivation** comes from within, and no one can give you the motivation you need to start, work on, or complete a project. The motivation itself depends on the reward and whether it satisfies your needs or wants.

LO2 Explain the benefits of having engaged employees and the problems organizations face when employees are not engaged. *(pp. 119–120)*

An **engaged employee** is one who is fully involved in and enthusiastic about his or her work, and thus will act in a way that furthers the organization's interests. Both employers and employees benefit from a motivated workforce. Employers find workers are more productive, more creative, and have much better retention levels when care is taken to provide a motivating environment and tasks. Employees often spend the majority of their waking day at their jobs, and their quality of life and overall happiness are enhanced when they feel excited about the work they contribute. The Global Workforce Study found that firms with the highest percentage of engaged employees collectively increased operating income by 19 percent and earnings per share by 28 percent year to year, so highly engaged employees improve productivity for the company. Not only does employee disengagement hurt companies financially, but it may also lead to poor company reputation, poor customer service, and lower quality output.

LO3 Describe the intricacies of Maslow's hierarchy of needs, McClelland's "three needs" theory, and Herzberg's motivator–hygiene theory. *(pp. 120–123)*

Maslow's hierarchy of needs suggests that our primary needs are met first before our higher-level needs are addressed.

McClelland's "three needs" theory suggests there are three main motivators: (1) the need for achievement (to accomplish something difficult on your own), (2) the need for affiliation (to form close personal relationships), and (3) the need for power (to be able to control the behaviour of others).

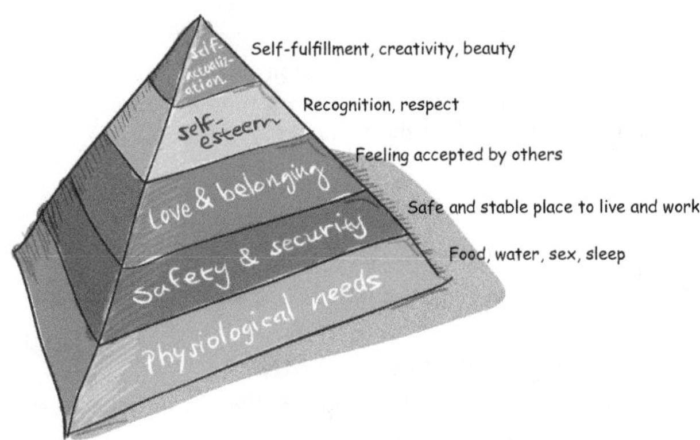

Maslow's Hierarchy of Needs

Herzberg's motivator–hygiene theory suggests that two factors influence a person's motivation: hygiene factors (which cause job dissatisfaction) and motivation factors (which cause job satisfaction).

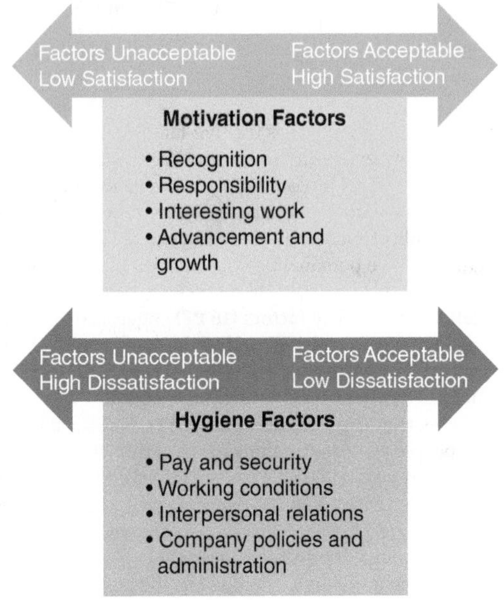

Herzberg's Motivator–Hygiene Theory

LO4 Distinguish between extrinsic and intrinsic motivators. *(pp. 123–124)*

In the workplace, managers can control some external motivating factors. These motivators, called **extrinsic motivators**, include such things as pay, promotion, and verbal praise. Other factors, called **intrinsic motivators**, are outside the set of factors under a manager's control because they are internal to each individual employee.

LO5 Summarize the implications of Theory X, Theory Y, Theory Z, and the Vroom models. *(pp. 124–128)*

McGregor's Theory X suggests that people inherently dislike work and want to avoid it. **Theory X management** proposes that employees have to be coerced and controlled by management to be productive. This leads to an authoritarian, hardline management style.

In contrast, **McGregor's Theory Y** suggests that people view work as being as natural as playing and resting. People are naturally motivated and will direct themselves to work for the aims of the organization if they are satisfied with their jobs. **Theory Y management** assumes that, on average, people will accept and seek out responsibility. Such managers have a softer style of management that involves the participation of many.

Theory Z management is a combination of American and Japanese management philosophies characterized by long-term employment security, consensual decision making, and slow evaluation and promotion procedures, with an emphasis on individual responsibility within a group context.

Vroom's expectancy theory suggests an individual's motivation in any given situation can be described by the relationship among three psychological forces, illustrated in the following formula:

Motivation = Expectancy × Instrumentality × Valence

The Vroom formula can be used to analyze factors including how satisfied employees are at their jobs, how likely it is they will remain at their jobs, and how hard they will work at their jobs.

LO6 Describe the various tools employers can use to assess personality traits and explain how this knowledge can improve employee satisfaction and productivity. *(pp. 128–131)*

The **Big Five**, also referred to as the five-factor model, categorizes most human personality traits into five broad dimensions and then assigns people a score for each dimension: openness, conscientiousness, extraversion, agreeableness, and neuroticism (emotional stability). Generally, there is a significant link between the Big Five personality traits and job performance in many jobs.

Cattell 16 personality factors (16 PF) suggests that each of us has a consistent and constant underlying personality. If we can understand our basic personality type, this model suggests, we can make better use of our natural strengths and weaknesses.

The **Thematic Apperception Test (TAT)** shows a subject pictures of people participating in various activities, such as riding a bike or playing a guitar. The subject is asked to make up a story about the individuals in the pictures to explain why those pictured are engaged in the particular acts shown. These stories are supposed to reveal the subject's needs.

While no one model is recognized as the perfect tool, all these personality tests can help give us a better understanding of the traits that form the foundation of successful leadership. Personality assessment tools can help employers determine whether a candidate will "fit" the corporate culture and work well with the team. Personality assessments can help leaders determine their personality tendencies; once identified, they can consciously adjust their leadership style as the situation dictates.

LO7 Explain the advantages of using teams in the workplace and outline the best practices to create and manage effective teams. *(pp. 132–133)*

A **team** comprises a group of people linked in a common purpose. Teams are especially appropriate for conducting tasks high in complexity with many interdependent subtasks. In good, working teams there's agreement on the objectives at hand and the best approach to solve a problem. Teammates depend on one another's ideas and efforts to successfully complete tasks. There is a sense of accountability, and members are committed to one another's success.

Group flow occurs when a group knows how to work together so that each individual member can achieve flow. Some important aspects a manager should consider in forming a team include the following:

- *Size.* A team that is too large may struggle with cohesiveness. At the same time, a large group can offer the benefit of diverse perspectives.
- *Time frame.* Some teams may be formulated to work on a specific problem or project within a short time frame, while others may work together for longer time periods on everyday tasks.
- *Status.* A team that is formally created by a company may be required to provide progress reports and updates, and it often has access to company resources. Less formal teams may need to take initiative in maintaining lines of communication.

Effective teams comprise people with diverse skills, talents, and points of view. Team members' respective skills and talents should complement one another so the team can perform at an optimum level.

LO8 Describe the roles that members of effective teams play to help the team achieve its goals. *(pp. 134–135)*

Belbin's Nine Team Roles

Role	Personality Traits
Plant	Creative and imaginative
Resource investigator	Extraverted and communicative
Coordinator	Mature and confident
Shaper	Challenging and dynamic
Monitor evaluator	Serious and strategic
Teamworker	Cooperative and diplomatic
Implementer	Disciplined and reliable
Completer finisher	Painstaking and conscientious
Specialist	Dedicated and self-starting

LO9 Explain what you can do to become a more valuable team member. *(pp. 135–136)*

There are many skills that you can develop to enhance your success as a member of a team. One way to organize these skills is the **Seven Habits model** developed by famed management author Stephen Covey. He has found that successful people exhibit the following seven habits of behaviour:

1. Be proactive.
2. Begin with the end in mind.
3. Put first things first.
4. Think win-win.
5. Seek first to understand and then to be understood.
6. Synergize.
7. Sharpen the saw.

Work to develop and use these habits in your role on teams and you will find that your teams become more successful—and that you are in demand for the next team.

MyBizLab Study, practise, and explore real business situations with these helpful resources:

- **Interactive Lesson Presentations:** Work through interactive presentations and assessments to test your knowledge of business concepts.
- **Study Plan:** Check your understanding of chapter concepts with self-study quizzes.
- **Dynamic Study Modules:** Work through adaptive study modules on your computer, tablet, or mobile device.
- **Simulations:** Practise decision-making in simulated business environments.

KEY TERMS

Big Five *(p. 128)*
Cattell 16 personality factors (16 PF) *(p. 130)*
cross-functional teams *(p. 134)*
engaged employee *(p. 119)*
equity theory *(p. 126)*
extrinsic motivators *(p. 123)*
flow state *(p. 119)*
group flow *(p. 133)*
groupthink *(p. 132)*
Hawthorne effect *(p. 127)*
Herzberg's motivator-hygiene theory *(p. 122)*
industrial psychology *(p. 127)*
intrinsic motivators *(p. 123)*
management by objectives (MBO) *(p. 126)*
Maslow's hierarchy of needs *(p. 121)*
McClelland's "three needs" theory *(p. 122)*
McGregor's Theory X *(p. 124)*
McGregor's Theory Y *(p. 125)*
organizational psychology *(p. 119)*
participative management and empowerment *(p. 126)*
personal motivation *(p. 118)*
scientific management *(p. 127)*
Seven Habits model *(p. 135)*
strength-based management *(p. 127)*
team *(p. 132)*
Thematic Apperception Test (TAT) *(p. 130)*
Theory X management *(p. 125)*
Theory Y management *(p. 125)*
Theory Z *(p. 125)*
Theory Z management *(p. 125)*
virtual teams *(p. 134)*
Vroom's expectancy theory *(p. 125)*

CRITICAL THINKING QUESTIONS

1. What factors are the most important to creating a team that works efficiently together? What problems have you seen in your own academic career when working in group settings, and how could they be prevented?
2. Are there personality differences between genders? Between generations? Explain your answers.
3. Stephen Covey's Seven Habits model is focused on making you a more successful, efficient person. What impact would these seven habits have on your relationships with your friends and family?

TEAM TIME

Forming a Successful Team

A shoe retailer's sales and earnings have a history of lagging during the spring and summer months. The company wants to reverse this trend by appealing to young people, a rapidly growing consumer base with increasing amounts of disposable income. The company has decided to give one team almost unlimited resources and freedom to develop a flip-flop sandal for modern youth. You need to apply the principles of best practices in team formation to determine the personalities and strengths of each member and assign roles in which the members will be motivated and contribute to the goal.

PROCESS

Step 1. Break up into teams of three or four individuals.
Step 2. Begin by deciding what tool you will use to evaluate each member for personality traits, strengths, and weaknesses.
Step 3. Develop a strategy for assessing what work needs to be done and then how your team will assign appropriate responsibilities to each member.
Step 4. How will you evaluate the level of motivation and creativity for the team? What changes can be made if the team's performance is not adequate?
Step 5. Present your findings to the class for discussion.

CONCLUSION

Teamwork can lead to creative, exciting results, but only if the team is designed and managed well. It takes a combination of technical skills, emotional intelligence, and leadership to create a team that motivates people to contribute and thrive.

ETHICS AND RESPONSIBILITY

Ethics in Teamwork

Being a member of a team means that you are accountable for your actions and the actions of your fellow teammates. Review the following scenario.

SCENARIO

Imagine you work at an advertising firm. You're on a team that is developing an ad campaign proposal for a chain of fitness centres. The firm has been struggling and needs your team to land this account. At a meeting, one of your teammates reveals that he has hacked into a competing firm's network and has a draft of its proposal for the same account. Your teammate wants to steal the idea and use it in your team's proposal. Most of your teammates agree with this idea, but you think it is unethical.

DISCUSSION QUESTIONS

1. How would you handle this situation? Would you voice your objection or go along with the team?
2. If you decide to voice your objection, do you address the entire team or speak to members individually? Why?
3. How would you reconcile your role as a loyal employee and team player with your need to uphold ethical standards?

CLOSING CASE

Toyota Teamwork and the Prius

If you watch a movie set in the future, you may see cars that are fuelled by the sun, water, or even garbage. Those scenarios seemed improbable, and even laughable, 10 years ago, but the birth of the Toyota Prius has changed the way we think about alternative power for vehicles. When the Prius hit the market in 2000, it became the car of the future: a gasoline-electric hybrid that could be purchased at the consumer level. Creating this futuristic car was no easy feat. The Toyota Prius design team realized early on that it was on its own. "We had to invent something completely original," states Satoshi Ogiso, the team's chief power train engineer. "We'd have to build it from scratch, blueprint and all."[51] The team knew it would take countless hours and strong teamwork to create this innovative piece of machinery.

The Prius might not have existed were it not for the tenacity of its engineering team. For years Toyota had toyed with idea of creating a car with a gasoline-electric motor. However, the idea was a continuous source of conflict. Engineers believed that this type of car would be the solution to the world's problem with carbon emissions. The executives saw other issues. They believed that the premium price, about US$25 000, would not be worth it to their average consumer. Akihiro Wada, Toyota's executive vice-president, sided with the engineers. He asked the team to develop a concept model of the Prius for the 1995 Toyota Motor Show. It was a lofty goal to achieve, especially in only 12 months.

Wada's decision to listen to the engineers instead of the executives may be unusual in most corporate settings, but it is a common practice at Toyota. In fact, in Toyota's list of guiding principles, "foster a corporate culture that enhances individual creativity and teamwork value, while honouring mutual trust and respect between labour and management" is listed as number five.[52] The confidence Wada showed in his design team provided the motivation the team needed to have the concept model ready on time. Impressed with the results, Toyota president Hiroshi Okuda put the Prius into production.

The original 10-person Prius design team quickly grew to thousands. The team encountered many problems while trying to turn a concept into a fully functional product. The battery was the main issue. The team had to come up with a way to make a battery that was big enough to power a car engine but not so big that it would overheat. The production of the engine became an ongoing process of trial and error. The first prototype wouldn't even start. The second only went 330 feet (100 metres) before puttering to a stop. However, the constant stream of failures and setbacks did not thwart the design team's mission. After gathering vital input from all engineers involved and testing meticulously for months, all the design kinks were worked out. In October 1997, Toyota revealed the Prius: a five-passenger car that could get 66 miles per gallon (almost 4 litres per 100 kilometres).

The car was not an immediate success during its first few years on the market. However, after celebrities such as Leonardo DiCaprio and Cameron Diaz purchased the Prius, sales gained tremendous momentum. "It's the hottest car we've ever had," stated Jim Press, president of Toyota Motor North America.[53] The Prius design team proved it could lower carbon emissions while raising Toyota's sales. The team's hard work and innovation even prompted *Time* magazine to name it "Heroes of the Environment."

DISCUSSION QUESTIONS

1. Why do you think the Toyota Prius design team was so motivated to create the car? What needs were being fulfilled in the development and production process? Where do you think it would fall in Herzberg's motivator–hygiene model of the workplace?
2. Review Toyota's guiding principle above. What style of leadership does this principle encourage?
3. Since the design of the Toyota Prius was completely new to all members of the design team, how do you think the phenomenon of groupthink affected the process? Why do you think the Toyota Prius design team was ultimately successful?

7 Human Resource Management

Rafal Olechowski/Shutterstock

LEARNING OBJECTIVES

After studying this chapter, you should be able to:

- **LO1** Define human resource management (HRM) and discuss how the functions of HRM support an organization. (pp. 143–144)
- **LO2** Explain how organizations determine and plan for human resource needs. (pp. 144–145)
- **LO3** Describe some of the methods used and issues faced by companies when recruiting, selecting, and hiring employees. (pp. 145–149)
- **LO4** Discuss some of the ways employees are trained and how performance can be evaluated. (pp. 150–153)
- **LO5** Describe how employees can be compensated and some of the different kinds of work schedule arrangements that are used to meet the needs of employees and the company. (pp. 153–158)
- **LO6** Explain how employees transition through a company over time by way of promotions, transfers, retirement, and termination. (pp. 158–161)
- **LO7** Identify the ways in which Canada's demographics are changing and how this affects the workforce. (pp. 161–164)
- **LO8** Outline the objectives of unions and the process of collective bargaining. (pp. 164–167)
- **LO9** Describe some of the key legislation regulating the hiring, compensating, and managing of employees in today's workplace. (pp. 167–168)

OPENING DISCUSSION: EMPLOYEE RETENTION

How Can Employers Keep Their Top Performers?

Employees who produce quality work and enhance a company's image are prized assets to any organization. Employers want to keep their top performers because the costs of replacing them are high. When experienced employees leave a company, they take valuable skills and knowledge with them, possibly to a competing company, and are usually replaced with new employees who require significant training and time before they become productive. Training and time cost the company money, and if the new employee is not successful in the job role, the costs incurred by the company are even greater. Due to Canada's shrinking available workforce (because of an aging population) and talent mismatch (job seekers skilled in areas where jobs are not available), companies may not only have difficulty finding right-fit employees, but are also in continuous competition to hire these employees before their competitors do. Employers may have a difficult time retaining top-performing employees if they don't understand what employees want. Further, managers do not always motivate employees in a fashion that aids retention. Studies repeatedly show that the number-one reason employees choose to stay at or leave their current employer is their relationship with their supervisor or manager.[1] Employers need to offer incentives that motivate and encourage employees to stay with the company.

One company that has successfully created a working environment that engages employees and supports the creative experience is SAS, the world's largest privately held software company, with more than 12 000 employees in 400 offices worldwide.[2] By providing employees amenities such as health care, subsidized childcare, a recreation and fitness centre, numerous wellness programs, flexible work hours, free car parking, a religious observance room, profitsharing, tuition subsidies, and a number of other wonderful benefits, the company boasts one of the lowest employee turnover rates in the industry: 2.6 percent, while the info-tech industry average is 22 percent.[3] The company welcomes employees to provide confidential feedback on their manager's performance and each year contracts independent consultants to conduct confidential employee satisfaction and engagement surveys.

Selected multiple times over the past few years as one of *Fortune*'s 100 Best Companies to Work for,[4] SAS believes that happy, healthy employees drive the innovation that keeps SAS in a leadership position among business analytics vendors; such an atmosphere is in part thanks to the policies of SAS CEO Jim Goodnight. According to Goodnight, SAS fosters a creative environment by[5]

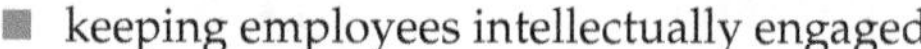

- keeping employees intellectually engaged
- removing distractions so employees can do their best work
- making managers responsible for sparking creativity
- eliminating the arbitrary distinctions between administrative "suits" and more abstract "creatives"
- engaging customers as creative partners

Andres Rodriguez/Alamy

In addition to encouraging strong professional lives, SAS supports its employees in their private lives, too. "The corporate philosophy is, if your fifth grader is in his first school play, you should be there to see it," says Goodnight.[6] Such a philosophy has placed SAS on *Working Mother* magazine's list of best companies multiple times.

DISCUSSION QUESTIONS

1. What would make you want to quit your job?
2. Besides the costs involved in hiring and training a new employee, what other losses might a company incur when a new employee does not work out and is asked to leave?
3. What do you think is the biggest motivator for most employees: money, interesting work, recognition on the job (employee of the month), or something else? Which incentives most appeal to you?

HIRING FOR OPTIMAL ORGANIZATIONAL PERFORMANCE

LO1 Define human resource management (HRM) and discuss how the functions of HRM support an organization.

The Importance of Managing Human Resources

Why are people considered valuable company resources? When you think about the resources required to run a business, you probably think about money, space, equipment, supplies, and so on. Although financial and material resources are important, the resource often taken for granted but that is arguably the most important is the "human" resource—or people. People are valuable to a company because they provide the ideas, creativity, knowledge, and ingenuity that make a business run. An organization can have all the money and materials in the world, but without the right people doing the right things it will not be successful.

What is human resource management? **Human resources (HR)**—the people in an organization—need to be managed just as carefully as the material and financial resources of a business. **Human resource management (HRM)** is the organizational function that deals with the people in the business, from the executives and the managers to the front-line production, sales, and administrative staff. HRM aims to ensure that the organization is correctly staffed at all times by the right number of employees with the right skills required to meet company goals. Proper management of human assets builds value in the company and ensures time and money are not wasted.

What are the functions of HRM? **HRM functions** encompass every aspect of the "human" in a business, including planning, recruiting, selecting and hiring, training, evaluating, compensating, scheduling, motivating, and transitioning employees. HRM also oversees employee–management relations and must always work to ensure that the company operates within the law (see **Figure 7.1**). HRM works through the many challenges in today's society, such as diversity issues, work and lifestyle preferences, and global business considerations. Human resource managers work with people, but they are also deeply involved in planning, record keeping, and other administrative duties. In recent years, HRM has become more focused on aligning its core responsibilities with the organization's vision, goals, and strategies for success. This alignment will allow HRM to take advantage of applicants' unique qualifications, which will enable it to provide strategic value to the company and the company's customers. Most HRM functions are shared between the professional human resource manager and the other managers.

What is the purpose of an HR department? **The human resources department**, working with other department managers, is responsible for the people in an organization and helps to maximize organizational productivity by optimizing the effectiveness of employees. A company may create an HR department to establish, develop, maintain,

human resources (HR) The people in an organization; they need to be managed just as carefully as the material and financial resources of a business.

human resource management (HRM) The organizational function that deals with the people in the business, from the executives and the managers to the front-line production, sales, and administrative staff.

HRM functions Encompass every aspect of the "human" in a business, including planning, recruiting, selecting and hiring, training, evaluating, compensating, scheduling, motivating, and transitioning employees. HRM also oversees employee–management relations and must always work to ensure that the company operates within the law.

human resources department Working with other department managers, this department is responsible for the people in the organization and helps to maximize organizational productivity by optimizing the effectiveness of employees.

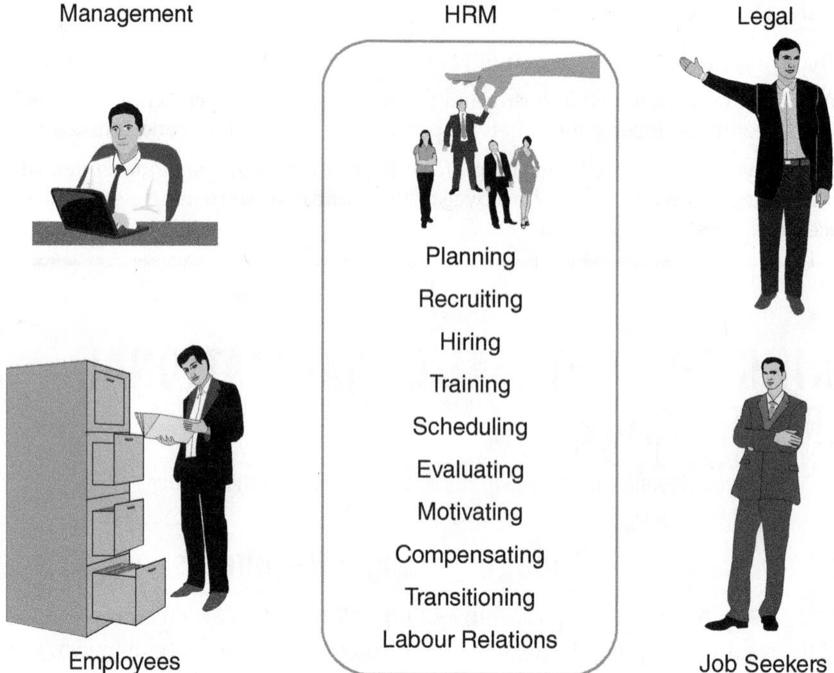

Figure 7.1 The Functions of Human Resource Management

and communicate company policies throughout the organization or to facilitate communication between management and employees. This is fairly easy to do in small companies and may not require a dedicated department; however, for large companies a department specializing in human resource functions and solutions is required.

The HR department represents employees and offers them advice while keeping the overall best interests of the company in mind. An HR department

- develops hiring plans and recruiting policies
- handles compensation and salary administration
- handles employee relations, transitions, contracts, performance reviews, benefits, and pension plans
- develops official documentation, workplace ethics and codes of conduct, employee handbooks, employee training programs, award/reward programs, and community connections[7]

Determining and Planning Human Resource Needs

LO2 Explain how organizations determine and plan for human resource needs.

Why is it important for a company to plan for its human resource needs?

human resource planning The creation of a strategy for meeting future human resource needs within an organization.

When an entrepreneur starts up a business, he or she may initially serve as the company's chief executive officer and financial manager, as well as the sales executive and marketing director. As a business expands, new people are brought into the organization. At that point, the owner may still serve as the HR director, hiring, firing, and realigning employees to fill the growing needs of the expanding business. Although keeping track of HR needs at small businesses can be fairly simple, companies that add employees and continue to grow require more specific HR planning. **Human resource planning** is creating a strategy for meeting future human resource needs within an organization. Poor staff planning can be costly. Being overstaffed burdens a company with the unnecessary expense of maintaining salaries, benefits, and training for surplus employees. But an understaffed organization can lead to loss of sales and competitiveness if customer needs are not met. Planning staffing needs therefore involves (1) assessing the supply of and demand for current and future employee resources and (2) evaluating job requirements.

How does a company determine how many employees it needs? First, managers need to determine what jobs are required within the organization so that the company can meet its organizational goals. For instance, a company may be growing and additional jobs need to be created for the company to maintain quality standards or increase production levels. Managers review trends in the company's human resource usage over time, economic trends that may affect the supply of available workers, trends that may increase or decrease possible future sales revenues, and future organizational goals before making any decisions about whether an increase or decrease in the number of employees is required. Many organizations use an **employee information system (EIS)** to create a workforce profile, in which a company can record and track their employees' skills and abilities, creating a "personnel inventory." Then, when a promotion, special project, or transfer position is available, the EIS can be searched to find an internal candidate who possesses the skills required to do the job. The skills inventory may include information such as an employee's education, training, experience, specialized skills, and current and previous positions held within the company.

employee information system (EIS) Creates a workforce profile, in which a company can record and track employee skills and abilities to generate a "personnel inventory."

Forecasting—an essential part of HR planning—is the process of determining the future demand for employees as well as the future supply of employees. Forecasting demand for employees is based on several factors, such as predicted sales of the company's goods or services, current workforce skill level, the effect of technology changes on staff needs, and changes in employment practices (such as using more or less temporary staff). In addition, staffing changes expected through normal turnover, retirement, and any planned reassignments are taken into consideration. Forecasting internal supply means tracking the number of current employees who will be available to fill various jobs at some future time. Forecasting external supply means examining labour market trends. If forecasting indicates an imbalance between the supply and demand for employees, further action must be taken. Such actions may include recruitment, training, retraining, labour reductions, or changes in workforce utilization.

forecasting The process of determining the future demand for employees as well as the future supply of employees.

Video: Holiday Jobs: Where to Find Them

How do companies identify the skills needed to perform a particular job? Human resource planners analyze the tasks being performed in specific jobs throughout the organization. A **job analysis** identifies and defines in detail the particular duties and requirements of the tasks and responsibilities an employee is required to perform. In a job analysis, each task is defined by a **job description**, a formal statement summarizing what the employee will do in that job role. It includes the job responsibilities, the conditions under which the job will be performed, and the job's relationship to other functions in the organization. Job descriptions are important because they define job objectives used later in performance appraisals. They also can become a part of the legal contract between the employee and the employer. To assist in recruiting the right person to fulfill the job's requirements, job specifications are also defined during the job analysis. **Job specifications** are the skills, education, experience, and personal attributes that candidates need to possess to successfully fulfill the job role. **Figure 7.2** shows a sample job description and job specifications.

job analysis Identifies and defines in detail the particular duties and requirements of the tasks and responsibilities an employee is required to perform.

job description A formal statement summarizing what the employee will do in that job role. It includes the job responsibilities, the conditions under which the job will be performed, and the job's relationship to other functions in the organization.

job specifications The skills, education, experience, and personal attributes that candidates need to possess to successfully fulfill the job role.

Recruiting

LO3 Describe some of the methods used and issues faced by companies when recruiting, selecting, and hiring employees.

What is the recruitment process? Finding and attracting capable applicants for employment depends on a well-devised recruiting plan. The **recruitment process** provides the organization with a pool of potentially qualified job candidates from which thoughtful selection can be made to fill vacancies. The recruitment process begins when new recruits are sought and ends when their applications are submitted. Usually, the process starts when a manager initiates an employee requisition for a specific vacancy or an anticipated vacancy. **Internal recruiting**—filling job vacancies with existing employees from within the business—is the first choice of many companies. Often, companies post job openings on the company intranet, staff notice boards, in-house newsletters, and in staff meetings. Internal recruitment has several

recruitment process Provides the organization with a pool of potentially qualified job candidates from which thoughtful selection can be made to fill vacancies.

internal recruiting The process of filling job vacancies with existing employees from within the business.

Company: Nelson Wireless	
Position title: Marketing manager	
(a) Job description	**(b) Job specifications**
Join a team of marketing professionals focused on mobile technologies in the consumer market segment. The marketing manager is responsible for coordinating and/or implementing marketing projects designed for the consumer market segment. Working in cooperation with the sales team, product offers, and other headquarters marketing teams, the marketing manager will coordinate public relations projects and other promotional activities to drive Nelson Wireless brand awareness and product demand and generate consumer purchases. The marketing manager will provide strategic oversight for regional-level industry events, and be responsible for planning and executing customer events. The marketing manager will be responsible for coordinating budgets and timelines, maintaining accurate records of expenditures, and compiling reports of activity results. Additionally, he/she will be responsible for managing a team of 8-10 marketing associates. The marketing manager role will also include administrative elements such as invoice processing, event scheduling, and maintenance of a promotional calendar.	• College degree required with emphasis in marketing, business administration, or communications preferred • 3+ years marketing/communications experience required • Excellent demonstrated verbal and written communication skills • Demonstrated experience in event execution • Demonstrated ability to coordinate cooperative working relationships across multiple parties • Ability to work well under pressure • Extremely well organized, strong project management and time management skills, and strong ability to multitask • Proven ability to operate in a fast-paced, high-growth professional environment

Figure 7.2 Sample (a) Job Description and (b) Job Specifications

advantages. It tends to be a morale booster for employees because they know that the company has an interest in promoting their own. And because the employer and employee have established a working relationship, there is a reduced risk of selecting an inappropriate candidate for the desired position. Finally, choosing from within is potentially quicker and less costly because it reduces costs associated with outside recruiting and shortens the length of training time.

However, there are disadvantages to not considering outside sources. This includes the possibility of not getting the best candidate because of a limited search process. In addition, another internal vacancy is created that must be subsequently filled. Moreover, relying on internal employees may discourage new perspectives and ideas and eventually make the business resistant to change. As a result, businesses also rely on external recruiting to meet staffing needs. **External recruiting** looks outside the business to fill vacancies using various resources and methods (see **Figure 7.3**).

external recruiting Looking outside the business to fill vacancies using various resources and methods.

employment agencies Agencies that help with external recruiting by providing a screened pool of candidates, which reduces the hiring company's administrative burden of recruitment.

Depending on the type of position, companies may try to recruit candidates by posting ads in local newspapers, on Internet job sites, or in specialized trade magazines. These can be advantageous methods because they are inexpensive and reach a wide audience. For more specialized positions, some companies use employment agencies or recruitment consultants. **Employment agencies**, which often specialize in accounting, sales, or clerical services, provide a screened pool of candidates, which reduces the hiring company's administrative burden of recruitment. However, these agencies can be costly.

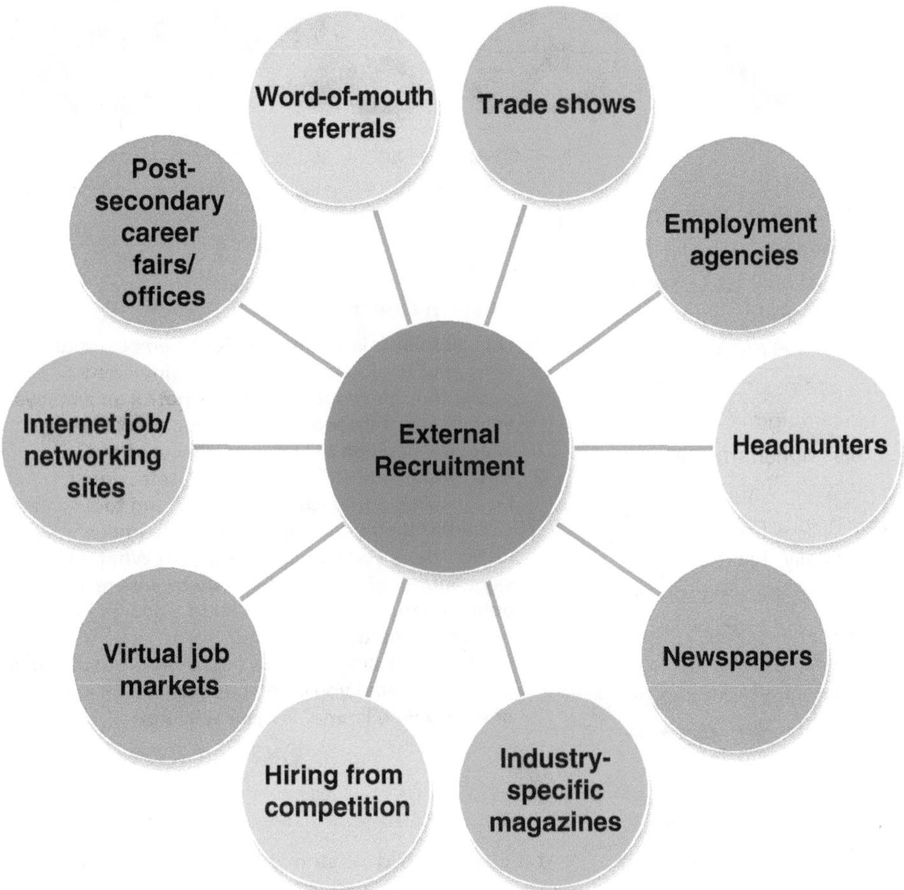

Figure 7.3 External Recruitment Resources

Recruitment consultants, often referred to as "headhunters," conduct specialized searches, usually for senior management or key employees. Recruitment consultants are often expensive, but the costs of finding the wrong candidate can be even higher.

What are the challenges in recruiting? One of the newer challenges facing recruiting specialists is the use of technology. Online job and résumé posting sites, Web and video blogs, virtual job fairs, podcasts, and other online media are all being used by both those looking to find a job and those looking to fill a position. While online job postings yield many responses and thus a large pool of candidates, sifting through these responses to find the right person for the job can be timeconsuming for HR professionals. Therefore, HR managers must know how to use technology skillfully. At a basic recruiting level, this means learning how to make a posted job description appeal to the most qualified candidates as well as stand out from competitors in the online environment so the right person can find the open position more readily. It also means becoming familiar with the new social networking technologies and Web 2.0 techniques to post jobs and find recruits.

Video: Lululemon Searches for CEO with Help Wanted Signs

Aslysun/Shutterstock

Finding the right person for a job opening is extremely difficult, but it is also extremely important.

One of the greatest recruiting challenges cited is the difficulty finding qualified

What Is Recruiting 2.0?

You're probably familiar with social networking sites such as Myspace and Facebook. The same concept is applied to the professional community through sites such as LinkedIn (www.linkedin.com), ZoomInfo (www.zoominfo.com), and Spoke (www.spoke.com). LinkedIn is an online network of more than 135 million experienced professionals worldwide whose connections are made through college and university, graduate school, or professional affiliations.[8] Most people would like to hire or work with someone they know, and LinkedIn can provide helpful colleague and customer recommendations. Additionally, LinkedIn may assist job seekers by providing insiders' information on companies and employees. If you've scheduled an interview, you might find a LinkedIn page for the person you are meeting with. This can give you some information on that person's professional background, including where he or she went to school, as well as information on hobbies. Knowing these details may provide for good conversation starters during the interview.

Discussion Questions

1. **Do you think it is appropriate for an employer to view your Facebook page before an interview or before they hire you? Why or why not? If an employer viewed your Facebook page, do you think it would affect the decision to hire you? Why or why not?**
2. **Have you established an online "professional" image using a professional networking tool such as LinkedIn? If you don't have an online image now, do you think you should create one? What will it say about you? What can you do to ensure your online image is portraying you in a positive way to potential employers?**
3. **Some people say they don't care what others think of them. Should you care about what others think of your online image? Why or why not?**

candidates for critical positions.[9] At the 2010 World Economic Forum, Manpower Inc. identified several top concerns for business leaders, including that many aging employees will be retiring soon, taking with them much talent, and new employees with similar skills and abilities will be difficult to find. Another concern was that job seekers who do have sought-after skills will have the power to choose which company they will work for and, as a result, companies will have to define jobs differently and adapt how they recruit and retain scarce talent.[10]

Video: Building Careers and Writing Résumés-Giant Robot Magazine

Selecting and Hiring

How do employers select potential job candidates from many job applicants?

The large group of applicants that has been identified at the beginning of the recruitment process needs to be narrowed down into a smaller pool of qualified candidates. **Selection** entails gathering information about candidates, evaluating their qualifications, and choosing the ones that best fit the job specifications. Some companies use special applicant-tracking system software to sort through résumés and job applications quickly. Through the selection process, HR personnel, in collaboration with department managers, compare the candidates' qualifications to the job specifications. Every employer is looking for a specific set of skills from job seekers that match the skills necessary to perform the particular job.

Beyond the job-specific technical skills, employers also demand certain critical employability skills. The Conference Board of Canada developed an employability skills profile based on input from employers and validated by a wide range of stakeholders. This profile is used by businesses to identify skills that potential employees require to enter, stay in, and progress in the world of work. These skills are grouped into three main areas: fundamental skills (communication, problem solving, mathematics, and technology), personal management skills (positive attitudes and behaviours), and teamwork skills (working with others).[11]

selection Entails gathering information about candidates, evaluating their qualifications, and choosing the ones that best fit the job specifications.

job interview A one-on-one meeting of the company and the job candidate through which the company is able to gauge the candidate's personality, clarify information in the candidate's résumé, and determine whether the candidate is the best match for the position.

behavioural interviews Interviews conducted to evaluate a candidate's experience and behaviours so the employer can determine the applicant's potential for success in the job.

What happens when an appropriate candidate is found?

After identifying a small pool of appropriate candidates, department and HR managers meet with each candidate to conduct a **job interview**, a meeting between the company and the job candidate in which the company attempts to gauge the candidate's personality, clarify information in the candidate's résumé, and determine whether the candidate is the best match for the position. At the same time, the interview is an opportunity for the candidate to evaluate whether the company is right for him or her. The candidate may also be asked to complete one or more skills-related or behavioural tests. More and more organizations are hiring candidates who show they have the most "trainable fit." Employers look for and test candidates for the ability to fit in with the organization's culture and values, as well as the ability to learn quickly and adapt to new challenges. **Behavioural interviews** are conducted to evaluate a candidate's experience and behaviours so the employer can determine the applicant's potential for success in the job. In certain types of jobs, such as those in which a candidate may be handling money, working in safety-sensitive positions, or giving care to others, a candidate may be asked to undergo drug testing, get bonded, or obtain a police record check. Interviews may be conducted by one interviewer or a panel of interviewers, and the candidate may be asked to attend a single interview or several interviews before a hiring decision is reached.

Before offering a candidate a position, it is important that the company complete thorough background and reference checks. It is not uncommon to hear stories about companies that failed to conduct background checks and hired someone who falsified his or her educational or professional experiences or who had been in trouble with the law. For example, the Treaty Group Inc. hired a person to assist with bookkeeping functions who ended up defrauding the company of more than $250 000. It was discovered later that the hired bookkeeper had been convicted of defrauding a former employer prior to joining Treaty.[12]

Video: Applying and Interviewing for Employment

The 10 Skills Employers Most Want in 20-Something Employees

Here are the 10 skills employers say they seek, in order of importance:

1. Ability to work in a team
2. Ability to make decisions and solve problems
3. Ability to plan, organize, and prioritize work
4. Ability to communicate verbally with people inside and outside an organization
5. Ability to obtain and process information
6. Ability to analyze quantitative data
7. Technical knowledge related to the job
8. Proficiency with computer software programs
9. Ability to create or edit written reports
10. Ability to sell and influence others

Source: Susan Adams, "The 10 Skills Employers Most Want in 20-Something Employees," *Forbes*, accessed February 2, 2014, http://www.forbes.com/sites/susanadams/2013/10/11/the-10-skills-employers-most-want-in-20-something-employees/.

What happens after an applicant has progressed satisfactorily through all the selection steps? If an applicant progresses satisfactorily through all the selection steps, a decision to hire the individual is made. The manager of the new employee is usually involved in the decision to hire.

As shown in **Figure 7.4**, hiring is a multistep process. The **hiring process** begins with developing the job requirements and ends when a job offer is made. Where a company has a collective labour agreement (a union contract with its employees), the selection process must also follow the provisions of that agreement. When hiring for full-time, permanent employees, companies often hire on a probational condition. **Probation** is a specific timeframe (typically three to six months) during which the new hire proves his or her skills and worth on the job. If the employee proves himself or herself on the job, he or she moves from probational employee status to permanent employee status.

hiring process Begins with developing the job requirements and ends when a job offer is made.

probation A specific timeframe (typically three to six months) during which the new hire proves his or her skills and worth on the job.

Simulation: Human Resource Management

Figure 7.4 Hiring Process

DEVELOPING EMPLOYEES FOR OPTIMAL PERFORMANCE

LO4 Discuss some of the ways employees are trained and how performance can be evaluated.

Training

Why is it important to train employees? Training employees can enhance the success of a business and ensure that employees stay in top form. Companies that emphasize training and development experience greater productivity, loyalty, and retention. Employee training is important for many reasons, as it often contributes to[13]

- increased job satisfaction, motivation, and morale among employees
- greater efficiency in work, resulting in financial gain
- more effective use of new technologies and methods
- development of new strategies and products
- lower employee turnover
- fewer interpersonal conflicts and better communication

What kind of training do new employees receive? When an employee is hired, most organizations use an **orientation program** to introduce the employee to the company's people, policies, and procedures. Orientation can be as simple as an overview of the organization and the distribution of basic information, such as company procedures and expectations. Employees should be introduced to associates in their department as well as the associates in other departments with whom the employee will be interacting; this will help them feel at ease so they can quickly become as productive as possible. The employee should be shown their workspace; given IDs and passwords necessary to log in to computers, printers, phones, and faxes; and provided information about company policies and procedures and employee benefits. Orientation is more effective if it becomes a means of familiarizing the employee with the company's mission and discussing how the new employee's contribution can add to the company's success. Over the first few weeks, the manager should schedule brief daily meetings with the new employee to review expectations and responsibilities and answer any questions the new employee may have. Failure to integrate new hires into a company adequately leads to low retention rates.

What other training is required of new and present employees? Training begins where orientation ends. Training should teach employees skills or ways to improve on existing skills. For example, a salesperson may know how to sell a product but may not know all the intricacies of selling a new product. Often, other employees in the department or the recent hire's mentor can conduct on-the-job training. In **on-the-job training**, employees learn skills by performing them. **Mentoring** is a form of on-the-job training whereby an experienced employee provides direction and information to the new employee as he or she learns the job. **Mentors** are experienced individual employees who help a less-experienced person by explaining how to perform specific tasks, creating opportunities to learn new skills, and counselling about the consequences of particular actions and decisions. Like other forms of training, mentoring increases employee performance, satisfaction, and loyalty. Sometimes, however, an apprentice training program is required. An **apprentice training** program trains individuals through classroom or formal instruction and on-the-job training.

Some companies use **off-the-job training and development** techniques that require employees to participate in outside seminars, university-conducted programs, and corporate universities. Hamburger University, McDonald's corporate training facility, aligns training with employees' specific career paths, including development paths for crew, restaurant managers, mid-managers, and executives. Their curriculum is delivered using a combination of classroom instruction, hands-on lab activities, goal-based scenarios, and computer e-learning modules. Management hopefuls enroll in extensive classroom and field instruction and can earn credit that can even be applied toward a two- or four-year degree.[14]

orientation program Used to introduce the employee to the company's people, policies, and procedures.

on-the-job training When employees learn skills by performing them.

mentoring A form of on-the-job training whereby an experienced employee provides direction and information to the new employee as he or she learns the job.

mentors Experienced individual employees who help a less-experienced person by explaining how to perform specific tasks, creating opportunities to learn new skills, and counselling about the consequences of particular actions and decisions.

apprentice training A program that trains individuals through classroom or formal instruction and on-the-job training.

off-the-job training and development Techniques that require employees to participate in outside seminars, university-conducted programs, and corporate universities.

simulation training Provides realistic job-task training in a manner that is challenging but does not create the threat of failure.

vestibule training A type of simulation most suitable to airline pilots, astronauts, and surgeons, for whom making mistakes during training is not an option or is too costly.

online training Allows employees to take college or university classes on the Internet at their convenience, enabling them to obtain specific job-related education or to pursue a degree. Also called distance learning.

What kind of impact has technology had on training? Improvements in technology provide companies with other training options such as simulated training and interactive multimedia training. **Simulation training** provides realistic job-task training in a manner that is challenging but does not create the threat of failure. **Vestibule training** is a type of simulation most suitable to airline pilots, astronauts, and surgeons, for whom making mistakes during training is not an option or is too costly.

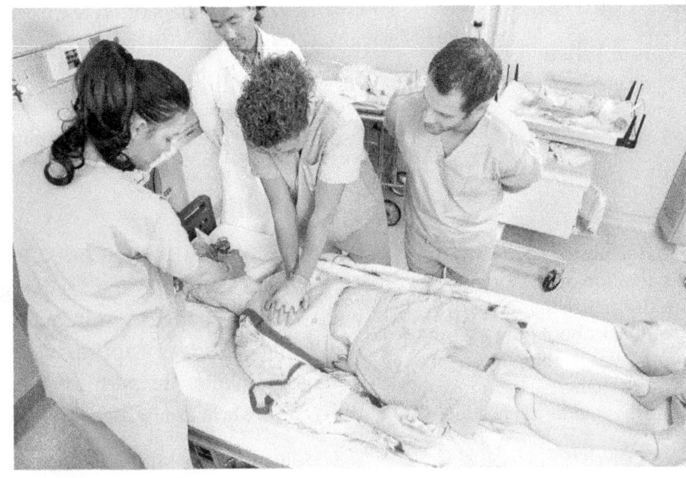

Tyler Olson/Shutterstock

Robots are used in simulation training for medical students.

Online training (or *distance learning*) allows employees to take college or university classes on the Internet at their convenience, enabling them to obtain specific job-related education or to pursue a degree. Other forms of Internet-based distance training have instructors in a centralized location teach groups of employees at remote locations via television hookups (teletraining) or a combination of audio/video equipment (videoconferencing). **Games-based learning (serious games)** is a training method whereby employees play virtual reality games that simulate real-life events. SubSafe is a recent example of a games-based training system for submarine safety and spatial awareness, providing end users with a real-time, interactive, three-dimensional model of part of a Trafalgar class submarine.[15] The Canadian Forces is using games-based training for air traffic control to increase the speed with which trainees gain experience.[16] SAP, which creates enterprise resource planning (ERP) software, introduced games-based training in France and in several African countries "to drive adoption of business strategies and increase employees' business skills."[17] Colleagues split into teams to compete on a live SAP ERP system to manage a mock company. According to SAP's South African education director, Johan Pretorius, "The simulation game won wide acclaim for achieving these goals through a fun, interactive, and informative process."[18]

Pavel L Photo and Video/Shutterstock

Two pilots training on a helicopter flight simulator. This type of training is ideal for jobs where making a mistake is not an option.

games-based learning (serious games) A training method whereby employees play virtual reality games that simulate real-life events.

How are managers trained? Because of their roles in the organization, managers require different training than their front-line co-workers. **Management development training** focuses on leadership, communication, teamwork, and relationship-building skills. In addition, managers need to keep abreast of the changes in employment laws such as discrimination and harassment, as well as updates in the use of electronic communication resources. In addition to training for current managers, many companies offer management development programs that prepare management trainees to become managers within the organization. These programs may have the trainees participate in an on-the-job training program, which may include **job rotation**, in which the employee rotates through different departments to learn first-hand the various aspects of the business, or a **coaching/understudy program**, in which the employee works directly with senior management in planning and other managerial functions. **Action learning**, another management development training approach, focuses on solving real problems on actual work projects. Action learning allows trainees to work together in teams to analyze real-time corporate problems that extend beyond their areas of expertise. Companies such as General Electric and Johnson & Johnson have successfully implemented action-learning teams as part of their management development programs.[19]

management development training Training that focuses on leadership, communication, teamwork, and relationship-building skills.

job rotation When the employee rotates through different departments to learn first-hand the various aspects of the business.

coaching/understudy program When the employee works directly with senior management in planning and other managerial functions.

action learning A management development training approach that focuses on solving real problems on actual work projects.

Video: Wilson Learning: Training

Senior managers often use executive coaches to further develop their effectiveness. Executive coaches identify the manager's strengths and weaknesses by interviewing those who work closely with the manager. They then meet with the manager to work on eliminating weaknesses and further developing strengths. Mentoring is another option that companies use to enable their experienced managers to work closely with inexperienced managers.

Evaluating

performance appraisal An evaluation of an employee's performance that gives feedback about how well the employee is doing as well as where changes and improvements are needed.

How is employee performance evaluated? A **performance appraisal** is an evaluation of an employee's performance that gives feedback about how well the employee is doing as well as where changes and improvements are needed (see **Figure 7.5**). Managers use the results of performance appraisals in decisions about promotions, raises, additional training, or reassignments. The performance appraisal process is important for both employees and the organization as a whole. The process includes

1. determining standards that employees should aim for in their work
2. evaluating the employee's performance in comparison with these standards
3. providing feedback to reduce and eliminate poor performance and improve or enhance positive performance

When employees are hired, they should have a good understanding of what is expected of them. These expectations become the performance standards upon which they'll be measured. Appraisals act as a confirmation of these standards and help employees establish quantifiable and measurable goals for improvement in the upcoming year.

performance management An approach that combines goal setting, performance appraisal, and training and development into a unified and ongoing process.

Are performance appraisals effective? When conducted properly, performance appraisals are very helpful to the employee and ultimately the organization. Unfortunately, since appraisals often lead to criticism, many managers shy away from them because they are uncomfortable handing out bad or harsh comments. Despite the fact that annual raises are often tied to the performance evaluation, managers avoid doing them as long as possible. This results in unmotivated employees who feel that the manager does not care about them enough to facilitate their annual raise. Additionally, some managers have a difficult time quantifying performance and fear not being able to defend their ratings if questioned. Although performance appraisals often suggest means to improve weak performance or to enhance solid performance, the process does not always offer the opportunity to follow up and ensure that such means have been acted on. Often it's not until the next performance appraisal that it is recognized that such training and development have not happened. And when the next appraisal can be a year away, the benefits of appraisals become diluted.

Annual Employee Performance Evaluation

Employee's Name:		Supervisor:	
Job Title:		Date Hired:	
Department:		Date of Review:	

Evaluation

This form is design to assess your current performance and to help in setting goals for the future. This form is considered confidential and will only be reviewed by you and your supervisor(s).

Overall Job Knowledge/Experience Level

	Consistently meets requirements
	Generally meets requirements
	Does not meet requirements

Comments:

Quality of Work

	Exceeds expectations
	Meets expectations
	Does not meet expectations

Comments:

Attendance

	Rarely tardy or absent
	Sometimes tardy or absent
	Frequently tardy or absent

Comments:

Cooperation

	Consistently participates and contributes to the team
	Generally participates and contributes to the team
	Does not participate or contribute to the team

Comments:

Future Goals:

Figure 7.5 A Sample Performance Appraisal

Is there an alternative to performance appraisals? An alternative to a performance appraisal is performance management. **Performance management** is an approach that combines goal setting, performance appraisal, and training and development into a unified and ongoing process. As such, it is more of a cyclical and fluid process than the single occurrence

Table 7.1 Aspects of Performance Management

Direction sharing	Communicating the organization's higher-level goals such as vision, mission, values, and strategy
Role clarifying	Defining roles in terms of daily work tasks
Goal setting and planning	Redefining organizational or departmental goals into specific employee goals, which include the employee's development of the steps necessary to achieve goals
Ongoing performance monitoring and feedback	Periodic performance reports regarding progress on meeting goals as well as feedback regarding progress toward goals
Coaching and support	Ongoing as part of the feedback process
Performance assessment (appraisal)	An element in the performance management process that offers specific, defined knowledge on how the employee's performance is improving company results
Rewards, recognition, and compensation	Given as appropriate to motivate the employee toward achieving current and future goals
Workflow, process control, and return on investment management	Making sure the employee's measurable performance is linked to measurable goals of company

Source: *Gary Dessler,* Human Resource Management, *11th ed.(Upper Saddle River, NJ: Prentice Hall, 2007), 338.*

of a performance appraisal. Employees are constantly receiving feedback and given opportunities for training and development to ensure that they have the right tools with which to perform their job. The vibrancy and performance of the organization is ensured because managers focus on developmental plans and opportunities for each staff member. Thus, it is much more effective than the traditional method of using performance appraisals. **Table 7.1** summarizes several aspects of the performance management process. The concept, while often applied to employees, is also applicable to other components of the organization, including an entire department, a product or service, or the organization as a whole. Performance management, appraisals, and training can play a significant role in keeping a business productive and efficient.

COMPENSATING, SCHEDULING, AND TRANSITIONING EMPLOYEES

LO5 Describe how employees can be compensated and some of the different kinds of work schedule arrangements that are used to meet the needs of employees and the company.

Compensating

What is compensation? In today's workplace, **compensation**, payment for work performed, comes in a variety of forms, including money, bonuses, work–life benefits, health insurance, and retirement plans. Having the right pay system in place is important for a company to become and remain competitive. A fair and comparable compensation package attracts high-quality employees and keeps them from leaving. Moreover, employees have a greater incentive to work harder and more efficiently if they know their compensation is tied to their efforts and to the overall success of the company. A low turnover rate and a productive workforce help to keep costs low, which has a positive impact on the company's profits. Because there are many ways to structure compensation, the decision is not an easy one. It is often a delicate balance between paying to attract and keep the best and not jeopardizing the financial security of the company.

compensation Payment for work performed, which comes in a variety of forms, including money, bonuses, work–life benefits, health insurance, and retirement plans.

Are all employees compensated in the same way? Employers have to consider many factors when determining an employee's pay rate. Employees are evaluated on prior work experience and education as well as contribution to the company. The employer considers how competing companies are compensating their employees and in

Table 7.2 Various Types of Compensation

Wages	Compensation based on the number of hours or days worked. Each province has a minimum hourly wage that varies depending on the positions and job market.
Salary	Fixed annual compensation usually paid on a weekly, biweekly, or monthly basis. The employee's compensation level has the potential to increase based on the results of employee evaluations, which usually occur on an annual basis. Many companies pay employees a base salary plus some sort of incentive-based payment.
Piecework	Compensation based on the number of items produced or sold. For instance, employees may receive $1 for every pie they make, so the more pies they make, the more money they make. Many assembly line workers are paid by the number of pieces they produce. Although this method may motivate workers to work faster, quality of work may suffer.
Commissions	Some salespeople are paid a percentage of the amount they sell. This is called a commission on sales (compensation based directly on employee performance).
Accelerated commissions	Increased commission based on levels. For instance, a salesperson may receive 2 percent commission on the first $75 000 they sell, plus 4 percent commission on the next $75 000 they sell, and so on.
Bonuses	Extra pay for reaching certain goals in work performance, lifelong learning, or other predetermined targets. Bonus may be money or gifts, trips, time off, and so on.
Profit sharing	Bonuses based on total corporate profits, which help tie employees' efforts to the company's bottom line. Higher corporate profits mean higher bonuses.
Gain sharing	Bonuses paid to employees when company costs are reduced through greater work efficiency, such as improving quality measures or production targets.
Stock options	Stock option plans offer shares of company stock to employees for purchase on a set date. The shares can be purchased at the value of the stock when it was originally offered or at an agreed-upon price. Employee stock purchase plans allow employees to buy company stock at a discount (usually 85 percent of market value). Companies typically provide payroll deductions for these purchases and limit amounts to 10 percent of total pay. An advantage of providing employees with ownership in the company via stock transactions is that employees feel more connected to the business and are motivated to ensure that the business succeeds. Starbucks uses stock options to give its employees a sense of ownership in the business.[20]

so doing may find the company needs to offer more wages or benefits to attract top talent. Not all company employees receive the same amount of pay, nor are they paid by the same methods. Pay varies depending on the type of job role and the industry an employee is working in. Regarding specific individuals and positions, companies typically determine the type and amount of compensation on a balance of the following: federal and provincial legislation (the law), what the company can afford, what competitors are paying, and what skills and talents each employee brings to the company.

There are many ways to pay workers for their time and effort. The most common types of compensation in Canada today are wages and salary. In addition to wages and salary, many companies compensate employees based on performance. Refer to **Table 7.2** for descriptions of various types of compensation.

In what other ways are employees compensated? An important part of the business planning and management process is determining the type and amount of employee benefits, or indirect financial and nonfinancial payments, an employer offers that supplement cash compensation. Benefit compensation often enables a company to attract, motivate, and retain the best employees. **Benefits** come in many forms and provide additional compensation to employees beyond base wages. Some benefits are required by law, such as employment insurance (EI) and the Canada and Quebec Pension Plans (CPP/QPP)—each paid partially by the employer—paid vacations, statutory holiday pay, and maternity leave. Other benefits come voluntarily from the employer or as a result of

benefits Come in many forms and provide additional compensation to employees beyond base wages.

employer–union agreements and may include health and disability insurance plans (dental, eyewear, massage, etc.), company pension plans (retirement plans), sick leave, bonuses, maternity leave top-up pay, termination pay, retirement packages, paid professional development (training), and paid time off.

Some companies offer **flexible benefits plans** (or *cafeteria plans*) that permit the employee to pick from a "menu" of several choices of taxable and nontaxable forms of compensation. Flexible benefit plans allow employees to choose the benefits most important to them while reducing the cost of offering all benefits to all employees. Vacation, holidays, and pensions constitute a significant percentage of total compensation. Other non-cash benefits help employees balance the demands of their professional and personal lives, also known as work–life benefits.

Work–life benefits help an employee achieve a balance between the demands of life both inside and outside the workplace. Work–life benefits include flexible schedules, relaxed atmospheres, free meals, childcare, fitness/gym programs, and much more. For example, you'll recall from the chapter-opening discussion that SAS offers employees a range of amenities, including an onsite fitness club with indoor pool, onsite car detailing, massages, and a hair salon. Although seemingly expensive, this strategy of keeping its employees happy saves the company approximately $70 million per year because it experiences low turnover. Offering an employee discounted prices, free merchandise, or a sabbatical (leave from work with or without pay) are other types of work benefits (also known as job perks). Procter & Gamble offers up to 12 weeks unpaid leave, while McDonald's offers 8 weeks paid leave, and Nike offers 5 weeks paid leave.[21] The sabbatical is thought to rejuvenate employees and increase their passion for their jobs.

Newscom

The Googleplex, Google's Mountain View, California, campus, has several pools, 11 free gourmet cafeterias, volleyball courts, and massage services.

Compensating, motivating, scheduling, and promoting employees compose an important part of HR management. Companies identified as "The Best Companies to Work for" have revolutionized the way that businesses approach these issues with their implementation of innovative work–life benefits and a dynamic, employee-friendly work environment. Many of the highest-quality applicants nowadays expect companies to offer these perks.

flexible benefits plans Permit the employee to pick from a "menu" of several choices of taxable and nontaxable forms of compensation. Also called cafeteria plans.

work–life benefits Help an employee achieve a balance between the demands of life both inside and outside the workplace.

Do most employers offer medical, pension, and wellness benefits? Employers are becoming more concerned with employee wellness, both physical and mental. They are recognizing that happy, healthy employees are more productive and more likely to stay with the company. Low productivity, absenteeism, and high employee turnover rates cost companies money. **Employee assistance programs (EAPs)** are employee benefit programs offered by many employers, typically in conjunction with a health insurance plan. EAPs are intended to help employees deal with personal and workplace problems that may adversely affect their work performance. According to the Sun Life Financial Canadian Health Index, "employers with highly effective workplace wellness programs have performed more than 55% better than their industry peers, achieved higher average revenue per employee and seen less absence, disability, total turnover and lower annual medical costs."[22]

Video: Best Boss Ever Pays Employees to Go on Vacation

employee assistance programs (EAPs) Employee benefit programs offered by many employers, typically in conjunction with a health insurance plan. EAPs are intended to help employees deal with personal and workplace problems that may adversely affect their work performance.

A competitive group benefits plan allows employers to help attract and retain employees by satisfying their needs and demands. But employers need affordable benefits plans. As the population ages, they spend more on health care. The government already spends a substantial portion of its revenue on health care and is likely to continue to limit and eliminate health services to shift costs to private plans.[23] Statistics Canada projects that by about 2031, seniors will compose between 23 and 25 percent of the total population. Bell Canada, Ford Motor Company of Canada, and Sears Canada, among others, are taking steps toward the growing concern over the rising costs of retiree health benefits. For example, Bell plans to phase out all post-retirement benefits for those retiring after 2017.[24]

Multinational corporations need to understand the cultural and legal standards in the countries in which they operate. The variances between each country's human resource practices and laws make managing employees and their benefits especially complicated. As the world continues to engage in global business, Canadian human resource practices will be influenced by conditions in other countries and cultures.

Scheduling

What is the traditional workweek schedule? An increasing number of employees are finding that managing the demands of work and personal life results in doing neither well. The added stresses that face employees today from childcare, elder care, commuting, and other work–life conflicts have led to a decrease in productivity and an increase in employee absenteeism and tardiness. As a result, more and more employers are offering alternatives to the traditional 9:00 a.m. to 5:00 p.m., Monday to Friday workweek. Creating work schedules requires meeting the needs of the company while satisfying the needs of the employees.

Some companies have flexible scheduling policies in place and others approach scheduling issues on an individual basis. Flexible schedules provide employees with many benefits, such as

- reduced childcare costs (e.g., when parents are home, childcare is not needed)
- additional personal time (e.g., to attend appointments, work out at the gym, or get the shopping done)
- additional savings (e.g., money saved by a decreased frequency in dry cleaning or purchasing business attire)
- opportunity to pursue other interests (e.g., community involvement, volunteerism, or academic goals)

flexible work schedule Can take many different forms, yet not every job is well suited for an alternative structure. Flexible work schedules help people juggle work and family responsibilities, making them happier with their jobs, which can be measured in increases in productivity and morale and decreases in stress, absenteeism, and burnout.

A **flexible work schedule** can take many different forms, yet not every job is well suited for an alternative structure. Flexible work schedules help people juggle work and family responsibilities, making them happier and more satisfied with their jobs, which can be measured in increases in productivity and morale and decreases in stress, absenteeism, and burnout.

State Farm believes employees are more engaged and productive when they work a schedule best suited for their individual work style and personal circumstances. State Farm offers several flexible scheduling options (compressed workweek, flextime, telecommuting, and job sharing) to help employees balance their personal and professional responsibilities.[25] IBM, Sun Microsystems, and Best Buy, among others, have successfully fostered ROWE (Results Only Work Environment), which debunks the old theory that the longer employees stay at the office, the higher their productivity. Instead, ROWE suggests that employees be paid for the work they accomplish, regardless of the hours it took or the work location. Best Buy's former chief executive, Brad Anderson, stated, "Orders processed by people who are not working in the office are up 13% to 18% over those who are."[26]

Martin Allinger/Shutterstock

More working Canadians are caring for both their children and aging parents, making it difficult to balance work and life demands.

What alternate work arrangements are there? The most popular flexible work arrangements include the following:

David R Frazier/Alamy

UPS offers a permanent part-time package handler position in which employees work about four hours per day, Monday through Friday, with no weekend or evening work required. In addition to traditional health insurance, vacations, and a stock purchase plan, UPS offers tuition assistance as an additional benefit.

1. *Flextime.* In flextime scheduling, management defines a total number of required hours as a core workday and is flexible with starting and ending times. Managers must rise to the challenge of ensuring that required hours are met and monitoring employee performance. However, overall, flexible arrangements allow for increased productivity because of reductions in absenteeism and tardiness. For example, some employees may work 8:00 a.m. to 4:30 p.m., others 9:00 a.m. to 5:30 p.m., and so on. Of course, flextime may not be feasible in some types of jobs where everyone must work at the same time or when there are shiftwork schedules in place.
2. *Permanent parttime.* Permanent part-time employees are hired on a permanent basis to work a part-time week. Unlike temporary part-time workers who are employed to fill short-term needs, permanent part-time employees enjoy the same benefits that full-time employees receive.
3. *Job sharing.* Job sharing is an arrangement in which two employees work parttime sharing one full-time job. Those who share a job have been found to be very motivated to make this flexible situation work, so productivity and employee satisfaction increase. On the other hand, conflicts may arise if the job sharers don't have a clear understanding of who is in charge of what or if there is confusion from other employees about whom to contact and when. Therefore, job sharers must carefully coordinate and communicate both with one another and with their employer to ensure that all responsibilities are met.
4. *Compressed workweek.* A compressed workweek allows employees to work fewer but longer days: four 10-hour days per week or 9-hour days with one day off every two weeks. Such arrangements can reduce worker overtime, make more efficient use of facilities, and provide employees with longer blocks of personal time and less commuting time. The disadvantages are a potential increase in employee fatigue and possible conflicts with labour laws that cite overtime requirements for hours worked in excess of eight a day.
5. *Telecommuting.* Telecommuting allows employees to work in the office parttime and work from home parttime, or to work completely from home, making only occasional visits to the office. Telecommuting reduces commuting costs and allows employees to take care of home needs while also fulfilling work responsibilities. Telecommuting arrangements are also necessary for those employees dealing with clients, colleagues, or suppliers who are on the other side of the globe. Taking calls at 2:00 a.m. is much easier at home than at the office. The disadvantages of telecommuting include monitoring employees' performance at a distance, servicing equipment for offsite employees, and communication issues. Additionally, employees who telecommute may become isolated from other employees.

Yeko Photo Studio/Shutterstock

Working from home has many benefits for both employees and employers.

Shiftwork is not considered as flexible as some of the flexible scheduling options discussed above because it doesn't give employees much say over their schedules. There are advantages, however. One advantage may be that employees don't waste time and fuel sitting in traffic as they may if all employees poured out of work at the same time. It also means

Video: Patagonia: Human Resource Management

that employees are not working 9:00 a.m. to 5:00 p.m. each day of the week, thus giving some flexibility in personal time to schedule medical or other personal appointments. Employees may work the 8:00 a.m. to 4:00 p.m. shift, the 4:00 p.m. to 12:00 a.m. shift, or 12:00 a.m. to 8:00 a.m. shift (or some variation of this pattern). Often employees will cycle through the shifts, working an entire week on each.

contingent workers (temporary employees) Individuals who are hired on an as-needed basis; therefore, they lack the status that comes from being a regular, full-time employee.

independent contractors and consultants Contingent workers who are generally self-employed and are hired on a temporary basis to perform specific tasks.

Why does a company hire contingent workers? **Contingent workers (temporary employees)** are hired to fill in for absent employees (e.g., maternity leave) or to augment the staff during busy periods (e.g., holidays, promotions, events). Long-term temporary staff is often hired for indefinite periods to work on specific projects. In many cases, temporary staffing is part of a company's human resource "temp to perm" strategy.

Independent contractors and consultants are contingent workers who are generally self-employed and are hired on a temporary basis to perform specific tasks. Often contractors are hired for those jobs that are commonly hard to fill that involve state-of-the-art skills in construction, financial activities, and professional and business services. For example, it may be most cost efficient to hire a webpage developer as an independent contractor rather than keeping one on staff permanently. Consultants are hired to assist with long-term projects, often at a strategic level, but also with a specific end in sight. For example, a company that is reviewing its executive management compensation arrangements may hire a compensation consultant.

Transitioning: Promoting, Transferring, Retiring, and Terminating

LO6 Explain how employees transition through a company over time by way of promotions, transfers, retirement, and termination.

promotion An upward or lateral move into a new position that allows employees to develop and display new skills and to learn more about the company overall.

What is meant by transitioning employees? Employees don't always stay in the same position for which they were hired. Sometimes they transition into different positions within the company or sometimes they leave the company (by their own choice or by the employer's choice). HRM performs various functions to help transition employees through changing job roles.

Ways to Get Promoted

1. Get a mentor.
2. Learn outside of work.
3. Self-promote your successes.
4. Volunteer.
5. Ask questions.
6. Be consistent.
7. Help your colleagues.
8. Tell your boss you want to be promoted.
9. Be a team player.
10. Create your own opportunities.

How can employees increase their level of responsibility in the firm? After performing successfully in a position, many employees look to increase their level of responsibility and stature in the firm or department through a promotion. A **promotion** may be an upward or lateral move into a new position that allows employees to develop and display new skills and to learn more about the company overall. Promotions from within the company to well-qualified, deserving candidates improve employee morale because when employees know that management is going to promote based on merit, they are more likely to work hard and feel satisfied with the fair method of promotions, which creates a positive work environment and boosts morale. Promotions from within are also cost effective in that the promoted employees are already familiar with the corporate culture and business procedures, do not need to spend valuable time on basic orientation, and are already registered in the HR system as an employee. Employers like to promote from within because they can reward exceptional behaviour and fill positions with tested employees. However, promotion may not always result in a positive situation if it is seen as being draped in secrecy, unfairness, or arbitrariness. Therefore, management must ensure that promotions are based on a distinct set of criteria such as seniority or competency.

transfer Occurs when an employee is appointed to the same or a similar position elsewhere within the organization. Transfers usually refer to a lateral move (a horizontal job assignment).

Why do employees transfer within a company? A **transfer** occurs when an employee is appointed to the same or a similar position elsewhere within the organization. Transfers usually refer to a lateral move (a horizontal job assignment).

Better Business Better World

The Home Depot Canada Foundation[27]

The Home Depot Canada Foundation is committed to putting an end to youth homelessness in Canada.

On any given night, more than 6 000 young people are without a place to call home, making youth homelessness one of the most urgent social issues facing Canadians today.

Courtesy of The Home Depot Canada Foundation

Over the next three years, through **The Orange Door Project** initiative, the Foundation has pledged **$10-million** to support renovation and repair projects and programs that provide vulnerable youth with access to safe, stable housing and support services.

This includes the support of Team Depot, The Home Depot's associate-led volunteer program. Through this program associates are encouraged and empowered to take a leadership role in their community by organizing small-scale improvement projects for local charities. Annually, The Home Depot associates contribute more than 60 000 volunteer hours to community projects across Canada.

Learn more: www.homedepot.ca/foundation.

Courtesy of The Home Depot Canada Foundation

Discussion Questions

1. **What advantages might Home Depot or any other organization gain by engaging in philanthropy (goodwill, charity)? Are there any disadvantages to doing so?**
2. **With Team Depot, employees volunteer their time and talents to work on community projects. How might this lead to improved employee motivation and job satisfaction?**
3. **How do philanthropic initiatives influence the employee–employer relationship? Do you think employees would view such a volunteer program as a positive or negative workplace initiative? Why?**

Organizations transfer employees either to satisfy organizational requirements or to meet employee requests. Employees may request a transfer to a different department or a different position because they are not satisfied with their current work or manager. When vertical advancements are not available or possible, employees can transfer laterally to another department to develop new skills and learn more about the company. Employers may transfer employees because of a need for an employee's specific talent elsewhere in the organization. Also, a transfer may occur when the employee's current position is eliminated from restructuring or reclassification. Multinational corporations sometimes transfer specific managers to new sites in foreign countries to help get the new location up and running.

CREATISTA/Shutterstock

Many older adults are choosing to stay at work past the age of 65.

When do employees retire? It used to be that employees retired when they reached the age of 65, but the current Canadian labour laws do not specify a retirement age.[28] **Retirement** is the point in a person's life when he or she stops participating fulltime in his or her career. The average retirement age in Canada is 62. About 6 percent of workers continue to work fulltime after the age of 65.[29] Reasons for staying on the job after age 65 include financial need as well as a desire to remain active and enjoy office camaraderie. For employers, an aging workforce may present other challenges, such as decreasing morale among workers or age-discrimination lawsuits if they aggressively lay off older workers. Therefore, to encourage older (and more expensive) workers to retire, companies have offered financial incentives, known as worker buyouts, early retirement plans, or severance pay. Retiring senior workers increase promotion opportunities for younger employees. For instance, in 2010, General Motors offered US$60 000 buyouts (with full benefits) to several thousand skilled trades workers when the company estimated that it had 2000 more skilled trades workers than it needed.[30] Ford also reduced its workforce with buyouts and early retirement offers as part of a massive restructuring plan in 2009.[31] The term *golden parachute* or golden handshake is sometimes used to refer to the package bestowed on top-level managers who retire or otherwise leave the company. For example, when Citigroup CEO Charles Prince retired after four years and a poor third-quarter performance, he took nearly US$100 million with him.[32]

retirement The point in a person's life when he or she stops participating fulltime in his or her career.

Why do employees leave their jobs? Even the most attractive benefits package and high wage incentives don't always retain valuable employees. Some employees leave their jobs to work for another company and some leave for personal reasons (possibly to raise a family). Others may quit their jobs because they do not feel motivated by or satisfied with their work tasks, co-workers, or manager. Employees are free to resign voluntarily from work at any time. Employees resigning on good terms would choose to give their employer notice of leave, mainly because they wish to keep a good working relationship with the employer, to obtain a positive reference, and to keep future opportunities open. Employers may accept an employee's notice or may ask the employee to leave immediately. Note that if an employee quits without just cause, he or she may not be eligible to collect employment insurance.

Companies are always looking for experienced, talented employees, and they will offer higher wages and more incentives in an effort to find them. Sometimes that may even mean luring talented employees away from their competitors. Learning about the reasons employees leave can give valuable insight to an employer and may help prevent the loss of additional employees in the future. **Exit interviews** are often conducted (in person, online, or on the telephone) by an outside contractor or by HR department personnel to gather feedback before employees leave the company. The **turnover rate** tracks the number of employees that leave the company each year. Companies monitor the turnover rate to compare it to previous years as an aid in analyzing and determining staffing needs and trends.

exit interviews Often conducted to gather feedback before employees leave the company.

turnover rate Tracks the number of employees that leave the company each year.

Why do companies terminate employment? At times it is necessary to re-evaluate an employee's contribution or tenure at the company, or to re-evaluate the composition and size of the workforce altogether. Companies that find themselves struggling to survive in the business world may be forced to reduce the size of their workforce (downsize). Downsizing and restructuring, the growth of outsourcing and offshoring, the pressures of global competition, and the increased uses of technology are all reasons companies look to reduce the number of employees. **Termination** of employment reduces the number of employees by permanently laying off workers due to poor performance or a discontinued need for their services. Companies may offer outplacement services such as résumé writing and career counselling to help employees transition out of the company. When large numbers of employees have been laid off (either permanently or temporarily), the employees who remain often feel insecure and uncertain about the future of their own jobs with the company. Insecurity undermines motivation, so HRM must deal with the issue.

Rommel Canlas/Shutterstock

Constantly being late for work can become a reason for dismissing an employee for just cause; punctuality is important in the business world.

Terminating employment because of an employee's poor performance or illegal activities can be a rather complex process. It is imperative for employers to have a good record-keeping system in place regarding poorly performing employees. In general, employment standards legislation requires that notice of termination be given to workers who have been employed for three consecutive months or more unless the employee is dismissed for just cause.[33] In some cases, employers may give pay in lieu of notice of termination.

termination Reduces the number of employees by permanently laying off workers due to poor performance or a discontinued need for their services.

Before firing an employee for wrongful doings or incompetence, managers must take steps to avoid a wrongful dismissal lawsuit. These steps include maintaining solid records so that they can build a case for dismissal with sufficient documentation and evidence. Courts have sided with the terminated employee, especially when not enough evidence of poor behaviour is brought forth. Written evidence is the only material evidence accepted, which makes building an employee's personnel file with documented proof of poor performance critical. Hearsay and rumours do not stand up in legal proceedings. It is always up to the employer to prove to the judge that the dismissal was for just cause.

Video: Gordon Law Group: Employee Separation

Some reasons considered just cause include dishonesty, absenteeism or lateness, wilful disobedience, sexual harassment, insolence, and conflict of interest.[34] In addition, companies cannot terminate employees because of whistleblowing, filing a worker's compensation claim, jury duty, or testifying against the company in a legal proceeding. Traditionally, U.S. employers have possessed the right to discharge their employees at will for any reason. The United States is the only major industrial nation that maintains a general employment-at-will rule. Canada, France, Germany, Great Britain, Italy, Japan, and Sweden all have statutory provisions that require employers to show cause before discharging employees.[35]

Reasons Employees Get Fired

1. Dishonesty, evasion, or lack of integrity on the job
2. Lying on a résumé
3. Refusing to follow directions and orders
4. Talking too much and conducting personal business at work
5. Inconsistency—unreliable work and behaviours
6. Inability to get along with other people
7. Inability to actually do assigned job tasks
8. Performing tasks slowly with numerous errors
9. High absenteeism rate
10. Drug or alcohol abuse

Source: Patty Inglish, "Top 10 Reasons Employees Get Fired, Among Surveyed Companies 2008–2012," HubPages.com, accessed January 12, 2011, http://hubpages.com/hub/Fired. Used by the permission of the author.

MANAGING WORKPLACE DIVERSITY

LO7 Identify the ways in which Canada's demographics are changing and how this affects the workforce.

Demographic Projections

What are the demographic changes occurring in the Canadian workforce?

Look around you. Most likely you work, study, and socialize with people of different genders, ages, religions, races, sexual orientations, mental and physical abilities, and educational backgrounds. Several demographic changes have brought forth HR challenges—some new and some that have existed for many years—and Canada will continue to grow in human diversity (see **Table 7.3** for Statistics Canada's diversity projections).

Table 7.3 Statistics Canada: Diversity Projections

For year 2017*	For year 2031[†]
• Between 19% and 23% of Canadians will be a visible minority person. • The number of people whose mother tongue is neither English nor French will be between 21% and 25% of the total population in Canada. • For every 100 visible minority persons at the age to exit the labour force there willbe 142 at the age of entry. In the rest of the population there willbe only 75 potential entries for every 100 potential exits. • Alberta's Aboriginal population is expected to grow by 39%.** • 75% of visible minority persons will be living in one of Canada's three largest metropolitan areas—Toronto, Vancouver, and Montreal.	• Between 25% and 28% of the population could be foreign born. About 55% of this population will be born in Asia. • Visible minority groups will comprise 63% of the population of Toronto, 59% in Vancouver, and 31% in Montreal. • In Toronto, 24% of the population will be South Asian, which will continue to be its largest visible minority group. • Chinese residents will be the largest visible minority group in Vancouver, at 23% of the population. • 14% of people in Canada will be of non-Christian religion.

**Statistics Canada, "Study: Canada's Visible Minority Population in 2017,"* The Daily, *March 22, 2005, accessed November 12, 2011, http://www.statcan.gc.ca/daily- quotidien/050322/dq050322b-eng.htm.*

[†]Statistics Canada, "Study: Projections of the Diversity of the Canadian Population," The Daily, *accessed January 24, 2011, http://www.statcan.gc.ca/daily-quotidien/100309/dq100309a-eng.htm.*

***Human Rights, Citizenship and Multiculturalism Education Fund, "A Snapshot of Demographic Trends in Alberta," accessed November 12, 2011, http://justice.alberta.ca/programs_services/humanrights/hremf/Documents/Trends.pdf.*

workplace diversity Encompasses all the ways in which employees differ.

diversity-friendly organizations Organizations that are very inclusive. They don't just tolerate those who are different but instead celebrate their members' differences.

Workplace diversity encompasses all the ways in which people differ (keep in mind that people are often more similar than they are different). **Diversity-friendly organizations** are very inclusive. They don't just tolerate those who are different but instead celebrate their members' differences. These companies realize that by fostering an environment of involvement, respect, and inclusion, they create business value. Their diverse workforce equips them to understand evolving markets, connect with their global customer base, develop innovative solutions, and attract and retain the best talent.

Technological advancements have made it possible for businesses to operate with relative ease on a global basis. It is not unusual to read about companies offshoring work to other countries to lessen labour costs or establishing operations in other countries to broaden their market reach. Moreover, companies are hiring workers who have emigrated from other countries to Canada, where greater opportunities exist. European and Middle Eastern companies are experiencing similar increases in immigration. Many companies are seeking to increase the cultural diversity of their workforce because it has been proven to have positive results on the bottom line.

What challenges come from hiring a culturally diverse workforce? The workforce today comprises employees from many different cultures and religions, which can lead to challenges in helping employees understand one another. Companies need to address diversity with training and other initiatives to be successful. Failure to do this can lead to lawsuits and embarrassment.

A more culturally diverse population naturally brings about a wider variety of religious beliefs and practices, with more employees trying to integrate their religious practices into their workday. As employers struggle to accommodate workers' religious needs, they must also try to avoid the potential friction that open demonstrations of religious practices may provoke. Many employers strike a balance by allowing employees to take prayer breaks, enabling employees to take time off to observe religious holidays, catering to dietary requirements, and permitting differences in dress. Some companies have set up quiet prayer rooms for their employees, and some employers encourage workers to form religious-based support groups.

What challenges come from hiring a gender-diverse workforce? More women are entering the workforce than ever before. However, statistically, relatively few females hold top executive positions. High-performing women don't have the sponsorship they need to reach the top—there is an absence of male advocacy. Many women underestimate the impact sponsorship may play in their advancement and fail to cultivate it. Others feel that hard work alone should be the basis of advancement and not the "connections" they make. Sponsorship can be misconstrued as sexual interest, so ambitious women and top executive men avoid it. The *Financial Post* 500 Catalyst Census states that "from 2005 to 2009, the number of female seats on corporate boards in the top 500 Canadian companies increased by half a percentage point per year, from 12% to 14%."[36] At that rate, Canadian women won't hold half the board seats in these companies until 2082. Unfortunately, this snail's pace does not reflect women's educational qualifications; for example, in 2010, 71 percent of women aged 25 to 44 years had completed post-secondary education as compared to 65 percent of men of the same age.[37] Companies that foster sponsorships of their standout women will gain a competitive advantage in talent markets around the world.

What challenges come from hiring an age-diverse workforce? Baby boomers (those born between 1945 and 1964) represent about one-third of the Canadian workforce. Many baby boomers indicate that they would like to, and need to, work beyond the traditional retirement age. This aging demographic group creates several workforce challenges. Compared with younger workers in the same position, older workers often expect higher salaries and better benefits. Health care costs, for example, are higher with an older workforce. However, many employers find that hiring and retaining older employees has several benefits, including less turnover and absenteeism, lower training costs, and a willingness to learn new skills and to help and train younger coworkers. These benefits offset the higher costs of retaining senior workers. Companies that hire an age-diverse workforce have a unique opportunity to use the insight of different generations and capitalize on the unique attributes each age group brings to the workplace.

Diversity-Friendly Organizations

How is a diverse workforce beneficial? As discussed earlier, diversity is an important component of the modern workplace. For many companies, hiring to diversify the workforce initially meant complying with a government requirement by filling positions with a certain number of Aboriginal peoples, women, visible minorities, or persons with disabilities. Some criticized this strategy as unfair and bad for the company if the best candidate was not hired in favour of meeting such a requirement. Over time, however, many companies have come to embrace the idea of diversity beyond just satisfying a requirement. It is now becoming clear that companies should embrace diversity as a strategy and a resource to become more competitive in the global market. Promoting diversity in the workplace is more than abiding by the law; diversity should be aggressively pursued as a means to improve a company's competitiveness and its bottom line.

Stockbyte/Thinkstock/Getty Images

Harley-Davidson realized that to remain competitive it needed to understand the needs and wants of customers beyond the traditional stereotype of the white male. Since then, the motorcycle manufacturer has made a significant effort to hire and retain women and minority managers.[38]

A diverse workforce benefits organizations by supplying a broad range of viewpoints necessary to compete in a globalized marketplace. Such variety promotes creativity in problem solving with improved results. Products and services need to cater to customers

On Target

One Diversity Training Program Does Not Fit All

Because promoting diversity is a priority for most companies in today's global marketplace, so too is the implementation of diversity training programs. These often-costly programs typically involve workshops and seminars that teach managers about the benefits of a diverse workforce. Yet researchers found that most of them simply don't work.[39] While training was by far the most popular approach, it was also the least effective at getting companies to hire and promote women and minorities. Why? Some theorize that mandatory training inevitably leads to backlash; others say altering people's inner biases is a nearly impossible task. Hope for promoting diversity in the workplace is not lost, however; researchers also found that two techniques had significant, beneficial effects on workplace diversity. The first, the appointment of a specific person or committee specifically accountable for addressing diversity issues within the company, led to 10-percent increases in the number of women and minorities in management positions. The second, creating minority mentoring programs in which executives are designated a protégé to mentor, increased the number of women and visible minorities in leadership positions by 23.5 percent. A combination of several approaches leads to the best results.

Discussion Questions

1. **What might happen to companies that don't diversify their workforce?**
2. **Are most people unbiased and unprejudiced by nature or is this something they have to work at?**
3. **Why do you think a combination of approaches to diversity training seems to work best?**

and clients with diverse backgrounds, and if a company's workforce does not understand the nuances of different cultural needs, it may be missing some opportunities.

PepsiCo's Frito Lay launched a Doritos Guacamole-Flavoured Tortilla chip to appeal especially to Latino consumers. The Latino Employee Network at PepsiCo's Frito Lay division provided valuable feedback on taste and packaging to ensure that these chips would be regarded as authentic in the Latino community. The product generated more than US$100 million in sales in its first year, making it the most successful product launch in the company's history. Additionally, a diverse staff helps strategize ways to handle markets that have become segmented, both culturally and demographically.[40]

EMPLOYER–EMPLOYEE RELATIONS

LO8 Outline the objectives of unions and the process of collective bargaining.

Labour Unions

employer–employee relations The communication that takes place between employers and employees.

What is meant by employer–employee relations?

Employer–employee relations refer to the communication that takes place between employers and employees. Much of employee relations involve employers and employees working together. Discussions between employers and employees typically cover the following areas: work schedules, bonuses, compensation, the work environment, hours of work, safety, production targets, and disputes. Employer–employee relations are affected by a number of factors, including labour organizations, labour market, government policy, the structure of the economy, labour law, technical change, and the collective bargaining power of the union (explained below).

labour union A legally recognized group dedicated to protecting the interests of workers.

Employers and employees seem to approach employment from vastly different perspectives. So how can the two sides reach any sort of agreement? One answer lies in labour unions. A **labour union** is a legally recognized group dedicated to protecting the interests of workers. They negotiate employment issues such as salary, benefits, and working hours with corporations, businesses, and other organizations on behalf of union members (workers).

Olivier Le Moal/Shutterstock

What are the objectives of labour unions? Labour unions began as a means to protect workers from the terrible injustices employers inflicted on their workers in the nineteenth century during the Industrial Revolution. During that time, employers took advantage of workers, subjecting them to long hours, low pay, and health risks. Women and children were often treated worse and were paid less than men. Labour unions formed to fight for better working conditions and employee rights. These individual labour unions, by joining, proved to be more effective in bettering working conditions.

Unions have played a role in the employer–employee dialogue for centuries. Historically, unions were formed in manufacturing and resource companies, companies operating in steel mills, textile factories, and mines. Over time, unions have grown into other industries. Today, large memberships can be found in transportation, construction (e.g., roofers, plumbers, engineers), government (e.g., teachers, hospitals, firefighters), and utilities. Entertainers and supporting industries, such as actors and writers, also have unions. Nearly 30 percent of Canadian workers belong to unions.[41] Canada's largest labour unions include the Canadian Union of Public Employees (CUPE), the United Food and Commercial Workers Canada (UFCW Canada), and Unifor, which is a recent merger of the Canadian Auto Workers (CAW) and the Communications, Energy, and Paperworkers (CEP) union.

How are labour unions structured? To form a union, a group of workers must either have their employer voluntarily recognize them as a group or have a majority of workers form a bargaining unit for union representation. A **bargaining unit** is a group of employees who negotiate with the employer for better working conditions or pay. When a union forms, workers join and pay membership dues. Most unions have paid full-time staff as well as a substantial number of volunteer workers. In addition to dues, some unions create strike funds that help support workers in the event of a strike. Union members elect **officers and shop stewards**, who make decisions for the entire body and represent the members in dealings with management. There are three main functions of the local union: collective bargaining, member services and worker relations, and community and political activities.

bargaining unit A group of employees who negotiate with the employer for better working conditions or pay.

officers and shop stewards Elected by union members to make decisions for the entire body and represent the members in dealings with management.

collective bargaining A process in which workers (through a union) negotiate with employers for better work conditions and terms of employment.

collective bargaining agreement The result of union–employer negotiations that forces the employer to abide by the conditions specified in the agreement. Change can only be made through subsequent negotiations.

Collective Bargaining

What is the collective bargaining process? One of the main tasks performed by a union is **collective bargaining**, a process in which workers (through a union) negotiate with employers for better work conditions and terms of employment. Negotiation is between union representatives and employers usually over concerns including wages, benefits, working hours, and grievance procedures. In recent decades, unions have experienced limited growth because of a shift from manufacturing and large companies to small and medium-sized companies outside of manufacturing. A **collective bargaining agreement** is the result of union–employer negotiations and forces the employer to abide by the conditions specified in the agreement. Change can only be made through subsequent negotiations.

If management violates some part of the collective bargaining agreement, employees or the union may file a **grievance**, which is a formal complaint by an employee, employees, or the union usually brought to the supervisor's attention either in person or in writing. If the problem is not resolved, the grievance is put in writing and perhaps a union official, the employee, and one or more managers discuss the grievance. If top management and the local union cannot resolve the grievance, it goes to arbitration.

Video: UPS: Union-Management Relations

grievance A formal complaint by an employee, employees, or the union usually brought to the supervisor's attention either in person or in writing.

mediation A process that involves a neutral third party who assists the two parties both privately and collectively to identify issues and develop proposals for resolution.

arbitration A process in which the disputing parties present their case to a third-party intermediary who examines all the evidence and then makes a decision (usually binding) for the parties.

boycott Occurs when union members and their supporters refuse to buy or handle the company's products or services.

lockout Occurs when management refuses to allow union members to enter the work premises.

strike Occurs when union workers agree to stop work until certain demands are met.

strikebreakers (or scabs) Replacement personnel hired by management during a strike.

Video: Fast Food Workers Walk Out, Demanding Higher Pay

What happens if an agreement cannot be reached through collective bargaining? If negotiating does not produce a collective bargaining agreement, and both parties seem to be at an impasse, then other means to settle the dispute are used before workers go on strike. **Mediation** is a process that involves a neutral third party who assists the two parties both privately and collectively to identify issues and develop proposals for resolution.[42] The mediator works with both sides to understand their genuine interests and helps each side generate proposals that address those interests. **Arbitration** is a process in which the disputing parties present their case to a third-party intermediary (or a panel of arbitrators) who examine all the evidence and then make a decision (usually binding) for the parties. Sometimes, arbitration is nonbinding, meaning that neither party is required to accept the arbitrator's decision.

What happens when negotiations break down? When negotiation reaches an impasse, union workers can take several actions to prompt management to accept union demands. Union members and those sympathetic to their cause can stage a **boycott**, in which supporters refuse to buy or handle the company's products or services. On the other hand, companies can use a **lockout** in which management refuses to allow union members to enter the work premises. Lockouts are legal only if negotiations have come to an impasse and the company is defending a legitimate position.

A **strike** occurs when union workers agree to stop work until certain demands are met. As a last resort, union workers may vote to go on strike and agree to stop working. Strikes jeopardize the productivity of the organization, so they are used to force management into making concessions that they may not have made otherwise. Strikes also gain considerable media publicity, especially when the workers picket the workplace by walking outside the company's entrances with signs that reflect the employees' grievances. Workers do not easily make the decision to strike, as they risk losing income throughout the strike period. For example, a six-week strike would cost a worker earning $700 a week a total of $4200 in lost wages. Assuming the new contract negotiated an hourly wage increase of $1, it would take about two years to recover the lost wages. Additionally, strikers may be temporarily replaced during a strike, as management has the authority to hire replacement personnel, known as **strikebreakers (or scabs)**. Some public service workers such as police officers, firefighters, and hospital workers are prohibited from going on strike because these services are deemed essential to society. In these cases, workers often have "sick-outs," during which union members are not officially on strike but instead call in sick, refusing to come to work.

The summer of 2009 saw the longest strike in Toronto's history, as 24 000 city workers walked off the job after six months of unsuccessful contract bargaining, bringing a halt to garbage collection, 57 city-run daycares, public swimming pools, ferries, and a host of other public services. One of the main reasons for the contract dispute was an existing perk allowing workers to bank unused sick days and cash them in when they retired, which the City of Toronto wanted to abolish because it would cost hundreds of millions in payouts. Job security was another major issue.[43] After39 days on strike, the two sides reached an agreement. The deal phased out banked sick days by ending the practice for new hires and giving the 18 000 current workers a choice to sell their sick days or hold on to them. In the end, this deal saved the city well over $100 million. An agreement over wage increases was also made.[44]

David Cooper/Getstock

When employees go on strike it can cause major inconvenience for people who rely on the company's services. This is what happened when Toronto city workers went on strike in July 2009, when garbage piled up on city streets.

What is the future of unions and employer–labour relations? In response to a more globalized working community, unions have begun to build alliances worldwide. They recognize that when multinational corporations make decisions to move production abroad, for example, there may be a negative impact on local and international workers. Consequently, in an effort to protect their interests, they must broaden their reach and make a commitment to international labour solidarity. Unions will need to transform themselves to survive the effects of globalization.

Human Rights and Labour Laws

LO9 Describe some of the key legislation regulating the hiring, compensating, and managing of employees in today's workplace.

How do laws and regulations affect human resource management? Several federal, provincial, and territorial labour laws—aimed at safeguarding employee rights and mediating many aspects of the relationship between employers, unions, and employees—must be observed in HRM. In Canada, laws related to unionized workplaces (collective labour law) differ from those relating to nonunionized workplaces. (In most countries, however, no such distinction is made.[45]) There is a constitutional division between the federal government and the governments of Canada's 10 provinces and three territories. Only 10 percent of all Canadian employees are working in jobs covered by the federal labour law. The remaining 90 percent of Canada's employees are covered by provincial or territorial statutes.[46] Industries such as banks, broadcasting and telecommunications, airlines, railways, pipelines, uranium mines, and marine transport and related services are regulated by the federal government. Most other industries fall under provincial or territorial jurisdiction.

Legislation affects all areas of HRM, from hiring and training to compensating and transitioning employees. There have been many court cases where employees have accused employers of wrongful dismissal, and most often the courts decide in favour of the employee. Terminating an employee's employment because the employee is a certain race, nationality, religion, sex, or age may constitute wrongful dismissal. A court-proven wrongful dismissal tends to result in either a reinstatement of the dismissed employee or financial compensation for the wrongfully dismissed.[47] Similarly, employers must use equitable practices and offer equal opportunities to all when hiring for a position to avoid discrimination.

To ensure a company is in compliance with the laws governing HRM, managers need to know the regulations pertaining to human rights, employment standards, occupational health and safety, labour, privacy, and workers' compensation. A few essential topics include wrongful termination, discrimination or harassment, rules on drug testing, rules on accommodating employees with disabilities, personal liability, and various provincial laws within the provinces the company operates.[48] Such standards protect the rights of workers, foster a positive workplace environment, enhance the relationship between managers and employees, and ultimately benefit the bottom line of any business.

The **Canada Labour Code** (at the federal level) and the provincial **employment standards acts and labour codes** (at the provincial level) define the rights and obligations of individuals as workers, union members, and employers in the workplace.[49]

Canada Labour Code Together with the provincial employment standards acts and labour codes (at the provincial level), this federal law defines the rights and obligations of individuals as workers, union members, and employers in the workplace.

employment standards acts and labour codes Together with the Canada Labour Code (at the federal level), these provincial standards define the rights and obligations of individuals as workers, union members, and employers in the workplace.

Gunnar Pippel/Shutterstock

Equitable employment practices are important for all companies to follow to avoid discriminating against potential employees or those already working for the company.

The Canada Labour Code applies to federally regulated employers with 100 or more employees and contains three parts:

1. *Industrial relations.* Certification of unions, labour–management relations, collective bargaining, and unfair labour practices.
2. *Workplace health and safety.* Ensures health and safety of employees by preventing accidents and injury to health arising out of, linked with, or occurring in the course of employment. All workers in Canada have the right to work in a safe and healthy environment. WHMIS (Workplace Hazardous Materials Information System) is an amendment to the Occupational Health and Safety Act and dictates that information must be shared with employees on hazardous materials in the workplace.
3. *Employment standards.* Deals with the terms and conditions of employment such as general holidays, annual vacations, leaves, working hours, unjust dismissals, minimum wage, layoff procedures, and severance pay. Labour law prohibits companies from terminating employment because of whistleblowing, filing of a worker's compensation claim, jury duty, or testifying against the company in a legal proceeding.

How does the Canadian Human Rights Act affect recruiting practices? The Canadian Human Rights Act promotes equal opportunity and prohibits discrimination and a wide variety of practices in recruiting, selecting, promoting, and dismissing employees or prospective employees. An ability genuinely needed to perform a job is called a **bona fide job requirement**. A person who lacks such a necessary ability can be legitimately denied employment (e.g., a person with a visual impairment will be denied employment as a bus driver).

bona fide job requirement An ability genuinely needed to perform a job. A person who lacks such a necessary ability can be legitimately denied employment (e.g., a person with a visual impairment will be denied employment as a bus driver).

Does employment equity mean that every employee receives the same pay? While employers must ensure they compensate employees equally for equal work and equal qualifications, the act pertaining to employment equity is about correcting an imbalance in the workforce that has occurred over time. The Employment Equity Act applies to federally regulated industries. The act states that no person shall be denied employment opportunities or benefits for reasons unrelated to ability. It seeks to improve the employment conditions experienced by women, Aboriginal peoples, persons with disabilities, and members of visible minorities.[50] Equitable treatment does not mean preferential treatment, nor does it mean treating everyone the same. It means treating people as equals through the reasonable accommodation of their differences or using special measures designed to remedy past discrimination.

Are employers expected to provide employees with a safe work environment? The **Occupational Health and Safety (OHS) acts and regulations** are enabled at the federal, provincial, and territorial levels and are designed to secure workers and self-employed persons from risks to their safety, health, and physical well-being arising out of or in connection with activities in their workplaces. OHS legislation outlines the general rights and responsibilities of the employer, the supervisor, and the worker. Employers are required to provide a safe environment for workers as well as provide safety equipment and training where necessary. For example, **WHMIS (Workplace Hazardous Materials Information System)** is a comprehensive plan for providing information on hazardous materials to employees. Employees are required to conduct themselves in accordance with safety procedures and regulations and have the right to refuse work on a job if they believe it is unsafe; a legal procedure exists for resolving any disputes in this area. In most provinces, the Ministry of Labour appoints inspectors to enforce health and safety regulations. For instance, working at heights without proper fall protection is a primary safety issue in the commercial construction sector, and if OHS officers find a violation of this during an inspection they will issue a "stop work" order.[51]

Occupational Health and Safety (OHS) acts and regulations Enabled at the federal, provincial, and territorial levels and are designed to secure workers and self-employed persons from risks to their safety, health, and physical well-being arising out of or in connection with activities in their workplaces.

WHMIS (Workplace Hazardous Materials Information System) A comprehensive plan for providing information on hazardous materials to employees.

HR managers are responsible for knowing the legislation in detail and for ensuring that management throughout the organization implements the legislation effectively. In addition, managers must be sensitive to union contracts as well as social standards and expectations. HR managers can stay abreast of what is happening in the HR world by networking, joining relevant associations, subscribing to HR publications, and reviewing labour and employment laws.

Video: Woman on Track to Become First Female NFL Ref

CHAPTER SYNOPSIS

LO1 Define human resource management (HRM) and discuss how the functions of HRM support an organization. *(pp. 143–144)*

Human resources (HR)—the people in an organization—need to be managed just as carefully as the material and financial resources of a business. **Human resource management (HRM)** is the organizational function that deals with the people in the business, from the executives and the managers to the front-line production, sales, and administrative staff. HRM aims to ensure that the organization is correctly staffed at all times by the right number of employees with the right skills required to meet company goals. Proper management of human assets builds value in the company and ensures time and money is not wasted.

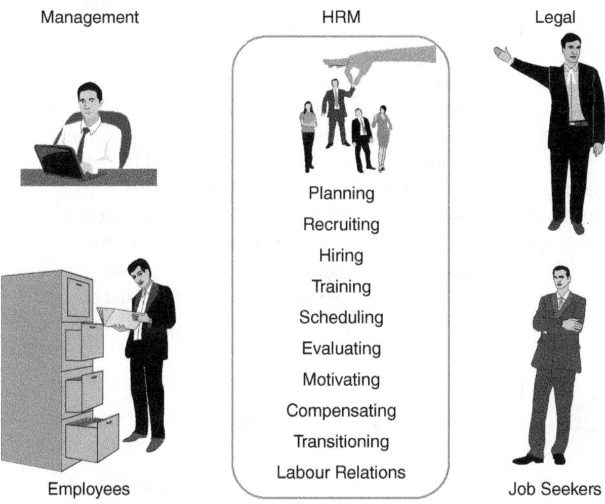

Functions of Human Resource Management

HRM functions encompass every aspect of the "human" in a business, including planning, recruiting, selecting and hiring, training, evaluating, compensating, scheduling, motivating, and transitioning employees. HRM also oversees employee–management relations and must always work within the limits of the law. HRM works through the many challenges in today's society, such as diversity issues, work–lifestyle preferences, and global business considerations. Most HRM functions are shared between the professional human resource manager and other managers.

The **human resources department**, working with other department managers, is responsible for the people in the organization and helps to maximize organizational productivity by optimizing the effectiveness of employees.

LO2 Explain how organizations determine and plan for human resource needs. *(pp. 144–145)*

Human resource planning is creating a strategy for meeting future human resource needs within an organization. Poor staff planning can be costly. Being overstaffed burdens a company with unnecessary expenses for salaries, benefits, and training for surplus employees. An understaffed organization can lead to loss of sales and competitiveness if customer needs are not met. Planning staffing needs therefore involves (1) assessing the supply of and demand for current and future employee resources and (2) evaluating job requirements.

Forecasting is the process of determining the future demand for employees as well as the future supply of employees.A **job analysis** identifies and defines in detail the particular duties and requirements of the tasks and responsibilities an employee is required to perform. A **job description** is a formal statement summarizing what the employee will do in that job role. It includes the job responsibilities, the conditions under which the job will be performed, and the job's relationship to other functions in the organization. **Job specifications** are the skills, education, experience, and personal attributes that candidates need to possess to successfully fulfill the job role.

LO3 Describe some of the methods used and issues faced by companies when recruiting, selecting, and hiring employees. *(pp. 145–149)*

The **recruitment process** provides the organization with a pool of potentially qualified job candidates from which thoughtful selection can be made to fill vacancies. The recruitment process begins when new recruits are sought and ends when their applications are submitted. **Internal recruiting**—filling job vacancies with existing employees from within the business—is the first choice of many companies. Often, companies post job openings on the company intranet, staff notice boards, in-house newsletters, and in staff meetings. Internal recruitment has several advantages. It tends to be a morale booster for employees because they know that the company has an interest in promoting their own. **External recruiting** looks outside the business to fill vacancies using various resources and methods (see figure). **Employment agencies**—which often specialize in accounting, sales, or clerical services—provide a screened pool of candidates, which reduces the hiring company's administrative burden of recruitment.

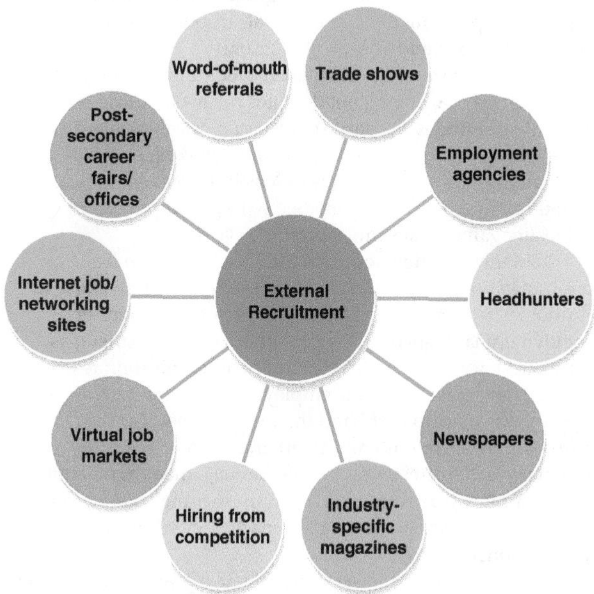

External Recruitment Resources

One of the newer challenges facing recruiting specialists is the use of technology. Online job and résumé posting sites, Web and video blogs, virtual job fairs, podcasts, and other online media are all being used by both those looking to find a job and those looking to fill a position. One of the greatest recruiting challenges cited is the difficulty finding qualified candidates for critical positions.

The **hiring process** begins with developing the job requirements and ends when a job offer is made. **Selection** entails gathering information about candidates, evaluating their qualifications, and choosing the ones that best fit the job specifications. After identifying a small pool of appropriate candidates, department and HR managers meet with each candidate to conduct a **job interview**, a one-on-one meeting between the company and the job candidate, in which the company is able to gauge the candidate's personality, clarify information in the candidate's résumé, and determine whether the candidate is the best match for the position. The candidate may also need to complete one or more skills-related or behavioural tests. **Behavioural interviews** are conducted to evaluate a candidate's experience and behaviours so the employer can determine the applicant's potential for success in the job.

Probation is a specific timeframe (typically three to six months) during which the new hire proves his or her skills and worth on the job. If the employee proves him- or herself on the job, he or she moves from probational employee status to permanent employee status.

LO4 Discuss some of the ways employees are trained and how performance can be evaluated. *(pp. 150–153)*

An **orientation program** is used to introduce a new employee to the company's people, policies, and procedures. **On-the-job training** occurs when employees learn skills by performing them. **Off-the-job training and development** techniques require employees to participate in outside seminars, university-conducted programs, and corporate universities.

Mentoring is a form of on-the-job training whereby an experienced employee provides direction and information to the new employee as he or she learns the job. **Mentors** are experienced individual employees who help a less-experienced person by explaining how to perform specific tasks, creating opportunities to learn new skills, and counselling about the consequences of particular actions and decisions. Mentoring increases employee performance, satisfaction, and loyalty. Sometimes, however, an apprentice training program is required. An **apprentice training** program trains individuals through classroom or formal instruction and on-the-job training.

Simulation training provides realistic job-task training in a manner that is challenging but does not create the threat of failure. **Vestibule training** is a type of simulation most suitable to airline pilots, astronauts, and surgeons, for whom making mistakes during training is not an option or is too costly. **Games-based learning (serious games)** is a training method whereby employees play virtual reality games that simulate real-life events.

Management development training focuses on leadership, communication, teamwork, and relationship-building skills. In addition, managers need to keep abreast of the changes in employment laws such as discrimination and harassment, as well as updates in the use of electronic communication resources. **Job rotation** occurs when the employee rotates through different departments to learn first-hand the various aspects of the business. **Coaching/understudy programs** occur when the employee works directly with senior management in planning and other managerial functions. **Action learning**, another management development training approach, focuses on solving real problems on actual work projects.

A **performance appraisal** is an evaluation of an employee's performance that gives feedback about how well the employee is doing, as well as where changes and improvements are needed. **Performance management** is an approach that combines goal setting, performance appraisal, and training and development into a unified and ongoing process. As such, it is more of a cyclical and fluid process than the single occurrence of a performance appraisal. Employees are constantly receiving feedback and given opportunities for training and development to ensure that they have the right tools with which to perform their job. The vibrancy and performance of the organization is ensured because managers put focus on developmental plans and opportunities for each staff member. Thus, it is much more effective than the traditional method of using performance appraisals.

LO5 Describe how employees can be compensated and some of the different kinds of work schedule arrangements that are used to meet the needs of employees and the company. *(pp. 153–158)*

Compensation, payment for work performed, comes in a variety of forms, including money, bonuses, work–life benefits, health insurance, and retirement plans. **Work–life benefits** help an employee achieve a balance between the demands of life both inside and outside the workplace.

Regarding specific individuals and positions, companies typically determine the type and amount of compensation on a balance of the following: federal and provincial legislation (the law), what the company can afford, what competitors are paying, and what skills and talents each employee brings to the company.

The methods of compensating employees include wages, salary, piecework, commissions, accelerated commissions, bonuses, profit sharing, gain sharing, and stock options. Vacation, holidays, and pensions constitute a significant percentage of total compensation. Other noncash benefits help employees balance the demands of their professional and personal lives.

Creating work schedules requires meeting the needs of the company while satisfying the needs of the workers.The most popular **flexible work schedules** include flextime, permanent parttime, job sharing, compressed workweek, and telecommuting. Despite the costs associated with designing and implementing flexible working arrangements, employers can expect positive bottom-line results because of increases in employee satisfaction, decreases in absenteeism, increases in worker productivity, and reduced turnover. At times companies must schedule **contingent workers** or **independent contractors and consultants** to help with various business activities.

LO6 Explain how employees transition through a company over time by way of promotions, transfers, retirement, and termination. *(pp. 158–161)*

A **promotion** may be an upward or lateral move into a new position that allows employees to develop and display new skills and to learn more about the company overall. A **transfer** occurs when an employee is appointed to the same or similar position elsewhere within the organization. Transfers usually refer to a lateral move (a horizontal job assignment). **Retirement** is the point in a person's life when he or she stops participating fulltime in his or her career.

Some employees leave their jobs to work for another company and some leave for personal reasons (possibly to raise a family). **Termination** of employment because of an employee's poor performance or illegal activities can be a rather complex process. It is imperative for employers to have a good record-keeping system in place regarding poorly performing employees. **Exit interviews** are often conducted (in person, online, or on the telephone) by an outside contractor or by HR department personnel to gather feedback before employees leave the company.

The **turnover rate** tracks the number of employees that leave the company each year. Companies monitor the turnover rate to compare it to previous years as an aid in analyzing and determining staffing needs and trends.

LO7 Identify the ways in which Canada's demographics are changing and how this affects the workforce. *(pp. 161–164)*

Workplace diversity encompasses all the ways in which people differ (keep in mind that people are often more similar than they are different). **Diversity-friendly organizations** are very inclusive. They don't just tolerate those who are different but instead celebrate their members' differences.

The workforce today comprises employees from many different cultures and religions, which can lead to challenges in helping employees understand one another. Companies need to address diversity with training and other initiatives to be successful. Failure to do this can lead to lawsuits and embarrassment.

A more culturally diverse population naturally brings about a wider variety of religious beliefs and practices, with more employees trying to integrate their religious practices into their workday. More women are entering the workforce than ever before. However, statistically, relatively few females hold top executive positions. Baby boomers (those born between 1943 and 1960) represent about one-third of the Canadian workforce. Many baby boomers indicate that they would like to (or need to) work beyond the traditional retirement age.

A diverse workforce benefits organizations by supplying the broad range of viewpoints necessary to compete in a world that is more globalized.

LO8 Outline the objectives of unions and the process of collective bargaining. *(pp. 164–167)*

A **labour union** is a legally recognized group dedicated to protecting the interests of workers. They negotiate employment issues such as salary, benefits, and working hours with corporations, businesses, and other organizations on behalf of union members (workers). A **collective bargaining agreement** is the result of such negotiations and forces the employer to abide by the conditions specified in the agreement. Change can only be made through subsequent negotiations. If negotiating does not produce a collective bargaining agreement, and both parties seem to be at an impasse, then other means to settle the dispute are used—usually mediation or arbitration and sometimes boycotts or lockouts and, in the most extreme cases, worker strikes. A **grievance** is a formal complaint by an employee, employees, or the union usually brought to the supervisor's attention either in person or in writing.

Mediation is a process that involves a neutral third party that assists the two parties both privately and collectively to identify issues and develop proposals for resolution. **Arbitration** is a process in which the disputing parties present their case to a third-party intermediary (or a panel of arbitrators) who examine all the evidence and then make a decision (usually binding) for the parties. Sometimes arbitration is nonbinding, meaning that neither party is required to accept the arbitrator's decision.

A **boycott** occurs when union members and their supporters refuse to buy or handle the company's products or services. A **lockout** occurs when management refuses to allow union members to enter the work premises. A **strike** occurs when union workers agree to stop work until certain demands are met. Strikes jeopardize the productivity of the organization, so they are used to force management into making concessions that they may not have made otherwise.

LO9 Describe some of the key legislation regulating the hiring, compensating, and managing of employees in today's workplace. *(pp. 167–168)*

Several federal, provincial, and territorial labour laws must be observed in HRM. Legislation affects all areas of HRM, from hiring and training to compensating and transitioning employees. Mainly the laws affecting HRM focus on issues of equity in the workplace, equal opportunity, human rights, and discrimination. They include but are not limited to the Canadian Human Rights Act, Canada Labour Code, and the provincial and territorial employment standards acts and labour codes.

The **Canada Labour Code** (at the federal level) and the provincial **employment standards acts and labour codes** (at the provincial level) define the rights and obligations of individuals as workers, union members, and employers in the workplace.

The **Occupational Health and Safety (OHS) acts and regulations** are enabled at the federal, provincial, and territorial levels and are designed to secure workers and self-employed persons from risks to their safety, health, and physical well-being arising out of or in connection with activities in their workplaces.

MyBizLab Study, practise, and explore real business situations with these helpful resources:

- **Interactive Lesson Presentations:** Work through interactive presentations and assessments to test your knowledge of business concepts.
- **Study Plan:** Check your understanding of chapter concepts with self-study quizzes.
- **Dynamic Study Modules:** Work through adaptive study modules on your computer, tablet, or mobile device.
- **Simulations:** Practise decision-making in simulated business environments.

KEY TERMS

action learning *(p. 151)*
apprentice training *(p. 150)*
arbitration *(p. 166)*
bargaining unit *(p. 165)*
behavioural interviews *(p. 148)*
benefits *(p. 154)*
bona fide job requirement *(p. 168)*
boycott *(p. 166)*
Canada Labour Code *(p. 167)*
coaching/understudy program *(p. 151)*
collective bargaining *(p. 165)*
collective bargaining agreement *(p. 165)*
compensation *(p. 153)*
contingent workers (temporary employees) *(p. 158)*
diversity-friendly organizations *(p. 162)*
employee assistance programs (EAPs) *(p. 155)*
employee information system (EIS) *(p. 145)*
employer–employee relations *(p. 164)*
employment agencies *(p. 146)*
employment standards acts and labour codes *(p. 167)*
exit interviews *(p. 160)*
external recruiting *(p. 146)*
flexible benefits plans *(p. 155)*
flexible work schedule *(p. 156)*
forecasting *(p. 145)*
games-based learning (serious games) *(p. 151)*
grievance *(p. 165)*
hiring process *(p. 149)*
HRM functions *(p. 143)*
human resource management (HRM) *(p. 143)*
human resource planning *(p. 144)*
human resources (HR) *(p. 143)*
human resources department *(p. 143)*
independent contractors and consultants *(p. 158)*
internal recruiting *(p. 145)*
job analysis *(p. 145)*
job description *(p. 145)*
job interview *(p. 148)*
job rotation *(p. 151)*
job specifications *(p. 145)*
labour union *(p. 164)*
lockout *(p. 166)*
management development training *(p. 151)*
mediation *(p. 166)*
mentoring *(p. 150)*
mentors *(p. 150)*
Occupational Health and Safety (OHS) acts and regulations *(p. 168)*
off-the-job training and development *(p. 150)*
officers and shop stewards *(p. 165)*
online training *(p. 150)*
on-the-job training *(p. 150)*
orientation program *(p. 150)*
performance appraisal *(p. 152)*
performance management *(p. 152)*

probation (p. 149)
promotion (p. 158)
recruitment process (p. 145)
retirement (p. 160)
selection (p. 148)
simulation training (p. 150)
strike (p. 166)
strikebreakers (or scabs) (p. 166)
termination (p. 161)
transfer (p. 158)
turnover rate (p. 160)
vestibule training (p. 150)
WHMIS (Workplace Hazardous Materials Information System) (p. 168)
work–life benefits (p. 155)
workplace diversity (p. 162)

CRITICAL THINKING QUESTIONS

1. Discuss how human resource management can help a company achieve or maintain a competitive advantage. How does human resource management help a company maintain a healthy bottom line?
2. Discuss the various types of training you have had as an employee or student. What suggestions would you make to improve the training? What parts of the training did you find to be most effective? How important is training employees to a company's overall goals and strategies? Why not just let employees learn their jobs as they perform them?
3. Describe the "perfect" benefits package that would be most important to you when applying for a job. What kinds of questions could you ask to determine how and when those benefits will be offered to you? How does salary/pay level affect your decision? Would you accept a lower salary/pay level for better benefits?
4. When Leslie was given the task of finding a new senior account executive, she weighed her options carefully. To fill such a senior position required patience. She hired a recruiter to find outside candidates to interview for the position, and, to keep her options open, she also placed job postings online and in newspapers.
   a. What are the benefits of outsourcing the recruitment process?
   b. What other methods could Leslie have used to fill the position?
   c. What else is involved in the hiring process?
5. Look at the following statements and think about what your reactions to the statements tell you about yourself:
   - Everyone, including white males, benefits from diversity training.
   - Diversity training only includes race and gender.
   - Certain ethnic groups are smarter than others.
   - Talking about diversity just makes people uncomfortable.
   - Some professions are not suited for older people.

   Have your feelings on the importance of diversity changed after reading this chapter? What challenges and benefits have you encountered or do you anticipate encountering in the workplace related to diversity?

APPLICATION EXERCISES

1. **Job description.** Create a job description and job specification for a job of your or your professor's choosing. Start with a job analysis. You'll probably need to ask your professor some questions.
2. **Staffing agency.** Locate a staffing agency near you and phone them and ask for information about their recruitment and placement services. Enquire about the processes the agency uses to register, interview, test, and place (find a suitable job for) a job applicant. Does it cost money to register for a job with the agency? What skills must you have? What does the interview process entail? What types of tests do they use? Do you notice similarities between the procedures the agency uses and those discussed in this chapter? Did you notice processes that were different from those discussed in this chapter? Do you think you might be interested in registering with a staffing agency once you graduate? Why or why not?
3. **Wrongful dismissal.** Find a recent case (within the past one to five years) of wrongful dismissal at a company in Canada or the United States. Read about it and gather some details. Determine what went wrong. Where did either the employer or employee make mistakes? Could this situation have been resolved earlier, before the employee was fired? Is the employer or employee right? What did the courts say? Summarize your findings.
4. **Organized labour.** The Canadian Labour Congress represents the interests of more than 3 million affiliated workers in every imaginable occupation. Explore the Canadian Labour Congress website (www.canadianlabour.ca). What are its current concerns and causes? How does one become involved in this organization? What about its history? Which historical, political, and social forces propelled the organized labour movement?
5. **Legal matters.** Visit the Canadian Civil Liberties Association (http://ccla.org) to find information about current cases concerning employee rights, anti-discrimination laws, or other HR concerns. What are the circumstances of these cases? What is your opinion on them?

TEAM TIME

Seeing Both Sides

Walmart has been both praised and criticized for many of its human resource policies. Assemble into teams of four students. Break each team into two subgroups.

Subgroup 1: Good HR Practices: Going back no more than five years, research articles about the positive human resource policies and practices Walmart has implemented. Prepare a summary paper outlining your findings.

Subgroup 2: Bad HR Practices: Going back no more than five years, research articles about the negative human resource policies and practices Walmart has implemented. Prepare a summary paper outlining your findings.

PROCESS

As one group, compile your findings, comparing the positive and negative policies.

Were there instances where a policy started out as a positive and ended up as a negative, or vice versa? How do the policies work with Walmart's strategic goals? How have the policies affected Walmart's stock price and bottom line? Did Walmart's treatment of its human resources affect the business or the company's reputation either negatively or positively? Did it affect morale? Do Walmart employees have a union or want to form one? Why?

If you were employed as an HR consultant for Walmart, what kind of advice would you give the company based on your findings? What can Walmart do to improve its employees' loyalty? What can it do to help motivate its workers? What effects on business (stock price and bottom line) will these changes have?

ETHICS AND RESPONSIBILITY

The Ethics of Interviewing
The interview and hiring process is fraught with ethical concerns. Form a small group and discuss the ethical implications of the following scenario.

SCENARIO

Where does a candidate's right to privacy end and a company's right to know begin? As you learned in this chapter, federal laws protect potential employees from discrimination. Hiring managers must observe these laws by refraining from asking certain questions during the interview process, such as direct questions about age and physical disabilities. However, to find out about these topics while still staying within the bounds of legality, managers have devised alternative questions.[52] For example:

Instead of asking:	They ask this legal alternative:
Which religious holidays do you observe?	Can you work our required schedule?
Do you have kids?	What is your experience with "X" age group?
Do you have any disabilities?	Are you able to perform this position's specific duties?

PROCESS

With your group, discuss your opinions on the use of these "legal alternatives" as an HR strategy. They are legal, but are they ethical? Do managers undermine the laws by finding ways around them? Or does the company have a right to know about these topics to make the best hiring decision?

CLOSING CASE

The Toyota T-Ten Program

Toyota's responsibility to its customers does not end once the buyer drives the car off the lot. Toyota must maintain promises made in its warranties and assist customers with annual maintenance. Most of these activities are performed at Toyota dealerships by Toyota-certified technicians. Finding employees with expertise on Toyota vehicles might be a difficult task if it were not for Toyota's T-Ten program.[53] The T-Ten program is a one-stop shop for Toyota recruitment, training, and hiring. The one- to two-year program trains potential employees to be automotive technicians who specialize in cars from the Toyota family.

Toyota aims to build its cars to exceptional standards, but the company recognizes that mechanical malfunctions are inevitable at some point in every car's life. Having automotive technicians who are familiar with the car and have the proper training helps customers resolve these problems quickly and effectively. This fulfills Toyota's mission to make dependable cars and provide outstanding service. Car maintenance and service is also a huge profit area for Toyota dealerships, so it is critical that Toyota has a strong group of trained technicians.

T-Ten is a unique concept in the sense that it is a training program set up like a university or college. In fact, T-Ten works in conjunction with a number of vocational schools and community colleges. The curriculum includes classroom training and hands-on experience. Those enrolled in the program can earn a professional certificate, one-year certificate, two-year certificate, or two-year associate degree. Certifications are earned by T-Ten graduates for completing Toyota-designed courses and for passing National Institute for Automotive Service Excellence (ASE) certification tests. These certificates, along with a passing score on the ASE certification tests, allow T-Ten graduates to pursue a career at a Toyota, Lexus, or Scion dealership.[54]

The Toyota T-Ten program is not free, and it does not guarantee a graduate a job. So what makes this program appealing to students? It's the opportunity to work for the world's largest automaker. As Toyota's market share continues to grow, employees can gain a sense of job security.

Education and training do not end once a student graduates from the T-Ten program. Toyota dealerships use the T-Ten school to keep current and even veteran employees up to date on all the latest automotive technologies, such as hybrid engines and GPS devices. Toyota considers itself a technological trailblazer, so ongoing employee education and training is a top priority. Veteran employees also serve as mentors to students during their internship or apprentice training.

By streamlining the recruiting, hiring, and training process of automotive technicians, dealerships are able to choose from a group of extremely qualified candidates. Highly trained and highly specialized employees are desirable in any industry, especially when dealing with a product as intricate as automotives. The Toyota's T-Ten program brings those employees to the workplace prepared on day one.

DISCUSSION QUESTIONS

1. Other car companies, such as GM and Ford, have similar training and technical schools. Why is it so important for companies in the automotive industry to generate qualified potential employees?
2. The text mentions that apprentice training programs are common for occupations such as electricians, roofers, plumbers, as well as auto mechanics. Why do you think the apprentice style of training is important to individuals in those fields? How can workers in those vocations benefit from both on-the-job training and classroom training?
3. Why is ongoing employee education important to Toyota? Why should it be important to any company in the automotive industry? Does the idea of ongoing education apply to all companies in all industries? Why or why not?

8 Marketing and Consumer Behaviour

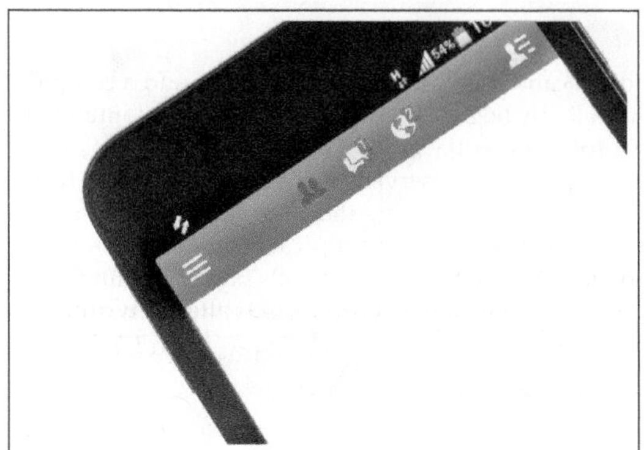

(left) New photo/Shutterstock; (right) Naito8/Shutterstock; (bottom) Sarawut Aiemsinsuk/Shutterstock

LEARNING OBJECTIVES

After studying this chapter, you should be able to:

LO1 Summarize how marketing has evolved over the production concept era, sales concept era, marketing concept era, and customer relationship era. (pp. 176–178)

LO2 Outline the benefits of marketing to various stakeholders and summarize the criticisms of marketing. (pp. 178–180)

LO3 Describe the 4 Ps of the marketing mix and explain the five steps of the marketing process to implement a marketing strategy. (pp. 180–184)

LO4 Describe how the various factors in the marketing environment influence a firm's ability to manipulate its marketing mix. (pp. 184–186)

LO5 Identify the five steps of the marketing research process and the four elements of a good marketing plan. (pp. 186–190)

LO6 Describe how target markets are determined and how a firm attempts to satisfy a target market. (pp. 190–192)

LO7 Describe the purchase decision process and the major influences affecting a consumer's buying decision. (pp. 192–194)

LO8 Compare the buying decisions and marketing processes in business-to-business markets to those in the consumer market. (pp. 194–195)

OPENING DISCUSSION: MARKETING BUZZ

Facebook Turns the "Like" into Its Newest Ad

"People are naturally interested in things their friends care about," says Facebook, which is why its News Feed is a key feature of the social networking site.[1] Clicking Facebook's ubiquitous "Like" button allows you to share online what you like with your friends as your "likes" appear in their News Feed, updating them on what you're saying and doing. Essentially, Facebook is an electronic version of the in-person, word-of-mouth model we might use to tell our friends about the newest and coolest things in our lives—where we like to shop, what products we like to buy, or how good the service is at our favourite restaurant.

Marketers refer to this word-of-mouth advertising as *guerrilla marketing*, which is typically unexpected, unconventional, and potentially interactive. Its goal is to generate buzz (getting people to talk about a company's product or service) and sales: minimal resources achieving maximum results. Companies hope that by generating buzz, their guerrilla marketing campaigns will turn viral. Viral marketing uses pre-existing social networks (i.e., you tell two friends, and they tell two friends, and so on) to increase brand awareness and generate more sales. The term *viral* describes how the ad reaches the masses. Companies want interest in their products and services to spread like a virus: One person reads an ad and likes it (is infected), then that person shares the ad with one or more other people and they like it (are infected), and so on exponentially. These types of marketing techniques have been further enhanced by the Internet's networking strength. Getting someone to "like" your company or product on Facebook is an endorsement and may generate additional business for a company.[2]

More and more companies are using social media and mobile devices to engage consumers and create a memorable brand experience. In 2011, Facebook launched a new ad format called "Sponsored Stories," which presents a friend's actions in the News Feed (likes, check-ins, etc.) as promoted content (ads) in the right-hand column of Facebook. Because, says Facebook, "a lot of impressions do get lost because there's so much content coming through," Sponsored Stories will give brand-related user action much more visibility. Users will be more likely to learn about places to go, apps to use, games to play, and organizations their friends like.[3] Launch partners included Starbucks, Coca-Cola, Levi's, Anheuser-Busch, Amnesty International, RED, and UNICEF.[4]

Jim Squires, Facebook product marketing lead, says, "The advertiser is not controlling the message; it's about actions."[5] For example, if Starbucks buys a Sponsored Story and one of your friends "liked" Starbucks, the ad would run twice: once in your friend's News Feed and again as a paid ad clearly titled Sponsored Story.[6] These relatively inexpensive ads yield a generally higher engagement rate because they target people who are already engaged. A potential area for concern exists should users become dissatisfied with the fact that they cannot stop their Facebook actions from becoming sponsored ads broadcast to all their connections. Friends may gain some control over the viewing of Sponsored Stories by setting their privacy options to hide their activities from each other, but doesn't that defeat the purpose of being a Facebook user?

A check-in post will show up in the Sponsored Story exactly as the user wrote it, which means that a dissatisfied customer could post a negative comment about a company or product. Facebook has obviously anticipated this possibility, providing a "flag" button for "inappropriate content" and giving advertisers the option to avoid any negative postings by limiting their ad purchases to "likes" only.

TBG Digital conducted a test of about 2 billion ad impressions (whenever an ad is displayed on a website), which showed that Sponsored Stories performed better in click-through rate and cost-per-click (measurement of cost on a per-click basis) than standard Facebook ads—in fact, there was a 46 percent higher click-through rate.[7] Click-through rate measures the success of an online advertising campaign and is calculated by dividing the number of mouse clicks the ad received by the number of times the ad was shown (impressions).

Historically, it has been very difficult for companies to buy word-of-mouth advertising, but Sponsored Stories allow companies to leverage their investment in Facebook further by amplifying their brands so they are noticed—which, ultimately, is what companies want.

DISCUSSION QUESTIONS

1. Would you like your posts to be used as ads? Do you think Facebook users will decrease the amount of "likes" they do knowing that their "likes" and other activities may become a Sponsored Story? Why or why not?
2. Do you think that Facebook users who do post a Sponsored Story should be paid for it? Why or why not? Do you think Facebook users may turn away from Facebook because they feel "spammed" on? Why or why not? Do you think businesses will consider that their Sponsored Stories may be viewed by Facebook users as "spam," which might in turn create a negative image of the company instead of the intended positive one? Why or why not?
3. Use the Internet to locate information on why some businesses have failed when trying to implement a social media campaign. Why did they fail? Are these factors present in the Facebook Sponsored Stories strategy?

MARKETING FUNDAMENTALS

LO1 Summarize how marketing has evolved over the production concept era, sales concept era, marketing concept era, and customer relationship era.

The Evolution of Marketing

marketing "A set of business practices designed to plan for and present an organization's products or services in ways that build effective customer relationships." (Canadian Marketing Association)

product Any good, service, or idea available for purchase in a market, as well as any intangible benefits derived from its consumption.

How does the Canadian Marketing Association (CMA) define marketing? CMA members follow a code of ethics to ensure that their marketing practices are fair to consumers. But how responsible are marketers who work with products that may do a disservice to society? For example, what is the moral responsibility for a caffeinated energy drink called Cocaine? Does this glamorize drug use or is it just a cheeky, attention-grabbing name created by marketers to generate buzz?

The CMA defines **marketing** as "a set of business practices designed to plan for and present an organization's products or services in ways that build effective customer relationships."[8] Marketing departments serve a variety of functions. First, marketers are responsible for keeping an eye on what people need and want, then communicating these desires to the rest of the organization. Marketing departments help establish desirable pricing strategies and promote the organization by persuading customers that their products are the best. A **product** is any good, service, or idea available for purchase in a market, as well as any intangible benefits derived from its consumption. Marketing departments are also responsible for distributing products to customers at a place and time most suitable to the customer. But perhaps the most important aspect of marketing is to establish meaningful relationships with customers to instill loyalty and ensure repeat business. Marketing is one of the most visible functions of any organization; however, the public only sees the tip of the iceberg.

ZUMA Press, Inc./Alamy

Is there a moral dilemma with choosing the name "Cocaine" for a caffeinated energy drink, or is it just an example of good marketing?

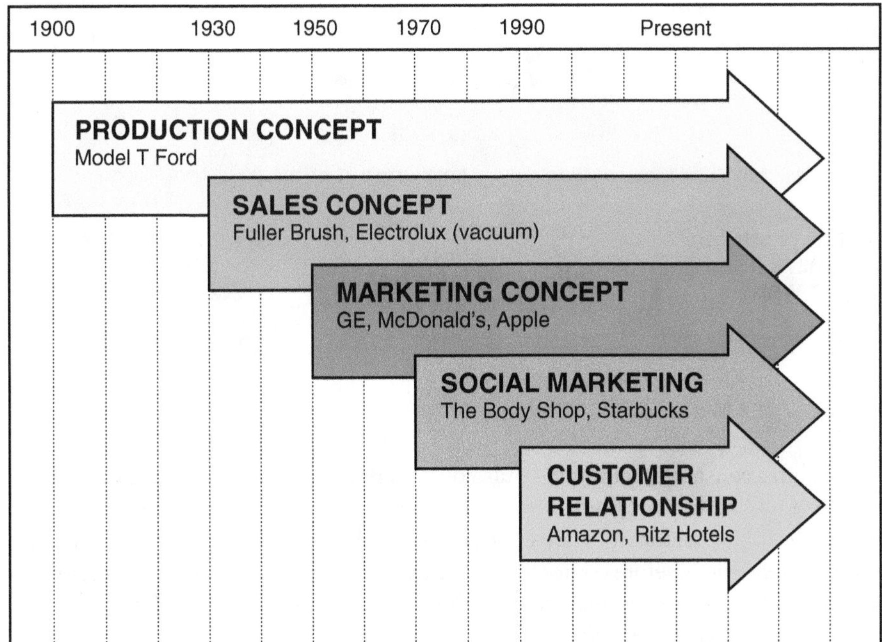

Figure 8.1 The Evolution of Marketing

Adapted from the figure entitled "The Alternative Business Philosophies" in "Overview of the Alternative Business Philosophies" by Dr. Kenneth M. Thompson. Introduction to Marketing course site. http://courses.unt.edu/kt3650_1/

How has marketing evolved over time? The nature of marketing has evolved over four general eras, which are discussed below and outlined in **Figure 8.1**.

The Production Concept Era From the Industrial Revolution until the 1920s, most companies focused solely on production. The prevailing mindset was that a good-quality product would simply sell itself. This approach worked for many organizations during this era because of a strong demand and a limited supply of products. Whenever demand outstrips supply, it creates a "seller's market."

The Sales Concept Era From the mid-1920s through the early 1950s, technological advances meant that production increased more sharply than demand for goods and services. The competition for customers became more intense, and businesses began to undertake aggressive sales tactics to sell or "push" their products. The use of heavy public advertising in all available forms of media became prevalent. During this era, marketing generally took place after the product was developed and produced. Heavy emphasis was placed on selling existing products. Even today, many people associate marketing with selling or advertising; however, it has become much more than that.

The Marketing Concept Era By the 1950s, production continued to expand more quickly than the growth in demand for goods and services, creating a "buyer's market." Soldiers returning from World War II were getting married, starting families, and were willing to spend their money on goods and services. Businesses began to realize that simply producing quality products and pushing them onto customers through clever advertising and promotional campaigns didn't guarantee sales. Companies needed to determine what customers wanted and then produce products, as opposed to producing products and then trying to convince customers to buy them.

The **marketing concept** changed the focus from finding the right customer for a product to producing the right product for a customer and doing it better than the competition (see **Figure 8.2**). More specifically, the marketing concept focuses on:

marketing concept A philosophy that changed the focus from finding the right customer for a product to producing the right product for a customer and doing it better than the competition.

1. Identifying customer needs before the product is designed and produced
2. Aligning all functions of the entire organization to meet or exceed these customer needs through superior products and customer service
3. Realizing a profit (not just sales) by satisfying customers over the long term

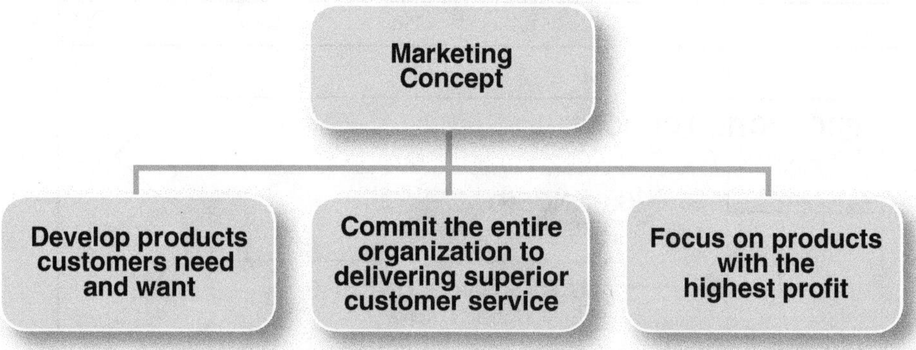

Figure 8.2 The Marketing Concept

This requires constantly taking the pulse of changing customer needs and wants and then quickly adapting to meet them. Moreover, it may mean anticipating customers' changing preferences—before they are expressed or even known by consumers—and satisfying these preferences before competitors. For example, Apple has become a master of anticipating customers' desires and fulfilling them with its range of iPods, iPhones, iPads, and all the accessories that go with each.

customer relationship management (CRM) The process of establishing long-term relationships with individual customers to foster loyalty and repeat business.

The Customer Relationship Era Since the late 1990s, organizations have tried to build on their marketing concept successes by intensifying the entire organization's focus on *customer satisfaction* over time. The result has been the creation of **customer relationship management (CRM)**, the process of establishing long-term relationships with individual customers to foster loyalty and repeat business. The marketing concept is good for *acquiring* customers by offering customized products, among other things, but CRM goes one step further by trying to please customers *after the sale*. It combines computer information technology with customer service and marketing communications to *retain* customers to stimulate future sales of similar or supplementary products. For example, after a customer makes a purchase, retailers such as Winners and Shoppers Drug Mart are increasingly handing out receipts that give customers a chance to enter post-purchase information online for a chance to win a prize. Several popular retail stores, including American Eagle Outfitters, Bath & Body Works, and Menchie's Frozen Yogurt, offer coupons to customers who join their mailing lists. Customers on the list also receive information about sales and promotions to keep them up to date on the latest deals at the store.

The idea is to learn as much as possible about customers and create a meaningful one-on-one interaction with each of them. In practice, CRM often involves the sales force gathering information about specific customers to create a customer database. CRM software allows email or other communications to be personalized. It enables the company to offer products tailored to these specific customers' needs and desires. CRM databases also mean that customers visiting the organization's website or calling the customer service centre can be recognized quickly and easily, and offerings can be adapted to their preferences. Customer relationship management is part of why airlines offer frequent flyer programs to selected customers and why credit card companies offer customized services and low-interest balance transfers to certain targeted customers.

Although each of these concepts has experienced a peak in popularity during a specific period, some companies still use marketing concepts from an earlier era. Today's most successful marketing campaigns are a sophisticated combination of the best of each of these times.

Benefits and Criticisms of Marketing

LO2 Outline the benefits of marketing to various stakeholders and summarize the criticisms of marketing.

How does marketing benefit stakeholders? *Stakeholders*, or interested parties, include customers, sellers, investors, employees, and society. Each group of stakeholders has a different set of motives for their interest in the success of the business. Through marketing, companies sell products and services that satisfy human needs and wants (the product or service has value and offers **utility**). There are five kinds of utility that marketing provides to customers (see **Figure 8.3**):

- *Form utility.* When a company produces a product from raw materials, such as creating a swimsuit from fabric and supplies. The product takes on a form that pleases the customer.
- *Task utility.* When someone performs a service for someone else, such as when a seamstress alters a swimsuit.
- *Time utility.* When a business makes a product available at a time when it is most needed, such as having a swimsuit available for purchase in time for summer.
- *Place utility.* When the product is made available for purchase at a place that is convenient for buyers, such as when a swimsuit is stocked and placed on display at your local department store.
- *Ownership utility.* When a store transfers ownership of a product to the customer, such as by selling you the swimsuit.

Form Utility
- Creating a finished product

Task Utility
- Performing a desired service

Time Utility
- Delivering a product when customers want it

Place Utility
- Delivering a product where customers want it

Ownership Utility
- Freedom to use the product as needed

Figure 8.3 Marketing Generates Five Types of Utility for Customers

Image sources, top to bottom: Africa Studio/Fotolia; wolfelarry/Fotolia; marinini/Fotolia; auremar/Fotolia; Lorelyn Medina/Fotolia

Businesses that are most successful in satisfying customers generate higher profits, and investors benefit from the profits earned. Below are some of the benefits to various stakeholders:

utility The power of a product to satisfy a human want or need; that is, to add something of value to the person.

- *Customer and seller benefits.* As consumers, we have many needs—food, clothing, housing, medical care, and transportation, among others. Marketers don't *create* needs, they *respond* to them. Indeed, many businesses have become extremely profitable by finding a need and satisfying it. Although marketers do not create needs, they do work very hard to convince you to choose their product over competing products. Hence, sellers, as stakeholders, benefit from successful marketing because their profits enable the organization not only to sustain itself but also to prosper and continue to provide value to customers.
- *Investor and employee benefits.* Investors, as stakeholders, receive profits to reward them for devoting their financial resources to organizations that are successful. Employees benefit from successful marketing as well because their jobs and livelihoods are more secure. In addition, new job opportunities are created as production expands to satisfy the growing demand for high-value products.
- *Societal benefits.* Society benefits from successful marketing because scarce resources are more efficiently allocated to the production of goods and services that are most desired by society. When resources are used more efficiently, society is able to consume more products, increasing the standard of living.

What is nontraditional marketing? To understand nontraditional marketing, let's first be clear about the meaning of traditional marketing. The objective of traditional marketing is to generate a *profit*. However, many nonprofit organizations also have an interest in marketing. Rather than looking to market a product or service, these organizations market an event, cause, place, or person. This is nontraditional marketing.

For example, environmental organizations such as the Sierra Club, the National Wildlife Federation, and the Nature Conservancy of Canada and other nonprofits such as the Red Cross and the Canadian Cancer Society rely on marketing to raise awareness of and increase donations to their causes. Likewise, churches and other civic organizations market their missions to attract new membership. Countries, provinces, and cities also run marketing campaigns to attract tourists and businesses to their locations. Museums and zoos also undertake "place marketing" by emphasizing the value of visiting their locations. For example, Joe Torzsok, the chair of the Toronto Zoo board, said that the zoo's unconventional marketing campaign, referring to the "Cute Fight" Toronto Zoo commercial, boosted attendance numbers for the first five months of 2012 by 46 percent. As a result the zoo brought in $8.3 million in the first five months of the year—$1.6 million more than the projected revenue in the 2012 budget.[9]

Other examples include politicians and political parties marketing candidates for elected office. Agents for athletes, movie stars, television personalities, and musicians market their clients. We market ourselves when we interview for a job. You may have marketed yourself for acceptance to your college or university. To a certain extent, we're all marketing ourselves every day at work and play. Regardless of what is being marketed—an event, a cause, a place, a person, a good, or a service—the essence of marketing remains the same. The only difference between nontraditional and traditional marketing practices is the stakeholders involved and their objectives.

What are the criticisms of marketing? Certain social shortcomings have emerged from marketing techniques. Some of the questionable tactics used by marketing that have created criticism include price gouging (asking for a price that is widely considered unfair), high-pressure selling, the production of shoddy or unsafe products, planned obsolescence (the product becomes obsolete after a period of time that is planned by the manufacturer), poor customer service, misuse of customer information, confusing and deceptive labelling, and other deceptive practices such as hidden fees and charges.

Let's consider a few examples of the costs to society of questionable marketing:

- *Misuse of personal information.* Marketing often involves collecting personal information about customers. Companies conduct marketing surveys to find out the marital status, annual income, age, sex, race, and other characteristics of their primary customers. Many of us feel violated when this personal information is not adequately protected or is resold without our permission, especially in the age of identity theft.
- *Hidden fees.* Many of us feel taken advantage of when we must pay "hidden" fees and charges not included in the advertised price. Products that require additional parts or shipping and service fees often make customers upset. For example, an advertisement for the sale of a Canon digital SLR camera brings customers into the store to make their purchase. Once there, they discover the camera does not include a lens, memory card, or battery. The purchase of these additional items brings up the cost of the camera significantly and typically leaves the customer feeling taken advantage of.
- *Consequences of purchase.* Unscrupulous marketing may take advantage of less sophisticated members of society. To what extent is it reasonable to hold buyers responsible for being aware of the consequences of their purchases? This is especially important when purchasing expensive or sophisticated goods and services, such as a car or a mortgage on a home. Similar concerns emerge when marketing is directed at children.

The many criticisms of marketing should not be taken lightly. These concerns may help explain the strong support for consumer protection laws and other regulations governing business behaviour. Too often, the social costs of marketing stem from unethical business behaviour.

marketing strategy Consists of two major elements: the *target market* and the *marketing mix*, which is designed to meet the needs of that market.

target market The specific group of consumers, who have similar needs and wants, a firm directs its marketing efforts toward.

Koodo uses a unique and appealing character to develop brand recognition.

The Marketing Mix (4 Ps of Marketing)

LO3 Describe the 4 Ps of the marketing mix and explain the five steps of the marketing process to implement a marketing strategy.

What is a marketing strategy? A **marketing strategy** consists of two major elements: the organization must determine its *target market* and then develop a *marketing mix* to meet the needs of that market. The **target market** is the specific group of consumers, who

Better Business Better World

Canadian Marketing Association's (CMA) Code of Ethics and Standards of Practice[10]

Marketers need to inform themselves about the relevant laws in their jurisdiction, including but not limited to the federal Competition Act and federal, provincial, and territorial consumer, privacy, and language laws. Marketing activities in Canada are governed by the federal Competition Bureau and Office of Consumer Affairs while consumer protection is regulated by the provincial and territorial governments.

CMA's Code of Ethics and Standards of Practice is the marketing community's cornerstone of self-regulation, but it does not replace legal advice nor provide legal guidance. It establishes and maintains standards for the conduct of marketing in Canada. Unlike many other codes that serve only as guidelines, CMA's code is compulsory for members and as such is a comprehensive regulatory framework governing members' conduct. A series of guidelines assist members to understand their obligations under the code, providing practical information relevant to today's marketing practices, technologies, and channels.

Some of the code's guidelines include the following:

- Marketing communications must be clear and truthful. Marketers must not knowingly make a representation to a consumer or business that is false or misleading.
- Organizations selling abroad are governed by this code unless doing so contravenes the laws of foreign jurisdictions.
- Marketers must not knowingly exploit the credulity, lack of knowledge, or inexperience of any consumer, taking particular care when dealing with vulnerable consumers. The term "vulnerable consumer" includes, but is not limited to, children, teenagers, people with disabilities, the elderly, and those for whom English or French is not their first language.
- All consumer marketers must abide by the Personal Information Protection and Electronics Documents Act (PIPEDA), and/or applicable provincial privacy laws and the 10 Privacy Principles from the National Standard of Canada and five additional CMA requirements.
- Marketers recognize and acknowledge a continuing responsibility to manage their businesses to minimize environmental impact.

Marketers know they have a core responsibility to the public to establish and maintain high standards of practice, which are also essential to winning and holding consumer confidence. CMA members are obligated to conduct themselves according to the highest standards of honesty, accuracy, fairness, and professionalism not only to serve consumers and businesses but also to preserve the integrity of the discipline in which they operate and to each other.

Discussion Questions

1. **Visit the CMA website and review the Code of Ethics and Standards of Practice documentation. Who does the code apply to? How are "must" and "should" used in the code? What do you think of the areas covered in the code? Is this a legal requirement? Will companies abide by the terms? Why or why not?**
2. **How will a CMA member company ensure that their employees follow the membership guidelines? Would a company lose membership if an employee were in noncompliance with the Code of Ethics and Standards of Practice? Can you find a case of a company having been in a situation of noncompliance? If so, summarize the situation and outcome.**
3. **Compare the CMA's code and standards to those in other countries. Did you find a country that does not seem to have a marketing association? If so, does this country have laws pertaining to marketing strategy and tactics? Do you think other countries should have a similar association? Why or why not?**

have similar needs and wants, that a firm directs its marketing efforts toward. The **marketing mix** is the combination of four factors, called the "4 Ps" of marketing, designed to serve the target market: product, price, promotion, and place (the marketing mix will be discussed in detail in Chapter 9). A marketing strategy must not only define the target market, it must define the goals and outcomes, timeline, resources, and opportunities as well.

marketing mix The combination of four factors, called the "4 Ps" of marketing, designed to serve the target market: product, price, promotion, and place.

Does effective marketing require a blend of the 4 Ps? The idea is to provide the *product* that customers need and want at an appropriate *price* and to *promote* its sale and

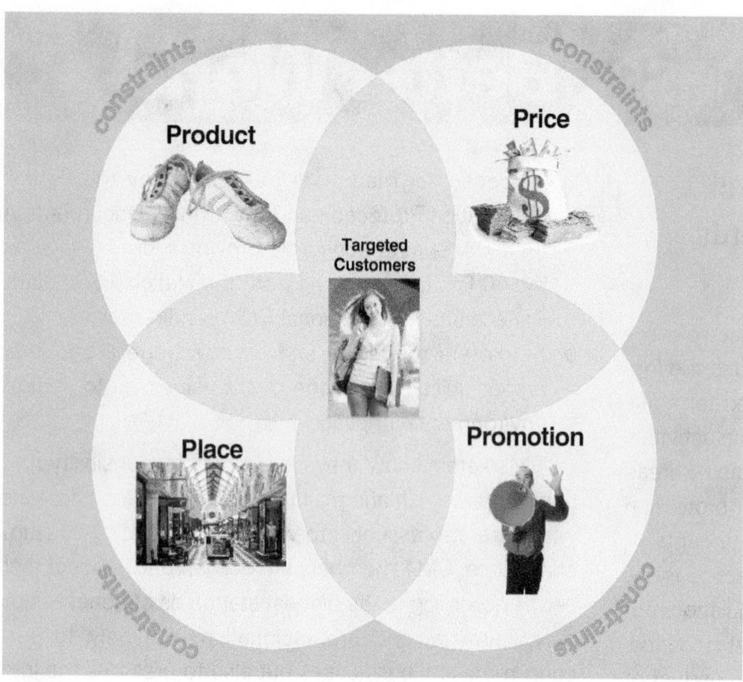

Figure 8.4 The Marketing Mix

Image Sources: (top left) Ingvald Kaldhussater/Shutterstock; (top right) Hurst Photo/Shutterstock; (middle): Stephen Coburn/Shutterstock; (bottom left) Kaspars Grinvalds/Shutterstock; (bottom right) Yanik Chauvin/Shutterstock.

place or distribute the good or service in a convenient location for the customer to purchase (see **Figure 8.4**). Effective marketing requires the appropriate blend of the 4 Ps directed at targeted customers. This blend is constrained by forces outside the firm's control that are found within the broader market environment.

Product Distinguishing your product from that of your competitors is critical. If you don't do something that's different from and superior to the competition, why should customers buy from you? **Product differentiation** is the creation of a real or perceived difference in a product designed to attract customers. Product differentiation is one of the most critical ingredients to success for most businesses. Product differentiation can take the form of functionality, styling, quality, safety, packaging, warranty, accessories, or brand name image. A brand is a name, term, symbol, or design that distinguishes a company and its products from all others.

Price There is a lot to consider when deciding on the price for a product. Of course, the price will have to be sufficient to cover costs if you wish to make a profit. However, the product must also be competitively priced to appeal to customers.

product differentiation The creation of a real or perceived difference in a product designed to attract customers.

Promotion The promotion part of the marketing mix consists of all the methods available to inform and persuade targeted customers to buy a product and to build positive customer relationships. Communicating the benefits of your good or service to customers includes advertising, sales promotions, personal selling, public relations, direct marketing, and publicity.

Place The place (or distribution) component of the marketing mix refers to all the methods involved in getting the product into the hands of customers. A product isn't beneficial to a customer if it can't be purchased when and where it is needed. When a business is providing a good instead of a service, the delivery component is often more complicated. Many goods, such as grocery store items, go through a distribution channel, which is a series of firms or individuals that participate in the flow of a product from manufacturer to consumer. The intermediaries in a distribution channel are sometimes called distributors or wholesalers. Some goods, such as food products, go through many wholesalers before reaching a retail outlet (such as a grocery store) and, finally, the consumer. Other goods, such as automobiles, typically move from the manufacturer to just one wholesaler, the car dealership, and then on to the consumer. Still other goods bypass wholesalers altogether and move from the manufacturer directly to the consumer. Today, many of these "direct to consumer" manufacturers have convenient websites whereby consumers can make purchases online and have the products delivered directly to them.

Jeff Greenberg/PhotoEdit

Costco offers its warehouse members a more direct distribution channel and therefore saves them money.

Is There a Fifth P?

Although the "4 Ps" of marketing are the accepted criteria for the marketing mix, there has been some discussion of adding a fifth "P" to the mix. In today's competitive business world, some say it is necessary to have a "purple cow" factor—something that makes your business or product stand apart from the competition. A company that has attained success using a "purple cow" is the Geek Squad computer service. An affiliate of Best Buy, Geek Squad provides a wide range of technical services to customers. What makes it stand apart is its image. Geek Squad employees make house calls, driving black-and-white Volkswagen Beetles with the Geek Squad logo on the door. The IT world is considered a nerdy field, and Geek Squad embraces that image and runs with it. Because of its unique marketing approach, Geek Squad is one of the most recognizable technical service businesses.

Discussion Questions

1. **Have you ever seen a "purple cow" marketing campaign? If so, what was it that made it a purple cow?**
2. **Are there other "Ps" you think are missing from the traditional four "Ps" of marketing?**
3. **Seth Godin, author of *Purple Cow*, has a special term for early adopters who love a product and tell all sorts of people about it: sneezers. Have you ever been a sneezer for a particular product or service?**

Dario Sabljak/Shutterstock

What are the steps in the marketing process? There are five steps in the marketing process, as outlined in **Figure 8.5**.

1. *Identify a market need.* Is there a need for pool cleaning services in your area? To identify a new business, new product, or new service need, you must observe your potential customer base. For example, if there are many pools in the area in which you wish to run your pool cleaning business and there are not too many other businesses already servicing those pools, then yes, there is probably a need.
2. *Conduct market research and develop a marketing plan.* The next step is to conduct research on the profitability of a potential business, product, or service. (How to conduct market research and develop a marketing plan are discussed later in this chapter.)
3. *Identify target customers.* The third step is to select a target market. Without this focus, you will waste effort and money promoting a product or service to individuals not interested in your product or service. When selecting a target market, visualize your ideal customer. What does your ideal customer need or want, and how will you provide this? Are you targeting customers who are individual/household consumers or other businesses for which you will be a supplier?
4. *Implement the 4 Ps.* Once you have selected a target market, the fourth step is to implement the marketing mix, or the 4 Ps of marketing—product, price, promotion, and place.

Figure 8.5 The Five Steps in the Marketing Process

Once an unfilled customer need has been identified, it is important to develop a product that not only meets that need but also fulfills it better than the competition. Start by coming up with a memorable brand to distinguish your business and services from all others. Having a memorable brand name will make it easier to find investors and to attract customers.

Having developed a set of goods and services and a brand that distinguishes your business from all others, you will now want to contemplate a pricing strategy. What price are people willing to pay, and how sensitive are customers to price changes? Will different hourly rates be charged on weekends as compared to weekdays? Will seasonal differences influence prices?

Promotion is the most visible part of the marketing mix. It can be very expensive, yet very fruitful. How should your business be promoted?

The place component of the marketing mix often involves finding the best location for the business. You will want to be within a reasonable distance of your customers. Whether providing products or services, the "place" (or delivery) component of the marketing mix is equally important.

5. *Nurture customer relationships.* The final step in the marketing process is to manage customer relationships. As we noted earlier, the goal of customer relationship management (CRM) is to establish long-term, trusting relationships with individual customers to foster loyalty and repeat business. You must develop a rapport with customers by learning which ones are returning customers and note any particular preferences they may have. You might even offer discounts for repeat customers. You should not only solicit but also respond to suggestions by customers on how to improve products or services. To build customer trust, you should also offer customers their money back if they are unsatisfied. To maintain and foster interest in your products or services, you may want to create a mailing list for select customers. You will want to establish relationships with suppliers. Above all, it is critical to personalize and maintain good customer relationships. Marketing is an ongoing process of tweaking a business to satisfy customers to ensure quality, value, and repeat business.

Is the marketing process easy to implement? The marketing process may seem simple when it's written on the page, but it's as much art as it is science. For instance, a mobile pool-cleaning service would have a completely different marketing strategy than a non-mobile standalone pool business selling goods and offering cleaning services. Each product needs to be looked at individually to tailor an appropriate marketing plan.

Common ingredients for marketing success include producing a high-quality product (with a unique brand that is properly promoted) that consistently delivers value to customers at a "fair" price, where they want it, and when they want it.

THE MARKETING ENVIRONMENT

LO4 Describe how the various factors in the marketing environment influence a firm's ability to manipulate its marketing mix.

The Competitive Environment

Why is analyzing the competitive environment important? Assessing the competitive environment, or the degree of competition facing a firm, is critical to creating an effective marketing mix. You may recall from Chapter 2 the four basic market environments with respect to the varying degrees of competition facing firms: perfect competition, monopolistic competition, oligopoly, and monopoly. The degree of competition affects the firm's production, pricing, promotion, and place (distribution) strategies in many ways. A successful business must be aware of competition and always try to stay one step ahead.

How do marketing managers control the competitive environment? Generally, the marketing mix (the blend of the 4 Ps) can be controlled by marketing managers;

however, the **marketing environment** includes environmental influences outside the firm's control that constrain the organization's ability to manipulate its marketing mix. These external environmental influences (see **Figure 8.6**) include the competitive environment as well as the political, economic, sociocultural, and technological (PEST) environment (discussed in Chapter 2).

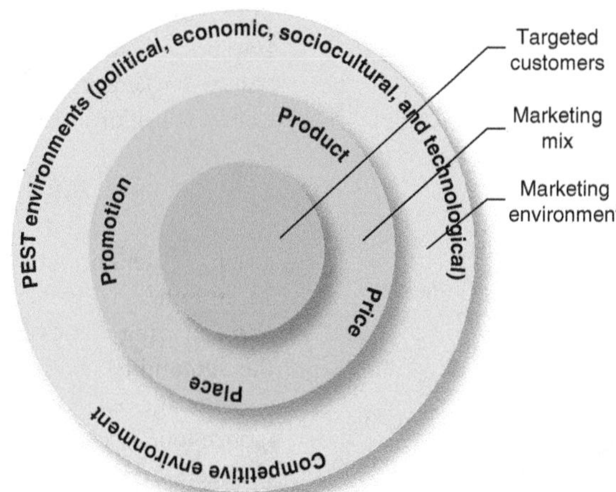

Figure 8.6 The Marketing Mix and the Marketing Environment

Scanning the Environment

How do companies stay informed about changes in the external marketing environment? Marketers must be keenly aware of the marketing environment when selecting their marketing mix. In fact, one of the key responsibilities of managers in any organization is to undertake **environmental scanning**, the process of surveying the market environment to assess external threats and opportunities. A successful business detects changes in the market environment and adjusts its marketing mix (product, price, promotion, and distribution) quickly and appropriately, inasmuch as the overall market environment will allow it to do so. Let's look at each of the elements of the marketing environment in a bit more detail.

marketing environment Includes environmental influences outside the firm's control that constrain the organization's ability to manipulate its marketing mix.

environmental scanning The process of surveying the market environment to assess external threats and opportunities.

How does the competitive environment affect marketing? Assessing the competitive environment, or the degree of competition facing the firm, is critical to creating an effective marketing mix. The degree of competition affects the firm's production, pricing, promotion, and place (distribution) strategies in many ways. A successful business must be aware of competition and always try to stay one step ahead.

How does the political environment affect marketing? It has been said that in a democracy, the squeaky wheel gets the grease. Special-interest groups try to influence the political process in various ways, and businesses are no exception. They try to wield political influence through contributions to political parties, individual candidates, and political action committees (PACs) because government laws and regulations significantly influence business interests. In addition, several agencies enforce laws and regulations constraining marketing efforts, such as Environment Canada, Health Canada, and the Federal Trade Commission. Businesses are forced to consider the political (and legal) environment in making marketing decisions, as these factors can play a major role in overall success.

How does the economic environment affect marketing? The economic environment can affect customers' willingness and ability to spend their money on a firm's product. Therefore, marketers must keep abreast of changes in inflation, interest rates, unemployment, and economic growth rates over the course of the business cycle. Part of this is keeping up with changes in consumer confidence levels and government fiscal and monetary policies. Moreover, because of globalization, prudent firms follow global economic trends as well. This is especially important if the firm is involved in international business.

The economic environment affects the firm's marketing strategy in many ways. For example, a rising inflation rate reduces the purchasing power of money, and sales may fall. A recession reduces consumer demand generally. In 2009, for example, average household spending in Canada declined by 0.3 percent to $71 177 following the economic slowdown that began in the fall of 2008.[11] Even the best-laid marketing plans will fail when customers can no longer afford to buy your product. If interest rates are high then the cost of borrowing is up, and consumers who buy on credit will purchase less and your sales may fall. As a final example, suppose the value of the dollar falls (gets weaker) in foreign exchange markets. This will cause imported goods to become more expensive. Importing firms may need to raise their prices, which could significantly reduce sales. Savvy marketers try to keep their fingers on the changing pulse of the economy to forecast looming problems or potential opportunities and make the necessary adjustments.

How does the sociocultural environment affect marketing? Domestic, and to a stronger extent multinational, businesses must realize that culture is dynamic, and effective marketers must be able to adapt to different attitudes and keep up with changing social trends. Demographic shifts—such as age, gender, ethnicity, and marital status—and changing values can signal opportunities for businesses. For example, we can expect the demand for medical care, pharmaceuticals, and nursing homes to increase as the average age of the population increases. We've also observed greater demand for convenience foods, restaurant services, and cellphones over the years as lifestyles have changed. Products like the Wii Fit attempt to deal with society's concern about children's lack of exercise.

Video: H&M CEO: Our Models Are Too Skinny

How does the technological environment affect marketing? The technological environment can also influence the marketing mix. Indeed, advances in communications and transportation technologies may be one of the most influential factors affecting modern business. The Internet alone has enabled many small businesses to compete with large corporations around the world by marketing and selling their products online. Moreover, modern, sophisticated manufacturing innovations have enabled many firms to customize their products more easily and to offer them at dramatically reduced prices to satisfy the varying tastes of targeted customers. Successful marketing requires use of the latest technologies to reach and satisfy target customers wherever they may be. This also includes the use of computer databases to enhance customer relationship management. Technological advances over the past decade have changed the way we work, live, and do business.

MARKETING RESEARCH AND PLANNING

LO5 Identify the five steps of the marketing research process and the four elements of a good marketing plan.

The Marketing Research Process

What is involved in researching the market? For a business example, let's look at Tiara Watson's salon supply business. Tiara thinks the business will be a great investment because the next closest supplier is more than 100 kilometres away, so salons have to pay unnecessarily high shipping costs. Tiara started researching and found more than 30 salons around the city, so she has a strong target market. She's already met with a few of the owners to see whether they'd be willing to switch suppliers, and they seem interested. She knows she can't start out selling supplies to every salon in the city, but she isn't sure where to start. How can she figure out which salons to target for her startup?

Look back at the five-step marketing process shown in Figure 8.5. You'll notice that after a market need is identified, a firm needs to conduct *market research* to determine the profitability of a venture, develop a marketing plan, and determine its target market. In this section, we'll explore each of these processes in more detail.

market research The process of gathering and analyzing market information for making marketing decisions.

Market research is the process of gathering and analyzing market information for making marketing decisions. The marketing research process consists of five steps:

1. *Define the need, problem, or objective.* Marketing managers and researchers need to work together to clearly define the objective of the research. They should determine the exact nature of the business need, problem, or opportunity, and the information desired. They should also determine why that information would be helpful to the manager. This step will help the researcher collect relevant and appropriate data for analysis. Tiara has defined the need for a salon supply company that is in close proximity to city salons.

2. *Collect relevant data.* Determining which types of data will be collected and how the information will be collected is the next step. Two general types of data exist: primary and secondary. **Primary data** are raw data collected by the researcher. The data are frequently collected through observation, questionnaires, surveys (via mail, email, or telephone), focus groups, interviews, customer feedback, samples, and controlled experiments. A **focus group** is typically a group of eight to ten potential customers who are asked for feedback on a good or service, advertisement, idea, or packaging.

   Secondary data have already been collected and processed. An example of secondary data is census data. This information is usually much cheaper to obtain. Tiara Watson has collected secondary data about the location of the closest salon supply companies and primary data about the interest of the salon owners in changing to a closer, cheaper supplier. Examples of primary and secondary data sources are summarized in **Table 8.1**.

primary data Raw data collected by the researcher. The data are frequently collected through observation, questionnaires, surveys (via mail, email, or telephone), focus groups, interviews, customer feedback, samples, and controlled experiments.

focus group Typically a group of eight to ten potential customers who are asked for feedback on a good or service, advertisement, idea, or packaging.

secondary data Data that have already been collected and processed. An example of secondary data is census data.

Simulation: Product Development

Table 8.1 Examples of Sources of Primary and Secondary Data

Primary Sources of Data	Secondary Sources of Data
• Observation • Questionnaires • Surveys • Focus groups • Interviews • Customer feedback • Sampling • Controlled experiments	**Government Resources** • Industry Canada—Economic research and analysis; company directories; trade and investment • Statistics Canada—census; labour statistics; demographics • *CIA World Fact Book* (U.S.) • Employment and Social Development Canada (ESDC) • Foreign Affairs, Trade, and Development Canada • Bank of Canada
	Company, Industry, and Product Resources • Ipsos Canada—marketing research • Euromonitor International—marketing research • Marketing Resources Links—by Decision Analyst, Inc. at SecondaryData.com • Canadian Business Resource—www.cbr.ca • Hoover's Online—listings include 12 million companies worldwide • *Frasers Canadian Trade Directory* • *Moody's Industry Review* • Standard & Poor's Industry Surveys
	Trade Publications Chamber of Commerce, Board of Trade, Canadian Marketing Association, Retail Council of Canada, Conference Board of Canada, Dun and Bradstreet Canada
	Magazines *Businessweek, Canadian Business, Fortune, Fast Company, Entrepreneur, Forbes, Marketing Magazine*
	Newspapers *The Globe and Mail, National Post, The Wall Street Journal*
	Internal sources Accounting records, annual reports, prior research reports, company records

3. *Analyze data.* Analysis of data requires knowledge of appropriate statistical techniques beyond the scope of this textbook. Nevertheless, honest analysis is necessary. You should never adjust your data to get the results you want. For example, Apple's honest assessment of marketing data led the company not to introduce the iPod wristwatch.
4. *Interpret results.* Statistics never speak for themselves. Careful analysis will lead to conclusions about marketing strategies that have more favourable benefits in relation to their costs. For example, a company's profit numbers for the previous year might appear to indicate a lack of growth, but when inflation and the falling value of the dollar are taken into account, the statistics may actually show that the company expanded its business.
5. *Act on conclusions.* The whole purpose of marketing research is to point managers toward better marketing decisions. Marketing research should therefore be ongoing. Changing market conditions require businesses to continually adapt and constantly search for better ways to provide value to customers. Part of acting on the conclusions of marketing research is creating a marketing plan (discussed in the next section).

Simulation: Market Research Matters

How is social media used in market research? For brands, reputation is a key foundation to building a successful fan-driven online community. Social media sites such as Facebook, Google+, LinkedIn, and Pinterest are becoming invaluable sources of information for company research. Companies can follow posts on Pinterest to find out what people are saying about their company, brand, products, and services. The value social media has over focus groups is in breadth, the great number of people that can be surveyed, and the speed at which people can be surveyed. Facebook has partnered with three data-mining companies (Acxiom, Datalogix, and Epsilon) that collect mounds of data on users related to purchase history and lifestyle. Facebook uses this information to let advertisers do powerful ad targeting with more than 500 categories.[12] Not every company or marketing research project will lend itself to social media tools, but if a fit is there, then social media gives marketers valuable, inexpensive, broad-ranging, and speedy tools for obtaining consumer insight. Of all people identified as marketers in Twitter, 15 percent follow more than 2000 people, compared with 0.29 percent of all Twitter users who follow more than 2000 people.[13]

Video: Finding, Evaluating, and Processing Information – MELT

The Marketing Plan

marketing plan A written document that specifies marketing activities designed to reach organizational objectives.

What is a marketing plan? A **marketing plan** is a written document that specifies marketing activities designed to reach organizational objectives. It is a critical component of a business plan. A marketing plan is typically a *written* document because details about tasks to be performed by employees can be lost easily if communicated orally. Moreover, written objectives can be compared with actual measurements to see whether objectives are being met.

What are the elements of a good marketing plan? Four elements emerge from all good marketing plans:

- a clearly written marketing objective
- performance of situational analysis
- selection of a target market
- implementation, evaluation, and control of the marketing mix (the 4 Ps)

marketing objective A clearly stated goal to be achieved through marketing activities. It should be realistic, quantifiable, and time specific.

Why is a marketing objective necessary? A **marketing objective** is a clearly stated goal to be achieved through marketing activities. It should be realistic, quantifiable, and time specific.[14] The objective is the starting point for the marketing plan. A marketing objective of having every home in Canada purchase a specific product is unrealistic. Selling 100 000 units in a year is a more realistic, quantifiable, and time-specific marketing objective. When objectives are realistic, they are attainable and can motivate employees toward their goal. When they are measurable, the firm can determine

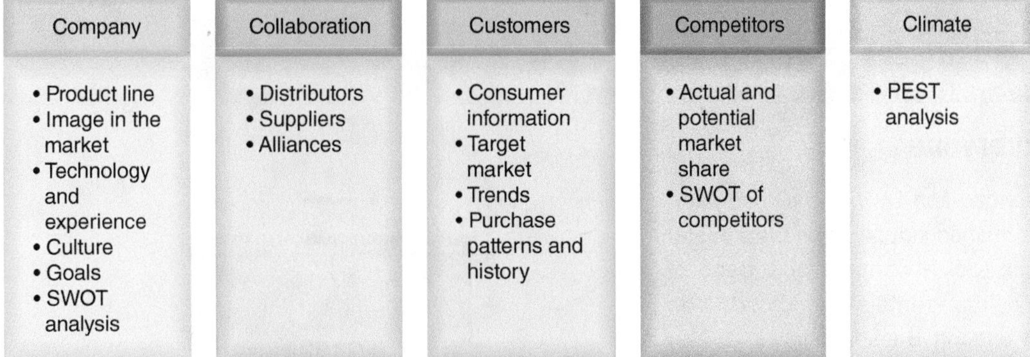

Figure 8.7 Situational Analysis: 5 Cs of Marketing

whether they are being achieved. If deadlines are also imposed, then firms know whether they are reaching their goals in a timely manner.

What is a situational analysis? Creating clearly stated objectives is the first step in any good marketing plan. The next step is conducting a *situational (or SWOT) analysis*. As you learned in Chapter 5, this is an evaluation of the organization's internal *strengths* and *weaknesses*, as well as the *opportunities* and *threats* found in the external environment. Scanning the environment by analyzing the **5 Cs of marketing** (company, collaborators, customers, competitors, and climate) is another useful situational analysis framework that can be used alone or in conjunction with a SWOT analysis (see **Figure 8.7**). It covers the internal, the micro-environment, and the macro-environment situations (these environments were discussed in Chapter 2). By combining regional and market analysis with knowledge of the firm's own capabilities and partnerships, the firm can select more favourable opportunities to provide value to the customer. The 5 C analysis is an extension of the 3 C analysis (company, customers, and competitors), with the addition of collaborators and climate (which is a macro-environmental analysis, or PEST analysis).[15]

5 Cs of marketing A situational analysis framework that includes analyzing the company, collaborators, customers, competitors, and climate.

What do we mean by internal strengths? In terms of marketing, a company's internal strengths refer to the competitive advantages or core competencies that the company has at its disposal to meet a specified marketing objective. Core competencies provide customer benefits and are not easily imitated by other companies, setting the company apart from the competition.

How does a company assess its weaknesses? Assessing internal weaknesses means that a company must perform an audit of current managerial expertise, manufacturing and financing capabilities, and the organization's execution of the 4 Ps in the marketing mix. By honestly assessing its weaknesses, a company can determine a realistic marketing objective. For example, a company that makes handmade watches and has only three employees cannot expect to produce 75 000 watches a week.

Why look to the external environment? The dynamic and ever-changing external environment offers many opportunities and creates many threats. Changes in the degree of competition facing firms; the economic, technological, and sociocultural forces; as well as changes in the political, legal, and regulatory environments have caused some firms to thrive while damaging others. This is especially true for international businesses because the number of market environments compounds the analysis. Rapid changes in technology create new opportunities, such as expanding sales over the Internet, but pose new threats, such as requiring additional technological expertise to protect against hackers. Successful companies continually evaluate environmental factors as part of their SWOT analysis to match their strengths with opportunities and to address their weaknesses to avoid threats.

Off the Mark

Netflix Angers Everyone

Netflix, the streaming video and DVD-by-mail company, was a major factor that pushed industry icon Blockbuster into bankruptcy. Netflix took advantage of a trend of streaming video and by-mail rentals that Blockbuster didn't recognize quickly enough. But seemingly as quickly as Netflix gained market share, it lost it. In one year, Netflix share price grew from $100 to nearly $300, and in half that time the share price plummeted to lows near $60.

Beyond the pure financial impact of this downward spiral is the pure tragedy that this debacle was entirely Netflix's own doing. What caused this self-inflicted nightmare? Netflix lost sight of its customer and the importance of the customer relationship. In an effort to deemphasize the more expensive DVD-by-mail component and focus on the more profitable streaming video component of the business, Netflix decided to create two separate service lines. The DVD-by-mail would be rebranded as Qwikster, while the streaming video component would continue as Netflix. Customers would have two separate logins to access two separate websites. Netflix completely violated the 4 Ps in the new marketing mix by misunderstanding the customer's needs and wants, the overall cost and lack of convenience the split businesses would have on the consumer, and also by poorly communicating the change to its customer base.

Beginning with a quick apology within days of the blunder, CEO Reed Hastings has since been trying to make amends. In the months that followed, attention to customer service and quality recouped many who had left in protest and pushed Netflix back to the top in market share.

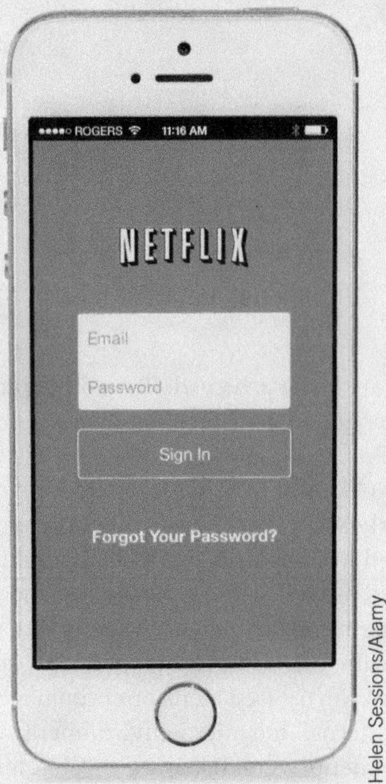

Helen Sessions/Alamy

Discussion Questions

1. **Who was the target market for this company's products?**
2. **What are some of the real and imagined errors this company's management made?**

Target Markets

LO6 Describe how target markets are determined and how a firm attempts to satisfy a target market.

How are target markets determined? Once an organization has evaluated its internal strengths and weaknesses, as well as the external opportunities and threats of the market environment, then it is ready to select its target market. If a business doesn't focus its marketing efforts, it will likely waste time and money promoting its product to individuals who are not interested.

market segmentation The process of separating the broader market into smaller markets (or market segments) that consist of similar groups of customers.

How do you find a target market? The marketing concept's recognition of consumers' various needs and wants leads marketing managers to think in terms of target markets. As mentioned earlier, a target market is the specific group of consumers who have similar needs and wants that a firm directs its marketing efforts toward. Finding a target market begins with **market segmentation**, the process of separating the broader market into smaller markets (or market segments) that consist of similar groups of customers. A **market segment** is a subgroup of potential customers who share similar characteristics and therefore have similar product needs and preferences. Some firms focus so much on one specific market that they undertake **niche marketing**, or marketing a product to a narrowly defined set of potential customers. A company that sells specialized gear shifters for racing bicycles is operating in a niche market.

Marketers choose those market segments that offer the greatest profit potential, and these become the target markets. For each target market, the company tries to blend the 4 Ps of the marketing mix to best satisfy the targeted customers. The process of developing a unique marketing mix that best satisfies a target market is known as **positioning**.

market segment A subgroup of potential customers who share similar characteristics and therefore have similar product needs and preferences.

niche marketing Occurs when a product is marketed to a narrowly defined set of potential customers.

positioning The process of developing a unique marketing mix that best satisfies a target market.

Video: Jones Soda: Marketing & Consumer Behaviour

How are consumer markets segmented? Consumer markets can be segmented based on many variables or characteristics of consumers. Four of the most common consumer market segmentation classifications are geographic, demographic, psychographic, and behavioural (summarized in **Table 8.2**).

Geographic segmentation is market segmentation according to geographic characteristics. For example, clothing apparel, skis, snow blowers, four-wheel-drive vehicles, air conditioning, and heating needs differ based on regional climate differences. Taste in food products also varies by region.

geographic segmentation Market segmentation according to geographic characteristics.

Demographic segmentation is market segmentation according to age, race, religion, gender, ethnic background, and other demographic variables. Few businesses want to miss a growing market segment. For example, it is now common to find product labels, television stations, and newspapers published in languages other than English. The number of people whose mother tongue is neither English nor French will be between 21 and 25 percent of the total population in Canada by 2017.[16] (Canadian demographics were discussed in Chapter 7.)

demographic segmentation Market segmentation according to age, race, religion, gender, ethnic background, and other demographic variables.

Automobile companies also use demographic segmentation. They are keenly aware of how important it is to position their models to appeal to different age groups, income levels, and differences in gender.

Psychographic segmentation is market segmentation based on lifestyles, personality traits, motives, and values. Cat food advertisements are cleverly focusing on "cat lover" personalities, whereas many beer commercials target specific personality types. When motives are used to determine the appropriate market, marketers focus on why consumers make a purchase. For example, Volvo has been successful in selling cars to consumers motivated by safety concerns, and Gold's Gym sells memberships to customers concerned with their health. Sophisticated marketers closely examine their customers' lifestyles, personality traits, motives, and values because, unlike geographic and demographic variables, these psychographic variables can be manipulated by marketing efforts. Whatever consumers may value, whether it be quality, social status or affiliation, safety, health, privacy, technology, or appearance, you can bet that businesses will offer a good or service to satisfy that real or perceived need. And they will be rewarded with profits for doing so.

psychographic segmentation Market segmentation based on lifestyles, personality traits, motives, and values.

Video: Abercrombie and Fitch Under Fire "Exclusionary" Tactics

Table 8.2 Consumer Market Segmentation

Geographic	Demographic	Psychographic	Behavioural
• Region	• Age	• Lifestyle	• Benefit sought
• Suburban	• Race	• Personality traits	• Volume usage
• Rural	• Religion	• Motives	• Brand loyalty
• City	• Family size	• Values	• Price sensitivity
• County	• Ethnicity		• Product end use
• Population density	• Gender		
• Climate	• Income		
• Terrain	• Education		

Joel_420/Fotolia

What personality traits and motives would marketers target when marketing an electric car?

Behavioural segmentation is market segmentation based on certain consumer behaviour characteristics, such as the benefits sought by the consumer, the extent to which the product is consumed, brand loyalty, price sensitivity, and the ways in which the product is used. For example, a company that produces herbal supplements is appealing to the specific benefits sought by its consumers.

Brand loyalty is another kind of behavioural segmentation. It can influence price sensitivity—the more loyal the customer, the less sensitive he or she is to a price increase. For example, if a customer has been using the same brand of toothpaste for 12 years and has had no cavities in that time, a small price increase will most likely not be an issue. Finally, knowing how the product is actually used can help companies develop packages that appeal to customers. For example, when pills are taken daily, having pills placed in a package where the day of the week is written below each pill can be useful for consumers.

behavioural segmentation Market segmentation based on certain consumer behaviour characteristics, such as the benefits sought by the consumer, the extent to which the product is consumed, brand loyalty, price sensitivity, and the ways in which the product is used.

CONSUMER BEHAVIOUR

LO7 Describe the purchase decision process and the major influences affecting a consumer's buying decision.

Consumer Markets

Why study consumer behaviour? Knowledge of consumer behaviour helps marketers select the most profitable target markets and guides the implementation, evaluation, and control of the marketing mix (the 4 Ps) for selected targeted markets. For example, consumers are becoming increasingly concerned about gas mileage. Automobile companies that realize this can create more gas-efficient cars or drop the prices on less-efficient models to compensate for poor gas mileage.

consumer behaviour The ways individuals or organizations search for, evaluate, purchase, use, and dispose of goods and services.

consumer market A market in which individuals purchase goods and services for personal consumption.

business-to-business (B2B) markets A market in which businesses purchase goods and services from other businesses.

Consumer behaviour refers to the ways individuals or organizations search for, evaluate, purchase, use, and dispose of goods and services. Notice that consumer behaviour involves the study of individual consumers or business organizations as buyers in the market. Most of us intuitively think of a market as being a consumer market because consumer markets are the markets we, as consumers, are most familiar with. In a **consumer market**, individuals purchase goods and services for personal consumption. But there are also business-to-business markets. In **business-to-business (B2B) markets**, businesses purchase goods and services from other businesses. In this section, we'll explore both markets and examine the buying behaviour differences between consumer markets and business-to-business markets.

How does a consumer make a buying decision? The consumer buying process involves five steps:

1. need recognition
2. information search
3. evaluation of alternatives
4. purchase or no purchase decision
5. post-purchase evaluation

Not all consumers go through each step in the process, and the steps do not need to be completed in the same order. As well, the process can be interrupted at any time with a "no purchase" decision.

Consider your decision to purchase the educational services of your college or university. You first recognized the need for higher education. You likely obtained information about schools from many sources, including your friends, family, counsellors, and the Internet. You may have also visited a few campuses to gather first-hand information. You then evaluated your choices based on a number of factors, including the tuition (price), geographic location, or maybe where your friends were going to school. Your final choice may have been based on "rational analysis" or the result of an emotional decision (based on some "gut feeling"). After making a purchase, we also evaluate our decision in terms of how well our expectations are being met. You'll likely continue to evaluate your college or university choice long after you graduate.

Video: Target to Sell 99-Dollar Wedding Dresses

SELF CHECK Answer the following questions to test your consumer behaviour IQ.

1. In a consumer market, who is the primary buyer of goods?
   a. Businesses
   b. Households
2. Which of the following is a major influence on what people buy?
   a. Education
   b. Income
3. Which step comes first in the buying decision process?
   a. Information search
   b. Evaluation of alternatives
4. Which product is a result of psychological influences on society?
   a. Hybrid cars
   b. Bottled water
5. Which of the following statements is true?
   a. Consumer behaviour doesn't help marketers identify target markets.
   b. The marketing process is the same for all markets.

Answers: 1. B; 2. B; 3. A; 4. A; 5. B

What influences consumer decision making? The five-step consumer decision-making process is part of a broader environmental context that influences each step. Effective marketing attempts to help consumers with their information search and the evaluation of alternatives. These environmental influences are shown in **Figure 8.8.**[17]

1. *Sociocultural influences.* Sociocultural influences on buying decisions include the buyer's culture, subculture, social class, family, and peers. Culture is the set of learned attitudes, beliefs, and ways of life that are unique to a society and are handed down through generations. Subcultures are specific groups within a culture that share attitudes and life experiences. Some examples of subcultures include churches, community organizations, and online communities such as Facebook and Myspace. Cultural values change over time. For example, many people today value healthier lifestyles. Social class refers to a combination of factors, such as education, income, wealth, and occupation, that are common to a group of people. Social class can have an impact on purchasing decisions because some possessions are considered status symbols.
2. *Personal influences.* Personal influences on a buyer's consumption choices are often shaped by his or her age, economic situation, lifestyle, and personality. A person who enjoys spending time outdoors hiking is more likely to purchase a tent than a person who spends time playing video games.

Figure 8.8 Major Influences Affecting a Consumer's Buying Decision

Hottest Product Searches (week ending December 14, 2013)

1. UGGs
2. PS4
3. Xbox One
4. Fitbit
5. iPhone 5s
6. iPad Air
7. Rainbow Loom
8. Kindle Fire HD
9. iPhone 5c
10. Call of Duty: Ghosts

While UGGs led the list for the most searched products overall, tech gadgets won seven of the top ten spots, including the PS4, Xbox One, Fitbit, iPhone 5s, iPad Air, Kindle Fire HD, and iPhone 5c.

Source: Experian Marketing Services, "Hot Holiday Products and Trends," December 14, 2013, accessed July 22, 2014, http://www.experian.com/marketing-services/hot-holiday-products.html.

Losevsky Pavel/Shutterstock

There are many influences that affect consumer buying decisions. A family with young children will purchase different grocery items than a university student living in a dorm room with limited kitchen space and a limited budget!

3. *Psychological influences.* Psychological influences include differences in the buyer's motivation, perception, attitudes, and learning. One goal of marketing is to shape the perception of a product in the minds of consumers. Attitudes toward a product put customers in a frame of mind that either predisposes them to view the product favourably or not. For example, changing attitudes toward the environment have increased the demand for hybrid cars. Learning refers to changes in buying behaviour based on experience. Good experiences with brands result in repeat business; bad experiences stunt future sales.
4. *Situational influences.* Situational influences include the physical surroundings, social surroundings, and the type of product purchased. Complex, expensive, and infrequently purchased products, like a new home, will elicit a greater degree of information searching and evaluation of alternatives than a frequently purchased product that has few substitutes, such as table salt.
5. *Marketing mix influences.* Marketing mix (the 4 Ps) influences include the product, price, promotion, and place (distribution) aspects of purchases. As stressed throughout this chapter, marketing is interested in producing a product that buyers want at an affordable price, promoting awareness of the attributes of the product, and placing the good or service in a timely and convenient location for consumers to buy.

Knowledge of consumer buying behaviour and the influences on the buying decision is critical to effective marketing. Some of these influences, such as personal influences, are outside the control of marketers, while other influences, such as psychological influences, can be affected by businesses. All these influences should be kept in mind when selecting a target market; implementing, evaluating, and controlling the marketing mix; and building customer relationships.

Business-to-Business (B2B) Markets

LO8 Compare the buying decisions and marketing processes in business-to-business markets to those in the consumer market.

What is the difference between consumer markets and business-to-business markets? The difference between consumer and B2B markets hinges on who's doing the buying. If a good or service is purchased in a B2B market, it is purchased by a business for further processing or for resale or to facilitate general business activity. The B2B market is significantly larger compared to consumer markets because virtually all consumer products go through a number of distributors or wholesalers before reaching the final consumer at a retail outlet. In fact, each time an unfinished product is bought and sold through the many stages of a product's development, a separate B2B market exists. Think of all the transactions involved in producing a car. Most of the components are produced by separate firms. Moreover, each of these firms derives its inputs from different businesses.

There are several key differences between consumer and B2B markets.[18] The more important characteristics of B2B markets include the following:

1. *A few buyers that purchase in large quantities.* Business-to-business markets typically involve a few buyers that purchase very large quantities. For example, only a few airline companies buy most of Boeing's jets.
2. *Highly trained buyers.* Most business purchasing agents are highly skilled at their jobs. They often weigh the benefits and the costs in a more systematic fashion and are less influenced by emotional factors than buyers in consumer markets. This requires sellers to pitch their products at a much more sophisticated level.
3. *Group purchasing decisions.* A team of individuals within purchasing departments usually collaborate in making a purchasing decision in B2B markets. This means

Table 8.3 Differences between Business-to-Business and Consumer Markets

	Business-to-Business Market	Consumer Market
Market Structure	• Few customers • Large-volume purchases • Geographically concentrated	• Many customers • Small-volume purchases • Geographically dispersed
Nature of the Buying Unit	• More professional and rational purchase decision	• Less sophisticated and more emotional purchase decision
Purchasing Process	• Highly trained buyers • Group purchasing decisions • Complex buying decisions • Formalized buying procedures • Close relationship between marketer and buyer • Personal selling • Geographically concentrated	• Untrained buyers • Individual purchasing decisions • Relatively simple buying decisions • Informal buying decisions • Impersonal relationship between marketer and buyer • Mass advertising • Geographically dispersed

marketers must be prepared to be patient and mindful of all decision-makers' concerns to seal a deal.

Video: Eaton

4. *Close customer relationships.* Because there are only a few sophisticated buyers that purchase large quantities, marketers find it necessary to establish a much closer relationship with customers compared to the relationship with buyers in consumer markets. As a result, B2B marketing is more focused on personal selling compared to the mass advertising campaigns that typify consumer markets.
5. *Geographically concentrated buyers.* Most buyers in B2B markets are concentrated in a few of the most industrialized areas where most large businesses are located. This reduces the costs of reaching buyers.
6. *Direct purchasing.* Often buyers in B2B markets purchase directly from sellers, as opposed to consumer markets, where products typically go through many wholesalers before the product arrives to the end user.

These key differences between consumer and B2B markets are summarized in **Table 8.3**. These differences can be organized by differences in market structure, the nature of the buying unit, and the purchasing process.

How does a business make a buying decision, and what influences that decision? The five-step consumer decision-making process is equally applicable to business purchasing decisions. Businesses begin by recognizing a need, they seek out information to aid them in the purchase decision, they evaluate alternatives, they decide to either purchase or not to purchase, and they undertake a post-purchase evaluation. However, business purchases are generally more rational, reasoned, and objective decisions that are based on influences such as the state of the economy, technological factors, the degree of competition, political and regulatory concerns, and organizational objectives, policies, and procedures.

Is the marketing process different for B2B markets? The marketing process remains the same for all markets: identify a need, undertake research to come up with a marketing plan, select a target market, implement and control the marketing mix, and nurture customer relationships.

Think back to the quiz you took at the beginning of this section. Would you ace the quiz now based on what you've learned? Understanding consumer behaviour and the buying and marketing process are essential for marketers when selecting a target market and managing the marketing mix.

CHAPTER SYNOPSIS

LO1 Summarize how marketing has evolved over the production concept era, sales concept era, marketing concept era, and customer relationship era. *(pp. 176–178)*

During the production concept era (from the Industrial Revolution until the 1920s), most companies focused solely on production. Demand was often greater than supply, and the prevailing mindset was that a good-quality product would simply sell itself.

During the sales concept era (from the mid-1920s through the early 1950s), technological advances meant that production increased more sharply than demand for goods and services. The use of heavy public advertising in all available forms of media became prevalent.

During the marketing concept era (from the 1950s through the 1990s), production continued to expand more quickly than the growth in demand for goods and services. The **marketing concept** changed the focus from finding the right customer for a product to producing the right product for a customer and doing it better than the competition.

During the customer relationship era (from the late 1990s to the present), organizations have worked to establish long-term relationships with individual customers to foster loyalty and repeat business (referred to as **customer relationship management, CRM**).

LO2 Outline the benefits of marketing to various stakeholders and summarize the criticisms of marketing. *(pp. 178–180)*

Stakeholders, or interested parties, include customers, sellers, investors, employees, and society. Each group of stakeholders has a different set of motives for their interest in the success of the business. Through marketing, companies sell products and services that satisfy human needs and wants (the product or service has value and offers **utility**). The five types of utility are form, task, time, place, and ownership. Businesses that are most successful in satisfying customers generate higher profits, and investors benefit from the profits earned. Employees benefit from successful marketing as well because their jobs and livelihoods are more secure. Society benefits from successful marketing because scarce resources are more efficiently allocated into the production of the goods and services most desired by society.

Criticisms of marketing include price gouging, the production of shoddy or unsafe products, and confusing and deceptive practices. The criticisms of marketing should not be taken lightly. All companies should have a code of ethics and policies in place to curb unethical behaviour within their organizations.

LO3 Describe the 4 Ps of the marketing mix and explain the five steps of the marketing process to implement a marketing strategy. *(pp. 180–184)*

A **marketing strategy** consists of two major elements: the organization must determine its *target market* and then develop a *marketing mix* to meet the needs of that market. The **target market** is the specific group of consumers, who have similar needs and wants, a firm directs its marketing efforts toward. The **marketing mix** is the combination of four factors, called the "4 Ps" of marketing, designed to serve the target market: product, price, promotion, and place.

The idea is to provide the *product* that customers need and want at an appropriate *price* and to *promote* its sale and *place* or distribute the good or service in a convenient location for the customer to purchase. Effective marketing requires the appropriate blend of the 4 Ps directed at targeted customers. This blend is constrained by forces outside the firm's control that are found within the broader market environment.

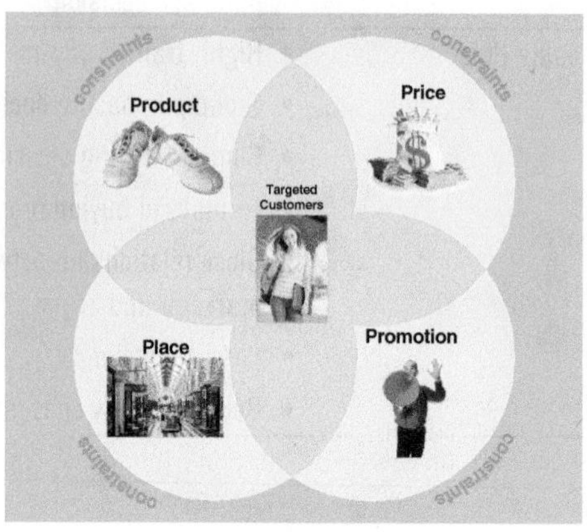

The Marketing Mix

The Five Steps in the Marketing Process

The marketing process may seem simple when it's written on the page, but it's as much art as it is science. Common ingredients for marketing success include producing a high-quality product (with a unique brand that is properly promoted) that consistently delivers value to customers at a "fair" price, where they want it, and when they want it.

LO4 Describe how the various factors in the marketing environment influence a firm's ability to manipulate its marketing mix. *(pp. 184–186)*

The **marketing environment** includes environmental influences such as the competitive environment (discussed in Chapter 2) and the political, economic, sociocultural, and technological (PEST) environment (also discussed in Chapter 2). Because these factors are outside the firm's control, they constrain the organization's ability to manipulate its marketing mix.

LO5 Identify the five steps of the marketing research process and the four elements of a good marketing plan. *(pp. 186–190)*

Market research is the process of gathering and analyzing market information to make marketing decisions. The marketing research process consists of five steps: (1) define the need, problem, or objective; (2) collect the relevant data (primary and secondary sources); (3) analyze the data; (4) interpret the results; and (5) act on the conclusions.

A **marketing plan** is a written document that specifies marketing activities designed to reach organizational objectives. Four elements emerge from all good marketing plans: (1) a clearly written marketing objective, (2) a thorough situational analysis (e.g., SWOT and the 5 Cs), (3) selection of a target market, and (4) implementation, evaluation, and control of the marketing mix (the 4 Ps).

LO6 Describe how target markets are determined and how a firm attempts to satisfy a target market. *(pp. 190–192)*

Once an organization has evaluated its internal strengths and weaknesses, as well as the external opportunities and threats of the market environment, then it is ready to select its target market. A target market is the specific group of consumers, who have similar needs and wants, a firm directs its marketing efforts toward. Finding a target market begins with **market segmentation**, the process of separating the broader market into smaller markets (or market segments) that consist of similar groups of customers. A **market segment** is a subgroup of potential customers who share similar characteristics and therefore have similar product needs and preferences. Four of the most common consumer market segmentation classifications are **geographic**, **demographic**, **psychographic**, and **behavioural**. For each target market, the company tries to blend the 4 Ps of the marketing mix to best satisfy the targeted customers. The process of developing a unique marketing mix that best satisfies a target market is known as **positioning**.

LO7 Describe the purchase decision process and the major influences affecting a consumer's buying decision. *(pp. 192–194)*

The consumer buying process involves five steps:

1. need recognition
2. information search
3. evaluation of alternatives
4. purchase or no purchase decision
5. post-purchase evaluation

Not all consumers go through each step in the process, and the steps do not need to be completed in the same order. As well, the process can be interrupted at any time with a "no purchase" decision.

The five-step consumer decision-making process is part of a broader environmental context that influences each step. Effective marketing attempts to help consumers with their information search and the evaluation of alternatives.

Major Influences Affecting a Consumer's Buying Decision

LO8 Compare the buying decisions and marketing processes in business-to-business markets to those in the consumer market. *(pp. 194–195)*

In a **consumer market**, buyers are households that purchase final consumer goods. In a **business-to-business (B2B) market**, businesses buy from other businesses. There are many more B2B markets compared to consumer markets. In B2B markets, purchases are often undertaken by a small group of highly trained individuals who buy in large volumes and have a much closer relationship with marketers. B2B buyers are also more geographically concentrated and often avoid distributors.

MyBizLab Study, practise, and explore real business situations with these helpful resources:

- **Interactive Lesson Presentations:** Work through interactive presentations and assessments to test your knowledge of business concepts.
- **Study Plan:** Check your understanding of chapter concepts with self-study quizzes.
- **Dynamic Study Modules:** Work through adaptive study modules on your computer, tablet, or mobile device.
- **Simulations:** Practise decision-making in simulated business environments.

KEY TERMS

5 Cs of marketing *(p. 189)*
behavioural segmentation *(p. 192)*
business-to-business (B2B) markets *(p. 192)*
consumer behaviour *(p. 192)*
consumer market *(p. 192)*
customer relationship management (CRM) *(p. 178)*
demographic segmentation *(p. 191)*
environmental scanning *(p. 185)*
focus group *(p. 187)*
geographic segmentation *(p. 191)*
market research *(p. 186)*
market segment *(p. 191)*
market segmentation *(p. 190)*
marketing *(p. 176)*
marketing concept *(p. 177)*
marketing environment *(p. 185)*
marketing mix *(p. 181)*
marketing objective *(p. 188)*
marketing plan *(p. 188)*
marketing strategy *(p. 179)*
niche marketing *(p. 191)*
positioning *(p. 191)*
primary data *(p. 187)*
product *(p. 176)*
product differentiation *(p. 182)*
psychographic segmentation *(p. 191)*
secondary data *(p. 187)*
target market *(p. 179)*
utility *(p. 179)*

CRITICAL THINKING QUESTIONS

1. Can you think of an example of how a specific organization (for-profit or nonprofit) tried to establish a better customer relationship with you? What did the organization do? Was it effective? Why or why not? What recommendations would you make to these organizations?
2. Select a product or service you use regularly, such as a cosmetic or toiletry item, a snack food, article of clothing, cellphone, laptop, and so on. Explain how the 4 Ps of the marketing mix (product, price, promotion, and place) relate to this product. Who is the target market for this product? How can this product be changed or the marketing strategy be adjusted to appeal to other market segments?
3. You're interested in starting a limousine service in your community. How might you best segment the market for your services? What is your target market and why? What marketing mix strategies would you employ? How would you nurture customer relationships?
4. Retailers such as the Real Canadian Superstore and Canadian Tire offer loyalty programs. Walmart has a loyalty program now with its own credit card that offers consumers Walmart bucks that can be used toward future purchases. What other such programs can you think of? What are companies trying to do by offering such programs?
5. Think of the last major purchase you made. Discuss how the sociocultural, personal, psychological, situational, and marketing mix influences influenced this purchase.

TEAM TIME

Tobacco Wars

Divide into two even teams, one to represent each of the following:

a. tobacco company employees; pro-cigarette advertising in magazines
b. anti-tobacco advertising activists

SCENARIO

Does a company have a fundamental right to market its products wherever it wishes? Cigarette advertising in magazines has been a topic of great controversy. The large tobacco companies provide publications with a great deal of revenue by purchasing expensive advertising space, but many anti-smoking groups and some magazine publishers are questioning the ethical nature of this. Anti-smoking groups argue that these advertisements appeal to children and glamorize smoking. Tobacco companies claim that they are merely making attractive advertisements with no intention of encouraging children to use their products. The European Union has banned tobacco advertisements from magazines entirely, and many U.S. publications have stopped selling ad space to tobacco companies. The Canadian government has also taken bold steps to control tobacco marketing. Do tobacco companies have the right to advertise their products as they see fit? Is it morally wrong to advertise a product that is known to cause health problems?

PROCESS

Step 1. Collaborate with team members to discuss both sides of the issue, analyzing the arguments from each perspective.
Step 2. Prepare the most effective argument for your team's perspective and think about counterpoints to arguments that the other team may raise.

ETHICS AND RESPONSIBILITY

Daily Deal Sites: Groupon Settles Class Action Lawsuit

Who doesn't love a bargain? Sales, coupons, BOGOs, and other discount promotions have been a common way for companies to get you to try something you may not purchase otherwise. Daily deal sites like Groupon, LivingSocial, and Google Offers have merged the concept of discount promotions with social networking and have caught on like wildfire. The question is whether or not they are working—either for the consumer or for the business promoting its product. Perhaps the only party winning is the discounting site, but even that is undecided.

The enticement for a company to offer its product on a daily deal site is that its promotion reaches a large group of people quickly. And, unlike other promotions, the "deal" doesn't take place unless there is a significant mass of interest. The downside that many companies experience is an initial surge of interest surrounding the deal but little or no repeat business, which they had hoped would result. One would also think consumers benefit by being able to try something for nearly half the cost. But many have been caught in the fine print that restricts the time, place, or type of offering. In fact, Groupon was hit with a class action lawsuit that claimed the expiration dates on the deals are in violation of consumer protection laws.

The outcome of the lawsuit was favourable for Canadian consumers. Anyone using Groupon prior to March 8, 2013,

John Konstantaras/AP Images

received notice that the $500 000 settlement approval for the class action lawsuit against Groupon Inc. had gone through, giving close to 1 million Groupon deal hunters the chance to redeem vouchers that were previously considered expired. If any of the members of the class action lawsuit did not want to redeem their vouchers, they had to submit a claim for a refund by January 27, 2014.[19]

The daily deal sites themselves have grown to become a multibillion dollar industry and may be the only ones receiving long-term benefits. But will they begin to experience growing pains, or can they continue their rapid success?

DISCUSSION QUESTIONS

1. Do you feel that it is unethical to offer deals with limited expiry dates or dates that are written in fine print and not obvious to the online buyer? Or do you feel that consumers are responsible for apprising themselves of the terms of use when they purchase a voucher?
2. As a business owner offering deals through Groupon, are you responsible for the expiration dates on those deals or do you think that Groupon is responsible and should be making better efforts to be transparent with expiry dates?
3. How does the fact that the customer is purchasing a *voucher*, not a good or service, impact your thoughts about responsibility in question 2?
4. What consumer protection laws are being violated in the case of expired Groupon deals?

CLOSING CASE

The iPod Started a Love Affair[20]

Today, the original Mac 128k computer is likely viewed more as a technological dinosaur than as an innovative machine. However, when Apple introduced it in 1984, the Mac 128k began a revolutionary way of developing and marketing new technology. Its simple design, easy-to-use operating system, and accessible cost made it the first personal computer created with the consumer in mind. Apple continued to produce successful products in its first decade but fell into a bit of a slump starting in the late 1980s. The company lost its grip on its target market and had difficulty competing with companies such as IBM and Hewlett-Packard. It took the dawning of a new millennium and the return of a founding member to turn Apple around.

In 1997, Steve Jobs's return to Apple Computer Inc. as interim chief executive officer sparked a sort of renaissance for the company. Jobs wanted to revive what had made Apple a flourishing company in the first place: making products based on the customer's needs. The key to Apple's success was marketing to a specific target audience: a young, creative demographic who valued advanced technology and sleek design. The true brilliance of this marketing strategy was that Apple didn't just identify its target audience—it actually predicted what the target audience wanted. "A lot of times, people don't know what they want until you show it to them," Jobs told *Businessweek* in 1998. And what Jobs showed the world three years later was exactly what his target audience wanted.

Generation Y (those born between 1982 and 2000) was already accustomed to getting its music digitally through websites such as Napster and Lycos, but it needed a way to take music from the computer to the streets. In 2001, Apple introduced the iPod, a portable digital music player that fulfilled this need. The iPod's sleek geometric design and durability made it easy to slide in a pocket or toss in a backpack. The iPod also met the customer need to have creative control over the media outlet. The iPod allowed music files to be organized in a variety of ways, and customers could make playlists of their favourite songs.

When the iPod was introduced, it was not an immediate worldwide success, but that was to be expected. Jobs knew he could not market to everyone. He was willing to alienate some consumers to appeal to the core group of people for which the product was designed. He knew it would take time to turn some skeptics into customers. In 2003, Apple announced the second-generation iPod and iTunes, a digital music store that allowed customers to buy song files. It was then that the iPod/iTunes juggernaut emerged. The iPod was no longer just a product. Part status symbol, part entertainment, the iPod created a love affair between young adults and all things Apple. "Apple's products often elicit an emotional response and connection with customers that is extremely unique and very rewarding," states Apple's marketing department.[21]

That emotional connection translates into big numbers for Apple. Currently, the iPod holds a majority market share for digital music players.[22] Its presence in the market is so dominant that, like Kleenex, Xerox, and Post-it, the brand name has become synonymous with the product, which makes all competing brands look generic. Jobs's decision to streamline Apple's customer base proved that a focused marketing strategy could dominate a target market, whereas an expansive strategy must submit to the many needs of a broad market. With his keen ability to anticipate future trends, Jobs (who passed away October 5, 2011) helped Apple become a giant in the digital markets. As Apple continues to improve upon the iPod with its many iterations, such as the iPod shuffle, iPod nano, and iPod touch, it's inevitable that the original iPod will join the ranks of the Mac 128k as a technological fossil, but Apple's marketing methods behind these and other products, including the iPhone and the iPad, will likely influence Apple's success for decades to come.

DISCUSSION QUESTIONS

1. What was Apple's target demographic for the iPod? Why do you think that Apple chose to market specifically to this audience? How would Apple have to change its product if it wanted to appeal to a broader market?
2. How did Apple meet the sociocultural, personal, psychological, and behavioural needs of its target audience?
3. Consider what you've learned about marketing to audiences in this chapter. What methods do you think companies should use to help them establish a target market?

9 Marketing Mix: Product, Price, Promotion, and Place

Michael Neelon/Alamy

LEARNING OBJECTIVES

After studying this chapter, you should be able to:

LO1 Define various concepts applied to the term *product* as they apply to marketing and explain the role of product differentiation in product development. (pp. 202–204)

LO2 Outline the steps in new product development, the application of the product life cycle, and describe classifications of consumer products and business-to-business products. (pp. 204–210)

LO3 Explain why branding is beneficial to both buyers and sellers and describe some different types of brands. (pp. 210–216)

LO4 Describe three major approaches to pricing strategy and outline some pricing tactics used to launch a new product, to adjust prices, and to affect price perceptions. (pp. 216–220)

LO5 Define a promotional mix and explain its function in a promotional campaign. (pp. 220–222)

LO6 Explain the advantages and disadvantages of the various types of media used for advertising and discuss the role of public relations in a company. (pp. 222–227)

LO7 Describe the six steps in the personal selling process. (pp. 227–229)

LO8 Describe the two main types of sales promotions and the types of tools commonly used as incentives. (pp. 229–231)

LO9 Define marketing intermediaries and distribution channels and explain why these are important elements in marketing. (pp. 231–237)

OPENING DISCUSSION: PRODUCT PROMOTION

Kraft Is a Champion Marketer

Kraft Foods Group Inc. is a food, beverage, and confectionery company that is ranked number one in North America and number two (after Nestlé) in the world. Revenues in 2012 were US$18.3 billion, approximately 14 percent of which is generated in Canada.[1] According to its 2012 annual report, Kraft sells its products in the United States and Canada and exports to 35 countries and territories worldwide. Two of its brands—Kraft cheeses, dinner, and dressing, and Oscar Mayer meats—have annual revenues exceeding US$1 billion annually worldwide. Kraft produces over 25 well-known brands with annual net revenues in the range of $100 million–$1 billion each. Kraft Canada brands include Kraft cheeses, dinners, and dressings; Caramilk chocolate; Christie cookies and crackers; Kool-Aid and Del Monte beverages; Maynards candy; and Stride and Dentyne gum.[2] People around the world consume about 900 million servings of Kraft products daily.

Kraft's marketing efforts include consumer marketing in print, on-air, outdoor, and digital media; consumer incentives such as contests and coupons; and trade promotions (e.g., gifts, demonstrations, special pricing, and display).[3] It is essential to Kraft's business success to continue to extend its brands into new markets, expand its brand image by developing new products, and maintain its brand image for existing products. This is done through product innovation and marketing investments in advertising and consumer promotions. Kraft ranked number 62 on *Advertising Age's* 100 Leading National Advertisers ranking published in June 2013, spending $683 million on measured-media advertising in 2012.[4]

Kraft's marketing services division is a collection of teams that supply marketing strategies to Kraft's business divisions. Positions include market research analysts, consumer promotion coordinators, and Kraft Kitchens members. The market research team helps transform consumer data and demographic information into business-building initiatives. The consumer promotions team develops and executes consumer awareness programs such as in-store promotions, couponing, contests, and loyalty programs. The Kraft Kitchens team develops recipes and provides ideas about entertaining, healthy eating, and other cuisine tips.[5]

A few of Kraft's recent marketing strategies include the following:

- *Mobile marketing.* "Big Fork Little Fork" is an iPad app that helps parents teach kids smart eating habits and an appreciation for food. It offers recipes, how-to videos, and educational games to encourage the whole family to cook together, eat together, and live well together. It targets parents in their 20s and 30s and aims to teach users healthy eating while promoting love and loyalty for Kraft's brands, such as Kraft Singles, Ritz Crackers, Jell-O, and Kraft Dinner.[6]
- *Epic campaign.* "The Real Women of Philadelphia" cream cheese contest asked women to invent their own dishes and shoot and upload instructional videos to the contest's website. Aligning itself with a popular television personality who was already using Philadelphia cream cheese on her cooking show, Paula Deen, the campaign tapped into an existing network rather than having to start from scratch. Intended to run for only one year with an estimated 400 responses, "The Real Women of Philadelphia" received about 6000 entries and blossomed into a thriving social network of more than 30 000 women. And it sold 5 percent more cream cheese.[7]
- *Product innovation.* When Post, a division of Kraft, launched the "Diamond Shreddies" campaign, it positioned a historic product prominently in people's minds without changing the product. The campaign compared how the old square Shreddies were "boring" and the new Diamond Shreddies were "exciting." Customers laughed along with the light-hearted notion that by turning old Shreddies 45 degrees, new Diamond Shreddies could be made exciting![8] The advertising industry seemed to appreciate Post's "innovation" too, as the campaign won several awards, including a Grand Clio, a Bronze Pencil at the One Show, and a finalist spot in Cannes in the Integrated category.[9]

- *Power brand.* Increased marketing and new packaging in regions including Latin American and Asia Pacific have seen Kraft's Tang sales grow remarkably. Kraft's strategy is to grow 10 of its key brands overseas. In China, market research showed that children thought water was boring and bland, while mothers believed their children needed about six glasses of water per day; this led to the campaign and slogan: "Tang makes water more exciting." Kraft's market research also showed that Chinese consumers preferred drinks by the glass rather than by the pitcher, so single-serve powder sticks were created for sale in China instead of pitcher packs.[10]
- *Positive image and social media.* Since 2006, Kraft Canada has sponsored an annual Kraft Hockeyville program along with the Canadian Broadcasting Corporation (CBC), the National Hockey League (NHL), and the National Hockey League Players' Association (NHLPA) to find Canada's "most passionate" hockey community. Each year the winner receives $100 000 for arena upgrades and earns a spot as guest host for a preseason NHL game. The marketing program has become one of Kraft's most successful, with sales of products featured in the program—such as Kraft Dinner, Maxwell House coffee, Ritz crackers, Oreo cookies, and Cracker Barrel cheese—increasing between 4 percent and 6 percent. Kraft Hockeyville is supported by TV, in-store materials, Facebook, Twitter, and YouTube.[11]

Over the years, Kraft has launched numerous successful marketing campaigns. Kraft joins mainstay marketers such as Campbell, General Mills, Heinz, and Kellogg in boosting ad spending, launching new products, and restaging old favourites.[12]

DISCUSSION QUESTIONS

1. You may recall the TV commercial about college students cooking Kraft Dinner on a hot water radiator in their dorm room. Choose a different Kraft advertisement or commercial you can recall and research the specific gains or losses incurred by the company from this marketing effort. What were they?
2. Review Kraft's online annual and sustainability reports. What types of projects, practices, initiatives, or endeavours is Kraft working on that will help build its good reputation and at the same time market its company and brands to potential consumers?
3. Which Kraft products do you use? Why do you choose Kraft? Are Kraft products more expensive than generic products? Do you prefer the Kraft brand over other brands? Why or why not?

THE MARKETING MIX (4 Ps): PRODUCT

LO1 Define various concepts applied to the term *product* as they apply to marketing and explain the role of product differentiation in product development.

The Total Product Offer

Which do you prefer: Diet Coke or Coke Zero? Some may not have a preference, believing that they are basically the same beverage, but they're not. They have different flavours, marketing strategies, and targeted demographics. After having moderate success with flavoured versions of Coke products, the company came up with an idea to differentiate Diet Coke to appeal more to men.[13] Coke Zero's marketing strategy reflects this new target market. The can is darker to convey a bigger flavour, and advertisements for the beverage are male dominated, with advertising plots built around sports like auto racing. The website for Coke Zero also includes pages with information about NCAA and NFL football. Coke Zero shows it is not only important to differentiate products from their competitors, but also to differentiate current products to meet the needs of a broader market.

The application of the marketing process is as much an art as a science. Making a high-quality product with a unique, properly promoted brand that consistently delivers value to customers at a "fair" price, when and where they want it, presents significant challenges to marketers all over the world.

Mediablitzimages(uk) Limited/Alamy

Coke Zero is not the same product as Diet Coke. Differentiating a company's products from those of competitors is important, but sometimes companies have to differentiate their own products, too.

What is the total product offer? As you'll recall from Chapter 8, a product is any good, service, or idea available for purchase in a market, as well as any intangible benefits derived from its consumption. An Apple iPad Air, a GMC Acadia, a college or university education, E*Trade financial services, a doctor's advice, and even a Caribbean vacation package are all products. Consumers buy products for a number of tangible and intangible benefits. The **total product offer** (or *value package*) consists of all the benefits associated with a good, service, or idea that affect a consumer's purchasing decision. When you buy a car, you're not just buying a mode of transportation; you're also buying some intangible benefits, such as style or an image. Marketers know this, and when planning a total product offering they think about products on three levels: the *core product*, the *actual product*, and the *augmented product*. Each level adds more value to a product.

total product offer Consists of all the benefits associated with a good, service, or idea that affect a consumer's purchasing decision. Also called a value package.

- The *core product* provides the core benefit or service that satisfies the basic need or want that motivates the consumer's purchase. For a car, that core benefit is the convenient transportation it provides. For a soft drink, it is the product's thirst-quenching capability. For a camera, it is the ability to capture and share memories. Notice that the core product is *intangible*—it relates to what it does for you, and you can't touch it. This is because the core product is the basic *benefit* the product provides. Companies use the benefits of their products to lure customers. That is why car companies such as Toyota use "Moving Forward" as an advertising slogan. Similarly, the soft drink Sprite uses "Obey Your Thirst," and Shutterfly, the Internet-based image publishing service, uses "Memories You Can Hold" to draw in customers.
- Of course, an *actual product* must be developed to provide the core benefit or service desired. The actual product is the *tangible aspect* of the purchase that you can touch, see, hear, smell, or taste. It provides core benefits when it is used. Consumers often assess the tangible benefits of actual products by comparing brands, quality (often associated with a brand's reputation), features, styling, or packaging. For a car, the actual product is the automobile itself. Benefits of an actual product such as a Volvo station wagon could be a high-quality brand, numerous safety features, seating for seven passengers, or leather seats. For a soft drink, the actual product might provide a refreshing taste, desirable colour, or pleasant aroma. The product could even provide the "pick-me-up" caffeine buzz that consumers are looking for when they purchase some soft drinks. For a camera, the actual product may provide features such as an LCD screen or a lightweight design.
- The *augmented product* consists of the core product and the actual product *plus* other real or perceived benefits that provide additional value to the customer's purchase. These benefits might include customer service and support, delivery, installation, a warranty, or favourable credit terms. The value-enhancing elements of an actual product are an important part of the total product offering because they help provide a more satisfying customer experience. For a product such as a car, augmented benefits might include a reasonable price, an easy payment plan, a 10-year warranty, or just the security of owning a brand new car.

NC1/ZGLR WENN Photos/Newscom

Ben & Jerry's Homemade Ice Cream differentiated itself from other ice cream makers by offering original and unique flavours and product names such as "Goodbye Yellow Brickle Road," "Cherry Garcia," and "Phish Food."

Figure 9.1 summarizes the three levels of a product. Remember that when developing products, marketers must begin with a basic customer need or want to be satisfied by a product. Then marketers develop an actual product to satisfy that need for targeted customers. Successful product developers then augment the product to create a total product offering that provides a benefit package superior to that of the competition. This is the essence of successful *product differentiation*, which we'll discuss next.

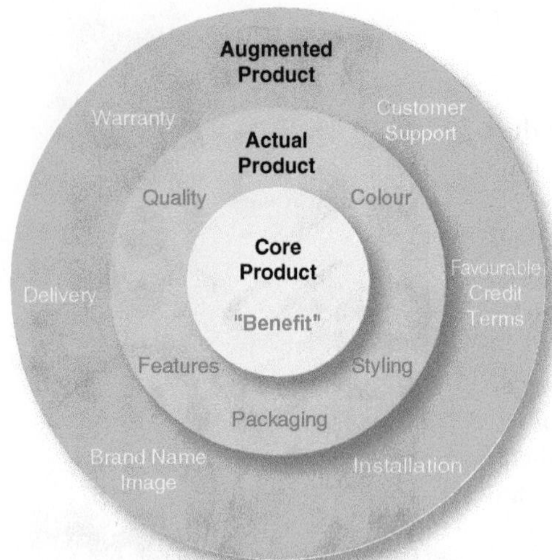

Figure 9.1 Three-Ring Model

The three levels of a product define the benefits to be derived from a total product offering.

Product Differentiation

How important is product differentiation? **Product differentiation** is the creation of a real or perceived difference in a product designed to attract customers. A company can distinguish a product from its competitors by establishing concrete or intangible differences between similar products. For example, a luggage company might offer suitcases in unique colours or shapes. It might also offer a lifetime guarantee on certain models. Product differentiation is critical for a product's success. If a product doesn't possess qualities that make it stand out, then customers will not be motivated to buy that product instead of a competitor's product.

How does consumer input affect product development? Companies rely on customer input and feedback to help shape their products. Listening to customers and incorporating their suggestions are effective ways to foster good customer relationships, which are a critical component in establishing repeat business and long-term success. In fact, listening to customers is one of the most important elements of sound customer relationship management. You have to know what your customers want to tailor a product offering that best satisfies their needs.

product differentiation The creation of a real or perceived difference in a product designed to attract customers.

Video: High-End Designers Embrace Plus-Size Market

Consumer input often provides information that prompts companies to segment a large market and focus on narrowly defined targeted customers. For example, a breakfast cereal company might find that most consumers buy its cereal because it is high in fibre. That company can differentiate its product from competing products by labelling the cereal "a good source of fibre" and target the product to health-conscious adults. Today's health-conscious consumers look for products that are fat free, cholesterol free, or gluten free, and companies can use this knowledge to differentiate their products by improving an existing product or creating an entirely new product and marketing these products on that basis. Product differentiation is the result of carefully segmenting markets into clearly defined targeted customers and developing a variety of total product offerings that best meet these varying customer needs—and doing it better than the competition.

New Product Development

LO2 Outline the steps in new product development, the application of the product life cycle, and describe classifications of consumer products and business-to-business products.

new product development The five steps for developing a new product: idea generation, idea screening, product analysis, product development and concept testing, and commercialization.

What are the steps in developing a new product? As outlined in **Figure 9.2**, **new product development** involves five steps:

1. *Idea generation.* Ideas for entirely new products or improved versions of existing products are often obtained by listening closely to customers or focus groups. In fact, customer complaints may signal a need for a new product. Suppliers, employees, and salespeople also generate ideas by assessing the competition and through trade shows.
2. *Idea screening.* The objective of idea screening is to eliminate unsound concepts before devoting costly resources to their development. Screening involves estimating the level of consumer demand for the product, its profitability, and its production feasibility given the company's current technical capabilities.
3. *Product analysis.* Product analysis estimates costs of production, selling price, sales volume, and profitability. Costs of production depend on the features of the product deemed necessary to meet the targeted customers' needs. The selling price, sales volume, and profitability may depend on the degree of competition in the market.
4. *Product development and concept testing.* At this stage, product ideas that survive the screening and analysis steps are analyzed further. This often begins with a physical prototype of the good. Computer-aided design systems are helpful in quickly making design changes even before a physical prototype is manufactured. In the testing phase of a new service offering, management determines the details concerning staffing needs and equipment requirements to ensure the service is delivered properly.

Stephen Finn/Shutterstock

By listening to consumers and discovering what they want, such as today's health-conscious consumers who want food products that are fat free, cholesterol free, and so on, companies can created products that are differentiated on these qualities to target these consumers.

Idea Generation
- Brainstorm new product ideas
- Think of ways to improve an existing product

Idea Screening
- Ask yourself: Will my target market benefit from this product?
- Ask yourself: Can this product be competitive with similar products?

Product Analysis
- Determine a desired sale price
- Assess the cost of production

Product Development and Concept Testing
- Produce a prototype
- Get feedback from potential customers

Commercialization
- Introduce the product to the market
- Begin the rollout process

Figure 9.2 The Five Steps in the New Product Development Process

Concept testing involves soliciting customer responses to a new product idea. Potential targeted customers are asked to evaluate different features, prices, packages, and a host of other factors surrounding the product. The idea is to come up with the best, most profitable total product offering.

5. *Commercialization.* If a product makes it this far in the process, it is ready to be launched. Commercialization is the decision to market a product. Introducing a new product can be costly because of manufacturing investments, advertising, personal selling, and other promotional activities. The returns from such investments can take time. This may explain why many companies introduce their new products in one region at a time—sometimes called *rolling out the product*.

Video: Subaru America: New Product Development and Life Cycle Strategy

Despite the scientific nature of new product development, a large proportion of new products still fail. In contrast to the success of Coke Zero discussed earlier, one of the most interesting cases of a new product failure was Coca-Cola's "New Coke" launched in 1985. In an attempt to revitalize its brand, the company toyed with the formula of its popular beverage and almost destroyed it. People didn't want their favourite soft drink to be modified, and New Coke was pulled from the shelves only three months after the product was introduced.[14] Coca-Cola returned to its original formula and renamed the cola Coca-Cola Classic.

What is a product's life cycle? Once a product is developed, it begins the product life cycle. A **product life cycle** is a theoretical model describing a product's sales and profits over the course of its lifetime. During this cycle, a product typically goes through four stages: an introductory stage, a growth stage, a maturity stage, and a declining stage. The product life cycle can be applied to a specific product or to an entire product category. However, like all models, it is a simplified version of reality and should not be used prescriptively because the duration of a product's entire life can be as short as a few months, as is often the case for fad items such as the Rainbow Loom. The product's life can also be as long as a century or more for such products as baking soda. In addition, not all products strictly follow these stages. Some products are introduced but never grow in sales, whereas others never seem to decline.

product life cycle A theoretical model describing a product's sales and profits over the course of its lifetime.

You can see how the theory works if you consider the life cycle of vinyl music recordings. Vinyl records were first introduced in 1930 by RCA Victor but became popular in the 1950s as a replacement for the brittle and easily broken 78-rpm records. This

lululemon athletica was originally marketed as high-performing running and yoga wear, but in 2010 it gained popularity as everyday casual wear. lululemon might have been considered a fad, but only time will tell if this product will continue to grow or hit a declining stage.

was their introductory stage. Sales grew rapidly in the 1950s and through the 1960s, representing the product's growth stage. They came in 33⅓-rpm long-playing records, or LPs, and 45-rpm single records. In the early 1970s, vinyl records hit their maturity stage. By the late 1970s and early 1980s, cassette tapes gained wide acceptance, which caused sales of vinyl records to drop drastically, representing their declining stage. After compact discs (CDs) were introduced, the decline continued. For many years, vinyl records were sold mostly as collectors' items but have been making a small comeback in recent years among avid music fans who believe the sound quality is better than digital formats.

How do marketing decisions affect the product's life cycle? The product life cycle model may be useful as a general description of a product's sales and profits over time, but it should be used with caution when forecasting or predicting future sales and profits. Not all products strictly follow these stages, and the period involved with each stage can vary dramatically. In fact, marketing decisions can affect each of the phases of a product's life cycle, while knowledge of a product's life cycle stage also helps determine the appropriate marketing mix strategy for that stage. **Figure 9.3** summarizes the characteristics, marketing objectives, and strategies for each of the four stages of a product's life cycle.

Because most products eventually decline and may have to be withdrawn from the market, companies must continuously seek to develop new products to replace older ones. At the same time, marketers work hard to extend the life of existing products to milk as much profit from them as possible. Some auto companies have used discounted prices, rebates, and low-interest loans to extend the life of their models. Arm & Hammer, a company that produces baking soda, extended its product's life by advertising and *creating a new use* for its product as a refrigerator deodorizer. The Home Depot and Lowe's tried to *create new markets* for their businesses by expanding into do-it-yourself training on home projects within their stores. Jell-O extended its knowledge (*extended technology*) of raw gelatin to create puddings and other snacks. *Repackaging*, or using new labels or different container types, is another popular method to extend a product's life. For example, in a nod to Taylor Swift, Diet Coke created a collector's edition can in celebration of extraordinary individuals. The limited-time Diet Coke Taylor Swift can six-pack was available in the United States from October to December 2013. The can features the singer's logo along with a handwritten quote from Swift that circles the can. Diet Coke has embarked on a multiyear partnership with Swift as part of the company's "Stay Extraordinary" campaign. In-store and point-of-sale advertising inspired by Swift will also support the launch of the new can. In addition, visitors to MyCokeRewards.com can redeem "double points" from their collector's edition six-packs for exclusive access to Taylor Swift prizes, gear, and insider information about the extraordinary global superstar.[15]

As you've just learned, developing a high-quality product is not so much an end in itself as it is a beginning. After a product is developed, the product life cycle begins and appropriate marketing strategies must be conceived and implemented accordingly.

Product Lines and the Product Mix

product line A group of similar products intended for a similar market.

product mix The combination of all product lines offered for sale by a company.

What term describes a group of similar products? Customer feedback guides product development and product differentiation. It also gives rise to the creation of a **product line**, a group of similar products intended for a similar market. A **product mix** is the combination of all product lines offered for sale by a company. For example,

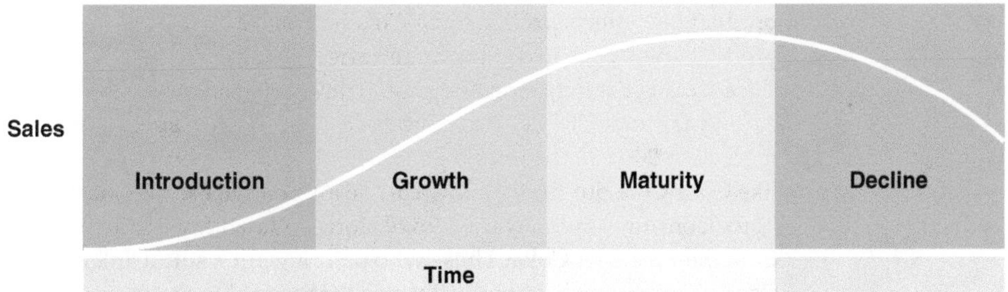

Sales

	Introduction	Growth	Maturity	Decline

Time

Characteristics

	Introduction	Growth	Maturity	Decline
Sales	Low sales	Radically rising sales	Peak sales	Declining sales
Costs	High cost per customer	High cost per customer	Low cost per customer	Low cost per customer
Profits	Negative	Rising	High	Declining
Customers	Innovators	Innovators	Middle majority	Laggards
Competitors	Few	Growing number	Stable number beginning to decline	Declining number

Marketing Objectives

	Introduction	Growth	Maturity	Decline
	Create product awareness and trial	Maximize market share	Maximize profit while defending market share	Reduce expenditure and milk the brand

Strategies

	Introduction	Growth	Maturity	Decline
Product	Offer a basic product	Offer product extensions, services, warranty	Diversify brands and models	Phase out weak items
Price	Charge cost-plus	Price to penetrate market	Price to match or beat competitors	Cut prices
Distribution	Build selective distribution	Build intensive distribution	Build more intensive distribution	Go selective; phase out unprofitable outlets
Advertising	Build product awareness among early adopters and dealers	Build awareness and interest in the mass market	Stress brand differences and benefits	Reduce to level needed to retain hard-core loyals
Sales Promotion	Use heavy sales promotion to entice trial	Reduce to take advantage of heavy customer demand	Increase to encourage brand switching	Reduce to minimal level

Figure 9.3 The Product Life Cycle Model

Coca-Cola has many product lines, including its soft drinks, energy drinks, and sports drinks, which collectively make up its product mix. General Motors offers a full line of automotive products, which can be broken down into various product lines, including its cars, minivans, trucks, SUVs, ATVs, and vehicle-related parts and accessories. General Motors also offers a financial services product line to dealers and their customers for the purchase or lease of GM vehicles. General Motor's combined activities constitute its product mix.

product line length The number of items in any given product line. Product line length is determined by how the addition or removal of items from a product line affects profits.

How long can a product line be? An important marketing decision involves product line length. **Product line length** is the number of items in any given product line. Product line length is determined by how the addition or removal of items from a product line affects profits. Coca-Cola has found it very profitable to pursue a long product line length given the huge variety of drinks it offers for sale. Although Coca-Cola is the biggest-selling soft drink in history, the company still offers more than 500 brands and 3500 beverage products to satisfy the specific tastes of the customers in more than 200 countries who purchase 1.7 billion servings per day.[16] Consumers who like Coca-Cola but desire a low-calorie alternative can purchase Diet Coke or Coke Zero. Consumers who want a low-calorie soda without caffeine can purchase Caffeine-Free Diet Coke. Those who do not want a soft drink can choose from one of Coca-Cola's many beverage offerings that appeal to the various wants and needs of the company's wide consumer base.[17]

product mix width The number of different product lines a company offers.

How do companies decide how many product lines to offer? **Product mix width** refers to the number of different product lines a company offers. This, too, is determined by profitability. General Electric (GE) has hundreds of product lines, ranging from light bulbs and home appliances to jet engines and medical machinery.[18] GE aims to achieve maximum profitability by stretching the company's capabilities across multiple markets. Product line length and product mix width are the result of companies striving to offer differentiated products to satisfy targeted customers.

Consumer and Business-to-Business Products

consumer products Goods and services purchased by households for personal consumption.

business-to-business (B2B) products Goods and services purchased by businesses for further processing or resale or used in facilitating business operations. Also called industrial products.

Video: Konica/Minolta: Advancing in the Digital Age

consumer product classifications Four classifications that emerge from strategic marketing mix plans for consumer products: convenience, shopping, specialty, and unsought goods and services.

What is the difference between consumer products and business-to-business products? In Chapter 8 we explored the differences between consumer markets and business-to-business (B2B) markets; now we'll explore the differences between consumer products and B2B products. **Consumer products** are goods and services purchased by households for personal consumption. They are traded in consumer markets. **Business-to-business (B2B) products** (sometimes called *industrial products*) are goods and services purchased by businesses for further processing or resale or are used in facilitating business operations. They are traded in B2B markets.

Most products can be classified as either consumer or B2B products. The distinction depends on their use. For example, if a homeowner purchases a lawn mower for personal use, then it would be a consumer product. If a landscaper purchases the same lawn mower but uses it for his business, then it would be a B2B product. It is convenient for marketers to classify various consumer and B2B products because the buying behaviour is different between these two categories. This behaviour affects how the marketer prices, promotes, and distributes the product.

How are consumer products classified? Four **consumer product classifications** emerge from strategic marketing mix plans for consumer products: convenience, shopping, specialty, and unsought goods and services. Let's look at each in more detail.

- *Convenience goods and services* are those that the customer purchases frequently, immediately, and effortlessly. Convenience goods are typically *nondurable goods*—goods normally used or consumed quickly. Gum, soap, tobacco, and newspapers are all considered convenience goods, as are common grocery items such as ketchup and milk. A car wash is an example of a convenience service. These purchases are usually based on habitual behaviour, meaning consumers routinely purchase a particular brand with which they're familiar and comfortable. Convenience goods and services are relatively low-priced items. They're usually promoted through brand awareness and image (which we'll discuss shortly) and are widely distributed through convenience stores or local grocery stores. Consumers make purchasing decisions for these goods based on the convenience of location and brand name image.
- *Shopping goods and services* are products purchased less frequently than convenience goods and services and typically require more effort and time for comparison. Consumers usually base their comparison on attributes such as suitability, quality, price, and style. Shopping goods are typically *durable goods*—goods that can be used

repeatedly over a long period. Examples of shopping goods include clothes, shoes, televisions, cameras, stereos, bicycles, lawn mowers, furniture, and major appliances. These products are often sold at shopping centres that allow for easy comparison between stores, such as Future Shop, Sears, and Home Depot. Examples of shopping services include hotels and airline services. Since consumers carefully compare brands, companies that sell shopping services compete based on price, quality, and brand name image.

- *Specialty goods and services* are unique to the point that buyers are willing to spend a considerable amount of time and effort searching for particular brands or styles. Customers know exactly what they want and they will not accept substitutes. Examples of specialty goods and services include Ferrari sports cars, Rolex watches, high-fashion designer clothing, and the services of prestigious legal experts. Because there are no suitable substitutes, buyers of specialty products do not comparison shop. They already know the specific good or service they want, and they are willing to seek it out regardless of its price and location. Businesses that successfully differentiate their product to the point that it is considered a specialty good or service can set a much higher price than similar products considered shopping goods or services.
- *Unsought goods and services* are products buyers don't usually think about buying, don't know exist, or buy only when a specific problem arises. We don't usually think about or want to think about buying some products such as life insurance or cemetery plots. These goods and services require a lot of persuasive advertising and personal selling to encourage consumers to buy products that will help them prepare for life's uncertainties. Other unsought goods and services are products that are completely new to consumers. New and innovative products, such as pharmaceutical drugs, must be introduced to consumers through promotional advertising before consumers can actively seek out these products. Automobile repairs are also unsought purchases where prepurchase planning is rarely considered. In these cases, resolving the immediate problem is more important than comparison shopping based on price or other features. Notice that sales of unsought products require personal selling or promotional advertising, and price may not be an important consideration if the good or service is urgently needed.

How are business-to-business products classified? Five **business-to-business product classifications** (or industrial product classifications) emerge from strategic marketing mix plans for B2B products: equipment; maintenance, repair, and operating (MRO) products; raw and processed materials; component parts; and specialized professional services. Each of these types of products has unique pricing, promotion, and distribution strategies. Let's look at each in more detail.

business-to-business product classifications Five classifications that emerge from strategic marketing mix plans for B2B products: equipment; maintenance, repair, and operating (MRO) products; raw and processed materials; component parts; and specialized professional services. Also called industrial product classifications.

- *Equipment,* also known as *installations* or *capital items,* includes all the physical facilities of a business, such as factories, warehouses, office buildings, heavy equipment, and other less costly equipment, such as computers, printers, and copiers. Many of these capital items are expensive, unique, and intended to last for a long time; therefore, they may require special negotiations involving top management that can stretch over many months or even years. Marketers frequently offer a variety of services to help sell this type of equipment, including financial assistance with the purchase, maintenance, and repairs after the sale.
- *Maintenance, repair, and operating (MRO) products* facilitate production and operations but do not become a part of the finished product. They include printer paper, pens, cleaning materials, tools, and lubricants for machines. They are often marketed based on convenience, just like consumer convenience goods and services.
- *Raw and processed materials* are the basic inputs that become part of a finished good. Many raw products and some processed farm products, such as eggs or butter, go into the production of our grocery items. Raw materials such as wood and processed

materials such as steel are used to make a variety of products, such as buildings or bridges. Raw and processed materials are usually purchased in large quantities at prices based on the quality of the materials.

- *Component parts* are assembled portions of the finished product. Examples include brakes, engines, transmissions, and steering columns for a car, or lumber, cement, drywall, and electrical wire for a house. Businesses purchasing component parts make their decisions based on quality and brand name recognition because, ultimately, the quality of a business's product will be based on the quality of its component parts.
- *Specialized professional services* help support a firm's operations. They include advertising, management consulting, legal, accounting, and information technology services. Managers compare the costs and the quality of these specialized services with their in-house operations before deciding whether to *outsource* these activities. For example, a local grocery store owner might assess his or her ability to handle the business's financial records before hiring an outside accounting firm.

Considering the variety of types and classifications of products, it is clear that product development is an exciting yet challenging area of business. As Coca-Cola showed with the development of Coke Zero, new product development can lead to great success. The key is considering and understanding the many complex factors involved in creating a differentiated product.

logos Representations of brands that help build an image for a company.

brand A name, term, symbol, or design that distinguishes a company and its products from all others.

brand loyalty The degree to which customers consistently prefer one brand over all others.

brand insistence The highest degree of brand loyalty. It can turn a product into a specialty good or service that can command a much higher price.

brand equity The overall value of a brand's strength in the market.

brand awareness The extent to which a particular brand name is familiar within a particular product category.

brand association Involves connecting a brand with other positive attributes, including image, product features, usage situations, organizational associations, brand personality, and symbols.

Branding

LO3 Explain why branding is beneficial to both buyers and sellers and describe some different types of brands.

Why do companies use logos? **Logos** are representations of brands that help build an image for a company. Many logos are trademarked so the company alone has rights to the symbol. Which logos do you remember best? What does the logo say about the brand? What are the benefits of a brand? These questions are important components of another complex aspect of product development: branding.

What are the benefits of branding? A **brand** is a name, term, symbol, or design that distinguishes a company and its products from all others. Branding is one of the most important tools of product differentiation, and it benefits both buyers and sellers. For buyers, well-recognized brands reduce the shopping time necessary to find the quality and consistency they desire in a product. Branding also reduces the risks involved in some purchases for which buyers are unable to determine quality objectively. We rely on established brand names to deliver an expected level of quality consistently. Imagine the frustration you'd feel if all the products in your grocery store were packaged with generic labels. How would you decide what type of peanut butter or frozen pizza to buy? Comparing product descriptions and ingredients takes a lot longer than simply picking up your favourite brand. Consumers are also able to express themselves by buying brand names with which they wish to be identified. For example, some buyers seek prestige by buying exclusive brands such as Mercedes-Benz, Rolex, or Grey Goose Vodka.

Iain Masterton/Alamy

Branding is extremely important. Twitter uses the simple image of a bird, which is a representation of a "tweet," and Instagram uses the image of a camera, which succinctly depicts what their company is all about.

Branding also helps sellers define their products' special qualities, thus promoting repeat purchases as well as new sales at higher prices. Because certain brands, like Coca-Cola, are associated with quality and value, these companies are able to introduce new products quickly and at a relatively low cost. In doing so, they add length to their product lines, widen their product mix (also known as *brand extension*), and enhance their profitability. Because Coca-Cola has a large amount of diversity in its product mix, the company can market its brand to just about any person in the world. To those who don't enjoy cola, Cola-Cola claims it is "so much more than soft drinks. Our brands also include milk products, soup, and more so you can choose a Coca-Cola Company product anytime, anywhere for nutrition, refreshment or other needs."[19] Well-branded companies usually establish a trademark so their products are easily identifiable.
A trademark (a legally protected brand) can also benefit sellers by distinguishing them from competitors' *knockoff brands*, or illegal copies or cheap imitations of a product.

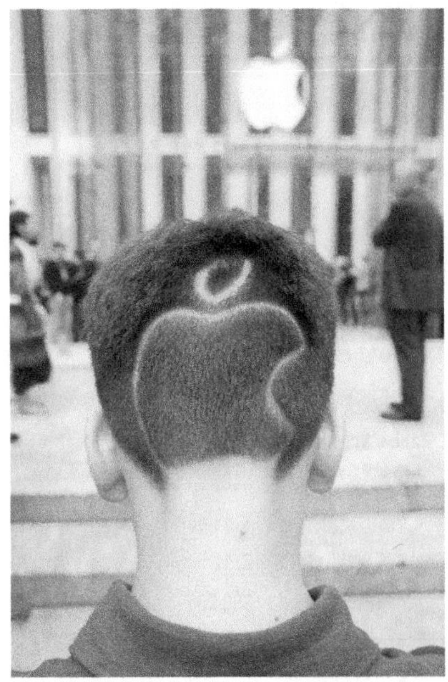

James Leynse/Corbis

One benefit of branding for sellers is brand loyalty, such as that displayed by many users of Apple products.

Brand Loyalty and Brand Equity

Does customer satisfaction create loyalty to a brand? Another major benefit of branding for sellers is the creation of **brand loyalty**, the degree to which customers consistently prefer one brand over all others.
In fact, companies hope their brands are not just recognized (*brand recognition*) and then preferred (*brand preference*), but that customers will eventually insist on their brand name (*brand insistence*). **Brand insistence** is the highest degree of brand loyalty. It can turn a product into a specialty good or service that can command a much higher price. Ultimately, the degree of brand
loyalty depends on satisfied customers. Perhaps the most significant contemporary example of brand loyalty is the passionate devotion of many Mac users to Apple and its products.

Video: Gogurt

How do companies build equity in their brands? Strong brand loyalty contributes to **brand equity**, the overall value of a brand's strength in the market. Perceptions of quality contribute significantly to brand equity. Quality products are not just free from defects; they consistently perform at high levels. For example, many of Apple's customers will purchase another Apple product because of the brand's high quality. This adds significantly to Apple's brand equity.

Perceptions of *brand awareness* and *brand association* also contribute to brand equity. **Brand awareness** refers to the extent to which a particular brand name is familiar within a particular product category. Companies participate in mass advertising as a way to help their product's brand name become synonymous with the actual name of the product. For example, what brand first comes to mind when you think of facial tissues? If it's Kleenex, then Kimberly-Clark has succeeded in its brand awareness campaigns for its tissues.

Brand association involves connecting a brand with other positive attributes, including image, product features, usage situations, organizational associations, brand personality, and symbols. Hiring celebrities to endorse a product can be an effective tool for nurturing brand associations. Professional tennis player Rafael Nadal has appeared in television commercials for PokerStars.com: The "girl next door" is playing online poker on her tablet in a library against none other than Rafael Nadal, world champion tennis player and multimillionaire, who is soaking in his bathtub! Another example is Red Bull's involvement with Formula One

Rick Maiman/Polaris/Newscom

Rafael Nadal has one of the biggest Nike deals in tennis, and he has been with Nike since the start of his career.

Video: DC Shoes: Product Development & Pricing Strategies

Top 10 Most Valuable Global Brands (2013)

Rank	Brand	Brand Value (US$ millions)
1.	Apple	$185 071
2.	Google	$113 669
3.	IBM	$112 536
4.	McDonald's	$90 256
5.	Coca-Cola	$78 415
6.	AT&T	$75 507
7.	Microsoft	$69 814
8.	Marlboro	$69 383
9.	Visa	$56 060
10.	China Mobile	$55 368

Source: Millward Brown, "Brandz Top 100 Most Valuable Global Brands 2013," accessed January 18, 2014, http://www.millwardbrown.com/brandz/2013/Top100/Docs/2013_BrandZ_Top100_Chart.pdf.

Mandoga Media/Alamy

Mark Webber of Infiniti Red Bull Racing F1 team. The Red Bull brand has associated itself with Formula One racing and the desired values of speed and excitement.

racing, which began in 1995. In 2005, Red Bull became the main sponsor, and the team was called Red Bull Racing. In 2013, the team name changed to Infiniti Red Bull Racing when Infiniti became the team's main sponsor.

What does a brand manager do? Branding has become such an important part of marketing that businesses have created brand manager positions within their organizations. A **brand manager** (or *product manager*) is responsible for the 4 Ps of marketing a specific product or product line. Brand managers attempt to increase the product's perceived value to customers to increase brand equity. Brand managers are also responsible for new product development.

Brand You: Creating a Personal Brand

What do Lady Gaga and Donald Trump have in common? They both are their own brands. Each celebrity has a unique image that is as much of a brand as are Nike, Apple, and Starbucks. But celebrities are not the only ones who can create a personal brand. Everyone, including you, can create a personal brand. Personal branding is the process by which we market ourselves to others. If we develop our personal brand carefully, it can build brand equity similar to well-known corporate brands.

Business management guru Tom Peters actually coined the phrase personal branding. "We are CEOs of our own companies: Me Inc.," he writes. "To be in business today, our most important job is to be head marketer for the brand called You. It's that simple—and that hard. And that inescapable."[20] Enhancing your own personal brand is important to your success; it's what will give you a competitive edge in almost everything you do.

There are a variety of ways you can create your own personal brand, and many of them are similar to the ways companies promote their own brands. For example, you can start by using social media tools, such as Facebook, LinkedIn, and Twitter. Make sure your brand image is consistent and professional within all these tools. Write a blog or have a website with your own name in the title or domain name and establish your brand in your email address by using something like firstname.lastname@email.com. Take charge of your brand. It's the first step you can take toward your own success.

Discussion Questions

1. **How might personal branding help you establish your career?**
2. **Discuss how your personal brand will build brand equity. Can you give an example of the kind of "equity" you might be able to build?**
3. **Suppose you have been able to effectively develop a personal brand and are beginning to establish some brand equity. How might an inconsistent message, say between how you market yourself on LinkedIn and how you appear on Facebook, affect your image?**

Packaging and Labelling

How does packaging affect a product and the brand? How a product is packaged sends a message about the product and the brand. Packaging serves four functions:

1. to contain and protect the product
2. to facilitate use and convenience
3. to promote the product
4. to be environmentally friendly

Effective packaging is crucial to the success of a product, because the customers typically see the packaging before they see the product.

The Dieline is an organization dedicated to the progress of the package design industry. Established in 2007 by Andrew Gibbs, the purpose of the organization is to define and promote the world's best packaging design and provide a place where the package design community can connect on the latest industry trends and design projects. The Dieline has become the most visited website on package design in the world, with readership spanning millions of people across hundreds of countries. The Dieline Package Design Awards represent a global competition devoted exclusively to the art of brand packaging. The 2013 competition received over 1100 entries from 61 countries. Categories for the awards span an incredible array of products, including fresh foods, packaged foods, wine and champagne, water and juice, personal care

Marzetti

The Association for Dressings and Sauces named the T. Marzetti Company's Marzetti Simply Dressed Salad Dressing bottle the 2013 package of the year.[21]

brand manager A manager who is responsible for the 4 Ps of marketing a specific product or product line. Brand managers attempt to increase the product's perceived value to customers in order to increase brand equity. Also called a product manager.

Photo Courtesy of The Dieline

Bzzz Honey's super-premium, all-wood packaging was developed as a pack that becomes a permanent piece of one's kitchenware. It gives a totally new spin on the idea of a household honey pot. Developed originally a gift for VIP banking clients in Russia, the response has been so positive that the brand is currently producing a full-scale international rollout.

top 10

Characteristics of a Good Brand Name

1. Evokes positive associations
2. Easy to remember
3. Suggests product benefits
4. Easy to pronounce
5. Unique within its industry
6. Copyright protected
7. Promotes company image
8. Timeless
9. Transferable to other products
10. Recognizable and meaningful

Source: Brighter Naming, "Top 10 Characteristics of a Good Name," accessed January 22, 2012, http://www.brighternaming.com/namebase/articles/top-10-characteristics-of-a-good-name/; and Tutor2u, "Brands and Brand names," accessed January 22, 2012, http://tutor2u.net/business/marketing/brands_names.asp.

Photo Courtesy of The Dieline

Swedish research company Innventia developed a sustainable package customized for freeze-dried food. The instant food package combines different aspects of sustainability. It saves space in transportation because it is compressed and it is made out of a 100 percent biodegradable material made from renewable sources.

products, healthcare products, and office supplies, to name just a few. A new Sustainable Packaging Award was created to highlight innovative contributions to the field of sustainable package design.

How does packaging affect the environment? A growing concern among many consumers is whether a product and its package are environmentally sound. Landfills contain discarded products and packaging materials, which often are not biodegradable. Some packaging, especially the single-serve packages, can be considered wasteful and environmentally unfriendly. Consequently, many companies are going green and placing increased effort on reusing, recycling, and developing new products that are eco-friendly. For example, Puma has developed a new eco-friendly packaging concept for its shoes. Instead of the traditional cardboard shoebox that has been criticized as wasteful, Puma is packaging its shoes in cardboard frames wrapped in reusable shoe bags. This repackaging saves nearly 8500 tonnes of paper and reduces the resources required for production and transportation.[22] Even companies that are selling services are trying to go green. For example, Kimpton Hotels has instituted an EarthCare Program that is run by employees with support of management. In keeping with the green mission of the program, the hotel chain uses environmentally friendly practices such as using green cleaning products, installing recycling bins in every room, switching to water-saving fixtures, and providing local and organic ingredients for their restaurants. They even give parking discounts for guests with hybrid cars.[23] This type of service "packaging" will appeal to those who share a concern for the environment.

Why is convenient packaging so important? Packaging should facilitate use and convenience. Sellers want packages that are easy to ship, store, and stock on shelves. More importantly, consumers want products that handle easily, open and reseal, store conveniently, and have a long shelf life. We dislike bulky, heavy packages that are difficult to handle and open. Packages that don't reseal or result in easy spoilage are also unpopular.

Packages that are convenient to use and physically attractive sell better. Heinz ketchup experienced a significant increase in sales when it began offering ketchup in a squeezable bottle. Hellman's mayonnaise now offers a similar squeezable bottle for its product. Campbell's soup is responding to changing consumer tastes and preferences for greater convenience and healthier foods by offering sippable soups, microwave soup lines, and ready-to-serve soups. For example, Campbell's Healthy Request microwavable bowls come in six varieties, and their Soup on the Go sippable soups are low in calories, saturated fat, and cholesterol.[24] This shift toward healthy eating has helped the company gain 70 percent market share of the microwavable, ready-to-go soup category.[25] Many sellers also offer different-sized packages dependent on frequency of use. For example, salt, sugar, and breakfast cereal packages come in many different sizes for added convenience.

Off the Mark

Q-tips Brand Cotton Swabs

Branding acts as a tool to help differentiate a product from other similar products. However, what happens when the brand itself becomes the category? When was the last time you purchased a box of cotton swabs? How about Q-tips? Well if you bought cotton swabs that didn't display the brand name Q-tips, then you didn't buy Q-tips. The Q-tips brand has been so effective in establishing itself that the brand name has become synonymous with its product category. Someone shopping for Q-tips may actually buy another brand of cotton swabs. The competitor's price or packaging could convince a consumer to choose that particular brand over the Q-tips brand. Perhaps the issue Q-tips hasn't made clear is explaining why a box of Q-tips cotton swabs is better than a competitor's brand. Nevertheless, all companies want to guard against their brand name becoming a generic description for a product category because then their brand name becomes public property, which means the owner loses all rights to it!

Companies hope that consumers will think of their brand name before all others, and they spend billions to turn their products into "household names." With that said, they also spend millions trying to prevent these household names from being applied to products other than their own. Coca-Cola and Xerox are probably the best-known examples of companies fighting to ensure their brand name is not used generically. Although Coke has lost the proprietary right to the name *cola* because it is considered descriptive of the product, it has won lawsuits against restaurants who serve another brand of cola when their customers ask for a Coke.[26]

Some products that have retained their registered trademarks despite the generic use of their names include Q-tip, Band-Aid, Jell-O, Frisbee, Kleenex, Play-Doh, and Scotch Tape. Former trademarks that have been legally declared as descriptive words and are therefore no longer owned by the companies or individuals who invented them include aspirin, cellophane, raisin bran, thermos, yo-yo, and zipper.[27]

Through obtaining trademarks for their brands, companies can help prevent their brand names from becoming public property and preserve their product differentiation.

Discussion Questions

1. **Can you think of any other brand names now used as generic descriptors? If so, which ones?**
2. **How can having your brand name used as a generic descriptor be a good thing for your company?**
3. **How can a company get their brand known but not have it become a generic description?**

How does packaging help promote the product? Getting the consumer to notice a product and pick it up from crowded shelves is extremely important. The package design, shape, colour, and texture all influence buyers' perceptions and buying behaviour. Luxury items such as jewellery or high-end cosmetics typically package their products to create an impression of extravagance, sophistication, and exclusiveness.

Video: 'Extreme Couponing' Expert Tips: Name Brand vs. Generic

What does the government have to say about product labels? Labelling serves two functions: to inform and to persuade. The Consumer Packaging and Labelling Act and Regulations requires companies to identify[28]

- the product name or function
- the name and place of business of the manufacturer, packer, or distributor
- the size, age, material content, or information about the nature of the contents

Administration and enforcement of the act and regulations, as they relate to nonfood products, is the responsibility of the Competition Bureau. Labelling of food products enforcement is the responsibility of the Canadian Food Inspection Agency (CFIA). Clearly, labels should inform consumers about the product, its uses, and any safety concerns. However, labels can be confusing and misleading. For example, what does the label "organic product" really mean? Are all ingredients in that product organic, or just one ingredient? Businesses that wish to foster good customer relationships must be careful to label their products ethically.

Why is labelling important to establishing a brand image? Labels are also used to promote and to persuade customers to buy the product. Labels can educate consumers about the features and other benefits of the product. Many companies label their products with their brand logo to distinguish their product from that of their competitors. If the label comes to represent consistent quality and dependability, then the label can perpetuate a positive brand name image.

THE MARKETING MIX (4 Ps): PRICE

LO4 Describe three major approaches to pricing strategy and outline some pricing tactics used to launch a new product, to adjust prices, and to affect price perceptions.

Revenue-Generating Component

price The only revenue-generating component of the marketing mix—product, promotion, and place (distribution) strategies are all cost components.

Why is price an important component in the marketing mix? Pricing is so important to consumers and producers alike that it ranks as one of the 4 Ps in the marketing mix. Prices are sometimes called *fees, fares, tolls, rates, charges*, or *subscriptions*. **Price** is the only revenue-generating component of the marketing mix—product, promotion, and place (distribution) strategies are all cost components. In fact, *revenue* to a business equals the price multiplied by the number of units sold or services performed. *Profit* equals total revenue minus total costs. So, you can see that the pricing decision has a huge impact on profitability.

Trying to set the right price can be a real challenge for marketers. The price of a product has to be low enough to generate enough value to customers to motivate sales, yet high enough to enable the company to cover costs and earn a profit. Setting the right price is challenging because market conditions are always changing. As a result, companies must constantly tweak prices to remain competitive. Moreover, some companies operating in very competitive markets may have little to no control over their price. Instead, price is determined in the market through the interaction of demand and supply. These companies may therefore be *price takers* (not *price setters*). For example, farmers have virtually no control over the prices of their agricultural commodities. However, most companies have at least some control over the price they charge.

What are some pricing objectives? Some of the most common pricing objectives include the following:

- *Maximizing profits.* This occurs when price is set so that total revenue exceeds total cost by the greatest amount.
- *Achieving greater market share.* A company's market share is the percentage of total industry sales or revenues it is able to capture. Unfortunately, achieving greater market share does not always translate into higher profits.
- *Maximizing sales.* Maximizing sales often means charging low prices that can result in losses. Firms cannot survive for long with losses. However, maximizing sales may be an appropriate short-run objective to rid the company of excess inventory, such as last year's models.
- *Building traffic.* Many retail stores, such as grocery stores, pharmacies, hardware stores, and department stores, may advertise a sale price on a few goods to increase traffic in their stores and build a stronger customer base. They also hope customers will purchase other, more profitable items while they are shopping for the bargains.
- *Status quo pricing.* The objective of status quo pricing is simply to match competitors' prices, possibly to avoid a price war that could be damaging to everyone. The airfare wars of the past hurt all the airline carriers, so they have chosen to compete on non-price factors instead.
- *Survival.* If a company is struggling to build a customer base, it may choose to set prices to generate just enough revenues to cover costs. However, this is not a suitable long-term objective. Survival prices might generate sales, but they will not generate profits.

- *Creating an image.* Some products are priced high because firms hope that consumers will associate high prices with high quality. This is the case for many specialty goods such as luxury cars, perfume, and designer jewellery.
- *Achieving social objectives.* Some companies may charge low prices to enable the poor to afford their products. For example, many governments have been involved in ensuring that staple food products such as grains are affordable to all.

Marketers must develop their pricing strategies in coordination with their product branding, packaging, promotion, and distribution strategies as well. Indeed, price is only one element in the marketing mix.

Pricing Strategies

What are the major pricing strategies? Although there is no one right way to determine the price of a good or service, there are a number of strategies a seller can use. The most common **pricing strategies** include *cost-based pricing, demand-based pricing,* and *competition-based pricing.*

pricing strategies Strategies sellers use to set prices. The most common include *cost-based pricing, demand-based pricing,* and *competition-based pricing.*

What is cost-based pricing? **Cost-based pricing** (or *cost-plus pricing*) is charging a price in relation to the costs of providing the good or service. It is the simplest and one of the more popular pricing strategies. Suppose you manufacture 100 units of a product at a total cost of $2000. The per unit cost would be $20. If you want to make a unit profit margin, or *markup*, of 20 percent, which is $4 (0.20 × $20), you would price the product at $24. Total revenue would equal $2400 and profit would equal $400, or 20 percent above costs.

cost-based pricing Charging a price in relation to the costs of providing the good or service. Also called cost-plus pricing.

There are many advantages of cost-based pricing. Besides being easy to calculate and easy to administer, it requires a minimum amount of information. However, it has several disadvantages as well. It ignores whether the price is compatible with consumer demand or expectations and the prices charged by competitors. It also provides little incentive to be efficient and to hold costs down. Many pharmaceutical companies undertake cost-based pricing to recoup their expensive research and development costs associated with a new drug and to earn a targeted profit level. The monopoly power granted by patents on new drugs means there is no competition, and pharmaceutical companies find little need to consider consumer demand when setting prices on drugs.

Cost-based pricing can be facilitated by **break-even analysis**, which determines the production level for which total revenue is just enough to cover total costs. Total costs equal total fixed costs plus total variable costs. **Fixed costs** (or *overhead costs*) are any costs that do not vary with the production level. Total fixed costs typically include salaries, rent, insurance expenses, and loan repayments. **Variable costs** are costs that vary with the production level. Examples include wages, raw materials, and energy costs. *Average variable costs* (or *per unit variable costs*) equal total variable costs divided by the production level. A convenient formula for calculating the break-even production level is

break-even analysis Determines the production level for which total revenue is just enough to cover total costs.

fixed costs Any costs that do not vary with the production level. Total fixed costs typically include salaries, rent, insurance expenses, and loan repayments. Also called overhead costs.

$$\text{Break-even volume of production} = \frac{\text{Total Fixed Costs}}{\text{Price} - \text{Average Variable Costs}}$$

variable costs Costs that vary with the production level. Examples include wages, raw materials, and energy costs. Average variable costs (or per unit variable costs) equal total variable costs divided by the production level.

For example, suppose that total fixed costs equal $600, the selling price is $24, and average variable costs are $14. The break-even volume of production is therefore $600/($24 – $14), or 60 units. Any production level below the break-even volume will result in losses, and any production level above the break-even level will result in profits. Any changes in fixed or variable costs, as well as changes in the price, will affect the break-even volume of production. Many book publishers use this strategy.

What is demand-based pricing? **Demand-based pricing** (or *value-based pricing*) is pricing a good or service based on the demand for the product or its perceived value. A high price will be charged when demand or the perceived value of the product is high, and a lower price will be charged when demand or perceived value is low. This pricing strategy assumes firms can accurately estimate perceived value or the demand for their

demand-based pricing Pricing a good or service based on the demand for the product or its perceived value. Also called value-based pricing.

goods or services. Sometimes this is the case, but it is usually very difficult to do in practice. Nevertheless, many firms try.

target costing A demand-based pricing strategy that estimates the value customers receive from a product and therefore the price they are willing to pay, and then subtracts an acceptable profit margin to obtain a desired cost.

price discrimination A demand-based pricing strategy that involves charging different prices to different customers when these price differences are not a reflection of cost differences.

One of the specific demand-based pricing strategies that firms employ is target costing. **Target costing** estimates the value customers receive from a product and therefore the price they are willing to pay, and then subtracts an acceptable profit margin to obtain a desired cost. Firms then work to get costs down to this targeted level. Boeing, Caterpillar, Chrysler, and Continental Teves (a supplier of automotive brake systems) have successfully used target costing as a pricing strategy.[29]

Another demand-based pricing technique is **price discrimination**, charging different prices to different customers when these price differences are not a reflection of cost differences. Successful price discrimination charges higher prices to targeted customers who are price insensitive and lower prices to other targeted customers who are more price sensitive. Price discrimination requires firms to be able to segment customers successfully based on their differences in demand and price sensitivity, and it requires that the product cannot be easily resold among customers. One example of price discrimination includes hotels and resorts charging different rates based on different days of the week or seasonal variations. Movie theatres may also charge higher prices to view a movie during the evening showing as opposed to the matinee viewing time. Airline companies also price discriminate on the airfares they charge. Those who place their reservations well in advance pay less than those who book a flight on short notice. Restaurants price discriminate with early bird specials and discounted happy hour rates. Grocery stores price discriminate by offering clip-out coupons that price-sensitive customers may use to buy grocery items at lower prices. In some cases, even salespeople charge different prices to customers based on their perceived demand for big-ticket items such as cars and furniture, so don't tell them how much you value or love their good or service! Many organizations price discriminate because it is profitable to do so.

competition-based pricing A pricing strategy based on what the competition is charging. Revenues and costs are secondary.

Video: Fast Food Chains Beef Up Dollar Menus

What is competition-based pricing? **Competition-based pricing** is a pricing strategy based on what the competition is charging. Revenues and costs are secondary. The degree of competition in markets affects a company's price-setting ability. *Monopolistically competitive markets*, markets in which many firms compete based on doing something unique, have some firms that charge higher prices if they are successful in their product differentiation strategies. Other companies may charge lower prices to get an edge on the competition. *Oligopolies*, a market with a few dominant sellers such as those in the airline and oil industries, often avoid competing based on price to avoid price wars. Instead, they compete aggressively on product differentiation and charge higher prices if their total product offerings are unique. However, periodically a *price leader* may charge a different price and all other firms follow with similar price changes. Finally, a *monopoly*, a market that is controlled by one dominating firm, possesses the greatest price-setting ability because there is no competition. In some extreme cases, monopolies may have captured their markets through *predatory pricing*, the practice of charging very low prices with the intent to destroy the competition. Predatory pricing is illegal, but that hasn't prevented it from occurring. Most real-world competition rests on product differentiation and customer's perception of value. For example, a company like Harley-Davidson has successfully differentiated its products and can charge higher prices than for comparable models produced by Honda, Yamaha, and Kawasaki.

price skimming A pricing strategy that involves charging a high price for a product initially, then lowering the price over time.

Are there alternate pricing strategies? When launching a new product, companies may need to use a different type of pricing strategy than they would on an existing product. One pricing strategy for introducing a new product is **price skimming**. It involves charging a high price for a product initially, then lowering the price over time. Price skimming coincides with the introductory stage of a product's life cycle during which there are few, if any, competitors. The idea is to skim off as high a price as possible to recoup the expensive new product development costs. However, the high price may encourage competitors to enter the market at a lower price.

At the other end of the spectrum is **penetration pricing**, a strategy of charging the lowest possible price for a new product. This pricing strategy is designed to build market share for the product quickly. If the increased production to satisfy growing sales results in lower per unit costs, then profits can actually rise even though the price is lower. Penetration pricing is appropriate during the growth stage of a product's life cycle and when customers are price sensitive. It may also create goodwill among consumers and inhibit competitors from entering the market. Its drawbacks include the establishment of low-price expectations or a poor-quality image for the brand and the company. This may make it difficult to raise prices later.

penetration pricing A strategy of charging the lowest possible price for a new product.

What are the common types of price adjustments? Most businesses adjust their prices to promote their products. Several tactics are used. One way to adjust prices is to use **discounts**, a deduction from the regular price charged. Discounts come in many forms:

- quantity discounts (a lower price for buying in large quantities)
- cash discounts (a reduced price for paying with a method that does not require processing)
- seasonal discounts (a price reduction if you buy out of season)
- forms of allowance, such as a trade-in allowance (a reduced price if you trade your old good for a new good)

Another way to adjust prices is to use rebates. **Rebates** are partial refunds on what a customer has already paid for a product. An example is mail-in rebates, where the manufacturer writes a cheque to the customer after the customer provides proof of purchase.

Bundling is another type of price adjustment. In **bundling**, two or more products that usually complement one another are combined and sold at a single price. To be attractive, the single price is usually lower than the sum of the individual products' prices. Bundling is quite common in the fast-food industry where products are bundled to make a complete meal. Bundling also occurs with cable or satellite TV sales, when a package of channels is sold at a single price. Many vacation packages are also bundled products consisting of airfare, car rental, hotel accommodations, and other amenities bundled together.

Dynamic pricing is another price-adjustment technique. In **dynamic pricing**, prices are determined directly between the buyer and seller, unlike the more traditional fixed pricing in which prices are set by the seller. Auctions are a traditional form of dynamic pricing. More recent examples exist in ecommerce, such as eBay and Priceline.com. Dynamic pricing often results in quick price adjustments.

Finally, some retail stores choose not to adjust their prices at all, but instead offer **everyday low pricing (EDLP)**, a strategy of charging low prices with few, if any, special promotional sales. Walmart has successfully used this strategy because it has been able to give the impression that its brand means everyday low cost. However, it risks taking the excitement out of shopping for bargain hunters.

discounts Deductions from the regular price charged.

rebates Partial refunds on what a customer has already paid for a product.

bundling When two or more products that usually complement one another are combined and sold at a single price.

dynamic pricing A pricing strategy where prices are determined directly between the buyer and seller, unlike the more traditional fixed pricing in which prices are set by the seller.

everyday low pricing (EDLP) A strategy of charging low prices with few, if any, special promotional sales.

prestige pricing The practice of charging a high price to invoke perceptions of high quality and privilege. Also called premium pricing.

Simulation: Pricing Strategies and Objectives

Video: Smashburger

What are some strategies used to affect price perceptions? For many consumers, a high price indicates good quality. Although this is not always the case, many consumers make this association when products are complex, do not have a strong brand identity, or are services with which they are unfamiliar. **Prestige pricing** (or *premium pricing*) is the practice of charging a high price to invoke perceptions of high quality and privilege. For those brands for which prestige pricing may apply, the high price itself is a motivator for consumers. The higher perceived value because of the higher price actually increases demand and creates a higher price that becomes self-sustaining. Some people have called this the

Vicki Beaver/Alamy

In dynamic pricing, prices are determined directly between the buyer and the seller, a practice seen in online auctions such as eBay and Priceline.com.

Ian Pilbeam/Alamy

Mercedes-Benz uses the pricing strategy known as prestige pricing to invoke perceptions of high quality and privilege.

snob effect. Examples of this strategy include the pricing of cars made by Mercedes-Benz, Lexus, and Rolls-Royce.

Another pricing strategy that affects price perceptions is **psychological pricing** (or *odd* or *fractional pricing*), the practice of charging a price just below a whole number to give the appearance of a significantly lower price. For example, charging $9.99 as opposed to $10.00 is an example of psychological pricing. Gas stations often use psychological pricing.

A **loss leader** is a product priced below its cost. Stores use loss leaders to attract customers and motivate them to buy items that are more expensive as well. Reference pricing is another strategy used to attract customers. **Reference pricing** refers to listing an inflated price (the "regular retail price" or "manufacturer's suggested retail price") that is then discounted to appear as if it is a good value. A variation of this strategy occurs when stores provide both a more expensive "gold-plated" version of a product and a lower-priced alternative. This makes the alternative appear to be a bargain.

These are just a few pricing strategies—many others exist. Indeed, the pricing component of the marketing mix is one of the most difficult for marketers to grapple with.

psychological pricing The practice of charging a price just below a whole number to give the appearance of a significantly lower price. Also called odd or fractional pricing.

loss leader A product priced below its cost. Stores use loss leaders to attract customers and motivate them to buy items that are more expensive as well.

reference pricing Refers to listing an inflated price (the "regular retail price" or "manufacturer's suggested retail price") that is then discounted to appear as if it is a good value.

promotion A part of the marketing mix that consists of all the methods marketers use to inform and persuade targeted customers to buy a product and to build positive customer relationships.

THE MARKETING MIX (4 Ps): PROMOTION AND THE PROMOTIONAL MIX

LO5 Define a promotional mix and explain its function in a promotional campaign.

Promotion

What does it mean to "promote" a product? Few products—no matter how well developed, priced, and distributed—will sell well if they are not properly promoted. The **promotion** part of the marketing mix consists of all the methods marketers use to inform targeted customers of the benefits of a product and to persuade them to buy a product, service, or idea. Promotion is designed to build positive customer relationships and increase brand awareness, brand loyalty, and sales, and is therefore one of the most visible components of the marketing mix. Finding the best way to communicate the benefits of a product and to persuade consumers to buy it is a critical job of marketers. Should the product be advertised, or is personal selling more appropriate? If advertising is used, is it best to advertise through newspapers, magazines, radio, television, or another source? Beyond advertising and personal selling, what types of public relations activities might be most appropriate? These are just a few of the questions that marketers must ask themselves when promoting a product.

promotional tools The tools marketers use to promote a good or service, including advertising, public relations, personal selling, and sales promotions.

promotional mix The strategic combination of promotional tools used to reach targeted customers to achieve marketing objectives.

What are the most popular tools marketers use to promote a product? Four basic **promotional tools** are used to promote a good or service: advertising, public relations, personal selling, and sales promotions. The **promotional mix** is the strategic combination of promotional tools used to reach targeted customers to achieve marketing objectives. These elements are illustrated in **Figure 9.4**. Notice that the product itself can be a promotional tool because its features may be promoted by giving away free samples of the good or service.

Efficient organizations search for the optimal or most cost-effective promotional mix given their marketing objectives and budgetary constraints. If a firm's major objective is to maximize profits, then it will juggle the amounts of advertising, public relations, personal selling, and sales promotion until a mix is found that maximizes profits, given the company's limited promotional budget. The optimal, or best, promotional mix for a given product will vary depending on the goals of the business.

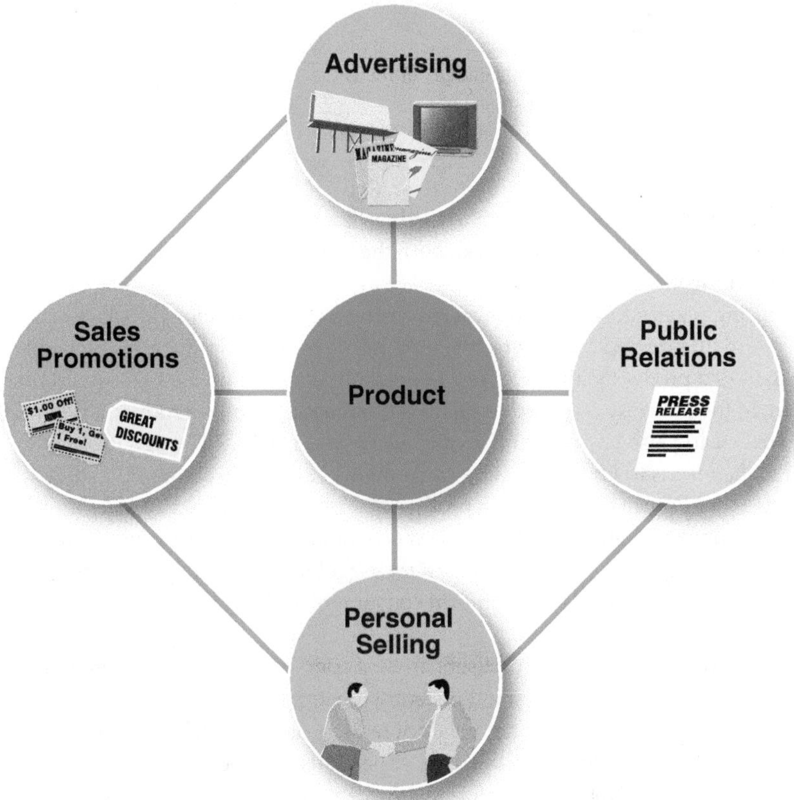

Figure 9.4 The Promotional Mix

What are the steps involved in a promotional campaign?

Six steps emerge from all **effective promotional campaigns**:

effective promotional campaigns Include six steps: identify the target market, determine marketing objectives, design the message, determine the budget, implement the promotional mix, and evaluate and adjust as needed.

1. *Identify the target market.* The first step in any promotional campaign is to identify the specific group of potential customers on which to focus marketing efforts.
2. *Determine marketing objectives.* Is the business trying to maximize profits, sales, or market share? Is the goal to build traffic, brand awareness, or brand image? Is the business trying to introduce a new product or respond to an attack by a competitor? Whatever the marketing objective is, the goal should be clearly understood and measurable.
3. *Design the message.* The message should inform customers of the benefits of the business's product and be echoed by all elements of the promotional mix to give a unified message.
4. *Determine the budget.* The best combination of promotional activities can be determined by finding that mix with the biggest bang for the buck.
5. *Implement the promotional mix.* Businesses must always integrate and coordinate all promotional efforts. For example, public relations, sales promotions, and direct marketing efforts should try to produce results at the same time advertisements are scheduled to appear.
6. *Evaluate and adjust as needed.* The effectiveness of any promotional mix depends on clearly understood and measurable objectives. Each element of the mix, as well as the entire combination of the mix, will need to be adjusted as necessary for growth, for changing marketing objectives, or to correct ineffective promotional techniques.

How do companies create consistency across an entire promotional campaign?

An **integrated marketing communication (IMC)** is a strategy to deliver a clear, consistent, and unified message about the company and its products to customers at all contact points. Consistency nurtures good customer relations and repeat business. It is essential that all members of the marketing team—whether they are involved with advertising, public relations, personal selling, or sales promotions—work together to foster and sustain a consistent and compelling message to create a positive brand image. In short, everyone in the organization needs to be on the same page and communicate with one voice.

integrated marketing communication (IMC) A strategy to deliver a clear, consistent, and unified message about the company and its products to customers at all contact points.

Promotional Mix: Advertising

LO6 Explain the advantages and disadvantages of the various types of media used for advertising and discuss the role of public relations in a company.

advertising Paid, impersonal mass communication from an identified sponsor to persuade or influence a targeted audience.

How do companies persuade consumers to buy their products? **Advertising** is paid, impersonal mass communication from an identified sponsor to persuade or influence a targeted audience. When we think of advertising, many of us first think of television commercials, such as those that air during the Super Bowl. But as we shall see, advertising is much more than this.

Advertising plays a huge role in business as one of the promotional tools designed to communicate with targeted customers. It is especially important in the introduction and growth stages of a product's life cycle, as it helps build mass brand awareness and brand association. In the maturity stage, advertising is often used to stress product differentiation. Effective advertising also builds brand loyalty and brand equity. Although it is costly, advertising often leads to lower prices for consumers because advertising is a mass-marketing tool. The more people know about a product and like it, the higher its sales and the greater its production level. Given the frequent economies of scale associated with increased volumes of production, we, as consumers, get lower per unit costs and lower-priced products. Advertising can also inform consumers of the value inherent in products and educate the public in their uses.

However, critics argue that advertisers are less concerned about informing or educating consumers and are instead more interested in misleading the public into perceptions of value that may not really exist. This debate continues. It echoes the need for ethical business behaviour and can explain the existence of government laws and regulations that constrain advertising and other marketing practices.

Advertising also affects the economy because of the huge sums of money spent on it. This creates many jobs in advertising agencies as well as related and supporting industries. Companies spend so much on advertising because it is economically in their best self-interest to do so. It doesn't just cost, it pays! For example, a business that advertises online with Google can exponentially increase traffic to its company website, leading to more sales.

What are the different types of advertising? Advertising is undertaken by virtually all organizations in one form or another. Different organizations use different types of advertising. The following are some of the more common types of advertising:

- *Product advertising.* Advertising that promotes a specific product's uses, features, and benefits. This is the type of advertising we most often think of.
- *Corporate (or institutional) advertising.* Advertising that focuses on creating a positive image toward an organization or an entire industry as opposed to a specific product (e.g., "Got Milk?"). Government entities can also undertake institutional advertising. For example, provincial governments do it when they run advertisements that promote tourism in their provinces.
- *Comparative advertising.* Advertising that compares a brand's characteristics with those of other established brands. Examples include television commercials comparing toothpaste, pain relievers, and detergents.
- *Retail (or local) advertising.* Advertising that focuses on attracting customers to a fixed location such as a department store or a grocery store.

SELF CHECK Below are some of the most successful advertising campaigns of all time. Can you connect each advertising campaign to its product?

1. "Have it your way" 1973	A. Maxwell House coffee
2. "When it rains it pours" 1912	B. AT&T
3. "Takes a licking and keeps on ticking" 1950s	C. Morton Salt
4. "Good to the last drop" 1959	D. Campbell's Soup
5. "Ring around the collar" 1968	E. Burger King
6. "Reach out and touch someone" 1979	F. Hallmark
7. "Breakfast of champions" 1930s	G. Wisk Detergent
8. "Mmm mm good" 1930s	H. Timex
9. "When you care enough to send the very best" 1930s	I. Kellogg's Rice Krispies
10. "Snap! Crackle! Pop!" 1940s	J. Wheaties

Answers: 1. E; 2. C; 3. H; 4. A; 5. G; 6. B; 7. J; 8. D; 9. F; 10. I

Source: Bob Garfield, "The Top 100 Advertising Campaigns of the Century," AdAge.com, accessed May 29, 2011, http://adage.com/century/campaigns.html.

How did you do? Did these campaigns succeed in making a lasting impression on you? Some of these campaigns date back more than 50 years and are still used today. Can you think of others?

- *Business-to-business advertising.* Advertising directed to other businesses rather than to consumers. For example, Caterpillar, the earth-moving equipment company, advertises to construction companies.
- *Nonprofit advertising.* Advertising that focuses on promoting nonprofit organizations such as the Red Cross and the Nature Conservancy of Canada.
- *Public service advertising.* Advertising that communicates a message on behalf of a good cause, such as the prevention of wildfires.
- *Advocacy advertising.* Advertising that promotes an organization's position on a public issue, such as global warming or immigration. We are familiar with advocacy advertising undertaken during political campaigns by organizations independent of a political party or candidate.
- *Interactive advertising.* Advertising that uses interactive media, such as interactive video catalogues on the Internet or at kiosks in shopping malls, to connect directly with consumers in a personal and engaging way.
- *Internet advertising.* Advertising that uses popup and banner ads and other techniques to direct people to an organization's website. Internet advertising is growing rapidly. Revenues to businesses from this type of advertising are expected to continue to grow.[30]

What are the different types of advertising media? Advertising media are the means of conveying a message about a product. Media conveying informative and persuasive messages exist all around us, including on seats of grocery carts, on sides of buses and trucks, on billboards, in magazines, in newspapers, and in brochures. Advertisements are also heard on telemarketing and telephone hold messages, on in-store public address systems, and on the radio. And of course we see ads on television, on the Internet, in movies, in video games, and in our mailboxes every day. Advertising is pervasive and has been around for many years. Some of the more modern, traditional media for advertising include television, newspapers, magazines, radio, the Internet, and outdoor media. Outdoor media include billboards; signs in sports arenas; ads painted on the sides of cars, trucks, and buses; and even skywriting.

Beyond these advertising media, *direct mail advertising* remains one of the largest forms of advertising. You're probably familiar with direct mail advertising, you just have a different name for it—junk mail. Direct mail advertising comes in many forms, ranging from coupon offers to brochures and catalogues. However, it continues to and may even grow because it's generally a very effective advertising tool.[31] Direct mail advertising allows companies to target their advertising dollars to the customers most likely to buy their products and to offer customized product offerings to these customers.

What are the advantages and disadvantages of the different types of advertising media? Many advantages and disadvantages accompany each of these advertising media. For example, television advertising reaches a huge audience but is very expensive. In fact, TV commercials are so effective that networks can command huge sums of money for commercial airtime during popular or prime-time TV events. For example, as of 2013, a 30-second spot during the Super Bowl would cost around US$4 million.[32] But remember, the marketer's task is to find the most effective and efficient medium for transmitting his or her message to targeted customers—given marketing objectives and budget constraints. **Table 9.1** lists some of the advantages and disadvantages of each major medium.

What are some important recent trends in advertising? One of the most important trends to emerge from modern advertising has been the development of Internet advertising. In fact, it is one of the fastest-growing media in part because it allows firms to focus their advertising dollars on targeted customers. Other trends include the use of social media, mobile marketing, product placement, infomercials, and global advertising.

Table 9.1 Advantages and Disadvantages of Advertising Media

Media	Advantages	Disadvantages
Television	Good mass-market coverage; low cost per contact; combines sight, sound, and motion; good attention span	High cost; low recall; channel surfing or digital video recorders skip over ads; short exposure
Newspaper	Timing and geographic flexibility; good local market coverage; high credibility and acceptability	Short lifespan; lots of competition for attention; poor-quality reproductions
Magazine	High market segmentation; high-quality colour; long life; longer attention span; high credibility	Declining readership; lots of competition for attention; high cost; long ad-purchase lead time
Radio	High geographic and demographic selectivity; low cost; creative opportunities with sound	Low attention span; short exposure time; information overload; limited coverage
Internet	Global and interactive possibilities; ease of segmentation; high audience interest; easy to measure responses	Audience controls exposure; clutter on each site; skewed demographically to Web surfers
Outdoor	Able to select key geographic areas; low cost per impression; high frequency on major commuter routes	Short exposure time; brief messages; creative limitations; little segmentation possible
Direct Mail	High levels of segmentation; allows personalization; high flexibility; ad can be saved; measurable impact	High cost; can be rejected as "junk mail" and viewed as a nuisance

Internet Advertising Internet advertising includes spam ("junk" email), popups, banner ads, and other links found at websites to attract potential customers to a company's webpage. Google, Yahoo, and other search engine sites can determine customers' perceived needs and wants based on their searches. If you search for a vacation package, for example, then Disney or Norwegian Cruise Line may pay Google or Yahoo to have its banner ad appear in your search. Once customers have been persuaded to visit a firm's website, the company can learn a lot about potential customers depending on where and how many times they click within the company's website. Businesses then attempt to interact with their customers through videos or even through starting a chat based on their perceived needs and wants. The idea is to work with customers to create a customized product offering that best meets the customers' unique tastes and preferences. If the business is able to deliver consistently high-quality value using these modern techniques, then Internet advertising can help businesses maintain positive customer relations. However, on July 1, 2014, Canada's new anti-spam laws (CASL) came into effect. Any business that uses electronic channels to reach their customers or market their product has to have express consent from each individual to continue to communicate with him or her using electronic forms like email.

Social Media The emergence of Web 2.0 technologies—tools that allow users to connect, share information, communicate, and collaborate with each other online—has caused many companies to rethink how they can connect and communicate with their customers. Social media is a part of many IMC plans. Using social networks such as Facebook and Pinterest, companies are building customer support and gaining better insight into their customers and competitors. Companies create blogs and tweets to announce new products or corporate developments, post help tutorials and product demonstration videos on YouTube, and create fan pages on Facebook that prompt interactions with their customers.

Video: Kmart Goes from 'Shipping Pants' to 'Big Gas Savings'

Mobile Marketing Changes in advertising, technology, and consumer behaviour have influenced the explosive growth of mobile advertising.[33] Specifically, the mobile gaming space has experienced the penetration of many forms of advertising for brands and publishers. Advertising within mobile games presents many advantages, including an opportunity to directly reach the targeted demographic—young males. Mobile game advertising also motivates creative flexibility, where publishers are encouraged to think outside of the box when creating the interactive visuals and experience for their brand message. Compared to other forms of mobile ads, those contained within mobile games offer a superior experience. Users are actively engaged in game play and are in a leisure state of mind—an optimal environment for captivating the attention of your audience.[34] Given the ubiquitous market penetration of mobile phones, they make the best platform for advertisers. Companies are embracing technologies such as QR codes, text messages, and mobile app platforms to connect with their customer base nearly 24/7.

Product Placement and Infomercials The placement of products in TV shows, movies, and video games where they will be seen by potential customers has increased vastly in recent years. This is known as **product placement**. For example, the superhero in the movie *Iron Man* drives an Audi R8, while his leading lady cruises around in an Audi S5.[35] The advent of digital video recorders (DVRs), which allow viewers to record shows and then fast-forward through advertisements, has driven product placement on TV. Another variant of strategic placement is the banners of brand names, symbols, and slogans found on the walls of professional sports stadiums so that camera shots of the televised games will frequently display the banners' messages.

product placement The placement of products in TV shows, movies, and video games where they will be seen by potential customers.

Another significant trend on TV is the use of **infomercials**, television commercials that run as long as regular TV programs. Infomercials typically appear as actual television programs, often in the form of a talk show, with little direct reference to the fact that they are actually advertisements. Unlike normal commercials, infomercials are designed to elicit a specific, direct, and quantifiable response from viewers. The pitches are similar to "call this toll-free number and order yours today" or "if you call within the next few minutes we will also . . ." Infomercials often use "experts" or celebrities as guests or hosts to endorse and push their products. Infomercials have the advantage of showing the features of the products in detail. Some of the most successful infomercials include Bowflex Home Gym, Proactiv Plus Acne Treatment, Ronco Showtime Rotisserie Oven, and Ionic Breeze Air Purifier.[36]

infomercials Television commercials that run as long as regular TV programs.

Global Advertising The globalization of advertising is another important trend. Most products have to be customized to satisfy foreign customers. This means that products are tailored to meet the unique local tastes, preferences, and cultural sensitivities of foreign customers or to satisfy the regulatory standards of different governments around the globe. Likewise, some advertising campaigns can be exported intact, while others have to be changed. Advertisers prefer to use the same message because it is cheaper, it allows for a more globally integrated communication message, and it allows for the pooling of talent to design the most compelling advertising message. But transferring domestically successful advertising messages abroad can be tricky. Marketers have to consider the interpretations of their messages carefully in the underlying cultural context of the foreign market. Increasingly, marketers are realizing that customized advertising campaigns to globally segmented markets work much better, just as domestic market segmentation is more effective.

Promotional Mix: Public Relations

How much control do businesses have over their public image? Another important part of the promotional mix is public relations. **Public relations** is the management function that establishes and maintains mutually beneficial relationships between an organization and its stakeholders.[37] Stakeholders for businesses include all interested parties, including consumers, shareholders, employees, suppliers, the government, and the public in general. All organizations—for-profits, nonprofits, and even governments—are interested in public relations.

public relations The management function that establishes and maintains mutually beneficial relationships between an organization and its stakeholders.

The idea behind public relations is to create and maintain a positive image of the organization in the minds of stakeholders. This begins with assessing public attitudes and perceptions of the organization. Sometimes public opinion may be based on perceptions that have little to do with facts. Nevertheless, an honest audit of public opinion is necessary before specific public relations programs can be implemented to shape the image and reputation of the organization. Once an organization has listened carefully to public concerns and interests, it needs to respond by changing its behaviour or by correcting misperceptions. Finally, the organization needs to inform the public of any changes it has made or educate the public about the facts associated with the organization.

Several specific types of public relations tools exist to build a positive business image. They can be classified by whether the news transmitted is controlled, semi-controlled, or uncontrolled by the organization.[38] The degree of control hinges on how and when the message is delivered. **Controlled messages** include corporate (or institutional) advertising, advocacy advertising, and public service advertising. An organization may also disseminate annual reports, brochures, flyers, and newsletters or provide films or speakers to send a controlled message to targeted audiences. **Semi-controlled messages** are placed on websites, in chat rooms, and on blogs. In these forums, what people say about the company is not strictly regulated. Other forms include sporting or special events sponsorships because participation by the press and stakeholders is not under the control of the sponsoring company. A company may also use **uncontrolled messages**, which generally take the form of publicity.

controlled messages Public relations messages that include corporate (or institutional) advertising, advocacy advertising, and public service advertising.

semi-controlled messages Public relations messages that are placed on websites, in chat rooms, and on blogs and are not strictly regulated. Other forms include sporting or special events sponsorships because participation by the press and stakeholders is not under the control of the sponsoring company.

uncontrolled messages Public relations messages that generally take the form of publicity.

publicity Information about an individual, organization, or product transmitted through mass media at no charge.

Publicity is information about an individual, organization, or product transmitted through mass media at no charge. Publicity has two advantages over advertising. First, it is free. Second, it is more believable because it is often presented as a news story. However, publicity is *not* controlled by the seller—it is controlled by the media, and this is its disadvantage. If, when, and how a news release, a press conference, a captioned photograph, an appearance on a talk show, or a staged event will be covered by the media is outside the control of public relations managers.

How does a company generate positive publicity? Naturally, keeping friendly relations with the press increases the probability that a "newsworthy" story will be covered and treated with a favourable spin. This was precisely how the lawsuit filed by Canada Goose against International Clothiers was treated in the press. In January 2012, Canada Goose filed suit against International Clothiers for trademark violations over using a similar logo. International Clothiers was aware that Canada Goose objected to its Super Triple Goose jacket, but didn't stopped any of its "deceptive trade practices," Canada Goose alleged.[39] The company also sometimes published print ads promoting its jackets as Canada Goose products, but did nothing more than apologize and didn't dissuade customers from thinking they were buying Canada Goose jackets, it's alleged in the lawsuit. The suit was later settled, but the terms were not disclosed.

Jonny White/Demotix/Corbis

Companies like the Canadian Imperial Bank of Commerce (CIBC) generate positive publicity through philanthropic efforts such as hosting a Run for the Cure for Breast Cancer.

Canada Goose chief executive officer, Dani Reiss, received positive attention in an interview with the *Financial Post*'s Hollie Shaw about how the brand's goodwill was built through grassroots marketing and a made-in-Canada strategy. Shaw asked Reiss: "What has counterfeiting done to the brand from a marketing perspective? Does the controversy help in any way, or does it always hurt? Is the resulting publicity good for you?" Reiss responded: "The fact that we are being counterfeited speaks to the presence that our brand has in the global marketplace. I think that it is up to us to turn it into a positive thing however we can. The most important thing we can do is to educate consumers about counterfeiting."[40]

It also appears that green business is good business. For example, Home Depot, the world's largest seller of lumber, now gives preference to vendors that offer FSC-certified wood. The FSC

(Forest Stewardship Council) determines whether lumber is grown and harvested responsibly to preserve environmental integrity. Shoppers can identify FSC-certified lumber by its green tree logo. IKEA, based in Sweden, where nearly half the forests are certified, produces as much furniture as possible from FSC-certified wood. These companies received a lot of publicity when the documentary *Buyer Be Fair* first aired on public television in March 2006, and you can bet these companies appreciate the publicity for their efforts.

Another example of positive publicity is the favourable press McDonald's Ronald McDonald House Charities receives for providing families with temporary living quarters while their children are in the hospital. Corporate philanthropy is generally good publicity, especially if it results in getting your name on a building, an annual event, a scholarship, or volunteer programs visible to the community. Many smaller companies give to local schools, hospitals, and arts programs. Some of the larger corporations renowned for their philanthropic and charitable efforts include Microsoft, Target, Avon, Hewlett-Packard, CIBC, and Timberland.[41]

Whether motivated by publicity needs or a sense of social responsibility, giving back to the community doesn't just *cost* companies, it *pays* them. Most of us like buying products from companies if we believe that some of our money will be used to give back to the community or to reward companies for doing the right thing.

Video: Mountain Dew Ad Called 'Most Racist Commercial Ever'

How does a company respond to negative publicity? A final role of public relations personnel is managing a crisis. **Damage control** is a company's effort to minimize the harmful effects of a negative event. Negative publicity, in a matter of days, can tear down a firm's image that took decades to build up. For example, Exxon-Mobil still suffers from the *Exxon Valdez* oil spill accident that occurred more than two decades ago. Sometimes, bad news doesn't come from the media but from word of mouth. In the event of bad news, a company must stand ready to react, and react quickly. No easy remedies exist for crises, but being honest, accepting responsibility, and making other ethical responses are the first steps toward regaining credibility and re-establishing a positive image.

damage control A company's effort to minimize the harmful effects of a negative event.

Advertising, public relations, and publicity are important elements in the promotional mix. Review the self-check quiz earlier in the chapter. You're probably familiar with many of the ads, which means that they were highly successful, well-crafted campaigns. These campaigns were effective because they resonated with customers, created memorable brand awareness, and made people want to buy the products. In doing so, they demonstrated the power of promotion.

Video: Kmart Has Web Shipping Their Pants from Laughter

Promotional Mix: Personal Selling

LO7 Describe the six steps in the personal selling process.

What is "personal" selling and why is it an important promotional technique?

Personal selling is direct communication between a firm's sales force and potential buyers to make a sale and to build good customer relationships. For example, a laboratory supplies company may deploy a representative to a research facility to demonstrate new products. Good salespeople don't just want to sell their products, they want to serve customers. A salesperson should help customers with their buying decisions by understanding their needs and presenting the advantages and disadvantages of a product. Sales-people most effectively represent their companies by establishing good customer relationships that foster repeat business and long-term company success.

personal selling Direct communication between a firm's sales force and potential buyers to make a sale and to build good customer relationships.

The sales staff is often the first contact point for many customers. To build good customer relationships, a salesperson should be customer oriented, competent, dependable, honest, and likeable. Good salespeople are also able to listen carefully to customer needs. They possess knowledge of the company's total product offerings and make the buying process as easy as possible for the customer. In many business-to-business or industrial sales, millions of dollars may be involved in a single purchase, such as buying an airplane or constructing an office building.

Obtaining and keeping good salespeople is expensive. This helps explain why personal selling is the most expensive part of the promotional mix for most companies, along with the fact that sales, unlike advertising, is labour intensive and deals with only one

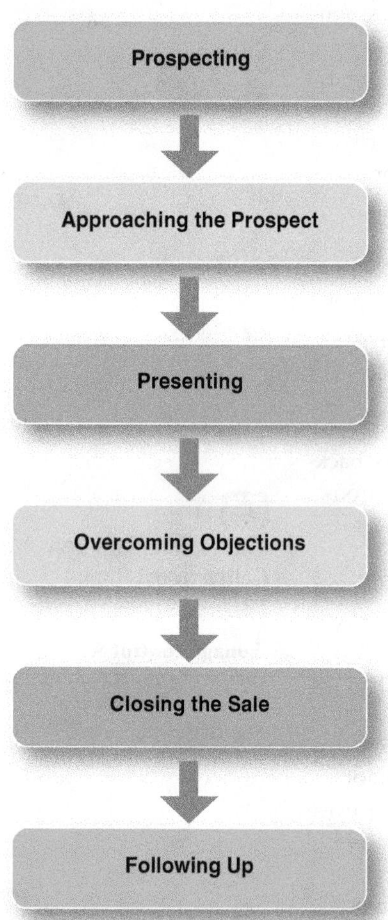

Figure 9.5 The Personal Selling Process

buyer at a time. Generally, personal selling is preferred over advertising when selling a high-value, custom-made, or technically complex product. Advertising is more cost effective when selling a low-value, easily understood, standardized product.

What are the steps in the selling process? The best way to understand the personal selling process is to look at an example. Suppose your company sells a sophisticated global positioning system (GPS) for use in the trucking industry. Your latest model allows trucking firms to keep track of their tractor-trailer rigs via a password-protected website that features a digital map display of vehicle locations and speed, engine use, refrigerated load temperature, door alarms or other motion-sensing devices that have been activated, cargo weight, and odometer reports. You can imagine the benefits of such a system for trucking companies. Although this is a business-to-business (B2B) example, the steps involved in the selling process are essentially the same for selling a consumer product, even though selling a B2B product is usually more complex. In all cases, the salesperson has to be knowledgeable about his or her product and competitors' products.

No two salespeople are alike, and no two selling situations are the same. However, six steps emerge from all personal selling: prospecting, approaching the prospect, presenting, overcoming objections, closing the sale, and following up. This six-step personal selling procedure is outlined in **Figure 9.5**.

STEP 1: Prospecting. The first step in the personal selling process is to identify qualified potential customers. This is known as prospecting. Notice that businesses need not only to find potential customers, they need to identify those who are qualified to buy. To be qualified to buy means that the potential customer has the ability and the authority to purchase, plus the willingness to listen to the sales message. Prospecting can be a daunting task. Good salespeople find leads at trade shows from those who have scouted the company's website or, better yet, from currently satisfied customers willing to recommend the salespeople to others for their superior product and service.

Video: Medtronic: Personal Selling and Sales Promotion

STEP 2: Approaching the prospect. This step divides into two parts: the pre-approach and the actual approach. The pre-approach involves salespeople doing their homework. This is especially critical if they are trying to sell a B2B product such as the GPS device described earlier. Salespeople must learn as much as possible about their potential customers to determine their likely needs and think about how they might be able to satisfy those needs. In our trucking example, you would need to determine the people in the trucking firm who would be most interested in buying your GPS product and learn as much about them as you can. Are they currently using a GPS system? If so, what brand is it? How is your product better? You should also decide on the best approach. Should you phone them, send a letter, or make a personal visit? The timing decision of the actual approach should also be carefully planned not to catch the prospect at a busy time.

In the actual approach, the idea is to meet, greet, and put the prospect at ease. First impressions are lasting impressions! This is the salesperson's first chance at building a long-lasting relationship. Good salespeople present themselves as knowledgeable and friendly professionals who are genuinely interested in serving customers. The first impression is followed by asking some questions to learn about the potential customers' needs. Then the salesperson must listen carefully to those responses. In our example, because GPS hardware and software are often complicated, you may want to remind buyers that your product is not only superior, but your service is better than that of the competition as well. You can offer to help install the system, train employees in its use, and offer free 24-hour service and upgrades when necessary.

STEP 3: Presenting. In the actual presentation of the GPS technology, you'll need to tell your product's "story" and detail how your product can help the trucking firm. You should demonstrate the product and let the prospect use it as well. Your presentation should be carefully planned using the most advanced presentation technologies that allow for the full use of multimedia effects. Most importantly, you should ask probing questions during your presentation and listen carefully to answers. Listening is more important than talking. You can't serve the customer until you fully understand his or her needs or problems.

STEP 4: Overcoming objections. Objections to buying are common. Good salespeople anticipate them and are prepared to counter them. Once objections surface, you should use this opportunity to provide more information on your GPS product and turn these objections into reasons to buy. You may invite others from your company to join in at this point to address any objections via a teleconference or a virtual meeting. This provides an opportunity to establish a rapport based on trust among you, your company, and the prospect. Overcoming objections can be the beginning of a mutually beneficial and lasting relationship.

STEP 5: Closing the sale. After overcoming objections, the next step is to close the sale and ask for a purchase. You should look for physical cues, comments, or questions that signal the time to ask the buyer for an order. You may want to review points of agreement, ask the buyer which model he or she prefers, ask how many units are needed, or sweeten the deal by offering more favourable credit terms or by throwing in an extra quantity free of charge. Closing the sale is an art that is learned with practice.

STEP 6: Following up. To ensure a long-term relationship and repeat business, be sure to follow up with the customer to ensure he or she is happy with his or her new GPS product. Stand ready to help him or her with any problems promptly after the sale. Ask for feedback. Relay that feedback to your company as input for improving existing products or for designing new ones. Periodically check up on customers by phone or by sending birthday cards. Good follow-up service and rapport can give rise to referrals or testimonials that can be used to enhance future sales. Following up is all about building and nurturing relationships.

Promotional Mix: Sales Promotions

LO8 Describe the two main types of sales promotions and the types of tools commonly used as incentives.

How can a company generate interest in a product? The final element of the promotional mix is sales promotion. **Sales promotions** are short-term activities that target consumers and other businesses for generating interest in a product. Sales promotions encompass all those activities designed to inform, persuade, and remind targeted customers about the product—and that have not already been undertaken by advertising, public relations, or personal selling. As consumers, we see sales promotions almost everywhere: from clip-out coupons in our newspaper, to rebate offers on a new car purchase, to email announcements offering discounted prices on airline tickets, to end-of-aisle displays of potato chips at our local grocery store tempting impulse purchases.

sales promotions Short-term activities that target consumers and other businesses for generating interest in a product.

What are two general types of sales promotions? Most companies' products go through a distribution system before they ever reach the final consumer. These companies encourage the intermediaries (such as wholesalers) to push their products on through the distribution channel to end users. Any incentives to push a product through the distribution system to final consumers are called **trade sales promotions** (or *business-to-business sales promotions*). In addition, **consumer sales promotions** are incentives designed to increase final consumer demand for a product. The whole idea behind all sales promotions is to generate interest and excitement around a product. Businesses need to create a reason why stores should not only carry their product, but also encourage its purchase by consumers. Companies want consumers to be so excited about their products that they seek the products out and ask for them by name. In short, companies want to create a tipping point so that all involved will opt for their products instead of the competitors' alternatives.

trade sales promotions Incentives to push a product through the distribution system to final consumers. Also called business-to-business sales promotions.

consumer sales promotions Incentives designed to increase final consumer demand for a product.

Trade Sales Promotional Tools If you want other businesses to become interested in and excited about carrying your product, then you must first generate in-house enthusiasm. You will need to educate your entire staff, especially your sales staff, about your product and its many uses, features, and benefits. This may require some formal training of your sales staff on how to best present your product. To generate leads, you may need to send your sales staff to trade shows equipped with sophisticated multimedia presentations; full-colour brochures; shirts, hats, and coffee mugs with your product logo; and a lot of excitement. You have to create some internal buzz and excitement for your product before you can ever expect other businesses to be interested in carrying and promoting your product. Once your staff is energized, then you can work on creating the same level of energy and excitement for distributors. Some of the specific trade sales promotion tools include the following:

- trade shows and conventions
- trade allowances (deals and price reductions to wholesalers, dealers, and retailers)
- cooperative advertising (a manufacturer agrees to pay for some of the advertising costs of the retailer)
- free merchandise
- sales contests (e.g., a free trip to Hawaii for those who sell the most)
- dealer listings (advertisements of your product that mention retail outlets where it can be found)
- catalogues and store demonstrations
- in-store displays
- quantity discounts
- training and support programs

When it comes to trade sales promotional techniques, firms have many options to choose from. If one doesn't work, they can easily adopt new strategies until they find the best combination.

Consumer Sales Promotion Tools Consumer sales promotions are aimed at the end users, or final consumers. Consumer sales promotions are intended to increase demand for a good or service, or at least provide that extra incentive to tip consumers in favour of a specific brand. Sales promotions are also aimed at providing customers with another reason to feel good about their purchases. Timing of consumer sales promotions is important to get maximum impact. They need to be strategically coordinated with the other elements in the promotional mix. Some of the most common consumer promotional tools include the following:

- *Coupons.* Coupons are discount certificates that reduce the price of a product and are redeemable at the time of purchase. Coupons are found in print ads, on packages, in direct mail, at checkout counters, and on the Internet. They are used to encourage the purchase of a new product or to generate repeat sales. Coupons are the most common consumer promotional tool. They are popular because consumers like the sense of getting a bargain.
- *Rebates.* Rebates provide for a reduced price if the rebate form is mailed in along with a proof of purchase. Unlike coupons, the discounted price is not realized at the point of purchase. Because most people do not redeem the rebates, they are an inexpensive way for businesses to promote sales.
- *Frequent-user incentives.* Some credit card companies encourage customers to use their credit cards for purchases that accumulate points redeemable for merchandise. Airlines sometimes offer frequent-flyer miles redeemable for free tickets for additional travel. Hudson's Bay has a rewards program whereby customers accumulate points for the purchases they make that are redeemable for merchandise or store credit. These incentives encourage customer loyalty and repeat business.
- *Point-of-purchase (POP) displays.* These are displays strategically located to draw attention and encourage impulse purchases. Examples are items placed in racks close to checkout counters at grocery stores and end-of-aisle stacks of soft drink bottles. Studies indicate that POP displays really work.[42]
- *Free samples.* Free samples are an effective way to introduce a new product, to get nonusers to try it, or to get current users to use it in a new way—especially if the samples are made available where the product is sold. Most of us have sampled small portions of foods at our local grocery stores. Some companies also mail samples of products such as cereal and shampoo directly to consumers.
- *Contests and sweepstakes.* Many companies use contests and sweepstakes to increase the sales of their products. As a reward for participating, consumers might win cash, free products, or vacations.

Table 9.2 The Advantages and Disadvantages of Promotional Tools

Promotional Tool	Advantages	Disadvantages
Advertising	• Builds brand awareness and brand loyalty • Reaches a mass audience	• Expensive • Impersonal • Not good at closing a sale
Public Relations	• Often seen as more credible than advertising • Inexpensive way of reaching many customers	• Risk of losing control • Cannot always control what other people write or say about your product
Personal Selling	• Highly interactive communication between the buyer and seller • Excellent for communicating a complex product, information, and features • Good for building customer relationships and closing a sale	• Expensive • Not suitable if there are thousands of buyers
Sales Promotions	• Can stimulate quick increases in sales by targeting promotional incentives on particular products • Good short-term tactical tool	• If used over the long term, customers may get used to the effect • Too much promotion may damage the brand image

- *Advertising specialties.* Companies frequently create and give away everyday items such as bottle or can openers, hats, and key rings with their names and logos printed on them. Companies prefer to use inexpensive handouts that will yield constant free advertising when used by the recipient.

Other consumer sales promotion tools include bonuses (buy one, get one free), catalogues, demonstrations, special events, lotteries, premiums, and cents-off deals. Consumer sales promotions are becoming more common because they help segment markets and they are cost effective.

Video: Nestlé

What are the advantages and disadvantages of the promotional mix? When developing the best promotional mix for a product, companies must weigh the advantages and disadvantages of each of the four main options—advertising, public relations, personal selling, and sales promotions. **Table 9.2** summarizes some of these key advantages and disadvantages.

Simulation: Promoting a Product

THE MARKETING MIX (4 Ps): PLACE (DISTRIBUTION)

LO9 Define marketing intermediaries and distribution channels and explain why these are important elements in marketing.

Marketing Intermediaries and Distribution Channels

How do companies get their products into the hands of customers? Imagine walking through a drugstore, looking for cough syrup. Did you ever wonder how far the products on the shelves have travelled? Consider that cough syrup you're looking for. After it was bottled, it had to travel to a wholesaler and then to the retailer. If you cut out all the travelling and intermediaries, how much would the cough syrup actually cost? What are wholesalers and intermediaries? Why are they needed? And how do they affect the price of a product?

place A component of the marketing mix that refers to all the methods involved in getting the product into the hands of customers. Also called distribution.

The **place** (or *distribution*) component of the marketing mix refers to all the methods involved in getting the product into the hands of customers. Distribution is the process that makes products available to consumers when and where the consumers want them. Managing the entire process of getting products out the door and eventually into the

Video: Beyond Food Carts: Building a Mobile Business

hands of final consumers is known as *supply chain management* (discussed in Chapter 10). Although somewhat limited in scope, this is still a very complicated process in the real world of business today. Most of us don't think about the transfer and storage of the products we buy—unless something goes wrong and we are unable to get the products we want, when and where we want them. You can imagine the challenges companies face trying to guarantee that customers have access to the products at the right time and in the right quantity and place. Despite proper distribution being critical and extremely complicated in practice, the distribution function of the 4 Ps of marketing is often overshadowed by the more visible product, pricing, and sales promotional strategies.

marketing intermediary A business firm that operates between producers and consumers or business users. Also often called a middleman.

distribution channel A series of firms or individuals that participate in the flow of a product from manufacturer to consumer.

distributors The intermediaries in a distribution channel. Also called wholesalers.

wholesalers Intermediaries that buy and resell products to other wholesalers, retailers, or industrial users.

A **marketing intermediary** is a business firm that operates between producers and consumers or business users. Intermediaries are sometimes referred to as *middlemen* or *resellers* because they pass along products from manufacturers to end users.

Many goods, such as grocery store items, go through a **distribution channel**, which is a series of firms or individuals that participate in the flow of a product from manufacturer to consumer. The intermediaries in a distribution channel are sometimes called **distributors** (or *wholesalers*).

What are the different types of intermediaries? There are three types of intermediaries:

- **Wholesalers** are intermediaries that buy and resell products to other wholesalers, retailers, or industrial users. For example, your local grocery store probably purchased the Tide laundry detergent on its shelves from a wholesaler who bought it from Procter & Gamble, the manufacturer.
- **Agents/brokers** are intermediaries that facilitate negotiations between buyers and sellers of goods and services but never take title (ownership) of the products traded. Examples include real estate agents and brokers, stockbrokers, and agricultural brokers. Even eBay, which never owns the various items it sells, can be considered an agent/broker because the company facilitates the transfer of ownership from sellers to buyers.
- **Retailers** are intermediaries that buy products for resale to ultimate consumers. As consumers, we buy most of our products from retail outlets, such as the Tide laundry detergent from our local supermarket.

Why are intermediaries needed? You might wonder why we need all these intermediaries and whether they only serve to drive up prices. It is certainly true that each link in the distribution channel incurs costs, and intermediaries must cover these costs and earn a profit to remain in business. However, these costs and the higher prices we must pay are usually less than the time and money we would otherwise spend to obtain the products directly from the manufacturer. In short, intermediaries add costs, but these costs are offset by the value added.

To examine the efficiencies provided by intermediaries, review **Figure 9.6**, which shows five manufacturers and five retail outlets. Without an intermediary, each retailer

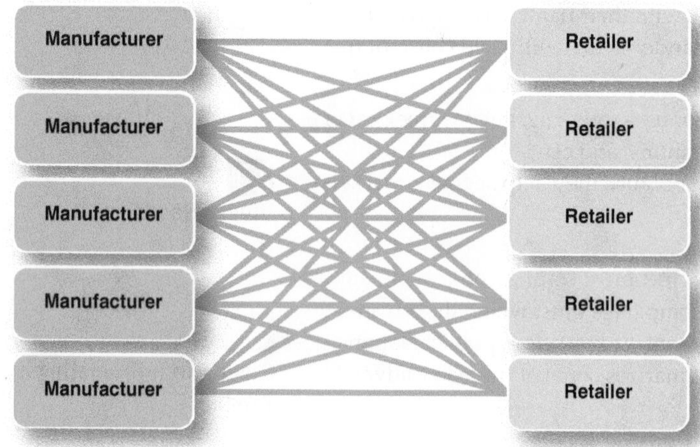

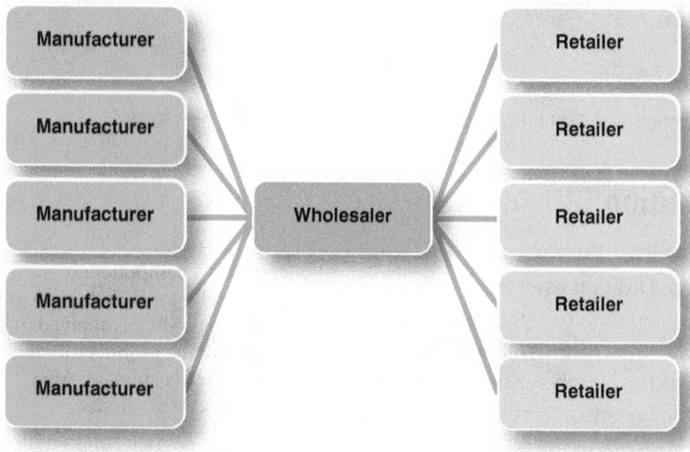

Figure 9.6 The Efficiencies of Intermediaries

The introduction of an intermediary reduces the number of exchange relationships between manufacturers and retailers.

would have to contact each manufacturer to order desired goods. That would entail 25 (5 × 5) exchange relationships. Now suppose a wholesaler is established to stock and resell each of the five manufacturers' products to each of the five retailers. Now the five manufacturers and five retailers have only one intermediary to deal with. This reduces the number of exchange relationships from 25 to 10. Intermediaries reduce the time and costs of providing products to customers. Of course, the wholesaler will incur some costs that will be pushed onto the consumer. But these costs are less than the costs without the involvement of the intermediary. The most efficient intermediaries get most of the business and survive in a competitive environment. This is why intermediaries are always looking for more advanced technologies to facilitate their operations. The modern distribution system is high-tech business.

agents/brokers Intermediaries that facilitate negotiations between buyers and sellers of goods and services but never take title (ownership) of the products traded.

retailers Intermediaries that buy products for resale to ultimate consumers.

What are the different types of distribution channels? Many distribution channels exist, as illustrated in **Figure 9.7**. As you can see, the type of distribution channel used varies depending on the type of product being brought to the consumer. The number of intermediaries depends on whether greater efficiency or adding value is possible by adding another link to the chain in the distribution system. If greater efficiency is possible, then another link will be added to increase profits. Competitive markets determine what number of intermediaries will be most efficient.

An important recent development in the distribution of products has been the increased use of ecommerce, buying and selling on the Internet. It is now possible for consumers to buy thousands of products online. Businesses are also using the Internet to buy and sell to other businesses. For example, customer relationship software can be purchased and downloaded online for sales to other businesses. These direct channels (channels 1 and 6 in Figure 9.7) bypass all intermediaries.

Ecommerce is prevalent in all distribution channels, not just the direct channel. Almost all firms—manufacturers, agents, brokers, wholesalers, or retailers—have websites

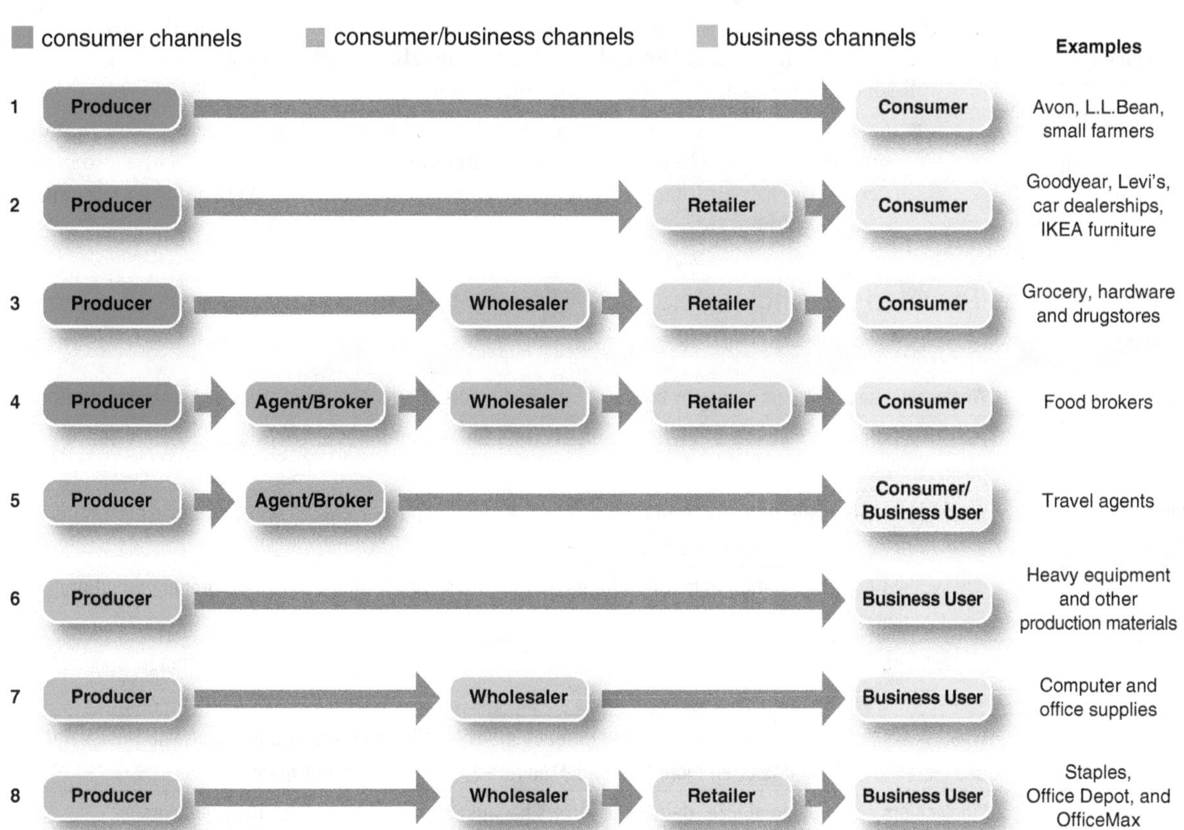

Figure 9.7 Different Channels of Distribution

that allow customers to shop, place an order, and pay. Many sites also use interactive videos to enable customers to explore the features of products from their homes or offices. Ecommerce is expected to continue to grow because of the convenience it provides.

Remember the questions you had about the cough syrup in the drugstore? You now know that the cough syrup likely travelled from the manufacturer to a wholesaler and then to a retailer before landing in your hands. You also know that although intermediaries do add costs to products, these costs are offset by the value they add. As you purchase your cough syrup, consider that while it may seem at first cheaper to buy products directly from the producer, the time and money it would take to do so would ultimately make it more expensive.

Wholesalers, Agents, and Brokers

What services do wholesalers provide? As we've already discussed, wholesalers are intermediaries that buy and resell products to other wholesalers, retailers, or industrial users. They are different from retailers because retailers only sell products to final consumers. It can be confusing because some of us, as households, purchase products at wholesale distributors, such as Costco or Staples, which also sell to other businesses. One of the most effective ways to distinguish wholesalers from retailers is to remember that wholesalers *primarily* sell business-to-business products, while retailers sell *only* consumer products. Nevertheless, wholesalers provide a host of services to their customers. Some of these are listed in **Table 9.3.**[43]

What are the different types of wholesalers? Wholesalers are technically known as merchant wholesalers, independently owned businesses that take ownership (title) of the products they handle. They are sometimes called *jobbers, mill supply firms,* or *distributors.* Merchant wholesalers include *full-service wholesalers* and *limited-service wholesalers.* **Full-service wholesalers** provide a full line of services: carrying stock, maintaining a sales force, offering credit, making deliveries, and providing management assistance. There are two types: *wholesale merchants* who sell primarily to retailers, and *industrial distributors* who sell to manufacturers and institutions such as hospitals and the government. As intermediaries, **limited-service wholesalers** offer fewer services than full-service wholesalers. There are four major types:

full-service wholesalers Provide a full line of services: carrying stock, maintaining a sales force, offering credit, making deliveries, and providing management assistance.

limited-service wholesalers Offer fewer services than full-service wholesalers. There are four major types: cash-and-carry wholesalers, truck wholesalers, drop shippers, and rack jobbers.

- *Cash-and-carry wholesalers* carry a limited line of fast-moving goods and sell to small retailers for cash. They normally do not deliver. For example, a small fish store may drive to a cash-and-carry fish wholesaler, buy fish for cash, and bring the merchandise back to the store.

Table 9.3 Services Provided by Wholesalers

Service	Description
Bulk Breaking	Wholesalers save retailers money by buying in bulk and breaking bulk packages down into smaller quantities.
Financing	Wholesalers finance retailers by giving credit, and they finance manufacturers by ordering early and paying bills on time.
Management Services and Advice	Wholesalers often help retailers train their sales clerks, improve store layouts and displays, and set up accounting and inventory control systems.
Market Information	Wholesalers give information to manufacturers and retailers about competitors, new products, and price developments.
Risk Bearing	Wholesalers absorb risk by taking title to merchandise and bearing the costs of theft, damage, spoilage, and obsolescence.
Selling and Promoting	Wholesalers' sales forces help manufacturers reach many smaller retailers at a low cost. The wholesaler has more contacts and is often more trusted by the retailer than the distant manufacturer.
Transportation	Wholesalers can provide quicker delivery to buyers because they are closer than the producers.
Warehousing	Wholesalers hold inventories, thereby reducing the inventory costs and risks of suppliers and retailers.

- *Truck wholesalers* (or *truck jobbers*) perform primarily a selling-and-delivery function. For example, soft drink trucks that deliver to supermarkets and restaurants are truck wholesalers.
- *Drop shippers* don't carry inventory or handle the product. On receiving an order, they select the manufacturer, who ships the merchandise directly to the customer. Drop shippers assume title and risk from the time of the order to delivery. They operate in bulk industries such as lumber, coal, and heavy equipment.
- *Rack jobbers* serve grocery stores and drug retailers, mostly in nonfood items. They send delivery trucks to stores, where the delivery people set up racks or displays within the stores. Rack jobbers retain title to the goods and bill the retailer only for the goods sold to consumers.

Because of their limited functions, these limited-service wholesalers usually operate at a lower cost than wholesale merchants and industrial distributors.

Video: Pet Food Express: Marketing

What are some common types of agents? Agents and brokers are unique among intermediaries because they do not take title to the products traded. They merely facilitate the buying and selling of products and earn a commission on the selling price. What distinguishes agents from brokers is that agents represent the buyers or sellers who hired them on a more permanent basis than brokers do. Three common types of agents are manufacturers' agents, selling agents, and purchasing agents:[44]

- *Manufacturers' agents* represent two or more manufacturers of complementary lines. A formal written agreement with each manufacturer covers pricing, territories, order handling, delivery service and warranties, and commission rates. Manufacturers' agents are often used in such lines as apparel, furniture, and electrical goods. Most manufacturers' agents are small businesses with only a few skilled salespeople. Small manufacturers may hire an agent if they cannot afford their own field sales force, while larger manufacturers rely on agents to open new territories or to cover territories that cannot support full-time salespeople.
- *Selling agents* have contractual authority to sell a manufacturer's entire product line. The manufacturer is either not interested in the selling function or feels unqualified to sell. The selling agent serves as the sales department for the manufacturer. Selling agents are common in the industrial machinery and equipment businesses as well as for coal, chemicals, and metals.
- *Purchasing agents* generally have long-term relationships with buyers and make purchases for them, often receiving, inspecting, warehousing, and shipping the merchandise to the buyers. They provide helpful market information to clients and help them obtain the best goods and prices available.

Retailers

What are three important retail strategies? Retailers primarily sell their products to final consumers. All companies need to decide how intensively they wish to cover any geographic market. Undertaking an **intensive distribution** entails selling the product through all available retail outlets. This seems most appropriate when selling convenience goods such as tobacco, newspapers, soft drinks, chewing gum, potato chips, bread, and milk. Companies want these products to obtain the widest possible exposure in the market. As a result, they try to make these products convenient for purchase at as many convenience stores and supermarkets as possible.

intensive distribution Entails selling the product through all available retail outlets.

Selective distribution uses only a portion of the many possible retail outlets for sale of a product. This approach is appropriate for the sale of shopping products and durable goods such as stereos, TVs, and furniture. Buyers spend more time comparing competitors' prices and features when buying shopping products. A sale often depends on providing buyers with information on these features to successfully differentiate one brand's product from another. Naturally, producers want to determine selectively where their products will be sold to ensure successful differentiation. Moreover, customers often want other services such as installation to be properly distributed. Again, producers are selective in determining outlets and may provide training to outlets to ensure the best service.

selective distribution Uses only a portion of the many possible retail outlets for sale of a product.

Table 9.4 Types of Retail Stores

Type of Store	Description	Examples
Specialty Store	A retail store that carries a wide selection of products in one category	Payless ShoeSource, Foot Locker, EB Games
Department Store	A retail store that carries a wide variety of products organized by departments	Sears, Hudson's Bay, Target
Supermarket	Large, low-cost, high-volume grocery stores that also sell household products	Loblaws, Metro, Safeway
Convenience Store	Small stores located near residents that are open long hours seven days a week and carry the most frequently purchased convenience goods	Mac's Convenience Stores, 7-Eleven
Discount Store	Stores that offer lower prices by accepting lower profit margins and selling at a higher volume than department stores	Giant Tiger, Walmart
Category Killer	Large specialty stores that specialize in selling a particular product line and are staffed by knowledgeable sales staff	Toys "R" Us, Best Buy, Indigo, Bass Pro Shops
Factory Outlet	Stores owned and operated by a manufacturer that normally carry surplus, discontinued, or irregular goods	Nike Factory Store, Under Armour Outlet
Warehouse Club	Stores that sell a limited selection of brand name food and nonfood items at deep discounts that usually require an annual membership fee	Costco

exclusive distribution The use of only one outlet in a geographic area.

Video: Nike

At other times, sellers want to undertake **exclusive distribution**, the use of only one outlet in a geographic area. This is most appropriate when selling specialty products such as expensive, high-quality sports cars, jewellery, or high-fashion clothing. Because these products carry a certain degree of prestige, sellers often require distributors to carry a full line of inventory, offer distinguished high-quality service, and meet other exclusive requirements. Another common form of exclusive distribution exists with franchises such as McDonald's and Subway. Only one outlet is chosen in a given geographic area, and the retail distributors are required to meet strict quality and service standards to protect brand name integrity.

What are the different types of retailers? Retailing constitutes a major sector of our economy. You're likely familiar with retail distributors because most of your personal shopping experiences have occurred at retail stores. **Table 9.4** describes the major types of retail stores and lists some examples of each.

What is nonstore retailing? Little has drawn as much attention in modern retailing as the growth of nonstore retailing. Nonstore retailing is a form of retailing in which consumer contact occurs outside the confines of a traditional brick-and-mortar retail store. Examples include the use of electronic shopping, vending machines, at-home personal selling, and catalogue buying. For example, Best Buy has placed vending machines in several major airports that stock frequently forgotten consumer electronics.

The rapid growth of technology and especially the Internet has made it possible for consumers to shop online—comparing prices, ordering, and paying for a product from the convenience of their homes. Electronic retailing, or the selling of consumer goods and services over the Internet, is a fast-growing trend. This poses many risks for some businesses that haven't adapted to this trend. Online shopping offers many benefits as well. In fact, many small businesses have found the Internet to be the great equalizer. They can establish websites offering an interactive environment that allows for the full use of state-of-the-art multimedia to attract sales.

Many other forms of nonstore retailing exist beyond electronic retailing. You have seen vending machines, kiosks, and carts before. Vending machines provide many convenience goods, like soft drinks, at locations where they are most often desired, such as airports, swimming pools, and college dorms. Kiosks are familiar in shopping malls. They are an inexpensive way to sell many goods, as are carts that often sell food on the street. Here are some other important nonstore retailers:

- *Telemarketing* is selling products over the phone. Sometimes the sales pitches are recorded messages. Many people, annoyed by telemarketers, have signed up for the National Do Not Call List. However, many consumers do use the telephone to place orders, even though these sales may not have been solicited by phone.
- *Direct selling* is selling goods and services door to door at people's homes and offices, or at temporary or mobile locations. Avon and Mary Kay cosmetics, Pampered Chef kitchen products, and PartyLite candles are sold through direct selling.
- *Direct marketing* refers to any aspect of retailing a good or service that attempts to bypass intermediaries. It includes catalogue sales, direct mail, and telemarketing.

Jeff Greenberg/The Image Works

Mall kiosks are a relatively inexpensive way to sell goods and services in a nonstore retail environment.

Physical Distribution

How important are warehousing and inventory control? **Warehousing**, or storing products at convenient locations ready for customers when they are needed, is critical for customer service. It is often much easier to sell products than to get them to their destinations. This is especially true when selling products globally. There are tradeoffs between maximizing customer service and minimizing physical distribution costs. Increasing customer service requires rapid delivery and large inventories to reduce the probability of being understocked. But this is expensive. On the other hand, lowering distribution costs can cause slower deliveries and lower inventory levels that increase the risk of being out of stock of a desired product. Given these tradeoffs, the goal of any physical distribution system should be to first determine the desired level of customer service and then work toward achieving that level of customer service at the lowest cost. Those companies that are most efficient at this survive and prosper. Inefficient businesses lose market share and risk failure.

warehousing Storing products at convenient locations ready for customers when they are needed.

Two types of warehouses emerge from marketing products. *Storage warehouses* store goods from moderate to long periods. *Distribution warehouses* (or distribution centres) are designed to gather and move goods quickly to consumers. Warehousing today uses sophisticated technologies to effectively store and distribute products. A host of technologies allows companies to manage their entire supply chain systems more effectively. As you will see in Chapter 10, one of the challenges in managing a supply chain is managing inventory levels to ensure there is neither too much nor too little inventory on hand.

What are the benefits and costs of various transportation methods? Transportation is the most expensive distribution cost. If a company wants one of its products to remain price competitive, then the selection of the most effective transportation mode is obvious. When deciding on transportation modes, companies also have to consider other factors beyond cost—such as speed, dependability, flexibility in handling products, frequency of shipments, and accessibility to markets. As you will see in Chapter 10, there are benefits and costs associated with each of the five major types of transportation—railroads, trucks, waterways, airways, and pipelines. Businesses have to weigh these benefits and costs carefully in making a mode-of-transportation decision. It is often the job of the supply chain manager to find the most efficient combination of these forms of transportation.

CHAPTER SYNOPSIS

LO1 Define various concepts applied to the term *product* as they apply to marketing and explain the role of product differentiation in product development. (pp. 202–204)

A product is any good or service, along with its perceived attributes and benefits, that creates value for the customer. Consumers buy products for a number of tangible and intangible benefits. The **total product offer** (or value package) consists of all the benefits associated with a good, service, or idea that affects a consumer's purchasing decision. When you buy a car, you're not just buying a mode of transportation—you're also buying some intangible benefits, such as style or an image.

Product differentiation is the creation of a real or perceived difference in a product designed to attract customers. A company can distinguish a product from its competitors by establishing concrete or intangible differences between similar products. For example, a luggage company might offer suitcases in unique colours or shapes. It might also offer a lifetime guarantee on certain models. Product differentiation is critical for a product's success. If a product doesn't possess qualities that make it stand out, customers will not be motivated to buy that product instead of a competitor's product.

LO2 Outline the steps in new product development, the application of the product life cycle, and describe classifications of consumer products and business-to-business products. (pp. 204–210)

As outlined in the figure below, **new product development** involves five steps: idea generation, idea screening, product analysis, product development and concept testing, and commercialization.

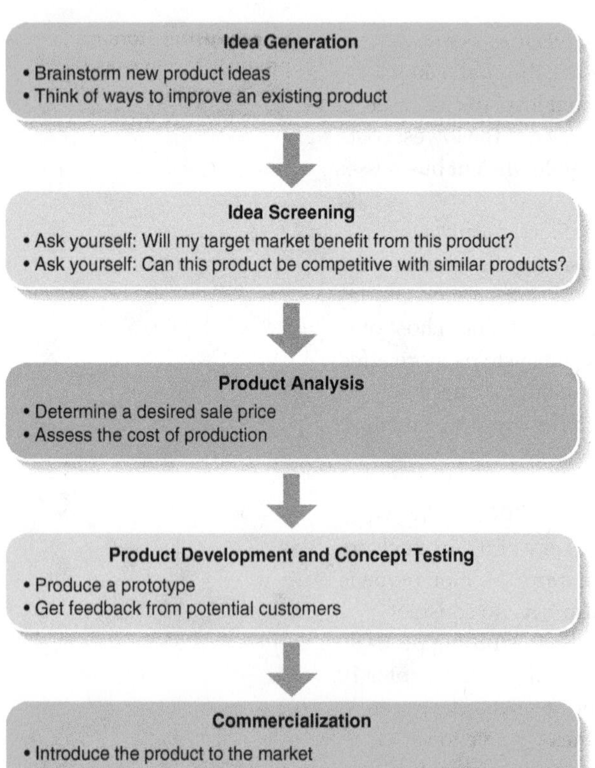

The Five Steps in the New Product Development Process

A **product life cycle** is a theoretical model describing a product's sales and profits over the course of its lifetime. During this cycle, a product typically goes through four stages: an introductory stage, a growth stage, a maturity stage, and a declining stage.

Four **consumer product classifications** emerge from strategic marketing mix plans for consumer products: convenience, shopping, specialty, and unsought goods and services.

Five **B2B product** (or industrial product) **classifications** emerge from strategic marketing mix plans for B2B products: equipment; maintenance, repair, and operating (MRO) products; raw and processed materials; component parts; and specialized professional services. Each of these types of products has unique pricing, promotion, and distribution strategies.

LO3 Explain why branding is beneficial to both buyers and sellers and describe some different types of brands. (pp. 210–216)

A **brand** is a name, term, symbol, or design that distinguishes a company and its products from all others. Branding is one of the most important tools of product differentiation, and it benefits both buyers and sellers. For buyers, well-recognized brands reduce the shopping time necessary to find the quality and consistency they desire in a product. Branding also reduces the risks involved in some purchases for which buyers are unable to determine quality objectively.

Branding also helps sellers define their products' special qualities, thus promoting repeat purchases as well as new sales at higher prices. Because certain brands, such as Coca-Cola, are associated with quality and value, these companies are able to introduce new products quickly and at a relatively low cost. In doing so, they add length to their product lines, widen their **product mix** (also known as *brand extension*), and enhance their profitability.

LO4 Describe three major approaches to pricing strategy and outline some pricing tactics used to launch a new product, to adjust prices, and to affect price perceptions. (pp. 216–220)

There are three major **pricing strategies** companies can use: (1) **Cost-based pricing** (or cost-plus pricing) is charging a price in relation to the costs of providing the good or service; (2) **demand-based pricing** (or value-based pricing) is pricing a good or service based on the demand for the product or its perceived value; and (3) **competition-based pricing** is a pricing strategy based on what the competition is charging. Revenues and costs are secondary.

One pricing strategy for introducing a new product is **price skimming**. It involves charging a high price for a product initially, then lowering the price over time. Price adjustments may consist of **discounts**, a deduction from the regular price charged; **rebates**, which are partial refunds on what a customer has already paid for a product; and **bundling**, when two or more products that usually complement one another are combined and sold at a single price.

Prestige pricing (or premium pricing) is the practice of charging a high price to invoke perceptions of high quality and privilege. Another pricing strategy that affects price perceptions is **psychological pricing** (or odd or fractional pricing), the practice of charging a price just below a whole number to give the appearance of a significantly lower price. A **loss leader** is a product priced below its cost. Stores use loss leaders to attract customers and motivate them to buy items that are more expensive as well. **Reference pricing** refers to listing an inflated price (the "regular retail price" or "manufacturer's suggested retail price") that is then discounted to appear as if it is a good value.

LO5 Define a promotional mix and explain its function in a promotional campaign. *(pp. 220–222)*

Four basic **promotional tools** are used to promote a good or service: **advertising, public relations, personal selling,** and **sales promotions**. The **promotional mix** is the strategic combination of promotional tools used to reach targeted customers to achieve marketing objectives. Six steps emerge from all effective promotional campaigns: identify the target market, determine marketing objectives, design the message, determine the budget, implement the promotional mix, and evaluate and adjust as needed.

LO6 Explain the advantages and disadvantages of the various types of media used for advertising and discuss the role of public relations in a company. *(pp. 222–227)*

The following table outlines the advantages and disadvantages of the various types of media used for advertising:

Advantages and Disadvantages of Advertising Media

Media	Advantages	Disadvantages
Television	Good mass-market coverage; low cost per contact; combines sight, sound, and motion; good attention span	High cost; low recall; channel surfing or digital video recorders skip over ads; short exposure
Newspaper	Timing and geographic flexibility; good local market coverage; high credibility and acceptability	Short lifespan; lots of competition for attention; poor-quality reproductions
Magazine	High market segmentation; high-quality colour; long life; longer attention span; high credibility	Declining readership; lots of competition for attention; high cost; long ad-purchase lead time
Radio	High geographic and demographic selectivity; low cost; creative opportunities with sound	Low attention span; short exposure time; information overload; limited coverage
Internet	Global and interactive possibilities; ease of segmentation; high audience interest; easy to measure responses	Audience controls exposure; clutter on each site; skewed demographically to Web surfers
Outdoor	Able to select key geographic areas; low cost per impression; high frequency on major commuter routes	Short exposure time; brief messages; creative limitations; little segmentation possible
Direct Mail	High levels of segmentation; allows personalization; high flexibility; ad can be saved; measurable impact	High cost; can be rejected as "junk mail" and viewed as a nuisance
Yellow Pages	Inexpensive; commonly used and accessible; good local coverage and segmentation possible; long life	Costly for very small businesses; lists the competition as well

Publicity is information about an individual, organization, or product transmitted through mass media at no charge. Naturally, keeping friendly relations with the press increases the probability that a "newsworthy" story will be covered and treated with a favourable spin. Nevertheless, public relations managers need to ensure that publicity releases are timely, interesting, accurate, and in the public interest. Corporate philanthropy is generally good publicity, especially if it results in getting your name on a building, an annual event, a scholarship, or volunteer programs that are visible to the community.

Damage control is a company's effort to minimize the harmful effects of a negative event. Negative publicity, in a matter of days, can tear down a firm's image that took decades to build up. In the event of bad news, a company must stand ready to react, and react quickly. No easy remedies exist for crises, but being honest, accepting responsibility, and making other ethical responses are the first steps toward regaining credibility and re-establishing a positive image.

LO7 Describe the six steps in the personal selling process. *(pp. 227–229)*

No two salespeople are alike, and no two selling situations are the same. However, six steps emerge from all personal selling: prospecting, approaching the prospect, presenting, overcoming objections, closing the sale, and following up.

LO8 Describe the two main types of sales promotions and the types of tools commonly used as incentives. *(pp. 229–231)*

Any incentives to push a product through the distribution system to final consumers are called **trade** (or business-to-business) **sales promotions**. In addition, **consumer sales promotions** are incentives designed to increase final consumer demand for a product.

Some of the specific trade sales promotions tools include trade shows and conventions, trade allowances (deals and price reductions to wholesalers, dealers, and retailers), cooperative advertising (a manufacturer agrees to pay for some of the advertising costs of the retailer), free merchandise, sales contests (e.g., a free trip to Hawaii for those who sell the most), dealer listings (advertisements of your product that mention retail outlets where it can be found), catalogues and store demonstrations, in-store displays, quantity discounts, and training and support programs.

Some of the most common consumer promotional tools include coupons, rebates, frequent-user incentives, point-of-purchase (POP) displays, free samples, contests and sweepstakes, advertising specialties, bonuses (buy one, get one free), catalogues, demonstrations, special events, lotteries, premiums, and cents-off deals.

LO9 Define marketing intermediaries and distribution channels and explain why these are important elements in marketing. *(pp. 231–237)*

A **marketing intermediary**, or middleman, is a business firm that operates between producers and consumers or business users. Many goods, such as grocery store items, go through a **distribution channel**, which is a series of firms or individuals that participate in the flow of a product from manufacturer to consumer. Intermediaries reduce the time and costs of providing products to customers. Of course, the **wholesaler** will incur some costs that will be pushed onto the consumer, but these costs are less than the costs of sourcing the product without the involvement of the intermediary.

KEY TERMS

CRITICAL THINKING QUESTIONS

1. What types of consumer products are sold by a gas station? By an automotive repair shop? By a shoe store? By an orthodontist? How might these goods and services be best differentiated in terms of the product and price components of the marketing mix?
2. What are the differences among cost-based pricing, demand-based pricing, and competition-based pricing?
3. Describe the conditions when it might be appropriate to use each of the following pricing strategies: discounting, rebates, bundling, dynamic pricing, prestige pricing, psychological pricing, loss leader pricing, and reference pricing.
4. Describe which distribution strategy—intensive, selective, or exclusive—would be most appropriate for each of the following products, and explain why: laundry detergent, cigarettes, Mercedes sports cars, and Snickers chocolate bars.
5. Suppose you are the distribution manager for a high-tech producer of big-screen televisions. Which mode of transportation would you select in distributing your products to customers and why?
6. How might fresh food packaging be adapted to be more environmentally friendly? Can you think of methods that a consumer electronics manufacturers might use to reduce the degree of nonrecyclable material in their packaging?

TEAM TIME

Developing a Promotional Mix

The company you work for, FitFoods, is launching a new product: Shine Breakfast Bars, all-natural, vitamin-fortified granola bars. The company has enlisted you and your teammates to design an optimal promotional mix for this product.

PROCESS

Step 1. Assemble into teams of four. Each team member should be assigned as the "lead" for one of the four components of the promotional mix—advertising, public relations, personal selling, and sales promotions.

Step 2. Use the knowledge gained from this chapter to develop a promotional mix for Shine Breakfast Bars that integrates each of the four components. What will be the key aspects of the advertising campaign? What media will be used? What public relations tools will be used? What will a sales pitch for this product consist of? How will sales promotions be implemented?

Step 3. Summarize the key points of the promotional mix plan in a poster or PowerPoint presentation.

Step 4. Present your findings to the class for discussion.

ETHICS AND RESPONSIBILITY

The Ethics of Rx

The pharmaceutical drug industry is an ethical minefield. The development of prescription medications is one topic among many that can present significant ethical challenges. Consider the questions raised by the following scenario. If possible, discuss your thoughts with a classmate or participate in a group debate on the topic.

You are an executive at the top pharmaceutical company in Canada, Johnson & Johnson. At the most recent product development meeting, two teams of scientists reported that each is within one year of having a new drug ready for clinical trials. Team A is developing a drug to cure a rare but fatal bone disease. Team B is developing a drug to treat a common, non-life-threatening skin condition. To make the deadline, however, both teams need an additional $10 million in funding. You know that the company can only afford to fund one team. According to the product analysis, Team A's drug will be expensive to produce, difficult to market, and will yield only modest profits. Team B's drug has the potential to yield massive profits.

1. Which team would you recommend the company fund? Why?
2. How do the potential profits of Team B's drug affect your position, from both financial/business and medical/ethical perspectives?
3. What about pricing? How might you reconcile the need to keep the drug company profitable and your responsibility to shareholders with the ethical responsibility to make medications affordable for those in need?

CLOSING CASE

The iPhone: Revolutionary Product or Rip-off?

Then entire auditorium was buzzing with excitement as the crowd waited for Steve Jobs, CEO of Apple, Inc. and keynote speaker, to take the stage at the 2007 Macworld Conference and Expo.[45] Executives, reporters, and Apple enthusiasts alike were anxiously anticipating the introduction of Apple's latest advancement in portable technology: the iPhone. Rumours about the iPhone's capabilities floated around for months, but few people had actually seen the product. Jobs's presentation of the iPhone wowed the audience. Its touchscreen design and Web browsing capabilities were nothing short of revolutionary.[46]

On June 29, 2007, thousands of people stood in line for hours at the retail stores of AT&T, the iPhone's exclusive wireless carrier, to get their hands on the first iPhone.[47] The hefty price of US$599 for the 8-gigabyte device did not deter customers. The premium cost seemed a small price to pay for some tech junkies, many of whom were eager to be the first person in their school or office to hold the cutting-edge miracle. Apple sold an impressive 270 000 iPhones within the first 30 hours it was available for purchase.[48] Just 74 days after its initial release, on September 10, Apple sold its one millionth iPhone.[49]

Although Apple's millionth iPhone sale should have been a celebrated milestone, Apple, Inc. and Jobs were busy dealing with a much bigger issue involving iPhone sales. On September 5, less than 10 weeks after the product hit the market, Apple announced that it would drop the price of the popular 8-GB iPhone from US$599 to US$399. The $200 reduction was intended to boost iPhone sales during the 2007 holiday season. "We've clearly got a breakthrough product, and we want to make it affordable for even more customers as we enter this holiday season," said Jobs. The price cut made the iPhone accessible to a larger market, but it enraged many of Apple's loyal customers. Many felt betrayed by the reduced price, believing that Apple had ripped off its most devoted supporters. Early iPhone owners let Jobs know how they felt about his sales decision by flooding his inbox with heated emails.

Jobs did not shy away from the price-drop backlash. After reading hundreds of emails from iPhone customers,[50] Jobs decided to offer anyone who purchased an iPhone within 14 days of the price drop a US$100 credit toward other Apple products. Jobs defended his initial decision to cut the iPhone price, stating, "It benefits both Apple and every iPhone user to get as many new customers as possible under the iPhone 'tent.'" Jobs explained that the purpose of this credit was to mend ties with loyal customers. "Our early customers trust us, and we must live up to that trust with our actions in moments like these," he continued. The $100 credit not only helped repair the image of the iPhone, but of Apple in general.

Although the lower price of the iPhone may have ruffled feathers among Apple aficionados, this pricing strategy is a customary practice in the specialty goods market. The latest video game, luxury car, and designer handbag often have inflated prices when they are first released. The snob appeal alone can be most alluring for customers who want something that only a select few can afford. What is different for Apple is that their products are tailored so tightly to their customers' needs that customers feel personally connected to the products. If that personal connection is broken, Apple can lose its greatest asset—brand loyalty.

DISCUSSION QUESTIONS

1. What do you think might have happened if Apple originally set its price at US$399? Would this have increased or decreased sales of the iPhone in the end? What do you think might have happened if Steve Jobs had not issued the $100 credit?
2. Why is brand loyalty so important to a company like Apple? How does regaining the trust of iPhone customers affect all Apple brands?
3. Consider what you've learned about the different types of product pricing. Do you think it was ethical for Apple to practise price skimming with the iPhone? Do you think price skimming is always unfair to the customer, or is it a legitimate way of doing business?

10 Operations Management: Goods and Services

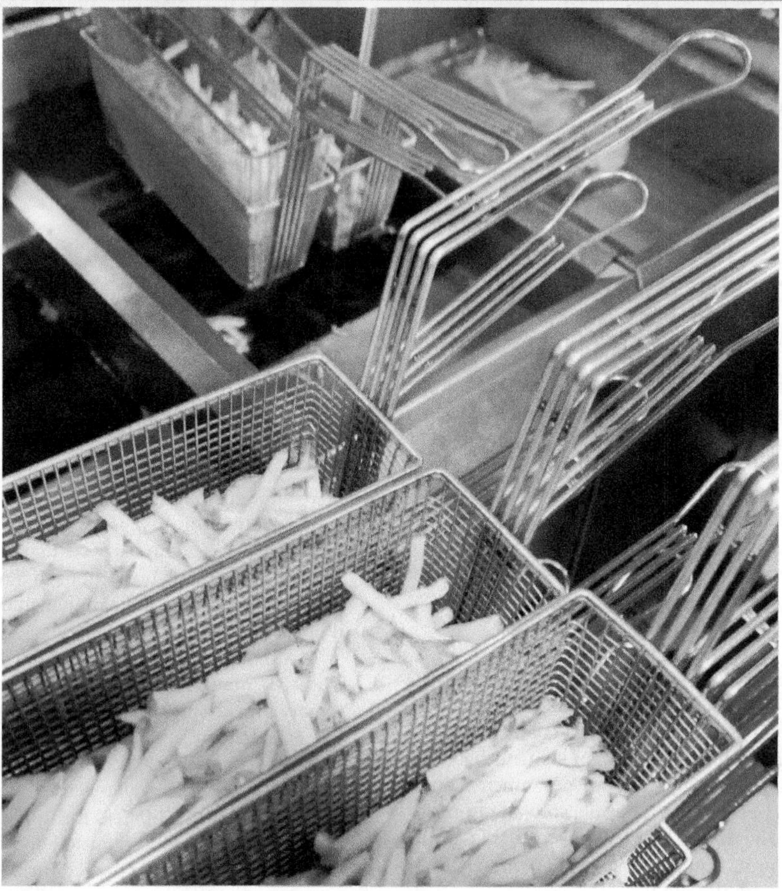

KAKIMAGE/Alamy

LEARNING OBJECTIVES

After studying this chapter, you should be able to:

- **LO1** Explain how operations management produces finished goods that provide utility to consumers, and differentiate between goods and service operations. (pp. 244–247)
- **LO2** Describe mass production, mass customization, flexible manufacturing, and lean production and the benefits and challenges of each, including how technology influences the production process. (pp. 247–251)
- **LO3** Summarize the factors involved in choosing a manufacturing location, a facility layout, and how green manufacturing integrates sustainability into the supply chain. (pp. 251–256)
- **LO4** Explain how a company determines that it requires a supplier, selects a supplier, and strives to manage its supply chain. (pp. 256–258)
- **LO5** Describe what value-stream mapping is and what its benefits are. (pp. 259–261)
- **LO6** Explain the benefits of just-in-time (JIT) production and enterprise resource planning (ERP). (pp. 261–262)
- **LO7** Describe quality control, how ISO standards help companies produce high-quality goods and services, and the application of sustainability to operations management. (pp. 262–266)

OPENING DISCUSSION: SUPPLY CHAIN

McDonald's . . . From Farm to Front Counter

The quality of every item on a McDonald's menu begins with the quality of its ingredients—where they come from, how they are processed, and how they are prepared in each restaurant determine the taste and quality of the finished product. According to J.C. Gonzalez-Mendez, senior vice-president of global corporate social responsibility, sustainability, and philanthropy, "We always strive to be better tomorrow than we are today. This, more than anything, speaks to who McDonald's is as a company. The overarching goal of our sustainability efforts is focused on continuous improvement through our five focus areas: Nutrition and Well-Bring, Sustainable Supply Chain, Environmental Responsibility, Employee Experience, and Community.[1] Let's take a closer look at those famous shoestring fries to examine how McDonald's accomplishes this mission.

Potato Suppliers and Social Responsibility

Farms around the world comply with a set of good agricultural practices (GAP) developed by McDonald's employees, suppliers, and outside consultants to plant, grow, and harvest potatoes. Among the hundreds of potato varieties that exist, only four types (following strict requirements for size, shape, and consistency) are used to achieve the perfect appearance and texture of McDonald's fries. Working with the National Potato Council, the Integrated Pest Management Institute, and growers in the United States and Canada, McDonald's developed a comprehensive process to analyze the use of pesticides, fertilizer, and water on potato crops. McDonald's USA has initiated a plan to reduce pesticide use among potato growers in its supply chain. According to John Keeling of the National Potato Council, "Growers now have a state-of-the-art tool to benchmark their performance and learn from the efficient production of high quality potatoes. McDonald's has been a real leader in identifying a path forward that is truly a win/win for all involved."[2]

The Production Process and Quality Control[3]

Potatoes are brought into the processing plant by conveyor belts, shakers, slides, or flumes (small stainless steel canals that use water to move the potatoes along). A combination of steaming and tumbling peels the potatoes, followed by a rinsing to remove any particles. The potatoes are separated by size, conforming to McDonald's strict length specifications, and inspected for blemishes, which are trimmed away. After being precooked in boiling water for three minutes to soften them, they are then pushed along by water pressure into a series of blades that cuts them into shoestring-style strips. These strips are inspected, blanched in hot water, dried, and inspected again before being partially fried in pure vegetable oil for 50 seconds (at 182°C). They continue along the conveyor to the de-oiler shaker, which does exactly as the name suggests: shakes off the excess oil. After the fries cool for six minutes they are transferred to the blast freezer for six chilly minutes (at −10°C). The frozen fries move down the conveyor for another quality inspection and length check before being packaged in bags (3 kilograms, or 6 pounds, each). The bags are packed six to a case, sealed by a glue press, and then placed on pallets (36 cases to a pallet), dated, shrinkwrapped, and moved on rollers to the freezers. Refrigerated trucks deliver the fries to McDonald's restaurants where they are stored in walk-in freezers until use. Fries are then cooked in pure vegetable oil at 182°C temperature for three and a half minutes, salted, and served crisp, hot, and fresh to customers. Each restaurant could quite possibly use 120 cases of fries every four days. McDonald's developed a next-generation "low oil volume" (LOV) fryer that uses about 40 percent less cooking oil and 4 percent less energy than regular fryers. Electric and gas fryers are available in McDonald's around the world.

Environmental Sustainability[4]

In partnership with Conservation International, McDonald's developed an Environmental Scorecard—measuring energy, water, air, and waste impacts—for potato suppliers to complete each year. For example, one of the restaurant chain's largest suppliers, McCain Foods, began using the scorecard in 2005 to track the use of "biogas" (a wastewater treatment byproduct that replaces fossil fuels in plant boilers to generate "green" electricity). McCain was able to identify opportunities that increased biogas usage from about 65 percent to more than 86 percent (which is a good thing). As a result, this increase generated enough clean, renewable energy to power a city of about 20 000 people for one year. Using fewer natural resources makes McDonald's supply chain more efficient and cost effective.

McDonald's also achieves environmental sustainability in the area of packaging. McDonald's has implemented a global packaging scorecard to better inform packaging decisions. The scorecard builds on best practices from both European and North American markets, as well as advice from outside experts and nongovernmental organizations such as the Environmental Defense Fund.[5] McDonald's is one of the world's largest purchasers of recycled paper. It is used extensively in the restaurants, including tray liners, napkins, bags, sandwich containers and other restaurant materials. Today, approximately 79 percent of the consumer packaging used in the eight largest markets is made from renewable (paper or wood-fibre) materials, and nearly 30 percent of consumer packaging is made from recycled materials.[6]

DISCUSSION QUESTIONS

1. Do you think McDonald's has the power to prompt changes in standards used around the world (technology, environmental, employment, agricultural)? Why or why not?
2. How do McDonald's operational methods show evidence of quality control? Is it necessary to have so many steps in the production of french fries? Why or why not?
3. How do you think McDonald's attempts to keep input costs low while continuing to supply consumers with quality products and services?
4. In addition to implementing a packaging scorecard, how else might McDonald's incorporate sustainability practices into their global business?

OPERATIONS OVERVIEW

LO1 Explain how operations management produces finished goods that provide utility to consumers, and differentiate between goods and service operations.

Producing Goods and Services

production The process of getting a good or service to the customer; it is a series of related activities, with value being added at each stage.

Why is the production of goods and services a critical component of any business? Every business that produces goods or provides services has a unique production process. **Production** is the process of getting a good or service to the customer; it is a series of related activities, with value being added at each stage. Both businesses that produce manufactured goods ("things")—such as bicycles, automobiles, and computers—and businesses that offer services—such as restaurants, schools, and retail stores—require an efficient production process. General Electric and IBM, for example, are considered manufacturing companies, and both are also considered among the largest, most competitive service operations in the world. All businesses have a service component to their operations.

Companies strive to make a profit by providing goods and services to consumers. To increase their profits and decrease production costs, businesses must find the most efficient production process possible. Increasing global competition, rising resource prices (particularly that of labour), and changing customer needs are just a few of the issues that require companies to scrutinize the efficiencies of their production process. If a business uses a production process that's inefficient, the company might go bankrupt, even if there is demand for its product. Companies that spend too much on production have to increase prices to break even, which can drive consumers away. A cost-effective, efficient, innovative, and flexible production process is crucial to the success of a business. For example, in 1908 the Model T Ford was less expensive than most other cars on the market. However, it still wasn't affordable "for the great multitude,"[7] which was Henry Ford's ultimate goal. The changes that Ford introduced during the production process—division of labour, interchangeable parts, precise speed and motions, and most notably the use of an assembly line—allowed the Ford Motor Company to produce an automobile that truly was affordable for a great number of people.

How a company handles its production processes can dramatically impact its chance of success. Swedish furniture manufacturer IKEA is a great example of a company using intelligent production management to enhance its business. What sets IKEA apart from the competition is that it purchases mass quantities of production resources worldwide and most of its products are shipped in flat packs for assembly at the consumer's home, which minimizes storage and transportation costs. Ultimately, these processes result in high-quality products at a low cost.[8]

Is there a difference between production and operations? **Operations management** (or *production management*) refers to the organized direction and control of the processes that transform resources (inputs) into finished goods and services (outputs). As shown in **Figure 10.1**, the act of production gives these finished products and services *value*. Whenever a business satisfies a need or want, it creates *value* for the customer. The **value** of a product equals the ratio of the product's benefits to its costs (value = benefits/costs). With a high-value product, its benefits far exceed its costs. Businesses that offer the highest-value products gain the most customers and thrive.

operations management The organized direction and control of the processes that transform resources (inputs) into finished goods and services (outputs). Also called production management.

value The value of a product equals the ratio of the product's benefits to its costs (value = benefits/costs).

Products and services provide businesses with economic results (profits, wages, suppliers) and provide customers with utility, which is the power of a product or service to satisfy a human want or need—that is, provide something of value to the person. Utility was discussed in Chapter 8.

To buy groceries, for example, most of us go to the grocery store. As a customer, you expect the shelves to be stocked with fresh products (task utility), the store to be open at

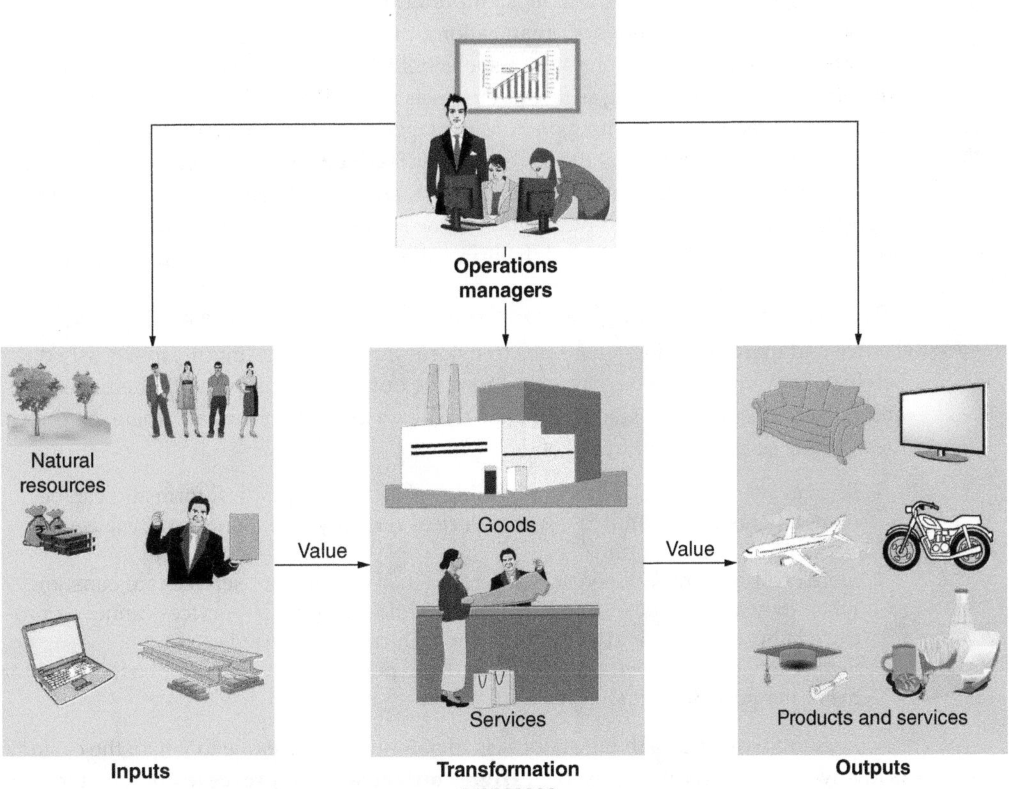

Figure 10.1 The Transformation Process

convenient times (time utility), be conveniently located (place utility), offer quality food products (form utility) that you can take home to eat (ownership utility), all at reasonable prices (value). As a consumer, you affect the operations process because the manager sets the store hours to meet customer requirements, orders food supplies to meet customer demand, and so on.

Operations Management

How do firms manage and control the creation of products and services? The business plans and forecasts developed by top managers guide operations planning. Planning and controlling operation processes are critical to business success. There are four decisions that must be made in **operations planning**: (1) the type of production process, (2) the facility location, (3) the facility layout, and (4) resource planning. To ensure that a product provides utility, production managers must successfully develop and carry out a **production plan**, which helps ensure a smoothly run operations process. **Operations managers** are responsible for managing and supervising all the activities that occur when transforming resources into goods or services, such as setting schedules, making buying decisions, and overseeing quality control. Managers who plan effectively are able to increase productivity, reduce costs, and improve customer satisfaction.

operations planning Includes four decisions: (1) the type of production process, (2) the facility location, (3) the facility layout, and (4) resource planning.

production plan When well developed and efficiently executed, ensures a smoothly run operations process and a product that provides utility.

operations managers Managers who are responsible for managing and supervising all the activities that occur when transforming resources into goods or services, such as setting schedules, making buying decisions, and overseeing quality control.

Operations control means that managers check to ensure that production decisions are being implemented. If schedules or quality standards are not being met, managers need to take corrective action. Through operations management—controlling production processes—managers can ensure schedules are met and production goals are fulfilled, in both quality and quantity. We'll examine these concepts later in this chapter.

What is meant by "a company must be effective" to stay in business? Operations management includes forecasting, purchasing, inventory management, information management, production scheduling, quality control, distribution, and more. For instance, in your school, operations management takes inputs—such as information, professors, students, supplies, buildings, offices, and computer systems—and creates outputs—co-op placements, job opportunities, and most importantly graduates. The operations function is one of three primary functions of organizations; the other two are marketing and finance. Operations management involves the responsibility of ensuring that business operations are efficient (in terms of using as few resources as needed) and effective (in terms of meeting customer requirements). In operations management, **efficiency** means completing a task or producing a product at the lowest cost. **Effectiveness** means completing tasks and producing products that create the greatest value. Both effectiveness and efficiency are important, but a firm may produce a good at the lowest cost, thereby being efficient, but if no one wants to purchase that good the firm will not be effective and won't be in business.

efficiency Completing a task or producing a product at the lowest cost.

effectiveness Completing tasks and producing products that create the greatest value.

What are the differences between service and manufacturing operations? Both service and manufacturing operations transform raw materials (inputs) into finished products (outputs), but in service operations the outputs are people with their needs met and possessions serviced. Goods are produced; services are performed. There are three areas where services differ from goods:

1. *Services are intangible.* Goods are tangible—they have a physical form and can be seen, touched, and handled—while services can only be experienced because they do not have a physical form.
2. *Services are unstorable.* Goods can be stored in inventory, but services are consumed when they are produced. Trash collection, childcare, or mail services cannot be produced ahead of time and then stored for high-demand periods.
3. *Services are more customizable than goods.* Each person receives service customized for his or her specific needs.

A useful way of classifying services is to determine the degree to which the customer is involved in the production system. **High-contact service processes** require the customer to be present, such as a public transit system, a hair salon, or a dentist. Companies offering high-contact services, where the customer is present, must ensure

high-contact service processes Services that require the customer to be present, such as a public transit system, a hair salon, or a dentist.

their locations are clean and inviting. **Low-contact service processes** do not require the customer to be present, such as a utility company, an auto-repair shop, or the chequing processes at a bank. Since customers are not present while the service is occurring, the attractiveness and atmosphere of the location are not of much concern.

low-contact service processes Services that do not require the customer to be present, such as a utility company, an auto-repair shop, or the chequing processes at a bank.

There are some inherent differences between the industrial sector and the service sector. Service providers have more contact with their customers than manufacturers do. In addition, services are usually customized to satisfy the specific needs of a customer. For example, a house painter applies the colours chosen by the customer, and a doctor treats each patient's specific symptoms. However, despite these differences, the ultimate goal of providing a quality product in a cost-efficient manner is similar to manufacturers and service providers.

OPERATIONS PLANNING

LO2 Describe mass production, mass customization, flexible manufacturing, and lean production and the benefits and challenges of each, including how technology influences the production process.

The Production Process

What types of production processes are usually used by businesses? Businesses can use several types of production processes. The type chosen depends on the business and what types of goods or services it produces. The most common types of production processes and techniques include the following (see **Figure 10.2**):

- mass production
- mass customization
- flexible manufacturing
- lean production

The production process plays a major role in determining the profitability of a business. Efficiency and low production costs are essential in successfully producing any product. Let's examine each type of production process in detail.

mass production A method of producing large quantities of goods at a low cost; relies on machines and automated assembly lines to mass produce goods that are identical and adhere to certain standards of quality.

assembly line Used to move partially complete products from one worker to the next on a conveyor belt. Also called a production line.

What production process results in large quantities of goods? The method of producing large quantities of goods at a low cost is called **mass production**. This method relies on machines and automated assembly lines to mass produce goods that are identical and adhere to certain standards of quality. Mass produced goods are usually manufactured along an **assembly line** (or *production line*) in which partially complete products are moved from one worker to the next on a conveyor belt.

The cost to run an assembly line is kept low because machines do the majority of the work and the labourers don't need to be especially skilled to perform their repetitive tasks. This method also cuts down on production time, allowing a large quantity of goods to be produced very quickly. Because machinery is the main component, risk of human error is virtually eliminated. A major disadvantage, however, is that mass production is inflexible. After a production line is established, it's very difficult to change or alter the process if an unexpected problem occurs.

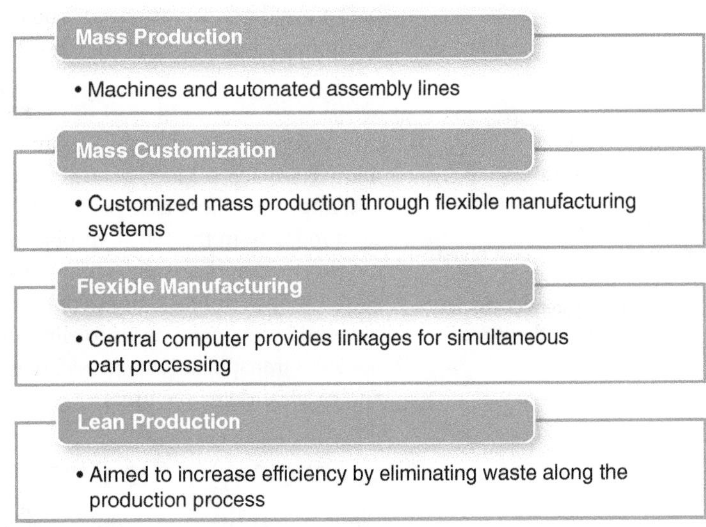

Figure 10.2 Common Production Processes and Techniques

Can product customization be done with mass production? When mass production was first implemented, if any customization of product design was desired the process had to be stopped

Scott Olson/Staff/Getty Images

A flexible manufacturing system includes four components: processing machines, a material-handling system, a central computer, and human labour.

or slowed down to do so in small batches. With advances in technology, customization is now accessible and affordable to a wide variety of markets. **Mass customization** combines the low unit cost of mass production processes with the flexibility of producing goods or services tailored to meet individual customer's needs. More and more manufacturers are learning to customize their products. For example, Dell permits customers to customize their computer design (i.e., laptop colour) and specifications (i.e., hard drive space) online when ordering new computer systems.[9] At Walmart Photo Centres, you can not only customize your photo prints with borders and text but also purchase calendars, mugs, or photo albums that feature your photos in the style and layout of your choice.[10] You can even order personalized M&Ms.[11]

mass customization Combines the low unit cost of mass production processes with the flexibility of producing goods or services tailored to meet individual customer's needs.

flexible manufacturing system (FMS) Uses one central computer to link together several machines that can process different part types simultaneously.

How is mass customization achieved? A solution to the rigid system of mass production is *flexible* production, also known as a **flexible manufacturing system (FMS)**. An FMS uses one central computer to link together several machines that can process different part types simultaneously. Unlike a mass production system, an FMS can adapt to changes in schedules and product specifications. There are four components to a flexible manufacturing system: processing machines, a material-handling system, a central computer, and human labour.[12]

Can mass customization be used in service industries? The technologies of mass customization have also enabled many service-based organizations—such as the fast-food industry—to meet the individual needs of their customers. When you think about Burger King, McDonald's, and Wendy's, for example, realize that they are using a mass customization process every time you choose a specific drink or side dish with your order or even a certain salad dressing. The hospitality industry is also enhancing customer service through mass customization. Hotel chains note unique habits, likes, and dislikes of each guest in their database, so that the next time the same guest visits one of the hotel chain's locations, staff retrieve these preferences to provide a more individualized, customized service. For example, a guest may have his or her favourite newspaper waiting in the room or have nonallergenic pillows on the bed. Hotel staff seem to anticipate a customer's every need. The result of this type of customized program at the Ritz-Carlton, for instance, has shown a 23 percent increase in guest retention.[13]

lean production A set of principles concerned with reducing waste and improving flow that evolved from the original Toyota production system (TPS) first used in Japan in the 1980s.

What type of production focuses on efficiency? Although efficiency has always been a concern, the success of lean production has made efficiency a primary focus for many companies. **Lean production** is a set of principles concerned with reducing waste and improving flow that evolved from the original Toyota production system (TPS) first used in Japan in the 1980s. Its objective is to focus all resources and energies into producing products and services with value-added characteristics (utility to the consumer) while eliminating activities that are of no value.[14] Lean production can be used in goods- or service-producing companies to eliminate wasteful overproduction, unnecessary wait time, needless transportation, excess inventory, superfluous motion, redundant overprocessing, and careless defective units.

Technology in the Production Process

What is the role of technology in the production process? With thousands of goods to produce at a given time, you might guess that technology plays an integral role in facilitating the flow of any production process. When managed efficiently, the technological aspect of a production process should lead to increases in production and reductions in costs. Technology may also improve the quality and increase the variety of products, which influences the customer's buying decisions. Customers are more likely to buy a product that is not only low priced compared to other similar products but also of high quality and readily available in many varieties. It is essential for businesses in today's globally competitive environment to be up to date on new technologies that can improve any or all aspects of the production process.

Supergenijalac/Shutterstock

Robots play a big part in automobile manufacturing, but they are also used to weld, paint, assemble, package, inspect, and test many other types of products.

What has helped automate the production process? Humans are sometimes at a disadvantage when it comes to performing a task repetitively for many hours and with great precision and accuracy. This is where robots come in; an industrial robot is any device that performs automatically, typically completing repetitive tasks.[15] Not only can robots work around the clock tirelessly and with accuracy, but they can also work in potentially hazardous conditions, thereby protecting human workers from dangerous environments.

Robots offer consistency in reducing production costs, raising productivity, and producing high-quality products. Industrial robots may take away some jobs, but they also create many new jobs for technicians and engineers. Companies that can effectively apply robotic technology in their production process are more likely to gain an economic advantage in the global marketplace.

How has technology improved the design process? **Computer-aided design (CAD)** refers to the use of a computer to create two-dimensional or three-dimensional models of physical parts. With CAD systems, the models displayed onscreen can be modified in size or shape, viewed internally, and rotated on any axis. CAD also enables testing of a part by simulating real-world environments. CAD, however, cannot design a model of a product on its own. A designer must first translate the design into a geometrical model for the CAD system to display. Once the model data are received, the CAD system provides the designer with tools and a flexible environment. By programming a simple design change into the CAD system, a manufacturer can produce custom-designed products such as clothing and cars without incurring higher costs. CAD is not only used to design smaller products, it can also be used to design houses, machinery, tools, and commercial structures.

computer-aided design (CAD) The use of a computer to create two-dimensional or three-dimensional models of physical parts.

Some manufacturing processes that are more complicated, such as those for motor vehicles, airplanes, and ships, need more than one CAD program to design and incorporate all the different model parts. For instance, the design of a ship may require one CAD application for the steel structure and another CAD program for the propeller. A disadvantage to this method is that it requires knowledge of all the different software applications used as well as knowledge of how to integrate them in the end. On the other hand, Boeing's 757 model is a good example of how integration can be achieved. Because the 757 model is composed of parts from 50 different firms, Boeing's CAD system effectively integrates all the parts, ensuring a precise fit. This system effectively reduces the number of prototypes needed and the working hours for assembly.[16]

Syda Productions/Fotolia

CAD uses computer technology for the design of objects in two or three dimensions.

computer-aided manufacturing (CAM) Uses the design data to control the machinery used in the manufacturing process.

How is CAD information incorporated into the manufacturing process? Once a design is approved, **computer-aided manufacturing (CAM)** uses the design data to control the machinery used in the manufacturing process. The integration of the CAD and CAM systems with the various aspects of a firm's production process is referred to as *simultaneous engineering*. Ford Motor Company's engine division, for example, successfully integrated all its production and design systems into one database that could be accessed by PCs and workstations of employees and suppliers involved with design and production.[17] This type of facilitated communication is a huge benefit for firms with complex systems. One of the main disadvantages of using CAD/CAM systems is that they require considerable time and investment to set up and to learn the necessary software, hardware, communications, and integration.

Video: Blackbird Guitars: Organizational Culture

computer-integrated manufacturing (CIM) Combines design and manufacturing functions with other functions such as order taking, shipment, and billing.

Can an entire facility be automated? Yes, and **computer-integrated manufacturing (CIM)** takes it even further by combining design and manufacturing functions with other functions such as order taking, shipment, and billing. For example, printing company VistaPrint uses CIM not only to manufacture its products but also to help customers create and place orders for custom-designed business cards, brochures, T-shirts, and more. Using CIM, the company has expanded its business and is able to serve more customers while continuing to offer affordable prices.[18]

What effect has automation had on the production process? CAD, CAM, and CIM have dramatically improved the process of producing goods by reducing the time between design and manufacturing, thus making a sizable impact on productivity. These

Technology: It's Hard to Tell What's Real and What's Fake

Creating IKEA's catalogue is a massive undertaking. Every picture of an IKEA product you've ever seen was taken in IKEA's 8700 square metre photo studio in Älmhult, Sweden. Over 10 months, 285 photographers, carpenters, and interior designers craft, decorate, photograph, and take down whole kitchens, porches, and bathrooms. Even then, there was no way IKEA was able to keep up with its growing catalogue.

Enter photorealistic rendering. In 2005, IKEA tasked a few interns trained in computer graphics to create an image of an IKEA product without the aid of a camera. When no one noticed that a "fake" chair had been placed in their catalogue, IKEA began hiring teams to render more of their products. Fast forward to 2012, and 12 percent of all content was a virtual realization of the product's CAD file. By 2013 it was 25 percent.

The net benefit is less studio space, less time, and less physical waste being created—no perfectly good bathrooms have to be thrown away. Renderings can be tweaked to suit regional styles, such as darker tones for North American buyers and lighter tones for Scandinavian or Japanese consumers. Ultimately the aim is lower costs of business without sacrificing anything. So far few customers have noticed, so IKEA is moving full steam ahead with virtualizing as much of their product lines as possible.[19]

JFP/Alamy

Discussion Questions

1. **As a whole, do you think technology plays a positive or negative role in our society? Why?**
2. **In what ways can technology make you more productive? Less productive?**
3. **How long do you think you could live comfortably without a cellphone? Your iPad? A laptop/PC? Access to the Internet?**

systems have also increased the scope of automated machinery usage in the production process. Through the rapid pace of technological advancement, the use of CAD, CAM, and CIM is not limited to large mass production facilities; they are entering smaller companies as well.

How has social networking affected production? Social media capabilities enable consumers to have a direct influence on what products and services companies bring to market. They also permit customers and potential customers to give companies instant feedback, which enables companies to gather market statistics and use consumer feedback to enhance processes in the hopes of obtaining greater profits. For example, Adidas created miadidas, which is a custom-design extension of its product line. It has a company Twitter account (@miadidas) and blog (Adidas Group), as well as an interactive website that helps announce and discuss new styles.[20] Social media helps Adidas to better understand which product features are most attractive to customers and to collect information that will help it make future product decisions.

Best Buy Canada's community page on its website invites customers to participate in blog discussions and forums related to brands and products. It also provides online support from its Geek Squad and includes some common troubleshooting Q&As. Twelpforce Best Buy (on Twitter) is a collective force of Best Buy technology pros offering technical advice in Tweet form.[21] Starbucks has a My Starbucks Ideas site and Dell has an Idea Storm site where they invite customers to share product development ideas.[22] Third-party sites, such as Engadget Web magazine, have been running "How Would You Change or Improve" topics that give users a place to voice their insights and suggestions about products.[23] The Internet and social media have created a virtually new world of opportunities.

Facility Location Planning

LO3 Summarize the factors involved in choosing a manufacturing location, a facility layout, and how green manufacturing integrates sustainability into the supply chain.

What factors must be considered when determining the location of facilities? The location of a factory, office, or retail business affects its production costs and flexibility, so sound location planning is crucial. In goods-producing operations, facility location decisions are influenced by the availability and proximity of raw materials; transportation costs; labour availability; physical factors such as electrical power, water, and communication capabilities; local regulations and taxes; and community living conditions. In low-contact service-producing operations, facilities can be located near resource supplies, labour, or transportation outlets. In high-contact service-producing operations, facilities must be located near customers. For example, businesses such as restaurants, supermarkets, and hair salons choose their locations based on their *proximity to market*—they need to be close to their potential customer base. A restaurant easily visible to passing motorists and pedestrians has more of an advantage in attracting business than a restaurant tucked away in a remote part of town where few people visit.

What are the transportation factors a company must consider? Transportation costs are one of the major expenses that many manufacturing companies must consider. In fact, transportation costs for supplies coming in and goods going out can be as much as five times the costs of operating a production facility.[24] Therefore, locating a facility with easy access to natural resources or suppliers helps a business keep transportation costs low. Many automotive companies outsource their transportation systems to logistics companies that plan and execute this complex operation through logistics networks.

Transportation systems become more complex and costly when a company's supply chain is global. A **supply chain** is the sequence of organizations—their facilities and activities—that are involved in producing (right from the raw materials) and delivering (all the way to the consumer) a good or service. Supply chain facilities include warehouses,

supply chain The sequence of organizations—their facilities and activities—that are involved in producing (right from the raw materials) and delivering (all the way to the consumer) a good or service.

Comstock/Getty Images

Transportation costs are a major consideration for many manufacturing companies.

factories, processing centres, office buildings, distribution centres, and retail outlets (see **Figure 10.3**).

Businesses look to different transportation methods when receiving materials from suppliers and delivering orders to customers. A business might rely on one method of transportation or a combination of methods. Each type of transportation comes with advantages and disadvantages.

- The most common transportation mode used by suppliers and businesses is *road transport.* Not only is this method cheaper than other transportation modes, the delivery time is relatively quick and the goods can be tracked easily by communicating with the driver. This method is especially ideal for delivering perishable goods such as fresh fruit and vegetables. The disadvantages of transporting by road include possible damage to goods from rough driving, delays due to heavy traffic or bad weather, the effects of high gas prices, and the risk of late delivery if a vehicle breaks down or is involved in an accident.
- Another cost-effective transportation mode is *rail transport*, which is generally a superior choice for delivering heavy goods such as coal or steel. Railroads provide a quick and safe mode of transportation. However, rail schedules may be inflexible and wrought with unexpected delays. Rail stations are often isolated from major business areas, meaning longer delivery times and higher costs because of the need for additional forms of transportation to and from the rail station.
- When businesses receive supplies from abroad or when they export goods to foreign markets, *sea transportation* is usually the preferred mode for heavy, bulky goods such

Video: 'Made in America': Shipping to China

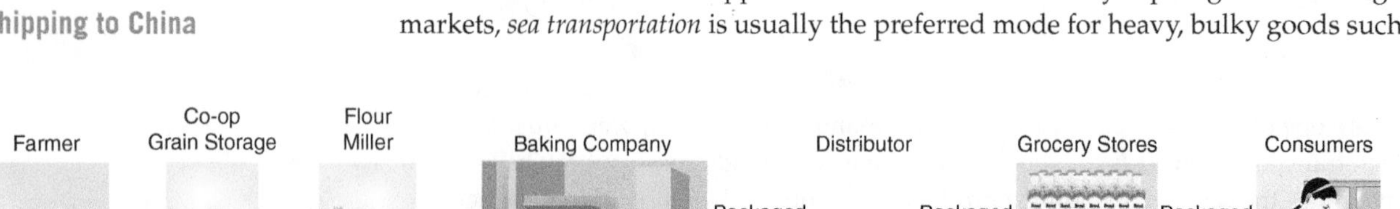

Figure 10.3 Supply Chain for Bread

as stone slabs. Sea tankers are also used to carry goods such as oil and coal. Transportation by water naturally takes more time, entails higher costs, and is subject to delays from bad weather.

- Another transportation option for companies with distant suppliers and customers is *air transport*. Although this option may not be ideal for huge or bulky goods, businesses that want to transport fragile goods are likely to use transportation by air as opposed to land. The rapid delivery time also improves service, satisfying customers who are in a rush. This method is usually the most costly. Like other transportation modes, it can be affected by bad weather, which can cause flights to be cancelled or delayed.
- Advantages of using *pipeline* as a transportation mode include its low cost, but disadvantages include slow speed and the fact that not many products can travel by pipeline.

How can organizations incorporate sustainability into the supply chain?

The goal of supply chain management is to maximize value and achieve a sustainable competitive advantage. Moreover, supply chain management helps companies reduce their carbon footprint by critically looking at each component of the supply chain (see **Figure 10.4**). Until recently, companies didn't consider the chain of activities that ultimately delivered their product to the final customer when they looked at their environmental impact. Stakeholders today are demanding business take responsibility for their impact on the environment.

Video: PTC: Green Management

As you read in the opening case, McDonald's has identified a sustainable supply chain as a focus for its sustainable operations. Their supply chain focus areas include the following:[25]

Video: Method: Operations Management & Quality

- *Sustainable land management commitment.* McDonald's aims to begin purchasing verified sustainable beef in 2016. Globally, McDonald's is committed to responsible coffee sourcing. In 2012, about 25 percent of total coffee bean purchases were from Rainforest Alliance, Fair Trade USA, or UTZ Certified farms.

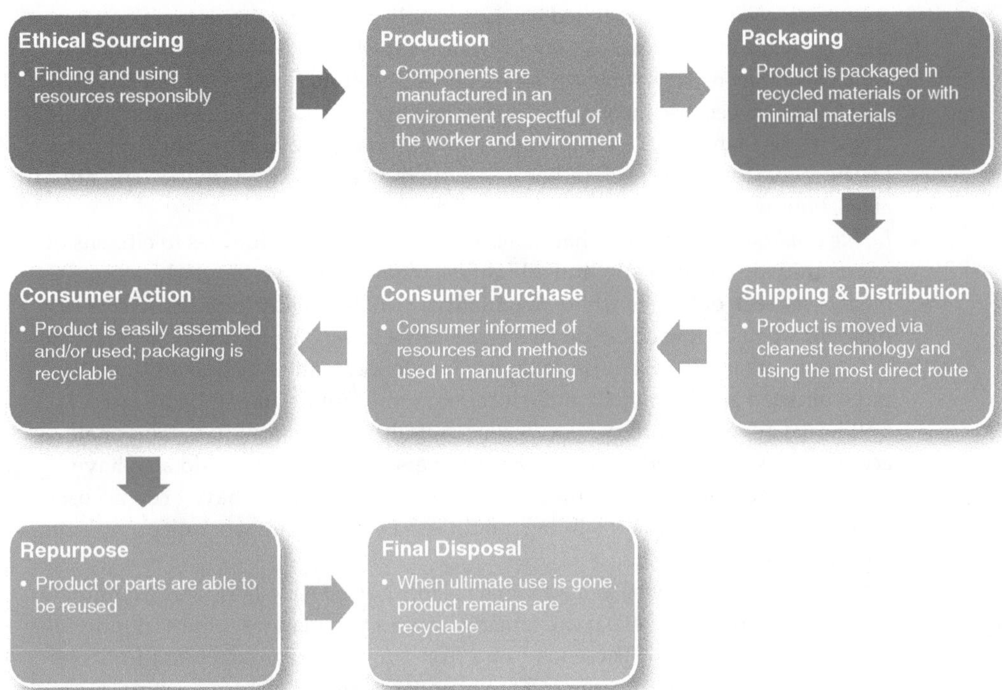

Figure 10.4 Green Supply Chain Management

As companies try to reduce their carbon footprints, they need to take a closer look at each component of the supply chain.

- *Animal health and welfare.* In 2012, McDonald's formed a new global Animal Health & Welfare Team. This group has an expanded scope that encompasses the health and welfare of animals raised for food production.
- *Supplier workplace accountability.* McDonald's puts a commitment to supply chain workers into action through the Supplier Workplace Accountability Program, which promotes a unified set of global workplace standards for *all* workers who touch the restaurant's supply chain—ensuring everyone is treated fairly and provided with a safe and healthy work environment.
- *Sustainable fisheries.* Over the past 10 years, McDonald's commitment to sustainable sourcing has been best exemplified by their global Sustainable Fisheries Program which includes global purchasing standards and annual assessments of all suppliers by the Sustainable Fisheries Partnership. As a result, 100 percent of McDonald's fish worldwide currently comes from Marine Stewardship Council–certified fisheries.

There are several initiatives in the manufacturing sector that demonstrate how today's successful organizations are embracing green manufacturing, and North American automobile manufacturers are leading the way. These companies have responded to stakeholder demands with progress in the development of electric cars and engines with much higher fuel efficiency than ever before. In General Motors's 2013 Sustainability Report,[26] the implementation of six environmental principles is facilitated by a set of environmental performance criteria (EPC) that are applied to its manufacturing facilities (and, in specific cases, to nonmanufacturing sites as well) on a global basis. These EPCs addresses common environmental issues that affect its facilities worldwide and help to develop common strategies.

human factor Refers to how a company's location decision affects the people in a surrounding community and vice versa.

What else affects location selection? The second consideration when deciding on a location for production is the **human factor**, which refers to how the location decision affects the people in a surrounding community and vice versa. Companies need to hire employees to maintain their operations, but they also need to be aware of how their presence affects the community overall. The human factor has three separate, though interrelated, components:

- *Labour availability.* Seeking skilled workers is only part of the decision-making process. Many businesses need to find a workforce that they can financially afford as well. One of the reasons some corporations send their manufacturing operations outside Canada is because those countries contain highly skilled workers who require lower wages than their Canadian counterparts. India is the number-one destination for outsourced high-tech labour because it offers an experienced, skilled, and affordable labour pool.[27]
- *Living conditions.* On the one hand, a business brings opportunities to citizens of a community by creating jobs and a higher standard of living. Similarly, many businesses seek out areas where the quality of life is already high (good schools, pleasant weather, low crime rates, etc.) before settling on a location. Some social entrepreneurs might take it upon themselves to locate their businesses in an impoverished area to revitalize the local economy. Environmentally aware politicians advocate "green collar" jobs precisely for their ability to rejuvenate economically depressed communities. Conversely, a business could also have negative effects on the surrounding area. Some corporations have been accused of worsening a community's living conditions by exploiting workers or polluting the environment.
- *Laws and regulations.* To try to maintain a balance between business and community interests, governments have created many laws and regulations to protect individuals and the environment. These may vary from province to province and from one country to another; companies need to understand which business practice laws affect their business operations and then determine whether the location is right for the company.

What are the physical factors a company must consider? When selecting a location for production, a company must also consider physical factors such as hazardous waste disposal and supply of utilities. These factors are often determined by local ordinances that may vary from province to province—and even from city to city. The **utility supply** refers to the availability of public infrastructure services such as power, water, and communications. For example, a company establishing a large facility—like a bottling plant or a warehouse—wouldn't want to situate it in a remote location with little public infrastructure, even if the land is cheap. Because such a large facility requires ample amounts of electricity or running water to operate properly, the cost to establish this infrastructure could be enormous. Moreover, locating manufacturing operations in an area where easy access to these utilities and resources is inexpensive greatly reduces costs. Another common public utility—waste management—is also essential for business operations. Just as being "off the grid" wouldn't make much sense in terms of selecting a business location, a remote location would also render waste disposal and treatment difficult.

utility supply Refers to the availability of public infrastructure services such as power, water, and communications.

Knowing how to handle hazardous waste is essential. Regardless of the type of business, understanding how to dispose of unwanted material—and the regulations involved—is an important factor to consider when selecting a location. Even everyday materials such as paint and cleaning fluids are considered hazardous waste and must be disposed of properly.[28] Many businesses, as part of their day-to-day operations, create large amounts of hazardous waste. The proper disposal of this waste has ramifications on a business's immediate vicinity. Each municipality, region, and province will have its own guidelines and procedures for dealing with hazardous waste. Responsible organizations must be aware of the disposal options available in their areas.

Taking transportation, human, and physical factors into consideration, businesses ultimately choose a manufacturing location that will enable them to remain competitive. These decisions are influenced and measured by their efficiency and practicality.

Facility Layout and Capacity Planning

Why is facility layout important? A production manager is responsible for determining the layout of a facility. **Facility layout** is the physical arrangement of resources, the people in the production process, and how they interact. The design of a facility's layout is important to maximize efficiency and satisfy employees' needs. It involves everything from the arrangement of cubicles in an office space to the position of robotic arms in an automobile manufacturing plant. When determining or renovating a facility layout for maximum effectiveness and efficiency, business owners must also consider many operational factors. For example, facilities should be designed so that they can be easily adjusted to meet changing production needs. Having to undergo extensive renovations or completely relocate as a company's operations change or expand can be a costly endeavour; therefore, managers need to be prepared to factor in possible growth at the planning stage. Additionally, the facility layout must be in accordance with Canada's Occupational Health and Safety Act and regulations to ensure worker safety. Service organizations are concerned with how the layout affects customers' behaviour, while manufacturers are concerned with efficient processes that will reduce costs.

facility layout The physical arrangement of resources, the people in the production process, and how they interact.

capacity The amount of a product or service that a company can produce under normal working conditions in a given time period.

How big should the facility be? **Capacity** is the amount of a product or service that a company can produce under normal working conditions in a given time period. Capacity is dependent on the size of the facility, the number of workers employed, and the technology and processes used. When managers plan for capacity, they must consider that if capacity is too

Nataliya Hora/Fotolia

When planning a facility's layout, every detail is important, including the space workers have to complete their tasks and where robotic arms or machines are located.

small to meet demand, the company will have to turn customers away and forgo profits; yet if capacity is too large, the firm wastes money by having employees, space, and equipment underutilized. For manufacturing facilities, capacity is determined by the extent of the production processes, whereas for service facilities, capacity is determined by peak demand and fluctuations in demand.

How does facility layout affect production? A facility layout should be able to handle materials in an orderly and efficient way to ensure a smooth flow of production. To do so, designers need to use available space effectively. Warehouses, for instance, need to have enough space to stack goods, and products need to be easily accessible for workers using equipment such as forklifts and conveyor belts.

The distance that a work in progress must travel within a facility must also be taken into account. This is not only true for the production of goods but in service industries as well. For example, the layout of a fast-food restaurant can help the employees involved in the different parts of the process—preparing food and serving customers—to work in a more integrated fashion.

What are the most common types of facility layouts? Different manufacturing processes require different types of facility layouts based on the following four common types:

- **Process layout** (or *job-shop* or *functional layout*) is a format in which workers who perform similar tasks on similar equipment are grouped together. The partially assembled product travels from one work area to the next, but not necessarily to all work areas, for workers to perform a particular process on the product. Each work area is one step in the production process. For example, all painting of parts would be done in one work area, all welding of parts in another, and all assembling in yet another, but not all products require welding so they would skip over that functional area.
- **Product layout** (or *flow-shop layout*) arranges equipment or work processes according to the progressive steps by which the product is made. It is used mostly when large quantities of a product must be produced. Products move along a straight line (assembly line) with the workstations arranged along the line. Production of toilet paper, shoes, chemicals, and candy, as well as services such as car washes, all use product layout.
- **Fixed-position layout** is a format in which the product stays in one place (fixed position) while workers and machinery move to the product to complete tasks rather than vice versa. Fixed-position layouts are ideal for manufacturing large items, such as ships, airplanes, and modular homes. Examples of fixed-position layouts in the services might include house cleaning, landscaping, and interior painting.
- **Cellular layout** (or *group technology layout*) combines aspects from both product and fixed-position layout. Workers are arranged into self-contained, stand-alone production units (or *cells* of small work teams). Each cell completes all tasks necessary to complete a manufacturing order. Each team is equipped with the machinery, parts, and tools necessary to produce a product from start to finish. Clothing manufacturing often use cellular layout.

process layout A format in which workers who perform similar tasks on similar equipment are grouped together. Also called job-shop or functional layout.

Simulation: Improving a Business

product layout A format in which equipment or work processes are arranged according to the progressive steps by which the product is made. It is used mostly when large quantities of a product must be produced. Also called flow-shop layout.

fixed-position layout A format in which the product stays in one place (fixed position) while workers and machinery move to the product to complete tasks rather than vice versa.

cellular layout A format that combines aspects from both product and fixed-position layout: Workers are arranged into self-contained, stand-alone production units (or *cells* of small work teams). Also called group technology layout.

Resource Planning

LO4 Explain how a company determines that it requires a supplier, selects a supplier, and strives to manage its supply chain.

How are materials acquired? One of the challenges in production planning is to ensure that the resources needed, such as raw materials, parts, and equipment, will be available at strategic moments in the production process. Resource planners create a **bill of material** for each product in the production process that lists the items and the number

bill of material Lists the items and the number of each required to make a specific product.

of each required to make that specific product. **Purchasing** (or *procurement*) is the task of buying the materials and services needed in the production process. Production managers need to find reliable suppliers who can provide high-quality resources at the best price.

Robert Puglia/epa/Corbis

When Mattel had to recall close to 1 million toys because of a problem with one of its suppliers, the company paid a hefty price—both financially and in damaged reputation.

purchasing The task of buying the materials and services needed in the production process. Also called procurement.

make-or-buy decision A decision about what needs to be manufactured and what needs to be purchased from outside suppliers.

Video: Olympic Athletes' Outfits Made in China

Video: Olympic Uniform Uproar Riles U.S. Manufacturers

What is a make-or-buy decision?

When starting the production process, one of the first decisions that must be made is a **make-or-buy decision**: deciding what needs to be manufactured and what needs to be purchased from outside suppliers. If a company plans to manufacture a product that will carry both the company's name and reputation, it has to decide if it will make the entire product in-house or if the product will be assembled from a combination of parts manufactured in-house and other parts purchased from suppliers. It is not always necessary for a company to make everything in-house, so how does a company decide what to make and what to buy? A company needs to consider factors such as cost and quality. If it is less expensive to outsource the production of certain parts elsewhere, that may be the best decision. However, it is important that a manager can trust the quality of any parts produced elsewhere and that appropriate quantities are delivered in a timely manner.

How does a company decide which suppliers to use?

Selecting suppliers is a significantly less complicated task than making a make-or-buy decision, but that doesn't mean that deciding which suppliers to use should receive any less consideration. After all, establishing a business relationship with a supplier is like entering into a partnership. Customers don't see a product that is supplied by one company with parts provided by different suppliers; they see a total product. Customers will hold the company responsible even if an individual supplier is to blame for making a faulty part or missing a deadline and causing a delay. For example, Mattel had to recall close to 1 million toys because its supplier in China had coated the toys in lead paint. Mattel was later fined $US2.3 million by the Consumer Product Safety Commission.[29] Such recalls can be costly and damaging to a company's reputation. So having a good supplier that meets the company's needs and cares about the company's customers as if they were its own is an invaluable asset.

A company's first step in finding suppliers involves clearly defining and understanding its needs so that it can find suppliers that truly fit its requirements. Cost is always a factor, but it should never be the sole factor. For example, if several potential suppliers offer similar products with similar prices, other factors will come into play: The company may need a supplier that is reliable or one that is fast. Likewise, one supplier may offer a part for significantly less but of such poor quality that later repairs or recalls would end up costing the company more than the cost of quality parts; its reputation would also be affected. Understanding these needs before choosing a supplier will make the process easier and more beneficial in the end.

There's a vast collection of resources designed to help businesses connect with suppliers. These resources include the Better Business Bureau, the local chamber of commerce, exhibitions, trade magazines, the Internet, and old-fashioned recommendations

supply chain management Involves the logistics of obtaining all the necessary inputs that go into a production process (*inbound logistics*), managing the actual production process (*materials handling* and *operations control*), and managing the physical distribution (*outbound logistics*) of getting the proper quantities of produced products to customers when and where they want them.

e-procurement An online purchasing system connecting companies and their business processes directly with suppliers while managing all interactions between them.

from friends and business acquaintances. The challenge is finding the best people for the job and determining which of those suppliers offer optimal solutions for production needs.

Supply chain management involves the logistics of obtaining all the necessary inputs that go into a production process (*inbound logistics*), managing the actual production process (*materials handling* and *operations control*), and managing the physical distribution (*outbound logistics*) of getting the proper quantities of produced products to customers when and where they want them. When applying supply chain management, companies are trying to reduce costs, increase flexibility and speed, and improve quality and customer service. It is crucial that companies develop tighter bonds with suppliers, as many suppliers play an important role in supporting the operations of their business customers, offering suggestions for reducing costs, and even contributing to new product design.

E-procurement is an online purchasing system connecting companies and their business processes directly with suppliers while managing all interactions between them. For example, authorized Canada Post employees have access to an e-procurement system that gives them a single portal for the acquisition of goods and services from suppliers.[30]

Better Business **Better World**

Ethical Standards for Suppliers

Many multinational companies now demand that their suppliers enforce legal and ethical business practices before they will order from them. While the notion of what is ethical varies around the globe, as do the laws, multinational companies in North America and other developed nations are putting pressure on global suppliers to do business legally and ethically or forgo the business relationship.

According to Walmart's "Standards for Suppliers," the chain has "fundamental expectations from its suppliers regarding their activities in relation to the workers producing merchandise for sale by Walmart and the impact of their manufacturing practices on the environment."[31] Standards include, but are not limited to

- abiding by the law
- not employing workers through forced or involuntary labour practices
- hiring and compensating employees in accordance with labour laws
- not giving gifts or entertainment to Walmart associates
- not using bribery or corruption in dealings with public officials or individuals in the private sector
- adhering to local environmental laws for air emissions, water discharges, toxic substances, and hazardous waste disposal

In the "Ethical Standards" section of Home Depot's *Supplier Reference Manual*, it states that the company "expects that all suppliers will abide by all applicable local laws, rules and regulations"[32] as well as adhere to the company's ethical standards. The *Supplier Reference Manual* outlines key contractual obligations suppliers need to follow to conduct business with Home Depot. The obligations include, but are not limited to

- providing transparent operations, policies, processes, and relevant records
- not employing any persons under the age of 16
- not employing workers through forced or involuntary labour practices
- abiding by the law
- compensating employees in accordance with labour laws
- not discriminating against employees
- providing safe workplaces
- providing workplaces free from corruption and fraud

Discussion Questions

1. **When multinational companies put pressure on developing countries' governments and businesses to improve workplace conditions and ethical practices are they making a difference? Why or why not?**
2. **By creating rules that suppliers must follow are companies possibly chasing away potential low-cost suppliers?**
3. **What problems might you foresee with this type of ethical procurement? How can companies ensure their suppliers are ethical?**

OPERATIONS CONTROL

LO5 Describe what value-stream mapping is and what its benefits are.

Operations Scheduling

How does routing shape the production process? **Routing** is the way in which goods are transported via water, rail, truck, or air. It includes transporting goods to a client, transporting materials from suppliers, or any of the other many combinations. Routing is actually the first step in production control. It sets out workflow, the sequence of machines and operations through which a product or service progresses from start to finish. The management of routing ensures that any transportation of goods, from the supplier, through the facility, and to the customer, is done at a minimum of cost, time, and distance without sacrificing quality. One useful tool for routing is **value-stream mapping**, which identifies all the flows and resources required to deliver a product: people, technologies, physical facilities, communication and transportation channels, policies, and procedures. It enables a company to identify and eliminate waste, thereby streamlining work processes, cutting lead times, reducing costs, and increasing quality. Anything that does not add value to the end customer is waste.

routing The way in which goods are transported (to a client, from a supplier, or any other combination) via water, rail, truck, or air.

value-stream mapping Identifies all the flows and resources required to deliver a product: people, technologies, physical facilities, communication and transportation channels, policies, and procedures.

How does scheduling shape the production process? Related to routing is scheduling. **Scheduling** involves specifying and controlling the time required for each step in the production process as well as making the most efficient use of equipment, facilities, labour, and materials. There are two different types of scheduling: *forward* and *backward*. With *forward scheduling*, you start with the date that materials are available, create the most efficient schedule, and then determine a shipping date based on that schedule. *Backward scheduling* is the exact opposite, where you are given a shipping or due date and you have to determine the start date and the most efficient schedule based on when everything has to be finished.

Two major components go into making an effective schedule: loading and sequencing. *Loading* is assigning a job to a specific machine or work centre. *Sequencing* is assigning the order in which jobs are processed. A **master production schedule** shows the resources that will be used to produce specific products during the scheduled time. There are numerous tools designed to help managers ensure that all the right resources are working on the right jobs at the right times. Two of the most commonly used tools are *Gantt charts* and *PERT charts.*

scheduling Involves specifying and controlling the time required for each step in the production process as well as making the most efficient use of equipment, facilities, labour, and materials.

master production schedule Shows which products will be produced, when production will occur, and what resources will be used during the scheduled time.

What is a Gantt chart? One method for monitoring the progress of a given project is a Gantt chart, a tool developed by Henry Gantt in the 1920s. A **Gantt chart**, formatted similarly to a horizontal bar graph, is used to lay out each task in a project, the order in which these tasks must be completed, and how long each task should take. **Figure 10.5** shows an example of a Gantt chart for a remodelling project. Originally used for large-scale construction projects, such as building the Hoover Dam between Nevada and Arizona in the 1930s, Gantt charts are still used today to manage a variety of both large-scale and small-scale projects. At any point in the process, project managers and manufacturers can see at a glance which tasks have been completed and whether these tasks were completed on schedule.

Gantt chart A chart that is formatted similarly to a horizontal bar graph and is used to lay out each task in a project, the order in which these tasks must be completed, and how long each task should take.

What is a PERT chart? The **program evaluation and review technique (PERT)** was first used in the development of submarines in the 1950s. This method maps out the various steps involved in a project, differentiating tasks that must be completed in a certain order from tasks that may be completed simultaneously. The result is a web-like diagram similar to the example shown in **Figure 10.6**.

In creating a PERT chart, time estimates are assigned to each task. Creating the chart helps identify the *critical path*, or the path of sequential tasks that will take the longest amount of time to complete. This helps managers determine an overall timeline for completing a project or, from a manufacturing standpoint, producing a particular good or service. However, because delays can cause the critical path in a project to change, PERT charts are limited in their ability to predict project completion times.

program evaluation and review technique (PERT) Maps out the various steps involved in a project, differentiating tasks that must be completed in a certain order from tasks that may be completed simultaneously.

Remodelling Project

Remodelling Project Job No.: 980015.05	Jul '15			Aug '15				Sep '15					Oct '15	
	15	22	29	5	12	19	26	2	9	16	23	30	7	14
Project Summary														
Soft Demo														
Soft Demo-Structural														
Structural Steel-Fab														
Framing-Rough														
Skylights														
Roof Curbs & Patch														
Electrical-Rough/Finish														
Overhead Doors														
Inspection-Structural Rebar														
Structural Concrete-Pour														
Service/Repair Elevator														
Plumbing Rough														
Data/Phone Cabling														
Structural Steel-Install														
T-bar Grid Repair														
Inspection-Walls														
Inspection-Drywall Screw														
Mud & Tape														
Mezzanine Demo														

Figure 10.5 Sample Gantt Chart

Created with KIDASA Software, Inc's Milestones Software. Reprinted by permission.

Is scheduling for service operations the same as scheduling for production operations? In low-contact service operations, schedules may be based either on the desired completion date or on the time of order arrival. For example, an auto-repair shop may schedule various customer jobs on different days of the week and at different times; although you'd like your car serviced today, you may be on the schedule for tomorrow. In such businesses, appointment systems help to balance demand. In high-contact service

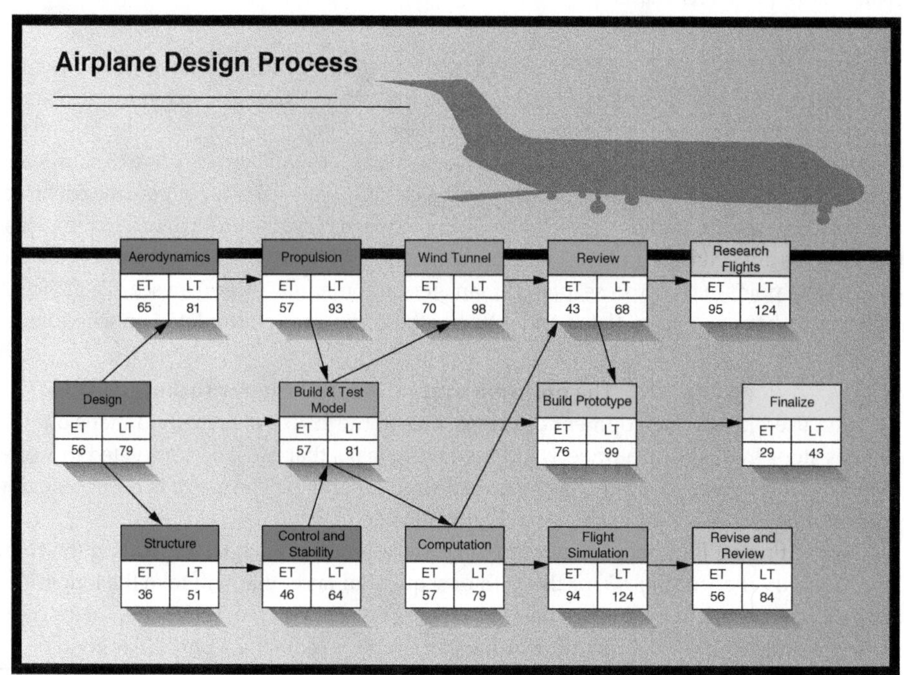

Figure 10.6 Sample PERT Chart

operations, precise scheduling of services may not be possible because it is difficult to balance. For example, some health clinics take appointments as well as accommodate walk-in patients. If a patient with an appointment cancels at the last minute or does not show up, then the appointment time is wasted unless there is a walk-in patient to take that time slot. Walk-in patients don't want to have long wait times, nor do scheduled patients, but if the doctor sees too many walk-in patients throughout the day then scheduled patients will have longer wait times and may begin to look for another clinic to use in the future. If the doctor does not see enough walk-in patients throughout the day, then this group will have longer wait times or may not be seen at all, and they will also begin to look for another clinic to use in the future. Due to the difficulty of balancing the schedule, some clinics do not accept walk-in patients.

Inventory Control

LO6 Explain the benefits of just-in-time (JIT) production and enterprise resource planning (ERP).

What's the best way to manage inventory? **Inventory control** includes the receiving, storing, handling, and tracking of everything in a company's stock, from raw materials to finished products. Inventory often makes up a large portion of a business's expenses. Therefore, proper management is not only a way to stay informed, it's necessary to keep costs low while ensuring that all necessary materials are in stock and stored in the proper place. There are four main types of stock: raw materials, unfinished products, finished products, and consumables (such as pens and paper). Maintaining each of these kinds of stock helps determine where money should and shouldn't be spent. Proper maintenance keeps track of things such as products that have shelf lives that could deteriorate or products that have become obsolete or where more stock than necessary is being purchased. Ensuring an adequate supply of finished products or other types of stock is further complicated when customer demand is variable.

inventory control Includes the receiving, storing, handling, and tracking of everything in a company's stock, from raw materials to finished products. Inventory often makes up a large portion of a business's expenses.

Managing stock can be achieved in a number of different ways, and no single method works best for every business. Factors such as the size of the business, the amount of inventory necessary, the amount of inventory storage space, and the proximity to suppliers all contribute to which inventory control method will work best for an individual company. The least involved way to manage inventory is simply to estimate it. This method works really well for smaller companies or companies that don't maintain large amounts of stock. When accuracy is a necessity, a *stock book solution*, where stock on hand is tallied in a book along with stock on order and stock that has been sold, would probably work best. Another less complicated management system is called the *reserve stock system*. This is where stock is set aside in reserve so that it cannot be used. The company goes through its inventory as it regularly would, and when it has to dip into the reserve stock it knows it is time to reorder that item. It is important for managers to keep in mind when using this system that however much stock is in reserve should be enough to last the amount of time it takes to resupply.[33]

Whereas these systems can work well with smaller businesses, larger businesses generally require a more complicated inventory management system. A **just-in-time (JIT) inventory control** system keeps the smallest amount of inventory on hand as possible, and everything else that is needed is ordered so that it arrives just in time to be used. Storing fewer items and using items right away can reduce storage costs. Dell Computers adopted JIT inventory control. By manufacturing computers to customer specifications, Dell orders only the specific parts needed to complete those orders, thereby reducing expenses (less storage, fewer damaged parts, fewer obsolete parts).[34]

just-in-time (JIT) inventory control An inventory control system that keeps the smallest amount of inventory on hand as possible, and everything else that is needed is ordered so that it arrives just in time to be used.

This system, however, is not without its drawbacks. To work properly, a company must have a very good relationship with its suppliers to ensure that appropriate quantities arrive on time and where they are needed. Even then, if a supplier is far away there may be shipping delays caused by bad weather. The shipping costs, too, may become quite high.

Video: Toyota: Outsourcing and Logistics

How is technology used to streamline inventory control? Many organizations rely on a computerized inventory system that uses a barcode or **radio frequency identification (RFID)** tag on each item, allowing a computer to keep track of the status

radio frequency identification (RFID) A tag that allows a computer to keep track of the status and quantity of each item.

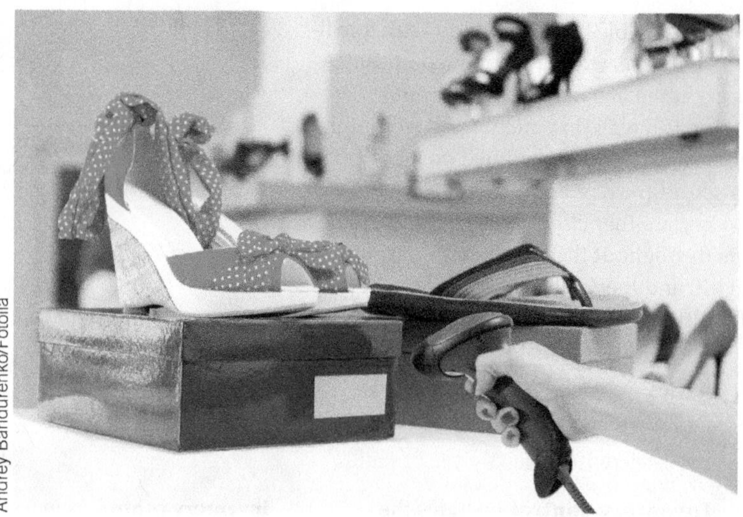
Andrey Bandurenko/Fotolia

With the use of barcodes and RFIDs, items can be scanned and inventory can be monitored electronically.

and quantity of each item. Each item is logged and classified when it is stocked and an identifying barcode or RFID is attached to the item. Both barcodes and RFIDs store all the specific information for each item, such as cost, stock number, and storage location. Using these systems, items in inventory can be scanned when they are used or sold, and the computer can continuously update the information for each item. Depending on the system used, computerized inventory makes it easier to analyze the quantitative factors of managing stock, such as how quickly each item is sold, how much really needs to be held in inventory at one time, and when it's time to restock items.

What is materials requirement planning (MRP)? **Materials requirement planning (MRP)** is a type of software system used to schedule and monitor the use of components and other materials in a manufacturing operation. When an order is made, the specifics of that order are put into the MRP. The MRP then determines which parts will be needed to finish the job and compares these findings to the current inventory. Based on this information, it highlights what needs to be obtained, either through production or a supplier, as well as when the parts will be needed. It uses previous manufacturing data to break the job into parts. A process is input into the system, and the MRP portion of the system determines which components are needed when to meet customers' order quantities and due dates. The result should be the best estimate based on previous data. Knowing these estimates helps determine both part and labour shortages before a project even starts. There are many limitations to MRP, though, the biggest being that it is only as effective as its data. So if its data are not well maintained, the estimates that it provides will only become increasingly useless. Another limitation to MRP is its scope: It only focuses on the management of needed component parts in the *manufacturing* processes of a company.

materials requirement planning (MRP) A type of software system used to schedule and monitor the use of components and other materials in a manufacturing operation.

While MRP is concerned primarily with manufacturing materials, **manufacturing resource planning (MRPII)** is concerned with integrating and coordinating data from many departments, including manufacturing, finance, marketing, and human resources. MRPII can not only generate a production plan but also various management reports, forecasts, and financial statements.

manufacturing resource planning (MRPII) Uses software to integrate data from many departments, including manufacturing, finance, marketing, and human resources.

Enterprise resource planning (ERP) systems give companies the ability to streamline the various workflows and share information across departments by consolidating information into a central database accessible to various system modules (company departments). This allows for improved productivity from all employees. With an ERP system in place, the various aspects of an organization can work together without worrying about compatible software. Unfortunately, there are disadvantages for a business that fails to invest fully in an ERP system. These problems can range from inadequate tech support to limited customization of the system. Companies that specialize in ERP systems include Oracle, SAP, and Microsoft.

enterprise resource planning (ERP) systems Give companies the ability to streamline the various workflows and share information across departments by consolidating information into a central database accessible to various system modules (company departments).

Quality Control

LO7 Describe quality control, how ISO standards help companies produce high-quality goods and services, and the application of sustainability to operations management.

Has quality control always been part of the production process? The use of techniques, activities, and processes to guarantee that a certain good or service meets a specified level of quality is referred to as **quality control**. Quality control is essential in maintaining both the reputation of a business and consumer safety. Customers demand quality and expect products they purchase to be reliable, safe, and provide utility (value). They also expect quality service from the company employees they interact with. If

quality control The use of techniques, activities, and processes to guarantee that a certain good or service meets a specified level of quality.

customers do not perceive that they have received a quality product or service, they will not make a repeat purchase. Customer loyalty is an important element to company success, and to create a satisfied customer a company must deliver a high-quality product or service as well as excellent customer service.

The old method of quality assurance was to delegate quality control to a separate department that would inspect and test products for flaws after the product had been manufactured. This inspection method of quality control involves checking work at the *end* of the process before products are delivered. Unfortunately, several problems arise using this method, including the expense in terms of time, labour, and employee confidence. Because inspection is performed by outside people instead of by the workers, each inspector can pass or fail a product using his or her own standards and procedures. Moreover, inspecting finished products and discovering defects means some of these defects have to be scrapped or reworked, which can be costly.

What methods are used to improve quality? Merely controlling for quality through inspection and monitoring employees is like visiting the doctor for treating symptoms as opposed to the source of an illness. Since the 1980s firms have been focusing on building quality into every step of the production process instead of merely taking actions to scrap or fix defects. This concept of "total quality" at every stage of a production process was only embraced in North America after Japanese manufacturers implemented company-wide quality improvement methods and strengthened their presence in the global market.[35] Unlike the old inspection method of quality control, in which products are reviewed at certain points of the process (usually the end), total quality management involves every factor in producing high-quality goods—management, customers, employees, and suppliers. At any point, employees and leaders are aiming to produce high quality.

total quality management (TQM) Emphasizes the use of quality principles in all aspects of a company's production and operations.

Total quality management (TQM) involves ongoing improvement of products, services, and processes. This can be accomplished by undertaking a Plan, Do, Check, Act (PDCA) cycle, created by American statistician W. Edwards Deming (see **Figure 10.7**).[36] Using the PDCA, organizations first formulate a plan to reduce potential errors, carry out

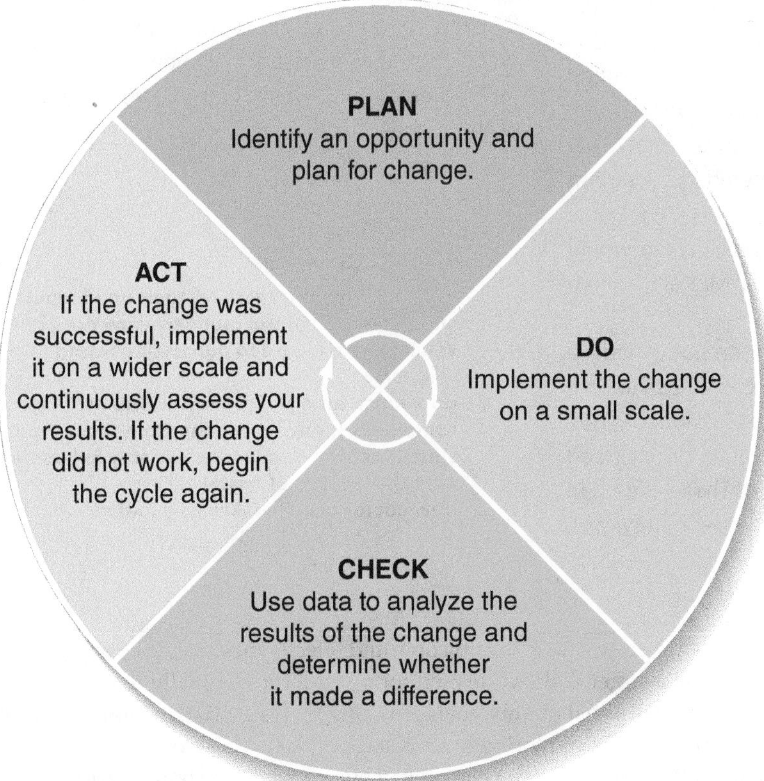

Figure 10.7 Quality—PDCA

Off the Mark

Quality Catastrophes

There was a time when people would buy Toyota vehicles solely based on the automaker's reputation for excellent quality and durability, but its longstanding reputation has been heavily questioned in the last few years. While trying to recover from a painful public relations blow over the "sticky" accelerator pedal recall, among 16 others in 2010 (involving more than 700 000 vehicles), Toyota Canada took yet another hit in 2011 when it had to notify 11 700 Lexus owners about the possibility of improperly installed fuel pressure sensors that could eventually leak. The Lexus recall in Canada was part of a larger Lexus recall in Japan (affecting 1.3 million models), a sedan and station wagon recall in Europe and New Zealand, and a Daihatsu Motors truck recall. Toyota Canada officials said the recalls have hurt sales, but the company has put teams in place around the world to address customer concerns and resolve problems quickly.[37]

In 2007, Mattel's long history of producing safe, high-quality toys also came into question. Two weeks after the toymaker recalled more than 1 million Chinese-made toys in the United States because of excessive lead in the paint (lead is toxic if ingested), it had to recall another 18 million toys worldwide because of small magnets that posed a swallowing hazard *and* excessive lead in the paint. Mattel stated that it did not know whether the contracted Chinese manufacturer substituted paint from a noncertified supplier or if a certified paint supplier caused the problem, but it would ensure that Chinese-made toys are safe for North American consumers. Mattel offered replacement products to all consumers who had purchased the recalled products and estimated that the first recall alone would cost US$30 million in profits. This was Mattel's seventeenth recall in 10 years.[38]

The Bridgestone/Firestone tire company had to endure a major crisis because of poor quality assurance. In 2000, millions of its ATX, ATX II, and Firestone Wilderness radial tires had to be recalled because of tire tread separation, which caused SUV rollovers. These tires had not been adequately tested for quality and safety, and they caused numerous accidents because of their defects. Many people were injured and some were killed because of this lack of quality management, and Bridgestone/Firestone had to pay the Ford Motor Company US$240 million to settle claims from injured motorists.[39] This crisis could have been prevented had the company taken greater quality control measures in the production of these tires.

FORD MOTOR CO./AP Images

Discussion Questions

1. **How do companies recover their good reputation after a quality control blunder? How does it make you feel with regard to purchasing from these companies?**
2. **How much time and money do you estimate companies spend recovering from these types of situations? How do companies stay in business after these types of mistakes?**
3. **How could such mistakes be avoided?**

statistical quality control (SQC) The continual monitoring of each stage of the entire production process to ensure that quality standards are being met at every stage.

the plan on a small scale, check the outcome and effectiveness of the change, then implement the plan on a larger scale while monitoring results continually. One popular tool used to check or measure if quality goals are being met is **statistical quality control (SQC)**, or the continual monitoring of each stage of the entire production process to ensure that quality standards are being met at every stage. **Statistical process control (SPC)** uses statistical sampling of products at every phase of production and displays the results on a graph to show potential variations that need to be corrected. A common SPC tool is **Six Sigma**, a method that seeks to eliminate defects by removing variation in outcomes and measuring and analyzing manufacturing processes to see if standards are being met. A company with Six Sigma quality produces at a low defect rate of just 3.4 defects per million opportunities.

statistical process control (SPC) Uses statistical sampling of products at every phase of production and displays the results on a graph to show potential variations that need to be corrected.

Six Sigma A method that seeks to eliminate defects by removing variation in outcomes and measuring and analyzing manufacturing processes to see if standards are being met.

How does TQM cater to the customer? It is not enough simply to implement quality management tools. A significant aspect of TQM is catering to the customer's needs and desires. SGL Carbon, a manufacturer of graphite specialties, emphasizes adherence to a TQM approach by giving its customers the final say in determining whether a product meets the requirements of high-quality standards. Although firms may define in the beginning what makes their products high quality or low quality, those companies that learn how to simultaneously emphasize quality throughout the production process and incorporate the desires of customers will make a greater presence in the global marketplace.

What is the ISO? The **International Organization for Standardization (ISO)** is an organization dedicated to creating worldwide standards of quality for goods and services. ISO was established in 1947 and is headquartered in Geneva, Switzerland. The organization has published more than 18 500 International Standards and more than 1000 new ISO standards are published every year.[40] ISO standards facilitate trade, spread knowledge, share technological advances, and share good management and leadership practices. The ISO standards apply not to the products themselves, but to the production methods and systems used to manufacture them, as well as other areas, such as communication within the company and leadership. Such a standardized system is necessary to avoid trying to comply with various conflicting systems.

International Organization for Standardization (ISO) An organization dedicated to creating worldwide standards of quality for goods and services.

What is the ISO certification process? The **ISO 9000** is a set of five technical standards of quality management created by the International Organizations for Standardization to provide a uniform way of determining whether organizations conform to sound quality procedures. Since then, more than 90 countries have adopted these standards, and thousands of companies require their products to be ISO 9000 certified. Some industries have even developed their own industry-specific set of ISO standards. Certification is usually done by a third-party registrar who assesses the company's quality assurance manuals and practices. First, a pre-assessment must be conducted, during which the registrar reviews the documents that outline the company's standards and processes. If the manual and other printed documents pass the review, the company can proceed with the rest of the assessment. If the registrar finds errors in these documents, further review will have to be delayed until the mistakes are corrected.

ISO 9000 A set of five technical standards of quality management created by the International Organizations for Standardization to provide a uniform way of determining whether organizations conform to sound quality procedures.

During the formal assessment, the registrar reviews the corrected documents and interviews the employees and administrators of the company. The goal of this part of the assessment is to ensure that written policies and procedures are being implemented in the company's production methods. Finally, the registrar issues an audit report summarizing the results of the assessment and listing any areas that need improvement. If corrections are required at this stage, the company can make them and document them in a report to the registrar. After satisfactory corrections have been made, the registrar can then award certification to the company. Once it has earned certification, the company can put the ISO 9000 seal in advertising and on its letterhead.

After certification, the registrar returns to the company twice a year to make sure the company complies with the ISO standards. These spot

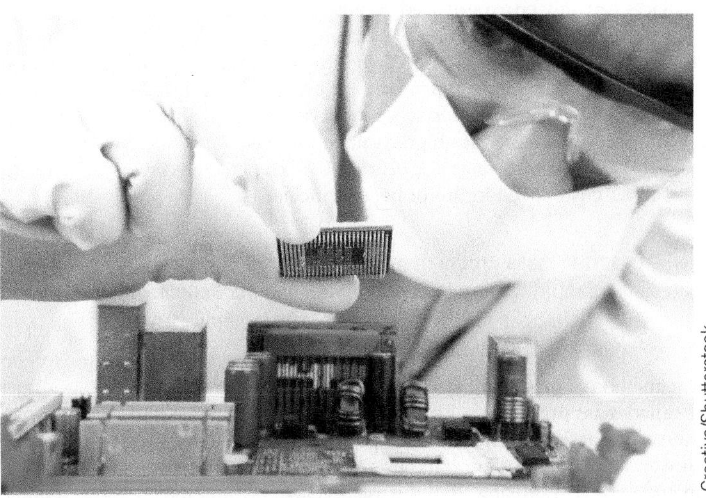

Creativa/Shutterstock

ISO 9000 standards were designed to ensure companies adhere to strict quality control measures. Once a company has been certified, they are able to use the ISO 9000 seal on company materials.

checks are conducted without advance warning, and the registrar focuses on areas that were notably weak during the initial assessment. Every three years the registrar will complete another assessment and issue a new audit report. The company must also establish an internal auditing program that is responsible for keeping the ISO standards in practice.

ISO 14000 Launched after ISO 9000, a set of standards designed to promote clean production processes in response to environmental issues such as global warming and water pollution.

The **ISO 14000**, launched after ISO 9000, is designed to promote clean production processes in response to environmental issues such as global warming and water pollution. Requirements for certification include documenting an environmental policy, invoking an environmental management system, and keeping control records pertaining to both. ISO 14000 ensures that "environmental management" is a continuously improving process to minimize harmful environment affects.[41]

In 2010, over 30 billion tonnes of carbon dioxide were released into the atmosphere worldwide—that is an enormous amount of the greenhouse gas emissions that cause global warming. The International Standard ISO 14067, *Carbon footprint of products—Requirements and guidelines for quantification and communication*, is being developed to increase transparency in quantifying and reporting carbon dioxide emissions over the entire life cycle of products and services—from production to recycling or waste disposal.[42]

CHAPTER SYNOPSIS

LO1 Explain how operations management produces finished goods that provide utility to consumers, and differentiate between goods and service operations. *(pp. 244–247)*

Operations management (or production management) refers to the organized direction and control of the processes that transform resources (inputs) into finished goods and services (outputs). The act of production gives these finished products and services **value**, or *utility*. Products and services provide businesses with economic results (profits, wages, suppliers) and provide customers with utility, which is the power of a product or service to satisfy a human want or need.

Both service and manufacturing operations transform raw materials (inputs) into finished products (outputs), but in service operations the outputs are people with their needs met and possessions serviced. Goods are produced; services are performed. There are three areas where services differ from goods:

1. *Services are intangible.* Goods are tangible—they have a physical form and can be seen, touched, and handled—while services can only be experienced because they do not have a physical form.
2. *Services are unstorable.* Goods can be stored in inventory, but services are consumed when they are produced. Trash collection, childcare, or mail services cannot be produced ahead of time and then stored for high-demand periods.
3. *Services are more customizable than goods.* Each person receives service customized for his or her specific needs.

LO2 Describe mass production, mass customization, flexible manufacturing, and lean production and the benefits and challenges of each, including how technology influences the production process. *(pp. 247–251)*

The method of producing large quantities of goods at a low cost is called **mass production**. This method relies on machines and automated **assembly lines** to mass produce goods that are identical and adhere to certain standards of quality. The advantages include low costs arising from the use of machines, automated processes and low-skilled labour, less production time, and elimination of human error. The major disadvantage is inflexibility. **Mass customization** combines the low unit cost of mass production processes with the flexibility of producing goods or services tailored to meet individual customer's needs.

A solution to the rigid system of mass production is flexible production, also known as a **flexible manufacturing system (FMS)**. An FMS uses one central computer to link together several machines that can process different part types simultaneously. Unlike a mass production system, an FMS can adapt to changes in schedules and product specifications.

Lean production is a set of principles concerned with reducing waste and improving flow. Its objective is to focus all resources and energies into producing products and services with value-added characteristics (utility to the consumer) while eliminating activities that are of no value.

Technology plays an integral role in facilitating the flow of any production process. When managed efficiently, the technological aspect of a production process should lead to increases in production and reductions in costs. Technology may also improve the quality and increase the variety of products, which influences the customer's buying decisions. **Computer-aided design (CAD)** refers to the use of a computer to create two-dimensional or three-dimensional models of physical parts. Once a design is approved, **computer-aided manufacturing (CAM)** uses the design data to control the machinery used in the manufacturing process. **Computer-integrated manufacturing (CIM)** takes it even further by combining design and manufacturing functions with other functions such as order taking, shipping, and billing.

LO3 Summarize the factors involved in choosing a manufacturing location, a facility layout, and how green manufacturing integrates sustainability into the supply chain. *(pp. 251–256)*

In goods-producing operations, facility location decisions are influenced by the availability and proximity of raw materials; transportation costs; labour availability; physical factors such as electrical power, water, and communication capabilities; local regulations and taxes; and community living conditions. In low-contact service-producing operations, facilities can be located near resource supplies, labour, or transportation outlets. In high-contact service-producing operations, facilities must be located near customers.

The goal of supply chain management is to maximize value and achieve a sustainable competitive advantage. Moreover, supply chain management helps companies reduce their carbon footprint by critically looking at each component of the supply chain (see the figure below). Until recently, companies didn't consider the chain of activities that ultimately delivered their product to the final customer when they looked at their environmental impact. Stakeholders today are demanding businesses take responsibility for their impact on the environment—which is bringing green manufacturing or sustainable manufacturing to the forefront of corporate social responsibility strategies.

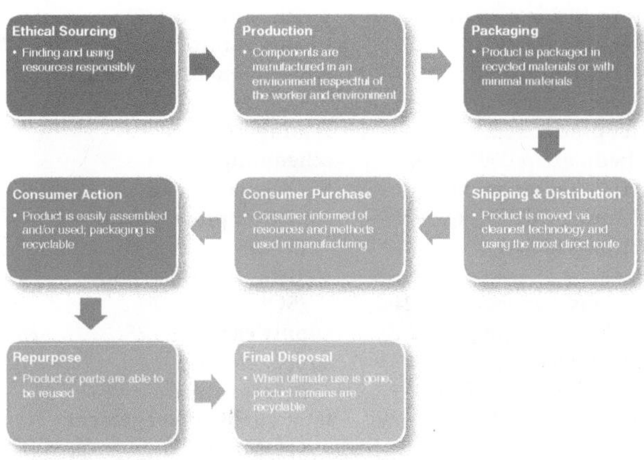

Green Supply Chain Management

Facility layout is the physical arrangement of resources, the people in the production process, and how they interact. When determining or renovating a facility layout for maximum effectiveness and efficiency, business owners must also consider many operational factors. The facility layout should be in accordance with Occupational Health and Safety Act and regulations to ensure worker safety. Service organizations are concerned with how the layout affects customers' behaviour, while manufacturers are concerned with efficient processes that will reduce costs. Four common types of layouts are **process**, **product**, **cellular**, and **fixed position**.

Capacity is the amount of a product or service that a company can produce under normal working conditions in a given time period. Capacity is dependent on the size of the facility, the number of workers employed, and the technology and processes used. For manufacturing facilities, capacity is determined by the extent of the production processes, whereas for service facilities, capacity is determined by peak demand and fluctuations in demand.

LO4 Explain how a company determines that it requires a supplier, selects a supplier, and strives to manage its supply chain. *(pp. 256–258)*

If a company plans to manufacture a product that will carry both the company's name and reputation, it has to decide if it will make the entire product in-house or if the product will be assembled from a combination of parts manufactured in-house and other parts purchased from suppliers. This is known as the **make-or-buy decision**. A company needs to consider factors such as cost and quality. If it is less expensive to outsource the production of certain parts elsewhere, that may be the best decision. However, it is important that a manager can trust the quality of any parts that are produced elsewhere and that appropriate quantities are delivered in a timely manner.

A company's first step in finding suppliers involves clearly defining and understanding its needs so that it can find suppliers that truly fit its requirements. Cost is always a factor, but it should never be the sole factor.

Supply chain management involves the logistics of obtaining all the necessary inputs that go into a production process (*inbound logistics*), managing the actual production process (*materials handling* and *operations control*), and managing the physical distribution (*outbound logistics*) of getting the proper quantities of produced products to customers when and where they want them. When applying supply chain management, companies are trying to reduce costs, increase flexibility and speed, and improve quality and customer service. It is crucial that companies develop tighter bonds with suppliers, as many suppliers play an important role in supporting the operations of their business customers, offering suggestions for reducing costs, and even contributing to new product design.

LO5 Describe what value-stream mapping is and what its benefits are. *(pp. 259–261)*

One useful tool for **routing** is **value-stream mapping**, which identifies all the flows and resources required to deliver a product: people, technologies, physical facilities, communication and transportation channels, policies, and procedures. It enables a company to identify and eliminate waste, thereby streamlining work processes, cutting lead times, reducing costs, and increasing quality. Anything that does not add value to the end customer is waste.

LO6 Explain the benefits of just-in-time (JIT) production and enterprise resource planning (ERP). *(pp. 261–262)*

A **just-in-time (JIT) inventory control** system keeps the smallest amount of inventory on hand as possible, and everything else needed is ordered so that it arrives just in time to be used. Storing fewer items and using items right away can reduce storage costs.

Enterprise resource planning (ERP) systems allow companies the ability to streamline the various workflows and share information across departments by consolidating information into a central database accessible to various system modules (company departments). This allows for improved productivity from all employees. With an ERP system in place, the various aspects of an organization can work together without worrying about compatible software. Unfortunately, there are disadvantages for a business that fails to invest fully in an ERP system. These problems can range from inadequate tech support to limited customization of the system. Companies that specialize in ERP systems include Oracle, SAP, and Microsoft.

LO7 Describe quality control, how ISO standards help companies produce high-quality goods and services, and the application of sustainability to operations management. *(pp. 262–266)*

The use of techniques, activities, and processes to guarantee that a certain good or service meets a specified level of quality is referred to as **quality control**. The **International Organization for Standardization (ISO)** is an organization dedicated to creating worldwide standards of quality for goods and services. ISO standards facilitate trade, spread knowledge, share technological advances, and share good management and leadership practices. The ISO standards apply not to the products themselves, but to the production methods and systems used to manufacture them, as well as other areas, such as communication within the company and leadership. Such a standardized system is necessary to avoid trying to comply with various conflicting systems.

MyBizLab Study, practise, and explore real business situations with these helpful resources:

- **Interactive Lesson Presentations:** Work through interactive presentations and assessments to test your knowledge of business concepts.
- **Study Plan:** Check your understanding of chapter concepts with self-study quizzes.
- **Dynamic Study Modules:** Work through adaptive study modules on your computer, tablet, or mobile device.
- **Simulations:** Practise decision-making in simulated business environments.

KEY TERMS

assembly line *(p. 247)*
bill of material *(p. 256)*
capacity *(p. 255)*
cellular layout *(p. 256)*
computer-aided design (CAD) *(p. 249)*
computer-aided manufacturing (CAM) *(p. 250)*
computer-integrated manufacturing (CIM) *(p. 250)*
effectiveness *(p. 246)*
efficiency *(p. 246)*
enterprise resource planning (ERP) systems *(p. 262)*
e-procurement *(p. 258)*
facility layout *(p. 255)*
fixed-position layout *(p. 256)*
flexible manufacturing system (FMS) *(p. 248)*
Gantt chart *(p. 259)*
high-contact service processes *(p. 246)*
human factor *(p. 254)*
International Organization for Standardization (ISO) *(p. 265)*
inventory control *(p. 261)*
ISO 9000 *(p. 265)*
ISO 14000 *(p. 266)*
just-in-time (JIT) inventory control *(p. 261)*
lean production *(p. 248)*
low-contact service processes *(p. 247)*
make-or-buy decision *(p. 257)*
manufacturing resource planning (MRPII) *(p. 262)*
mass customization *(p. 248)*
mass production *(p. 247)*
master production schedule *(p. 259)*
materials requirement planning (MRP) *(p. 262)*
operations management *(p. 245)*
operations managers *(p. 246)*
operations planning *(p. 246)*
process layout *(p. 256)*
product layout *(p. 256)*
production *(p. 244)*
production plan *(p. 246)*
program evaluation and review technique (PERT) *(p. 259)*
purchasing *(p. 257)*
quality control *(p. 262)*
radio frequency identification (RFID) *(p. 261)*
routing *(p. 259)*
scheduling *(p. 259)*
Six Sigma *(p. 265)*
statistical process control (SPC) *(p. 264)*
statistical quality control (SQC) *(p. 264)*
supply chain *(p. 251)*
supply chain management *(p. 258)*
total quality management (TQM) *(p. 263)*
utility supply *(p. 255)*
value *(p. 245)*
value-stream mapping *(p. 259)*

CRITICAL THINKING QUESTIONS

1. What are the advantages and disadvantages of mass production and the mechanized assembly line? Did this shift to machines and robots eliminate jobs, or did it create new ones?
2. What are the resources (inputs) needed and the finished products (outputs) for each of the following service companies: a childcare centre, a bank, an auto-repair shop?
3. A sports equipment company is known for a special grip on its tennis racquets that is imported from South America. The cost of shipping these grips has grown steadily more expensive, and the business would like to produce the grips in-house. What factors does the business need to consider before adding another step to the production process?
4. How does a business decide what the best method of shipment is for its products? What factors, other than cost, are important in this decision?
5. Give an example of what the process of total quality management (TQM) would involve in the production of automobiles. What steps can manufacturers take to ensure that a high level of quality is maintained consistently in their production processes?

TEAM TIME

To Outsource or Not to Outsource . . . That Is the Question

Divide into two teams to represent both sides of the issue.

a. Your group thinks the company should make the component.
b. Your group thinks the company should outsource the component.

SCENARIO

The Fathertime Supply Company of Manitoba is attempting to expand its manufacturing of large wall clocks. In years past, the company has outsourced the manufacturing of clock springs to a company in Newfoundland. This has been cost effective in the past, but now that demand for the springs has increased, Fathertime is considering manufacturing the springs in-house. Although the cost of producing the springs in-house is lower, it is unclear whether it will be profitable in the end, as the manufacturing process will change greatly. New machines for the production of springs will be needed, as the factory works exclusively in wood and plastic. With the new machines comes the need for new technicians to monitor and service them. Should the Fathertime Supply Company alter its manufacturing process to include the production of clock springs, or should it continue outsourcing to Newfoundland as it has in the past? What factors contribute to this decision? Will this be more profitable in the end? How will it affect employee morale and relations?

PROCESS

Step 1. Record your ideas and opinions about the issue presented in the scenario above. Be sure to consider the issue from your assigned perspective.

Step 2. Meet as a team and review the issue from both perspectives. Discuss together why the position of your group is the best decision.

ETHICS AND RESPONSIBILITY

Environmental Shipping Concerns

You have just been promoted to head of the shipping department for your office supply company, and it is now your responsibility to determine routing. The company is located on the west coast, near major highways as well as the ocean. In the past, trucking has been the preferred method of shipping, as it was deemed the most cost effective. Shipping the freight by boat, however, would greatly reduce the negative effects on the environment caused by truck emissions. After calculating the cost on paper, you realize that shipping by sea would have a negative effect on the overall profit margin, but the company would still generate solid profits.

DISCUSSION QUESTIONS

1. What decision would you make in this situation: land or sea?
2. If you were told that you would take a personal pay cut from switching to the more environmentally friendly route, how would that affect your decision?
3. What kind of impact do you think one company switching to less environmentally damaging practices could have on the general atmosphere of the shipping world?

CLOSING CASE

Just in Time for Toyota

Since Toyota Motor Corporation's inception, it has prided itself on having a lean production system that manages equipment, people, and materials in the most effective manner. Toyota builds this system from two main principles: *jidoka* and just-in-time production. *Jidoka* is a Japanese term that refers to the power given to an employee to stop a production line if he or she detects a problem. Just-in-time production refers to the manufacturing of only "what is needed, when it's needed."[43] Toyota feels that these principles emphasize the company's philosophy that "good thinking means good production."

Toyota's desire for lean production dates back to the early 1900s with Sakichi Toyoda, the founder of the Toyota Group. When it came to producing goods, whether by hand or by machine, Toyoda knew that there was a difference between being quick and being efficient. He came to this conclusion after observing the automatic looms being used in Japanese textile mills. The looms formed fabrics quickly; however, threads would snap in the process, and the defective fabric would continue in the production line. Toyoda invented an automatic loom that would stop whenever a thread snapped so the problem could be fixed before the product moved on.[44] Toyoda used the word *jidoka* to describe this process, and his son, Kiichiro Toyoda, applied it to the company's automobile manufacturing operations when they began in the 1930s.

The *jidoka* philosophy focuses on quality. It means a machine will safely stop if it encounters a quality or equipment problem. A production line operator can fix the problem before any materials are passed down the production line. Operators are notified of any problems through the *andon*, or problem display board, which gives details about where and when the problems occurred. By stopping any potentially defective materials from continuing on in the production process, Toyota can guarantee that all products are made to the highest standards of quality.

Producing quality parts through *jidoka* allows the just-in-time system to function. This system strives to produce quality products efficiently through the complete elimination of waste, inconsistencies, and unreasonable requirements on the production line.[45] To achieve this, Toyota stocks its assembly line with only a small number of the parts needed to make different types of cars. For example, Toyota may have four different types of rear-view mirrors and only stock three of each type on the assembly line. When one type of rear-view mirror is used, a message is sent to the parts production department to construct a new rear-view mirror of that particular type. Then that mirror is sent back up to the assembly line to replenish the stock. By not mass producing parts, Toyota minimizes the chance of having a large inventory of unneeded materials. Toyota also uses this process with parts it orders from outside suppliers. The company only orders parts on an as-needed basis and receives them "just in time" for the parts to be configured. Therefore, Toyota avoids being bogged down by excess inventory and can run its assembly line more efficiently.

The intricate methods of Toyota's production system may seem cumbersome and possibly overwhelming to employees, but the results state otherwise. Toyota Motor Manufacturing Kentucky, Inc., Toyota's largest production facility outside of Japan, produces about 2000 vehicles a day. "An environment where people have to think brings with it wisdom, and this wisdom brings with it *kaizen* (continuous improvement)," states Teruyuki Minoura, Toyota's chief officer of the business development and purchasing group.[46] Toyota always looks to improve its *jidoka* and just-in-time production to make its production system as lean as possible, believing that wasted resources lead to wasted revenue.

DISCUSSION QUESTIONS

1. What lesson did Sakichi Toyoda learn from observing the Japanese looms? Why is it so important for a problem to be fixed when it happens instead of once it reaches the end of the assembly line?
2. What are the benefits of just-in-time production?
3. What problems might operators encounter with just-in-time production systems?

11 Financial Management and Accounting

A.Penkov/Shutterstock

LEARNING OBJECTIVES

After studying this chapter, you should be able to:

LO1 Summarize the implications of financial management and how financial managers fulfill their responsibilities. (p. 272)

LO2 Describe how financial managers plan for financial needs. (pp. 272–275)

LO3 Describe different short-term financing options available to finance business needs. (pp. 275–278)

LO4 Summarize the pros and cons of debt and equity financing and differentiate among different types of long-term financing options. (pp. 278–283)

LO5 Describe the functions of corporate accounting, managerial accounting, financial accounting, auditing, tax accounting, and government and nonprofit accounting. (pp. 283–286)

LO6 Explain how double-entry bookkeeping is used to maintain the balance of the fundamental accounting equation. (pp. 286–289)

LO7 Describe the functions of balance sheets, income statements, and statements of cash flows. (pp. 289–297)

OPENING DISCUSSION: PLANNING FOR FINANCIAL NEEDS

A Googol of Dollars for Google

Like many Silicon Valley success stories, Internet search engine Google arose from humble beginnings. The company started as a thesis project developed and refined by two students in their Stanford University dorm room. Larry Page and Sergey Brin wanted to organize the chaotic data on the Internet by developing a new way to search and retrieve information from the Web. Other Internet search engines already existed at the time, but Page and Brin wanted a system that was easy to use and could generate results in a split second. After leaving their Ph.D. studies behind, the two students formed Google Inc. The seemingly senseless company name was formed from the word *googol*, which is a mathematical term for a 1 followed by 100 zeroes. A googol, or Google, represented the vast amount of information on the Web and the company's mission to organize it. What Page and Brin did not know was that those zeroes also represented the amount of money their search engine would eventually generate.[1]

Originally, Page and Brin had no interest in starting their own company. They simply wanted to sell their technology to a second party. It was actually David Filo, friend and founder of Yahoo, who convinced the two young men to start a search engine company of their own. By the beginning of 1998, Page and Brin were ready to move forward, but they needed some long-term financing to get the company on its feet. The two students approached university faculty member Andy Bechtolsheim to be their first investor. Bechtolsheim provided Google with US$100 000. The initial investment was an encouraging start. By the end of 1998, Brin was able to acquire nearly US$1 million in funding for their company. Soon, a staff of eight was running a system that answered more than 500 000 queries a day. Google was proving to be a very wise investment. Later that year, Google announced that it had secured US$25 million in funding from two venture capital firms in Silicon Valley.

Now that Google had the funds to set up an office, they needed to start turning a profit. Selling search services to Internet giants such as AOL/Netscape and Virgin Net generated Google's initial revenue. However, it was advertising programs that catapulted Google's balance sheet into the black. By the end of 2000, Google was receiving 100 million hits a day, giving the company a larger audience than the Super Bowl. It was clear to Google's financial management team that an advertising program would be a lucrative venture. Google developed a keyword-target advertising program that allowed website owners to purchase keywords or phrases that potential customers might use in a search. If one of those keywords is typed into the Google search engine, the company is placed at the top of the search results page as a sponsored link.

To tailor to the needs of smaller businesses, Google established AdWord. The program allowed businesses to place a small advertisement along the edge of a search results page for certain keywords. Google advertising programs were so successful that by 2001, only three years after its incorporation, Google was a profitable company. The following year, Google looked to expand its advertising program to include AdSense. This program served as a way for advertisers to buy ad space on keyword-targeted sites outside Google and those site owners to profit from the sale of the space.

Over the last six years, Google has continued to make the majority of its revenue from advertising. In fact, in 2013 Google's advertising revenues totalled about US$50.5 billion, which accounts for 95 percent of the company's total revenue.[2] While Google continues to consider providing users with the ultimate search engine to be its primary goal, it strives to be a profitable business. Google uses the statement "You can make money without doing evil" (or simply put, "Don't do evil") as one of its business philosophies.[3] In following this philosophy, it does not use flashy or obtrusive advertisements and only provides users with advertisements that are relevant to their search. This sharp form of managerial accounting has allowed Google to stay true to Page and Brin's original mission, as well as achieve a net income of more than US$12.9 billion in 2013.[4]

DISCUSSION QUESTIONS

1. Since Google is an Internet service company and does not have to worry about the cost of goods sold, why would Page and Brin need to get long-term financial support to start their business? What operating expenses might they encounter during their first year?
2. Why did Google choose to incorporate advertising into its business plan? What do you think Google's bottom line would look like if it only sold search services?
3. How much of Google's success can be attributed to strong managerial accounting? Explain.

FINANCIAL MANAGEMENT

LO1 Summarize the implications of financial management and how financial managers fulfill their responsibilities.

The Financial Manager

financial management Involves the strategic planning and budgeting of short- and long-term funds for current and future needs.

What is financial management? Producing, marketing, and distributing a product are important aspects of generating a profit. Even more important, however, is the company's ability to *pay* for the resources required to accomplish these tasks. Without management of finances, there is no business! Without good financial controls and planning, a company will not be able to respond to unexpected challenges or planned expansion. **Financial management** involves the strategic planning and budgeting of short- and long-term funds for current and future needs. Tracking past financial transactions, controlling current revenues and expenses, and planning for future financial needs of the company are the foundation of financial management.

In most companies, the finance department comprises two divisions: accounting (which will be discussed later in the chapter) and financial management. Just as you might save money to ensure that you can pay next month's rent or make plans for a big purchase such as a car or home, businesses must also plan and save. To remain competitive, businesses must make large strategic investments such as buying or building a new factory or investing in more advanced machinery or technology. At the same time, they also must ensure that they can pay their monthly bills. Financial management involves setting up and monitoring controls to make certain the plans and budgets are monitored sufficiently so that the business can reach its financial goals.

financial manager Oversees the financial operations of a company. Also called a chief financial officer (CFO).

What is the role of a financial manager? A **financial manager** or *chief financial officer (CFO)* oversees the financial operations of a company. Generally, a financial manager assumes accounting responsibilities for the company. A financial manager is responsible for planning and managing the company's financial resources, including the following:

- developing plans that outline the company's financial short-term and long-term needs
- defining the sources and uses of funds that are needed to reach goals
- monitoring the cash flow of a company to ensure that obligations are paid in a timely and efficient manner and that funds owed to the company are collected efficiently
- investing any excess funds so that those funds can grow and be used for future development
- raising capital for future growth and expansion

Although not all companies have a CFO, all successfully run businesses have some person or persons designated to manage the financial needs of a company. In smaller companies, the financial manager may have other business-related responsibilities as well. Some entrepreneurs might serve as both owner and financial manager of a company.

Planning for Financial Needs

LO2 Describe how financial managers plan for financial needs.

How does the financial manager plan for financial needs? A company's financial needs are both short term and long term in nature, and a financial manager must plan for both. In addition, he or she must ensure that funds are used optimally and that the firm is ultimately profitable. To meet these objectives, a financial manager oversees three important processes: forecasting financial needs, developing budgets and plans to meet financial needs, and establishing controls to ensure that the budgets and plans are being followed.

What is involved in forecasting financial needs? In most large companies, the executive management team and the board of directors formulate a strategic plan that sets out corporate goals and objectives. For example, if one of a company's goals and objectives were to produce a new device to compete directly with a competitor's product, it would be the CFO's responsibility to manage revenues and expenses for this plan. In addition, the CFO would need to develop short- and long-term financial forecasts to ensure that the strategic goals and objectives were financially feasible. Financial managers coordinate with other areas of the company to formulate answers to certain questions: How much product do we need to sell? Do we need to expand to meet demand? Do we have the resources to expand our product line? Financial forecasts are especially important when strategic goals include large capital projects, such as acquiring new facilities, replacing outdated technology, or expanding into a new product line. It is critical that such forecasts are relatively accurate, as erroneous forecasts can have serious consequences.

Forecasts Forecasts predict revenue, costs, and expenses for a specific future period. Short-term **forecasts** would include predictions within the upcoming year, while long-term forecasts would include predictions for a period longer than one year into the future. In developing forecasts, the financial manager considers many factors, including the current and future plans of the company, the current and future state of the economy, and the current and anticipated actions of the competition. In addition, the financial manager must anticipate the impact such factors will have on the company's financial situation. If, for example, national economic forecasts predict a recession in six months, a financial manager knows such a forecast will affect the company in many ways. Therefore, additional planning is required during general economic downturns to handle the possibility that payments might be harder to collect or that sales could be lower. Because of the result from either or both of these possibilities, plans for expansion of buildings or equipment might need to be postponed.

forecasts Predict revenue, costs, and expenses for a specific future period.

How does a company know it has enough resources to meet forecasted needs? The accounting area of the finance department generates financial statements, such as the income statement, balance sheet, and statement of cash flows. Financial statements will be discussed in more detail later in the chapter, but generally they create a financial landscape that explains where the company has been over the current and past years. Moreover, they serve as a basis for management to develop expectations of where the company will be in future periods. Using these expectations, a financial manager puts together a **budget**, a financial plan that outlines the company's planned cash flows, expected operating expenses, and anticipated revenues. An **operating (master) budget** includes all the operating costs for the entire organization, including inventory, sales, purchases, manufacturing, marketing, and operating expenses. The operating budget maps out the projected number of units to be sold and estimated income for the coming year, in addition to all anticipated costs of operating the business to manufacture and sell the estimated level of business.

budget A financial plan that outlines the company's planned cash flows, expected operating expenses, and anticipated revenues.

Video: Big Apple Circus: Sources of Financing

operating (master) budget Includes all the operating costs for the entire organization, including inventory, sales, purchases, manufacturing, marketing, and operating expenses.

How are funds made available for large projects? Another component of the budgeting process is the **capital budget**, which considers the company's long-range plans and outlines the expected financial needs for significant capital purchases such as real estate, manufacturing equipment, plant expansions, or technology. Since capital projects are often financed with borrowed money or money raised through the sale of stocks or bonds, it is important to plan ahead to ensure that necessary funds are available when needed. During the capital budget process, each department in the organization puts together a list of its anticipated capital needs. Then senior management and the board

capital budget Considers the company's long-range plans and outlines the expected financial needs for significant capital purchases such as real estate, manufacturing equipment, plant expansions, or technology.

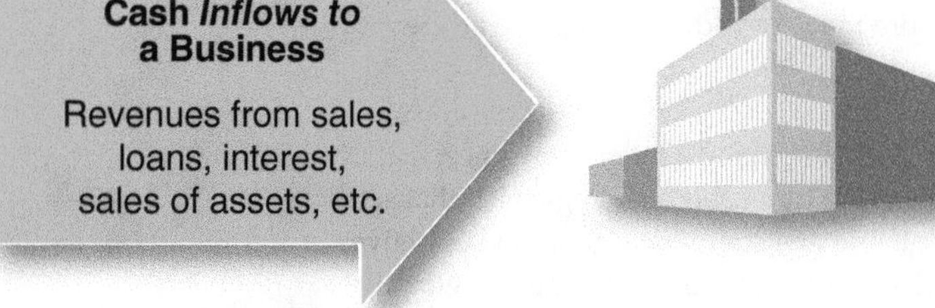

Figure 11.1 Business Cash Flow

evaluate these needs to determine which will best maximize the company's overall growth and profitability. Some requests are routine replacement of equipment or technology and may not need much evaluation. Other requests might be necessary to move the company in a new direction and should be evaluated closely.

Addressing the Budget

cash flow The movement of money in and out of a business over a defined period (weekly, monthly, or quarterly).

What helps plan for short-term needs? **Cash flow** is the movement of money in and out of a business over a defined period (weekly, monthly, or quarterly). If cash going out of the business exceeds the cash coming into the business, then the business has a negative cash flow (a gap). To create a positive cash flow, a company would need to generate more cash and collect the cash in a more timely fashion, and at the same time maintain or reduce expenses. The cash flow budget is a short-term budget that estimates cash inflows and outflows and can predict a business's cash flow situation (see **Figure 11.1**). Cash flow budgets help financial managers determine whether the business needs to seek outside sources of funds beyond sales to manage anticipated cash shortages. Cash flow budgets also indicate future investment opportunities from surges in cash inflow, as well as show whether a business will have enough cash to grow. Moreover, the financial manager uses the cash flow budget to help plan for debt repayment or to cover unusual operating expenses.

Why is monitoring cash flow important? A company can have the bestselling product on the market, but if the flow of funds coming in and going out of the company is not managed properly, the company can easily fail. Monitoring cash flow is important because it measures a company's short-term financial health and financial efficiency. Cash flow specifically measures whether there are sufficient funds to pay outstanding bills. For seasonal businesses such as ski shops and pool installation companies, cash management is critical to carry a business through the slow months. Although many investors focus on a company's profitability as an indicator of strength, a company's **liquidity**—how quickly assets can be turned into cash—is often a better indicator.

liquidity How quickly assets can be turned into cash.

How does a company know if it is staying on budget? A budget allocates the use of specific resources throughout the firm in accordance with management's expectations. After the budget is developed, it must be compared periodically to the actual performance of the company. It is important that management compare actual performance regularly to the budget. This generally occurs every month. Without such a comparison, it is hard to determine whether the company is actually performing as expected. For example, let's say you decide to save some money, and at the end of the month you have $50 in your savings account. Is that good or bad? It all depends on what you originally planned on saving. If you intended on saving only $35 and ended up with $50, that's great. If you intended on saving $75, then the outcome is not as good.

The same is true with the financial performance of a company. If the actual numbers generated by the company closely match the budget, this shows the company is fulfilling

Table 11.1 Sources of Short-Term and Long-Term Financing

Short-Term Financing	Long-Term Financing
Friends and family	**Debt Financing**
Credit cards	• Commercial banks (e.g., line of credit, loans)
Commercial banks (e.g., line of credit, loans)	• Commercial finance companies (e.g., loans)
Commercial finance companies (e.g., loans)	• Selling bonds
Trade credit	**Equity Financing**
Promissory note	• Selling stock
Factoring	• Venture capital
Commercial paper	• Retained earnings

its plans. On the other hand, if the actual numbers differ greatly from those projected by the budget, this indicates that corrective action must be taken. Businesses strive to stay on budget and fund needs through monies generated by business operations. However, there are many situations, even with the best planning, when a financial manager needs to consider funding operations by using internal cash sources or by finding outside sources (e.g., donations or grants to help fund large projects).

What must a financial manager consider when seeking outside funds? In your personal life, you most likely have different types of financing to help you manage your financial needs. For example, you may have a credit card to pay for expenses. In addition, you might also have loans to pay for bigger, long-term expenses such as school, a car, or your home. Like you, a company may have several different types of borrowing needs to finance small operating costs as well as large projects. There are many sources of outside funds available to a company. How does a financial manager evaluate the best financing option? The financial manager must first match the length of the financing to the length of the need. Then, the financial manager must evaluate the cost of obtaining the funds and determine whether it is best to finance by raising *equity*—ownership interest in the form of stocks—or issuing *debt*— funds borrowed that must be repaid.

Financial managers or CFOs have myriad responsibilities, some of which include controlling and collecting funds, managing taxes, auditing, and budgeting. To determine the feasibility of a company's project, CFOs develop short- and long-term financial forecasts. They take into account the state of the economy and the plans of the company. They also need to take a close look at the capital budget and evaluate funding options. The next section of this chapter discusses short-term and long-term funding options. **Table 11.1** lists the sources from which financial managers must choose when making decisions about financing both short-term and long-term business needs.

FINANCIAL NEEDS

LO3 Describe different short-term financing options available to finance business needs.

Financing Short-Term Business Needs

How are the operations of a company financed? When businesses, both large and small, find it necessary to expand, they must make some important decisions regarding financing. You may recall from Chapter 4 that different forms of business ownership have varying short-term needs. It is important that all companies have a plan to finance those needs. As was mentioned above, cash flow budgets are prepared to predict a company's cash flow gaps—periods when cash outflows are greater than cash inflows. When these gaps are expected, depending on the size of the business and the cash flow gap, there are several short-term sources available to help fill the temporary gap.

short-term financing Any type of financing repaid within a year or less.

Short-term financing is any type of financing repaid within a year or less. It is used to finance day-to-day operations such as payroll, inventory purchases, and overhead (utilities, rent, leases). As discussed in Chapter 4, smaller startup businesses often fund cash flow gaps first by appealing to friends and family. This is not a recommended strategy as it can lead to severed relationships if loans are not paid back promptly. However, when it is used it is important that both parties understand and agree to formal payment arrangements. Another approach that many smaller businesses take to fund cash flow gaps is the use of credit cards. Credit cards are a good way to defer payments, but they can become very expensive if credit balances are not paid off completely every month.

trade credit The ability to purchase inventory and supplies on credit without interest.

Larger businesses with good credit and an established relationship with their suppliers take advantage of another credit relationship to help bridge the temporary gap. Companies will often purchase inventory and supplies on trade credit. **Trade credit** is the ability to purchase inventory and supplies on credit without interest. Suppliers will typically request payment within 30, 60, or 90 days. Deferring payment with trade credit is a good strategy to bridge a temporary cash flow gap because it does not tie up cash unnecessarily. Moreover, using trade credit keeps debt levels down, which is always attractive to outside investors and lenders. However, there are disadvantages associated with using trade credit. Sometimes buyers are offered a discounted rate if they pay their creditor early. Trade credit will negate this early payment discount. Additionally, if payments extend beyond the trade credit period, delinquency penalties are charged and, if allowed to accrue, can be very costly.[5] Financial managers must weigh the costs and benefits of paying early for a discount or paying on time without a discount so that their cash is available longer. **Figure 11.2** illustrates this decision.

promissory note A written promise to pay a supplier a specific amount of money by an agreed-upon date.

Some suppliers hesitate to give trade credit to organizations with a poor credit history. In such cases, the supplier may insist that the customer sign a promissory note as a condition of obtaining credit. A **promissory note** is a written promise to pay a supplier a specific amount of money by an agreed-upon date. A supplier might decide to sell a promissory note to a bank at a discounted rate (the amount of the note less a fee for the bank's services in collecting the amount due).

Figure 11.2 Trade Credit

Using trade credit can be advantageous but must always be evaluated and monitored carefully.

In addition to trade credit, companies will often rely on commercial banks, savings and loans institutions, or other commercial lenders for interim credit arrangements and other banking services.

How do commercial banks help with financial management? **Commercial banks** are financial institutions that raise funds from businesses and individuals in the form of chequing and savings accounts and use those funds to make loans to businesses and individuals. Small startup businesses rely on commercial banks for savings and chequing services to pay bills and to store excess funds. Chequing and savings accounts are a form of demand deposit—funds that can be withdrawn (or demanded) at any time without prior notice.

commercial banks Financial institutions that raise funds from businesses and individuals in the form of chequing and savings accounts and use those funds to make loans to businesses and individuals.

As a business develops and establishes a good relationship with a bank, the business owners may seek to open a line of credit. You can think of a business **line of credit** as having available credit that a manager can access at any time up to an amount agreed upon between the bank and the company. The funds can be withdrawn all at once or in multiple withdrawals during the stated period. This is a common way of covering cash flow shortages, purchasing seasonal inventory, or financing unforeseen operating expenses.

line of credit Available credit that a manager can access at any time up to an amount agreed upon between the bank and the company.

Many commercial banks also offer loans for the purchase of equipment, property, or other capital assets. A **secured loan** requires collateral, which is generally the asset that the loan is financing, to guarantee the debt obligation. For example, if a bank were to give a loan to a company so it could purchase a building, the building would serve as the collateral. If the company were unable to pay down the loan, the bank would then take possession of the building as a substitute for the remaining loan payments. If the firm has an excellent credit history and solid relationship with the lending institution, it may get an **unsecured loan**, which does not require collateral.

secured loan A loan that requires collateral, which is generally the asset that the loan is financing, to guarantee the debt obligation.

unsecured loan A loan that does not require collateral.

Are there other short-term financing options? Sometimes a company is unable to secure a short-term loan from a commercial bank. In these cases, an alternative source of financing is a **commercial finance company**, a financial institution that makes short-term loans to borrowers who offer tangible assets as collateral. Commercial finance companies, such as General Electric Credit Corporation, provide businesses with loans but are not considered banks. Other nonbank or private lenders include credit unions, factors, and credit card companies. Nonbank lenders are becoming increasingly popular among entrepreneurs, particularly owners of startup businesses.

commercial finance company A company that is not considered a bank, but rather a financial institution that makes short-term loans to borrowers who offer tangible assets as collateral.

For example, soon after starting his own clothing manufacturing business, Ken Seiff needed additional short-term financing. He was looking to expand his product line for the next season, but he had no cash—it was tied up in receivables (money he is owed by customers) and business expenses. Commercial banks were not interested in helping him because of his perceived risk as a recent startup business. Being in the apparel industry added even more risk. On the advice of his accountant, Seiff turned to a commercial finance company, which ultimately helped him through his short-term cash crunch.[6]

One of the strategies that the commercial finance company used in Seiff's case was factoring. **Factoring** is the process of selling accounts receivable for cash. The finance company agreed to give Seiff money, and in exchange it would collect the accounts receivable and keep the money that was owed Seiff's company. The money given to Seiff was equal to the amount his company would have received had he waited to collect the funds directly, minus a fee charged by the factoring agent. The fee applied is dependent on how long the receivable has been outstanding, the nature of the business, and the economy. While costly at times, factoring can be an important strategy for companies to bridge cash flow gaps.

factoring The process of selling accounts receivable for cash.

Do larger corporations do anything differently for short-term financing? Large corporations have the advantage over smaller startup companies in that they have a greater ability to establish a credit or debt rating. Those companies who have a high-quality debt rating can issue commercial paper. When a company has a high-quality debt rating, it means it is looked upon favourably by lenders as being a company that has a good or excellent likelihood of paying off its debt. **Commercial paper** is an unsecured (i.e., it

commercial paper An unsecured (i.e., it does not need collateral) short-term debt instrument of $100 000 or more typically issued by a corporation to bridge a cash flow gap created by large accounts receivable, inventory, or payroll.

does not need collateral) short-term debt instrument of $100 000 or more typically issued by a corporation to bridge a cash flow gap created by large accounts receivable, inventory, or payroll. Commercial paper is a type of promissory note (promise to pay back) that comes due (matures) in 270 days or less and is not required to go through the same registration process as other longer-term debt and equity instruments, which we'll discuss next. When companies have extra cash, they may choose to buy commercial paper from other companies that need cash. The company that purchases the commercial paper will make money from the interest earned (the interest paid on the promissory note by the debtor). Therefore, commercial paper can be a means of short-term financing for companies in need of cash, and for other companies commercial paper can be a short-term investment.

Video: Johnny Cupcakes: Financial and Cash Flow Management

Financing Long-Term Business Needs

LO4 Summarize the pros and cons of debt and equity financing and differentiate among different types of long-term financing options.

Why do companies need long-term financing solutions? Remember that in order to grow, new or small companies need expansion projects such as establishing new offices or manufacturing facilities, developing a new product or service, or buying another company. These projects may cost millions of dollars and take several years to complete. Long-term financing is needed because it provides funds for a period longer than one year (often up to 10 years). In most cases, a company will use several sources of long-term financing, even for one project.

debt financing Occurs when a company borrows money that it is legally obligated to repay, with interest, by a specified time.

equity financing The generation of funds by the owners of the company rather than an outside lender. These funds might come from the company's own savings or partial sale of ownership in the company in the form of stock.

loan An arrangement in which a lender gives money to a borrower under the agreement that the borrower repays the loan amount, usually with interest, at some future point in time.

What are the different types of long-term financing? In general, a company can choose from two different types of long-term financing: debt financing and equity financing. **Debt financing** occurs when a company borrows money that it is legally obligated to repay, with interest, by a specified time. Contrary to debt financing, the funds for **equity financing** are generated by the owners of the company rather than an outside lender. These funds might come from the company's own savings or partial sale of ownership in the company in the form of stock. The choice depends on many factors, including the maturity and size of the company, the number of assets a company already owns, and the size and nature of the project being financed.

What kinds of debt financing are available? There are mainly two types of debt financing for companies to choose between to raise funds: loans and bonds.

Loans In our personal lives, when we want to buy something such as a house or a car that costs more than what we have saved, our best option is to borrow money. We take out a loan specifically to pay for an item, and that item is used as collateral, which permits the lender to claim ownership of the item in the event the loan is not repaid. A **loan** is an arrangement in which a lender gives money to a borrower under the agreement that the borrower repays the loan amount, usually with interest, at some future point in time. Similarly, when a company has a project or purchase that it cannot finance with existing company assets it can take out a business loan.

Sculpies/Shutterstock

Construction of large capital projects often requires long-term financing.

For larger projects that demand big loans with long payment terms, long-term financing is available from financial institutions such as insurance companies and pension funds, as well as large commercial banks and finance companies. Most long-term loans require some form of collateral, such as real estate, machinery, or stock. Often, as in a home mortgage, the asset being financed serves as the collateral. Large long-term loans usually have a higher interest rate (the rate charged for borrowing the money) because of the added risk associated with a large project and the longer term of the loan. The rate of interest is also determined by the prevailing market interest rates and the general financial worthiness of the borrower. Loans are easiest to obtain when a firm has established a relationship with a bank or other financial institution and has a good credit standing.

Bonds Some companies issue bonds when loans aren't obtainable or are not the most economical option; perhaps the rates are too high or the project requires a greater amount of financing than loans can provide. A **corporate bond** is a type of loan issued by a company and not a commercial bank or commercial finance company. It is a formal written agreement to reimburse a loan at a regular interest rate at a given date in time. Bonds are issued by companies or governments with the purpose of raising capital to finance a large project. The company issuing the bond is the borrower, who owes money to the lender, who is the investor and holder of the bond.

corporate bond A type of loan issued by a company, not a commercial bank or commercial finance company. It is a formal written agreement to reimburse a loan at a regular interest rate at a given date in time.

There are two types of payments made to bond investors: interest and principal. **Interest** is the payments the bond issuer makes to the bondholder for use of the borrowed money (most interest payments are semi-annual). At the end of the loan period, the company is responsible for paying back the entire initial amount of the bond (the principal). There is a legal contract between the company (borrower) and the investor (lender) that outlines the terms of the bond, the interest due, and the date when the principal amount of the loan must be paid back (the bond's maturity date). Corporate bonds are generally more risky to invest in than government bonds because companies can only stay in business as long as they remain profitable, while governments have a ready source of funds through taxes. Because they are riskier, corporate bonds often pay higher interest rates than government bonds to attract investors. To ensure there is enough money at the end of the loan period to pay off all the bondholders, companies use a **sinking fund**—a type of savings fund in which companies set aside money regularly to help repay a bond issue.

interest The payments the bond issuer makes to the bondholder for use of the borrowed money (most interest payments are semi-annual).

sinking fund A type of savings fund in which companies set aside money regularly to help repay a bond issue.

As attractive as bond financing sounds, financial managers must consider several factors before deciding to finance with bonds. First, the cost of the loan—the rate of interest the lender will demand—is an important consideration. If the interest rate is too high, it can force the cost of the project into something that is not affordable or that just doesn't make economic sense. The interest rate is determined by a combination of many factors, including *issuer risk*—whether the lender (bond purchaser) thinks the company can meet its obligations to pay back the loan. As the risk increases, so does the interest rate. Often bond issuers use *bond insurance* to help lower the risk. Although there is a cost to having such insurance, the amount of money saved by having a lower interest rate is greater than the cost of the bond insurance. In addition to issuer risk, the *length of the bond term* affects the rate. Bonds that have a longer length of term have a greater chance of default; therefore, they carry additional risk and a higher interest rate. Last, *the general state of the economy* affects the interest rate. Before making a final decision to issue bonds, a financial manager must also consider how this additional debt obligation affects the overall financial health of the company.

secured bonds Bonds that require some form of collateral pledged as security.

unsecured bonds Bonds that are issued with no collateral. Also called debenture bonds.

Secured bonds require some form of collateral pledged as security. The collateral is generally corporate-owned property that will pass to the bondholders (or be sold to reimburse bondholders) if the issuer does not repay the amount borrowed. **Unsecured bonds** (or *debenture bonds*) are issued with no collateral. They are only backed by the general creditworthiness and

Consignum/Alamy

This $1000 U.S. railroad bond was issued in 1900.

convertible bond A bond that gives the bondholder the right (but not the obligation) to convert the bond into a predetermined number of shares of the company's stock.

reputation of the issuer. A **convertible bond** gives the bondholder the right (but not the obligation) to convert the bond into a predetermined number of shares of the company's stock. Convertible bonds generally carry a lower interest rate since the investor will benefit from investing in the underlying stock.

What kinds of equity financing are available? The most common forms of financing for small businesses are personal savings or contributions from family, friends, or business associates. As a business grows, venture capital or funds from angel investors are also possible sources of new capital, but eventually those options are not sufficient to finance large capital needs. Without an established credit history, it is difficult to obtain a loan from a financial institution. Looking inside the company for long-term funding (equity financing) is an alternative to looking outside. Equity financing primarily takes three forms: (1) issuing common stock, (2) obtaining venture capital, or (3) retaining the company's earnings.

equity Money received in exchange for ownership in a business.

stock A unit of ownership in a company sold with the intention of raising capital to finance ongoing or future projects and expansions.

issuing common stock The process of selling common shares of ownership in the company to the general public—in other words, "going public"—which can be a great option to generate funds through equity financing.

initial public offering (IPO) The first time a company offers to sell new stock to the public.

Why finance with stock (equity)? Most companies issue stock (often referred to as equity) to finance long-term general funding and ongoing expansion rather than a specific project or need. **Equity** is money received in exchange for ownership in a business. There are two main types of stock that companies issue: *common* and *preferred.* **Stock** is a unit of ownership in a company sold with the intention of raising capital to finance ongoing or future projects and expansions. **Issuing common stock** by selling common shares of ownership in the company to the public—in other words, "going public"—can be a great option to generate funds through equity financing. A company can choose to go public when it feels it has enough public support to attract new shareholders. For instance, Google Inc. went public on the NASDAQ (National Association of Securities Dealers Automated Quotations) in 2004. The first time a company offers to sell new stock to the public is called an **initial public offering (IPO)**. Google's IPO was of 19.6 million shares of common stock at an opening price of US$85 per share (on March 4, 2014, the price per share was $1214.91).[7] In March 2006, Tim Hortons Inc. announced the pricing of its initial public offering of 29 million shares of common stock at a price of US$23.162.[8] More recent examples of initial public offerings include Twitter's IPO in November 2013 at $26 per share (on March 4, 2014, the price had risen to $54.28) and Facebook's IPO in May 2012 at a price of $38 per share (on March 4, 2014, the price was $68.80).[9] Imagine the funding these companies generated from selling shares to the public. Going public provides companies with equity financing opportunities to grow their businesses, from expansion of operations to buying other companies (acquisitions).

dividends A portion of a company's profits distributed to shareholders as either cash payments or additional shares of stock.

What are the disadvantages of financing with stock? Common shares are the most basic form of ownership, and shareholders have the right to (1) vote for the company board of directors and on important company issues and (2) share in the company profits through dividends. The biggest disadvantage of financing with stock is the dilution of ownership. Another disadvantage is the payment of dividends. **Dividends** are a portion of a company's profits distributed to shareholders as either cash payments or additional shares of stock. Legally, common share dividends and preferred share dividends (discussed next) never have to be paid if the company makes no profit, nor do they ever have to be repurchased by the company. Of course, if a company does not pay dividends, it would become difficult to entice new investors to purchase shares in the company. Paying dividends to shareholders is more expensive for a company than paying interest to bondholders, which is tax deductible, while paying dividends to shareholders is not (dividends are paid out of profit after taxes and are not an allowable income tax deduction). Shareholders do not have direct control over the day-to-day management of a company, but they do directly control who manages the company through voting rights. As a result, shareholders can have a strong influence on management's decisions.

preferred stock A hybrid investment because it has some of the features of common stock (i.e., it never matures) and some of the features of corporate bonds (i.e., payments on stock are for fixed amounts, such as $5 per share per year).

What are preferred stocks? **Preferred stock** is a hybrid investment because it has some of the features of common stock (i.e., it never matures) and some of the

Using Social Networks for Venture Capital

Businesses need money, and venture capitalists need investments. How do the two meet? You might find it surprising that today many connections are made online through social media sites, such as blogs and Twitter, and social networks like LinkedIn. For example, Chris Sacca of Lowercase Capital is always looking for new investment opportunities. In an off chance, he sent a tweet asking if there were any "bootstrapped, profitable startups with founders working late on a Friday night"[10] and, to his surprise, one replied. The connection was made, and the investment is still one of Chris' favourites.

Social media allows investors to get a sense of the personality of the startup founders of their potential investments before sinking a lot of time and effort into cultivating a relationship. Investors use social media to find deals and create relationships with entrepreneurs so they can close the deals that seem most attractive. Searching through Twitter streams can turn up valuable insight into a company's culture and viability, as well as the individual nature of the employees. Social networks can also help forge connections between investors and founders. If an investor doesn't know the management team of the potential investment, he or she can see if there are any common connections between them. If there are common connections, they can prove to be good sources of information—even if it's only about character and business acumen.

Twitter searches can be valuable to venture capitalists to see if users are having good experiences with a product or whether they are disgruntled. It helps to uncover the real-world problems that might otherwise be purposely ignored by a company's management team. But it's not just a one-way street. Investors also need to build their online reputations to differentiate themselves from other venture capitalists. Venture capitalists can also use the social web to build up a reputation for their investments.

features of corporate bonds (i.e., payments on stock are for fixed amounts, such as $5 per share per year). Preferred stock is a class of ownership in which the preferred shareholders have a claim to assets before common shareholders if the firm goes out of business. In addition, preferred shareholders receive a fixed dividend that must be paid before the payment of any dividend to common shareholders. A major advantage of preferred stock for the issuing company is that funds can be obtained without giving up control of the company because preferred shareholders usually do not have voting rights.

Video: Facebook Stock Falls to New Low

Why finance with venture capital? If a company does not feel it is ready to go public, it may look for long-term financing in the form of venture capital. Venture capital is an investment in the form of money that includes a substantial amount of risk for the investors. Because of the high level of risk, the group of outside investors, called venture capitalists (discussed in Chapter 4), command an active role in the management decisions of the company. Venture capitalists seek their return in the form of equity, or ownership, in the company. They anticipate a large return on their investment when the company is sold or goes public. Venture capitalists are willing to wait longer than other investors, lenders, or shareholders for returns on their investment, but they expect higher than normal results.

Why finance with retained earnings? A successful company that is making a profit could find long-term funding by simply looking at its balance sheet for retained earnings, or accumulated profits. **Retained earnings** represent the profits (money remaining after taxes and other expenses are paid) not paid out in dividends. Using retained earnings is an ideal way to fund long-term projects because it saves companies from paying interest on loans or underwriting fees on bonds. Unfortunately, not all companies produce enough retained earnings to fund large projects. In particular, startup businesses find themselves with few options for long-term financing. Each business owner can contribute

retained earnings Represent the profits (money remaining after taxes and other expenses are paid) not paid out in dividends.

money to the company for expansion, purchases, operations, and so on. However, at some point the individual owners contribute as much as they can or are willing to and still need additional funds to keep their business growing.

investment instruments Bonds (debt) or stock (equity) that are used for large capital-intensive projects or general expansion.

How do companies decide between debt and equity financing? For large capital-intensive projects or general expansion, business owners can use securities—**investment instruments** such as bonds (debt) or stock (equity). The choice between financing large projects with debt or equity is a decision managers reach by understanding the financing needs of the project itself and the impact the financing decision has on corporate earnings, cash flow, and taxes. In addition, a company must take into consideration how much debt it already has before issuing bonds or whether it wants to dilute ownership by issuing stock. Finally, the company must also consider external factors at the time of financing, such as the state of the bond or stock market, the economy, and the anticipated interest of investors.

leverage The amount of debt used to finance a firm's assets with the intent that the rate of return on the assets is greater than the cost of the debt.

Most companies use debt to finance operations, which increases the company's leverage. **Leverage** is the amount of debt used to finance a firm's assets with the intent that the rate of return on the assets is greater than the cost of the debt. One measure of a company's financial leverage is determined by its debt to equity ratio (or total liabilities divided by shareholders' equity—discussed in the next section). Using leverage wisely is beneficial because a company can invest in business operations without losing equity by increasing the number of owners in the company. For example, if a company formed with $3 million from five investors (who become the company's shareholders), the equity in the company is $3 million. If the company also uses debt financing to borrow $17 million, the company now has $17 million to invest in business operations without having to take on more shareholders. This creates additional opportunities for the original shareholders to make more money. Although there is a cost to borrowing, the intention is that the project or company expansion will ultimately have a positive rate of return after paying for the cost of the debt. However, it can be risky to take on too much debt, so lenders consider how much debt a company has relative to the amount of equity (or assets) a company owns before they issue a loan. A common leverage ratio is for a company to have at least twice the amount of equity (67 percent) as it has debt (33 percent).

If a company is unwilling or cannot take on additional debt, it must consider equity financing to meet its long-term business needs. Unlike bonds and other forms of debt, equity financing does not need to be repaid, even if the company goes bankrupt, and no assets need to be pledged as collateral. In addition, financing with equity enables the company to retain cash and profits in the company rather than using the funds to make interest and principal payments. In many instances, financing with equity can make the company look stronger, as high levels of debt can be problematic to lenders and investors.

optimal capital structure The optimal balance between equity and debt financing.

Financial planners try to find a mix between equity and debt financing that will maximize shareholders' wealth. The balance between debt and equity varies according to industry and size of the business. For example, capital-intensive manufacturing industries, such as car manufacturers, will have more debt than service industries, such as health care providers. Other industries that are expanding rapidly but have large capital reserves, such as computer hardware manufacturers, have a minimal need for debt or equity financing. Companies aim to achieve an **optimal capital structure**, which refers to the optimal balance between equity and debt financing. The most conservative strategy would be to use all equity financing and no debt because a company has no formal obligations for financial payouts. The riskiest strategy would be to use all debt financing because indebtedness increases the risk that the company will be unable to meet its obligations and will go bankrupt. See **Table 11.2** for a comparison of debt and equity financing.

Video: Capital Advisors: Securities and Investments

Companies that need large amounts of money in addition to profits gained through regular business operations often acquire funding through various investments and financing (debt and equity) options.

Table 11.2 Comparison of Debt and Equity Financing

Debt Financing	Equity Financing
What are the repayment obligations?	
Interest must be paid.	Not obligated to pay dividends
Principal must be repaid at maturity date.	Stock has no maturity date.
	Never required to repay equity.
What are the tax implications?	
Interest paid is tax deductible.	Dividends are not tax deductible.
What are the implications for management control?	
None, unless special conditions apply.	Common shareholders have voting rights.
	May cause challenge for corporate control.

ACCOUNTING FUNCTIONS

LO5 Describe the functions of corporate accounting, managerial accounting, financial accounting, auditing, tax accounting, and government and nonprofit accounting.

Accounting Fundamentals

What is accounting? **Accounting** is the recording, classifying, summarizing, and interpreting of financial events to communicate useful financial information. It involves tracking a business's income and expenses through a process of recording financial transactions. The transactions are then summarized into key financial reports that are further used to evaluate the business's current and expected financial status. Accounting is not just for large organizations—it is quite important for businesses of all sizes. Accounting defines the heart and soul of even the smallest business as it helps to "account for" what the business has done, what it is currently doing, and what it has the potential to do. While accounting involves a great deal of precision, there are also some degrees of interpretation in the process of accounting. This makes accounting both an art and a science.

accounting The recording, classifying, summarizing, and interpreting of financial events to communicate useful financial information. It involves tracking a business's income and expenses through a process of recording financial transactions.

Accounting is often called the language of business because it provides financial information used for decision making, planning, and reporting. When companies are small, it can seem relatively simple. However, as a company grows and diversifies, accounting becomes increasingly complex. For example, Arnold Sawyer was pretty good at handling figures. When his niece Josephine asked him to oversee finances for her vegan catering business, he figured he could handle it. Arnold's background was in sales, but he assumed he was smart enough to handle accounting. He used QuickBooks to create a basic bookkeeping system. Since the company only had a small but steady stream of clients, the accounting side didn't seem complicated. However, after Josephine appeared on a newscast to talk about the benefits of a vegan diet, sales skyrocketed. With the significant increase in catering contracts, the workload doubled. Josephine needed to increase her staff and supplies, but the company didn't have enough cash to cover the initial costs. Arnold needed to decide how his niece's catering business would acquire the extra funds it needed to keep the business moving. Arnold would need to review the company's financial information and possibly enlist outside consultants before making a decision.

In this section, the fundamentals of accounting, the types of accounting, and accounting standards and processes will be discussed.

Is there more than one type of accountant? It is critical for firms to keep accurate financial information. A company may employ a *private* accountant or hire the services of a *public* accountant. A **private accountant** is employed by an organization and may perform one or more different accounting functions. A **public accountant** provides a broad range of accounting, auditing, tax, and consulting activities for various corporate clients.

private accountant Employed by an organization and may perform one or more different accounting functions.

public accountant Provides a broad range of accounting, auditing, tax, and consulting activities for various corporate clients.

certified general accountant (CGA) Provides the financial information for use by shareholders, government, creditors, and others "outside" an organization.

certified management accountant (CMA) Provides financial information to managers and other corporate decision makers "inside" the corporation and helps formulate policy and strategic plans.

chartered accountant (CA) Provides financial information for use by shareholders, government, creditors, and others "outside" an organization. The CA can work in both public and private sector fields of business and finance.

Three professional accounting organizations have developed in Canada to certify accounting expertise:

1. *Certified General Accountants (CGA).* The Certified General Accountants Association of Canada grants the CGA designation. The duties of a CGA include accounting, auditing, taxation, and business consulting.[11] A **certified general accountant (CGA)** provides the financial information for use by shareholders, government, creditors, and others "outside" an organization.
2. *Certified Management Accountants (CMA).* The Society of Management Accountants of Canada grants the CMA certification. A **certified management accountant (CMA)** provides financial information to managers and other corporate decision makers "inside" the corporation and helps formulate policy and strategic plans.[12]
3. *Chartered Accountants (CA).* The Canadian Institute of Chartered Accountants (CICA) grants the CA designation. A **chartered accountant (CA)** provides the financial information for use by shareholders, government, creditors, and others "outside" an organization. A CA is widely recognized as the leading financial and accounting professional in Canada and has satisfied rigorous requirements; it is in no way less than the CGA or CMA. CA firms typically provide tax, audit, and management services.[13] The CA is a professional and can work in both public and private sector fields of business and finance.

Off the Mark

Department of Defence Makes Some Big Accounting Errors

In 2013, federal auditors from the Office of the Auditor General were performing a routine inspection of Canada's Department of National Defence's financial records from 2012. Their reports revealed $1.5 billion in "significant" accounting errors in the records, including the following:

- A $210 million error as a result of double counting the same anti-missile system.
- A $15 million mistake of listing an inaccurate price for torpedoes.
- A $27 million error resulting from failing to remove two defunct CF-18 fighter jets from inventory.

The Auditor General's Office also discovered an incorrect listing of $200 million for services that were never rendered. "The magnitude of errors listed above raises concern about the reliability of the department's accounts and its reported financial information," a letter from the auditors that was sent to senior Defence officials in December 2013 stated.

Since the federal government has been scrutinized in the media for its poor reputation for financial management, it is not surprising that the Defence Department disagreed with the report from the auditors. The audit reached the estimate of $1.5 billion worth of inaccuracies through a limited review, which revealed close to $700 million in problems. It appears that the department's inventory-tracking system was riddled with complications. Specifically, the department failed to remove $117 million worth of inoperable vehicles, either defunct or retired, from the books. The auditors noted the Defence Department's plans to implement a new inventory-tracking system, but that it was not going to be implemented until 2016 at the earliest.

This is not the first time the Defence Department has disagreed with the Auditor General's Office. In April 2012, the Auditor General's Office released a report stating that the Defence Department mishandled the F-35 project. The department conceded to one mistake—understating the true costs of the fighter—but otherwise it insisted it did nothing wrong. Nevertheless, the Conservative government froze the stealth fighter program. It also ordered officials to reanalyze potential options for replacing aging CF-18s.[14]

Discussion Questions

1. **How can such errors go on for years without being noticed? Is this any one person's fault?**
2. **How might the government prevent such errors from occurring? Is it important for the department to publicize and correct the errors? Why or why not?**
3. **Isn't this just a small oversight with nothing to be concerned about? After all, it is a government agency. What might be the effect on the Defence Department's public image?**

Types of Accounting

What are the types of corporate accounting?

Accounting is a general term, to say the least. Since different forms of business have varying needs, there is a multitude of specialty areas under the accounting umbrella.

As stated in the beginning of this chapter, financial managers must make many important decisions. Some decisions may involve determining whether the company's financial assets are working most efficiently (i.e., earning as much money as possible), evaluating what kind of financing strategy is best, or choosing a way to obtain needed funds. The answers to these decisions, and many more, are found in the reports and analysis done by corporate accountants. **Corporate accounting** is the part of an organization's finance department responsible for gathering and assembling data required for key financial statements. Corporate accounting has two separate functions: *managerial accounting* and *financial accounting*.

corporate accounting The part of an organization's finance department responsible for gathering and assembling data required for key financial statements.

Managerial accounting is used to provide information and analyses to managers within the organization to assist them in making good business decisions. More specifically, managerial accounting is responsible for tracking sales and the costs of producing the sales (production, marketing, and distribution). By doing so, it helps determine how efficiently a company is run. Moreover, managerial accountants help determine which business activities are most and least profitable. Based on their analysis, management is better equipped to make decisions about whether to continue with, expand, or eliminate certain business activities. Managerial accounting produces budgets so senior management can make informed decisions. For example, a managerial accounting budget can help management decide whether it should increase staff or institute layoffs. In addition, by monitoring the activities involved in planned budgets, managerial accountants help determine and anticipate in what areas the company strays from its budgeted expectations.

managerial accounting Used to provide information and analyses to managers within the organization to assist them in making good business decisions.

While individuals inside a company use managerial accounting to make decisions, interested parties outside a company depend on financial accounting to make financial decisions. **Financial accounting** produces financial documents to aid decision makers outside an organization in making decisions regarding investments and credibility. Investors and shareholders rely on financial accounting to help them evaluate a company's performance and profitability. Such information is generally found in key documents such as quarterly statements or **annual reports**—documents produced once a year that present the current financial state of a company and future expectations. These documents help investors determine whether it is wise to put funds into the company. Banks and other creditors analyze financial accounting statements to determine the business's financial health and creditworthiness.

financial accounting Produces financial documents to aid decision makers outside an organization in making decisions regarding investments and credibility.

annual reports Documents produced once a year to present the current financial state of a company and future expectations.

Is auditing considered an area of accounting?

Auditing is responsible for reviewing and evaluating the accuracy of financial reports. Large corporations may have private accountants on staff who work in-house to determine whether the company's financial information is recorded correctly and by using proper procedures. Generally, companies hire independent auditors from outside the company to ensure their financial reports have been prepared accurately and are not biased or manipulated in any way. Companies can avoid devastating budget problems, such as the one experienced by the Department of National Defence (described in the Off the Mark box above), by performing audits.

auditing Responsible for reviewing and evaluating the accuracy of financial reports.

Do businesses hire outside accounting firms to complete their income tax returns?

Paying taxes is an important part of running a business. Governments require individuals and organizations to file tax returns annually. **Tax accounting** involves preparing taxes and giving advice on tax strategies. The process for filing taxes can be complicated and is ever changing, so companies often have tax accountants on staff or hire an outside accounting firm such as H&R Block or BDO Canada to prepare their taxes.

tax accounting Involves preparing taxes and giving advice on tax strategies.

Do government and nonprofit organizations report financial activities?

Accounting is not only for organizations that strive to make money; government institutions and

government and nonprofit accounting Refers to the accounting required for organizations that are not focused on generating a profit, such as legislative bodies and charities.

nonprofit companies use accounting as well. **Government and nonprofit accounting** refers to the accounting required for organizations that are not focused on generating a profit, such as legislative bodies and charities. Governmental and nonprofit organizations need financial management expertise. Although their goal is not to make a profit, these organizations still must distribute and manage funds, maintain a budget, and plan for future projects. Government and nonprofit organizations must also report their financial activities so taxpayers and donors can see how funds are spent and used.

Accounting Standards and Processes

LO6 Explain how double-entry bookkeeping is used to maintain the balance of the fundamental accounting equation.

Are there specific standards accountants must adhere to? For any financial information to be useful, it is critical that the information is accurate, fair and objective, and consistent over time. Therefore, accountants in Canada follow standards defined by Financial Reporting and Assurance Standards Canada. Public companies (those who list their shares on a stock exchange) are required to follow International Financial Reporting Standards (IFRS). Private enterprises have a choice: They can either follow IFRS or they can follow the Accounting Standards for Private Enterprises (ASPE). Although ASPE and IFRS provide accountants with general rules, they are often subject to different interpretations, which can lead to problems. Companies such as WorldCom, Enron, and Tyco made headlines and fell into financial ruin in the early 2000s because of aggressive and fraudulent accounting practices. Hundreds of thousands of investors lost millions of dollars because of the accounting fraud that occurred in these companies' corporate financial disclosures, and one of the five big accounting firms, Arthur Andersen, was found guilty of criminal charges related to the firm's handling of its audit of Enron. The conviction was later reversed, but the damage to Arthur Andersen's image has subsequently made it difficult for the firm to return as a viable business.

Due to a series of major corporate scandals, the United States introduced the Sarbanes-Oxley Act (SOX) in 2002 to restore investor confidence in the markets and prevent future occurrences of corporate fraud. Given that 15 percent of Canadian firms listed on the Toronto Stock Exchange (TSX) were also listed on a U.S. stock exchange, Canadian regulators adopted similar reforms.[15] The regulatory reforms are an ongoing process, and in Canada, the Canadian Securities Administrators (CSA) have introduced a series of national instruments and policies to cover major SOX provisions. It is worth noting that Canada is the only industrialized country that still does not have a federal regulatory agency overseeing securities markets. In Canada, each market is governed by provincial authorities, such as the Ontario Securities Commission.

With the growing number of business-related investigations and the growing complexity of the business environment, the use of forensic accountants has increased. A **forensic accountant** provides investigative accounting services and litigation support. *Forensic* means "pertaining to or used in a court of law," and forensic accountants are often involved in investigating and analyzing financial evidence and assisting in legal proceedings by providing reports, advice, and evidence to clients, lawyers, and courts. This may include testifying in court as an expert witness and preparing visual aids to support trial evidence.[16]

forensic accountant Provides investigative accounting services and litigation support.

In an attempt to make accounting practices country-neutral and financial information comparable between countries, the International Accounting Standards Board (IASB) developed International Financial Reporting Standards (IFRS) (see this chapter's closing discussion). By doing so, multinational companies that have operations in Canada and other countries, such as Toyota, Walmart, Best Buy, and General Motors, may avoid the need to convert regional financial reports into foreign accounting specifications. As mentioned earlier, it is now mandatory in Canada for all public companies (even if they only operate within Canada) to follow IFRS.

What is the accounting process? When people think of accounting, most think of the systematic recording of a company's every financial transaction, which is a small but

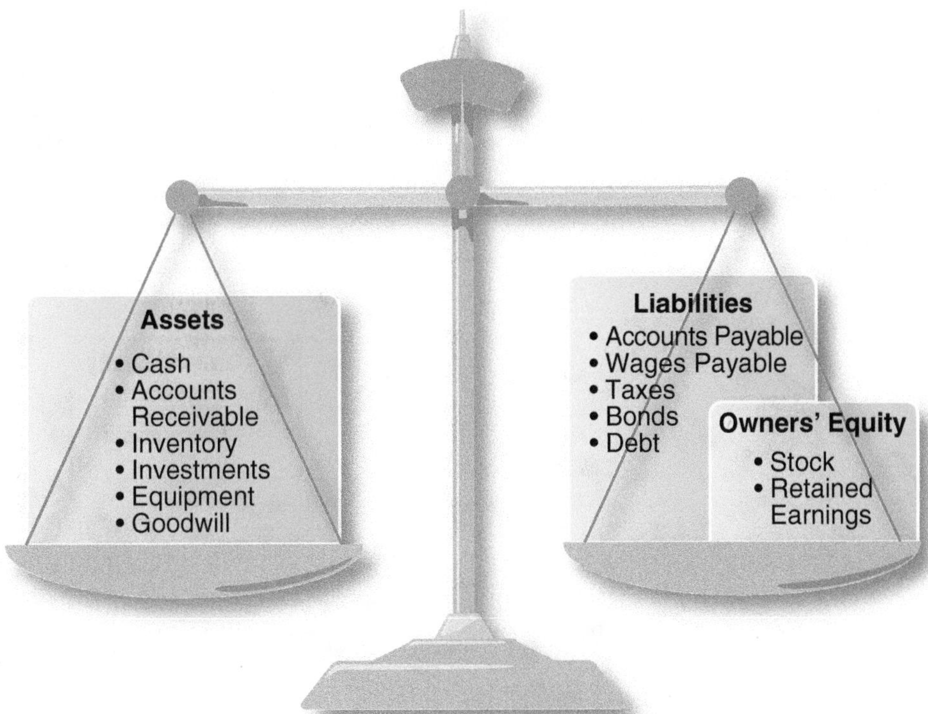

Figure 11.3 The Fundamental Accounting Equation

important part of accounting called **bookkeeping**. The process of bookkeeping centres on the fundamental concept that what a company owns (**assets**) must equal what it owes to its creditors (**liabilities**) plus what it owes to its owners (**owners' equity**). This balance is illustrated in **Figure 11.3** and is better described as the **fundamental accounting equation**: assets = liabilities + owners' equity.

bookkeeping The systematic recording of a company's every financial transaction.

assets What the company owns.

liabilities What the company owes to its creditors.

owners' equity What the company owes to its owners.

fundamental accounting equation Assets = liabilities + owners' equity.

double-entry bookkeeping Recognizes that for every transaction that affects an asset, an equal transaction must also affect either a liability or owners' equity.

Does the accounting equation always stay in balance? To maintain the balance of assets and liabilities plus owners' equity, accountants use a recording system called double-entry bookkeeping. **Double-entry bookkeeping** recognizes that for every transaction that affects an asset, an equal transaction must also affect either a liability or owners' equity. For example, say you were to start a business mowing lawns. Your initial assets are a lawn mower worth $500 and $1500 in cash that you have saved and are willing to use to start the business. Your assets total $2000. Because the cash and lawn mower were yours to begin with, you do not owe anyone any money, so you have zero liabilities. If you were to close the business tomorrow, the cash and the lawn mower would belong to you; therefore, they are considered owners' equity. The accounting statement for your lawn mowing business would look like the one in **Figure 11.4**.

Now imagine that the business is growing rapidly. You realize you need to buy another lawn mower and you also want to buy a snow blower so you can expand your business to include snow removal. Together these items cost $2500. You don't have enough cash to buy either outright, so you have to borrow the money. Although you are increasing your assets with a new riding lawn mower and a new snow blower, you are also adding a liability—the debt you have incurred to buy the new equipment. If the business closed tomorrow, your owners' equity would not change because you could sell the lawn mower and the snow blower to pay off the debt. The accounting statement for your lawn mower business would look like the one in **Figure 11.5**.

Accounting is necessary for businesses of all sizes to help figure out what they have the potential to do. Arnold Sawyer was able to handle finances for his niece's catering

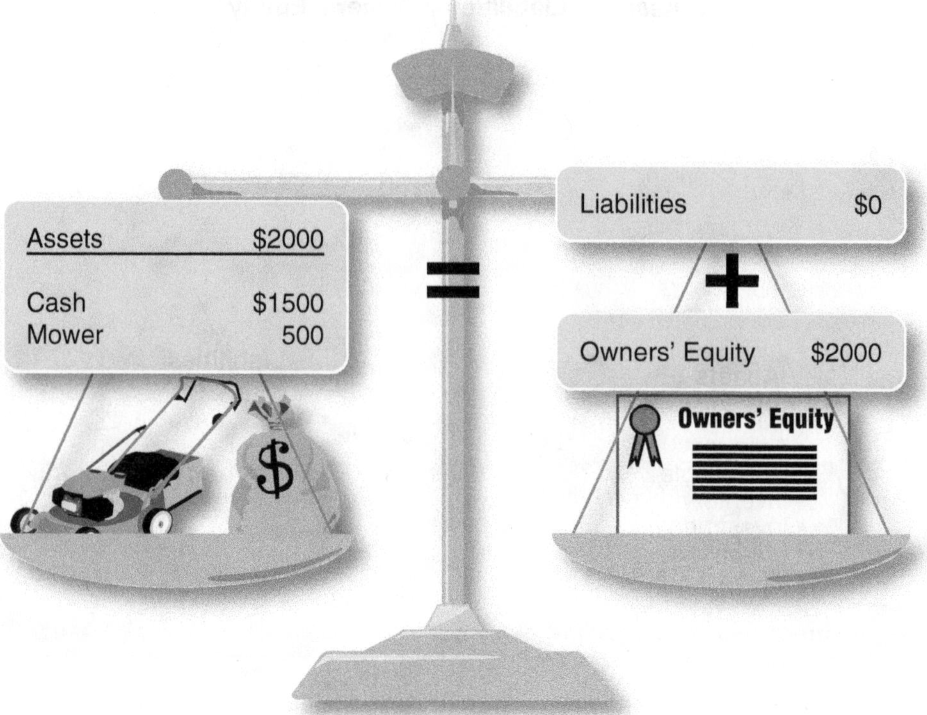

Figure 11.4 Business with No Liability

Without any liabilities, assets equal owners' equity.

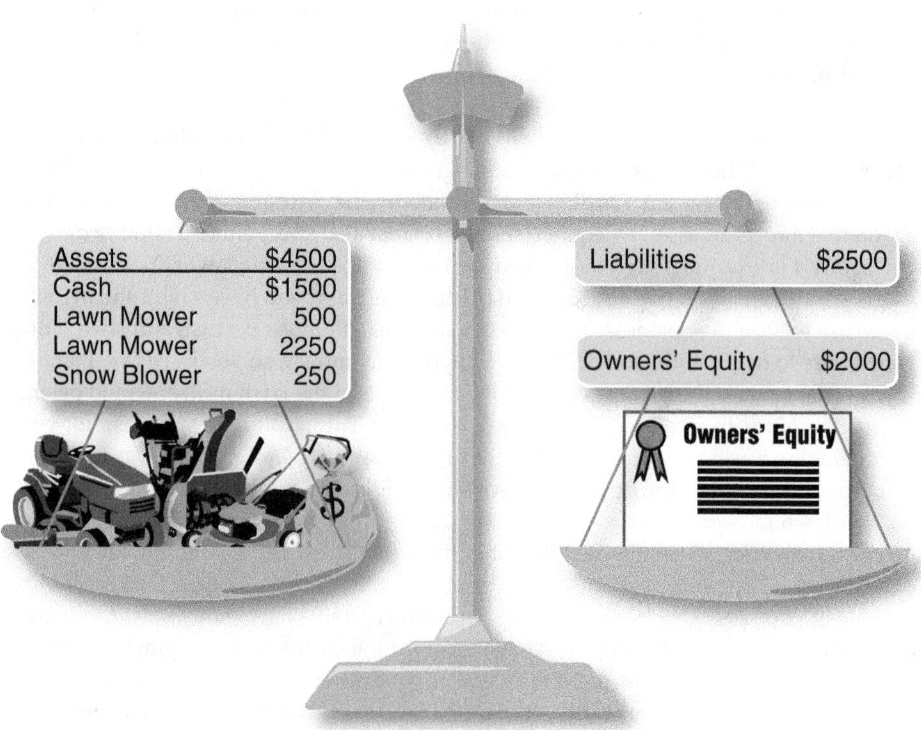

Figure 11.5 Business with Liability

Borrowing to buy assets increases assets and liabilities.

business for a while, but when business boomed he didn't know what to do. He realized he was in over his head and convinced his niece that she needed to hire an accountant to handle these important matters. Having someone on staff who is knowledgeable about accounting is vital to a company's success.

FINANCIAL STATEMENTS

LO7 Describe the functions of balance sheets, income statements, and statements of cash flows.

The Balance Sheet

Are companies required to publish financial information? **Financial statements** are the formal reports of a business's financial transactions that accountants prepare periodically. They represent what has happened in the past and provide management, as well as various outsiders such as creditors and investors, with a perspective of what is going to happen in the future. Publicly owned companies are required to publish three financial statements:

- A **balance sheet** shows what the company owns and what it has borrowed (owes) at a fixed point in time and shows the net worth of the business.
- An **income statement** shows how much money is coming into a company and how much money a company is spending over a period. It shows how well a company has done in terms of profit and loss.
- A **statement of cash flows** shows the exchange of money between a company and everyone else it deals with over a period. It shows where cash was used.

Let's look more closely at each of these financial statements.

financial statements The formal reports of a business's financial transactions that accountants prepare periodically.

balance sheet Shows what the company owns and what it has borrowed (owes) at a fixed point in time and shows the net worth of the business.

income statement Shows how much money is coming into a company and how much money a company is spending over a period. It shows how well a company has done in terms of profit and loss.

statement of cash flows Shows the exchange of money between a company and everyone else it deals with over a period. It shows where cash was used.

What is the balance sheet used for? A balance sheet is a snapshot of a business's financial condition at a specific point in time. It reflects what the company owns (assets), what it owes to its creditors (liabilities), and what it owes to the owners (owners' equity). At any point in time, the information in the balance sheet is used to answer questions such as "Is the business in a good position to expand?" and "Does the business have enough cash to ride out an anticipated slowdown in sales?" In addition, by analyzing how a balance sheet changes over time, financial managers can identify trends and then suggest strategies to manage accounts receivable and accounts payable in a way that is most beneficial to the company's bottom line. **Figure 11.6** is a condensed balance sheet for Google.

What does the balance sheet reveal? Balance sheets are based on the most fundamental equation in business accounting:

$$\text{assets} = \overbrace{\text{liabilities} + \text{owners' equity}}^{\text{claims on assets}}$$

It is important to remember that assets (the items on the left side of the balance sheet) must always equal claims on assets, which are liabilities plus owners' equity (the items on the right side of the balance sheet). Let's look at each of these components in a bit more detail, and then see how they all fit together on a balance sheet.

Assets Assets are the things a company owns, which include cash, investments, buildings, furniture, and equipment. On a balance sheet, assets are organized into three categories: current, fixed, and intangible. These categories are listed on the balance sheet in order of liquidity—the speed at which assets can be turned into cash.

- **Current assets** are those assets that can be turned into cash within a year. Examples of current assets include cash, accounts receivable, inventory, and short-term investments like money market accounts. **Accounts receivable** are amounts owed to the company from customers who have purchased goods or services on credit. As you can see in Figure 11.6, as of the end of 2013, Google had more than US$72.8 billion in current assets.

current assets Those assets that can be turned into cash within a year.

accounts receivable Amounts owed to the company from customers who have purchased goods or services on credit.

Google Inc.
Summary of Balance Sheet
as of December 31, 2013
(in millions of U.S. Dollars)

Assets		Liabilities	
Current Assets		Current Liabilities	
Cash and Cash Equivalents	18 898	Accounts Payable	11 837
Short-Term Investments	39 819	Short/Current Long-Term Debt	3 009
Net Receivables	10 916	Other Current Liabilities	1 062
Inventory	426	**Total Current Liabilities**	**15 908**
Other Current Assets	2 827		
Total Current Assets	**72 886**	Long-Term Liabilities	
		Long-Term Debt	2 236
Fixed Assets		Other Liabilities	3 381
Property, Plant, and Equipment	16 524	Deferred Long-Term Liability Charges	2 086
Total Fixed Assets	**16 524**	**Total Long-Term Liabilities**	**7 703**
Intangible Assets		**Total Liabilities**	**23 611**
Goodwill	11 492		
Long-Term Investents	1 976		
Other Intangible Assets	6 066	Common Stock	25 922
Total Intangible Assets	**19 534**	Retained Earnings	61 262
Other Assets	1 976	Other Stockholder Equity	125
		Total Owners' Equity	**87 309**
Total Assets	**110 920**	**Total Liabilities and Owners' Equity**	**110 920**

Figure 11.6 Condensed Balance Sheet for Google Inc.

Source: Based on Yahoo! Finance, "Google Inc. Balance Sheet," accessed January 19, 2014, https://ca.finance.yahoo.com/q/bs?s=googl&ql=1.

fixed assets Assets with long-term use, such as real estate, buildings, machinery, and equipment.

depreciation Spreads out the cost of the equipment over its useful life.

intangible assets Assets that do not have physical characteristics (you can't touch or see them), but they have value nonetheless. Trademarks, patents, and copyrights are examples of intangible assets, in addition to strong brand recognition and excellent customer or employee relations.

goodwill An accounting concept meaning the value of an entity over and above the value of its assets.

amortization The process of applying long-term expenses to intangible assets such as goodwill or patents.

- **Fixed assets** are assets with long-term use, such as real estate, buildings, machinery, and equipment. Often the value of a fixed asset, such as machinery or equipment, decreases over time because of usage or obsolescence. To compensate for such reduction in value over time, accountants use **depreciation** to spread out the cost of the equipment over its useful life. Depreciation helps keep the accounting equation in balance by matching the expense of the asset with the revenue that asset is expected to generate. As you can see in Figure 11.6, as of December 31, 2013, Google had approximately US$16.5 billion in fixed assets.
- **Intangible assets** do not have physical characteristics (you can't touch or see them), but they have value nonetheless. Trademarks, patents, and copyrights are examples of intangible assets, in addition to strong brand recognition and excellent customer or employee morale. Intangible assets are often reflected on financial statements and reports as *goodwill*. **Goodwill** is an accounting concept meaning the value of an entity over and above the value of its assets. **Amortization** is the process of applying those long-term expenses to intangible assets such as goodwill or patents. Sometimes the term *amortization* is used to indicate the length of time given to pay off the principal and interest of a debt, as with a mortgage or other loan. However, for accounting purposes, only the narrower definition applies. As you can see in Figure 11.6, Google's goodwill and intangible assets amounted to approximately US$17.5 billion.

Liabilities Liabilities are all debts and obligations owed by the business to outside creditors, suppliers, or other vendors. Liabilities are listed on the balance sheet in the order in which they will come due.

- **Current liabilities** (or *short-term liabilities*) are obligations a company is responsible for paying within a year or less and are listed first on the balance sheet. They consist of accounts payable, accrued expenses, and short-term financing. **Accounts payable** are obligations a company owes to vendors and creditors. They are similar to those bills you need to pay every month, such as cable fees, credit card payments, cellphone charges, and other obligations paid less frequently such as taxes and insurance. **Accrued expenses** include payroll, commissions, and benefits earned but not paid to employees. Trade credit and commercial paper make up short-term financing. As you can see in Figure 11.6, Google had approximately US$15.9 billion in current liabilities.

- **Long-term liabilities** include debts and obligations owed by the company and due more than one year from the current date, such as mortgage loans for the purchase of land or buildings, long-term leases on equipment or buildings, and bonds issued for large projects. As you can see in Figure 11.6, Google's long-term liabilities were approximately US$7.7 billion at the end of 2013.

current liabilities Obligations a company is responsible for paying within a year or less and are listed first on the balance sheet. Also called short-term liabilities.

accounts payable Obligations a company owes to vendors and creditors.

accrued expenses Include payroll, commissions, and benefits that have been earned but not paid to employees.

long-term liabilities Include debts and obligations owed by the company and due more than one year from the current date, such as mortgage loans for the purchase of land or buildings, long-term leases on equipment or buildings, and bonds issued for large projects.

Owners' Equity The easiest way to think of owners' equity is what is left over after you have accounted for all your assets and taken away all that you owe. For small businesses, owners' equity is literally the amount the owners in the business can call their own. Owners' equity increases as the business grows, assuming debt has not increased. It is often referred to as the owners' capital account.

For larger publicly owned companies, owners' equity becomes a bit more complicated. Shareholders are the owners of publicly owned companies. Owners' equity, in this case, is the value of the stock issued as part of the owners' (shareholders') investment in the business and retained earnings, which are the accumulated profits a business has held onto for reinvestment into the company. As you can see in Figure 11.6, the owners' equity (or stockholders' equity, because it is a public company) for Google was approximately US$87.3 billion.

Analyzing a Balance Sheet

How do you analyze a balance sheet?

A lot of information about a company can be determined by the balance sheet. For example, just looking at the amount of inventory a company keeps on hand can be an indicator of a company's efficiency. **Inventory** is the merchandise a business owns but has not sold. Inventory on hand is necessary to satisfy customers' needs quickly, which makes for good business. However, there are costs associated with keeping inventory, the most obvious being the money spent to purchase the merchandise. In addition to the initial cost, storing unused inventory incurs warehousing costs and ties up money that could be used elsewhere. An even worse situation can arise if the value of unused inventory decreases over time, causing the company to lose money. This is a big concern for computer companies like Apple, whose inventory consists of computer parts and other technology-related components that can quickly become obsolete. Generally, it is okay to have a lot of inventory on hand if it is being sold quickly enough to avoid becoming outdated or spoiled. Inventory turnover varies greatly by industry, and companies must always have enough inventory to keep business moving and keep up with competitors.

inventory The merchandise a business owns but has not sold.

Ratio Analysis Although looking at a balance sheet is a good way to determine the overall financial health of a company, the data presented on the sheet can be overwhelming and useless to investors if they are not organized. This is why ratio analysis is crucial when analyzing financial statements. **Ratio analysis** is a comparison of numbers and therefore is used to compare current data to data from previous years, competitors' data, or industry averages. Ratios eliminate the effect of size, so you can reasonably compare a large company's performance to a smaller company's performance. There are three main calculations one can do using information from a balance sheet to determine a company's financial health and liquidity:

1. *Working capital:* Current assets – current liabilities
2. *Current ratio:* Current assets ÷ current liabilities
3. *Debt to equity ratio:* Total liabilities ÷ owners' equity

Let's examine these measurements in more detail.

ratio analysis A comparison of numbers; it is used to compare current data to data from previous years, competitors' data, or industry averages.

Working Capital One of the most important reasons one looks at a company's balance sheet is to determine the company's working capital. **Working capital** tells you

working capital The amount left over if the company pays off its short-term liabilities with its short-term assets. It is a measure of a company's short-term financial fitness as well as its efficiency.

what is left over if the company pays off its short-term liabilities with its short-term assets. Working capital is a measure of a company's short-term financial fitness as well as its efficiency. Working capital is calculated as

$$\text{current assets} - \text{current liabilities} = \text{working capital}$$

If a company has positive working capital (its current assets are greater than its current liabilities), that means it is able to pay off its short-term liabilities. If a company has negative working capital (its current assets are less than its current liabilities), that means it is currently unable to offset its short-term liabilities with its current assets. In this case, even after adding up all of a company's cash, collecting all funds from accounts receivable, and selling all inventory, the company would still be unable to pay back creditors in the short term. When a company's current liabilities surpass its current assets, many financial difficulties develop, bankruptcy being the most severe. It is important to watch for changes in working capital, as a decline in positive working capital over time can be an indication that a company's finances are in trouble. For example, a company experiencing a decrease in sales will have a decrease in accounts receivable (current assets).

On the other hand, situations such as the one faced by Arnold Sawyer and his niece's catering company can arise when a company experiences a sudden spike in sales. It is possible to have positive working capital, but not have enough immediately available to handle a large, unexpected cash need. A good financial manager and accountant must maintain a balance between having enough cash on hand and keeping the available short-term assets from being idle. Because of this, working capital can also be an indicator of a company's underlying operational efficiency.

Current Ratio (Liquidity Ratio) Although working capital is an important measurement, it is hard to compare how efficient a company is to the rest of the industry or to its competitors, especially if companies vary significantly in size. The **current ratio** (or *liquidity ratio*) is a measurement used to determine the extent to which a company can meet its current financial obligations. Current ratio is calculated as

current ratio A measurement used to determine the extent to which a company can meet its current financial obligations. Also called the liquidity ratio.

$$\text{current ratio} = \frac{\text{current assets}}{\text{current liabilities}}$$

As you can see in Figure 11.6, Google's current ratio ($72 886/$15 908) equals 4.58, which means Google has US$4.58 of current assets for every US$1 of current liabilities. Usually a company with a current ratio of 2 or better is considered a safe risk for granting short-term credit to because it has two or more times current assets than current liabilities, so if need be the current assets could be converted to cash to pay off the current liabilities.

It is important for a company to compare its current ratio to that of the industry average as well. For example, if during 2013 the current ratio for automotive manufacturers was 1.68, and during the same year Toyota had a current ratio of 1.4, then Toyota would rank slightly below the industry average. Having a current ratio that is too high indicates the company may not be very efficient with its cash, but having a current ratio that is too low may indicate the company will face potential problems paying back its creditors.

Debt to Equity Ratio (Leverage Ratio) Another way to analyze the activities of a company is to use the debt to equity ratio. Although leverage can be beneficial by freeing up cash for other investments, too much debt can become a problem. Companies with too much long-term debt may end up financially overburdened with interest payments. The **debt to equity ratio** (or *leverage ratio*) measures how much debt a company has relative to its assets by comparing a company's total liabilities to its total owners' (or shareholders') equity. Debt to equity ratio is calculated as

debt to equity ratio Measures how much debt a company has relative to its assets by comparing a company's total liabilities to its total owners' (or shareholders') equity. Also called the leverage ratio.

$$\text{debt to equity ratio} = \frac{\text{total liabilities}}{\text{owners' equity}}$$

The debt to equity ratio can give a general idea of a company's financial leverage. As you may remember from the beginning of this chapter, *leverage* is the amount of debt used to finance a firm's assets. The debt to equity ratio will tell potential investors how

Table 11.3 Industry Comparison of Balance Sheet Data for Period Ending December 31, 2013*

Company	Working Capital	Current Ratio	Debt to Equity Ratio
	Current Assets – Current Liabilities	**Current Assets/Current Liabilities**	**Total Liabilities/Owners' Equity**
Google	$56 978	4.58	0.27
	($72 886 – $15 908)	($72 886/$15 908)	($23 611/$87 309)
Yahoo	$3686	3.75	0.29
	($5026 – $1340)	($5026/$1340)	($3730/$13 075)

**Numbers in US$mil.*

Sources: Yahoo! Finance, "Google Inc. Balance Sheet, accessed January 19, 2014, https://ca.finance.yahoo.com/q/bs?s=GOOGL; and "Yahoo! Inc. Balance Sheet," accessed January 19, 2014, http://finance.yahoo.com/q/bs?s=YHOO.

much a company is willing to go into debt with creditors, lenders, and suppliers over debt with shareholders. As you can see in Figure 11.6, Google's debt to equity ratio is 0.27, which means Google has 27 percent debt and 73 percent equity. A ratio above 1 (above 100 percent) shows that a firm has more debt than equity. Creditors and investors may perceive a company as quite risky if it has a very high debt to equity ratio. A lower debt to equity ratio number means that a company is using less leverage and has more equity. It is a good idea for a company to compare its debt to equity ratio with that of the industry standard, because having a high debt to equity ratio in some industries is quite acceptable.

To get a better idea of how ratio analysis is used as a comparison tool, see the information displayed in **Table 11.3**. In this case, both companies are in the same industry but Google is much bigger than Yahoo, so comparing absolute numbers is not effective. It appears that Google has a better current ratio than Yahoo, but the debt to equity ratios are about the same.

Income Statements

What does an income statement show? An income statement reflects the profitability of a company by showing how much money the company takes in (*revenue*) and how much money it spends (*expenses*). **Revenue** is any monies received by a company from sales of goods or services or from other sources such as licensing fees, rental fees, or interest earned. **Expenses** are the costs incurred (an outflow of money) while operating a business. The difference of money in and money out is the profit or loss, sometimes referred to as the **bottom line**. Besides showing overall profitability, income statements also indicate how effectively management is controlling expenses by pinpointing abnormal or excessive expenditures, highlighting unexpected increases in costs of goods sold, or showing a change in returns.

revenue Any monies received by a company from sales of goods or services or from other sources such as licensing fees, rental fees, or interest earned.

expenses The costs incurred (an outflow of money) to produce and sell the goods and services offered by a business.

bottom line Refers to the difference of money in and money out, the profit or loss.

What are the components of an income statement? Recall that the balance sheet relates directly to the fundamental accounting equation: assets = liabilities + owners' equity. Similarly, income statements also work around an equation:

revenues – expenses = profit (or loss)

The income statement is grouped into four main categories: revenues, costs of goods sold, operating expenses, and net income, which are arranged in the following formula:

[(revenue – cost of goods) – operating expenses] – taxes = net income or (loss)

Figure 11.7 shows an income statement for Google Inc. Let's look at each of these components in more detail, and then see how they all fit together on an income statement.

Revenue If a company has several different product lines or businesses, the income statement shows each product or division in categories to distinguish how much each

Google Inc.
Summary Income Statement
as of December 31, 2013
(in millions of U.S. Dollars)

Total Revenue	**$55 550**
Cost of Goods Sold	(25 858)
Gross Profit	**$29 692**
Operating Expenses	
Research Development	$7952
Selling General and Administrative	$12 049
Total Operating Expenses	**(20 001)**
Net Income Before Interest and Taxes	**$13 966**
Interest Income	530
Net income (loss) from discontinued operations	706
Less: Income Tax Expense	(2282)
Net Income	**$12 920**

Figure 11.7 Summary Income Statement for Google Inc.

Source: Based on Google Inc., "Consolidated Statements of Income," accessed January 19, 2014, https://investor.google.com/pdf/20131231_google_10K.pdf. Used by the permission of Google Inc.

generated in revenue. For example, Starbucks breaks down its revenue into two sources: retail and specialty. Revenue generated from retail sources is from sales made at all Starbucks stores. Specialty sales include revenue generated from licensing arrangements, food service accounts, and other initiatives related to core businesses.[17]

cost of goods sold (COGS) The variable expenses a company incurs to manufacture and sell a product, including the price of raw materials used in creating the good along with the labour costs used to produce and sell the items.

gross profit Calculated by subtracting cost of goods sold (or cost of sales) from revenue (total sales).

operating expenses The overhead costs incurred with running the business. They include sales, general, and administrative expenses. These costs may consist of items such as rent, salaries, wages, utilities, depreciation, and insurance.

operating income Determined when operating expenses are subtracted from gross profit.

Cost of Goods Sold An income statement delineates several categories of expenses. The first category of expenses, cost of goods sold (COGS), is a separate item on an income statement. **Cost of goods sold (COGS)** are the variable expenses a company incurs to manufacture and sell a product, including the price of raw materials used in creating the good along with the labour costs used to produce and sell the items. For Starbucks, obviously, the costs of coffee beans, cups, milk, and sugar are included in COGS. When you subtract cost of goods sold (or cost of sales) from revenue (total sales), the result is **gross profit**. Gross profit tells you how much money a company makes just from its products and how efficiently management controls costs in the production process. In addition, analysts use gross profit to calculate one of the most fundamental performance ratios used to compare the profitability of companies: *gross profit margin* (which will be discussed later in this chapter).

Operating Expenses Although it is certainly important to identify the costs associated with producing the product or service, it is also important to identify **operating expenses**, the overhead costs incurred with running the business. Operating expenses include sales, general, and administrative expenses. These costs may consist of items such as rent, salaries, wages, utilities, depreciation, and insurance. Expenses associated with research and development of new products also are included in operating expenses. Unlike costs of goods sold, operating expenses usually do not vary with the level of sales or production and are constant or "fixed." Outside interested parties (lenders and investors) watch operating expenses closely as an indication of managerial efficiency. Management's goal is to keep operating expenses as low as possible without negatively affecting the underlying business. The amount of profit realized from the business's operations (**operating income**) is determined when operating expenses are subtracted from gross profit.

Management focuses on operating income as they prepare and monitor budgets. Some feel that operating income is a more reliable and meaningful indicator of profitability than gross profit since it reflects management's ability to control operating expenses. But it is still not the "bottom line." Adding or subtracting any other income or expense, such as interest payments on outstanding debt obligations or earnings from investments, adjusts operating income further. Finally, taxes paid to local and federal governments are subtracted to determine net income (or net income after taxes). **Net income (or loss)** is the revenue remaining after all costs and expenses, including taxes, have been paid. It is the "bottom line" and is usually stated on the very last line of an income statement. For publicly owned companies, however, net income is further adjusted by dividend payments to shareholders, resulting in *adjusted net income*.

net income (or loss) The revenue remaining after all costs and expenses, including taxes, have been paid. It is the "bottom line" and is usually stated on the very last line of an income statement.

Analyzing Income Statements

How do I analyze an income statement? One of the main purposes of the income statement is to report a company's earnings to its shareholders. However, an income statement reveals much more about a company, such as how effectively management controls expenses or how the company's profits compare to others in its industry. Specifically, the measurements that reveal this information are

- gross profit margin
- operating profit margin
- earnings per share (EPS)

Let's look at each measurement in detail to understand the differences between them and learn how they are used to analyze a company's financial health.

How can I determine a company's overall profitability? A company's profitability and efficiency can be determined at two levels: profitability of production, and profitability of operations. The **gross profit margin** determines a company's profitability of production. It indicates how efficient management is in using its labour and raw materials to produce goods. A gross profit margin is calculated as

$$\text{gross profit margin} = \frac{(\text{total revenue} - \text{COGS})}{\text{total revenue}}$$

gross profit margin Determines a company's profitability of production. It indicates how efficient management is in using its labour and raw materials to produce goods.

The **operating profit margin** determines a company's profitability of operations. It indicates how efficiently management is in using business operations to generate a profit. An operating profit margin is calculated as

$$\text{operating profit margin} = \frac{(\text{total revenue} - \text{COGS}) - \text{operating expenses}}{\text{total revenue}}$$

operating profit margin Determines a company's profitability of operations. It indicates how efficiently management is in using business operations to generate a profit.

Gross profit margin and operating profit margin are equally important to management as to investors. You may notice they are both ratios, and, as you have learned in this chapter, ratios are best used when comparing two or more companies. Look at **Table 11.4**. Google's gross profit (revenue less cost of goods sold) for 2012 is US$29.7 billion. Yahoo's gross profit of US$3.3 billion seems to pale in comparison. However, you'll notice that while the two companies' gross profits are quite different, their gross profit margins are very close.

How much of the company's profit belongs to the shareholders? The portion of a company's profit allocated to the shareholders on a per-share basis is determined by calculating **earnings per share**. The general formula for earnings per share is calculated as

$$\text{earnings per share} = \frac{\text{net income}}{\text{outstanding shares}}$$

earnings per share Determines the portion of a company's profit allocated to the shareholders on a per-share basis.

Again, looking at the earnings per share number in isolation is not completely meaningful. For example, it might seem reasonable to assume that a company with higher

Table 11.4 Benefit of Ratio Analysis

Company	Based on Annual Income Statement Data for Fiscal Year 2012	
	Gross Profit*	Gross Profit Margin
	Revenue − Cost of Goods Sold	Gross Profit/Revenue × 100
Google	$29 692	53.5
	($55 550 − $25 858)	([$29 692/$55 550] × 100)
Yahoo	$3331	71.2
	($4680 − $1349)	([$3331/$4680] × 100)

** Numbers in US$mil.*

Sources: Based on Google Inc., "Consolidated Statements of Income," accessed January 19, 2014, https://investor.google.com/pdf/20131231_google_10K.pdf; and Yahoo! Finance, "Yahoo! Inc. Income Statement," accessed January 19, 2014, http://finance.yahoo.com/q/is?annual=&s=YHOO+Income+Statement.

shares outstanding Common shares authorized, issued, and purchased by investors.

earnings per share will be the better company to invest in than one with lower earnings per share. However, a highly efficient company—and potential good investment—can have a low earnings per share ratio simply because it has a large number of outstanding shares. **Shares outstanding** are common shares authorized, issued, and purchased by investors. Still, shareholders and prospective investors monitor earnings per share closely. In some instances, the pressure of maintaining a continued growth record in net income or earnings per share has led management to "cook the books" or misrepresent financial information so that the business's bottom line appears better than it actually is. Such fraudulent behaviour was the notable downfall of companies such as Enron, WorldCom, and Tyco, and it was the motivation for the Sarbanes-Oxley Act of 2002. Therefore, it is best not to rely on any one financial measure and to look at the financial statements and other information as a whole.

Statement of Cash Flows

What is the statement of cash flows? You have just looked at two important financial statements, the balance sheet and the income statement. The statement of cash flows (or cash flow statement) is the third important financial statement and gives some information that the other two financial statements do not show. The balance sheet is a snapshot of a company's financial position, and the income statement reflects a company's profitability over a specific period. A statement of cash flows is different because it does not reflect the amount of incoming and outgoing transactions that have been recorded on credit. Instead, it only displays cash transactions, similar to a chequebook register. As shown in **Figure 11.8**, the statement of cash flows organizes and reports cash generated in three business components:

1. *Operating activities* measure cash used or provided by the core business of the company.
2. *Investing activities* represent the cash involved in the purchase or sale of investments or income-producing assets such as buildings and equipment.
3. *Financing activities* show the cash exchanged between the firm and its owners (or shareholders) and creditors, including dividend payments and debt service.

Why is the statement of cash flows important? The statement of cash flows tells a story that the income statement does not. The income statement reports revenue receipts and expense payments. Because revenue and expenses are often accrued (earned but not paid), the income statement does not tell how efficiently management generates and uses cash. The statement of cash flows, because it focuses specifically on cash, provides this important information. It shows whether all the revenues booked on the income statement have actually been collected. Looking again at Figure 11.8, it is apparent that the bulk of Google's change in cash position came from operations (sale of advertising and

Google Inc.
Summary of Cash Flow Statement
as of December 31, 2013
(in millions of U.S. Dollars)

Net Income	**$12 920**
Operating Activities, Cash Flows Provided by or Used in	
Depreciation and Amortization of Property and Equipment	2781
Amortization of Intangible and Other Assets	1158
Adjustments to Net Income	1831
Changes in Accounts Receivables	(1307)
Changes in Liabilities	1805
Change in Inventories	(234)
Changes in Other Operating Activities	(295)
Total Cash Flow from Operating Activities	**$18 659**
Investing Activities, Cash Flows Provided by or Used in	
Capital Expenditures	($7358)
Investments	(7099)
Other Cash Flows from Investing Activities	778
Total Cash Flows from Investing Activities	**($13 679)**
Financing Activities, Cash Flows Provided by or Used in	
Dividends Paid	$0
Net Proceeds (Payments) from Stock-Based Award Activities	(781)
Excess Tax Benefits from Stock-Based Award Activities	481
Sale Purchase of Stock	0
Net Borrowings	(557)
Total Cash Flows from Financing Activities	**$(857)**
Effect of Exchange Rate Changes	(3)
Change in Cash and Cash Equivalents	**$4120**

Figure 11.8 Summary Statement of Cash Flows for Google Inc.

Source: Based on Google Inc., "Consolidated Statements of Cash Flows," accessed January 19, 2014, https://investor.google.com/pdf/20131231_google_10K.pdf. Used by the permission of Google Inc.

search engine technology), rather than its investments. This information is useful to creditors who are interested in determining a company's short-term health, particularly in its ability to pay its bills. In addition, it signals to investors that the business is generating enough money to buy new inventory and to make investments in the business. Accounting personnel, potential employees, or contractors may be interested in cash flow information to determine whether a company will be able to afford salary and other labour obligations.

How is a statement of cash flow analyzed? The bottom number, or change in cash and cash equivalents, reflects the overall change in the company's cash position. If it is positive, it means that the company had an overall positive cash flow. If it is negative, the company paid out more cash than it took in. Recall on the balance sheet in Figure 11.6 that the first line item under current assets is cash and cash equivalents. The difference between cash and cash equivalent figures between periods is the same value that appears at the bottom of the statement of cash flows for the same period. The rest of the balance sheet itemizes the broad categories that show what generated that positive cash flow.

Simulation: OBM and Financial Statements

As you've learned, financial statements, including balance sheets, income statements, and statements of cash flow, reveal a great deal about the health and prospects of a company. Although the abundance of numbers and figures might seem overwhelming at first, they can be analyzed and assessed once you know what they all mean and how they are calculated.

Video: POPS: Financial Information: Accounting & Financial Statements

CHAPTER SYNOPSIS

LO1 Summarize the implications of financial management and how financial managers fulfill their responsibilities. (p. 272)

Producing, marketing, and distributing a product are important aspects of generating a profit. Even more important, however, is the company's ability to *pay* for the resources required to accomplish these tasks. Without management of finances, there is no business! Without good financial controls and planning, a company will not be able to respond to unexpected challenges or planned expansion. **Financial management** involves the strategic planning and budgeting of short- and long-term funds for current and future needs. Tracking past financial transactions, controlling current revenues and expenses, and planning for future financial needs of the company are the foundation of financial management.

A **financial manager** or chief financial officer (CFO) oversees the financial operations of a company. Generally, a financial manager assumes accounting responsibilities for the company. A financial manager is responsible for planning and managing the company's financial resources, including the following:

- developing plans that outline the company's financial short-term and long-term needs
- defining the sources and uses of funds needed to reach goals
- monitoring the cash flow of a company to ensure that obligations are paid in a timely and efficient manner and that funds owed to the company are collected efficiently
- investing any excess funds so that those funds can grow and be used for future development
- raising capital for future growth and expansion

LO2 Describe how financial managers plan for financial needs. (pp. 272–275)

A company's financial needs are both short term and long term in nature, and a financial manager must plan for both. In addition, he or she must ensure that funds are used optimally and that the firm is ultimately profitable. To meet these objectives, a financial manager oversees three important processes: forecasting financial needs, developing budgets and plans to meet financial needs, and establishing controls to ensure that the budgets and plans are being followed.

Forecasts predict revenue, costs, and expenses for a specific future period. Short-term forecasts would include predictions within the upcoming year, while long-term forecasts would include predictions for a period longer than one year into the future. A **budget** is a financial plan that outlines the company's planned cash flows, expected operating expenses, and anticipated revenues. It is very important that management compare actual performance regularly to the budget. This generally occurs every month. Without such a comparison, it is hard to determine whether the company is actually performing as expected.

LO3 Describe different short-term financing options available to finance business needs. (pp. 275–278)

Short-term financing is any type of financing repaid within a year or less. It is used to finance day-to-day operations such as payroll, inventory purchases, and overhead (utilities, rent, leases). As discussed in Chapter 4, smaller startup businesses often fund cash flow gaps first by appealing to friends and family. This is not a recommended strategy as it can lead to severed relationships if loans are not paid back promptly. However, when it is used, it is important that both parties understand and agree to formal payment arrangements. Another approach that many smaller businesses take to fund cash flow gaps is the use of credit cards. Credit cards are a good way to defer payments, but they can become very expensive if credit balances are not paid off completely every month.

Trade credit is the ability to purchase inventory and supplies on credit without interest. Suppliers will typically request payment within 30, 60, or 90 days. Deferring payment with trade credit is a good strategy to bridge a temporary cash flow gap because it does not tie up cash unnecessarily. Moreover, using trade credit keeps debt levels down, which is always attractive to outside investors and lenders. Some suppliers hesitate to give trade credit to organizations with a poor credit history. In such cases, the supplier may insist that the customer sign a promissory note as a condition of obtaining credit. A **promissory note** is a written promise to pay a supplier a specific amount of money by an agreed-upon date.

A **line of credit** is available credit that a manager can access at any time up to an amount agreed upon between the bank and the company. A **secured loan** requires collateral, which is generally the asset that the loan is financing, to guarantee the debt obligation. An **unsecured loan** does not require collateral. A **commercial finance company** is not considered a bank, but rather a financial institution that makes short-term loans to borrowers who offer tangible assets as collateral. **Factoring** is the process of selling accounts receivable for cash. **Commercial paper** is an unsecured (i.e., it does not need collateral) short-term debt instrument of $100 000 or more typically issued by a corporation to bridge a cash flow gap created by large accounts receivable, inventory, or payroll.

LO4 Summarize the pros and cons of debt and equity financing and differentiate among different types of long-term financing options. (pp. 278–283)

Debt financing occurs when a company borrows money that it is legally obligated to repay, with **interest**, by a specified time. Contrary to debt financing, the funds for **equity financing** are generated by the owners of the company rather than an outside lender. These funds might come from the company's own savings or partial sale of ownership in the company in the form of stock.

A **corporate bond** is a type of loan issued by a company and not a commercial bank or commercial finance company. It is a formal written agreement to reimburse a bond at a regular interest rate at a given date.

Stock is a unit of ownership in a company sold with the intention of raising capital to finance ongoing or future projects and expansions. **Equity** is money received in exchange for ownership in a business. **Issuing common stock** by selling common shares of ownership in the company to the general public—in other words, "going public"—can be a great option to generate funds through equity financing. The first time a company offers to sell new stock to the public is called an **initial public offering (IPO)**. **Dividends** are a portion of a company's profits distributed to shareholders as either cash payments or additional shares of stock.

Sometimes companies can get money from venture capitalists (discussed in Chapter 4). Because of the high level of risk, venture capitalists command an active role in the management decisions of the company. They seek their return in the form of equity, or ownership, in the company, and they anticipate a large return on their investment when the company is sold or goes public. Venture capitalists are willing to wait longer than other investors, lenders, or shareholders for returns on their investment, but they expect higher than normal results.

Retained earnings represent the profits (money remaining after taxes and other expenses are paid) not paid out in dividends. Using retained earnings is an ideal way to fund long-term projects because it saves companies from paying interest on loans or underwriting fees on bonds. Unfortunately, not all companies produce enough retained earnings to fund large projects.

LO5 Describe the functions of corporate accounting, managerial accounting, financial accounting, auditing, tax accounting, and government and nonprofit accounting. *(pp. 283–286)*

Corporate accounting is the part of an organization's finance department that is responsible for gathering and assembling data required for key financial statements. **Auditing** is responsible for reviewing and evaluating the accuracy of financial reports. **Financial accounting** produces financial documents to aid decision makers outside an organization in making decisions regarding investments and credibility. **Managerial accounting** is used to provide information and analysis to managers within the organization to assist them in making good business decisions. **Annual reports** are documents produced once a year to present the current financial state of a company and future expectations.

Tax accounting involves preparing taxes and giving advice on tax strategies. The process for filing taxes can be complicated and is ever changing, so companies often have tax accountants on staff or hire an outside accounting firm such as H&R Block or BDO Canada to prepare their taxes.

Government and nonprofit accounting refers to the accounting required for organizations that are not focused on generating a profit, such as legislative bodies and charities. Government and nonprofit organizations need financial management expertise. Although their goal is not to make a profit, these organizations still must distribute and manage funds, maintain a budget, and plan for future projects. Government and nonprofit organizations must also report their financial activities so taxpayers and donors can see how funds are spent and used.

LO6 Explain how double-entry bookkeeping is used to maintain the balance of the fundamental accounting equation. *(pp. 286–289)*

The systematic recording of a company's every financial transaction is called **bookkeeping**. The **fundamental accounting equation** is assets = liabilities + owners' equity. **Assets** are what the company owns. **Liabilities** are what the company owes to its creditors. **Owners' equity** is what the company owes to its owners.

To maintain the balance of assets and liabilities plus owner's equity, accountants use a recording system called double-entry bookkeeping. **Double-entry bookkeeping** recognizes that for every transaction that affects an asset, an equal transaction must also affect either a liability or owners' equity.

LO7 Describe the functions of balance sheets, income statements, and statements of cash flows. *(pp. 289–297)*

A **balance sheet** shows what the company owns and what it has borrowed (owes) at a fixed point in time and shows the net worth of the business. At any point in time, the information in the balance sheet is used to answer questions such as "Is the business in a good position to expand?" and "Does the business have enough cash to ride out an anticipated slowdown in sales?" In addition, by analyzing how a balance sheet changes over time, financial managers can identify trends and then suggest strategies to manage accounts receivable and accounts payable in a way that is most beneficial to the company's bottom line.

Balance sheets are based on the most fundamental equation in business accounting:

$$\text{assets} = \overbrace{\text{liabilities} + \text{owners' equity}}^{\text{claims on assets}}$$

There are three main calculations one can do using information from a balance sheet to determine a company's financial health and liquidity:

1. **Working capital:** current assets – current liabilities
2. **Current ratio:** current assets ÷ current liabilities
3. **Debt to equity ratio:** total liabilities ÷ owners' equity

An **income statement** shows how much money is coming into a company (revenue) and how much money a company is spending (expenses) over a period. It shows how well a company has done in terms of profit and loss:

$$\text{revenues} - \text{expenses} = \text{profit (or loss)}$$

The income statement is grouped into four main categories: **revenues, costs of goods sold (COGS), operating expenses,** and **net income**, which are arranged in the following formula:

$$[(\text{revenue} - \text{cost of goods}) - \text{operating expenses}] - \text{taxes} = \text{net income or (loss)}$$

A **statement of cash flows** shows the exchange of money between a company and everyone else it deals with over a period. It shows where cash was used. The statement of cash flows tells a story that the income statement does not. The income statement reports revenue receipts and expense payments. Because revenue and expenses often are accrued (earned but not paid), the income statement does not tell how efficiently management generates and uses cash. The statement of cash flows, because it focuses specifically on cash, provides this important information. It shows whether all the revenues booked on the income statement have actually been collected.

MyBizLab Study, practise, and explore real business situations with these helpful resources:

- **Interactive Lesson Presentations:** Work through interactive presentations and assessments to test your knowledge of business concepts.
- **Study Plan:** Check your understanding of chapter concepts with self-study quizzes.
- **Dynamic Study Modules:** Work through adaptive study modules on your computer, tablet, or mobile device.
- **Simulations:** Practise decision-making in simulated business environments.

KEY TERMS

accounting *(p. 283)*
accounts payable *(p. 290)*
accounts receivable *(p. 289)*
accrued expenses *(p. 291)*
amortization *(p. 290)*
annual reports *(p. 285)*
assets *(p. 287)*
auditing *(p. 285)*
balance sheet *(p. 289)*
bookkeeping *(p. 287)*
bottom line *(p. 293)*
budget *(p. 273)*
capital budget *(p. 273)*
cash flow *(p. 274)*
certified general accountant (CGA) *(p. 284)*
certified management accountant (CMA) *(p. 284)*
chartered accountant (CA) *(p. 284)*
commercial banks *(p. 277)*
commercial finance company *(p. 277)*
commercial paper *(p. 277)*

convertible bond *(p. 280)*
corporate accounting *(p. 285)*
corporate bond *(p. 279)*
cost of goods sold (COGS) *(p. 294)*
current assets *(p. 289)*
current liabilities *(p. 290)*
current ratio *(p. 292)*
debt financing *(p. 278)*
debt to equity ratio *(p. 292)*
depreciation *(p. 290)*
dividends *(p. 280)*
double-entry bookkeeping *(p. 287)*
earnings per share *(p. 295)*
equity *(p. 280)*
equity financing *(p. 278)*
expenses *(p. 293)*
factoring *(p. 277)*
financial accounting *(p. 285)*
financial management *(p. 272)*
financial manager *(p. 272)*
financial statements *(p. 289)*
fixed assets *(p. 290)*
forecasts *(p. 273)*
forensic accountant *(p. 286)*
fundamental accounting equation *(p. 287)*
goodwill *(p. 290)*
government and nonprofit accounting *(p. 286)*
gross profit *(p. 294)*
gross profit margin *(p. 295)*
income statement *(p. 289)*
initial public offering (IPO) *(p. 280)*
intangible assets *(p. 290)*
interest *(p. 279)*
inventory *(p. 291)*
investment instruments *(p. 282)*
issuing common stock *(p. 280)*
leverage *(p. 282)*
liabilities *(p. 287)*
line of credit *(p. 277)*
liquidity *(p. 274)*
loan *(p. 278)*
long-term liabilities *(p. 291)*
managerial accounting *(p. 285)*
net income (or loss) *(p. 295)*
operating (master) budget *(p. 273)*
operating expenses *(p. 294)*
operating income *(p. 294)*
operating profit margin *(p. 295)*
optimal capital structure *(p. 282)*
owners' equity *(p. 287)*
preferred stock *(p. 280)*
private accountant *(p. 283)*
promissory note *(p. 276)*
public accountant *(p. 283)*
ratio analysis *(p. 291)*
retained earnings *(p. 281)*
revenue *(p. 293)*
secured bonds *(p. 279)*
secured loan *(p. 277)*
shares outstanding *(p. 296)*
short-term financing *(p. 276)*
sinking fund *(p. 279)*
statement of cash flows *(p. 289)*
stock *(p. 280)*
tax accounting *(p. 285)*
trade credit *(p. 276)*
unsecured bonds *(p. 279)*
unsecured loan *(p. 277)*
working capital *(p. 291)*

CRITICAL THINKING QUESTIONS

1. Jason worked in a deli for five years before starting his own sandwich delivery store. The business has been quite successful for two years. The quality of the service and the sandwiches has caused an increased demand for his products. Jason now thinks he needs to buy more cars to deliver the sandwiches. He is trying to decide on the most appropriate way of financing the acquisition of two cars.
   a. What methods of financing should Jason consider?
   b. What information will Jason need to have to help make his decision?
   c. How would the financing decisions change if Jason also decided to open another store at a new location?
2. What are the key financial statements, and what is the importance of financial statements? What information do they contain? Which statement do shareholders typically find most useful? Why? Which statements would independent contractors considering working with a firm find most useful?
3. Discuss the role of independent auditors for a company. Over the past decade, why have independent auditors been under scrutiny by the government?
4. Recall Arnold Sawyer from the third section of this chapter. What advice would you give to him? Why was recording the transactions in QuickBooks not enough?
5. What is the relationship between the balance sheet and the income statement?

TEAM TIME

Industry Analysis

Assemble into groups of four or five.

PROCESS

Step 1. As a group, decide on an industry. Alone or with a partner, pick a company in that industry. The company should be publicly traded so that financial records are easily available.
Step 2. Alone or with a partner, review the annual report and the three key financial statements for the company you chose and prepare a brief analysis of the company's financial situation. Then calculate the ratios covered in this chapter and find three other ratios that are meaningful to your analysis.
Step 3. When your report is completed, combine your information with the information from others members of your group into an industry analysis and determine how each company fits into the industry. Would the conclusions from your independent analysis change once you see the analyses of other companies in the industry?
Step 4. As a group, prepare a presentation summarizing your findings for the industry and each company in the industry and present it to the class.

ETHICS AND RESPONSIBILITY

Getting to the Bottom of the Sarbanes-Oxley Act
In 2002, U.S. president George W. Bush signed the Sarbanes-Oxley Act into law in the aftermath of some of the largest financial and accounting scandals in recent U.S. history. The intent of the law is to protect investors from accounting fraud.

Reports indicate that complying with the law's requirements has cost U.S. businesses tens of millions of dollars. In addition, critics state that complying with Sarbanes-Oxley has stripped CEOs of their creativity and is making U.S. companies less competitive internationally,[18] although support for the act's provisions is slowly gaining.

EXERCISE

Research the history behind the Sarbanes-Oxley Act as well as current compliance with the act's provisions. Then prepare a brief report summarizing your answers to the following questions:

1. What specifically are companies asked to do?
2. How might these requirements affect "CEO creativity" and international competitiveness?
3. What are your thoughts as to the need for and effectiveness of this act? Is it effective, or is it causing more harm than good? Why, and what other measures, if any, do you think should be taken to address these issues?

CLOSING CASE

2011 Was a Pivotal Year in Accounting History

For years, Canadian businesses used the generally accepted accounting principles (GAAP)—a common set of accounting principles, standards, and procedures—to compile their financial statements. GAAP gives investors a minimum level of consistency in the financial statements they use to analyze companies for investment purposes. While companies were expected to follow GAAP when reporting financial data, there was still room within GAAP for unscrupulous accountants to distort figures, so even when companies followed GAAP, investors still needed to scrutinize their financial statements.[19]

For fiscal years commencing in 2011 and thereafter, Canadian GAAP for most public companies transitioned to the International Financial Reporting Standards (IFRS)—a set of accounting standards developed by the International Accounting Standards Board (IASB) that has become a global standard for the preparation of financial statements of publicly accountable enterprises (PAEs). In general, PAEs are enterprises other than government, public sector, or nonprofit organizations that trade their debt or equity in a public market or that hold assets in a fiduciary capacity for a broad group of outsiders.[20] Approximately 120 nations (many in Europe) and reporting jurisdictions have for several years now required or permitted IFRS.[21] Using IFRS, a business's financial statements are presented on the same basis as its foreign competitors, which makes comparisons easier. Companies with subsidiaries in foreign countries that use IFRS may need only one accounting language company wide. Adopting IFRS does not only affect how items are accounted for but also calls for more extensive disclosures.

Since private companies are reporting to a much smaller user group than publicly traded companies, and investors may request additional information from the company if not satisfied with the annual financial statements, there is no need for private corporations to issue "general purpose" financial statements.[22] Separate accounting standards are still issued and maintained for private enterprises, nonprofit organizations, and public sector (government) organizations. Canada has developed its own standards for private enterprises called the Accounting Standards for Private Enterprises (ASPE), which are similar to IFRS but are usually simpler and may provide additional information for special industries (e.g., mining) that IFRS doesn't examine in detail. Canadian private companies may choose to use either the full IFRS, just like a public company, or ASPE for nonpublicly accountable enterprises. By not using the full IFRS, a private company takes a chance that potential capital providers (sources of money) may assess the company at a higher risk level because the company is not using IFRS, which may hinder the company's chances of obtaining capital.

In Canada, nonprofit organizations (including government organizations) are not publicly traded, so the typical primary user of the businesses financial statements is nonexistent. These organizations generally are required to follow ASPE standards, although larger nonprofits (such as hospitals, universities, and colleges) are usually required to get an audit and are often required to provide special-purpose financial statements for specific users (such as government ministries).

As of 2011, Canada had a four-pronged approach to accounting standards:[23]

1. Public (publicly traded enterprises) and publicly accountable enterprises (such as banks) will follow IFRS.
2. Private enterprises (not publicly traded) have an option to follow full IFRS or a less complex IFRS created specifically for small and medium enterprises (ASPE).
3. Nonprofit organizations have an option to follow IFRS or accounting standards for nonprofit organizations.[24]
4. The Public Sector Accounting Board (PSAB) will continue to make recommendations to all levels of government organizations (federal, provincial, territorial, and municipal).

When countries each used their own accounting standards, users were forewarned that financial statements were not comparable, but with IFRS a new concern is growing—that users will be misled into thinking that international comparison is simple. This is indeed not the case; there are three factors that limit comparability:[25]

1. IFRS standards are not accepted to the same extent in each country.
2. The quality of reporting under IFRS depends on the quality of the accounting profession within each country and the effectiveness of each country's financial reporting enforcement mechanism.
3. Even when IFRS standards are fully accepted, some standards will be applied differently in different nations because of local conditions (e.g., taxes, interest, ways of doing business, and economic and political factors).

DISCUSSION QUESTIONS

1. Do you think the move to IFRS was necessary? Why or why not? Whom does it benefit?
2. Do you think IFRS should apply to all businesses, not just those that are publicly traded? Why or why not?
3. Do you think foreign countries will follow IFRS? Why or why not?

12 Global Business

Mark Pearson/Getstock.com

LEARNING OBJECTIVES

After studying this chapter, you should be able to:

- **LO1** Understand how the globalization of markets and production has affected business. (pp. 304–306)
- **LO2** Explain why globalization has accelerated so rapidly. (pp. 306–309)
- **LO3** Explain the meaning of *comparative advantage* and *absolute advantage* and describe the benefits and costs of international trade. (pp. 309–311)
- **LO4** Define free trade and summarize the different types of trade barriers used to protect domestic industries from foreign competition. (pp. 311–314)
- **LO5** Describe the organizations that facilitate trade and attempt to eliminate trade barriers. (pp. 314–318)
- **LO6** Distinguish among the three basic strategies of international business. (pp. 318–319)
- **LO7** Outline the ways international firms can successfully enter foreign markets. (pp. 319–321)
- **LO8** Define exchange rates and explain how they affect international business. (pp. 321–325)
- **LO9** List the economic factors and challenges that play a role in conducting business on a global scale. (p. 325)
- **LO10** Summarize the sociocultural, political, legal, and ethical challenges to conducting business in a global marketplace. (pp. 325–328)

OPENING DISCUSSION: GLOBAL TRADE

Japan's Disaster Affects Imports, Exports, and Productivity around the Globe

On March 11, 2011, an 8.9-magnitude earthquake off the northeast coast of Japan's main island unleashed a seven-metre (23-foot) tsunami and generated more than 50 aftershocks, causing widespread ruin. In particular, these natural disasters damaged a nuclear power plant in Fukushima, triggering the worst nuclear crisis since Chernobyl in Ukraine. Most tragic, of course, was the heavy loss of human life and devastation of livelihoods in the affected regions. Authorities said more than 20 000 people were confirmed dead or missing in the weeks after the disaster. Countries around the world offered their sympathy for Japan's loss and took action by sending aid to the traumatized nation.

It was evident that Japan had been severely incapacitated and would need some time to clean up, rebuild, and re-establish a comfortable livelihood for its residents. Let's take a closer look at Japan's crisis and consider how it affected multinational and global business operations:

- Many organizations, businesses, and governments rushed to Japan's aid, donating time, people, and money to help the disaster victims. For example, the BMO Financial Group, among others, donated $100 000 to the Red Cross to support disaster relief efforts.[1] The Salvation Army provided hot drinks and packed meals to the many people whose homes were destroyed or left without power. Doctors Without Borders had teams working throughout the country, while World Vision focused on easing the emotional and psychological stress that children faced during this crisis. The Canadian government sent medical, biological, chemical, radiological, and nuclear expertise, supplies, and equipment.[2]
- Manufacturers across Japan shut down production lines or cut back on output because of damage, power shortages, and supply chain problems. The country's production of parts used by manufacturers around the world suffered major disruptions, with global car and technology industries particularly affected.[3]
- Japan accounts for some 60 percent of the global silicon wafer supply, and some of the biggest silicon manufacturing units in Japan were damaged in the disaster. Since silicon wafers are used in micro devices and a wide range of electronic equipment, a shortfall in their supply had a negative effect on global manufacturers.[4]
- Due to business closures, disruptions to ports, and slowed shipments from Japan, Western companies such as Molycorp Inc. and Avalon Rare Metals were struggling to restart idle rare earth metal mines. Rare earth metals are used in everything from computers and cellphones to armoured vehicles and wind turbines.[5]
- After the nuclear leak, the demand for anti-radiation drugs, specifically potassium iodine (KI) tablets, skyrocketed not only in Japan but also in the United States and Canada, where "radiated" rain and ocean water was feared.[6] Iodine tablets can prevent the body from absorbing radioactive iodine.[7] Cancer is a key long-term risk from radiation exposure, and officials will undoubtedly be monitoring the health outcomes of the population around Fukushima for many years. The radiation leak will have a psychological impact on people who live with the fear of radiation contamination as well as the stress of being displaced from their homes.
- Food shortages occurred in Japan when radioactive matter was found in food sources, thus creating an increased demand for imported foods and a decreased demand for exported foods. Fishing ports and vessels were damaged, and both aquaculture and wild seedbeds for key products such as scallops and oysters were washed away. Contamination of seawater caused Japanese consumers to avoid fresh local seafood and choose canned or imported products instead.[8] Japan allocated 700 million yen (more than CDN$9 million) to help pay for exporters' radiation screening costs.[9] Bans on importing food from Japan were imposed by Russia, China, Hong Kong, India, the United States, Taiwan, and Singapore. Seoul insisted that Japan provide safety certificates for food products from the radiated areas.[10] Restaurant

owners in Mumbai and New Delhi assured customers that the restrictions wouldn't take sushi off the menu immediately. Restaurants noticed an increase in supplier prices when ordering substitute goods from Thailand, Vietnam, or China and imported seafood from Scotland.[11]

- Japan suffered tremendously from a decline in tourism. As well, most Japanese people feel a sense of responsibility toward their country after such a national crisis and chose not to travel outside the country for the short term after the disaster. This reduced tourism, at least temporarily, around the world.[12] Japanese tourists are among the top international visitors to the United States, comprising almost 20 percent of the visitors to Hawaii alone. Hawaii projected a possible US$2 billion decline in tourism from Japan for 2011.[13] Australia, Nepal, and Indonesia also predicted lower tourism numbers to and from Japan.[14]
- Japan supplies 3 to 4 percent of the globe's jet fuel, including exports to Asia, and damage to fuel infrastructure facilities in Japan could push jet fuel prices higher.[15]

What other changes have occurred or may occur due to lessons learned from Japan's crisis? Think about regulations (nuclear risk), cooperation among nations, insurance companies (life, home, disaster, etc.), national debt, and increased government spending on roads and building repairs. While the insurance industry can handle many claims, the Japanese government had to set up several subsidy programs to help deal with the vast number of people affected by the disaster. Japan's recovery was also complicated by financial questions: How would it manage to pay the bills?

DISCUSSION QUESTIONS

1. How did these events increase business opportunities for the Japanese? How did these events increase business opportunities for foreigners?
2. How did these events decrease business opportunities for Japan with other countries? For business located in foreign countries, how did these events decrease business operations?
3. Do you think foreign countries were justified in banning imported food from Japan? Why or why not? How did such a ban affect global supply and demand for these food products? How did such a ban affect the productivity, employment rates, and gross domestic product (GDP) in Japan? Besides banning imported food from Japan, what other measures could foreign countries have taken? Would you have felt safe buying food exported from Japan in the months following the disaster? Why or why not?

GLOBALIZATION: WHAT'S IT ALL ABOUT?

LO1 Understand how the globalization of markets and production has affected business.

International Business

How does doing business globally affect you? In recent years, the rise of globalization has dramatically influenced the lives of people around the world. Canadians to Taiwanese to Argentinians are all connected and dependent on one another for a variety of goods and services. Canada and other nations are increasingly **importing**, or buying products from other countries, and **exporting**, or selling domestically produced products to other countries. This trend is why you'll notice that many products you own are made in countries other than Canada. Not only has globalization affected our personal lives, it has also affected the way companies conduct business around the world.

importing Buying products from other countries.

exporting Selling domestically produced products to other countries.

Studying international business will make you a better employee, business owner, person, and citizen. It will broaden your horizons, requiring you to think outside your own domestic economic, social, and political box. Because the world is truly a global village, studying international business can also help you understand and appreciate the complex nature of the global economy, the rich diversity of world cultures, and the intricacies of international politics. At the very least, studying international business will give you the tools to answer questions inherent in many of today's headline-grabbing issues. For example, what can people do to enhance their country's ability to compete in the global economy? What can a country do to provide well-paying jobs for its citizens? How can Canadian companies increase their profitability in the face of foreign competition at home or enhance their market share overseas? When Canada's dollar is stronger or weaker than other countries' currencies, how does it affect business in Canada? After studying this chapter, you'll be able to answer these and other questions.

As business students, the following exercise might not surprise you: Check the labels on the following personal belongings to determine where they were manufactured:

- shoes
- shirt or sweater
- pants
- purse or backpack
- electronic device (smartphone, laptop, tablet, headphones, etc.)

Calculate the number of countries, other than Canada, that are represented in your total. If your personal belongings represent 0 countries, then they are considered homegrown; 1–2 countries, then they have an international flair; and 3 or more countries, then they truly reflect the growing trend in globalization.

What is globalization? **Globalization**, the movement toward a more interconnected and interdependent world economy, may be one of the most profound factors affecting people around the globe.[16] Globalization has created the ultimate *worldwide consumer*. Changes in the Canadian economy impact business and economic activity in other countries. Similarly, our domestic economy is affected by business activity and the overall economic health in foreign countries Canada does business with.

globalization The movement toward a more interconnected and interdependent world economy.

One example of globalization can be seen in the booming economies of India and China, whose growth is a major reason for the increasing global demand for energy. Increased energy demand is a significant cause of the world's rising oil prices, which have created higher prices at the gas pump. As a result, people have less money to spend on other things, including entertainment. Local restaurants, for example, experience lower sales as a direct result of consumer decisions to rein in their conspicuous consumption. In response to lower demand, businesses curtail production and lay off employees.

As you can see, globalization implies that the business decisions and economic actions within one country influence other countries. Of course, markets have not only become more interconnected but also more *reliant* on one another. If you inspect the packaging of items you buy, you'll see that many products consumed in Canada today, such as laptop computers and cars, are made from parts manufactured in countries halfway around the world. Many domestic businesses rely on foreign companies to supply inputs into their production process, assemble components, or provide some other function in the production process.

How does globalization offer more marketing opportunities to businesses?

The concept of globalization includes two primary components: the globalization of markets and the globalization of production.[17] The **globalization of markets** is the movement away from the belief that the market is local or "domestic" (within one nation) to the view that the market includes the entire world. Although what sells in one country may not sell in another because of different consumer tastes, to some extent consumer preferences in different nations are beginning to converge, thereby helping to create a global market. Companies such as Apple, IKEA, General Electric, Dell, and Toyota are not just selling to customers in domestic markets, they are selling to customers all over the globe. Even some relatively small companies find it profitable to sell their products abroad.

globalization of markets The movement away from the belief that the market is local or "domestic" (within one nation) to the view that the market includes the entire world.

The globalization of markets has become so widespread that more and more businesses must "think globally and act locally." Companies often need to adjust their products or marketing campaigns to suit the unique preferences of their local customers, wherever they may be. For example, Coca-Cola often has to adjust its recipes to appeal to the tastes of consumers in different parts of the world. In India, Coca-Cola adapted its

Minute Maid orange soda recipe to suit the taste of the majority Indian population, who prefer a sweeter version of the drink than is sold in North America.[18] Similarly, many foreign-owned companies advertise or adapt their products for sale in Canada to attract consumers. For example, when Walmart first opened in Canada in 1994 it had to change the product mix it carried for Canadians: hockey equipment was prominently featured in stores across the country and halal foods were sold to meet the requirements of the Muslim market in Toronto.[19] As you will see later in this chapter, Walmart was not as successful in foreign markets such as India, China, and Brazil because of its inability to meet the needs and preferences of local customers.

globalization of production The trend of individual firms moving production to different locations around the globe to take advantage of lower costs or to enhance quality.

How does globalization make it easier to manufacture products? The **globalization of production**, the other component of globalization, is the trend of individual firms moving production to different locations around the globe to take advantage of lower costs or to enhance quality. When faced with intense foreign competition, firms may be forced to relocate at least some of their production to another country to realize lower costs so they can offer customers lower prices.

Globalization of markets and production is certainly nothing new. In fact, countries have been trading with one another since ancient times. What has changed in the last three decades is the rapid pace at which globalization has been accelerating.

The Rapid Acceleration of Globalization

LO2 Explain why globalization has accelerated so rapidly.

Why has globalization accelerated so rapidly? Two main factors underlie the trend toward greater globalization:[20]

trade and investment barriers Government barriers that prevent the flow of goods, services, and financial capital across national boundaries.

- *A dramatic decline in trade and investment barriers.* **Trade and investment barriers** are government restrictions that prevent the flow of goods, services, and financial capital across national boundaries. The lowering of trade barriers makes global business much cheaper and easier. For example, the North American Free Trade Agreement (NAFTA) of 1994 (discussed later in this chapter) made it easier for North American companies to shift work among Canada, the United States, and Mexico and opened the door to offshore expansion. It also allows international firms to move their production facilities to the least-cost location for that activity. A firm might design its product in one country, produce component parts in two or three other countries, assemble the product in yet another country, and then export it around the world.
- *Technological innovations.* Advances in technology have made it possible to manage the global production and marketing of products. There have been dramatic breakthroughs in communications, transportation, and IT in the last decade. Using Web conferencing tools, a business manager in Toronto can meet with contacts at a firm's European and Asian operations centres without ever leaving the office. This has significantly reduced the cost of doing business. Technological advancements have levelled the playing field for small companies, enabling them to access customers worldwide through their websites at negligible expense, so they can more effectively compete with huge global corporations.

Based on these and other factors, the globalization of markets and the globalization of production have resulted in some international firms becoming so large that they actually generate more revenue than the GDP of many nations. As you can see in **Figure 12.1**, several multinational corporations rank above many countries in the world in terms of the total revenue they generate.

Technology is changing where businesses are located, what goods are produced, how goods and services are marketed, and what will be expected of employees in the new global marketplace. One result of technology has been the increase in **offshoring**, a practice in which work is shifted from its original domestic location to other foreign (or offshore) locations. Traditionally, the practice of offshoring was common in production and manufacturing; however, as technology provided secure and simple means to transmit data files, *white-collar offshoring* increased. Workers in many economic sectors who had

offshoring A practice in which work is shifted from its original domestic location to other foreign locations.

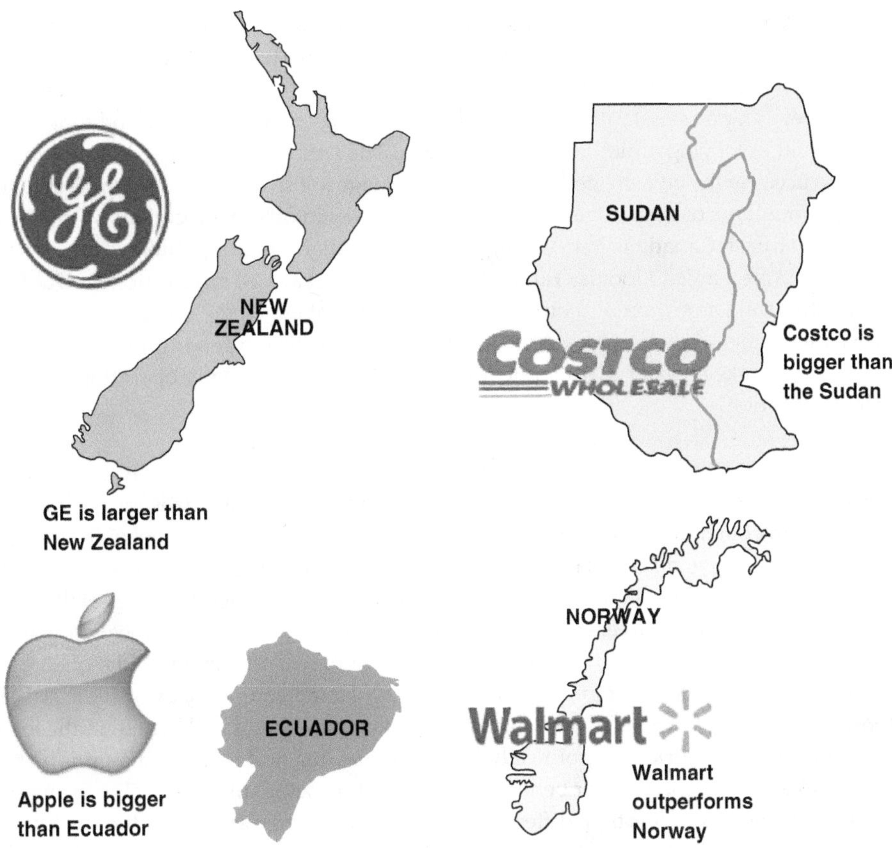

Figure 12.1 Company Revenue versus National Incomes

Today, many international businesses are larger than entire countries in terms of the economic activity they generate.

Data from Vincent Trivett, "25 US Mega Corporations: Where They Rank if They Were Countries," http://www.businessinsider.com/25-corporations-bigger-tan-countries-2011-6?op=1.

been insulated from foreign competition began to see change. In considering international offshoring, two trends stand out: (1) Many U.S. and Canadian firms are offshoring to China because it is quickly becoming the world's cheapest manufacturer, and (2) an increasing number of traded services, involving advanced, high-tech processes and employing well-paid white-collar workers, are being offshored. In the past, it was thought unlikely that low-cost countries such as India could export high-value-added services.[21] Today, it is common to find Indian software programmers customizing sophisticated software applications for businesses worldwide. In addition, the financial services industry—retail banking, investment banking, and insurance—has been very aggressive in moving call-centre jobs and clerical jobs offshore.

Location has become much less important, and countries with educated, English-speaking citizens can bid for work that has previously taken place in Canada or the United States. With a population of more than 1 billion, India graduates many more engineers each year than either Canada or the United States does. This outpouring has fuelled 10 years of double-digit increases in salary in India for many technology workers, as Canadian and American firms send a variety of programming and support positions to Indian companies. Although the income of Indian workers has risen, the economic advantage of offshoring to India is fading. Now China is beginning to show it has the necessary infrastructure and pool of talent to become an offshoring destination for knowledge work.

Although countries in Asia are seeing the most offshoring activity, some North American companies like to keep their business a little closer to home. **Near-shoring** is a form of offshoring in which a company moves jobs to a foreign location geographically

near-shoring A form of offshoring in which a company moves jobs to a foreign location that is geographically close or linguistically and culturally similar to its own country.

close or linguistically and culturally similar to its own country. Sending work from Canada to countries such as the United States, the United Kingdom, and Australia is considered near-shoring. Canadian lawyers are quietly starting to outsource legal work to India, where they can pay substantially less per hour and enjoy a faster turnaround time than they would by paying junior lawyers in Canada. The United States outsources work to Canada because the culture, geography, and language are so similar. As such, despite the stronger numbers of outsourcing firms and employees in offshore locations such as India and the Far East, Canada is performing well against overseas competitors, especially in high-end project areas. Google, Yahoo, and Hewlett-Packard all have offices in Dublin, where they send a portion of their IT work. Although labour in these countries may not be as low cost as labour in some Asian countries, similarities in geography, language, and culture make it easier to integrate foreign workers into the daily operations of the original location.

What changes might offshoring bring for Canadian companies and employees? The drastic difference in wages between offshore countries and Canada is the key ingredient in making offshoring profitable for a business. As the international pool of technical talent becomes the new marketplace, Canadian workers can expect to see a slowing of wage growth. It will be important for Canadian workers to have increased language skills and to shift their view of their careers and opportunities toward the reality of a global economy.

It is also useful to point out that Canadian workers will see benefits from offshoring. As middle-class jobs appear in India and other developing countries, the middle class in those countries will expand. Companies and workers in Canada will benefit in the long run when more countries are politically stable and the demand for Canadian products and services increases. Another benefit comes from time zone differences. For example, there is almost an 11-hour time difference between India and Canada. As the workday ends in Toronto, people begin to wake up and head to work in Bangalore and Hyderabad. By using teams of workers divided between both locations, companies can conduct business almost 24 hours a day.

outsourcing Occurs when a company contracts with an outside firm to handle a specific part of its business activities.

Video: Bringing Jobs Back to the United States

What is the difference between outsourcing and offshoring? **Outsourcing** occurs when a company contracts with an outside firm to handle a specific part of its business activities. For example, the college or university you currently attend probably outsources various functions such as security, maintenance, bookstore, and food services to outside organizations operating within the same city as your school. Another example of outsourcing would include a real estate company hiring a graphic design firm to create a special layout for a sales brochure (the graphic design firm might be located anywhere in the world). Most companies outsource work to outside firms that can do a job or project better, faster, or cheaper than the company could do on its own. Outsourcing to a foreign country is often referred to as offshore (outside the country) outsourcing. However, some people use the term *offshoring* to refer distinctly to the relocation of part of a business to a lower-cost location, typically a foreign country, and not simply as contracting work outside the country's borders.

Global Business Trends

Where will trends in global business take us? Four noteworthy global business trends will continue to impact our future:[22]

1. *A growing role for developing nations.* Over the last several decades, North American dominance of world output and world exports has declined in relative terms because of the rapid economic growth of several other countries, most notably Japan, China, and India. This trend is expected to continue as developing nations, such as Indonesia, Thailand, and many Latin American nations, continue to increase their presence on the world economic stage.
2. *A rise in non-U.S. foreign direct investment.* Over the previous 30 years, U.S. dominance in foreign direct investment (FDI), which is the purchasing of property and businesses in foreign nations, has declined. The direction of investment has switched, and now

many other countries have begun to undertake foreign direct investment. In fact, other countries have invested much of their money in companies in the United States. Not only is more foreign direct investment flowing into the United States than ever before, but also more and more foreign direct investment is flowing into developing nations.

Foreign direct investment by Canadian corporate enterprises is a cornerstone of Canada's engagement globally. The total stock of Canadian foreign direct investment abroad reached $711 billion in 2012. Canada's net FDI position (Canadian FDI abroad minus FDI in Canada) is approximately $77.7 billion, implying Canadian corporations invest more overseas than foreign corporations invest in Canada.[23]

3. *A rise in multinational enterprises.* Over the last several decades, there has been a rise in the importance of multinational enterprises, businesses that manufacture and market products in two or more countries. Moreover, mini-multinationals (small and medium-sized multinational enterprises) have become prominent on the world stage. There is an increase in the number of companies that can grow into an international presence.
4. *Increasing democratization.* With the movement toward democratization and the adoption of free market economies around the globe, many more nations are becoming involved in the global economy. If this trend continues, the opportunities for international business will be enormous as the global marketplace expands and more locations open as potential production sites.

INTERNATIONAL TRADE

LO3 Explain the meaning of *comparative advantage* and *absolute advantage* and describe the benefits and costs of international trade.

International Competition

What is the theory of comparative advantage? Many theories apply to international trade. The most popular theory is the *theory of comparative advantage*, which states that specialization and trade among countries benefit all who are involved. The theory of comparative advantage suggests that a country should sell to other countries the goods that it manufactures most efficiently and effectively, and buy from other countries the goods it cannot manufacture as efficiently or effectively. If this method is practised, each nation will have a greater quantity and variety of higher-quality products to consume at lower prices.

For this mutually beneficial system to work, each country must specialize in the production of those products for which it possesses a comparative advantage. To possess a **comparative advantage** means that a country can produce a good or service relatively more efficiently than any other country. A comparative advantage should not be confused with an **absolute advantage**, which is a country's ability to produce *more* of a good or service than any other country. Just because a large country can produce more of a good than a small country can doesn't necessarily mean it is relatively more efficient at producing that good. What matters is relative efficiency, or comparative advantage—not absolute advantage.

comparative advantage A country's ability to produce a good or service relatively more efficiently than any other country.

absolute advantage A country's ability to produce more of a good or service than any other country.

When all countries focus on producing those products for which they have a comparative advantage, collectively they all have more production to share. This, in turn, creates higher standards of living for these countries. As you've probably guessed, countries export those products for which they have a comparative advantage and import those products for which they do not have a comparative advantage.

Video: Comparative and Competitive Advantages in Global Competition

What can a country do to get ahead in world markets? In many nations, governments focus on improving the nation's resources—natural resources, labour, capital (plant, equipment, and infrastructure), technology, and innovation and entrepreneurialism—to improve competitiveness.

Governments can't do much to improve a nation's natural resources; they have to work with what they have. Nations with abundant natural resources will likely have a comparative advantage in the production of goods that require these raw materials. For example, if Brazilians can grow coffee more easily than they can produce dairy products, and Canadians can produce dairy products more easily than they can grow coffee, we would say that Canadians have a comparative advantage in producing dairy products and Brazilians have a comparative advantage in coffee production. Trading Canadian dairy products for Brazilian coffee would clearly benefit both groups.

However, governments can and do invest in health, education, and training designed to increase the productivity of their labour force. All international businesses are constantly looking for good workers, and each country wants to attract businesses to enhance employment opportunities for its citizens.

Many governments try to create incentives for private company investments in capital (plant and equipment). For example, governments may try to keep interest rates low so private companies will invest in the latest state-of-the art equipment, thereby giving them an edge over foreign competition. Governments also invest in *public capital,* which is sometimes called *infrastructure.* Infrastructure includes roads, bridges, dams, electric grid lines, and telecommunications satellites that enhance productivity. Governments also try to promote technological advances to give their nations a competitive edge. This can include investments in basic and applied research at government-funded higher educational institutions. Finally, governments might also promote innovation and entrepreneurialism.

What can businesses do to be more competitive? Can a business create a competitive or comparative advantage? The ingredients for national competitiveness are the same for business competitiveness. That is, successful firms try to gain access to cheap raw materials, invest in their workers' training, and purchase state-of-the-art capital (plant and equipment). Successful companies also invest in cutting-edge technology in their research and development (R&D) departments. Finally, they promote innovativeness throughout their organizations. Conversely, if a company, an entire industry, or even a nation has lost its comparative (or competitive) advantage, then it probably failed in one or more of these areas. It is the joint job of government and private business to determine where to focus improvements to compete more effectively. Remember, comparative advantage is really a relative advantage—relative to the competition.

Benefits and Costs of International Trade

What are the benefits of international trade? The theory of comparative advantage indicates that countries participating in international trade will experience higher standards of living because of the greater quantity and variety of higher-quality products offered at lower prices. These results stem from the increased competition associated with more open trade. But these benefits are not without their costs.

Lilac Mountain/Shutterstock

When foreign imports arrive in Canada, they increase the supply of the product, pushing its price down. Consumers welcome the competition and the lower prices, but domestic competitors are displeased.

What are the costs of international trade? The costs of international trade are borne by those businesses and their workers whose livelihoods are threatened by foreign competition. Some domestic businesses may lose market share to foreign companies, stunting their profitability and ability to create jobs. Other firms may not be able to compete and will be driven out of business entirely.

Do the benefits of international trade outweigh the costs? This is a difficult question to answer. The answer depends on the timing of the benefits and the costs, and the extent to which they are felt within any given period. The critics point out the costs—including lost jobs to foreign competitors—but the advocates point out the benefits—greater quantity and variety of higher-quality products available for purchase. However, the benefits may not be easily traced to increased international trade because they are often slow and subtle. People benefit from lower-priced products, although the price reductions may only save people a nickel here and a dime there. But the sum of these lower prices for the public at large can be dramatic—especially over time.

Although international trade happens all the time in today's society, companies still have to abide by certain rules and regulations. Governments often impose restrictions on the quantity and types of goods that can cross national borders.

Trade Barriers and Protectionism

LO4 Define free trade and summarize the different types of trade barriers used to protect domestic industries from foreign competition.

What is free trade? **Free trade** is the unencumbered flow of goods and services across national borders. That is, free trade is free from government intervention or other impediments that can block the flow of goods across borders. Virtually all economists are free trade advocates because they argue that over time the benefits far outweigh the costs for the nation as a whole.

Still, even if virtually all economists are free trade advocates, all real-world governments do have trade barriers in place to protect selected domestic industries from foreign competition.

free trade The unencumbered flow of goods and services across national borders.

Video: Government Intervention: Spotlight on China and Germany

What trade barriers can governments put in place? There are three types of trade barriers:

1. *Tariffs and subsidies.* The most common trade barrier is the **tariff**, a tax imposed on an imported good or service, such as French wine. Governments prefer to impose tariffs because they raise tax revenues. The opposite of a tariff is a **subsidy**; governments make payments to domestic producers. A subsidy can take many forms. It can be a direct cash grant or a payment in-kind that could include tax concessions or a low-interest loan.
2. *Quotas and embargoes.* A **quota** is a limitation on the amount of an import allowed to enter a country. For example, a quota on French wine might limit the quantity to 10 000 cases per day. The most heavy-handed government trade barrier is an **embargo**, a total restriction on an import (or an export). Since the 1960s, for example, the United States has imposed an embargo on most goods traded with Cuba. Embargoes may be used to achieve a political goal. In the case of Cuba, the American embargo has been used to apply pressure for change toward a more democratic system.[24]
3. *Administrative trade barriers.* Several other types of trade barriers can be lumped under the heading of **administrative trade barriers**—government rules designed to limit imports. One example is a **local content requirement**, which is a requirement that some portion of a good be produced domestically. This usually drives up the cost of the import. Administrative trade barriers may also require an import to meet some technical standard or bureaucratic rule (e.g., customer regulations that are different from generally accepted international standards), effectively shutting the import out of the domestic market. The European Union (EU) does not accept beef products that have been produced with growth hormones. Much of American and Canadian beef could not be sold in the EU. In 2010, Canada won some duty-free access (a quota) to the EU market; therefore, if Canadian producers choose to produce this type of beef, despite the higher costs of doing so, at least they see that a market does exist.[25] Although administrative trade barriers can be legitimate, they may be designed purely to protect domestic producers from international competition.

tariff A tax that governments impose on an imported good or service, such as French wine. Governments prefer to impose tariffs because they raise tax revenues.

subsidy A payment that governments make to domestic producers.

quota A limitation on the amount of an import allowed to enter a country.

embargo A total restriction on an import (or an export).

administrative trade barriers Government rules designed to limit imports.

local content requirement A requirement that some portion of a good be produced domestically.

Who benefits and who suffers from protectionist trade barriers? Without a doubt, trade barriers benefit domestic producers and their workers, and they hurt domestic consumers. How does this occur? Trade barriers increase costs to foreign companies or restrict the supply of imports, driving up their prices and reducing their sales in the

Table 12.1 Economic Benefits and Costs of Free Trade and Protectionism for a Nation

	Free Trade	Protectionism
Economic Benefits	A greater quantity and variety of higher-quality products at lower prices	Increased sales at higher prices improves the profitability of the protected domestic companies, creating greater job security for their workers
Economic Costs	Reduced sales and lower prices for domestic firms that find it difficult to compete	Lower quantity and variety of lower-quality products at higher prices internationally, which reduces their profitability and lowers job security for their workers

domestic market. As a result, the higher-priced imports increase the demand for domestically produced substitute goods or services. This higher demand also increases the domestically produced product's price, although it simultaneously increases domestic sales. And this is exactly what the trade barriers are designed to do—restrict sales of imports while stimulating sales for domestic firms. Because the domestic firms are selling more at higher prices, they are more profitable. This profitability also creates more job security for their employees. The undesirable outcome, however, is that both the imports and the domestically produced substitute products are now more expensive. Domestic consumers lose while domestic producers and their workers gain. Trade barriers also hurt consumers because the overall quantity, variety, and quality of products are lower because of curtailing foreign competition. **Table 12.1** summarizes the economic benefits and costs of free trade and protectionism for a nation.

What are common arguments in favour of protectionist trade barriers? Four main arguments exist for implementing protectionist trade barriers:

1. *National security.* The national security argument states that certain industries critical to national security should be protected from foreign competition. For example, Canada wouldn't want to become dependent on another nation for a critical component of national defence. However, rarely have protected industries using this argument proven critical to national defence.
2. *Infant industry.* The infant industry argument states that an undeveloped domestic industry needs time to grow and develop to acquire a comparative advantage in the global economy. The protected time to grow allows opportunities for the industry to make the investments needed to become innovative. Once the comparative advantage is captured, then protection from foreign competition will no longer be necessary. However, in practice it can be very difficult to determine whether an industry legitimately holds promise of developing a comparative advantage. In addition, rarely do infant industries ever grow up, and the government protection can become addictive.
3. *Cheap foreign labour.* The cheap foreign labour argument centres on the sometimes significantly lower wages paid to workers of foreign companies. How can domestic companies compete with these low wages? Sometimes they can't, but trying to protect these jobs creates still higher costs for the nation in the form of higher prices and a reduced quantity, quality, and variety of products from which to choose. Note also that what is relevant for costs of production is not just wages but productivity in relation to wages. A company's costs of production can be lower even when it pays its workers twice as much if the productivity of workers is at least twice as high. It's no surprise that if a country wants to maintain high wages in a global marketplace, it needs to find a way to increase the productivity of its labour force.
4. *Threat of retaliation.* The threat of retaliation (or the bargaining chip) argument says that if a trading partner increases its trade barriers on your exports, or fails to reduce trade barriers as you reduce yours, then an uneven, unfair playing field is created. Domestic companies may also be put at a disadvantage if a foreign firm is dumping its product. **Dumping** is selling a product at a price below the price charged in the producing country; it is illegal but can be difficult to prove. The intent of dumping is to dominate an industry and then control it. The threat of higher trade barriers can be a bargaining chip in retaliation for dumping or for negotiating lower trade barriers for exports. However, the threat of trade barriers can be a risky policy. If it fails, the result can be a trade war—nations would implement higher trade barriers and leave everyone at a disadvantage.

dumping Selling a product at a price below the price charged in the producing country; it is illegal but can be difficult to prove.

Off the Mark

How Does China's Internet Censorship Affect Global Business?

While many parts of the world, notably the Middle East, are undergoing dramatic political and social changes because of Internet access, China has become more restrictive with what its netizens are allowed to access.[26] Google and other tech companies have had difficulty doing business in China because of government censorship and regulations. Beijing's extensive censorship of online content—often called the "Great Firewall of China"—systematically removes material it deems harmful, including politically sensitive information, pornography, and violence.[27] Facebook had been blocked in China since mid-2009 when riots that broke out were condemned by authorities as being abetted by social networking sites. As of September 2013, a small selection of people living and working in the 17-square-mile free trade zone in Shanghai, China, have been able to access banned sites, including Facebook, Twitter, and other "politically sensitive" links.[28]

Google declared war on censorship and decided not to censor its Web searches in China any longer, so China started closing the doors on Google services, banning or highly restricting various services from the country. Microsoft, on the other hand, continued to comply with local regulations, including the censorship of some political material.

In 2011, one of China's largest social networks, Renren, was looking to raise US$500 million on the New York Stock Exchange. It may seem unusual that while a Chinese social network can tap U.S. capital markets, American social networks, especially Facebook, cannot tap Chinese consumer markets. If Facebook grew rice or manufactured textiles, it could be argued that China was putting up trade barriers, but that has yet to happen because China's Internet censorship is considered a human rights issue and not a trade problem.[29]

Some people are pushing the U.S. government to make Internet censorship a trade issue. The argument, which Google has made in congressional testimony, is that digital barriers to the free flow of information are equivalent to traditional trade barriers, which are illegal under World Trade Organization (WTO) rules. Google spokesperson Niki Fenwick says censorship is first a human rights issue, then adds, "When a government blocks the Internet, it is the equivalent of a customs official stopping goods at the border."[30]

Imaginechina/Corbis

Under order of Pakistan's high court, the Pakistan Telecommunication Authority (PTA) started to observe Google, MSN, YouTube, Yahoo, Hotmail, and other websites for any infringement of Muslim sentiments.[31] Spotflux, a free proxy service that allows people to access uncensored content on the Internet, was banned by the PTA in January 2014. Spotflux isn't the only Web application that has faced a ban in Pakistan. In 2012, PTA banned YouTube, blaming a controversial movie trailer for *Innocence of Muslims* to be the source of civil unrest in the country. Moreover, Skype and Viber have also been blocked temporarily over security concerns about an impending terrorist attack.[32] If the trend to block Internet access continues, what will happen to human rights and global trade? Where are we headed?

Discussion Questions

1. **How do you feel about censorship? Is it a violation of human rights or does it protect citizens, government, or society? Do you think the Chinese government will be pressured into providing open Internet access for all of its citizens if the use of social media in the free trade zone in Shanghai is without political incident? Why or why not?**
2. **Do you think the Chinese government's censorship is an attempt to control Internet usage in favour of its own domestic Baidu search engine (Baidu is the Chinese equivalent to Google)? What if other countries did the same? Could censorship become more prevalent?**
3. **How does Internet censorship affect global business? As more countries move toward market economies, do you think there will be a decline in Internet censorship by government? Should the Internet be kept "open" for all world citizens?**

How do economists feel about protectionist trade barriers? As noted earlier, most economists are free trade advocates because they believe that the economic benefits of free trade outweigh the economic costs. Economists insist that the best way to address the concerns of those industries and their workers whose livelihoods are threatened by foreign competition is *not* to impose protectionist trade barriers. Instead, these displaced individuals need to be equipped with the education, training, and skills necessary to smooth their transition into a line of business or work in which the nation has a comparative advantage and demand is rising. Although all governments have protectionist trade barriers in place, they have been working to reduce them because they believe the economic benefits of doing so generally outweigh the costs. This political position explains the recent trend toward reduced trade and investment barriers that have fuelled globalization.

International Organizations Promoting Free Trade

LO5 Describe the organizations that facilitate trade and attempt to eliminate trade barriers.

What are some international organizations that promote free trade? Countries realize that unilaterally reducing their trade barriers puts their businesses at an unfair disadvantage. The key for realizing the mutual benefits of international trade is to get all countries to lower their trade barriers simultaneously, which was the reason for creating organizations such as GATT and the WTO.

General Agreement on Tariffs and Trade (GATT) Created in 1948 with 23 member nations to provide rules for world trade; its membership grew to 123 countries by 1994.

The **General Agreement on Tariffs and Trade (GATT)** was created in 1948 with 23 member nations to provide rules for world trade; its membership grew to 123 countries by 1994. Although GATT was not an organization with any real enforcement powers, its eight rounds of negotiated agreements, or treaties, were very successful in reducing tariffs and other obstacles to free trade on goods. This, in turn, spurred significant world economic growth.[33] However, GATT was not as successful in reducing trade barriers on services, protecting intellectual property rights, or enforcing agreements among member nations. As a result, the WTO replaced GATT in 1995 during the eighth and final round of negotiations (called the Uruguay Round because it was launched in Punta del Este, Uruguay).

World Trade Organization (WTO) Strengthened the world trading system by extending GATT rules to services, increasing protection for intellectual property rights, and, perhaps most significantly, taking on the responsibility for arbitrating trade disputes and monitoring the trade policies of member countries.

The **World Trade Organization (WTO)** has strengthened the world trading system by extending GATT rules to services, increasing protection for intellectual property rights, and perhaps most significantly taking on the responsibility for arbitrating trade disputes and monitoring the trade policies of member countries (see **Figure 12.2**).[34] The WTO operates as GATT did—on the basis of consensus—in the area of dispute settlement. However, unlike GATT the WTO doesn't allow losing parties to ignore their arbitration reports. The WTO has the power to enforce decisions, which gives the WTO something that the GATT never had: teeth.

World Bank Offers low-interest loans, advice, and information to developing countries.

International Monetary Fund (IMF) Promotes trade through financial cooperation.

Two international financial organizations are instrumental in fostering global trade: the World Bank and the International Monetary Fund. Founded in 1944, the **World Bank** offers low-interest loans, advice, and information to developing countries. To receive loans, countries must agree to lower trade barriers and aid private enterprise. Founded one year after the World Bank, the **International Monetary Fund (IMF)** promotes trade through financial cooperation. The IMF makes short-term emergency loans to member nations and operates as a lender of last resort for troubled nations. In return for these emergency funds, borrowers must make significant commitments to address the problems that lead to the crises in the first place.

What more can be done to promote free trade? Advocates of free trade argue that much remains to be done to reduce trade barriers in the global economy. The first round of WTO talks was launched in Seattle in 1999, but anti-globalization protestors disrupted and derailed these talks. The meetings were relaunched in 2001 in Doha, Qatar, in the Persian Gulf, with an agenda to curtail dumping, reduce protectionist trade barriers, protect intellectual property rights, and reduce government barriers on foreign direct investment.[35] The Doha Round was slated to last three years, but the first changes were not realized until December 6, 2013. At the heart of the deal is an agreement on *trade facilitation*, or measures to reduce trade costs by more than 10 percent, raising annual global output by over $400 billion.[36]

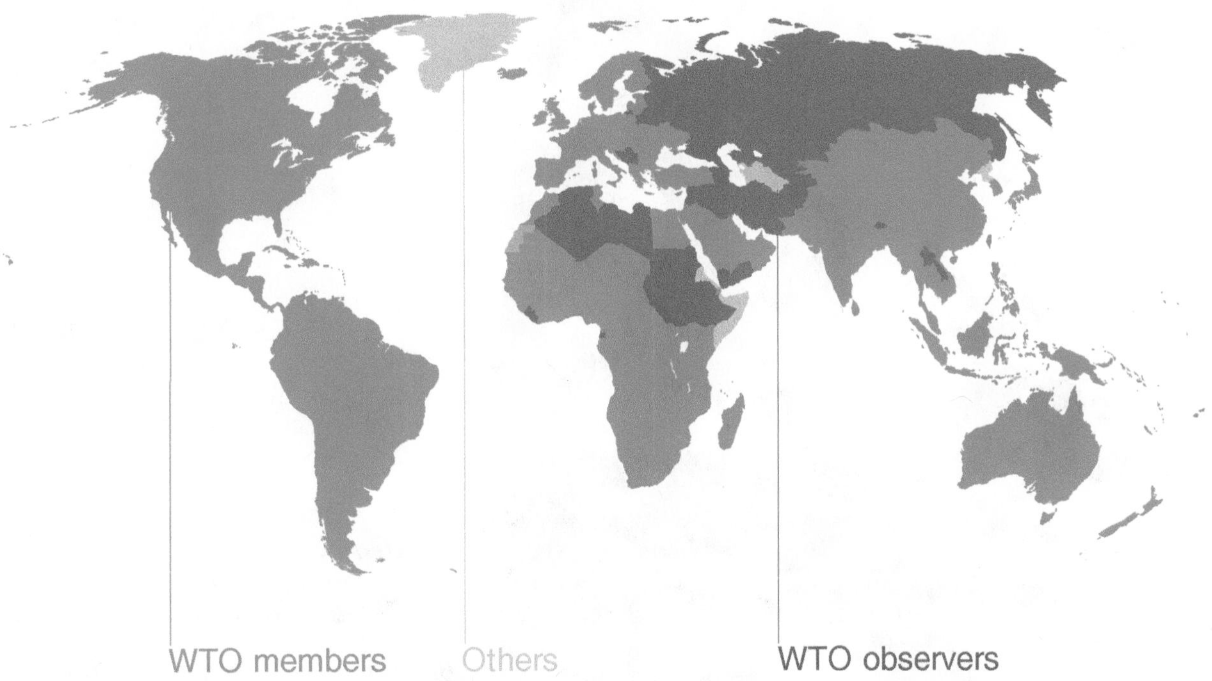

Figure 12.2 Countries in the WTO

Critics argue that exploitation of workers can contribute to the gap between the rich and poor. Environmentalists have also expressed a growing concern that expanded international trade encourages companies to move production to countries in which they are freer to pollute and degrade the environment, which contributes to global climate change and all the problems that may stem from global warming. These concerns highlight the fact that the economic perspective on the benefits and costs of free trade is not the only perspective. Important social, ethical, political, and environmental concerns are also important.

Regional Free Trade Agreements

What is a free trade agreement? Many nations have been so eager to achieve the higher standards of living associated with free trade that they have struck out on their own by creating **free trade areas or agreements (FTA)** to abolish trade barriers among member countries. Although all current free trade areas still have some obstacles to free trade among their members, many have made considerable headway in reducing these barriers.

free trade areas or agreements (FTA) Abolish trade barriers among member countries.

European Union (EU) With 28 member nations (including the accession of Croatia on July 1, 2013), the EU is the oldest and largest free trade area.

What is the largest free trade area in the world? The greatest free trade area exists among member nations of the **European Union (EU)**, which is the oldest and largest free trade area. The EU can trace its roots to 1957 with the creation of the European Economic Community (or Common Market), which consisted of the six founding countries of Belgium, France, Germany, Italy, Luxembourg, and the Netherlands. Although many obstacles had to be overcome, like the concern over the potential loss of national sovereignty, the EU has grown to its current membership of 28 countries, as shown in **Figure 12.3**. The EU's success is due, in large part, to its demonstrated commitment to the free flow of goods, services, capital, and people across borders in Europe.

Video: Regional Economic Integration: Outlook for the European Union

Video: Globalization and RIM

The EU is currently the world's largest single market. It accounts for approximately one-third of the world's total production. The EU is the largest exporter in the world and

Figure 12.3 The 28 Member Countries of the European Union

the second-largest importer.[37] In 1999, the EU also surpassed all other free trade areas with respect to economic integration by adopting a common currency—the euro. The euro is currently used by 23 of the 28 member countries and has become a major currency in global financial markets.[38] The EU has a population of nearly 500 million people and is likely to continue to grow as many other candidate countries, such as Turkey, Serbia, and Iceland, apply to join.

The EU's economic power and political clout has a huge influence on international businesses worldwide. For example, some international businesses have been motivated to invest in production facilities within the EU to hedge against any potential trade barriers. The EU has also established many legal, regulatory, and technical standards for imports to the EU market. In addition, the EU's anti-trust rulings have significantly affected businesses around the world. For example, on March 25, 2014, European anti-trust regulators raided a French car parts maker, a U.S.-based parts supplier, and several exhaust system manufacturers in a crackdown against suspected price fixing in the global auto industry.[39] It is alleged that the companies have participated in a cartel and abused their market power. The European Commission can fine companies up to 10 percent of their global turnover for breaching EU rules. It is investigating cartels involving more than 100 car parts by more than 70 automakers.[40]

Does Canada have a free trade agreement with the EU? The tentative free trade agreement between Canada and the EU, the Comprehensive Economic and Trade Agreement (CETA), was signed by Prime Minister Stephen Harper and the European Commission President Jose Manual Barroso in Brussels on October 18, 2013. The agreement will give Canada preferential market access to the 28-member EU and its more than 500 million consumers and $17 trillion in annual economic activity.[41]

Canadian Prime Minister Stephen Harper and European Commission President Jose Manuel Barroso shake hands after signing an agreement in principle on trade in Brussels. Harper tabled the agreement in the House of Commons in October 2013.

The agreement's finer details still need to be worked out, and full ratification will not likely occur until 2015. The CETA is expected to bring enormous opportunities to Canadian exporters by providing full access to EU markets. It will remove 98 percent of EU tariffs on a wide range of Canadian products, including agriculture, seafood, metals, and mineral products. The deal would also impact Canadian automobile exporters, allowing them greater access to new and larger markets. Canadian farmers will benefit because the agreement will permit larger exports of beef, pork, and bison. On the consumer side Canadians can expect to see lower prices on food, wine, and luxury European automobiles.

Financially, some have expressed concerns that CETA will end up costing Canada as the agreement will result in a loss of $670 million in tariff revenues for Canada. Europe currently exports more to Canada than Canada does to European markets. The agreement is expected to save Canadian exporters about $225 million annually in duty payments, significantly less than EU counterparts.

International Trade Minister Ed Fast said the federal government will more than make up for the lost $670 million in tariff revenues. "We expect that the gains on the economy will more than outstrip the tariff losses. At the end of the day, this will be a net fiscal benefit to Canada," he said.[42]

Does Canada have an existing free trade agreement? The **North American Free Trade Agreement (NAFTA)** is an ongoing agreement to move Canada, the United States, and Mexico closer to true free trade. NAFTA was established on January 1, 1994, after considerable political opposition. The experience of NAFTA so far indicates that earlier claims made by both advocates and critics were exaggerated. One big issue confronting NAFTA is the proposal to expand into a greater Free Trade Area of the Americas (FTAA), which would include most countries in the western hemisphere. Although meetings continue to create a workable FTAA, some countries such as Brazil and Venezuela stand in opposition. As a result, much progress in the near future toward more free trade within the framework of FTAA is unlikely.

North American Free Trade Agreement (NAFTA) An ongoing agreement to move Canada, the United States, and Mexico closer to true free trade.

Video: Made in America: Mexico

What other free trade areas exist around the world? Many other free trade areas exist in the world:

- Mercosur, which originated in 1988 as a free trade pact between Brazil and Argentina but was expanded in 1990 to include Paraguay and Uruguay. In July 2012, Venezuela also became a full member. Bolivia is in the process of becoming a full member (since December 2012), while Chile, Colombia, Peru, and Ecuador are associated states. The population of Mercosur's full membership totalled more than 260 million people in 2011; including Venezuela, it has a collective GDP of $2.9 trillion and is the world's fourth-largest trading bloc after the EU, NAFTA, and ASEAN.[43]
- The Association of Southeast Asian Nations (ASEAN), which includes Indonesia, Malaysia, the Philippines, Singapore, Thailand, Brunei, Vietnam, Laos, Myanmar, and Cambodia. Progress toward integration has been limited, but ASEAN has negotiated free trade agreements with China, Korea, Japan, Australia, New Zealand, and

India and is working to create a free trade agreement with the EU. In 2012, its combined nominal GDP had grown to more than S$2.3 trillion.[44] If ASEAN were a single entity, it would rank as the eighth-largest economy in the world.

- The Asia-Pacific Economic Cooperation (APEC), which was founded in 1989 at the suggestion of Australia and currently has 21 member countries, including economic powerhouses such as Canada, the United States, Japan, and China. The member economies of APEC account for approximately 40 percent of the world's population, approximately 55 percent of world GDP, and about 44 percent of world trade.[45]

Video: Emerging Markets: Spotlight on India and Mexico

Most free trade areas haven't had the kind of success in reducing trade barriers that the EU and NAFTA have experienced. However, it's clear that most countries are eager to come together to reduce trade barriers in an attempt to realize the economic benefits of greater free trade.

CONDUCTING BUSINESS ACROSS BORDERS

LO6 Distinguish among the three basic strategies of international business.

Strategies for International Business

What types of strategies can an international business follow? All business is undertaken within an economic, sociocultural, political, and legal environment wherever it operates. When doing purely domestic business, keeping up with environmental forces can be a huge challenge for even the savviest manager. However, managing an international business is even more complex because additional and different economic, social, and political environments must be considered. Two major factors determine an international firm's strategy. The first factor involves how important it is for a business to keep its costs down and, therefore, its prices low. The second factor is how necessary it is for a company to customize or differentiate its product to adapt to different customer tastes and preferences around the globe. Three basic strategies for international business are global, multidomestic, and transnational.

global strategy Involves competing primarily based on price while selling a standardized (or homogenous) product.

Can companies compete with low prices? One basic strategy of international business is the **global strategy**, which involves competing primarily based on price while selling a standardized (or homogenous) product. Standardized products are basic products that meet universal needs. Examples of standardized products include agricultural products, oil, and raw material commodities. These goods are essentially the same from company to company—they are homogenous—because they are universally recognized and appeal to consumers across many cultures. When selling standardized products, firms compete aggressively based on price. Firms pursuing a global strategy face strong cost pressures to keep their prices low because they are selling a standardized product. The company with the lowest price captures most market share. Sony and Boeing are companies that pursue a global strategy.

multidomestic strategy Involves competing primarily by customizing or differentiating the product to meet unique local needs, tastes, or preferences.

Video: Gawker Media: Business in a Global Economy

Can companies compete by customizing products? A second basic strategy of international business is the **multidomestic strategy**, which involves competing primarily by customizing or differentiating the product to meet unique local needs, tastes, or preferences. Firms pursuing a multidomestic strategy face relatively low pressures for cost reduction because the price is often of secondary concern to buyers. Instead, what is important to customers is whether the product meets their needs or is distinct from the product of competitors. Companies that pursue a multidomestic strategy, such as Procter & Gamble and General Foods, all work to make their respective products appeal to different customers around the globe.

transnational strategy Involves competing by offering a customized product while simultaneously selling at the lowest possible price.

Are companies able to compete with low prices and still customize products? A third basic strategy of international business is the **transnational strategy**, which involves competing by offering a customized product while simultaneously selling at the lowest possible price. The strong cost pressures and strong pressures for differentiation that motivate this type of strategy are typically at odds. Therefore, the successful pursuit of this type of strategy is extremely difficult in practice. Frito Lay, American Express, and British Airways all pursue a transnational strategy.

Entering Foreign Markets

LO7 Outline the ways international firms can successfully enter foreign markets.

How do international firms enter foreign markets? In addition to determining a business strategy, international businesses must decide how they will serve foreign customers. Companies may undertake one of six strategies to enter foreign markets:

1. Export their product.
2. Implement a turnkey project.
3. Undertake franchising.
4. Enter into a licensing agreement, a joint venture, or a strategic alliance.
5. Undertake contract manufacturing.
6. Establish a wholly owned subsidiary.

Let's look briefly at these options.

Exporting As noted earlier, exporting is the sale of a domestically produced good in a foreign market. Most businesses typically begin serving a foreign market by exporting and only later switch to another mode to expand sales abroad. Exporting has two advantages. First, exporting is relatively easy and inexpensive compared with establishing a physical presence in a foreign market. Second, exporting may help a firm realize lower costs because companies can move production to an inexpensive location and then export its product from that location around the world. Exporting also has a few disadvantages. It is not economical for heavy or bulky products with high transportation costs. Exporting may also become uneconomical if foreign trade barriers are unexpectedly imposed.

Turnkey Projects When firms export their technological expertise in exchange for a fee, they have implemented a **turnkey project**. Turnkey projects are common in the production of sophisticated and complex manufacturing facilities such as those involved in petroleum refining, steel, and hydroelectric energy production. Once the facility is up and running, the locals are trained, then the keys are turned over to the new foreign owners. Black & Veatch, an engineering firm in Kansas City, has built power plants in China as turnkey projects. Turnkey projects allow firms with specialized knowledge, like Black & Veatch, to earn higher profits from their technical expertise. The drawback is that the firm may create a viable competitor if its technological expertise is easily accessible.

turnkey project Implemented when firms export their technological expertise in exchange for a fee.

Franchising **Franchising** involves selling a well-known brand name or a proven method of doing business to an investor in exchange for a fee and a percentage of sales or profits. The seller is the franchisor and the buyer is the franchisee. Franchising, which was discussed in depth in Chapter 4, is popular both domestically and internationally. Examples of franchising abound in the fast-food and entertainment industries. McDonald's and KFC restaurants are now found all over the world. Walt Disney has recently franchised 150 stores in India.[46] As of February 2014, Domino's Pizza operates 390 company-owned units and franchises another 4596 locations in the United States. In addition, it franchises another 4986 restaurants in 70 international markets.[47] Undoubtedly, all of these franchises must be careful to adapt their goods and services to appeal to their different global customers.

The main advantage of franchising is that the franchisor shifts to the franchisee the costs and risks of opening a foreign market. Disadvantages include the enforcement of franchise contracts that ensure quality control over distant franchisees and ensuring that the product is properly adapted to appeal to customers.

franchising Selling a well-known brand name or a proven method of doing business to an investor in exchange for a fee and a percentage of sales or profits. The seller is the franchisor, and the buyer is the franchisee.

licensing An agreement in which the licensor's intangible property—patents, trademarks, service marks, copyrights, trade secrets, or other intellectual property—may be sold or made available to a licensee in exchange for a royalty fee.

Licensing **Licensing** is an agreement in which the licensor's intangible property—patents, trademarks, service marks, copyrights, trade secrets, or other intellectual property—may be sold or made available to a licensee in exchange for a royalty fee.

Video: Pirate Joe's Resells Trader Joe's Popular Products

Stringer/AFP/Getty Images

International franchising abounds in the fast-food industry.

The advantage of licensing is the speed with which the licensor can enter a foreign market and the assumption of risks and costs by the licensee. The disadvantage is the loss of technological expertise to the licensee and the creation of a potential competitor. SRI International is a company that licenses its vast array of intellectual property around the world. Its technological specialty is patents in the biosciences, computing, and chemistry-related materials and structural areas.[48]

Joint Ventures **Joint ventures** involve shared ownership in a subsidiary firm. International joint venture partners involve an international business teaming up with a local partner to enter a foreign market. The advantages of a joint venture include gaining local knowledge of the economic, social, and political landscape while sharing the costs and risks of accessing a foreign market. Due to restrictions on foreign investment in some countries, a joint venture may be the only way to penetrate some foreign markets. For example, because of many restrictions on shopkeeper businesses in India, Walmart tried to enter India through a joint venture with Bharti Enterprises. However, in October 2013 Walmart and Bharti Enterprises broke off their Indian joint venture. After having struggled to build a bigger presence in this foreign country, Walmart was now on its own. If it wants to set up its own retail stores in India, it will need to find another local partner to own 49 percent of the business under foreign investment rules.[49]

joint ventures Involve shared ownership in a subsidiary firm. International joint venture partners involve an international business teaming up with a local partner to enter a foreign market.

Entering a joint venture requires considerable thought in the selection of a complementary partner. The disadvantage of joint ventures is losing control over the company because compromise with the partner is inevitable. The risk of losing proprietary technology in the event of dissolution or divorce of the joint venture is also a major drawback.

strategic alliances Cooperative arrangements between actual or potential competitors. Unlike a joint venture, each partner retains its business independence.

Video: MyGym (Mexico): Entry Strategy and Strategic Alliances

Strategic Alliances **Strategic alliances** are cooperative arrangements between actual or potential competitors. Unlike a joint venture, each partner retains its business independence. Strategic alliances are typically agreements for a specific period or for only the duration of a particular project. The advantages of strategic alliances include the pooling of unique talents and expertise and the sharing of the costs and risks of a project for mutual benefit. The disadvantages include loss of technology and initial difficulty in finding a compatible partner. The Renault–Nissan Alliance is a Franco-Japanese partnership between automobile manufacturers. Renault is based in Paris, France, and Nissan is based in Yokohama, Japan. The two companies have been partners since 1999. As of December 2013, the Alliance is the world's leading electric vehicle manufacturer. The strategic partnership between Renault and Nissan exemplifies how their arrangement can increase economies of scale for both companies while allowing each to maintain their individual unique identities. Collaboration between Renault and Nissan focuses on capital-intensive research projects such as sustainable, zero-emission transportation and development of automobile manufacturing in emerging markets such as Brazil, Russia, and India.[50]

contract manufacturing Occurs when a firm subcontracts part or all of its goods to an outside firm as an alternative to owning and operating its own production facility.

Contract Manufacturing **Contract manufacturing** occurs when a firm subcontracts part or all of its goods to an outside firm as an alternative to owning and operating its own production facility. When doing international business, the subcontractor is a foreign firm. Therefore, contract manufacturing is really a form of offshore outsourcing. Contract manufacturing allows international business to enter a foreign market by placing its label on the good and selling it in the foreign market where it was produced. Contract manufacturing also enables a firm to test market its product in a foreign market with

Table 12.2 Advantages and Disadvantages of the Various Entry Modes

	Advantages	Disadvantages
Exporting	• Speed of entry • Production site in lowest-cost location	• High transport costs • Threat of trade barriers such as tariffs • Lack of access to local information
Turnkey project	• Increased profits for high-tech firms	• Loss of technical know-how to potential competitors
Franchising	• Costs and risks of opening the foreign market fall on the franchisee	• Difficulty in maintaining quality control over distant franchisees
Licensing	• Speed of entry	• Licensee may become competitor • Loss of knowledge to potential competitor
Joint venture	• High potential for learning • Benefit of combined resources	• Shared control of business • Risk of losing specialized technology to partner
Strategic alliance	• Pooled talents and expertise • Shared costs and risks	• Risk of losing specialized technology to partner • Difficulty in finding a compatible partner
Contract manufacturing	• Speed of entry • Low test-marketing costs	• Lack of quality control over distant subcontractor
Wholly owned subsidiary	• Total control over all operations • Preservation of proprietary technology	• Risks and costs of entering a foreign market

very little expense compared with the high startup costs of building its own facility. The disadvantage centres on the lack of quality control over the subcontractor.

Simulation: Going Global—Emerging Markets

Wholly Owned Subsidiaries A **wholly owned subsidiary** involves establishing a foreign facility that is owned entirely by the investing firm. For example, as its seventh expansion into foreign markets, South Korean automotive manufacturer Hyundai entered the Sao Paulo state of Brazil by opening Hyundai Motor Brasil (HMB) in November 2012, a wholly owned subsidiary of Hyundai.[51] The advantages of this entry choice include total control over foreign operations and technological expertise. The disadvantage is that the parent company must bear all of the costs and risks of entering a foreign market.

wholly owned subsidiary Involves establishing a foreign facility that is owned entirely by the investing firm.

Video: Airbus vs. Boeing

Video: Entering the Chinese Market

Which mode of entering foreign markets is optimal? The optimal entry mode depends on many factors, including the firm's strategy. Companies must weigh the advantages and disadvantages of each when making a decision. **Table 12.2** summarizes the advantages and disadvantages of the various entry modes.

INTERNATIONAL BUSINESS: ECONOMIC FACTORS AND CHALLENGES

LO8 Define exchange rates and explain how they affect international business.

The Effect of Exchange Rates

What are exchange rates? Foreign exchange markets determine **exchange rates**, the rates at which currencies are converted into another currency. Depending on a firm's perspective, it may prefer a strong or weak dollar. Canadian exporters prefer a weak dollar because their products will be more affordable to foreigners. However, Canadian importers prefer a strong dollar because the cost of importing foreign goods is cheaper. If goods are imported cheaply, then those savings can be either passed on to the consumer or kept as higher profits.

exchange rates The rates at which currencies are converted into another currency.

Businesses are affected by fluctuating exchange rates every day. Transactions between international companies not only have to specify what each side will be paid but also in which currency. In addition, multinational enterprises use foreign currency to pay foreign workers or to invest spare cash in other nations where interest rates may be more attractive.

How do exchange rates affect international business? Changes in exchange rates can have important implications for international businesses. Suppose that the value of the Canadian dollar rises or gets stronger against the Chinese yuan. What effect will this have on Canadian and Chinese businesses? Goods exported from Canada will become more expensive because the Chinese will now have to come up with more yuan to purchase each dollar. This means, for example, the cost of a $40 pair of jeans made in Canada will increase in price for the Chinese consumer. Chinese consumers will buy fewer Canadian goods, such as jeans, and exports to China will fall. Canadian businesses selling to China will be hurt through no fault of their own. At the same time, this stronger dollar will cause a decline in the relative price of goods from China for Canadian consumers because fewer dollars are required to purchase each yuan. Thus, due to the currency exchange rate change, Canada will import more goods from China and Canadian businesses will lose market share to Chinese companies. This example illustrates that **currency appreciation**, an increase in the exchange rate value of a nation's currency, causes the relative price of imports to fall as the relative price of exports rises. When currency appreciates, the currency becomes stronger. **Currency depreciation**, a decrease in the exchange rate value of a nation's currency, has the opposite effect on the relative prices of exports and imports. A weak currency causes exports to become cheaper and imports to become more expensive.

currency appreciation An increase in the exchange rate value of a nation's currency; causes the relative price of imports to fall as the relative price of exports rises.

currency depreciation A decrease in the exchange rate value of a nation's currency; causes exports to become cheaper and imports to become more expensive.

Changes in exchange rates create other challenges for international business. In fact, rapid changes in exchange rates can create huge losses for some businesses. In the 1980s, Japan Airlines purchased several 747 jumbo jets from Boeing and agreed to pay in U.S. dollars. In the interim period between signing the contract and the delivery of the jets for payment, the value of the dollar rose dramatically. Japan Airlines had to pay a lot more money than anticipated for the jets, and it almost went bankrupt. This story illustrates a currency exchange rule: Unanticipated exchange rate changes can pose huge risks for international businesses.

Changing exchange rates also affect multinational firms in other ways. Many companies, such as General Electric, feel competitive pressure to shift production to countries with weak or low-valued currencies to take advantage of lower costs of production. For example, a weak Chinese currency reduces labour costs in China. If a firm doesn't shift more of its production to China and its competitors do, then its costs will be higher and the company will lose global market share.

Trade Deficit and Trade Surplus The **balance of trade** is the difference between the value of a country's exports and the value of its imports during a specific time. A **trade deficit**, or unfavourable balance of trade, exists when the value of a country's imports exceeds the value of its exports. A strong Canadian dollar may cause a trade deficit because a strong dollar can cause export prices to rise and import prices fall. A **trade surplus**, or favourable balance of trade, occurs when the value of a country's exports exceeds the value of its imports. As **Figure 12.4** illustrates, the Canadian trade balance was last in an appreciable trade surplus in 2008, at the onset of the Great Recession. Since then the trade balance has fluctuated between a negligible surplus or deficit. With exports to the United States recovering somewhat in 2013, Canada recorded a smaller trade deficit of $1.66 billion in December 2013.[52]

balance of trade The difference between the value of a country's exports and the value of its imports during a specific time.

trade deficit An unfavourable balance of trade; exists when the value of a country's imports exceeds the value of its exports.

trade surplus A favourable balance of trade; occurs when the value of a country's exports exceeds the value of its imports.

The advantage of a trade deficit for a nation is that it enables the country to consume more than it produces. However, the disadvantage is that domestic assets such as real estate or stocks and bonds must be sold to foreigners to pay for the trade deficit. This is similar to an individual who spends more money than he or she makes. The individual will go into debt and eventually have to sell off assets to continue to live beyond his or her means.

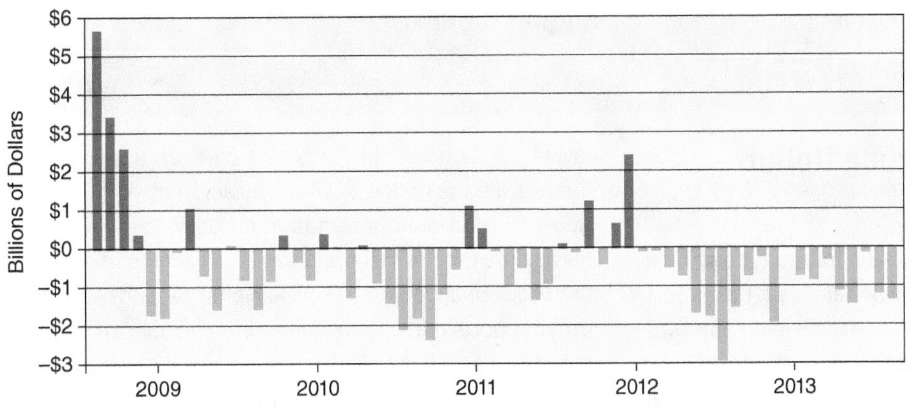

Figure 12.4 Canada Trade Balance: 2008–2013

Source: http://wpmedia.business.financialpost.com/2013/10/fp1009_canada_trade_balance_c_ab.jpeg?w=620&h=386

ANDREW BARR/NATIONAL POST

Canada's Top Export Destinations (2013)

Country	Exports (CDN$ billions)
1. United States	$357.5
2. China	$20.5
3. United Kingdom	$14.0
4. Japan	$10.7
5. Mexico	$5.4
6. Hong Kong	$4.9
7. Netherlands	$3.6
8. Germany	$3.5
9. South Korea	$3.4
10. France	$3.0

Source: Industry Canada, "International Trade Canadian Economy (NAICS 11-91)," accessed March 4, 2014, https://www.ic.gc.ca/app/scr/sbms/sbb/cis/internationalTrade.html?code=11-91&lang=eng.

Another measure of international trade is the **balance of payments**, which is a summary of a country's international financial transactions. The balance of payments includes imports and exports (balance of trade), government loans to and from other countries, long-term investments in overseas business operations, gifts and foreign aid, military expenditures made to other countries, and money transfers into and out of foreign banks. The balance of payments shows the difference between the country's total payments to and the total receipts from other countries.

balance of payments A summary of a country's international financial transactions.

Fixed and Flexible Exchange Rate Systems Exchange rates can be manipulated or fixed by governments. For example, China has fixed its currency to a rate that is weak compared to the Canadian dollar. The reason Chinese monetary authorities at the People's Bank of China do this is to make their exports relatively inexpensive and therefore attractive. This also means that Chinese imports from Canada are expensive. As a result, China's products are considered to be artificially cheap because the currency value is managed, which has a variety of negative effects on the rest of the world. This is one reason why manufacturing has been leaving North America and going to China.

Several countries are now calling upon the Chinese to allow their currency to "float," or to change in response to changing market conditions. Indeed, most countries use a **flexible (or floating) exchange rate system**, which uses the global supply and demand for currencies to determine exchange rates. Many specific factors affect the demand and supply of a nation's currency, such as changing interest rates, tax rates, and inflation rates. But generally, changes in exchange rates in a flexible exchange rate system reflect the country's current economic health and its outlook for growth and investment potential. The problems with floating exchange rates are that they can create relative price changes outside the control of international businesses, as well as engender risks of losses from rapid and unexpected changes in exchange rates.

flexible (or floating) exchange rate system Uses the global supply and demand for currencies to determine exchange rates.

Video: The G20 and the Global Monetary and Financial Systems

Canada's currency has undergone some variability over the years. After a weakening Canadian dollar under the flexible exchange rate system used in 1961–1962, the government, in agreement with the IMF, established a new par value for the Canadian dollar, fixing it at US$0.9250 where it remained until 1970.[53] At that time, in an effort to reduce inflation, the Bank of Canada reverted to a flexible exchange rate system. For most of the decade, the Canadian dollar rose in value and was valued in excess of the U.S. dollar, at one time reaching a high of US$1.0443 during that period. Over the next 30 years, the Canadian dollar fell in value against its U.S. counterpart and reached an all-time low of US$0.618 on January 21, 2002.[54] In 2003, the Canadian dollar began an upward climb that was unlike anything experienced in decades. On September 28, 2007, the Canadian dollar closed above the U.S. dollar for the first time in 30 years, at US$1.0052. **Figure 12.5** illustrates the appreciation of the Canadian dollar against the US dollar since December 2002.

Nonconvertible Currency and Countertrade Governments also reserve the right to restrict the convertibility of their currency. For example, many developing countries

Which Is Better—A Strong Dollar or a Weak Dollar?

The answer to this question depends on the type of business a firm undertakes. Companies that do a lot of exporting—such as auto companies, chemical manufacturers, and farmers—prefer a weak dollar because their products' prices are lower in the global marketplace so their sales and profits will be higher. On the other hand, companies that import components or finished goods for resale in the domestic market prefer a strong dollar because the relative price of their imports is lower.

From a consumer's perspective, a strong dollar is typically preferred because import prices are lower, which has a tendency to keep domestic competitors' prices low as well. As an employee, if you work for a company that exports much of its product, you would prefer a weak dollar to stimulate sales and ensure your job security.

The benefits of a strong dollar for a nation as a whole are lower-priced imports (such as oil), lower prices, and a lower inflation rate in general. However, a strong dollar creates a trade deficit. A weak dollar, on the other hand, is good for domestic international businesses because it stimulates employment and raises standards of living. The drawback of a weak dollar is the higher costs of energy and other imports that create higher rates of inflation. So which is better—a strong dollar or a weak dollar? Like most real-world issues, the answer depends on your perspective.

Discussion Questions

1. **As a person living in Canada, would you prefer a strong Canadian dollar or a weak dollar? Why?**
2. **If you were an importer in China, would you prefer a strong Canadian dollar or a weak one? Why?**
3. **Use the Internet to find a currency exchange converter and compare the value of the Canadian dollar to the Chinese yuan, Japanese yen, Indian rupee, Mexican peso, euro, and U.S. dollar. Based on your findings, which country would you most like to import goods from? How many Canadian dollars would it cost you to buy a Big Mac in each of these countries?**

nonconvertible currency A currency that can't be converted into another currency in the foreign exchange market.

capital flight The transfer of domestic funds into foreign currency held outside the country.

have a **nonconvertible currency**, a currency that can't be converted into another currency in the foreign exchange market. These governments often fear that allowing convertibility will result in **capital flight**, the transfer of domestic funds into foreign currency held outside the country. Capital flight would deprive the nation of much-needed funds for investment and development.

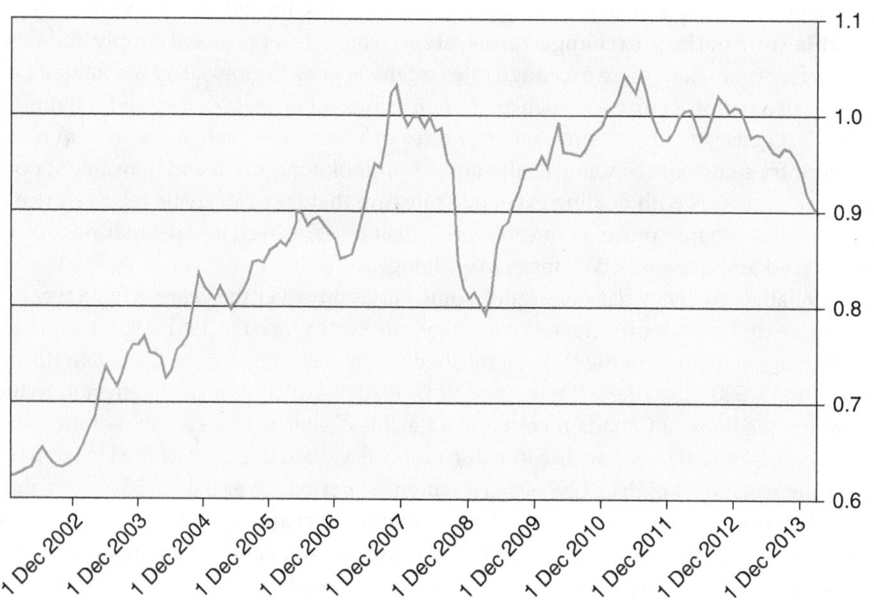

Figure 12.5 Canadian Dollar versus U.S. Dollar: 2002–2013

Source: Bank of Canada, "Canadian Dollar Versus American Dollar by Bank of Canada." Copyright © 2014 by Bank of Canada. Used by permission of Bank of Canada.

Global companies can still do business with countries that have nonconvertible currencies by using countertrade. **Countertrade** is a form of international barter—the swapping of goods and services for other goods and services. Currently, countertrade may account for as much as 10 to 15 percent of total world trade. Companies engage in countertrade because of necessity and profitability. Examples of companies that have undertaken countertrade include General Foods, Goodyear, General Electric, Westinghouse, 3M, General Motors, Ford Motor Company, Coca-Cola, and PepsiCo.[55]

countertrade A form of international barter—the swapping of goods and services for other goods and services.

Other Economic Challenges to Conducting International Business

LO9 List the economic factors and challenges that play a role in conducting business on a global scale.

What challenges does rapid growth of a nation pose to international business? Changing exchange rates and nonconvertible currencies are not the only economic challenges to conducting international business. Companies must also consider how to adapt their products for sale in developing nations, how certain government policies might affect their business, and how the socioeconomic factors of an area influence the types of products they sell.

Many developing countries are experiencing more rapid growth than advanced economies are, and they have hundreds of millions of eager new customers ready to put their money into the global market. It is also true that many developing countries still lack the basic infrastructure necessary for effective transportation of goods or lack access to dependable electricity. They may also be lacking in modern communications systems. The implications are obvious. For example, the types of food products offered for sale would have to be altered and packaged differently. Makers of electric can openers would need to produce manual can openers for sale. The modes of advertising would shift from television to radio, and marketing a product via the Internet wouldn't be effective because few customers would own a computer. It would be important for a business entering India, for example, to know the explosive growth there is not as much toward computer ownership as it is toward mobile phone ownership. Advertising delivered via mobile phones would be critical.

How does government intervention in the markets pose a challenge to international business? The degree to which markets are allowed to operate free from government intervention is another important economic consideration. International businesses prefer free-market economies to state-run or socialized economies because the bureaucratic hassles associated with government intervention drive costs up. Other economic factors include the debt load of a nation, its unemployment and inflation rates, and its fiscal and monetary policies. Unit labour cost—a measure that divides a worker's wages by the average productivity of that worker—is also important. Global companies are concerned with labour costs when looking for lowest-cost locations to establish production facilities. In addition, the degree of competition that exists in a nation is important because it's more attractive to relocate to places with fewer competitors.

How do socioeconomic factors affect doing business internationally? Several socioeconomic factors also need to be taken into account, such as the demographics of population density and age distribution. The birthrates of many developing countries are high and offer exciting opportunities to toy manufacturers such as Mattel. Other socioeconomic factors that firms must consider include income distribution, ethnicity, and the cultural behaviours of a community.

Sociocultural, Political, Legal, and Ethical Challenges

LO10 Summarize the sociocultural, political, legal, and ethical challenges to conducting business in a global marketplace.

What is culture? **Culture** is the complex set of values, behaviours, lifestyles, arts, beliefs, and institutions of a population that is passed on from generation to generation.

culture The complex set of values, behaviours, lifestyles, arts, beliefs, and institutions of a population that is passed on from generation to generation.

Culture affects all aspects of business, from managing workers and production techniques to marketing and beyond. When a business expands into an international market and lacks cross-cultural and political awareness, it is destined to fail. The role of government involvement in business is not universal, so knowing how specific government policies govern business activity is critical for business success. And because there is no global court to settle differences and disputes, businesses need to thoroughly study what is acceptable legally and ethically.

Walmart is a good example of a company struggling to understand international customers. For the year 2013, Walmart reported disappointing sales growth of a meagre 1.3 percent for its international division, compared to an 11.3 percent increase in retail sales in the United States. That same year, Walmart was forced to close 29 stores in China and another 26 stores in Brazil.[56] This was not Walmart's first defeat in foreign markets. In 2006 Walmart accepted defeat in both German and South Korean markets because of its inability to adapt to local customers. As you learned earlier, Walmart's failed attempt to penetrate markets in India through a joint venture with Bharti Enterprises exemplifies the dilemma faced by many multinational corporations—organizations attempting to gain a foothold in a foreign market must understand their local customers and the local customs in each and every market they wish to enter.

Why is the study of culture important for international business? Most international businesses that fail do so because they suffer from a lack of cross-cultural awareness. Attitudes toward time and work, aesthetics, religion, language, political systems, legal systems, and ethical ideals vary from country to country. **Cross-cultural awareness** is an understanding of, appreciation for, and sensitivity to foreign culture. **Ethnocentrism**, a belief that one's own culture is superior to all other cultures, is a guaranteed recipe for disaster when undertaking international business.

cross-cultural awareness An understanding of, appreciation for, and sensitivity to foreign culture.

ethnocentrism A belief that one's own culture is superior to all other cultures

Why do aesthetics matter when it comes to international business? *Aesthetics* is what is considered beautiful or in good taste and includes etiquette, customs, and protocol. Few things are more embarrassing than violating a sense of good taste. For example, a company selling eyeglasses in Thailand used ads featuring various cute animals wearing glasses. But because animals are considered a low form of life in Thailand and no Thai would wear anything worn by animals, the ads were a poor choice. Another example involves an American oil rig supervisor in Indonesia who yelled at an employee to take a boat to shore. Since it is considered rude to berate a worker in front of others, outraged workers brandishing axes chased the supervisor.[57]

How do different attitudes toward time and work affect international business? *Attitudes toward time* vary considerably around the world. Time is paramount to those in the Canada and the United States, where people in general expect promptness and often insist on getting down to business. Some cultures view this as pushy and impersonal—a cultural turnoff. In addition, the Canadian time horizon differs markedly from the Japanese perspective. A Canadian may consider a long-term view to be four to seven years into the future, while the Japanese may be preparing for decades in advance.

Attitudes toward work also vary. In Spain, business hours are generally from 9 a.m. to 2 p.m. and from 5 p.m. to 8 p.m., with an afternoon siesta (sleep or slowdown) in between. Sunday is still considered a holiday in Spain, so the majority of businesses are closed.[58] Of course, restaurants are open from 1 p.m. to 4 p.m. and after 8 p.m., when people are off work. A business person from Canada should not expect to hold a business meeting during siesta time. Business meetings in Germany should be scheduled two to three weeks in advance and are usually held between 11 a.m. and 1 p.m. and 3 p.m. and 5 p.m. Meetings on Friday afternoons or during the holiday months of July, August, and December are avoided.[59]

Video: CH2MHill: Management in the Global Environment

How do different religious beliefs affect international business? *Religion* plays a profound role in shaping a culture. International businesses are therefore well advised to educate themselves on varying religious value systems, customs, and practices if they don't wish to offend customers in marketing campaigns. For example, when Arabs interpreted a soft drink with a label that had six-pointed stars on it as pro-Israeli, they refused to buy it.[60]

Christine Schneider/Corbis

Should you bow or shake hands when you visit a Japanese client in Japan?

Can inaccurate language translation cost a company money? *Language*, both spoken and unspoken, is also extremely important. Consider a few more examples of international business blunders due to a lack of cross-cultural awareness. In Italy, Schweppes Tonic Water was translated as "Schweppes Toilet Water," and in Sweden, Kellogg had to rename its Bran Buds cereal when it discovered that the name roughly translated to "burned farmer."[61]

Unspoken language, or body language, also differs significantly around the world. Shaking your head side to side means "no" in Canada but "yes" in Bulgaria. In Asian cultures, it is considered rude to look someone in the eyes, yet in North American and other cultures, not looking at someone while speaking with them may be interpreted as disinterest, disrespect, or a sign that the person should not be trusted.

Although the world is getting smaller and a global culture is emerging, profound and significant cultural differences still exist. Cross-cultural awareness is a prerequisite to successful international business.

What are the political challenges to conducting international business? International businesses look for nations that have a stable government, a well-established educational system, and a well-maintained infrastructure. Political changes can create disruptive environments that affect business concerns. The political differences among nations can also pose a challenge when conducting international business.

Although companies are better equipped (and therefore prefer) to pursue their self-interests in market-based or capitalist economies, global companies often do business in government-controlled socialist economies such as China, Cuba, and North Korea. The differences between political systems can cause tensions. However, even in market economies, governments must address *market failures*, or shortcomings associated with free markets. The extent to which government is involved in addressing market failures can vary dramatically from country to country, which can have very important implications for international businesses. Many products that pollute the environment are deemed undesirable and have been regulated in one form or another by most governments around the world. The differences in these regulatory standards can impose big differences in costs of production for global businesses. There are also growing pressures on governments to address global climate change issues that will affect international business. **Table 12.3** summarizes the failures of markets and government attempts to address these shortcomings.

SELF CHECK Answer the following questions to determine your cultural IQ.

1. Between 1 and 4 p.m., business people in Spain are more likely to
   a. attend a lunch meeting with clients.
   b. return home for a family lunch and nap.
2. In Venezuela, it's common for business associates to
   a. maintain at least three feet of personal space.
   b. offer a handshake and pat on the shoulder upon greeting.
3. If you receive a business card from a Japanese business acquaintance, you should
   a. put it in your pocket without looking at it.
   b. receive the card with both hands and examine the information.
4. During a lunch meeting with a Muslim partner, you should avoid ordering
   a. lamb.
   b. pork.
5. If an Indian business acquaintance offers you a gift, you should
   a. politely decline the offer.
   b. open the present after your acquaintance has left.

If your answers are . . .
Mostly As—It is time to brush up on your cultural awareness.
Mostly Bs—Congratulations! With your high cultural IQ, you'll need to get your passport ready for global business encounters.

Video: Impact of Culture on Business: Spotlight on China

Table 12.3 Failures of Markets and Government Interventions

Market Failures	Government Interventions
Growth of monopoly power	Government enforces anti-trust laws
Undesirable and desirable social side effects from production and consumption	Government curtails the production and consumption of undesirable goods and promotes desirable products
Lack of public goods and services	Government provides them
Unfair distribution of income	Government redistributes income
Macroeconomic instability	Government uses fiscal and monetary policies to stabilize the business cycle

Just because governments intervene doesn't mean they succeed in improving market outcomes. Indeed, *government failure*—government intervention that fails to improve a market outcome—exists around the world. Government failure stems from corruption, ignorance, or pressure that special-interest groups place on politicians. International businesses prefer politically stable democracies because the probability of government failure is lower than for nondemocratic and unstable regimes.

What are the legal challenges to conducting international business? Laws, regulatory standards, and access to unbiased judicial systems based on a rule of law differ considerably around the world. No universal laws, regulatory standards, or global courts exist to settle disputes in the global economy. The different laws governing contracts, product safety and liability standards, and property rights are of particular importance when conducting global business. Property rights violations, including violations of patents and copyrights in the software, music, and publishing business, have cost businesses billions of dollars a year. Without adequate protection of intellectual property, technological developments would be too expensive and risky for companies to continue to fund long-term R&D.

Different laws also govern the use of bribery throughout the world. In Canada and the United States, offering bribes to foreign officials to gain contracts or other favours as a part of doing business is not only frowned upon, it is illegal. The Canadian government has concerns that Canadian businesses are at a disadvantage with many foreign companies that routinely pay bribes and are even able to deduct the cost of bribes from their taxes as legitimate business expenses. The Organisation for Economic Co-operation and Development (OECD), which currently consists of 30 member nations, is committed to combating bribery. In many places in the world, however, bribes are not uncommon and may even be necessary to do business.[62]

What are some ethical challenges to conducting international business? Bribery is just one of the many ethical dilemmas surrounding global business. But even when something isn't illegal, it doesn't mean it isn't unethical. Unique differences in economic conditions and cultural values give rise to many ethical dilemmas surrounding global business. For example, should a firm conform to its home country's environmental, workplace, and product safety standards—even though it is not legally required to do so—while operating in another country? Should a company do business with a repressive totalitarian regime? When conducting international business, companies must decide whether they're willing to defy their ethical codes to make a larger profit or even to survive.

Think back to the quiz that you took earlier in this section. It is truly important to realize that you can't assume that people will behave in similar ways in different cultures. Understanding and respecting these differences will help you in life, whether you're hoping to work for a large international company or planning to visit foreign countries as a tourist.

CHAPTER SYNOPSIS

LO1 Understand how the globalization of markets and production has affected business. (pp. 304–306)

The **globalization of markets** is thinking of the market as being the entire world rather than a local or national one. Companies often need to adjust their products or marketing campaigns to suit the unique tastes and preferences of their customers, wherever they may be.

The **globalization of production** occurs when companies move production to different locations around the globe (through **outsourcing** or **offshoring**) to take advantage of lower costs or to enhance quality. When faced with intense foreign competition, companies may be forced to relocate at least some of their production to another country to realize lower costs so they can offer customers lower prices.

The globalization of markets and production has resulted in some international firms becoming so large that they generate more revenue than the gross domestic product (GDP) of some nations.

LO2 Explain why globalization has accelerated so rapidly. (pp. 306–309)

Two main factors increase globalization: technological innovations and the dramatic decline in **trade and investment barriers** among countries since the end of World War II. For example, the North American Free Trade Agreement (NAFTA) of 1994 made it easier for companies to shift work among Canada, the United States, and Mexico and opened the door to expanding offshoring.

LO3 Explain the meaning of *comparative advantage* and *absolute advantage* and describe the benefits and costs of international trade. (pp. 309–311)

A country has a **comparative advantage** when it can produce a good or service relatively more efficiently compared with other countries. An **absolute advantage** is a country's ability to produce *more* of a good or service than any other country. Just because a large country can produce more of a good than a small country doesn't necessarily mean it is relatively more efficient at producing that good. What matters is relative efficiency, or comparative advantage—not absolute advantage.

The theory of comparative advantage indicates that countries participating in international trade will experience higher standards of living because of the greater quantity and variety of higher-quality products offered at lower prices. These results stem from the increased competition associated with more open trade.

The costs of international trade are borne by those businesses and their workers whose livelihoods are threatened by foreign competition. Some domestic businesses may lose market share to foreign companies, stunting their profitability and ability to create jobs. Other firms may not be able to compete with the foreign competition and be driven out of business entirely.

LO4 Define free trade and summarize the different types of trade barriers used to protect domestic industries from foreign competition. (pp. 311–314)

Free trade is the unencumbered flow of goods and services across national borders. A **tariff** is a tax on an imported good or service, such as French wine. Governments prefer to impose tariffs because they raise tax revenues. The opposite of a tariff is a **subsidy**, in which governments make payments to domestic producers. A **quota** is a limitation on the amount of an import allowed to enter a country. The most heavy-handed government trade barrier is an **embargo**, a total restriction on an import (or export).

Administrative trade barriers are government rules designed to limit imports. A **local content requirement** demands that some portion of a good be produced domestically, which usually drives up the cost of the import. Administrative trade barriers may also require an import to meet some technical standard or bureaucratic rule (i.e., customer regulations that are different from generally accepted international standards), effectively shutting the import out of the domestic market.

LO5 Describe the organizations that facilitate trade and attempt to eliminate trade barriers. (pp. 314–318)

The **World Trade Organization (WTO)** has strengthened the world trading system by extending **GATT** rules to services, increasing protection for intellectual property rights, and perhaps most significantly arbitrating trade disputes and monitoring the trade policies of member countries. The **World Bank** offers low-interest loans, advice, and information to developing countries. The **International Monetary Fund (IMF)** promotes trade through financial cooperation.

LO6 Distinguish among the three basic strategies of international business. (pp. 318–319)

The **global strategy** involves competing primarily based on price while selling a standardized (or homogenous) product. The **multidomestic strategy** involves competing primarily by customizing or differentiating the product to meet unique local needs, tastes, or preferences. Firms pursuing a multidomestic strategy face relatively low pressures for cost reduction because the price is often of secondary concern to buyers. The **transnational strategy** involves competing by offering a customized product while simultaneously selling at the lowest possible price. The strong cost pressures and pressures for differentiation that motivate this type of strategy are typically at odds.

LO7 Outline the ways international firms can successfully enter foreign markets. (pp. 319–321)

Companies may undertake one of six strategies to enter foreign markets:

1. Export their product.
2. Implement a **turnkey project**.
3. Undertake **franchising**.
4. Enter into a **licensing** agreement, a **joint venture**, or a **strategic alliance**.
5. Undertake **contract manufacturing**.
6. Establish a **wholly owned subsidiary**.

LO8 Define exchange rates and explain how they affect international business. (pp. 321–325)

Businesses are affected by fluctuating **exchange rates**—the rates at which currencies are converted into another currency—every day. Transactions between international companies not only have to specify what each side will be paid but also in which currency. **Currency appreciation**, an increase in the exchange rate value of a nation's currency, causes the relative price of imports to fall as the relative price of exports rises. **Currency depreciation**, a decrease in the exchange rate value of a nation's currency, has the opposite effect on the relative prices of exports and imports. A weak currency causes exports to become cheaper and imports to become more expensive.

LO9 List the economic factors and challenges that play a role in conducting business on a global scale. (p. 325)

A **trade deficit**, or unfavourable **balance of trade**, exists when the value of a country's imports exceeds the value of its exports. A strong Canadian dollar may cause a trade deficit because a strong dollar can cause export prices to rise and import prices fall. A **trade surplus**, or favourable balance of trade, occurs when the value of a country's exports exceeds the value of its imports.

Most countries operate under a **flexible (or floating) exchange rate system**, a system in which the global supply and demand for currencies determine exchange rates. Many developing countries have a **nonconvertible currency**, which is a currency that can't be converted into another currency in the foreign exchange market.

Companies must also consider how to adapt their products for sale in developing nations, how certain government policies might affect their business, and how the socioeconomic factors of an area influence the types of products they sell.

LO10 Summarize the sociocultural, political, legal, and ethical challenges to conducting business in a global marketplace. (pp. 325–328)

Culture—the complex set of values, behaviours, lifestyles, arts, beliefs, and institutions of a population passed on from generation to generation—affects all aspects of business, from managing workers and production techniques to marketing and beyond. Attitudes toward time and work, aesthetics, religion, language, political systems, legal systems, and ethical ideals vary from country to country. **Cross-cultural awareness** is an understanding, appreciation, and sensitivity to foreign culture. Most international businesses fail because they suffer from a lack of cross-cultural awareness.

KEY TERMS

absolute advantage *(p. 309)*
administrative trade barriers *(p. 311)*
balance of payments *(p. 323)*
balance of trade *(p. 322)*
capital flight *(p. 324)*
comparative advantage *(p. 309)*
contract manufacturing *(p. 320)*
countertrade *(p. 325)*
cross-cultural awareness *(p. 326)*
culture *(p. 325)*
currency appreciation *(p. 322)*
currency depreciation *(p. 322)*
dumping *(p. 312)*
embargo *(p. 311)*
ethnocentrism *(p. 326)*
European Union (EU) *(p. 315)*
exchange rates *(p. 321)*
exporting *(p. 304)*
flexible (or floating) exchange rate system *(p. 323)*
franchising *(p. 319)*
free trade *(p. 311)*
free trade areas or agreements (FTA) *(p. 315)*
General Agreement on Tariffs and Trade (GATT) *(p. 314)*
global strategy *(p. 318)*
globalization *(p. 305)*
globalization of markets *(p. 305)*
globalization of production *(p. 306)*
importing *(p. 304)*
International Monetary Fund (IMF) *(p. 314)*
joint ventures *(p. 320)*
licensing *(p. 319)*
local content requirement *(p. 311)*
multidomestic strategy *(p. 318)*
near-shoring *(p. 307)*
nonconvertible currency *(p. 324)*
North American Free Trade Agreement (NAFTA) *(p. 317)*
offshoring *(p. 306)*
outsourcing *(p. 308)*
quota *(p. 311)*
strategic alliances *(p. 320)*
subsidy *(p. 311)*
tariff *(p. 311)*
trade and investment barriers *(p. 306)*
trade deficit *(p. 322)*
trade surplus *(p. 322)*
transnational strategy *(p. 318)*
turnkey project *(p. 319)*
wholly owned subsidiary *(p. 321)*
World Bank *(p. 314)*
World Trade Organization (WTO) *(p. 314)*

CRITICAL THINKING QUESTIONS

1. The text explains that sometimes an international business needs to modify its product to adjust to the specific needs or tastes of the local market. How would a company such as Hewlett-Packard adjust its laptop computers to market them to families in developing nations like India?
2. Think about the technological advancements the world has embraced over the last 10 years. The World Wide Web, smartphones, tablets, and wireless connections have allowed businesspeople to have mobile offices. How does this technology reduce cultural distance and decrease business costs?
3. What are the advantages of increased competition in the global market? What are the disadvantages? Is foreign competition *always* good for the consumer? Is foreign competition *always* bad for the local business?
4. Review the three basic strategies of international business. Discuss the type of companies that would most likely pursue a global strategy, a multidomestic strategy, and a transnational strategy.
5. Imagine you own a furniture store in Canada that specializes in handcrafted dining room tables and chairs. You would like to sell your product to countries in Western Europe. What would be a good mode of entering the foreign market for your company?

TEAM TIME

The Devil's Advocate

Read the following Discussion Questions. Which side of the issue do you believe is correct? Form a group with other students in the class who share your belief. As a group, play devil's advocate by creating a case for the opposing side of the issue. Now that you've considered both sides, you're ready to debate the opposition.

DISCUSSION QUESTIONS

1. In the recent wave of globalization, developing countries have become the focus for many international businesses. Is this process of globalization the best way to strengthen developing countries and establish a level playing field, or does it keep them under the control of wealthy industries and drive income inequality?
2. Free trade versus protectionism is a heated debate in today's economy. Which is better for the health of the Canadian economy and domestic business owners over the next 10 years: free trade or protectionism?
3. What types of ethical concerns might a Canadian company be faced with when outsourcing work to foreign countries? What about child labour, fair wages, or safety in food and drugs? Is there need to be concerned? What is being done?

PROCESS

Step 1. Meet as a group to discuss the issue. Remember that you must build a case for the side you chose. Look for problems with your own personal beliefs to develop a case for your side.
Step 2. Prepare an individual response that supports your side of the issue.
Step 3. Share your response with your group. Think of possible rebuttals for each response. Then alter any responses that can produce a strong rebuttal.
Step 4. Determine who will be the group's primary spokesperson for the debate.
Step 5. Each group will be given five minutes to present its side of the issue. After each group has presented their argument, each team will be given five minutes to prepare a rebuttal and then three minutes to present the rebuttal.
Step 6. Repeat with other groups.
Step 7. After each group has debated, discuss whether anyone's personal view has changed after this assignment.

ETHICS AND RESPONSIBILITY

Outsourcing

Workers in Canada often view outsourcing in a negative light. Many people believe that this practice is used by companies wishing to increase their profits by lowering their labour costs. They feel that outsourcing eliminates Canadian jobs and that local workers suffer while the company enjoys greater profits from what is often argued to be an inferior product. However, outsourcing is sometimes necessary for the survival of a company. Review the following scenario.

SCENARIO

You are the owner of a company that makes industrial sewing machines. Currently, your company's profits are decreasing because your competitors have lower prices. You cannot lower the price of your machines without losing a significant amount of money. The majority of your costs come from labour. You have 2000 employees in your factory, and your company is a primary employer in the region. You could sell your product for one-third of the price if you outsourced half your production to a foreign country. However, this would eliminate 1000 jobs and devastate a community. Also, the country that you would be outsourcing to has a reputation for unsafe working conditions and practices. If you don't outsource some of your production, over time, your company may be unable to compete and you will have to shut down.

DISCUSSION QUESTIONS

1. As a business owner, what are the costs and benefits of moving half your production overseas?
2. Do the benefits of outsourcing outweigh the costs? Why or why not?
3. Are there any possible alternatives to consider? What other decision could you make so that each side (domestic and international) benefits?

CLOSING CASE

GE's Company-to-Country Strategy

When Jeffery R. Immelt stepped into the position of CEO of General Electric, he recognized that with the combination of growth in emerging countries with raw material inflation and changes in government, many opportunities were looming. By focusing on these emerging markets, Immelt and GE put themselves in a good position to provide this infrastructure and, eventually, other consumer needs.

While globalization is not a new concept for GE, the company-to-country strategy that Immelt implemented changed the way GE approached the global market. The goal of the company-to-country strategy is to form close business relationships with foreign governments and consumers and tailor products to their needs. GE's company-to-country strategy is exemplified by their involvement in the Olympic Games. GE's Olympic Games partnership was launched in January 2005 and continues through to the 2020 Summer Games, including the 2016 Games in Rio de Janeiro, the 2018 Winter Games in Pyeongchang, South Korea, and the 2020 Summer Games in Tokyo, Japan.[63]

GE provides a wide range of innovative products and services that are integral to successful Olympic and Paralympic Games. Immelt thought the Games would be a great way to combine the presence of GE's global entertainment franchise (NBC) with the value of its infrastructure technology.[64] GE works closely with host countries to provide infrastructure solutions for Olympic venues, including power, lighting, water treatment, transportation, and security.[65] GE's leadership position at the Beijing Olympics in 2008 created billions in revenues and decades of goodwill in China. GE hopes this goodwill will translate into big dollars when it comes to providing for China's increasing growth.

Likewise, in 2011, GE gained an important foothold in Russia. At that time, Immelt flew to Sochi to join Vladimir Putin in announcing two joint ventures—one to build industrial gas turbines with two Russian business partners and the other with state-backed Russian Technologies, or Rostec, to produce medical devices such as CT scanners for hospitals across the country.[66]

GE has focused a majority of its company-to-country efforts in China. As a country that has seen a significant increase in the population of urban areas, China has an extreme demand for new infrastructure. The company states on its website: "China is a market of tremendous opportunity for GE—particularly for our infrastructure businesses."[67] A growing China will also need more energy, water, security, and health care. GE hopes to build a relationship with China that will allow the company to be a one-stop shop for all of the country's needs.

GE is not only looking to globalize its market, it also wants to globalize its products. GE's goal is to create products in China for China. Instead of modifying existing products, GE has established a research centre in Shanghai to create innovative products that meet the most pressing needs of the emerging Chinese consumer. This method has been successfully used in GE's health care division. Now, GE can provide much-needed equipment such as mobile screening technology and low-cost diagnostic imaging tools to China and other major emerging markets.

GE's traditional customers, such as hospitals that buy defibrillators or car companies that buy lighting systems, cannot provide the type of double-digit growth that Immelt would like to see. By becoming a "familiar face" to consumers in emerging markets, GE is well positioned to become the go-to company for future ventures such as consumer finance. If and when the wealth in developing countries moves down to the working class, these people may look to GE to get financial products and services such as credit cards, loans, and financial advice. To GE, globalization isn't just about reaching more customers, it's about creating more opportunity.

DISCUSSION QUESTIONS

1. Why does GE feel that investing in emerging markets is a good idea? Do you agree with this approach? What problems could GE face by entering emerging markets?
2. What is unique about the company-to-country philosophy? How is it different from just selling GE products to emerging countries?
3. Consider what you've learned about market failure in this chapter. Do you think it is wise for GE to focus on infrastructure in emerging countries as opposed to, say, health care?

Glossary

absolute advantage A country's ability to produce more of a good or service than any other country.

accounting The recording, classifying, summarizing, and interpreting of financial events to communicate useful financial information. It involves tracking a business's income and expenses through a process of recording financial transactions.

accounts payable Obligations a company owes to vendors and creditors.

accounts receivable Amounts owed to the company from customers who have purchased goods or services on credit.

accrued expenses Include payroll, commissions, and benefits that have been earned but not paid to employees.

acquisition Occurs when one company or investor group buys a corporation and the identity of the acquired company might be lost.

action learning A management development training approach that focuses on solving real problems on actual work projects.

administrative trade barriers Government rules designed to limit imports.

advertising Paid, impersonal mass communication from an identified sponsor to persuade or influence a targeted audience.

affiliative (or laissez-faire) leader A leader who encourages employees to contribute ideas rather than specifically direct their tasks.

agents/brokers Intermediaries who facilitate negotiations between buyers and sellers of goods and services but never take title (ownership) of the products traded.

amortization The process of applying long-term expenses to intangible assets such as goodwill or patents.

angel investors Wealthy individuals who are willing to put their own money into your business in hopes of a profit return later on.

annual reports Documents produced once a year to present the current financial state of a company and future expectations.

apprentice training A program that trains individuals through classroom or formal instruction and on-the-job training.

arbitration A process in which the disputing parties present their case to a third-party intermediary who examines all the evidence and then makes a decision (usually binding) for the parties.

articles of incorporation Lay out the general nature of the corporation, the name of the corporation and its directors, the type and number of shares to be issued, and the location of the company's operations.

assembly line Used to move partially complete products from one worker to the next on a conveyor belt. Also called a production line.

assets What the company owns.

auction process A system that exemplifies price determination as bidders state their willingness to pay a price for an item based on demand. Supply factors into the price determination since multiple items available for sale will result in a lower price.

auditing Responsible for reviewing and evaluating the accuracy of financial reports.

autocratic leader A leader who makes decisions without consulting others.

balance of payments A summary of a country's international financial transactions.

balance of trade The difference between the value of a country's exports and the value of its imports during a specific time.

balance sheet Shows what the company owns and what it has borrowed (owes) at a fixed point in time and shows the net worth of the business.

Bank of Canada Acts as the federal government's financial adviser and is responsible for promoting the economic and financial well-being of Canada. It manages the country's money supply through its monetary policy to control inflation.

bargaining unit A group of employees who negotiate with the employer for better working conditions or pay.

bartering People trading goods or services without a medium of exchange. The "price" of something is determined by the needs of each person in the bartering exchange and what they are willing to trade.

behavioural interviews Interviews conducted to evaluate a candidate's experience and behaviours so the employer can determine the applicant's potential for success in the job.

behavioural segmentation Market segmentation based on certain consumer behaviour characteristics, such as the benefits sought by the consumer, the extent to which the product is consumed, brand loyalty, price sensitivity, and the ways in which the product is used.

benefits Come in many forms and provide additional compensation to employees beyond base wages.

Big Five One of the most widely accepted models of personality. The model categorizes most human personality traits into five broad dimensions and then assigns people a score for each dimension: openness, conscientiousness, extraversion, agreeableness, and neuroticism (emotional stability). Also called the Five-Factor Model.

bill of material Lists the items and the number of each required to make a specific product.

board of directors A group of people who are elected by shareholders to govern and handle the overall management of the corporation.

bona fide job requirement An ability genuinely needed to perform a job. A person who lacks such a necessary ability can be legitimately denied employment (e.g., a person with a visual impairment will be denied employment as a bus driver).

bookkeeping The systematic recording of a company's every financial transaction.

bottom line Refers to the difference of money in and money out, the profit or loss.

boycott Occurs when union members and their supporters refuse to buy or handle the company's products or services.

brand A name, term, symbol, or design that distinguishes a company and its products from all others.

brand association Involves connecting a brand with other positive attributes, including image, product features, usage situations, organizational associations, brand personality, and symbols.

brand awareness The extent to which a particular brand name is familiar within a particular product category.

brand equity The overall value of a brand's strength in the market.

brand insistence The highest degree of brand loyalty. It can turn a product into a specialty good or service that can command a much higher price.

brand loyalty The degree to which customers consistently prefer one brand over all others.

brand manager A manager who is responsible for the 4 Ps of marketing a specific product or product line. Brand managers attempt to increase the product's perceived value to customers in order to increase brand equity. Also called a product manager.

break-even analysis Determines the production level for which total revenue is just enough to cover total costs.

budget A financial plan that outlines the company's planned cash flows, expected operating expenses, and anticipated revenues.

budget deficit Occurs when the money being spent by the government exceeds the money coming into the government.

budget surplus Occurs when the money coming into the government exceeds the money being spent by the government.

bundling When two or more products that usually complement one another are combined and sold at a single price.

business Any activity that provides goods or services for the purpose of earning profit.

business cycle Describes how the economy fluctuates over time, going through periods of increased growth (expansion) and decreased growth (contraction).

business environment The forces outside the business that can affect the firm's industry and competitive environment.

business incubators Organizations that support startup businesses by offering resources such as administrative services, technical support, business networking, and sources of financing that a group of startup companies share.

business plan A formal document that states the goals of the business as well as the plan for reaching those goals.

business-to-business (B2B) markets A market in which businesses purchase goods and services from other businesses.

business-to-business (B2B) products Goods and services purchased by businesses for further processing or resale or used in facilitating business operations. Also called industrial products.

business-to-business product classifications Five classifications that emerge from strategic marketing mix plans for B2B products: equipment; maintenance, repair, and operating (MRO) products; raw and processed materials; component parts; and specialized professional services. Also called industrial product classifications.

bylaws The rules of a corporation, established by the board of directors during the process of starting a corporation.

Canada Labour Code Together with the provincial employment standards acts and labour codes (at the provincial level), this federal law defines the rights and obligations of individuals as workers, union members, and employers in the workplace.

capacity The amount of a product or service that a company can produce under normal working conditions in a given time period.

capital budget Considers the company's long-range plans and outlines the expected financial needs for significant capital purchases such as real estate, manufacturing equipment, plant expansions, or technology.

capital flight The transfer of domestic funds into foreign currency held outside the country.

capital Investments in the form of money, equipment, supplies, computers, and any other tangible thing of value.

capitalism An economic system that allows freedom of choice and encourages private ownership of the resources required to make and provide goods and services consumers enjoy. Also called a market economy, free market, or free enterprise.

cash flow The movement of money in and out of a business over a defined period (weekly, monthly, or quarterly).

Cattell 16 personality factors (16 PF) A theory that suggests each of us has a consistent and constant underlying personality.

cellular layout A format that combines aspects from both product and fixed-position layout: Workers are arranged into self-contained, stand-alone production units (or *cells* of small work teams). Also called group technology layout.

certified general accountant (CGA) Provides the financial information for use by shareholders, government, creditors, and others "outside" an organization.

certified management accountant (CMA) Provides financial information to managers and other corporate decision makers "inside" the corporation and helps formulate policy and strategic plans.

chartered accountant (CA) Provides financial information for use by shareholders, government, creditors, and others "outside" an organization. The CA can work in both public and private sector fields of business and finance.

circular flow An economic cycle in which businesses and households provide government with tax payments generated from revenue and wages, and government uses the tax money to provide businesses and households with incentives, programs, and services.

coaching/understudy program When the employee works directly with senior management in planning and other managerial functions.

collective bargaining A process in which workers (through a union) negotiate with employers for better work conditions and terms of employment.

collective bargaining agreement The result of union–employer negotiations that forces the employer to abide by the conditions specified in the agreement. Change can only be made through subsequent negotiations.

commercial banks Financial institutions that raise funds from businesses and individuals in the form of chequing and savings accounts and use those funds to make loans to businesses and individuals.

commercial finance company A company that is not considered a bank, but rather a financial institution that makes short-term loans to borrowers who offer tangible assets as collateral.

commercial paper An unsecured (i.e., it does not need collateral) short-term debt instrument of $100 000 or more typically issued by a corporation to bridge a cash flow gap created by large accounts receivable, inventory, or payroll.

communism An economic system in which government makes all economic decisions and controls all the social services and many of the major resources required for the production of goods and services.

comparative advantage A country's ability to produce a good or service relatively more efficiently than any other country.

compensation Payment for work performed, which comes in a variety of forms, including money, bonuses, work–life benefits, health insurance, and retirement plans.

competition When two or more businesses contend with one another to attract customers and gain an advantage.

competition-based pricing A pricing strategy based on what the competition is charging. Revenues and costs are secondary.

competitive environment The groups and organizations that have a direct relationship with the business and have an interest in the activities of the company because they are clearly affected by its actions.

computer-aided design (CAD) The use of a computer to create two-dimensional or three-dimensional models of physical parts.

computer-aided manufacturing (CAM) Uses the design data to control the machinery used in the manufacturing process.

computer-integrated manufacturing (CIM) Combines design and manufacturing functions with other functions such as order taking, shipment, and billing.

conceptual skills The ability to think abstractly, picture the organization as a whole, and understand its relationship to the rest of the business community.

consumer behaviour The ways individuals or organizations search for, evaluate, purchase, use, and dispose of goods and services.

consumer market A market in which individuals purchase goods and services for personal consumption.

consumer price index (CPI) A benchmark used to track changes in prices over time. It measures price changes by creating a "market basket" of a specified set of goods and services (including taxes) that represent the average buying pattern of urban households.

consumer product classifications Four classifications that emerge from strategic marketing mix plans for consumer products: convenience, shopping, specialty, and unsought goods and services.

consumer products Goods and services purchased by households for personal consumption.

consumer sales promotions Incentives designed to increase final consumer demand for a product.

contingency leadership A more adaptive style of leadership in which managers recognize that they need to be flexible and use whatever style works best for the particular situation.

contingency planning A set of plans that ensures that the organization will run as smoothly as possible during an unexpected disruption.

contingent workers (temporary employees) Individuals who are hired on an as-needed basis; therefore, they lack the status that comes from being a regular, full-time employee.

contract manufacturing Occurs when a firm subcontracts part or all of its goods to an outside firm as an alternative to owning and operating its own production facility.

contractionary fiscal measures Fiscal policy measures that include increasing taxes and decreasing government spending in an attempt to slow the economy.

controlled messages Public relations messages that include corporate (or institutional) advertising, advocacy advertising, and public service advertising.

controlling Ensures that the plans and strategies set in place by management are properly carried out.

convertible bond A bond that gives the bondholder the right (but not the obligation) to convert the bond into a predetermined number of shares of the company's stock.

cooperative A business owned and governed by members who use its products or services, not by outside investors.

core values The fundamental beliefs about what is important and appropriate when conducting company activities, which affect a company's overall planning processes and operations.

corporate accounting The part of an organization's finance department responsible for gathering and assembling data required for key financial statements.

corporate bond A type of loan issued by a company, not a commercial bank or commercial finance company. It is a formal written agreement to reimburse a loan at a regular interest rate at a given date in time.

corporate culture A collection of values, norms, and behaviour shared by management and workers that defines the character of the organization.

corporation A specific form of business organization that is a separate legal entity, that is liable for its own debts, and whose owners' liability is limited to their investment in the company.

cost of goods sold (COGS) The variable expenses a company incurs to manufacture and sell a product, including the price of raw materials used in creating the good along with the labour costs used to produce and sell the items.

cost of living The average monetary cost of the goods and services required to maintain a particular standard of living. It is closely related to the CPI.

cost-based pricing Charging a price in relation to the costs of providing the good or service. Also called cost-plus pricing.

countertrade A form of international barter—the swapping of goods and services for other goods and services.

cross-cultural awareness An understanding of, appreciation for, and sensitivity to foreign culture.

cross-functional teams Teams where members are selected across a range of critical functional divisions of a business.

Crown corporations Businesses owned by the federal government that provide important services to Canadians, such as Canada Post, the Canadian Broadcasting Corporation (CBC), and the Royal Canadian Mint.

culture The complex set of values, behaviours, lifestyles, arts, beliefs, and institutions of a population that is passed on from generation to generation.

currency A medium of exchange for the transfer of goods and services that provides a consistent and equitable standard, the value of which is based on an underlying commodity, such as gold.

currency appreciation An increase in the exchange rate value of a nation's currency; causes the relative price of imports to fall as the relative price of exports rises.

currency depreciation A decrease in the exchange rate value of a nation's currency; causes exports to become cheaper and imports to become more expensive.

current assets Those assets that can be turned into cash within a year.

current liabilities Obligations a company is responsible for paying within a year or less and are listed first on the balance sheet. Also called short-term liabilities.

current ratio A measurement used to determine the extent to which a company can meet its current financial obligations. Also called the liquidity ratio.

customer relationship management (CRM) The process of establishing long-term relationships with individual customers to foster loyalty and repeat business.

damage control A company's effort to minimize the harmful effects of a negative event.

debt financing Occurs when a company borrows money that it is legally obligated to repay, with interest, by a specified time.

debt to equity ratio Measures how much debt a company has relative to its assets by comparing a company's total liabilities to its total owners' (or shareholders') equity. Also called the leverage ratio.

decision-making skills The ability to identify and analyze a problem, examine the alternatives, choose and implement the best plan of action, and evaluate the results.

deflation A continuous decrease in prices over time.

demand How much of a product or a service people want to buy at any given time.

demand-based pricing Pricing a good or service based on the demand for the product or its perceived value. Also called value-based pricing.

democratic leader A leader who delegates authority and involves employees in decision making.

demographic segmentation Market segmentation according to age, race, religion, gender, ethnic background, and other demographic variables.

depreciation Spreads out the cost of the equipment over its useful life.

depression A severe or prolonged recession.

discounts Deductions from the regular price charged.

disinflation A decrease in the rate of inflation.

distribution channel A series of firms or individuals that participate in the flow of a product from manufacturer to consumer.

distributors The intermediaries in a distribution channel. Also called wholesalers.

diversity initiative Outlines a company's goals and objectives for managing, retaining, and promoting a diverse workforce. It might include a nondiscrimination policy, minority network, or diversity education.

diversity-friendly organizations Organizations that are very inclusive. They don't just tolerate those who are different but instead celebrate their members' differences.

dividends A portion of a company's profits distributed to shareholders as either cash payments or additional shares of stock.

double coincidence of wants A situation that requires all parties in the exchange to have an item that the other wants in order to accomplish trade.

double taxation Means that the corporation must pay income taxes on its profits, and the shareholders must pay personal income taxes on the dividends they receive from the corporation.

double-entry bookkeeping Recognizes that for every transaction that affects an asset, an equal transaction must also affect either a liability or owners' equity.

due diligence Researching and analyzing the business to uncover any hidden problems associated with it.

dumping Selling a product at a price below the price charged in the producing country; it is illegal but can be difficult to prove.

dynamic pricing A pricing strategy where prices are determined directly between the buyer and seller, unlike the more traditional fixed pricing in which prices are set by the seller.

earnings per share Determines the portion of a company's profit allocated to the shareholders on a per-share basis.

economic environment Consists of factors that affect consumer purchasing power and spending patterns.

economic indicators Indicators such as gross domestic product (GDP), consumer and producer price indexes (which measure inflation), and the unemployment rate are used by economists to determine how well businesses are performing overall.

economic system The organization or economic structure of a country; it refers to the way in which an economy allocates its scarce economic resources and how it produces and distributes its output.

economics The study of how individuals, businesses, and government make decisions about how to allocate limited (scarce) resources to best satisfy people's wants, needs, and desires.

effective promotional campaigns Include six steps: identify the target market, determine marketing objectives, design the message, determine the budget, implement the promotional mix, and evaluate and adjust as needed.

effectiveness Completing tasks and producing products that create the greatest value.

efficiency Completing a task or producing a product at the lowest cost.

embargo A total restriction on an import (or an export).

employee assistance programs (EAPs) Employee benefit programs offered by many employers, typically in conjunction with a health insurance plan. EAPs are intended to help employees deal with personal and workplace problems that may adversely affect their work performance.

employee information system (EIS) Creates a workforce profile, in which a company can record and track employee skills and abilities to generate a "personnel inventory."

employer–employee relations The communication that takes place between employers and employees.

employment agencies Agencies that help with external recruiting by providing a screened pool of candidates, which reduces the hiring company's administrative burden of recruitment.

employment standards acts and labour codes Together with the Canada Labour Code (at the federal level), these provincial standards define the rights and obligations of individuals as workers, union members, and employers in the workplace.

engaged employee An employee who is fully involved in and enthusiastic about his or her work, and thus will act in a way that furthers the organization's interests.

enterprise resource planning (ERP) systems Give companies the ability to streamline the various workflows and share information across departments by consolidating information into a central database accessible to various system modules (company departments).

entrepreneur Someone who assumes the risk of creating, organizing, and operating a business and who directs all the business resources.

environmental scanning The process of surveying the market environment to assess external threats and opportunities.

e-procurement An online purchasing system connecting companies and their business processes directly with suppliers while managing all interactions between them.

equilibrium price The market price at which supply is exactly equal to demand.

equity financing The generation of funds by the owners of the company rather than an outside lender. These funds might come from the company's own savings or partial sale of ownership in the company in the form of stock.

equity Money received in exchange for ownership in a business.

equity theory A theory that focuses on social comparisons—people evaluating their treatment by the organization relative to the treatment of others.

ethnocentrism A belief that one's own culture is superior to all other cultures.

European Union (EU) With 28 member nations (including the accession of Croatia on July 1, 2013), the EU is the oldest and largest free trade area.

everyday low pricing (EDLP) A strategy of charging low prices with few, if any, special promotional sales.

exchange rates The rates at which currencies are converted into another currency.

exclusive distribution The use of only one outlet in a geographic area.

exit interviews Often conducted to gather feedback before employees leave the company.

expansionary fiscal measures Fiscal policy measures that include decreasing taxes and increasing government spending to stimulate the economy and put money back into the hands of businesses and consumers, encouraging businesses to expand and consumers to buy more goods and services.

expenses Costs incurred to produce and sell the goods or services offered by a business.

expenses The costs incurred (an outflow of money) to produce and sell the goods and services offered by a business.

exporting Selling domestically produced products to other countries.

external recruiting Looking outside the business to fill vacancies using various resources and methods.

extrinsic motivators Motivating factors that are within managers' control, including such things as pay, promotion, and verbal praise.

facility layout The physical arrangement of resources, the people in the production process, and how they interact.

factoring The process of selling accounts receivable for cash.

factors of production The resources used to produce goods and services.

financial accounting Produces financial documents to aid decision makers outside an organization in making decisions regarding investments and credibility.

financial capital Money used to facilitate a business enterprise.

financial management Involves the strategic planning and budgeting of short- and long-term funds for current and future needs.

financial manager Oversees the financial operations of a company. Also called a chief financial officer (CFO).

financial statements The formal reports of a business's financial transactions that accountants prepare periodically.

first-line managers The managers who carry out operational planning.

fiscal policy The way in which the government determines the appropriate level of taxes and spending to smooth out fluctuations in the business cycle and stabilize the economy.

fixed assets Assets with long-term use, such as real estate, buildings, machinery, and equipment.

fixed costs Any costs that do not vary with the production level. Total fixed costs typically include salaries, rent, insurance expenses, and loan repayments. Also called overhead costs.

fixed-position layout A format in which the product stays in one place (fixed position) while workers and machinery move to the product to complete tasks rather than vice versa.

flexible (or floating) exchange rate system Uses the global supply and demand for currencies to determine exchange rates.

flexible benefits plans Permit the employee to pick from a "menu" of several choices of taxable and nontaxable forms of compensation. Also called cafeteria plans.

flexible manufacturing system (FMS) Uses one central computer to link together several machines that can process different part types simultaneously.

flexible work schedule Can take many different forms, yet not every job is well suited for an alternative structure. Flexible work schedules help people juggle work and family responsibilities, making them happier with their jobs, which can be measured in increases in productivity and morale and decreases in stress, absenteeism, and burnout.

flow state A state that happens when you are completely involved in and focused on what you are doing. Often people produce their best work, make the best use of their skills, and feel the most pleasure when they are in such a flow state.

focus group Typically a group of eight to ten potential customers who are asked for feedback on a good or service, advertisement, idea, or packaging.

forecasting The process of determining the future demand for employees as well as the future supply of employees.

forecasts Predict revenue, costs, and expenses for a specific future period.

forensic accountant Provides investigative accounting services and litigation support.

four degrees of competition The four levels of competition in business: monopoly, oligopoly, monopolistic competition, and perfect competition.

franchise A method of doing business whereby the business (the franchisor) grants the buyer (the franchisee) the right to use its brand name and to sell its goods and services for a specified time.

franchising Selling a well-known brand name or a proven method of doing business to an investor in exchange for a fee and a percentage of sales or profits. The seller is the franchisor, and the buyer is the franchisee.

free trade areas or agreements (FTA) Abolish trade barriers among member countries.

free trade The unencumbered flow of goods and services across national borders.

friendly takeover Occurs when the target company's management and board of directors support an acquisition.

full-service wholesalers Provide a full line of services: carrying stock, maintaining a sales force, offering credit, making deliveries, and providing management assistance.

functional areas Separate departments where business activities are grouped by similar tasks or skills.

fundamental accounting equation Assets = liabilities + owners' equity.

games-based learning (serious games) A training method whereby employees play virtual reality games that simulate real-life events.

Gantt chart A chart that is formatted similarly to a horizontal bar graph and is used to lay out each task in a project, the order in which these tasks must be completed, and how long each task should take.

GDP per capita Measures the country's total GDP divided by the country's population.

General Agreement on Tariffs and Trade (GATT) Created in 1948 with 23 member nations to provide rules for world trade; its membership grew to 123 countries by 1994.

general partners Partners who are full owners of the business and are responsible for all the day-to-day business decisions and remain liable for all the debts and obligations of the business.

general partnership A type of partnership that is similar to the sole proprietorship in that all the (general) partners are jointly liable for the obligations of the business.

geographic segmentation Market segmentation according to geographic characteristics.

global strategy Involves competing primarily based on price while selling a standardized (or homogenous) product.

globalization of markets The movement away from the belief that the market is local or "domestic" (within one nation) to the view that the market includes the entire world.

globalization of production The trend of individual firms moving production to different locations around the globe to take advantage of lower costs or to enhance quality.

globalization The movement toward a more interconnected and interdependent world economy.

globalization The movement toward a more interconnected and interdependent world economy.

goals Broad, long-term accomplishments an organization wants to achieve within a certain period.

goodwill An accounting concept meaning the value of an entity over and above the value of its assets.

goods Any physical products offered by a business.

government and nonprofit accounting Refers to the accounting required for organizations that are not focused on generating a profit, such as legislative bodies and charities.

grants Financial awards usually offered by federal and provincial governments and some private organizations.

green economy When ecological concerns are taken into account in business decisions.

grievance A formal complaint by an employee, employees, or the union usually brought to the supervisor's attention either in person or in writing.

gross domestic product (GDP) Measures economic activity—the overall market value of final goods and services produced in a country in a year.

gross national product (GNP) Attributes earnings to the country where the firm is *owned*, not where the product is manufactured.

gross profit Calculated by subtracting cost of goods sold (or cost of sales) from revenue (total sales).

gross profit margin Determines a company's profitability of production. It indicates how efficient management is in using its labour and raw materials to produce goods.

group flow A state that occurs when a group knows how to work together so that each individual member can achieve flow.

groupthink A type of narrow-mindedness that can emerge in a group situation if team members have not been carefully selected for a range of skills and attributes.

growth entrepreneurs Entrepreneurs who strive to create fast-growing businesses and look forward to expansion.

Hawthorne effect Describes the increase in productivity caused by workers being given special attention.

Herzberg's motivator–hygiene theory A theory that suggests two factors influence a person's motivation: hygiene factors (which cause job dissatisfaction) and motivation factors (which cause job satisfaction).

high-contact service processes Services that require the customer to be present, such as a public transit system, a hair salon, or a dentist.

hiring process Begins with developing the job requirements and ends when a job offer is made.

home-based entrepreneurs Entrepreneurs who run their businesses out of their homes.

horizontal organization An organization where the traditional managerial pyramid is flattened and the management layers are collapsed. Also called a flat organization.

hostile takeover Occurs when a takeover goes against the wishes of the target company's management and board of directors.

HRM functions Encompass every aspect of the "human" in a business, including planning, recruiting, selecting and hiring, training, evaluating, compensating, scheduling, motivating, and transitioning employees. HRM also oversees employee–management relations and must always work to ensure that the company operates within the law.

human factor Refers to how a company's location decision affects the people in a surrounding community and vice versa.

human resource management (HRM) The organizational function that deals with the people in the business, from the executives and the managers to the front-line production, sales, and administrative staff.

human resource planning The creation of a strategy for meeting future human resource needs within an organization.

human resources (HR) The people in an organization; they need to be managed just as carefully as the material and financial resources of a business.

human resources department Working with other department managers, this department is responsible for the people in the organization and helps to maximize organizational productivity by optimizing the effectiveness of employees.

importing Buying products from other countries.

income statement Shows how much money is coming into a company and how much money a company is spending over a period. It shows how well a company has done in terms of profit and loss.

independent contractors and consultants Contingent workers who are generally self-employed and are hired on a temporary basis to perform specific tasks.

industrial psychology The scientific study of how to manage employees and work optimally.

inflation A rise in the general level of prices over time.

infomercials Television commercials that run as long as regular TV programs.

information and knowledge Quickly becoming the key factors of production as the new competitive business environment places a premium on these factors.

initial public offering (IPO) The first time a company offers to sell new stock to the public.

intangible assets Assets that do not have physical characteristics (you can't touch or see them), but they have value nonetheless. Trademarks, patents, and copyrights are examples of intangible assets, in addition to strong brand recognition and excellent customer or employee relations.

integrated marketing communication (IMC) A strategy to deliver a clear, consistent, and unified message about the company and its products to customers at all contact points.

intensive distribution Entails selling the product through all available retail outlets.

interest The payments the bond issuer makes to the bondholder for use of the borrowed money (most interest payments are semi-annual).

internal recruiting The process of filling job vacancies with existing employees from within the business.

International Monetary Fund (IMF) Promotes trade through financial cooperation.

International Organization for Standardization (ISO) An organization dedicated to creating worldwide standards of quality for goods and services.

Internet entrepreneurs Entrepreneurs who create businesses that operate solely online.

interpersonal skills Skills that enable a manager to interact with other people to motivate them.

intrapreneurs Employees who work in an entrepreneurial way within the organizational environment.

intrinsic motivators Motivating factors that are outside managers' control because they are internal to each individual employee, such as the sense of purpose or value a person derives from his or her work.

inventory control Includes the receiving, storing, handling, and tracking of everything in a company's stock, from raw materials to finished products. Inventory often makes up a large portion of a business's expenses.

inventory The merchandise a business owns but has not sold.

investment instruments Bonds (debt) or stock (equity) that are used for large capital-intensive projects or general expansion.

ISO 14000 Launched after ISO 9000, a set of standards designed to promote clean production processes in response to environmental issues such as global warming and water pollution.

ISO 9000 A set of five technical standards of quality management created by the International Organizations for Standardization to provide a uniform way of determining whether organizations conform to sound quality procedures.

issuing common stock The process of selling common shares of ownership in the company to the general public—in other words, "going public"—which can be a great option to generate funds through equity financing.

job analysis Identifies and defines in detail the particular duties and requirements of the tasks and responsibilities an employee is required to perform.

job description A formal statement summarizing what the employee will do in that job role. It includes the job responsibilities, the conditions under which the job will be performed, and the job's relationship to other functions in the organization.

job interview A one-on-one meeting of the company and the job candidate through which the company is able to gauge the candidate's personality, clarify information in the candidate's résumé, and determine whether the candidate is the best match for the position.

job rotation When the employee rotates through different departments to learn first-hand the various aspects of the business.

job specifications The skills, education, experience, and personal attributes that candidates need to possess to successfully fulfill the job role.

joint ventures Involve shared ownership in a subsidiary firm. International joint venture partners involve an international business teaming up with a local partner to enter a foreign market.

just-in-time (JIT) inventory control An inventory control system that keeps the smallest amount of inventory on hand as possible, and everything else that is needed is ordered so that it arrives just in time to be used.

labour The human resource that refers to any physical or intellectual work people contribute to business production.

labour union A legally recognized group dedicated to protecting the interests of workers.

law of demand States that people will buy more of an item at a lower price than at a higher price.

law of supply States that there is a direct relationship between price and quantity: The amount supplied will increase as the price increases, and if the price is lower a lower quantity of the product will be supplied.

leading The process of influencing, motivating, and enabling others to contribute to the success and effectiveness of the organization by achieving its goals.

lean production A set of principles concerned with reducing waste and improving flow that evolved from the original Toyota production system (TPS) first used in Japan in the 1980s.

legal monopolies Monopolies that occur when a company receives a patent giving it exclusive use of an invented product or process.

leverage The amount of debt used to finance a firm's assets with the intent that the rate of return on the assets is greater than the cost of the debt.

liabilities What the company owes to its creditors.

liability The obligation to pay a debt such as an account payable or a loan.

licensing An agreement in which the licensor's intangible property—patents, trademarks, service marks, copyrights, trade secrets, or other intellectual property—may be sold or made available to a licensee in exchange for a royalty fee.

lifestyle entrepreneurs Entrepreneurs who look for more than profit potential when they begin a business.

limited liability Safeguards personal assets from being seized as payment for debts or claims.

limited partners Partners who don't participate actively in the business, and their liability is limited to the amount they invested in the partnership.

limited partnerships A type of partnership that consists of at least one general partner (who has unlimited liability) and one or more limited partners who cannot participate in the day-to-day activities of the business or they will risk losing their limited liability status.

limited-service wholesalers Offer fewer services than full-service wholesalers. There are four major types: cash-and-carry wholesalers, truck wholesalers, drop shippers, and rack jobbers.

line of credit Available credit that a manager can access at any time up to an amount agreed upon between the bank and the company.

liquidity How quickly assets can be turned into cash.

loan An arrangement in which a lender gives money to a borrower under the agreement that the borrower repays the loan amount, usually with interest, at some future point in time.

local content requirement A requirement that some portion of a good be produced domestically.

lockout Occurs when management refuses to allow union members to enter the work premises.

logos Representations of brands that help build an image for a company.

long-term liabilities Include debts and obligations owed by the company and due more than one year from the current date, such as mortgage loans for the purchase of land or buildings, long-term leases on equipment or buildings, and bonds issued for large projects.

loss A loss occurs when a company's revenue is less than its expenses.

loss leader A product priced below its cost. Stores use loss leaders to attract customers and motivate them to buy items that are more expensive as well.

low-contact service processes Services that do not require the customer to be present, such as a utility company, an auto-repair shop, or the chequing processes at a bank.

macro environment The external environment over which the organization can exert little influence. This environment is often referred to by the acronym *PEST* (political–legal, economic, sociocultural, and technological).

macroeconomics The study of the behaviour of the overall economy. Broader, aggregate variables, such as changes in the unemployment rate, interest rates, and prices, are considered in the study of macroeconomics.

make-or-buy decision A decision about what needs to be manufactured and what needs to be purchased from outside suppliers.

management by objectives (MBO) A performance goal-setting method in which management and employees work together to set goals and evaluate performance.

management development training Training that focuses on leadership, communication, teamwork, and relationship-building skills.

management The process of working with people and resources to accomplish the goals of the organization.

managerial accounting Used to provide information and analyses to managers within the organization to assist them in making good business decisions.

manufacturing resource planning (MRPII) Uses software to integrate data from many departments, including manufacturing, finance, marketing, and human resources.

market research The process of gathering and analyzing market information for making marketing decisions.

market segment A subgroup of potential customers who share similar characteristics and therefore have similar product needs and preferences.

market segmentation The process of separating the broader market into smaller markets (or market segments) that consist of similar groups of customers.

marketing "A set of business practices designed to plan for and present an organization's products or services in ways that build effective customer relationships." (Canadian Marketing Association).

marketing concept A philosophy that changed the focus from finding the right customer for a product to producing the right product for a customer and doing it better than the competition.

marketing environment Includes environmental influences outside the firm's control that constrain the organization's ability to manipulate its marketing mix.

marketing intermediary A business firm that operates between producers and consumers or business users. Also often called a middleman.

marketing mix The combination of four factors, called the "4 Ps" of marketing, designed to serve the target market: product, price, promotion, and place.

marketing objective A clearly stated goal to be achieved through marketing activities. It should be realistic, quantifiable, and time specific.

5 Cs of marketing A situational analysis framework that includes analyzing the company, collaborators, customers, competitors, and climate.

marketing plan A written document that specifies marketing activities designed to reach organizational objectives.

marketing strategy Consists of two major elements: the *target market* and the *marketing mix*, which is designed to meet the needs of that market.

Maslow's hierarchy of needs A theory that suggests our primary needs are met first before our higher-level needs are addressed.

mass customization Combines the low unit cost of mass production processes with the flexibility of producing goods or services tailored to meet individual customer's needs.

mass production A method of producing large quantities of goods at a low cost; relies on machines and automated assembly lines to mass produce goods that are identical and adhere to certain standards of quality.

master production schedule Shows which products will be produced, when production will occur, and what resources will be used during the scheduled time.

materials requirement planning (MRP) A type of software system used to schedule and monitor the use of components and other materials in a manufacturing operation.

McClelland's "three needs" theory A theory that suggests there are three main motivators: (1) the need for achievement (to accomplish something difficult on your own), (2) the need for affiliation (to form close personal relationships), and (3) the need for power (to be able to control the behaviour of others).

McGregor's Theory X A theory that suggests people inherently dislike work and want to avoid it.

McGregor's Theory Y A theory that suggests people view work as being as natural as playing and resting.

mediation A process that involves a neutral third party who assists the two parties both privately and collectively to identify issues and develop proposals for resolution.

medium of exchange Something such as money that is generally accepted in exchange for goods and services.

mentoring A form of on-the-job training whereby an experienced employee provides direction and information to the new employee as he or she learns the job.

mentors Experienced individual employees who help a less-experienced person by explaining how to perform specific tasks, creating opportunities to learn new skills, and counselling about the consequences of particular actions and decisions.

merger Occurs when two or more firms combine to form one new company, which often takes on a new corporate identity.

microeconomics The study of how individual businesses, households, and consumers decide to allocate their limited resources in exchange for goods and services.

micropreneurs Entrepreneurs who start their own business but are satisfied with keeping the business small in an effort to achieve a balanced lifestyle.

middle-level managers Top managers for only one division or a part of an organization.

mission statement A description of the organization's purpose, basic goals, and philosophies.

mixed economies A blend of market and planned economies with a mixed economy of privately owned businesses and government control of selected social programs, such as health care.

monetary policy The way in which the government manages the supply of money and interest rates to smooth out fluctuations in the business cycle and stabilize the economy.

monopolistic competition A form of competition where there are many buyers and sellers and little differentiation among the products, but consumers perceive there to be a difference so they favour one product offering over another.

monopoly A form of competition where there is only one provider of a service or product and no substitutes for the product exist.

multidomestic strategy Involves competing primarily by customizing or differentiating the product to meet unique local needs, tastes, or preferences.

national debt The accumulated total yearly deficits.

natural monopolies Monopolies that include public utilities, such as those that sell gas or water. These organizations require huge investments, and it would be inefficient to duplicate the products they provide.

natural resources The raw materials provided by nature and used to produce goods and services.

near-shoring A form of offshoring in which a company moves jobs to a foreign location that is geographically close or linguistically and culturally similar to its own country.

net income (or loss) The revenue remaining after all costs and expenses, including taxes, have been paid. It is the "bottom line" and is usually stated on the very last line of an income statement.

network organizations Collections of independent, mostly single-function firms that collaborate on a product or service.

new product development The five steps for developing a new product: idea generation, idea screening, product analysis, product development and concept testing, and commercialization.

niche marketing Occurs when a product is marketed to a narrowly defined set of potential customers.

nominal GDP A measure of economic activity that includes all of the changes that have occurred in market prices during the year from inflation and deflation.

nonconvertible currency A currency that can't be converted into another currency in the foreign exchange market.

nonprofit and voluntary sector Includes nongovernmental, nonprofit organizations that receive support from individual Canadians, governments, and businesses.

North American Free Trade Agreement (NAFTA) An ongoing agreement to move Canada, the United States, and Mexico closer to true free trade.

objectives The short-term targets designed to help achieve goals.

Occupational Health and Safety (OHS) acts and regulations Enabled at the federal, provincial, and territorial levels and are designed to secure workers and self-employed persons from risks to their safety, health, and physical well-being arising out of or in connection with activities in their workplaces.

officers and shop stewards Elected by union members to make decisions for the entire body and represent the members in dealings with management.

offshoring A practice in which work is shifted from its original domestic location to other foreign locations.

off-the-job training and development Techniques that require employees to participate in outside seminars, university-conducted programs, and corporate universities.

oligopoly A form of competition in which only a few sellers exist.

online training Allows employees to take college or university classes on the Internet at their convenience, enabling them to obtain specific job-related education or to pursue a degree. Also called distance learning.

on-the-job training When employees learn skills by performing them.

operating (master) budget Includes all the operating costs for the entire organization, including inventory, sales, purchases, manufacturing, marketing, and operating expenses.

operating expenses The overhead costs incurred with running the business. They include sales, general, and administrative expenses. These costs may consist of items such as rent, salaries, wages, utilities, depreciation, and insurance.

operating income Determined when operating expenses are subtracted from gross profit.

operating profit margin Determines a company's profitability of operations. It indicates how efficiently management is in using business operations to generate a profit.

operational plans Plans that determine the process by which tactical plans can be achieved.

operations management The organized direction and control of the processes that transform resources (inputs) into finished goods and services (outputs). Also called production management.

operations managers Managers who are responsible for managing and supervising all the activities that occur when transforming resources into goods or services, such as setting schedules, making buying decisions, and overseeing quality control.

operations planning Includes four decisions: (1) the type of production process, (2) the facility location, (3) the facility layout, and (4) resource planning.

opportunity niche A need in the marketplace that is not being adequately fulfilled.

optimal capital structure The optimal balance between equity and debt financing.

organizational chart A chart that shows how groups of employees fit into the larger organizational structure.

organizational psychology Studies how to create a workplace that fosters motivation and productivity among employees.

organizing The process of structuring the capital, personnel, raw materials, and other resources to carry out the organization's plans in a way that best matches the nature of the work.

orientation program Used to introduce the employee to the company's people, policies, and procedures.

outsourcing Occurs when a company contracts with an outside firm to handle a specific part of its business activities.

owners' equity What the company owes to its owners.

participative management and empowerment A management style that involves encouraging employees to become engaged in their jobs and remain loyal to the company by inspiring them to be self-motivated and giving them responsibility with the power (empowerment) to make decisions.

partnership A type of business entity in which two or more owners (or partners) share the ownership and the profits and losses of the business.

penetration pricing A strategy of charging the lowest possible price for a new product.

perfect competition A form of competition where there are many buyers and sellers of products that are virtually identical, and any seller can easily enter and exit the market.

performance appraisal An evaluation of an employee's performance that gives feedback about how well the employee is doing as well as where changes and improvements are needed.

performance management An approach that combines goal setting, performance appraisal, and training and development into a unified and ongoing process.

personal motivation What drives us internally and externally to succeed in our goals.

personal selling Direct communication between a firm's sales force and potential buyers to make a sale and to build good customer relationships.

PEST model A model used to measure changes in the external business environment that might affect the company's ability to prosper. Stands for political–legal, economic, sociocultural, and technological.

place A component of the marketing mix that refers to all the methods involved in getting the product into the hands of customers. Also called distribution.

planned economic system A system in which the government plays an important role in determining what goods and services are provided and how they are produced and distributed. Both *communism* and *socialism* are examples of planned economic systems.

planning The process of establishing goals and objectives and determining the best ways to accomplish them.

political–legal environment The government's relationship with business.

Porter's five forces model A model used to depict the five forces that affect industry competition: threat of new entrants, threat of substitutes, bargaining power of buyers, bargaining power of suppliers, and rivalry among existing competitors.

positioning The process of developing a unique marketing mix that best satisfies a target market.

preferred stock A hybrid investment because it has some of the features of common stock (i.e., it never matures) and some of the features of corporate bonds (i.e., payments on stock are for fixed amounts, such as $5 per share per year).

prestige pricing The practice of charging a high price to invoke perceptions of high quality and privilege. Also called premium pricing.

price discrimination A demand-based pricing strategy that involves charging different prices to different customers when these price differences are not a reflection of cost differences.

price skimming A pricing strategy that involves charging a high price for a product initially, then lowering the price over time.

price The only revenue-generating component of the marketing mix—product, promotion, and place (distribution) strategies are all cost components.

pricing strategies Strategies sellers use to set prices. The most common include *cost-based pricing*, *demand-based pricing*, and *competition-based pricing*.

primary data Raw data collected by the researcher. The data are frequently collected through observation, questionnaires, surveys (via mail, email, or telephone), focus groups, interviews, customer feedback, samples, and controlled experiments.

private accountant Employed by an organization and may perform one or more different accounting functions.

private business sector Includes goods and services produced and delivered by private individuals or groups as a means of enterprise for profit.

private corporations Companies whose shares of stock are held by only a few people and are not generally available for sale.

privatization The conversion of government-owned production and services to privately owned, profit-seeking enterprises.

probation A specific time frame (typically three to six months) during which the new hire proves his or her skills and worth on the job.

process layout A format in which workers who perform similar tasks on similar equipment are grouped together. Also called job-shop or functional layout.

producer price index (PPI) A benchmark used to track the average change in prices at the wholesale level (from the seller's perspective). Therefore, it tracks prices of goods sellers use to create their products or services, such as raw materials, product components that require further processing, and finished goods sold to retailers. The PPI excludes energy prices and prices for services.

product Any good, service, or idea available for purchase in a market, as well as any intangible benefits derived from its consumption.

product differentiation The creation of a real or perceived difference in a product designed to attract customers.

product layout A format in which equipment or work processes are arranged according to the progressive steps by which the product is made. It is used mostly when large quantities of a product must be produced. Also called flow-shop layout.

product life cycle A theoretical model describing a product's sales and profits over the course of its lifetime.

product line A group of similar products intended for a similar market.

product line length The number of items in any given product line. Product line length is determined by how the addition or removal of items from a product line affects profits.

product mix The combination of all product lines offered for sale by a company.

product mix width The number of different product lines a company offers.

product placement The placement of products in TV shows, movies, and video games where they will be seen by potential customers.

production plan When well developed and efficiently executed, ensures a smoothly run operations process and a product that provides utility.

production The process of getting a good or service to the customer; it is a series of related activities, with value being added at each stage.

productivity Measures the quantity of goods and services that human and physical resources can produce in a given time.

profit A profit is earned when a company's revenue is greater than its expenses.

program evaluation and review technique (PERT) Maps out the various steps involved in a project, differentiating tasks that must be completed in a certain order from tasks that may be completed simultaneously.

promissory note A written promise to pay a supplier a specific amount of money by an agreed-upon date.

promotion A part of the marketing mix that consists of all the methods marketers use to inform and persuade targeted customers to buy a product and to build positive customer relationships.

promotional mix The strategic combination of promotional tools used to reach targeted customers to achieve marketing objectives.

promotional tools The tools marketers use to promote a good or service, including advertising, public relations, personal selling, and sales promotions.

psychographic segmentation Market segmentation based on lifestyles, personality traits, motives, and values.

psychological pricing The practice of charging a price just below a whole number to give the appearance of a significantly lower price. Also called odd or fractional pricing.

public accountant Provides a broad range of accounting, auditing, tax, and consulting activities for various corporate clients.

public business sector Includes goods and services produced, delivered, and allocated by the government and public sector organizations (publicly controlled government business enterprises).

public corporations Companies whose shares of stock are widely held and available for sale to the public.

public relations The management function that establishes and maintains mutually beneficial relationships between an organization and its stakeholders.

publicity Information about an individual, organization, or product transmitted through mass media at no charge.

purchasing power parity (PPP) A measure to compare GDP between countries to determine living standards that takes into account the relative cost of living and the inflation rates of the countries, rather than just exchange rates, which might distort the real differences in income.

purchasing The task of buying the materials and services needed in the production process. Also called procurement.

quality control The use of techniques, activities, and processes to guarantee that a certain good or service meets a specified level of quality.

quality of life A subjective and intangible measure that takes into account not only a country's material standard of living, but also more intangible aspects that make up human life, such as environmental quality, good health, social interactions, leisure time, and a general belief that "life is good."

quota A limitation on the amount of an import allowed to enter a country.

radio frequency identification (RFID) A tag that allows a computer to keep track of the status and quantity of each item.

ratio analysis A comparison of numbers; it is used to compare current data to data from previous years, competitors' data, or industry averages.

real capital The physical facilities used to produce goods and services.

real GDP A measure of economic activity that attempts to remove the effects of inflation by using constant prices in some base year, thus allowing for comparisons against historical periods.

rebates Partial refunds on what a customer has already paid for a product.

recession A decline in the GDP for two or more consecutive quarters of a year.

recruitment process Provides the organization with a pool of potentially qualified job candidates from which thoughtful selection can be made to fill vacancies.

reference pricing Refers to listing an inflated price (the "regular retail price" or "manufacturer's suggested retail price") that is then discounted to appear as if it is a good value.

retailers Intermediaries that buy products for resale to ultimate consumers.

retained earnings Represent the profits (money remaining after taxes and other expenses are paid) not paid out in dividends.

retirement The point in a person's life when he or she stops participating fulltime in his or her career.

revenue Any monies received by a company from sales of goods or services or from other sources such as licensing fees, rental fees, or interest earned.

revenue The total amount of money received for goods and services provided.

routing The way in which goods are transported (to a client, from a supplier, or any other combination) via water, rail, truck, or air.

sales promotions Short-term activities that target consumers and other businesses for generating interest in a product.

scarcity The economic problem of how to reconcile unlimited human wants and desires with limited economic resources.

scheduling Involves specifying and controlling the time required for each step in the production process as well as making the most efficient use of equipment, facilities, labour, and materials.

scientific management A management theory that comprises methods aimed at determining the one best way for a job to be done.

secondary data Data that have already been collected and processed. An example of secondary data is census data.

secured bonds Bonds that require some form of collateral pledged as security.

secured loan A loan that requires collateral, which is generally the asset that the loan is financing, to guarantee the debt obligation.

selection Entails gathering information about candidates, evaluating their qualifications, and choosing the ones that best fit the job specifications.

selective distribution Uses only a portion of the many possible retail outlets for sale of a product.

semi-controlled messages Public relations messages that are placed on websites, in chat rooms, and on blogs and are not strictly regulated. Other forms include sporting or special events sponsorships because participation by the press and stakeholders is not under the control of the sponsoring company.

services Intangible products that are bought or sold.

Seven Habits model A model developed by Stephen Covey that lists the seven habits that successful people exhibits.

shareholders Investors in a corporation who buy shares of ownership in the form of stock.

shares outstanding Common shares authorized, issued, and purchased by investors.

shortage Occurs when sellers do not produce enough of a product to satisfy demand.

short-term financing Any type of financing repaid within a year or less.

simulation training Provides realistic job-task training in a manner that is challenging but does not create the threat of failure.

sinking fund A type of savings fund in which companies set aside money regularly to help repay a bond issue.

Six Sigma A method that seeks to eliminate defects by removing variation in outcomes and measuring and analyzing manufacturing processes to see if standards are being met.

Small Business Investment Companies (SBIC) Private venture capital firms that make equity capital or long-term loans available to small companies.

socialism An economic system in which the government plans and controls many important industries, but there does exist a form of capitalism whereby individuals are permitted ownership of resources and less crucial industries.

sociocultural environment An interconnected system of different demographic factors such as race, ethnicity, gender, age, income distribution, sexual orientation, and other characteristics.

sole proprietorship A business owned by one person and not protected by limited liability.

standard of living The level of wealth, comfort, material goods, and necessities available to a country's people. It is the ease by which people living in a time or place are able to satisfy their needs and wants. It is generally measured by standards such as income per person and poverty rate.

statement of cash flows Shows the exchange of money between a company and everyone else it deals with over a period. It shows where cash was used.

statistical process control (SPC) Uses statistical sampling of products at every phase of production and displays the results on a graph to show potential variations that need to be corrected.

statistical quality control (SQC) The continual monitoring of each stage of the entire production process to ensure that quality standards are being met at every stage.

stock A unit of ownership in a company sold with the intention of raising capital to finance ongoing or future projects and expansions.

strategic alliances Cooperative arrangements between actual or potential competitors. Unlike a joint venture, each partner retains its business independence.

strategic plan The main course of action created by top-level managers that sets the approach for achieving the long-term goals and objectives of the organization.

strength-based management A system based on the belief that, rather than improve weak skills, the best way to help employees develop is to determine their strengths and build on them.

strike Occurs when union workers agree to stop work until certain demands are met.

strikebreakers (or scabs) Replacement personnel hired by management during a strike.

subsidy A payment that governments make to domestic producers.

supply and demand A complicated process involving multiple factors, such as income levels, tastes, and the amount of competition in the market. The willingness and ability to purchase an item is called demand, and the willingness and availability to provide that item is called supply.

supply chain management Involves the logistics of obtaining all the necessary inputs that go into a production process (*inbound logistics*), managing the actual production process (*materials handling* and *operations control*), and managing the physical distribution (*outbound logistics*) of getting the proper quantities of produced products to customers when and where they want them.

supply chain The sequence of organizations—their facilities and activities—that are involved in producing (right from the raw materials) and delivering (all the way to the consumer) a good or service.

supply How much of a product or service is available for purchase at any given time.

surplus Occurs when sellers supply more of a product than buyers are willing to purchase.

SWOT (Strengths, Weaknesses, Opportunities, and Threats) analysis A situational analysis of strengths, weaknesses, and anticipated changes that helps determine the strategic fit between an organization's internal, distinctive capabilities, and external possibilities relative to the business and economic environments.

synergy The achieved effect when two companies combine and the result is better than each company could achieve individually.

tactical plans Plans that specifically determine the resources and the actions required to implement particular aspects of the strategic plan.

target costing A demand-based pricing strategy that estimates the value customers receive from a product and therefore the price they are willing to pay, and then subtracts an acceptable profit margin to obtain a desired cost.

target market The specific group of consumers, who have similar needs and wants, a firm directs its marketing efforts toward.

tariff A tax that governments impose on an imported good or service, such as French wine. Governments prefer to impose tariffs because they raise tax revenues.

tax accounting Involves preparing taxes and giving advice on tax strategies.

team A group of people linked in a common purpose.

technical skills The abilities and knowledge that enable an employee to carry out the specific tasks required of a job.

technological environment Includes human knowledge, work methods, physical equipment, electronics and telecommunications, and various processing systems used to perform business activities.

technology Includes human knowledge, work methods, physical equipment, electronics and telecommunications, and various processing systems used to perform business activities.

termination Reduces the number of employees by permanently laying off workers due to poor performance or a discontinued need for their services.

Thematic Apperception Test (TAT) A personality test that presents a person with a series of images and interprets his or her responses.

Theory X management A style of management that proposes employees have to be coerced and controlled by management to be productive. This leads to an authoritarian, hardline management style.

Theory Y management A style of management that assumes, on average, that people will accept and seek out responsibility. Such managers have a softer style of management that involves the participation of many.

Theory Z A theory based on a Japanese management style that relies heavily on collaborative decision making.

Theory Z management A style of management that is a combination of American and Japanese management philosophies characterized by long-term employment security, consensual decision making, and slow evaluation and promotion procedures, with an emphasis on individual responsibility within a group context.

time management skills The ability to achieve the maximum amount of productivity in a set amount of time.

top-level managers The corporate officers responsible for the organization as a whole.

total product offer Consists of all the benefits associated with a good, service, or idea that affect a consumer's purchasing decision. Also called a value package.

total quality management (TQM) Emphasizes the use of quality principles in all aspects of a company's production and operations.

total quality management An integrated approach focusing on quality from the beginning of the production process up through managerial involvement to detect and correct problems.

trade and investment barriers Government barriers that prevent the flow of goods, services, and financial capital across national boundaries.

trade credit The ability to purchase inventory and supplies on credit without interest.

trade deficit An unfavourable balance of trade; exists when the value of a country's imports exceeds the value of its exports.

trade sales promotions Incentives to push a product through the distribution system to final consumers. Also called business-to-business sales promotions.

trade surplus A favourable balance of trade; occurs when the value of a country's exports exceeds the value of its imports.

transfer Occurs when an employee is appointed to the same or a similar position elsewhere within the organization. Transfers usually refer to a lateral move (a horizontal job assignment).

transnational strategy Involves competing by offering a customized product while simultaneously selling at the lowest possible price.

turnkey project Implemented when firms export their technological expertise in exchange for a fee.

turnover rate Tracks the number of employees that leave the company each year.

uncontrolled messages Public relations messages that generally take the form of publicity.

unemployment rate Measures the number of people who are at least 15 years old, are seeking work, and are currently unemployed.

unlimited liability If business assets aren't enough to pay business debts, then personal assets, such as the sole proprietor's house, personal investments, or retirement plans, can be used to pay the balance.

unsecured bonds Bonds that are issued with no collateral. Also called debenture bonds.

unsecured loan A loan that does not require collateral.

utility supply Refers to the availability of public infrastructure services such as power, water, and communications.

utility The power of a product to satisfy a human want or need; that is, to add something of value to the person.

value The value of a product equals the ratio of the product's benefits to its costs (value = benefits/costs).

value-stream mapping Identifies all the flows and resources required to deliver a product: people, technologies, physical facilities, communication and transportation channels, policies, and procedures.

variable costs Costs that vary with the production level. Examples include wages, raw materials, and energy costs. Average variable costs (or per unit variable costs) equal total variable costs divided by the production level.

venture capitalists Investors who contribute money to your business in return for some form of equity—a piece of ownership.

vertical organization A company that is organized by specific function, such as marketing, finance, purchasing, information technology, and human resources. Also called a tall organization.

vestibule training A type of simulation most suitable to airline pilots, astronauts, and surgeons, for whom making mistakes during training is not an option or is too costly.

virtual teams Teams that comprise members located in different physical locations but working together to achieve a goal.

vision Identifies what the business wants to be in the future.

visionary leader A leader who is able to inspire others, believes in their own vision, and moves people toward a shared dream.

Vroom's expectancy theory A theory that suggests an individual's motivation in any given situation can be described by the relationship among three psychological forces, illustrated in the formula Motivation = Expectancy × Instrumentality × Valence.

warehousing Storing products at convenient locations ready for customers when they are needed.

WHMIS (Workplace Hazardous Materials Information System) A comprehensive plan for providing information on hazardous materials to employees.

wholesalers Intermediaries that buy and resell products to other wholesalers, retailers, or industrial users.

wholly owned subsidiary Involves establishing a foreign facility that is owned entirely by the investing firm.

working capital The amount left over if the company pays off its short-term liabilities with its short-term assets. It is a measure of a company's short-term financial fitness as well as its efficiency.

work–life benefits Help an employee achieve a balance between the demands of life both inside and outside the workplace.

workplace diversity Encompasses all the ways in which employees differ.

World Bank Offers low-interest loans, advice, and information to developing countries.

World Trade Organization (WTO) Strengthened the world trading system by extending GATT rules to services, increasing protection for intellectual property rights, and, perhaps most significantly, taking on the responsibility for arbitrating trade disputes and monitoring the trade policies of member countries.

Endnotes

Front Matter

1. Adapted from F.P. Robinson, *Effective Study* (New York, NY: Harper and Bros., 1946), Chapter II. ©Academic Skills Center, Dartmouth College 2001.
2. Metiri Group, "Multimodal Learning through Media: What the Research Says," 2008, accessed August 16, 2011, http://www.cisco.com/web/strategy/docs/education/Multimodal-Learning-Through-Media.pdf

Chapter 1

1. CareerBuilder.com, "Forty-five Percent of Employers Use Social Networking Sites to Research Job Candidates, CareerBuilder Survey Finds," accessed May 4, 2011, http://www.careerbuilder.com/share/aboutus/pressreleases-detail.aspx?id=pr519&sd=8%2f19%2f2009&ed=12%2f31%2f2009&siteid=cbpr&sc_cmp1=cb_pr519_&cbRecursionCnt=1&cbsid=4bbce0cfa8bc46909f7b09573e776c23-304007915-wy-6.
2. Patti Church and Andy Church, "Whyhire.me: Reveal Your Potential," Winter 2010, accessed November 11, 2011, http://beta.whyhire.me/images/media/RevealYourPotential_Winter2010.pdf.
3. Patti Church, "Whyhire.me Mission Statement," Interview Questionnaire, February 17, 2011. Used by permission of Whyhire.me.
4. Ibid.
5. United Nations Development Programme, "2013 Human Development Report: The Rise of the South: Human Progress in a Diverse World," accessed June 2, 2014, http://hdr.undp.org/en/2013-report.
6. Derek Abma and Peter O'Neil, "Canada Gets High Score on Quality of Life Index: Study," *National Post*, May 24, 2011, accessed June 20, 2011, http://news.nationalpost.com/2011/05/24/canada-scores-near-the-top-of-quality-of-life-index-study.
7. Human Resources and Skills Development Canada, "Support for the Not-for-Profit Sector," accessed June 18, 2011, http://www.hrsdc.gc.ca/eng/community_partnerships/voluntary_sector/index.shtml.
8. Statistics Canada, "Summary of the Findings of the National Survey of Non-profit and Voluntary Organizations," accessed February 6, 2011, http://www.statcan.gc.ca/pub/61-533-s/61-533-s2005001-eng.htm.
9. Habitat for Humanity, "Frequenty Asked Questions," accessed June 2, 2014, http://www.habitat.ca/faqp4227.php?articleID=8&iaCurrentCatID=2
10. Community Sector Council Newfoundland and Labrador, "The Voluntary Sector in Canada," *Envision.ca,* accessed June 18, 2011, http://www.envision.ca/templates/profile.asp?ID=54.
11. John Newman, personal interview, February 2014.
12. *CBC News,* "Canadians Spent $18.9B Online in 2012, StatsCan Says," October 28, 2013, accessed June 2, 2014, http://www.cbc.ca/news/business/canadians-spent-18-9b-online-in-2012-statscan-says-1.2254150
13. General Electric, "Thomas Edison & GE," accessed June 25, 2008. www.ge.com/company/history/edison.html.
14. General Electric, "A Tradition of Innovation," accessed June 25, 2008. www.ge.com/innovation/timeline/index.html.
15. General Electric, "We Are GE," accessed February 4, 2012, www.gelighting.com/au/company/brochure/we_are_ge_brochure.pdf.

Chapter 2

1. Coffee Association of Canada, "Canadian Coffee Drinking Study—2011 Highlights," accessed June 6, 2014, http://www.coffeeassoc.com/coffee-in-canada/canadian-coffee-drinking-study-2011-highights/
2. Jan McGirk, "Growing Coffee: It's Black, No Sugar," *NBC News,* accessed June 6, 2014, http://www.nbcnews.com/id/3072120/ns/news-special_coverage/t/growing-coffee-its-black-no-sugar/#.UyiY2f1te8o.
3. Eric Goldschien, "11 Incredible Facts about the Global Coffee Industry," *Business Insider,* November 14, 2011, accessed June 6, 2014, http://www.businessinsider.com/facts-about-the-coffee-industry-2011-11?op=1.
4. Global Exchange, "Coffee FAW," accessed June 6, 2014, http://www.globalexchange.org/fairtrade/coffee/faq.
5. McGirk, "Growing Coffee."
6. Isis Almeida, "Coffee Surplus Seen by CoffeeNetwork the Biggest in 4 Years," Bloomberg, "January 7, 2013, accessed June 6, 2014, http://www.bloomberg.com/news/2013-01-07/coffee-surplus-seen-by-coffeenetwork-the-biggest-in-4-years-1-.html.
7. Fairtrade International, "What Is Fairtrade?" accessed June 6, 2014, http://www.fairtrade.net/what-is-fairtrade.html.
8. Tim Hortons, "Tim Hortons Coffee Partnership," accessed June 6, 2014, http://www.timhortons.com/ca/en/difference/coffee-partnership.html; McDonald's, "McDonald's and Coffee Sustainability," accessed June 6, 2014, http://www.aboutmcdonalds.com/mcd/sustainability/signature_programs/coffee_story.html; Starbucks, "Responsibly Grown Coffee," accessed June 6, 2014, http://www.starbucks.ca/responsibility/sourcing/coffee.
9. Jessica Reid and David Hammond, "Tobacco Use in Canada: Patterns and Trends, 2013 Edition," Propel Centre for Population Health Impact, University of Waterloo, accessed June 6, 2014, http://www.tobaccoreport.ca/2013/TobaccoUseinCanada_2013.pdf.
10. MarketWatch, "Philip Morris International Inc., mCig, Inc." *Wall Street Journal,* February 3 2014, accessed June 6, 2014, http://www.marketwatch.com/story/e-cigarette-companies-scramble-while-tobacco-giants-pounce-lorillard-inc-nyse-lo-philip-morris-international-inc-nyse-pmi-vapor-corp-otcqb-vpco-mcig-inc-otcqb-mcig-2014-02-03.
11. Canadian Radio-television and Telecommunications Canada, "Checklist: Do You Know Your Rights as a Wireless Consumer?" accessed June 6, 2014, http://www.crtc.gc.ca/eng/info_sht/t15.htm.
12. Better Business Bureau, "BBB Structure," accessed February 10, 2011, www.bbb.org/canada/BBB-Structure.
13. Better Business Bureau, "BBB Code of Business Practices (BBB Accreditation Standards)," accessed February 20, 2011, www.bbb.org/canada/SitePage.aspx?id=e5c68728-5d54-4537-9e03-f33673a2e125.
14. David K. Foot, "Population Aging: Some Economic and Social Consequences of Population Aging," *Canadian Priorities Agenda,* accessed February 10, 2011, http://www.footwork.com/irpp_pop_aging.pdf.
15. CNBC, "American Boomers Now a $2 Trillion Market," September 28, 2006, accessed February 10, 2011, http://www.msnbc.msn.com/id/12288534.
16. Statistics Canada, "Demographic Change," accessed February 10, 2011, http://www.statcan.gc.ca/pub/82-229-x/2009001/demo/int1-eng.htm. Copyright 2014. Reproduced and distributed on an "as is" basis with the permission of Statistics Canada.
17. Statistics Canada, "Study: Projections of the Diversity of the Canadian Population," accessed February 10, 2011, http://www.statcan.gc.ca/daily-quotidien/100309/dq100309a-eng.htm.
18. Canada's Top 100 Employers, "Canada's Best Diversity Employers 2010," accessed February 10, 2011, http://www.canadastop100.com/diversity.

19. Ryan Z. Cortazar, "Diversity Training Fails to Boost Minorities into Management," *Harvard University Gazette* (online), September 14, 2006, accessed February 10, 2011, http://www.news.harvard.edu/gazette/2006/09.14/25-dobbin.html.
20. Andrea Cooper, "The Influencers: What Forces Will Affect Your Business in the Coming Year?" *Entrepreneur* (online), February 8, 2008, accessed February 10, 2011, http://www.entrepreneur.com/magazine/entrepreneur/2008/march/190234.html.
21. Daniel Gross, "Hummer vs. Prius," Slate.com, February 26, 2004, accessed February 10, 2011, http://www.slate.com/id/2096191.
22. Mark Kyrnin, "Upgrade or Replace a Desktop PC?" About.com, accessed February 10, 2011, http://compreviews.about.com/od/general/a/UpgradeReplace.htm.
23. Patty Azzarello, "How to Overcome IT's Credibility Challenges," CIOUpdate.com, September 25, 2007, accessed February 10, 2011, http://www.cioupdate.com/article.php/3701571.
24. Allan Schweyer, "Managing the Virtual Global Workforce," *Human Capital* (online), October 17, 2006, accessed February 10, 2011, http://www.hcamag.com/resources/hr-strategy/managing-the-virtual-global-workforce/113172.
25. Dave Roos, "The History of E-commerce," HowStuffWorks.com, accessed February 10, 2011, http://communication.howstuffworks.com/history-e-commerce.htm.
26. Scot Meyer, "Products Back by Popular Demand," Switch Yard Media, accessed June 21, 2014, http://www.switchyardmedia.com/images/stories/showcase/back_by_popular_demand/slideshow728.html.
27. Joe Wilcox, "Microsoft, Apple Alliance at Key Juncture," CNET News, February 2, 2002, accessed February 6, 2011, http://news.cnet.com/2100-1040-843145.html.
28. "Competition Bureau Denies Interac's Corporate Bid," *MONEY*, February 12, 2010, accessed February 21, 2011, http://money.canoe.ca/money/business/canada/archives/2010/02/20100212-160037.html; Competition Bureau Canada, "Competition Bureau Reaches Agreement in Principle in Real Estate Case," accessed February 21, 2011, http://www.competitionbureau.gc.ca/eic/site/cb-bc.nsf/eng/03293.html.
29. Competition Bureau, "Competition Bureau Issues a 'No Action Letter' to TELUS," November 29, 2013, accessed June 6, 2014, http://www.competitionbureau.gc.ca/eic/site/cb-bc.nsf/eng/03634.html.
30. Zach Pontz, "A Year Later, Amazon Kindle Finds a Niche," CNN.com, December 4, 2008, accessed June 6, 2014, http://www.cnn.com/2008/TECH/12/03/kindle.electronic.reader/index.html.
31. Bibhudatta Pradhan and Ketaki Gokhale, "India Asks RIM, Google, Skype, to Set Up Local Servers," Bloomberg.com, September 2, 2010, accessed February 3, 2011, http://www.bloomberg.com/news/2010-09-01/india-asks-rim-google-skype-to-set-up-local-servers-update1-.html.
32. Ibid.

Chapter 3

1. G20, "G20 Members," accessed January 14, 2014, http://www.g20.org/about_g20/g20_members.
2. Emma Dunkley, "China to Overtake US by 2018—PwC," *Investment Week*, January 13, 2011, accessed January 14, 2014, http://www.investmentweek.co.uk/investment-week/news/1936788/china-overtake-2018-pwc.
3. Tushar Dhara, "India to Top China as Fastest Growing Economy by 2015, Morgan Stanley Says," Bloomberg.com, August 16, 2010, accessed February 16, 2011, http://www.bloomberg.com/news/2010-08-16/india-to-top-china-as-fastest-growing-economy-by-2015-morgan-stanley-says.html.

4. PricewaterhouseCoopers, "Global Financial Crisis Accelerates Shift in Economic Power to Emerging Economics," pwc.com, January 7, 2011, accessed February 16, 2011, http://www.pwc.com/gx/en/press-room/2011/global-financial-crisis-accelerates-shift-eco-power.jhtml.
5. Legatum Institute, "The Legatum Prosperity Index Table Rankings," accessed January 14, 2014, http://www.prosperity.com/#!/ranking.
6. Denise Bedell, "Personal Income Tax Rates," *Global Finance,* November 19, 2012, accessed January 14, 2014, http://www.gfmag.com/tools/global-database/economic-data/12151-personal-income-tax-rates.html#axzz2qNwFoDZa.
7. Ibid.
8. James Gwartney, Robert Lawson, and Joshua Hall, "Economic Freedom of the World: 2013 Annual Report," Fraser Institute, accessed January 14, 2014, http://www.freetheworld.com/2013/EFW2013-complete.pdf, p. 7.
9. "Economic Freedom of the World: 2013 Annual Report," The Fraser Institute. Used by permission of The Fraser Institute. News release, September 18, 2013, accessed January 14, 2014, http://www.freetheworld.com/2013/091813_EFW_Canada.pdf.
10. Central Intelligence Agency, *World Factbook,* accessed January 14, 2014, https://www.cia.gov/library/publications/the-world-factbook/rankorder/2001rank.html?countryname=Italy&countrycode=it®ionCode=eur&rank=11#it.
11. Statistics Canada, "Labour Force Survey (LFS)," November 4, 2011, accessed March 19, 2011, http://www.statcan.gc.ca/cgi-bin/imdb/p2SV.pl?Function=getSurvey&SDDS=3701&lang=en&db=imdb&adm=8&dis=2.
12. Bank of Canada, "Inflation and Price Stability," April 2012, accessed July 9, 2014, http://www.bankofcanada.ca/wp-content/uploads/2010/11/inflation_price_stability.pdf.
13. Statistics Canada, "Chartered Bank Assets and Liabilities and Monetary Aggregates, Monthly Average, Seasonally Adjusted," Table 176-0025, accessed January 14, 2014, http://www5.statcan.gc.ca/cansim/pick-choisir?lang=eng&p2=33&id=1760025.
14. Bank of Canada, "The Bank Rate," September 2012, accessed July 9, 2014, http://www.bankofcanada.ca/wp-content/uploads/2010/11/bank_rate_sept2012.pdf.
15. Julian Beltrame, "Canada Household Debt Reaches Another Record High," *Huffington Post,* March 15, 2013, accessed January 14, 2014, http://www.huffingtonpost.ca/2013/03/15/household-debt-canada-net-worth_n_2883255.html.
16. Ibid.
17. http://www.ic.gc.ca/eic/site/bsf-osb.nsf/eng/br02347.html.
18. Teresa Sullivan, "Bankruptcy Statistics 1980–2010," BankruptcyAction.com, http://www.bankruptcyaction.com/USbankstats.htm.
19. Philip Demont, "Interest Rates: The Gamble in Canada's Debt Payment Plan," *CBC News,* February 25, 2010, accessed January 15, 2014, http://www.cbc.ca/news/business/taxes/interest-rates-the-gamble-in-canada-s-debt-payment-plan-1.912813.
20. Ibid.
21. *National Post,* "WFT: The Federal Budget and 50 Years of Canadian Debt," March 21, 2011, accessed January 15, 2014, http://news.nationalpost.com/2011/03/21/graphic-50-years-of-canadian-debt/.

Chapter 4

1. All quotes from a personal interview with Lee Renshaw.
2. Yahoo! Finance, "McDonald's Corp.," accessed May 3, 2011, http://finance.yahoo.com/q/pr?s=MCD+Profile.

3. Steven Almond, "Citizen Wayne—The Unauthorized Biography," *Miami New Times,* December 1–7, 1994, accessed May 3, 2011, http://www.corporations.org/wmi/huizenga.html.
4. Scott Allen, "Quotations from Famous Entrepreneurs on Entrepreneurship: Inspiring Words from the Best of the Best," About.com, accessed May 3, 2011, http://entrepreneurs.about.com/od/famousentrepreneurs/a/quotations.htm.
5. Ben & Jerry's Homemade, Inc., accessed May 3, 2011, http://www.benjerry.com/company.
6. Adapted from Jack Kaplan and Anthony Warren, *Patterns of Entrepreneurship,* 2nd ed. (New York, NY: John Wiley & Sons, Inc.), p. 27; and U.S. Small Business Administration Report, "The State of Small Business: A Report of the President" (Washington, DC: U.S. Government Printing Office, 1995), p. 114.
7. CEO Challenges, "Kennedy Featured in Daily Camera Business Plus Chat," February 29, 2008, accessed May 3, 2011, http://www.ceochallenges.com/news/2008/02/29/kennedy-featured-daily-camera-business-plus-chat.
8. Steam Whistle, "Steam Whistle's Awards," accessed January 27, 2014, http://www.steamwhistle.ca/ourbeer/awards.php.
9. Sheena Edwards, "About Us," Lizzie Lou Shoes, February 15, 2012, http://lizzieloushoes.com. Reprinted by permission of Sheena Edwards.
10. *New York Times,* "MeetMe Inc.," accessed January 25, 2014, http://topics.nytimes.com/top/news/business/companies/quepasa-corporation/.
11. John Case, "The Gazelle Theory," *Inc. Magazine,* May 15, 2001, accessed May 3, 2011, http://www.inc.com/magazine/20010515/22613.html.
12. Michael Arndt, "Creativity Overflowing," *Businessweek,* May 8, 2006, accessed May 3, 2011, http://www.businessweek.com/stories/2006-05-07/creativity-overflowing.
13. Michael Arndt, "How Whirlpool Defines Innovation," *Businessweek,* March 6, 2006, accessed May 3, 2011, http://www.businessweek.com/print/innovate/content/mar2006/id20060306_287425.htm.
14. Matt Bultman, "Facebook IPO to Make Dobbs Ferry's Mark Zuckerberg a $24 Billion Man," *Greenburgh Daily Voice,* May 15, 2012, accessed June 2, 2014, http://greenburgh.dailyvoice.com/news/facebook-ipo-make-dobbs-ferrys-mark-zuckerberg.
15. Jeff Macke, "Facebook Market Cap Tops $100 Billion: Is It Worth It?" Yahoo! Finance, September 4, 2013, accessed June 2, 2014, http://finance.yahoo.com/blogs/breakout/facebook-market-cap-tops-100-billion-worth-124317243.html.
16. Sam Gustin, "Facebook Blame-Game: Who's at Fault for IPO Debacle?" *Time,* September 6, 2012, accessed June 2, 2014, http://business.time.com/2012/09/06/facebook-blame-game-whos-at-fault-for-ipo-debacle/.
17. Donna Tam, "Facebook by the Numbers: 1.06 Billion Monthly Active Users," CNET, January 30, 2013, accessed June 2, 2014, http://news.cnet.com/8301-1023_3-57566550-93/facebook-by-the-numbers-1.06-billion-monthly-active-users/; Ross Kerber, "Bankers Conclude Facebook Is a Good Investment because They're Obsessed with It," *Huffington Post,* August 9, 2013, accessed June 2, 2014, http://www.huffingtonpost.com/2013/08/09/facebook-investment_n_3729706.html.
18. "The ASC Story," AnimatedSpeech.com, accessed June 2, 2014, http://www.animatedspeech.com/Story/story_founders.html.
19. Bruce Freeman, "Fired? Start a Business!" ProLine Communications, accessed June 2, 2014, http://www.prolinepr.com/Fired.html.
20. Industry Canada, Small Business and Tourism Branch, *Key Small Business Statistics: January 2009,* accessed June 2, 2014, https://www.ic.gc.ca/eic/site/061.nsf/vwapj/KSBS-PSRPE_Jan2009_eng.pdf/$FILE/KSBS-PSRPE_Jan2009_eng.pdf.

21. Wim Venter, "Your Own Business—Risks vs. Rewards," Ezinearticles.com, accessed May 4, 2011, http://ezinearticles.com/?Your-Own-Business---Risks-Vs-Rewards&id=1464351.
22. Stacy Perman, Jeffrey Gangemi, and Douglas MacMillan, "Entrepreneurs' Favorite Mistakes: Nina Riley, Water Sensations," *Businessweek,* accessed May 4, 2011, http://images.businessweek.com/ss/06/09/favorite_mistake/index_01.htm.
23. Canadian Franchise Association, "Frequently Asked Questions," accessed June 2, 2014, http://www.cfa.ca/FAQ/.
24. Tim Hortons, "Frequently Asked Questions," accessed July 22, 2014, http://www.timhortons.com/ca/en/team/franchise-ca-faq.php.
25. Financial Consumer Agency of Canada, "Credit Cards Interactive Tools," accessed June 2, 2014, http://www.fcac-acfc.gc.ca/Eng/resources/toolsCalculators/Pages/CreditCa-OutilsIn.aspx.
26. Centre for Small Business Financing, "Canadian Small Business Grants and Loans Can Be the Key to Success," accessed May 4, 2011, http://www.grants-loans.org/small-business-grants.php.
27. CBC News, "Suncor, Petro-Canada Announce Merger," March 23, 2009, accessed May 10, 2011, http://www.cbc.ca/news/business/story/2009/03/23/suncor-petro-canada-merge.html.
28. Competition Bureau, "The Competition Bureau's Letter to the Toronto-Dominion Bank and Canada Trust," January 28, 2000, accessed July 30, 2014, http://www.competitionbureau.gc.ca/eic/site/cb-bc.nsf/eng/01649.html.

Chapter 5

1. Eric Wheeler, "5 Predictions for Online Advertising," *Fast Company,* December 21, 2012, accessed May 13, 2014, http://www.fastcompany.com/3004173/5-predictions-online-advertising
2. EventSing Promotions, "Our Philosophy," accessed May 13, 2014, http://eventsing.com/about/
3. All quotes from a personal interview with Jon Holowachuk, March 2014.
4. Quoted in Pete Johnson, "Best Vision Statement," *Nerd Guru Wordpress Blog,* September 25, 2008, http://blog.nerdguru.net.
5. General Electric, "Past Leaders: John F. Welch Jr.," accessed July 27, 2014, http://www.ge.com/company/history/bios/john_welch.html.
6. Canadian Cancer Society, "Our Mission, Vision and Values," accessed March 30, 2011, http://www.cancer.ca/en/about-us/our-mission/?region=on.
7. Google, "Our Philosophy," accessed March 31, 2011, http://www.google.com/corporate/tenthings.html.
8. The Coca-Cola Company, "Workplace Culture," accessed March 31, 2011, http://www.thecoca-colacompany.com/citizenship/workplace_culture.html.
9. Volvo Car Corporation, "About Volvo," accessed March 31, 2011, http://www.volvocars.com/ly/top/about/values/pages/default.aspx.
10. Cara Foods, "Values & Principles," accessed March 31, 2011, http://www.dgp.utoronto.ca/~trendall/sfp/boycott/Cara_Values_and_Principles.html.
11. Canadian Tire, "Business Conduct Compliance," accessed March 31, 2011, http://corp.canadiantire.ca/EN/Investors/Governance/Pages/CodeofConduct.aspx.
12. Carter McNamara, "Strategic Planning (in Nonprofit or For-Profit Organizations)," *Free Management Library,* accessed March 30, 2011, http://managementhelp.org/planning/index.htm#anchor1384873.
13. Rie Ishiguro and Shinji Kitamura, "Japan Quake's Economic Impact Worse Than First Feared," Thomson Reuters, April 12, 2011, accessed July 25, 2014,

http://www.reuters.com/article/2011/04/12/us-japan-economy-idUSTRE73B0O320110412.

14. International Institute for Organization Research, "Horizontal Organization: A Brief Survey," accessed March 30, 2011, http://www.anarchy.no/horizon1.html.
15. Peter Drucker, "Quotation Details," The Quotations Page, accessed July 25, 2014, http://quotationspage.com/quote/26536.html.
16. James M. Kouzes and Barry Z. Posner, *The Leadership Challenge,* 3rd ed. (San Francisco: Jossey-Bass, 2003).
17. *Black Friday*, a 7-minute video on the *Toy Story* Blu-Ray Disc. Retrieved from YouTube, http://www.youtube.com/watch?v5bk8a_C0ao9Y.
18. Adapted from Carey Toane, "Overall Winner—Loblaw's Craig Hutchinson: Back to the Future," *Strategy*, December 1, 2009, accessed March 31, 2011, http://strategyonline.ca/2009/12/01/moyhutchison-20091201/?page=2.
19. Loblaw Companies Ltd., "Training Developer—Supply Chain: Company Description," LinkedIn.com, October 28, 2011, accessed November 5, 2011, http://www.linkedin.com/company/loblaw-companies-limited/careers?trk=job_view_topcard_company_name&trk=job_view_topcard_company_name.
20. Dana Flavelle, "Price Fight: Superstores take on Wal-Mart," *thestar.com*, October 2, 2009, accessed November 5, 2011, http://www.thestar.com/business/2009/10/02/price_fight_superstores_take_on_walmart.html.
21. Rick Wartzman, "Has Toyota Lost Its Way?" *Businessweek*, November 26, 2007, accessed May 15, 2008, http://www.businessweek.com/managing/content/nov2007/ca20071125_337938.htm; Charles Fishman, "No Satisfaction at Toyota" *Fast Company*, December 2006, accessed May 15, 2008, http://www.fastcompany.com/magazine/111/open_no-satisfaction.html; Toyota Motor Sales U.S.A., Inc., "Our Company," accessed May 15, 2008, http://www.toyota.com/about/our_values/index.html.
22. Toyota Motor Manufacturing Kentucky, Inc., "Toyota Production System Terms," accessed May 15, 2008, http://www.toyotageorgetown.com/terms.asp.
23. Katsuhiro Nakagawa, "The Toyota Way: Japanese Management in the Global Economy—Up Close and Personal," University of California, San Diego School of International Relations and Pacific Studies, September 27, 2004, accessed May 15, 2008, http://irps.ucsd.edu/news/speeches/the-toyota-way.htm.

Chapter 6

1. Achievers, "Past Winners," accessed June 10, 2014, http://www.achievers.com/engaged/winners.
2. 1-800-GOT-JUNK? "Our company RBDS, RUBBISH BOYS DISPOSAL SERVICE INC. D.B.A 1-800-GOT-JUNK?" Accessed June 10, 2014, http://www.1800gotjunk.com/ca_en/about/our_company.aspx.
3. "1-800-GOT-JUNK? Branding Professionalism, Industry Overview" from RBDS RUBBISH BOYS DISPOSAL SERVICE INC. D.B.A 1-800-GOT-JUNK? Accessed June 10, 2014, http://www.1800gotjunk.com/ca_en/about/gotjunk_industrycanada.aspx.
4. Brian Scudamore, "Pump Up Employee Passion," *Profit Guide,* Published by Rogers Publishing, October 13, 2010, accessed June 10, 2014, http://www.profitguide.com/manage-grow/human-resources/pump-up-employee-passion-29964.
5. Cynthia Clark, "Creating Lasting Employee Engagement," 1to1 Media, September 13, 2012, accessed June 10, 2014, http://www.1to1media.com/weblog/2012/09/creating_lasting_employee_enga.html.
6. Scudamore, "Pump Up Employee Passion."
7. 1-800-GOT-JUNK? "Branding Professionalism."
8. Mihaly Csikszentmihalyi, *Flow* (New York: HarperCollins, 1990).

9. Steve Crabtree, "Worldwide, 13% of Employees Are Engaged at Work," Gallup World, October 8, 2013, accessed June 10, 2014, http://www.gallup.com/poll/165269/worldwide-employees-engaged-work.aspx.
10. Towers Watson, *Closing the Engagement Gap: Towers Perrin Global Workforce Study 2007–2008,* accessed July 29, 2014, https://c.ymcdn.com/sites/www.simnet.org/resource/group/066D79D1-E2A8-4AB5-B621-60E58640FF7B/leadership_workshop_2010/towers_perrin_global_workfor.pdf.
11. Towers Watson, *Turbocharging Employee Engagement: Part 1—The Engagement Engine*, Two-Part White Paper, 2010, accessed November 7, 2011, http://www.towerswatson.com/en/Insights/IC-Types/Survey-Research-Results/2009/12/Turbocharging-Employee-Engagement-The-Power-of-Recognition-From-Managers-Part-1.
12. Towers Watson, "Key Findings: An Interview with Julie Gebauer on Towers Perrin's Just Released Global Workforce Study, Part 2," accessed November 7, 2011, http://www.towersperrin.com/tp/showhtml.jsp?url=global/publications/gws/key-findings_2.htm&country=global.
13. Towers Watson, *Closing the Engagement Gap.*
14. Towers Watson, "Key Findings: An Interview with Julie Gebauer."
15. Towers Watson, *Closing the Engagement Gap.*
16. Carnegie Management Group, "The Executor Mentor: The High Cost of Disengagement," accessed April 2, 2011, http://www.carnegiemg.com.au/blog/the-disengagement-crisis/.
17. Ian Tan, "Why Work for SAS," SAS.com, http://www.sas.com/offices/asiapacific/singapore/press/why-sas.html.
18. Beverly Brown, "SAS Achieves Double-Digit Growth, Rockets 12 Percent to Record $2.725 Billion," SAS.com, January 19, 2012, http://www.sas.com/news/preleases/2011financials.html.
19. James Goodnight, quoted in James Goodnight and Richard Florida, "Managing for Creativity," *Harvard Business Review* 83 (July/August 2005): 124–131.
20. Ibid.
21. Nash Popovic, "What Really Motivates Us?" BBC News in Video, accessed April 2, 2011, http://news.bbc.co.uk/nolavconsole/ukfs_news/hi/newsid_4760000/newsid_4764500/nb_rm_4764545.stm.
22. Victor Vroom, *Work and Motivation,* (New York: Wiley, 1964); and Craig Pinder, *Work Motivation* (Glenview, IL: Scott, Foresman, 1984).
23. WorldBlu, "The WorldBlu List, 2014," accessed June 10, 2014, http://www.worldblu.com/awardee-profiles/2014.php.
24. Charlton Communications, "The WestJet Story," accessed April 4, 2011, http://lin.ca/sites/default/files/attachments/vm091.pdf.
25. Gallup, "Strengths-Based Development," accessed April 2, 2011, http://www.gallup.com/consulting/61/strengths-development.aspx.
26. Ibid.
27. Fraya Wagner-Marsh, rev. Patricia A. Lanier, "Pioneers of Management," *Encyclopedia of Business*, 2nd ed., accessed April 4, 2011, http://www.referenceforbusiness.com/management/Or-Pr/Pioneers-of-Management.html.
28. Frank J. Landy and Jeffrey M. Conte, *Work in the 21st Century: An Introduction to Industrial and Organizational Psychology,* 2nd ed. (Malden, MA: Blackwell Publishing, 2007).
29. Daniel Pink, *Drive* (New York: Riverhead Books, 2009).
30. Ibid.
31. G. Scott Acton, "Great Ideas in Personality: Five-Factor Model," 1997, accessed April 3, 2011, http://www.personalityresearch.org/bigfive/costa.html; and Oliver D. John, "The Big Five Personality Test," 2009, accessed April 3, 2011, http://www.outofservice.com/bigfive/.
32. Adapted from Talya Bauer and Berrin Erdogan, "Organizational Behavior," FlatWorldKnowledge.com, accessed April 4, 2011, http://www.flatworldknowledge.com/node/34687#web-34687.

33. Sean Neubert, "The Five-Factor Model of Personality in the Workplace," Rochester Institute of Technology, accessed April 4, 2011, http://www.personalityresearch.org/papers/neubert.html.
34. *Professional's Feedback: Couple's Counseling Report*, 16PF Fifth Edition, accessed April 3, 2011, http://www.pearsonassessments.com/NR/rdonlyres/66658BFC-36EE-4D9F-9636-1B3DE8252644/0/16pf5couples.pdf.
35. John R. Katzenbach and Douglas K. Smith, *The Wisdom of Teams* (Cambridge, MA: Harvard University Press, 1993).
36. Matt Rosoff, "The Story Behind Kinect, Microsoft's Newest Billion Dollar Business," *Business Insider*, January 19, 2011, accessed June 10, 2014, http://www.businessinsider.com/the-story-behind-microsofts-hot-selling-kinect-2011-1?op=1.
37. "Teamwork Concept Questioned," National Association of College Stores, August 11, 2006, accessed June 10, 2014, http://www.nacs.org/news/081106-teamwork.asp?id5cm.
38. Neil Howe and William Strauss, *Millennials Rising: The Next Great Generation* (New York, NY: Vintage, 2000).
39. Stephanie Armour, "Generation Y: They've Arrived at Work with a New Attitude," *USA Today*, November 6, 2005, accessed June 10, 2014, http://www.usatoday.com/money/workplace/2005-11-06-gen-y_x.htm.
40. William Strauss, quoted in Matt Ehlers, "What's Up with Gen Y?" *The News & Observer*, February 5, 2006, accessed June 10, 2014, http://www.newsobserver.com/2006/02/05/53603/whats-up-with-gen-y.html.
41. George Anders, "Jeff Bezos Gets It," *Forbes*, April 25, 2012, http://www.forbes.com/global/2012/0507/global-2000-12-amazon-jeffbezos-gets-it.html.
42. David Robertson and Per Hjuler, "Innovating a Turnaround at LEGO," *Harvard Business Review* (September 2009), accessed June 10, 2014, http://hbr.org/2009/09/innovating-a-turnaround-at-lego/ar/1.
43. Queen's School of Business, "Queen's Executive MBA Program: Now Available on Your Desktop," January 24, 2011, accessed April 3, 2011, http://business.queensu.ca/news_blog/2011/queens-executive-mba-program--now-available-on-your-desktop; and "Virtual Teams a First in Canada," *Financial Post*, January 19, 2011, accessed April 3, 2011, http://business.financialpost.com/2011/01/19/mba-virtual-teams-a-first-in-canada/.
44. Kerith Nicholl, "Second Life Recreates Border Patrol at Loyalist," *Online Pioneer Plus*, accessed April 4, 2011, http://www.thepioneer.com/?q=node/3112.
45. J. S. Lurey and M. S. Raisinghani, "An Empirical Study of Best Practices in Virtual Teams," *Information & Management* 38 (October 2001): 523–544.
46. Stephen R. Covey, *The 7 Habits of Highly Effective People* (New York, NY: Free Press, 1989).
47. Geoffrey Colvin, "Why Dream Teams Fail," *Fortune*, accessed April 3, 2011, http://money.cnn.com/magazines/fortune/fortune_archive/2006/06/12/8379219/index.htm.
48. Yahoo Movies Canada, "Michael Ovitz Biography," accessed April 3, 2011, http://movies.yahoo.com/movie/contributor/1808503949/bio.
49. David Teather, "Investors Lose Battle with Disney over Ovitz's $140m," *The Guardian*, August 10, 2005, accessed April 3, 2011, http://www.guardian.co.uk/media/2005/aug/10/citynews.filmnews.
50. Colvin, "Why Dream Teams Fail."
51. Bryan Walsh and Toko Sekiguchi, "Heroes of the Environment: Toyota Prius Design Team," *Time*, October 17, 2007, accessed May 5, 2008, http://content.time.com/time/specials/2007/article/0,28804,1663317_1663323_1669899,00.html.
52. Toyota, "Contribution towards Sustainable Development," accessed May 5, 2008, http://www.toyota.com/about/our_values/index.html.

53. Alex Taylor III, "Toyota: The Birth of the Prius," *Fortune*, February 21, 2006, accessed May 5, 2008, http://money.cnn.com/2006/02/17/news/companies/mostadmired_fortune_toyota/.

Chapter 7

1. Nancy Germond, "Employee Retention Strategy Can Save Companies Millions," AllBusiness.com, accessed January 14, 2011, http://www.allbusiness.com/labor-employment/human-resources-personnel-management/14352477-1.html.
2. SAS, "About SAS," accessed June 29, 2011, http://www.sas.com/company/about/index.html.
3. "A Culture That Values Employees," Baldrige.com, February 22, 2011, accessed November 12, 2011, http://www.baldrige.com/criteria_workforce/a-culture-that-values-employees.
4. Canada's Top 100 Employers 2012, "Canada's Top 100 Employers," accessed November 12, 2011, http://www.canadastop100.com/national/; and "100 Best Companies to Work For 2011, 2010, 2009," CNN Money, accessed November 12, 2011, http://money.cnn.com/magazines/fortune/bestcompanies/2011/index.html, http://money.cnn.com/magazines/fortune/bestcompanies/2010/index.html, and http://money.cnn.com/magazines/fortune/bestcompanies/2009/full_list/.
5. Richard Florida and Jim Goodnight, "Managing for Creativity," *Harvard Business Review* (July–August 2005), accessed July 2, 2011, http://www.zuhl.com/~mikez/Info/Software/SoftwareEng/ManagingCreativity.html.
6. Ibid.
7. "Purpose of Having a Human Resource Department," *Small Business Bible*, accessed January 19, 2011, http://www.smallbusinessbible.org/purpose_having_humanr_department.html.
8. LinkedIn, "About LinkedIn," accessed November 3, 2011, http://press.linkedin.com/about.
9. JCSI, *The New Age of Recruiting: 2010 Recruiting Survey Results*, accessed January 15, 2011, http://documents.jdsupra.com/d8daebb9-5f66-465f-be24-013da3e48d22.pdf.
10. "Talent Mismatch Tops Manpower's Mega Trends," *Recruiter*, accessed January 27, 2011, http://www.recruiter.co.uk/archive/part-17/Talent-mismatch-tops-Manpower-s-mega-trends/.
11. Conference Board of Canada, "Employability Skills 2000+," accessed January 30, 2011, http://www.conferenceboard.ca/topics/education/learning-tools/employability-skills.aspx.
12. Stephane Thiffeault, "Poor Reference Check Results in Damages," McMillian Binch Mendelsohn, February 2006, accessed January 15, 2010, http://www.mcmillan.ca/Files/Poor%20Reference%20Check_0106.pdf.
13. Carter McNamara, "Employee Training and Development: Reasons and Benefits," Free Management Library, accessed January 1, 2011, http://www.managementhelp.org/trng_dev/basics/reasons.htm.
14. McDonald's, "Training & Education," accessed January 22, 2011, http://www.mcdonalds.com/us/en/careers/training_education.html.
15. Robert Stone, Antoinette Caird-Daley, and Kevin Bessell, "SubSafe: A Games-Based Training System for Submarine Safety and Spatial Awareness (Part 1)," *Virtual Reality* 13 (November 28, 2008), accessed January 26, 2011, http://www.springerlink.com/content/1p57h1h547734420.
16. "Next-Generation Training," *Military Simulation & Training News* 22 (Spring–Summer 2010), accessed November 9, 2011, http://www.cae.com/en/military/pdf/Newsletter22.pdf.

17. Tintswalo Baloyi, "SAP Introduces Games-Based Training in South Africa," *IT News Africa*, accessed January 25, 2011, http://www.itnewsafrica.com/?p=8902.
18. Ibid.
19. Human Resource Development Council, "Organizational Learning Strategies: Action Learning," accessed January 22, 2011, http://www.humtech.com/opm/grtl/ols/ols2.cfm.
20. Matt Andrejczak, "Starbucks Completes Employees Stock-Option Swap," MarketWatch.com, June 3, 2009, accessed January 22, 2011, http://www.marketwatch.com/story/starbucks-completes-employee-stock-option-swap-200963143100.
21. "Workplaces for Sabbaticals 2011," yourSABBATICAL.com, accessed January 23, 2011, http://yoursabbatical.com/learn/workplaces-for-sabbaticals/2011/.
22. "Canadians Don't Make Health a Priority," BenefitsCanada.com, January 18, 2011, accessed January 23, 2011, http://www.benefitscanada.com/benefits/health-benefits/canadians-don%E2%80%99t-make-health-a-priority-13854.
23. Jim Pearse, "Premium Value," BenefitsCanada.com, May 1, 2008, accessed January 23, 2011, http://www.benefitscanada.com/benefits/health-benefits/premium-value-8348.
24. Brooke Smith, "Out of Reach," BenefitsCanada.com, May 1, 2007, accessed January 23, 2011, http://www.benefitscanada.com/benefits/health-benefits/out-of-reach-8361.
25. State Farm Insurance, "Worklife & Wellness," accessed March 10, 2011, http://www.statefarm.com/careers/emp_worklife.asp.
26. Kelly Diels-Rostant, "Striving for the 'Clockless' Work Schedule," *Talent at Work* (blog), October 26, 2010, accessed January 23, 2011, http://www.goldbeck.com/hrblog/striving-for-the-clockless-work-schedule/.
27. The Home Depot Canada Foundation, accessed November 12, 2011, http://www.homedepot.ca/foundation.
28. Labour Canada, "Legislative Framework: Mandatory Retirement," accessed November 12, 2011, http://www.hrsdc.gc.ca/eng/lp/spila/wlb/aw/27retirement_legislative02.shtml.
29. *CBC News*, "Mandatory Retirement Fades in Canada," October 18, 2010, accessed March 10, 2011, http://www.cbc.ca/news/business/mandatory-retirement-fades-in-canada-1.799697.
30. "GM Offers Buyouts to Skilled Trades Workers," GazetteXtra.com, December 15, 2010, accessed January 23, 2011, http://www.gazettextra.com/news/2010/dec/15/gm-offers-buyouts-skilled-trades-workers/.
31. Associated Press, "Ford Offers Retirement, Buyout Packages to All 41,000 Factory Workers to Thin Ranks," *The Telegram*, December 22, 2009, http://www.thetelegram.com/Business/2009-12-22/article-823585/Ford-offers-retirement,-buyout-packages-to-all-41,000-factory-workers-to-thin-ranks/1.
32. Wallstats.com, "Golden Parachutes: How the Bankers Went Down," *Mint-Life*, February 24, 2009, accessed January 23, 2011, https://www.mint.com/blog/trends/golden-parachutes-how-the-bankers-went-down/.
33. Government of Canada Labour Program, *Terminations: Pamphlet 10—Labour Standards*, accessed November 12, 2011, http://www.labour.gc.ca/eng/standards_equity/st/pubs_st/terminations.shtml.
34. Lloyd Duhaime, "Wrongful Dismissal Law in Canada," Duhaime.org, accessed January 23, 2011, http://www.duhaime.org/LegalResources/EmploymentLabourLaw/LawArticle-104/Wrongful-Dismissal-Law-in-Canada.aspx.
35. "Employment at Will," TheFreeDictionary.com, accessed January 23, 2011, http://legal-dictionary.thefreedictionary.com/Employment+at+Will.

36. Sylvia Chrominska, Speech, Scotiabank, Investors & Shareholders: Investor Relations, November 2, 2010, accessed July 30, 2014, http://www.scotiabank.com/ca/en/0,,948,00.html.

37. Human Resources and Skills Development Canada, "Learning—Educational Attainment," accessed November 13, 2011, http://www4.hrsdc.gc.ca/.3ndic.1t.4r@-eng.jsp?iid=29.

38. Carol Hymowitz, "The New Diversity," *Wall Street Journal,* November 14, 2005, accessed January 23, 2011, http://www.tedchilds.com/files/TheNewDiversityWSJ.pdf.

39. Robert Rodriguez, "Diversity Finds Its Place," *HR Magazine,* August 1, 2006, accessed January 24, 2011, http://www.shrm.org/Publications/hrmagazine/EditorialContent/Pages/0806rodriguez.aspx.

40. Lisa Takeuchi Cullen, "Employee Diversity Training Doesn't Work," *Time,* April 26, 2007, accessed January 24, 2011, http://content.time.com/time/magazine/article/0,9171,1615183,00.html.

41. United Food and Commercial Workers Canada, "Facts About Unions," accessed November 13, 2011, http://www.ufcw.ca/index.php?option=com_content&view=article&id=29&Itemid=49&lang=en.

42. The Social Studies Help Center, "Collective Bargaining," accessed November 13, 2011, http://www.socialstudieshelp.com/Eco_collective_bargaining.htm.

43. *CBC News,* "Striking Toronto Workers Reach Tentative Deals," July 27, 2009, accessed January 24, 2011, http://www.cbc.ca/news/canada/toronto/striking-toronto-workers-reach-tentative-deals-1.812747; and Nina Lex and Frank Pingue, "Toronto Hopes for Quick End to City Workers' Strike," Reuters.com, June 22, 2009, accessed January 24, 2011, http://mobile.reuters.com/article/domesticNews/idCATRE55L2HN20090622.

44. Alison Haines, "Toronto on Strike: Council Approves Deal with Both Unions to End Strike," *National Post,* July 31, 2009, accessed January 24, 2011, http://network.nationalpost.com/np/blogs/toronto/archive/2009/07/31/toronto-on-strike-workers-return-to-jobs-as-city-council-votes.aspx.

45. The Lawyers & Jurists, "Labour Law," accessed November 13, 2011, http://www.lawyersnjurists.com/our-services/practice-areas-3/labour-law.

46. Ministry of Labour, *Canada Labour Code, Part II—Overview,* accessed June 27, 2011, http://www.labour.gc.ca/eng/health_safety/pubs_hs/overview.shtml.

47. World Law Direct, "Wrongful Termination," accessed November 13, 2011, http://www.worldlawdirect.com/forum/law-wiki/5940-wrongful-termination.html.

48. Bongarde, "HR Compliance," accessed November 13, 2011, http://www.bongarde.com/bongardeproducts/compliance/hr-compliance.

49. Government of Canada, *Canada Labour Code,* accessed January 26, 2011, http://laws.justice.gc.ca/eng/L-2/index.html.

50. Government of Canada, *Employment Equity Act,* accessed January 26, 2011, http://laws.justice.gc.ca/eng/E-5.401/page-1.html#anchorbo-ga:s_2.

51. Government of Alberta, *Occupational Health and Safety Focused Inspection Project: Commercial Construction,* December 13, 2010, accessed November 13, 2011, http://employment.alberta.ca/documents/WHS/WHS-PUB-Commercial-Construction-Focused-Inspection-Report-2010.pdf.

52. HR World Editors, "30 Interview Questions You Can't Ask and 30 Sneaky, Legal Alternatives to Get the Same Info," November 15, 2007, accessed May 5, 2008, http://www.hrworld.com/features/30-interview-questions-111507/.

53. Toyota Motor Sales, "About T-Ten," Toyota.com, accessed June 28, 2011, http://www.toyota.com/about/tten/whytten.html.

54. Toyota Motor Sales, "Certification You Will Receive," Toyota.com, accessed June 28, 2011, http://www.toyota.com/about/tten/certification.html.

Chapter 8

1. Facebook, "Sponsored Stories," accessed July 2, 2011, http://www.facebook.com/ads/stories/.
2. Cynthia Boris, "Facebook Adds Social Endorsement Stats," MarketingPilgrim.com, September 10, 2010, accessed November 19, 2011, http://www.marketingpilgrim.com/2010/09/facebook-adds-social-endorsement-stats.html.
3. Rob Pegoraro, "Facebook 'Sponsored Stories' Turn You into the Ad," *Washington Post*, January 27, 2011, accessed November 11, 2011, http://voices.washingtonpost.com/fasterforward/2011/01/facebook_sponsored_stories_tur.html.
4. Josh Costine, "Facebook's Sponsored Stories Turns News Feed Posts into Home Page Ads," InsideFacebook.com, January 24, 2011, accessed July 2, 2011, http://www.insidefacebook.com/2011/01/24/sponsored-stories-feed-ads.
5. Ben Parr, "Facebook Turns Friend Activity into New Ad Format," Mashable.com, January 25, 2011, accessed July 2, 2011, http://mashable.com/2011/01/25/facebook-sponsored-stories/.
6. Irina Slutsky, "Facebook Turns the 'Like' Into Its Newest Ad," *Advertising Age*, January 25, 2011, accessed June 30, 2011, http://adage.com/article/digital/facebook-turns-newest-ad/148452/.
7. Josh Constine, "Facebook Sponsored Stories Ads Have 46% Higher CTR, 18% Lower Cost Per Fan Says TBG Digital Test," InsideFacebook.com, May 3, 2011, accessed July 2, 2011, http://www.insidefacebook.com/2011/05/03/sponsored-stories-ctr-cost-per-fa/.
8. Canadian Marketing Association, *Code of Ethics and Standards of Practice*, accessed May 20, 2011, http://www.the-cma.org/regulatory/code-of-ethics.
9. Monika Warzecha, "The Toronto Zoo Figure Out That People Like Baby Animals," *Toronto Life*, July 4, 2012, accessed January 15, 2014, http://www.torontolife.com/informer/random-stuff-informer/2012/07/04/zoo-attendance-baby-animals/.
10. Canadian Marketing Association, "Regulatory Affairs," accessed May 27, 2011, http://www.the-cma.org/regulatory; and "Code of Ethics and Standards of Practice," accessed May 27, 2011, http://www.the-cma.org/regulatory/code-of-ethics.
11. Statistics Canada, "Average Household Expenditures by Province and Territory," accessed January 15, 2014, http://www.statcan.gc.ca/tables-tableaux/sum-som/l01/cst01/famil16a-eng.htm.
12. Jon Loomer, "How to Use Facebook Power Editor: A Detailed Guide," *Social Media Examiner*, August 6, 2013, accessed January 15, 2014, http://www.socialmediaexaminer.com/facebook-power-editor-guide/.
13. Alex Cheng and Mark Evans, "Inside Twitter: An In-Depth Look Inside the Twitter World," Sysomos.com, April 2014, accessed July 22, 2014, http://www.sysomos.com/docs/Inside-Twitter-BySysomos.pdf.
14. Charles W. Lamb, Jr., Joseph F. Hair, and Carl McDaniel, *Marketing*, 7th ed. (Stamford, CT: Thomson Publishing Company, 2004), p. 33.
15. Internet Center for Management and Business Administration, "Situational Analysis," NetMBA.com, accessed May 24, 2011, http://www.netmba.com/marketing/situation/; and Matt Winn, "Situation Analysis Continued—The 5 C's," Volusion's Ecommerce Blog, February 2, 2010, accessed May 24, 2011, http://onlinebusiness.volusion.com/articles/situation-analysis-the-5-cs.
16. Statistics Canada, "Study: Canada's Visible Minority Population in 2017," *The Daily*, March 22, 2005, accessed November 12, 2011, http://www.statcan.gc.ca/daily-quotidien/050322/dq050322b-eng.htm.
17. Philip Kotler and Gary Armstrong, *Principles of Marketing*, 12th ed. (Upper Saddle River, NJ: Pearson, 2008), pp. 131–147.

18. Philip Kotler and Kevin Lane Keller, *Marketing Management,* 12th ed. (Upper Saddle River, NJ: Pearson, 2006), pp. 211–212; and Kotler and Armstrong, *Principles of Marketing,* 12th ed., pp. 161–162.
19. Associated Press, "Groupon Settles Lawsuit for Expired Deals," *CBC News,* June 24, 2013, http://www.cbc.ca/news/canada/groupon-settles-lawsuit-for-expired-deals-1.1317587.
20. Andy Reinhardt, "Steve Jobs: 'There's Sanity in Returning,'" *Businessweek,* May 25, 1998, accessed June 30, 2011, http://www.businessweek.com/1998/21/b3579165.htm; Sohrab Vossoughi, "Apple: More than a Pretty Face," *Businessweek,* January 4, 2008, accessed June 30, 2011, http://www.businessweek.com/innovate/content/jan2008/id2008014_858681.htm; and Ina Fried, "Celebrating Three Decades of Apple," *CNET News,* March 28, 2006, accessed June 30, 2011, http://news.cnet.com/2009-1041-6054524.html.
21. Rehan Choudhary, "An Introduction to Apple Computer, Inc.," Suite101.com, March 30, 2010, accessed June 30, 2011, http://www.suite101.com/content/an-introduction-to-apple-computer-inc-a219539.
22. Sherilynn Macale, "Apple Has Sold 300M iPods, Currently Holds 78% of the Music Player Market," thenextweb.com, October 4, 2011, accessed November 19, 2011, http://thenextweb.com/apple/2011/10/04/apple-has-sold-300m-ipods-currently-holds-78-of-the-music-player-market.

Chapter 9

1. Kraft Foods Group, Inc., "Annual Report, 2012," accessed January 16, 2014, http://www.annualreports.com/HostedData/AnnualReports/PDF/KRFT%202012%2010-K%20-%20Final.pdf.
2. Kraft Foods, "Do You Like to Do It in Public or Keep It Private?" press release, February 2, 2011, accessed June 1, 2011, http://www.mononews.ca/news/1042/do-you-like-to-do-it-in-public-or-keep-it-private-this-valentines-day-dentyne-presents-the-great-kissing-debate-public-or-private.
3. Kraft Foods, *2010 Annual Report,* February 28, 2011, accessed June 1, 2011, http://global.mondelezinternational.com/SiteCollectionDocuments/pdf/KraftFoods_10K_20110228.pdf.
4. E. J. Schultz, "Kraft Foods Emerges Big Spender Post Company Split," *AdAge,* June 24, 2013, http://adage.com/article/news/kraft-foods-emerges-big-spender-post-company-split/242772/.
5. Kraft Foods, "Find a Job with Us," accessed November 20, 2011, http://www.kraftfoodscompany.com/Careers/Find_a_Job_With_Us/index.aspx; and Kraft Foods, "Kraft Kitchens Experts," accessed November 20, 2011, http://www.kraftcanada.com/en/about/experts/KraftKitchensExperts.aspx.
6. Giselle Tsirulnik, "Kraft Sets Bar for Food Marketing with New iPad App," MobileMarketer.com, July 12, 2010, accessed June 3, 2011, http://www.mobilemarketer.com/cms/news/advertising/6775.html.
7. Sarah Kessler, "Five Invaluable Marketing Lessons from an Epic Campaign for…Cream Cheese?" Mashable.com, November 17, 2010, accessed June 3, 2011, http://mashable.com/2010/11/17/cream-cheese-social-network.
8. Briana Southward, "Diamond Shreddies," TorqueCustomerStrategy.com, May 7, 2008, accessed June 3, 2011, http://www.torquecustomerstrategy.com/gallery_comments.php?gallery_id=42.
9. Jeromy Lloyd, "More Diamonds from Shreddies," *Marketing Magazine,* September 17, 2008, accessed June 3, 2011, http://www.marketingmag.ca/news/marketer-news/more-diamonds-from-shreddies-17677.
10. Duane D. Standford, "Kraft's Tang Makeover Led to 30% Sales Jump Abroad Last Year," Bloomberg.com, March 6, 2010, accessed June 3, 2011, http://www.bloomberg.com/apps/news?pid=newsarchive&sid=aRrQGB8IvwaM.

11. Chris Powell, "Kraft Brings Back Hockeyville to Showcase Canadian Passion for Hockey," *Marketing Magazine*, November 8, 2010, accessed November 17, 2011, http://www.marketingmag.ca/news/marketer-news/kraft-brings-backhockeyville-to-showcase-canadian-passion-for-hockey-5869.
12. Stuart Elliott, "Kraft Hopes to Encourage Adults to Revert to a Childhood Favorite," *New York Times*, May 26, 2010, accessed June 1, 2011, http://www.nytimes.com/2010/05/27/business/media/27adco.html.
13. Theresa Howard, "Coke Finally Scores Another Winner," *USA Today*, October 28, 2007, accessed May 27, 2011, http://www.usatoday.com/money/advertising/adtrack/2007-10-28-coke-zero_N.htm.
14. Michael E. Ross, "It Seemed Like a Good Idea at the Time," *NBC News*, April 22, 2005, accessed May 29, 2011, http://www.msnbc.msn.com/id/7209828.
15. "Diet Coke Introduces New Limited-Edition Taylor Swift Can Design," Yahoo! Finance, October 3, 2013, accessed February 2, 2014, http://finance.yahoo.com/news/diet-coke-introduces-limited-edition-144700411.html.
16. The Coca-Cola Company, "Growth, Leadership, Sustainability," accessed May 27, 2011, http://www.coca-colacompany.com/our-company/infographic-coca-cola-at-a-glance.
17. The Coca-Cola Company, "Product List," accessed May 27, 2011, http://www.thecocacolacompany.com/brands/brandlist.html.
18. General Electric Company, "Products and Services," accessed May 27, 2011, http://www.ge.com/products.
19. The Coca-Cola Company, "Products," http://www.thecoca-colacompany.com/brands/index.html, Accessed May 27, 2011.
20. Tom Peters, "The Brand Called You," *Fast Company*, August 31, 1997, accessed July 25, 2014, http://www.fastcompany.com/28905/brand-called-you.
21. "The Association for Dressings & Sauces Names 2013 Dressing, Sauce and Package of the Year Award Winners," PRWeb, October 7, 2013, accessed January 16, 2014, http://www.prweb.com/releases/2013/10/prweb11204815.htm.
22. Paul Harsh, "Puma Gives Up Wasteful Packaging in Favor of Eco-friendly Packages," Greenpacks.org, April 13, 2010, accessed July 28, 2014, http://www.greenpacks.org/2010/04/13/puma-gives-up-wasteful-packaging-in-favor-of-eco-friendly-packages.
23. Kimpton Hotels & Restaurants, "Environment: Kimpton Rolls Out the Green Carpet," accessed July 28, 2014, http://www.kimptonhotels.com/kimpton-cares/earthcare.aspx.
24. Campbell Company of Canada, "Soup on the Go," accessed November 20, 2011, http://www.campbellsoup.com/Products/Microwavable/Soup-At-Hand.
25. Wikinvest, "Campbell Soup Company (NYSE: CPB)," accessed November 20, 2011, http://www.wikinvest.com/stock/Campbell_Soup_Company_%28CPB%29.
26. Straight Dope, "Is There a Term for 'Trade Names That Become Generic'?" accessed August 12, 2011, http://www.straightdope.com/columns/read/1464/is-there-a-term-for-trade-names-that-become-generic.
27. Ibid.
28. Department of Justice, Consumer Packaging and Labelling Act, accessed November 20, 2011, http://laws.justice.gc.ca/eng/acts/C-38/page-3.html#h-5.
29. Dan Swenson, Shahid Ansari, Jan Bell, and Il-Woon Kim, "A Field Study of Best Practices in Target Costing," *Management Accounting Quarterly* (Winter 2003): 12–17.
30. Interactive Advertising Bureau and PricewaterhouseCoopers, "Internet Advertising Revenues Again Reach New Highs, Estimated to Pass $21 Billion in 2007 and Hit Nearly $6 Billion in Q4 2007," press release, February 25, 2008, accessed June 4, 2011, http://www.iab.net/about_th_iab/recent_press_releases/press_release_archive/press_release/195115.

31. John Zarwan, "Direct Mail Delivers," *American Printer*, August 2006, accessed June 4, 2011, http://www.johnzarwan.com/pubs/608APdir.pdf.
32. Alex Konrad, "Even with Record Prices, Expect a $10 Million Super Bowl Ad Soon" *Forbes,* February 2, 2013, accessed January 16, 2014, http://www.forbes.com/sites/alexkonrad/2013/02/02/even-with-record-prices-10-million-spot/.
33. Steve Sorge and Alice Luong, "Advantages to Advertising in Mobile Games," *Canadian Marketing Association*. November 13, 2012, accessed January 16, 2014, http://www.the-cma.org/about/blog/advantages-to-advertising-in-mobile-games.
34. Ibid.
35. "*Iron Man* and Audi: R8 Takes Leading Role in New Summer Blockbuster Movie *Iron Man* from Marvel Studios and Paramount Pictures," PRNewswire.com, April 8, 2008, accessed June 4, 2011, http://www.prnewswire.com/news-releases/iron-man-and-audi-r8-takes-leading-role-in-new-summer-blockbuster-movie-iron-man-from-marvel-studios-and-paramount-pictures-57301927.html.
36. Davide Dukcevich, "TV's Most Successful Products," *Forbes,* November 13, 2002, accessed June 4, 2011, http://www.forbes.com/2002/11/13/cx_dd_1113products.html.
37. Scott M. Cutlip, Allen H. Center, and Glen M. Broom, *Effective Public Relations,* 9th ed. (Upper Saddle River, NJ: Pearson Prentice Hall, 2009), 517–526.
38. Ibid.
39. Allison Jones, "Canada Goose Sues International Clothiers over Alleged Replicas of Parkas," *Toronto Star,* February 22, 2012, accessed January 17, 2014, http://www.thestar.com/business/2012/02/22/canada_goose_sues_international_clothiers_over_alleged_replicas_of_parkas.html. Used by the permission of Toronto Star.
40. Hollie Shaw, "Canada Goose's Made-in-Canada Marketing Strategy Translates into Success," *Financial Post,* May 18, 2012, accessed January 17, 2014, http://business.financialpost.com/2012/05/18/canada-gooses-made-in-canada-marketing-strategy-translates-into-success/. Material reproduced with the express permission of: Postmedia News, a division of Postmedia Network Inc.
41. Neal Santelmann, "Companies That Care," *Forbes,* accessed June 4, 2011, http://www.forbes.com/2004/09/29/cx_ns_0929feat.html.
42. Lisa Z. Eccles, "Point of Purchase Advertising," *Advertising Age* Supplement, September 1994, 1–6.
43. Philip Kotler and Gary Armstrong, *Principles of Marketing,* 12th ed. (Upper Saddle River, NJ: Pearson Prentice Hall, 2008), 386.
44. Ibid.
45. Peter Cohen, "Jobs Introduces iPhone, Apple TV," InfoWorld.com, January 9, 2007, accessed June 30, 2011, http://www.infoworld.com/article/07/01/09/HNiphoneappletv_1.html.
46. Associated Press, "Apple Unveils Cell Phone, Apple TV," *NBC News,* accessed June 30, 2011, http://www.nbcnews.com/id/16542805#.U9e30vldWSo.
47. Chris Barylick and Mathew Honan, "iPhone Release Brings Out the Crowds," Macworld.com, June 30, 2007, accessed June 30, 2011, http://www.macworld.com/article/58682/2007/06/iphone_crowds.html.
48. Jim Dalrymple and Jason Snell, "Apple Sets iPhone Sights on the Long Long Haul," PCWorld.com, July 26, 2007, accessed June 30, 2011, http://www.pcworld.com/article/id,135095-page,1/article.html.
49. Anna Lagerkvist, "Apple Sells One Millionth iPhone," Techradar.com, September 9, 2007, accessed June 30, 2011, http://www.techradar.com/news/phone-and-communications/mobile-phones/portable-devices/mp3-players/mobile-computing/tablets/internet/web/computing/apple/apple-sells-one-millionth-iphone-153982.

50. Ben Wilson, "Steve Jobs Posts Open Letter to iPhone Customers re: Price Drop: Offers $100 Credit," CNET, September 6, 2007, accessed July 27, 2014, http://www.cnet.com/news/steve-jobs-posts-open-letter-to-iphone-customers-re-price-drop-offers-100-credit/.

Chapter 10

1. J. C. Gonzalez-Mendez, Mission statement of McDonald's Corporation, McDonalds.com. Published by McDonald's Corporation.
2. McDonald's Corporation, *Worldwide Corporate Social Responsibility, 2010 Report*, accessed July 30, 2014, http://www.aboutmcdonalds.com/content/dam/AboutMcDonalds/Sustainability/Sustainability%20Library/2010-CSR-Report.pdf, p. 17.
3. "How McDonald's Fries Are Made," accessed May 19, 2011, http://www.associatedcontent.com/article/1386768/how_mcdonalds_fries_are_made_pg3.html?cat=22.
4. McDonald's Corporation, *Worldwide Corporate Social Responsibility, 2010 Report.*
5. McDonald's, "Corporate Social Responsibility and Sustainability."
6. Ibid.
7. PBS, "Ford Installs First Moving Assembly Line 1913," *A Science Odyssey: People and Discoveries Databank*, accessed May 11, 2011, http://www.pbs.org/wgbh/aso/databank/entries/dt13as.html.
8. Inter IKEA Systems B.V., "The IKEA Range," accessed May 12, 2011, http://franchisor.ikea.com/Theikeaconcept/Pages/The-IKEA-product-range.aspx.
9. Dell, "Laptop Deals," accessed May 11, 2011, http://www.dell.com/ca/business/p/laptop-deals?~ck=anav.
10. Walmart Canada, "Walmart Photo Centre," accessed May 11, 2011, http://www.walmartphotocentre.ca/.
11. Mars, "Personalize M&M's," accessed May 11, 2011, http://www.mymms.com.
12. "Flexible Manufacturing Systems," accessed July 30, 2014, http://www.nuigalway.ie/staff-sites/david_osullivan/documents/unit_15_flexible_manufacturing_systems.pdf.
13. Christopher W. Hart, "Creating Competitive Advantages through Mass Customization," accessed May 11, 2011, http://www.spiregroup.biz/pdfs/06-04-07%20Creating%20Competitive%20Advantage%20through%20Mass%20Customization.pdf.
14. "Intro to Lean," LeanProduction.com, accessed November 17, 2011, http://www.leanproduction.com/intro-to-lean.html.
15. "Robot," *Merriam-Webster Dictionary*, accessed May 11, 2011, http://www.merriamwebster.com/dictionary/robot?show=0&t=1305166216.
16. David Kucera, "Computer-Aided Design (CAD) and Computer-Aided Manufacturing (CAM)," *Encyclopedia of Business*, 2nd ed., accessed May 11, 2011, http://www.referenceforbusiness.com/encyclopedia/Clo-Con/Computer-Aided-Design-CAD-and-Computer-Aided-Manufacturing-CAM.html.
17. Ibid.
18. "Customer-Made," Trendwatching.com, May 11, 2011, http://trendwatching.com/trends/CUSTOMER-MADE.htm.
19. J.F. Brandon, "25% of IKEA Catalogues Will Have CAD Renders Instead of Real Products," GrabCAD, August 25, 2012, accessed June 19, 2014, http://blog.grabcad.com/2012/08/25-of-ikea-catalogues-will-have-cad-renders-instead-of-real-products/. Used with the permission of JF Brandon.
20. miadidas, "Getting Started," accessed November 18, 2011, http://www.miadidas.com/CustomizeShoe.action?ident=I1271855297882_ST; and Adidas Group Blog, accessed November 18, 2011, http://blog.adidas-group.com.
21. Best Buy Canada, accessed November 18, 2011, http://www.bestbuy.ca; and Twitter, "Twelpforce Best Buy," accessed November 18, 2011, http://twitter.com/#!/twelpforce.

22. Starbucks, "My Starbucks Idea," accessed November 18, 2011, http://mystarbucksidea.force.com; and Dell, "Idea Storm," accessed November 18, 2011, http://www.ideastorm.com.
23. Engadget, "Posts Tagged How Would You Change," accessed November 18, 2011, http://www.engadget.com/tag/how+would+you+change.
24. Tim Feemster, "A Step-by-Step Guide to Choosing the Right Site," AreaDevelopment.com, November 2007, accessed May 12, 2011, http://www.areadevelopment.com/siteSelection/nov07/stepByStep.shtml.
25. McDonald's, "Our Supply Chain," accessed June 19, 2014, http://www.aboutmcdonalds.com/content/mcd/sustainability/sourcing/priority-products.html
26. General Motors, "Connecting You to What's Important: 2013 Sustainability Report," accessed January 21, 2014, http://gmsustainability.com/report.html.
27. N. Shivapriya, "India Remains World's Top Outsourcing Destination," *Businessweek*, July 10, 2009, accessed May 12, 2011, http://www.businessweek.com/globalbiz/content/jul2009/gb20090710_974200.htm.
28. City of Toronto, "Garbage & Recycling," accessed May 12, 2011, http://www1.toronto.ca/wps/portal/contentonly?vgnextoid=03ec433112b02410VgnVCM10000071d60f89RCRD.
29. U.S. Consumer Product Safety Commission, "Mattel, Fisher-Price to Pay $2.3 Million Civil Penalty for Violating Federal Lead Paint Ban," press release, June 5, 2009, accessed May 15, 2011, http://www.cpsc.gov/cpscpub/prerel/prhtml09/09237.html.
30. Canada Post, "eProcurement," accessed May 16, 2011, http://www.canadapost.ca/cpo/mc/aboutus/suppliers/eprocurement.jsf.
31. Walmart, "Standards for Suppliers," October 2009, accessed November 21, 2011, http://corporate.walmart.com/global-responsibility/ethical-sourcing/standards-for-suppliers.
32. Home Depot, *Supplier Reference Manual*, September 21, 2010, accessed November 21, 2011, https://corporate.homedepot.com/en_US/Supplier_Center/Functional/SBA/Supplier_Reference_Manual.pdf.
33. SCORE (Counselors to America's Small Business), "Inventory Control," accessed May 15, 2011, http://www.ct-clic.com/Newsletters/customer-files/inventory0602.pdf.
34. Jonathan Byrnes, "Dell Manages Profitability, Not Inventory," Harvard Business School Working Knowledge (online forum), June 2, 2003, accessed May 15, 2011, http://hbswk.hbs.edu/archive/3497.html.
35. American Society for Quality, "The History of Quality—Total Quality," accessed November 18, 2011, http://asq.org/learn-about-quality/history-of-quality/overview/total-quality.html.
36. American Society for Quality, "Continuous Improvement," accessed May 16, 2011, http://asq.org/learn-about-quality/continuous-improvement/overview/overview.html.
37. Tony Van Alphen, "Toyota Recalls More Vehicles," TheStar.com, January 26, 2011, accessed May 17, 2011, http://www.thestar.com/business/2011/01/26/toyota_recalls_more_vehicles.html.
38. CBC News, "More than 18 Million Mattel Toys on Recall Globally," cbcnews.ca, August 14, 2007, accessed May 17, 2011, http://www.cbc.ca/news/story/2007/08/14/mattel-recall.html; and Louise Story, "Lead Paint Prompts Mattel to Recall 967,000 Toys," *New York Times*, accessed May 17, 2011, http://www.nytimes.com/2007/08/02/business/02toy.html.
39. Associated Press, "Bridgestone and Ford Settle Dispute Over Defective Tires," October 13, 2005, accessed May 17, 2011, http://www.nytimes.com/2005/10/13/business/13ford.html.
40. International Organization for Standardization, "ISO Standards," accessed May 16, 2011, http://www.iso.org/iso/home/standards.htm.

41. Bizmanualz, "ISO Standards," accessed May 16, 2011, http://www.bizmanualz.com/iso-9000-qms/ISO_Standards.html.
42. Herbert Hirner, "Greenhouse Gas Emissions—ISO14067 to Enable Worldwide Comparability of Carbon Footprint Data," International Organization for Standardization, press release, accessed June 19, 2014, http://www.iso.org/iso/home/news_index/news_archive/news.htm?Refid=Ref1643. Reproduced with the permission of the International Organization for Standardization, ISO.
43. Toyota Motor Manufacturing Kentucky, Inc., "Toyota Production System Terms," accessed June 25, 2008, http://www.toyotageorgetown.com/terms.asp.
44. Toyota Motor Manufacturing Kentucky, Inc., "History," accessed June 25, 2008, http://www.toyotageorgetown.com/history.asp.
45. Toyota Motor Corporation, "The Toyota Production System," accessed June 25, 2008, http://www.toyotageorgetown.com/tps1.asp.
46. Ibid.

Chapter 11

1. Google Inc., "Our History in Depth," Google.com, accessed June 30, 2011, http://www.google.com/corporate/history.html.
2. Google, "Investor Relations: 2014 Financial Tables," accessed January 19, 2014, http://investor.google.com/financial/tables.html.
3. Google Inc., "Ten Things We Know to Be True," Google.com, accessed June 30, 2011, http://www.google.com/about/company/philosophy/.
4. Google, "Investor Relations."
5. *Entrepreneur,* "Six Sources of Bootstrap Financing," Entrepreneur.com, accessed June 22, 2011, http://www.entrepreneur.com/article/80204.
6. Cynthia E. Griffin, "Breaking the Bank: Nonbank Lenders Are Pulling Ahead in Small-Business Financing. Here's What the Playing Field Looks Like," *Entrepreneur,* December 4, 2011, accessed June 22, 2011, http://www.entrepreneur.com/article/15294.
7. Google Inc., "Our History in Depth."
8. Tim Hortons, "Tim Hortons Announces Pricing for Its Initial Public Offering," press release, March 23, 2006, accessed January 19, 2014, http://www.timhortons.com/ca/en/about/news_archive_2006c.html. Published by permission of Tim Hortons Inc.
9. Alexis Xydias, "IPO Fund Gets Record Cash in Best Year Since '99 on Twitter," *Businessweek,* January 17, 2014, accessed January 19, 2014, http://www.businessweek.com/news/2014-01-16/ipo-fund-lures-record-money-in-best-year-since-99-with-twitter.
10. Jolie O'Dell, "How Venture Capitalists Are Using Social Media for Real Results," Mashable.com, May 17, 2010, accessed January 19, 2014, http://mashable.com/2010/05/17/vcs-social-media/.
11. "Difference between CA and CGA," DifferenceBetween.net, accessed November 21, 2011, http://www.differencebetween.net/business/finance-business-2/difference-between-ca-and-cga/.
12. "Managerial Accounting," *Encyclopedia of Business,* 2nd ed., accessed November 21, 2011, http://www.referenceforbusiness.com/encyclopedia/Man-Mix/Managerial-Accounting.html.
13. Chartered Accountants of Canada, "What Do CAs Do?" accessed November 21, 2011, http://www.cica.ca/about-the-profession/what-do-cas-do/index.aspx.
14. Mike White, "Canada: $1.5 Billion in Accounting Errors Found in Defence Dept.," *Digital Journal,* October 13, 2013, accessed January 19, 2014, http://digitaljournal.com/article/360023.
15. Automatic Data Processing Canada, "What Is the Sarbanes-Oxley Act and How Does It Affect Your Business?" TheJournalofFranchise.com, accessed June 24, 2011, http://www.thejournaloffranchise.com/art/article.cfm?id=3.

16. "Forensic Accounting Demystified," accessed November 21, 2011, http://www.forensicaccounting.com/four.htm.
17. Starbucks Corporation, *2010 Annual Report*, accessed June 25, 2011, http://phx.corporate-ir.net/External.File?item=UGFyZW50SUQ9NzkzODl8Q2hpbGRJRD0tMXxUeXBlPTM=&t=1.
18. Amey Stone, "SOX: Not So Bad After All?" *Businessweek,* August 1, 2005, accessed June 26, 2011, http://www.businessweek.com/stories/2005-07-31/sox-not-so-bad-after-all.
19. Investopedia, "Generally Accepted Accounting Principles (GAAP)," accessed November 20, 2011, http://www.investopedia.com/terms/g/gaap.asp#axzz1eJBd9eAO.
20. Chartered Accountants of Canada, "Definition of Publicly Accountable Enterprises," accessed June 26, 2011, http://www.cica.ca/ifrs/item2722.aspx.
21. American Institute of Certified Public Accountants, "International Financial Reporting Standards FAQs," accessed June 26, 2011, http://www.ifrs.com/ifrs_faqs.html#q3.
22. Thomas H. Beechy et al., *Advanced Financial Accounting*, 6th ed. (Toronto, ON: Pearson Canada, 2012), 21–22.
23. Ibid., 4.
24. Chartered Accountants of Canada, "New Accounting Standards for Not-for-Profit Organizations—Questions for Directors to Ask," March 2011, accessed November 21, 2011, http://www.rogb.ca/npo/npo-directors-series/director-alerts/item49752.pdf.
25. Beechy et al., *Advanced Financial Accounting*, 16.

Chapter 12

1. U.S. Chamber of Commerce/Business Civic Leadership Centre, "Corporate Aid Tracker—Japanese Earthquake and Tsunami, March 2011," accessed October 25, 2011, http://bclc.uschamber.com/site-page/corporate-aid-tracker-japanese-earthquake-and-tsunami-march-2011.
2. Foreign Affairs and International Trade, "Canada Provides Relief Supplies to Japan," March 15, 2011, accessed October 25, 2011, http://www.international.gc.ca/media/aff/news-communiques/2011/106.aspx?view=d.
3. BBC News "China, Japan, South Korea Seek Trade Pact," accessed April 25, 2011, http://www.bbc.co.uk/news/13184570.
4. Len Jelinek, "Japan Earthquake Suspends Supply of Raw Material Used in 25 Percent of Global Chip Production—Memory Segment Hit Hard," iSuppli, March 21, 2011, accessed October 25, 2011, http://www.rcrwireless.com/20110325/global/japan-earthquake-suspends-supply-of-raw-material-used-in-25-percent-of-global-chip-production-memory-segment-hit-hard.
5. Scott Malone, "Japan Disaster Called Temporary Hit for Rare Earth," Reuters, March 16, 2005, accessed April 25, 2011, http://www.reuters.com/article/2011/03/15/usa-rareearth-idUSN1527013820110315.
6. Laura Myers, "Japan Crisis Spurs Iodide Demand in U.S. and Canada," Reuters, March 15, 2011, accessed October 25, 2011, http://us.mobile.reuters.com/article/Deals/idUSTRE72E8Y920110315?irpc=932.
7. Ken Belson and Hiroko Tabuchi, "Japan Finds Tainted Food Up to 90 Miles From Nuclear Sites," *New York Times,* March 20, 2011, accessed April 25, 2011, http://www.nytimes.com/2011/03/20/world/asia/20japan.html?pagewanted=all&_r=0.
8. Rabobank Group, "Japan Food Trade Deficit Set to Rise after Earthquake," press release, April 7, 2011, accessed April 25, 2011, https://www.perscentrumrabobank.com/publications/food_agri/rabobank_says_japan_food_trade_deficit_set_to_rise_after_earthquake_.html.

9. Harumi Ozawa, "Trade Will Help Japan Quake Recovery: Ministers," Yahoo! Finance, April 24, 2011, accessed April 25, 2011, https://au.finance.yahoo.com/news/Trade-help-Japan-quake-afp-685840381.html.
10. Vittorio Hernandez, "China, South Korea Keep Japanese Food Import Restrictions," AHN News, April 25, 2011, accessed April 25, 2011, http://gantdaily.com/2011/04/25/china-south-korea-keep-japanese-food-import-restrictions/.
11. Kounteya Sinha, "Govt Bans Food Imports from Japan for 3 Months," *Times of India*, April 6, 2011, accessed April 25, 2011, http://timesofindia.indiatimes.com/india/Govt-bans-food-imports-from-Japan-for-3-months/articleshow/7879998.cms.
12. Bonnie Burgess, "Global Impact of Japan Earthquake Disaster," About.com, April 15, 2011, accessed April 24, 2011, http://tourism.about.com/od/globaltourismissues/a/Global-Impact-Of-Japan-Earthquake-Disaster.htm.
13. Ibid.
14. Ibid.
15. "IATA Sees Sharp Slowdown in Japan Air Traffic," *Space Mart*, March 18, 2011, accessed April 25, 2011, http://www.spacemart.com/reports/IATA_sees_sharp_slowdown_in_Japan_air_traffic_999.html.
16. Charles W. L. Hill, *International Business: Competing in the Global Marketplace*, 8th ed. (Burr Ridge, IL: Irwin/McGraw-Hill Publishing Co., 2010), 6–8.
17. Ibid.
18. Govindkrishna Seshan, "Fruit Punch," *Business Standard*, February 26, 2008, accessed April 26, 2011, http://www.business-standard.com/article/management/fruit-punch-108022601092_1.html.
19. Guy Stanley, "Wal-Mart in the NAFTA Market," GlobalStart.biz, accessed October 26, 2011, http://globalstart.biz/teaching-resources/wal-mart-nafta-market.
20. Hill, *International Business*, 6–8.
21. Daniel Trefler, "Policy Responses to the New Offshoring: Think Globally, Invest Locally," paper prepared for Industry Canada's March 30, 2005, Roundtable on Offshoring, accessed April 9, 2011, http://homes.chass.utoronto.ca/~trefler/Outsourcing_Final_TeX.pdf.
22. Hill, *International Business*, 18–24.
23. Canadian International Development Platform, "Canadian Foreign Direct Investment Abroad," accessed March 5, 2014, http://cidpnsi.ca/blog/portfolio/canadian-foreign-direct-investment-overseas-quick-review/.
24. U.S. Department of State, "U.S. Relations with Cuba: Fact Sheet," accessed April 28, 2011, http://www.state.gov/r/pa/ei/bgn/2886.htm.
25. Harley Richards, "Canada Lands Share of EU Beef Import Quota," *Red Deer Advocate*, November 23, 2010, accessed April 28, 2011, http://www.albertalocalnews.com/business/Canada_lands_share_of_EU_beef_import_quota_110287579.html?mobile=true.
26. Eric Eldon, "Facebook Hasn't Signed Any Deals to Enter China—At Least Not Yet," InsideFacebook.com, April 11, 2011, accessed April 24, 2011, http://www.insidefacebook.com/2011/04/11/facebook-hasnt-signed-any-deals-to-enter-china-at-least-not-yet/.
27. AFP, "China Warns Google Not to Stop Filtering Web Searches," Google News, March 12, 2010, accessed April 24, 2011, http://en.kioskea.net/news/15195-china-warns-google-not-to-stop-filtering-web-searches.
28. Victoria Woollaston, "China Lifts Ban on Facebook—But Only for People Living in a 17-Square-Mile Area of Shanghai," *Daily Mail*, September 25, 2013, accessed March 26, 2014, http://www.dailymail.co.uk/sciencetech/article-2431861/China-lifts-ban-Facebook--people-living-working-small-area-Shanghai.html#ixzz2x58ozxop.

29. Brendan Greeley and Mark Drajem, "China's Facebook Syndrome," *Businessweek*, March 10, 2011, accessed April 24, 2011, http://www.businessweek.com/magazine/content/11_12/b4220029428856.htm.
30. Ibid.
31. "Google Stops China Services," PoliticolNews.com, July 22, 2010, accessed April 24, 2011, http://www.politicolnews.com/google-stops-china-services/?utm_source=INK&utm_medium=copy&utm_campaign=share.
32. Basit Saeed, "Spotflux No More! Pakistan Telecommunication Authority Blocked Access to Spotflux in the Country," *Era of Technology* (blog), February 17, 2014, accessed March 26, 2014, http://eraoftechnology.wordpress.com/2014/02/17/spotflux-no-more-pakistan-telicommunication-authority-blocked-access-to-spotflux-in-the-country/. Used by permission of the author.
33. World Trade Organization, "The GATT Years: From Havana to Marrakesh," accessed May 1, 2011, http://www.wto.org/english/thewto_e/whatis_e/tif_e/fact4_e.htm.
34. World Trade Organization, "Understanding the WTO," accessed May 1, 2011, http://www.wto.org/english/thewto_e/whatis_e/tif_e/tif_e.htm.
35. World Trade Organization, "The Doha Round," accessed May 1, 2011, http://www.wto.org/english/tratop_e/dda_e/dda_e.htm.
36. "Doha Delivers," *The Economist,* December 9, 2013, accessed March 26, 2014, http://www.economist.com/blogs/freeexchange/2013/12/world-trade-organisation.
37. Central Intelligence Agency, "Rank Order: Exports," *The World Factbook*, accessed May 1, 2011, https://www.cia.gov/library/publications/the-world-factbook/rankorder/2078rank.html.
38. Matt Rosenberg, "Euro Countries," About.com, March 17, 2011, accessed May 1, 2011, http://geography.about.com/od/lists/a/euro.htm.
39. Reuters, "EU Antitrust Regulators Raid Faurecia, Tenneco, Car Exhause Suppliers," *Automotive News,* March 25, 2014, accessed March 26, 2014, http://www.autonews.com/article/20140325/COPY01/303259960/eu-antitrust-regulators-raid-faurecia-tenneco-car-exhaust-suppliers. Used by permission of Automotive News.
40. Ibid.
41. *CBC News,* "Summary of Canada–EU Free Trade Deal Tabled," October 29, 2013, accessed March 26, 2014, http://www.cbc.ca/news/politics/summary-of-canada-eu-free-trade-deal-tabled-1.2286695.
42. Ibid.
43. Joanna Klonsky, Stephanie Hanson, and Brianna Lee, "Mercosur: South America's Fractious Trade Bloc," Council on Foreign Relations, July 31, 2012, accessed March 26, 2014, http://www.cfr.org/trade/mercosur-south-americas-fractious-trade-bloc/p12762.
44. "ASEAN GDP Remains Robust, Backed by Services," ASEAN Secretariat News, October 21, 2013, accessed March 26, 2014, http://www.asean.org/news/asean-secretariat-news/item/asean-gdp-remains-robust-backed-by-services.
45. Asia-Pacific Economic Cooperation, "Frequently Asked Questions," accessed March 26, 2014, http://www.apec.org/faq.
46. Franchise International, "Disney Signs India Master," November 7, 2006, accessed May 1, 2011, http://www.franchise-international.net/page/walt-disney-company/disney-signs-india-master.php.
47. Mark Brandau, "Domino's Pizza Sees Record Unit Growth," *Nation's Restaurant News,* February 26, 2014, accessed March 26, 2014, http://nrn.com/international/domino-s-pizza-sees-record-unit-growth. Published by Penton Inc.
48. SRI International, "Products and Solutions," accessed May 1, 2011, http://www.sri.com/engage/products-solutions.

49. Nandita Bose, "Wal-Mart and Bharti Enterprises Call off India JV," Reuters, October 9, 2013, accessed March 26, 2014, http://www.reuters.com/article/2013/10/09/us-walmart-bharti-india-idUSBRE99804E20131009.
50. "Renault-Nissan Alliance on; Bets Big on India," *The Economic Times,* June 5, 2009, accessed March 26, 2014, http://articles.economictimes.indiatimes.com/2009-06-05/news/28492739_1_renault-nissan-alliance-renault-nissan-automotive-india-colin-dodge.
51. *Automotive World,* "Hyundai Motor Inaugurates New Brazilian Plant," news release, November 12, 2012, accessed March 26, 2014, https://www.automotiveworld.com/news-releases/hyundai-motor-inaugurates-new-brazilian-plant.
52. Trading Economics, "Canada Balance of Trade," accessed March 26, 2014, www.tradingeconomics.com/canada/balance-of-trade.
53. OANDA, "fxHistory Classic: results," accessed March 5, 2014, http://www.oanda.com/convert/fxhistory?lang=en&result=1&date1=12%2F21%2F01&date=02%2F21%2F02&date_fmt=us&exch=USD&exch2=CAD&expr=EUR&expr2=USD&margin_fixed=0&format=HTML&SUBMIT=Get+Table.
54. Ibid.
55. C.G. Alex and Barbara Bowers, "The American Way to Countertrade," *Barter News* 17 (1988), http://www.barternews.com/american_way.htm.
56. Walter Loeb, "Walmart's International Challenge: Trying to Understand Local Shoppers," *Forbes,* March 26, 2014, accessed March 27, 2014, http://www.forbes.com/sites/walterloeb/2014/03/26/walmarts-international-challenge-trying-to-understand-local-shoppers/.
57. Kwintessential, "Results of Poor Cross Cultural Awareness," accessed May 1, 2011, http://www.kwintessential.co.uk/cultural-services/articles/results-of-poor-cross-cultural-awareness.html.
58. Globerove, "Business Hours in Spain," accessed August 4, 2014, http://globerove.com/spain/business-hours-in-spain/9.
59. Kwintessential, "Doing Business in Germany," accessed May 2, 2011, http://www.kwintessential.co.uk/etiquette/doing-business-germany.html.
60. Kwintessential, "Results of Poor Cross Cultural Awareness."
61. Ibid.
62. Department of Justice, The Corruption of Foreign Public Officials Act, accessed May 2, 2011, http://laws-lois.justice.gc.ca/eng/acts/C-45.2/.
63. GE, "GE Extends Olympic Sponsorship through 2020," press release, accessed March 27, 2014, http://www.genewscenter.com/Press-Releases/GE-Extends-Olympic-Sponsorship-Through-2020-31d6.aspx.
64. Jeffrey Immelt, "Winning in the Essential Themes," GE 2007 Annual Report, accessed June 28, 2011, http://www.ge.com/ar2007/ltr_winning.jsp.
65. General Electric Company, "GE and the Olympic Games: A Legacy for Beijing," accessed June 28, 2011, http://www.ge.com/innovation/china/index.html.
66. Ted Mann, "For GE, Ukraine Roils Russia Strategy," *Wall Street Journal,* March 26, 2014, accessed March 27, 2014, http://online.wsj.com/news/articles/SB10001424052702304688104579463752543810262?mg=reno64-wsj&url=http%3A%2F%2Fonline.wsj.com%2Farticle%2FSB10001424052702304688104579463752543810262.html.
67. Immelt, "Winning in the Essential Themes."

Index

D

N